T0366507

THE I TATTI
RENAISSANCE LIBRARY

James Hankins, General Editor

POLIZIANO

MISCELLANIES

VOLUME I

ITRL 89

ANGELO POLIZIANO
✦ ✦ ✦
MISCELLANIES
VOLUME I

EDITED AND TRANSLATED BY

ANDREW R. DYCK

AND

ALAN COTTRELL

THE I TATTI RENAISSANCE LIBRARY
HARVARD UNIVERSITY PRESS
CAMBRIDGE, MASSACHUSETTS
LONDON, ENGLAND
2020

Series design by Dean Bornstein

First printing

Library of Congress Cataloging-in-Publication Data

Names: Poliziano, Angelo, 1454–1494, author. | Dyck, Andrew R.
(Andrew Roy), 1947– editor, translator. | Cottrell, Alan (Medievalist), editor,
translator. | Poliziano, Angelo, 1454–1494. Miscellaneorum centuria prima. |
Poliziano, Angelo, 1454–1494. Miscellaneorum centuria secunda. | Poliziano,
Angelo, 1454–1494. Miscellaneorum centuria prima. English. | Poliziano,
Angelo, 1454–1494. Miscellaneorum centuria secunda. English.
Title: Miscellanies / Angelo Poliziano, edited and translated by
Andrew R. Dyck and Alan Cottrell.
Other titles: I Tatti Renaissance library ; 89–90.
Description: Cambridge, Massachusetts : The I Tatti Renaissance Library :
Harvard University Press, 2020. | Series: The I Tatti Renaissance library; 89–90 |
Includes bibliographical references and index. | Text in Latin and Greek with
English translations; introduction and notes in English.
Identifiers: LCCN 2019028470 | ISBN 9780674049376 (v. 1 ; cloth) |
ISBN 9780674244962 (v. 2 ; cloth)
Subjects: LCSH: Classical literature—Criticism, Textual.
Classification: LCC PA3520 .P58 2020 | DDC 871/.04—dc23
LC record available at https://lccn.loc.gov/2019028470

Contents

❧❧❧

Introduction

1. *The Man and the Work*

"Pliny's text," wrote L. D. Reynolds, "is a tribute to the tenacity of humanism, the will to seek and to find."[1] The same could be said of many classical texts that trickled into Italy in the fourteenth and fifteenth centuries and sparked first curiosity and then a commitment on the part of scholars and men of letters to create some sort of order out of the chaos by comparing texts, publishing them via the new technology of printing, and exploiting their contents to achieve a better understanding of their authors and the ancient world in general. Angelo Poliziano (1454–94) was at the forefront of the movement, a man tenacious in the pursuit of information and sources, whom nothing pleased more than to find scraps of poetry despaired of by others (cf. *II* 31.3).

He was born Angelo Ambrogini in the Montepulciano region of central Tuscany, the origin of the name under which he became famous. His father, a jurist and supporter of the Medici, was murdered when Angelo was ten. In the aftermath, he was sent to Florence, where he lived with a relative and pursued studies of Greek and Latin, his mastery of which brought him the attention and patronage of the Medici and their circle. He benefited from a fine education in Latin (Cristoforo Landino), Greek (Theodore Gaza), and in Platonic and Aristotelian philosophy (Marsilio Ficino and John Argyropoulos). He was also exposed early on to the work of the Veronese scholar Domizio Calderini, the most prominent classical scholar of the previous generation, who much expanded the fund of texts used to explicate the ancient classics.[2] Blessed with an early start, privileged access to collections of manuscripts and antiquities made available by Lorenzo de' Medici, a sharp memory,

a subtle appreciation for the nuances of language, and a restless and probing intellect, Poliziano was positioned to carry classical philology to a level not seen since the critics of ancient Alexandria.[3] Like one of their number, Callimachus of Cyrene, Poliziano was a poet as well as a scholar, a further advantage in approaching poetic texts.[4]

2. A Visionary

By temperament and circumstance, Poliziano was so placed as to have a much more comprehensive picture of the ancient world and the sources of knowledge available for it, from both literature and antiquities, than others of his time. On this basis, he developed a critique of the scholarship of his day and pointed to what was needed in order to make progress.

Of fundamental importance were the texts themselves, but they had been transmitted for centuries by ignorant and/or careless copyists with a resulting accumulation of errors. Poliziano saw that the only way to get at the truth was to search diligently for the oldest available copies and base discussion or emendation on that evidence, not just any copy that happened to be conveniently available. In addition, commentaries on classical authors, which had begun to appear in print in the final quarter of the century, were an essential tool of scholarly inquiry. However, these were often hastily written by authors who lacked the knowledge to do their work properly and/or the time or resources to discover relevant information. The upshot was that, at best, the commentators drew inferences from the immediate context that more comprehensive knowledge revealed to be false or, even worse, made up information out of whole cloth to support an interpretation they had arrived at arbitrarily. Calderini is criticized on both grounds.[5]

So Poliziano pursues a double goal: to improve the base texts and also to provide information to make commentaries better

equipped (and to show paradigmatically how this can be done).[6] One of Poliziano's reforms involves raising the standard for the citation of evidence, both of texts (regularly citing authors by work and book number) and manuscripts (usually with indication of [relative] age and current location), in contrast to his predecessors, whose vague references can often be difficult or impossible to track down.[7]

3. The Miscellanea: Form and Content

Poliziano's chief claim to fame as a philologist rests on the work edited here, the *Miscellanea*, the first set published in 1489, the second left unfinished at his death and published for the first time in 1972. The form of the work was perhaps less original than Poliziano suggests, Calderini having published a miscellaneous volume (Rome, 1475) and Beroaldo his *Annotationes centum* (Bologna, 1488).[8] His essential model was the *Attic Nights* of Aulus Gellius (2nd century CE). Like Gellius, he produced individual chapters each on a set topic and with a corresponding title, with the titles listed at the beginning of the work as a guide to readers. Another model was the *Natural History* of the Elder Pliny, from which he borrowed the practice of listing at the beginning the sources he had used in the course of the project in order to ensure that the work would be taken seriously and could not be readily dismissed.[9] Like both authors, he preceded the work with a Preface. In addition, borrowing from and extending the usage of typographers of his day, he added a *coronis*, or tailpiece (which we might call an Epilogue) at the end of *Century I*, explaining the history of the preceding text and taking a stand on rival claims to priority. He does not explain exactly why he chose one hundred as the number of chapters for each set of the *Miscellanea* (several sets appear to have been planned from an early stage[10]). Possibly, he used the practice of the Greek paroemiographers as a model, who orga-

nized their materials century by century. He does, however, exploit the analogy to the organization of Roman troops by centuries when he depicts them as a combatant army.[11]

A miscellany was, in fact, the perfect form for Poliziano, because it enabled him to range widely over ancient literature and culture with a focus on particular problems, above all passages of ancient authors that were obscure and/or had been wrongly explained by predecessors, that seemed to contradict each other or one's notion of an author's knowledge or competence. He was able to bring to bear his wide reading of authors and acquaintance with antiquities as well as his dialectical skills[12] to shed new light on many such issues. In writing a commentary, however, he could have become bogged down by the need to give routine explanations where no particular problem existed.

4. The Genesis of the Chapters

The chapters of the *Miscellanea* did not spring fully formed from Poliziano's head. When he speaks of the hard work he devoted to the project (I Pref. 21; cf. I 90.9), he should be believed, even if he also speaks of the work as something he has been toying with (I Pref. 22: *ludicra*). Recent years have seen intense study of the marginalia in the books he owned, his manuscript papers, and the notes taken down by students during his lectures. Hence a clearer picture is emerging of his method of work.

Poliziano begins with intense reading and comparison of texts and jotting of manuscript readings and other notes in the margins of his printed copies. On occasion one can see a chapter of the *Miscellanea in nuce* in one of Poliziano's marginal notes (cf. on I 19, 53, 62, 98; II 35).[13] Usually, however, one finds that a process of refining and expanding the argument, adding examples, etc., has preceded inclusion in the *Miscellanea*.[14] The observations from Poliziano's reading formed the basis for the public lectures he

delivered starting in 1480 under the Florentine *Studio* (university).[15] Some of this material is then whittled down to provide content for chapters of the *Miscellanea*, notably *I* 18, 64, 65, 72; *II* 48.[16] Parallel with his reading, annotating, and lecturing, Poliziano made collections of various types of information.[17] Some chapters of the *Miscellanea* are transparently based on these collections, for example, words that are rare but not unique (*I* 30), the number of diphthongs (*I* 43), and the jurists and their works (*II* 44). The collections also feed into the *Miscellanea* in subtler ways.

5. A Typical Chapter

A typical chapter of the *Miscellanea* begins with a problem Poliziano has encountered, most frequently a particular passage of a classical text that, on its face, does not make sense grammatically, metrically, or in view of known facts about the author or his society. Poliziano will quote the offending passage together with previous attempts at exegesis, if relevant. After showing these to be inadequate, Poliziano proceeds to outline his solution and how he arrived at it, often with copious citations of parallel passages to illustrate the point of usage or the particular content he is arguing for. He may conclude the chapter with a brief summary, especially if the argumentation has been involved, or with a kind of footnote on some point of detail that he felt should be explained.[18] Occasionally, he will be moved to insert a kind of editorial preface ahead of the treatment of the problem in order to make a general point about scholarly procedure or the like.[19] A few of the chapters do not center on philological problems at all but incorporate information that he simply found interesting and wanted to share, such as the disquisition on lime-tree bark (*I* 72), the report of Severianus's views on the position of the sun and moon at the creation (*I* 94), or the testimonies for the poet Erinna (*II* 26).[20]

Some of his most striking contributions are, in fact, the discoveries he presents: the rediscovery of the Greek poet Nonnus in a manuscript that had belonged to Filelfo before being acquired by Lorenzo; the recovery of the Sibylline Oracle governing the Secular Games recorded by the Greek historian Zosimus, preserved in a Vatican manuscript; the *editio princeps* of Callimachus's hymn *On the Bath of Pallas*; the three Greek epigrams on famous springs Vitruvius had quoted but that had dropped out of his manuscripts and that Poliziano rediscovered in the manuscript of the "Florentine paradoxographer" recently acquired by Lorenzo.[21]

6. Poliziano's Method

Poliziano's wide acquaintance with manuscripts led him to formulate a theory of textual transmission that underlies many of his individual pronouncements: the best evidence for an author's text will be as close as possible to the author's own autograph.[22] He was prepared to search doggedly for the oldest recoverable reading, within the parameters of what was available to him in Italian libraries or from private book collectors of his acquaintance. This reading, once found, may itself provide the solution, correcting inferior readings widely circulated in later copies of the text. He supplements this "emendation by means of codices" (*emendatio ope codicum*) with conjectures of his own, as needed, with the oldest recoverable reading taken as the starting point. His best solutions of this type are ones that involve small changes to the transmitted text, for example, *sciamachiae* for *sciamachalae* (I 34). Here he is guided by a finely attuned sense of the kinds of errors scribes may fall into based on similarities of words or letterforms.[23] He has also developed a sense of the general areas where scribes are prone to err—not only in copying Greek words but also in copying proper names and numbers, since the grammar of the language provides no self-checking mechanism for these.[24] Poliziano also

saw that in evaluating manuscript evidence it was not simply a matter of "majority rules." In a famous formulation (*I* 39.2), he wrote that testimonies "must, I think, be not so much added up as weighed." Any number of manuscripts may forfeit a claim to consideration if they can be shown to have been copied from another extant manuscript, a demonstration that he conducts with reference to Cicero's *Letters to His Friends* and *On the Nature of the Gods* (Book 2), and the *Argonautica* of Valerius Flaccus.[25] In the last case, he anticipates the reconstruction of the physical characteristics of the archetype achieved by nineteenth-century philologists.[26] Alternatively, he establishes that a codex is an archetype by a close study of its internal structure and the character of its corrections, as he does with the Florentine *Pandects* at *I* 41. In general, it can be said that he pursued philology with a rigor, insight, and linguistic skill that were new in Renaissance Italy.

7. *The People of the* Miscellanea

At the center of the *Miscellanea* stands Poliziano himself. They are fueled by his intense drive to uncover the secrets of ancient culture and solve the problems posed by ancient texts. Here he is in dialogue with the reader, who is presented as a kind of ideal student, who, like Poliziano, is a keen explorer of the ancient world but is puzzled by some of the phenomena encountered along the way. Hence Poliziano intervenes to dispel the perplexity either by citing evidence of older manuscripts that correct the nonsense found in vulgate texts or by referring the reader to other texts that clarify the obscure point.[27] He treats his readers as partners, calling on them to join in the investigation (*I* 10.6, 59.3), submitting himself to their judgment (*I* Pref. 11), and being willing to accept that they may reach a different conclusion (*I* 73.4; *II* 48.9). In general, he shows the respect for truth that one expects from a scholar (*I* Pref. 14).

Third parties sometimes impinge on this basic teacher-student dialogue. Some are positive influences who encourage Poliziano and supply him with the materials he needs to carry on his work, above all the dedicatee, his patron Lorenzo de' Medici, who has provided access to books and antiquities in profusion, and so enabled Poliziano to build up the vast fund of knowledge on which he draws, as well as the decisive push toward publication.[28] There are others in supporting roles, above all Poliziano's close friend and fellow protégé of the Medici, Giovanni Pico della Mirandola, whose qualities are praised with superlatives and whose willingness to initiate Poliziano into sacred and philosophical studies is appreciatively recorded.[29] There are also the teachers who helped the young Poliziano grow into his current role, of whom Landino, Ficino, and Argyropoulos are mentioned, albeit the last-named is also a target of criticism.[30] Ermolao Barbaro appears as a leading philologist; he is particularly important in *Century II*, since his volume of Plinian emendations had recently been published,[31] but he is already dead when Poliziano writes *Misc. II*.[32] Others in minor supporting roles receive brief mention, such as the jurist Bernardino Valla, who gave Poliziano access to manuscript materials (*I* 23.1 and 81.1; *II* 10.2 and 35.2) or the Venetian Giovanni Lorenzi, who gave him a stimulating tip (*I* 47.1; cf. also *I* 74).[33]

On the other side are those whose obfuscations and false information stand in the way of progress. These adversaries are often cloaked in anonymity even as their views are refuted or their behavior deplored.[34] But Poliziano's principal bête noire is the aforementioned Domizio Calderini. Though he had admired Calderini in his youth, as he matured Poliziano came to see the senior scholar's influence as pernicious.[35]

A couple of scholars occupy an intermediate position, Giorgio Merula being commended for early opposition to Calderini, albeit his views are sometimes criticized without attribution.[36] In the

Epilogue to *Century I*, Poliziano warily circles around Filippo Beroaldo: while calling him a friend, he is clearly irritated at the man's claims to prior authorship of some readings Poliziano has also promoted (§§8–9 with notes).[37]

8. *Polemics*

If the *Miscellanea* put on display a good deal of learning and clear, goal-oriented thinking, they also engage in fierce polemics. This was a characteristic feature of Poliziano's time and place. Calderini, for instance, had been enmeshed in bitter controversies with rivals.[38] But it was also characteristic of Poliziano's approach: he needed to argue against an opponent or opponents in order to clear away prevailing false opinion and display his own dialectical skills. On occasion, his negative case is stronger than his positive.[39] His major target is, in fact, the already deceased Calderini, who serves as Poliziano's example of how *not* to do philology.[40] He also disagrees with the living, but with the name suppressed, a usual procedure in the Renaissance, with antique precedent.[41] A particular concern of his in *Misc. I* is to assert his priority in sponsoring certain readings or interpretations. Here he finds himself in a tricky position, since many of his ideas had previously been aired in the public lectures he had delivered in the *Studio* or elsewhere; they could thus have been leaked to others, though a charge of plagiarism would be difficult to prove on this basis. He repeatedly appeals to lectures or other public pronouncements of his to uphold a claim to priority over other scholars who had in the meantime published the same ideas in print.[42] He considered this essential to maintaining his reputation as an original critic, since charges of plagiarism were bandied very freely in scholarship of the period. Besides such specific criticisms, the *Miscellanea* also contain a general critique of the current state of culture: a new

Dark Age seems to be descending, and Poliziano depicts himself as engaged in a lonely struggle to ward it off.[43]

9. *Patterns*

While the *Miscellanea* have the quality Poliziano touts of not being linear or predictable (*I* Pref. 3), no doubt as a result of deliberate arrangement, certain patterns emerge nonetheless. One obvious tendency is for two (or on one occasion three) chapters in succession to take the same author or work as their starting point: *I* 9–10 (Juvenal), 14–15 (Ovid), 22–23 (Martial), 27–28 (Cicero, *Letters to Friends*), 39–40 (Ausonius), 47–48 (Pliny), 51–52 (Martial), 54–55 (Quintilian), 59–60 (Ovid), 68–69 (Catullus), 75–76 (Ovid), 80–81 (Propertius 4), 88–89 (Vergil), 90–91 (Theodore Gaza); *II* 32–33 (Pliny), 36–37 (Ovid), 38–39 (Cicero's *philosophica*), 48–49 (Statius), 50–51 (Aristotle, *Politics*), 53–55 (Aristotle). On the other hand, though Poliziano has a certain number of chapters devoted to the texts of the jurists, they tend to be scattered about, perhaps so as not to try the patience of readers who have no special interest in this area. There are also conjunctions of chapters based not on authors but on subject matter: *I* 6–7 (covert sexual allusions), 11–12 (the rose, dyed red with the blood of Venus, and the invention of purple dye), 15–16 (the luxuries of the Sybarites and of the Milesians); *II* 1–2 (restoration of texts to correct order), 3–4 (customs or behavior at symposia), 12–13 (technical terms explained), 35–36 (Greek words that had been misunderstood in the texts of Latin poets).[44]

10. *From* Misc. I *to* Misc. II

Misc. I was probably composed as ideas occurred to Poliziano during his intense occupation with classical texts as a professor in the Florentine *Studio* beginning in 1480. According to the Epilogue,

composition was complete approximately one year prior to the
date of publication (September 17, 1489). The interval between the
appearance of *Misc. I* and the beginning of work on *Misc. II* saw
several important changes.[45] Poliziano's great patron, Lorenzo,
died in the night of April 8, 1492, leaving a large void.[46] *Misc. II*
mentions no patron taking his place. Also missing from *Misc. II*
are the allusions to coins and other ancient artifacts from the
Medici collection that are prominent in *Misc. I*. Another new development was the publication in 1492–93 of Ermolao Barbaro's
detailed study of the text of the Elder Pliny. But there soon followed news of the death of Barbaro, whom Poliziano recognized
as a philologist of the first rank.[47]

Though the Epilogue to *Misc. I* might have led one to expect
Misc. II to exhibit a shift of interest to philosophy (*I Epil.* 6), this
is not, in fact, the case until we reach chapter 50, where a concen-
tration of topics based on Aristotle occurs (50–51, 53–55).[48] Another surprise is that, in spite of the threat of sharper polemics to
come (*I Pref.* 21), the criticism is actually more measured in *Misc.
II*, and indeed Poliziano is willing to concede that Barbaro should
receive credit for an idea he published but which Poliziano had
entertained privately (*II* 35).[49] In formal terms, the individual
chapters of *Misc. II* tend to be longer on average than those of the
previous installment: 560 words for *Misc. II* versus 433 for *Misc. I*.
However, the chapter titles tend to be shorter in *Misc. II*, those of
Misc. I more detailed. Though this is, on the whole, probably a
good thing, some of the material in *Misc. II* is as a result not
flagged in the chapter titles and may thus be hard to locate, for
example, one might not expect discussion of the epigrams on
Thermopylae in a chapter entitled "Homer's Polyphemus" (*II* 39).

The Greek-Latin cultural divide, emphatically invoked at *I* 1 is,
of course, still present, and Poliziano speaks of exercising general
responsibility for Latin culture (*II* 5.1), expressed, for example, in
his effort to prevent the disappearance of elegant Latin words

(*II* 11.2, 32), and he still shows an interest in pitting Greek poetry against Latin (*II* 47; cf. *I* 26, 27, 49). But the anti-Greek polemic is now muted. If in *Misc. I* he suggested that study of the Greek version of the Justinianic corpus could pay dividends (*I* 84.1), he continues that line in *Misc. II* (*II* 8.4) and even suggests that something can be learned from the Greeks about a special technical sense of the word *auctoritas* (*II* 12.1).

Programmatic emphasis in *Misc. II* is not devoted to cultural issues, but to method, *divination* in the sense of "conjecture" being the key word of the first chapter. Since the publication of *Misc. I* he has seen his rearrangement of the letters of the Ciceronian corpus *To His Friends* take hold in subsequent printed editions (*II* 1.1). With his self-confidence thus boosted, he is prepared to be a bit bolder and more speculative in *Misc. II*: he speaks at one point of "play[ing] Aristarchus" (*II* 50.4) and at another of "stepping back a bit from the traces of ancient codices" (*II* 32.3).

With greater self-confidence comes a willingness to lay his cards on the table even if he does not have a definitive solution. Hence certain chapters in *Misc. II* have an open-ended character, partly also conditioned by the incomplete state of the surviving manuscript:[50] at 8.2 *fin.* and 38.1 Poliziano evidently meant to add more examples, at 42.21 he expresses doubts about his own results, and at 44.1 he announces a plan for detailed work on the jurists.

11. *Poliziano's Limitations*

Poliziano clearly had greater insight into the history and mechanics of transmission than his contemporaries did, and this, together with his access to books and other antiquities collected by the Medici, and his powerful drive to exploit these advantages, gave him a leg up. He did, however, also have limitations, both personal ones and those of his historical position. The development

of a systematic science of codicology was still centuries in the future. He has, nevertheless, a kind of rough-and-ready sense of which codices are older, based on the script, rustic capitals and "Lombardic" (i.e., Beneventan) script being telltale signs of antiquity.[51] Though he did conduct some systematic collations, the sample available to him may be too small or the relations of witnesses may have been too complicated or investigated insufficiently to allow him to form a true picture of the tradition.[52] Another problem was his very uniqueness. He did not have others in his own field who could give him the kind of feedback he would have needed to improve some of his positions. This was reinforced by his own preference for extemporaneous jotting over critical reconsideration of what he had previously written. Hence the first *Century* lay in his drawer for a year before publication but without much in the way of revision; and though it was circulated to some of his friends (*I* Epil. 1), they were apparently unable to provide much usable critique.[53] When faced with criticism after publication, he tended to dig in his heels, albeit he did withdraw one ill-advised conjecture.[54]

Another limitation was shared by his age generally, namely that he put too much faith in the reliability of some of his sources and failed to consider their limitations. Though he shows awareness elsewhere that some ancient letter collections were not by their purported authors (see on *I* 51), this insight fails to appear in the *Miscellanea*, where the authenticity of letters of Heraclitus and of Androcydes, the physician of Alexander the Great, is not challenged (cf. *I* 51 and 61). Similarly, Poliziano cannot bring himself to believe, in spite of the evidence of all the manuscripts, that Macrobius confused *cicuta* (hemlock) with *conium* (poison: *I* 61.2), and he struggles to acquit Cicero of misreporting the content of Polyphemus's address to the ram in the *Odyssey* (*II* 39);[55] and when he disbelieves an ancient source, his reasoning can be less than cogent (cf. on *I* 63 apropos of Varro).

It can be said in general that Poliziano tends to view his materials as an antiquarian would, not as a historian. This, too, is in line with the emphasis of his age on collecting and organizing knowledge of the past, exemplified, for example, in the encyclopedic works of Biondo Flavio (1392–1463).[56] Hence, for instance, Poliziano's confusion at I 85 when he tries to combine a note about the aedileship at Dio 43.51.3 with information from a coin or coins in the Medici collection identifying a C. Memmius as founder of the Cerealia festival. He takes Caesar's action in appointing two patrician and four plebeian *aediles Cereales* to be the first invention of the aedileship and the C. Memmius in question to be the man who served as praetor in 58 with L. Domitius (Ahenobarbus). Here he betrays that he has too little understanding of the history of institutions (the aediles had existed long before Caesar's reform of 44), of political careers of the late Republic (a man who had been praetor in 58 would hardly be aedile in 44 or 43[57]), or of political propaganda and numismatic iconography (the bearded man with shaggy hair on the coin points to an ancestor of the moneyer who would have lived in the early Republic). Furthermore, if a conflict arises between sources, Poliziano tends to treat it as a philological problem, even if there is no obvious philological solution for it.[58] Hence he is sometimes constrained simply to juxtapose conflicting versions without attempting to explain or resolve the conflict.[59]

12. *Poliziano's Contribution*

Poliziano's particular advantage lay in his knowledge of the Greek language and literature, which surpassed that of other Italian humanists and enabled him to debate with the Greek immigrants.[60] In this respect, his learned contemporary Beroaldo could not compete, since the resources for Greek studies available to him in Bo-

logna were far inferior.[61] With characteristic insight, Poliziano recognized that Greek words embedded in Latin texts had often been corrupted or omitted altogether by medieval scribes ignorant of Greek; hence a wide field lay open for a philologist equipped with sufficient Greek to emend the corruptions or fill the lacunae. Many of his best solutions are of this type.[62] Similarly, he can defend a text against erroneous alteration by citing information from a Greek source.[63] He also uses his knowledge of Greek material to good effect to explicate otherwise obscure passages of Latin authors.[64]

Another advantage Poliziano had was his privileged access (arranged by Lorenzo) to the Florentine *Pandects*. This plus his analysis showing from internal evidence that this codex was the archetype gave him a dominant position as a philologist dealing with legal texts, and he repeatedly exploits it in the *Miscellanea*.[65] He also repeatedly exploits privileged access to collections of books and artifacts, not only those of the Medici but also, thanks to their influence, elsewhere, including use of the "private" Vatican library.[66]

Some of Poliziano's solutions were simply wrong (*I* 38, 56, 66, 68, 75, 81, 82), some partially right (*I* 23, 89); others may have been less fresh and original than he suggests (*I* 6, 18, 19, 24, 43). But a number of his conjectures and interpretations still hold the field in current editions and commentaries,[67] a testimony to his acuity. Others can claim status as diagnostic conjectures that highlight a problem even if they fail to provide a definitive solution: *I* 73, 76, 79; *II* 21, 50. Elsewhere, too, he sometimes called attention to anomalies without providing a wholly satisfying explanation: *I* 48, 63; *II* 56.

Even today, Poliziano's breadth of interests and depth of knowledge of texts and manuscript traditions seem remarkable, all the more so when one considers that he did not have the benefit of precollected information but had to build his formidable toolkit

(*instrumentum: I 2*) on his own.[68] He also had a vision of where classical philology needed to go in order to make progress and offered clear and convincing examples of how to go about it. For all these reasons, he can qualify as a pioneer and a prototype of the modern philologist.[69]

Cottrell would like thank to Dustin Mengelkoch, who provided extensive feedback on first portions of his translations as well as on challenging excerpts later. Elias Theodoracopoulos kindly reviewed his Greek translations. Fellow presenters and audience members at sessions on Poliziano at multiple annual conferences of the Renaissance Society of America provided illuminating critiques of specific excerpts or features or have otherwise informed his approach to this work, including in particular Francesco Caruso, Paola Megna, and Luigi Silvano.

A generous fellowship from the National Endowment for the Humanities provided Cottrell the *otium* that enabled him to pursue this project. (Views, findings, conclusions, or recommendations expressed in this publication do not necessarily reflect those of the National Endowment for the Humanities.) A Renaissance Society of America travel grant to Venice enabled him to examine Poliziano's autograph manuscript of the *Centuria secunda* conserved in the Biblioteche della Fondazione Giorgio Cini. The Library, and especially the collections director Lucia Sardo, went far beyond professional courtesy by allowing him access to the manuscript despite the closure of the facilities for renovation. The staff generously created workspace for him among themselves in the midst of the disruption. A Houghton Library fellowship principally to examine Harvard University's two copies of the *Centuria prima* annotated by Poliziano was crucial. The Houghton staff provided every imaginable assistance. Cottrell also thanks John Monfasani for providing a photocopy of the difficult-to-find H. Katayama text. Heartfelt gratitude goes above all to the series

editor, James Hankins. Cottrell dedicates his portion of these volumes to his son Andy.

Dyck would like to thank James Hankins for his encouragement and his wife Janis for her support, to whom he dedicates his portion of these volumes.

NOTES

1. Reynolds, *Texts*, 322. (Full references to titles referred to in brief form in this Introduction and in the Notes to the Translation may be found in the Bibliography.)

2. Calderini had achieved great visibility in the world of scholarship by his innovative use of the printing press to disseminate his results. There are well over a hundred incunabular editions of Calderini's commentaries and other philological writings, far outnumbering those of Poliziano. See Campanelli, *Polemiche e filologia*.

3. Aware of the possible analogy, he speaks of "play[ing] Aristarchus" at II 50.4.

4. A certain self-identification with his Cyrenean predecessor is suggested by the remarks at I 80. He criticizes inadequate metrical knowledge of predecessors at *Cent. I* 39, 44, 46, 68, and 71, and offers a sensitive comment on poetic language at *I* 100.4. Those who read Italian can find an attractive general account of Poliziano's life and work in Orvieto, *Poliziano e l'ambiente Mediceo*; cf. also Bigi, *La cultura del Poliziano*.

5. For false inference from context, cf. II 4 (and as a general tendency of commentators, II 52); for free invention, I 10, 33, 38, 58, 75; II 5, 8, 13.

6. Cf. his remarks at II 6.

7. Cf. I Pref. 17 with note.

8. Poliziano seems to imply that Beroaldo took the idea from him; see I Epil. 8 with note.

9. See the justification at I Pref. 16. He produced these lists for *Century I* only; he would presumably have done so for *Century II* as well had he been able to see it through the press.

10. See I Pref. 1 and 21.

11. See on I Pref. 2.

12. Cf. Vasoli, "Il Poliziano maestro di dialettica."

13. Cf. on II 46, where Poliziano's marginalia allow us to see how the chapter took a new direction as his research unfolded.

14. Cf. Gaisser, *Catullus*, 70.

15. Cf., for example, on I 65 and II 48.

16. Cf. Grazzini, "Osservazioni," 173–74, comparing Poliziano's lectures on Juvenal in the academic year 1485–86, as recorded by students, with the treatment of corresponding passages in the *Miscellanea*.

17. He referred to these as his *collectanea*; see further Lo Monaco, "On the Prehistoria," 60 n. 54 with citations.

18. For example, II 57, a summary of the preceding; II 29, on the different senses of *naumachia* in Greek and Latin; 42, on the different form of the cross in antiquity and in modern usage; 47, on Cicero's use of *exsequi*; 57, on orthography: Milax vs. Smilax.

19. Notable examples: I 1 (Argyropoulos), 9 (Calderini), 77 (critics of attention to minutiae), 90 (on suitable critics); II 5 (Calderini and Barbaro).

20. Albeit this last example leads to an emendation of a passage of Pliny.

21. See on I 11, 58, 80, and II 31.

22. Cf. I 89, where he prefers Quintilian's text of Vergil over Servius's, since the former had access to the author's autograph copy.

23. Errors described as easy: I 50, *pasto* to *pastore*; I 61, *conium* to *aconitum*; II 14, *noster Cocles* to *Stercodes*. He shows awareness of the ease of corruption of *l* to *i* at I 53 in restoring *cerula* from *ceruia*. He is not explicit about how he arrived at *expernata* or *Neritidae*, but his reasoning can in both cases be reconstructed; cf. on I 73 and II 21.

24. Cf. I 58.

25. Cf. I 25 and II 1–2.

26. On this and on the general characteristics of Poliziano's innovations, cf. Grafton, "On the Scholarship."

27. For example, *I* 70: "If anyone should find a coin of Brutus engraved with an image of him and besides a skullcap and two small daggers, lest he toil for a long time trying to explain the reason and cause, let him read Book 47 of Dio's *Histories*."

28. Preface 1 (push to publish); *I* 19, 43, 58, 67, 72, 77, 85 (access to coins and other antiquities); repeated references to the library at San Marco that the Medici opened to the public, but also access to their private library (cf. Index s.v. Library of the Medici), including one at Fiesole (*II* 7.4). Lorenzo also provided special access to the codex of the Florentine *Pandects* (*I* 41) as well as to an old codex of Cicero's *Letters to Friends* (*I* 87.2) and recent acquisitions from Greece (*II* 31). He pays his patron the compliment of citing his poetry at *I* 11.

29. General eulogies: *I* Pref. 22, *I* Epil. 5–6; sacred studies (*I* 14, 94); access to his unpublished work (*I* 1.11, 4.2); Pico's access to Poliziano's unpublished work (*I* 68.3) spurs Poliziano to translate Callimachus' *Bath of Pallas* (*I* 80); philosophical studies (*I* 90).

30. Landino, *I* 77; Ficino, *I* Pref. 22, *I* Epil. 4; Argyropoulos, *I* Pref. 22, *I* Epil. 4, but critique at *I* 1.

31. Barbaro, *Castigationes Plinianae* (Rome: Eucharius Argentius Germanus, 1492–93); see the modern edition edited by G. Pozzi listed in the Bibliography.

32. *I* 90; *II* 5 (obituary notice); *II* 35 (conceding priority to Barbaro on grounds of publication); *II* 42 (supports a reading put forward by Barbaro, though he is in doubt about Barbaro's general interpretation of the passage); *II* 57 (polite disagreement).

33. See the list by Branca and Stocchi, "La Biblioteca Vaticana," 141 n. 1.

34. *I* Pref.; criticism of anonymous targets: see Index s.v. Valla, Giorgio, as well as note 36 below.

35. In order to develop his own style of philology, Poliziano needed to react against a predecessor; cf. Krautter, "Der 'grammaticus' Poliziano," 111–12. He similarly tests his mettle against his sometime teachers Argyropoulos at *I* 1 and Theodore Gaza at *I* 90–91.

36. *I* 9; *II* 4, 20; tacit criticism, *I* 67, 85; *II* 32.2, 34.7. At *II* 24 he remains neutral on Merula's proposal; at *II* 42 he finds Merula's minimalist approach "safer" (*sc.* than Barbaro's) but partly hackneyed and implicitly less interesting.

37. Krautter, "Angelo Poliziano als Kritiker," 318–22, concludes that Poliziano's claims of plagiarism against Beroaldo are justified in some cases.

38. Cf. *I* 9 and on the Epilogue.

39. Cf., for example, *I* 38 and 98.

40. He wrote to Jacopo Antiquari: "I point out Domizio to students as one would a pit to travellers" (*Epist.* 3.19.4 = *Letters,* ed. Butler [ITRL 21], 201).

41. Thus Barbaro criticizes only Poliziano with the name suppressed; cf. Barbaro, *Castigationes,* 1:cxv. For ancient precedent, cf., for example, Juvenal, or Cicero's criticisms of P. Clodius, on which cf. C. Steel, "Name and Shame? Invective against Clodius and Others in the Post-Exile Speeches," in *Cicero on the Attack: Invective and Subversion in the Orations and Beyond,* ed. J. Booth (Swansea: The Classical Press of Wales, 2007), 105–28.

42. *I* 19 is an elaborate argument designed to assert priority for an interpretation of Catullus 84 based on presentations at Florence and Verona; *I* 81 claims that he previously knew a reading in Propertius 4.3.21, in the meantime published by Beroaldo. He seems to have softened this posture somewhat, at least as regards Barbaro, at *II* 35.

43. Most notably, *I* Pref. 12–13; *I* Epil. 6.

44. Martelli, "La semantica," pursues the connections that bind together the seemingly disparate chapters of *Misc. II.*

45. Composition of *Misc. II* is dated from summer 1493 to Poliziano's death, September 29, 1494; cf. Branca, *Poliziano,* 86 n. 18. The bodies of Poliziano and Pico, both of whom died in the fall of 1494, were exhumed in 2007 and subjected to forensic investigation by a team led by Giorgio Gruppioni, professor of anthropology at Bologna, with the finding that both died of arsenic poisoning. Cf. "Medici writers exhumed in It-

aly," *BBC News:* http://news.bbc.co.uk/go/pr/fr/-/2/hi/europe/6920443
.stm (July 28, 2007); Malcolm Moore, "Medici philosopher's mystery
death is solved," *The Telegraph:* http://www.telegraph.co.uk/news/world
news/1577958/Medici-philosophers-mystery-death-is-solved.html (February 7, 2008).

46. Cf. Poliziano's famous letter on Lorenzo's death addressed to Jacopo
Antiquari: *Letters* 4.2, ed. Butler (ITRL 21), 226–51.

47. Cf. *II* 5 with notes.

48. These seem to reflect the steady diet of Aristotelian lectures Poliziano
offered at the *Studio* from 1490 to 1494; cf. Maïer, *Ange Politien,* 432–35.

49. Pozzi, in Barbaro, *Castigationes* 1:cxiii, detects a more measured polemical tone in *Misc. II,* which he attributes to Barbaro's influence.

50. The one comparable phenomenon in *Misc. I* is the note in the *Emendationes* apropos of chapter 79 that further study may be required to
clarify the apparent contradiction of text and coinage.

51. See on *I* 23 and the respect accorded to the Vatican Vergil (R) on the
basis of its being written in rustic capitals (*I* 71, 77); similarly, *I* 41 apropos of the Florentine *Pandects.*

52. Cf. on *I* 23.

53. They did, however, prompt the *Emendationes* inserted in front of the
first edition.

54. See further on *I* 38.

55. Albeit he was prepared to accept that Cicero had misremembered
another Homeric passage at *I* 53.

56. See, for example, Biondo Flavio, *Rome Illuminated,* ed. and trans. Jef-
frey A. White, 2 vols., I Tatti Renaissance Library 20 and 75 (Cambridge, MA: Harvard University Press, 2005–16); idem, *Rome in Triumph,*
ed. and trans. F. Muecke, vol. 1, I Tatti Renaissance Library 74 (Cambridge, MA: Harvard University Press, 2016); F. Muecke and M. Campanelli, eds., *The Invention of Rome: Biondo Flavio's* Roma triumphans *and
Its Worlds* (Geneva: Droz, 2017).

57. For the controversy over the date of the implementation of Caesar's decree (44 vs. 43), cf. Maximilian Becker, "*Suntoque aediles curatores urbis . . .*" (Stuttgart: Steiner, 2017), 270.

58. Cf. *I* 58.8 with note.

59. Cf. *I* 48, contradictory identifications of a visitor to Apelles's workshop in Greek and Latin sources; *I* 79, an apparent conflict of numismatic and literary evidence finally left unresolved (in Poliziano's *Emendationes*).

60. Cf. *I* 1 and 90–91.

61. Cf. Krautter, "Angelo Poliziano als Kritiker," 322, 324–25.

62. For example, *I* 17, 20, 26, 32, 34, 46, 68, 87, 97; *II* 7, 8, 35, 36, 43. Restoring Greek quotations in Latin manuscripts was, however, a preoccupation that went back to the circle of Salutati and Chrysoloras around the turn of the fifteenth century.

63. For example, *I* 29, 69; *II* 10.

64. For example, *I* 10, 11, 13, 52, 83; *II* 3, 4, 6, 24, 57, 59.

65. *I* 41 (status as archetype), 77, 82, 93; *II* 8.

66. See the entries in the Index s.v. Library for evidence of Poliziano's access to collections and diligence in exploiting their contents.

67. *I* 5, 25, 31, 34, 44, 56, 66, 68, 75, 81, 82, 87; *II* 1–2, 14 (though Piero Vettori receives credit in modern editions), 26 (Gelenus receives credit), 35, 36, 49; cf. also *I* 69, where he defended the reading (*Oarion*) that maintains its place in current editions.

68. He makes it clear, for instance, that one of the reference works available at the time, the lexicon of the Neapolitan humanist Giuniano Maio, did not meet his standards (cf. on *I* 3).

69. Sebastiano Timpanaro, *The Genesis of Lachmann's Method* (Chicago: University of Chicago Press, 2005), 48, observes that "Poliziano . . . has the beginnings of a historical understanding of manuscript traditions."

ANGELI POLITIANI
MISCELLANEORUM CENTURIA
PRIMA

ANGELO POLIZIANO
FIRST CENTURY OF THE
MISCELLANIES

Ad Laurentium Medicem Praefatio

1   Cum tibi superioribus diebus, Laurenti Medices, nostra haec
Miscellanea inter equitandum recitaremus, delectatus arbitror novi-
tate ipsa rerum et varietate non illepida lectionis, hortari coepisti
nos ut unam saltem ex eis centuriam (nam centenis libri singuli
capitibus explicantur) publicaremus. Quod nunc utique simul auctoritate tua, qua maior nobis quidem nulla in terris est, simul ratione adducti facimus, quoniam nostra ista iam nonnulli vel cum
pulvisculo converrunt, sic ut aliis pridem sibique nostrorum titulo
laborum nimis placeant. Quanquam scimus invidia⟨m⟩ magna⟨m⟩[1]
fore hos libros et multum sermonis subituros, ut qui de magni
nominis auctoribus libere pronuntient. Sed non id nostrum exemplum. Nam scriptores ferme omnes sic suas tuentur partis ut alie-
nas oppugnent ac laudis occasionem plerunque de aliorum erratis
petant. Tum saepe a tenuioribus et gregariis velutique postremae
notae, qualis ego vel Cluvienus, etiam proceres illi (ut ita dixerim)
et antesignani quidam litterarum sugillantur.

2   Vetus est autem dictum: 'Conscientia mille testes.' Scit illa prorsus nihil hic odio datum, nihil stomacho, candide omnia et simpliciter, nihil aut insectanter aut malevole, nihil oblatrandi studio,
nihil ostentandi voto protulimus, animoque semper ad probandum
(si liceret) quam ad improbandum propensiore fuimus. Neque videlicet strophis aut cuniculis, sed libero examine, libera veritatis
fronte rem gessimus. Ac non id quaesivimus, ut aliquam doctis
hominibus veluti labeculam aspergeremus, sed id cavimus potius,

Preface to Lorenzo de' Medici

As I was reading these *Miscellanies*[1] of mine aloud to you, Lorenzo 1
de' Medici, some time ago while we were out riding, you were delighted, I think, at the very novelty of their content and the
charming variety of the text, and you began to urge me to publish
at least one "century" of them (for the individual books are laid out
in one hundred chapters each). I am now doing so without fail,
prompted by your authority (than which, as far as I am concerned,
there is none greater on earth) and also for the reason that some
individuals are already sweeping up all my material down to the
last particle, with the result that for some time now they have been
gratifying themselves and others all too much by laying claim to
my own toils. And yet we know that these writings will be subject
to tremendous envy and a lot of talk in that they openly hold forth
on famous authors. But I do not follow this model. For almost all
writers defend their own standpoints by attacking those of others
and often seek an opportunity for praise through others' errors.
Then again, it is often the case that those "generals" (so to speak)
and certain "battalion leaders" of literature are beaten back by insignificant common soldiers, those of the least fame, "such as Cluvienus and I."[2]

    There is an old saying: "Conscience is a thousand witnesses."[3] 2
My conscience knows that I have offered up absolutely nothing
herein out of hatred, nothing out of pique, with everything said
openly and straightforwardly, nothing with rancor or ill will, and
nothing out of zeal for ranting, nothing from a wish to show off;
and my intention was always more inclined toward proving (if I
could) than disapproving. Nor obviously have I acted by tricks or
deceit but with free inquiry and truthful candor. Nor have I
sought to cast the slightest of aspersions upon learned men, but

ne sub illorum auctoritate studiosorum fides periclitaretur. Denique in eos potissimum cuneus hic ex professo directus, in eos hic
aries ex destinato temperatus, qui contra veri faciem pro vernaculo
quidem sibi sed imaginario tamen sensu frontem durant, eos acie
stili maxime compungimus qui stilum vertere, hoc est qui sua errata dispungere, non didicerunt.

3   At[2] inordinatam istam et confusaneam quasi silvam aut farragi-
nem perhiberi, quia non tractim et continenter sed saltuatim scri-
bimus et vellicatim, tantum abest uti doleamus, ut etiam titulum
non sane alium quam *Miscellaneorum* exquisiverimus, in quis[3]
Graecum tamen Helianum, Latinum sequimur Gellium, quorum
utriusque libri varietate sunt quam ordine blandiores. Quanquam
ne Clementis quidem Alexandrini commentaria[4] quae *Stromatis*,[5]
quasi stragula picta dixeris, inscribebantur alium profecto nobis
titulum nisi varietatis istius insinuabant. Etenim de Aristoxeni
taceo commentariis, quos pari ferme titulo citat eo volumine Porphyrius quod in *Harmonica* Ptolemaei composuit. Denique si va-
rietas ipsa, fastidii expultrix et lectionis irritatrix, in *Miscellaneis*
culpabitur, una opera, reprehendi rerum quoque natura poterit,
cuius me quidem profiteor tali disparilitate discipulum.

4   Quod si ad omnem se minutiem demittunt, hoc vero apud Latinos exemplo etiam Caesaris, Varronis, Messalae, Ciceronis, Plini,
Quintiliani, aliorumque similium facere licet, quos aemulantibus
et errare honestum. Quare quod istos veluti patricios decuit, etiam
me quasi minorum gentium non dedeceat. Par adeo celebritas nominum, vel Graeca inserit, vel ex commodo interpretatur, idque
nunc ad sensum, nunc ad verbum, quod hic utrunque.

rather I took care that the trust of the students under their authority not be put at risk.[4] Finally, this phalanx has been overtly drawn up, this battering ram has intentionally been hardened for those who steel themselves against the face of truth on behalf of their own homegrown but nonetheless fanciful thinking,[5] I especially prick those persons with the point of my stylus who have not learned "to reverse their stylus," that is, to delete their own errors.[6]

I am so far from regretting that my work is called disordered   3
and jumbled like a forest or a mishmash, since I do not write in a smooth and even style but jump about here and there, that I have even chosen no other title than *Miscellanies*, for which I follow the Greek Aelian, and the Latin Gellius, both of whose books are the more enticing because of their variety rather than their orderliness.[7] And yet not even the books of Clement of Alexandria, which were entitled *Stromateis*, as if to say an embroidered coverlet, suggested to us any other claim than variety,[8] not to mention the books of Aristoxenus,[9] which Porphyry cites by virtually the same title in the volume he composed on Ptolemy's *Harmonics*.[10] Finally, if mere variety — that very feature that expels repugnance and stimulates reading — is to be found at fault in my *Miscellanies*, a single work, then the blame must lie with nature, whose student, by such variety, I profess myself to be.

Yet if these essays descend to minutiae, that is certainly allowed   4
among Latin writers by the precedent of Caesar, Varro, Messalla, Cicero, Pliny, Quintilian, and others like them; for those emulating these men, even to err is honorable.[11] Hence what was appropriate for those patricians, so to speak, would not be disgraceful for me either, being, as it were, from the lesser families.[12] The distinction of the words is the same whether one cites them in Greek or translates them for convenience, sometimes according to the sense, sometimes verbatim, both of which occur here.

5   Iam si cui parum quaepiam enucleata fortasse etiam nimis dura obscuraque videbuntur, certe is nec ingenio satis vegeto nec eruditione solida fidelique fuerit. Sicubi barbara quaedam et obsoleta deprehendentur, ea vero de industria dispersimus, etiam ut barbaris et ineruditis placeremus et fieret liber corrasa undique gratiola vendibilior. Si qui remotiora dicent hic inveniri vocabula quam ut sumpta credantur de medio, nae isti arbitror sententiam suam mutabunt cum adusque medium litteraturae promoverint. Nec enim desunt quibus etiam (ut ait M. Tullius) alabastrus[6] unguenti plena putere videatur.

6   Tum in hoc genus scriptionibus, quae non se populo venditant sed paucis modo parantur, usus istiusmodi reconditae supellectilis, praesertim verecundus, minime improbatur a bonis. Nec enim renovare sit probrum quae iam pene exoleverunt, si modo haec ipsa non vetustescere adhuc, sed veterascere de integro possint. Si quem nonnulla interim offendent eloquendi diverticula minus fortasse homini nota qui decem tantum Ciceronis paginas, nihil praeterea, lectitaverit, utique ab hoc ego ad eruditos provoco, praecipue credo laudaturos quae ab ipso improbabuntur. Nihil autem forsan intolerabilius quam ut de te sententiam ferat indoctus qui tamen sibi ipse doctissimus videatur. Si quis, ubi quid refellitur, multarum vel auctoritatum vel rationum moles desiderat, at victoriam sciat illic a nobis, non victoriae quaeri satietatem.

7   Si longiuscula capita alia, breviuscula rursus alia putabuntur, credamus hanc quoque esse legem novi operis, ut aequale habeat nihil, nusquam sibi sit par, semper dissimilitudine claudicet, unamque istam regulam tueatur, ne quid ad regulam, ne quid ad

If some points strike anyone as having been inadequately ex-   5
plained, or perhaps too difficult to understand or too obscure,
then that person does not have a quick enough mind or a sound
and reliable education. If ever you come across any barbarous or
obsolete usages, I deliberately sprinkled them in, so that my book
might be pleasing even to the uncultured and unlearned and more
marketable, its charms raked together from diverse sources. If
some say they find the vocabulary herein remote rather than
drawn from the common stock, they will change their minds, I
think, when they have advanced significantly through the corpus
of literature.[13] For there is no shortage of people to whom (as
Marcus Tullius [Cicero] says[14]) a perfume bottle full of ointment
seems putrid.

So then, in writings of this genre—which are not offered up for   6
sale to the masses but prepared for only the few—the use of this
sort of recherché furniture, especially in moderation, is counte-
nanced by good writers. For it would be a shame not to restore
those words that have now become nearly obsolete, provided that
they do not linger in decrepitude but can achieve full ripeness of
age.[15] If in the meantime some little deviations of style should of-
fend anyone, deviations perhaps not familiar to someone whose
reading was limited to only ten pages of Cicero and nothing beyond that, then certainly I appeal from him to the learned, who, I
believe, are bound to praise the very points that are condemned by
the other. But perhaps nothing is more intolerable than that an
unlearned man, who nonetheless considers himself the epitome of
learning, should pass judgment on you.[16] If, when a claim is refuted, anyone requires either a ton of sources or reasons, let him
know that I seek victory, not a glut of victory.

And if some chapters seem overlong, others too short, let us   7
think of this as the principle for the new study, that it have nothing equal, no homogeneity, that it be ever lopsided in its disparity,
and that it observe this single rule, namely, that it not be submit-

perpendiculum libellamque revocet. Si liberior stilus insolentis ex⟨is⟩timabitur[7] naturae, forsan benignior interpres simplicitati potius tribuet, quae nec ingenuos dedecet. Sicubi porro consuetudo refragabitur, at veritas, quae nugas non facit, aut veritatis vicaria consuetudo melior patrocinabitur. Nam et sumptum consuetudine dicitur quod adversus auctoritatem sit receptum, et error saepe consuetudinis obiectatur a doctis. Tum pulchre sic ait quidam: 'Consuetudo sine veritate vetustas erroris est.'

8   Denique si paucula respersimus interim scrupulosa et anxia, quodque verius subacida, vel ex philosophia, cuius iam pridem sumus candidati, vel ex orbe illo disciplinarum quae studio sapientiae famulantur, at ea stomachum tamen lectoris praedulcibus marcentem recreabunt fortassis et exacuent. Nam quo haec omnia grata sui vice conspirent et quodam velut antitheto foederentur, pene de calcaria (quod dicitur) in carbonariam decucurrimus, et id operam dedimus, ut alternatim deinceps inter se contraria quoque subsequerentur, quae nos querelae istiusmodi eximerent. Nec enim defieri apud nos etiam patimur quae sint amoena magis et oblectatoria, ne dixerim illecebrosa, quam vel utilia vel necessaria, siquidem est (ut ait Varro) aliud homini, aliud humanitati satis, etiamque citra emolumentum speciosa interim petuntur non hercle minus quam sine specie compendium.

9   Ergo ut agrestes illos et hircosos quaedam ex his impolita et rudia delectabunt, exasceataque magis quam dedolata, nec modo limam sed nec runcinas experta nec scobinas, ita e diverso vermiculata interim dictio et tessellis pluricoloribus variegata delicatiores hos capiet volsos et pumicatos, ne conflatis utrinque

ted to any rule, perpendicularity, and the plumb line. If an unrestrained pen is taken as a mark of arrogance, perhaps a friendlier critic will attribute it rather to simplicity, which does not disgrace ingenuous writers. Further, if usage might sometimes be thwarted, truth — which is no joking matter — or else, truth's proxy, better usage, will supply the defense.[17] For what has been received contrary to authority is said to have been adopted by usage, and an error of usage is often objected to by the learned. Besides, it has been elegantly said, "Custom apart from truth is the lineage of error."[18]

Finally, if I have sprinkled about here and there a few troublesome and meticulous points, or more precisely ones that are half-sour, whether from philosophy, for knowledge of which I have for a long time now been striving,[19] or from that circle of disciplines that serve the pursuit of wisdom,[20] then those savors will perhaps revive and sharpen the appetite of a reader jaded by cloying treats.[21] For in order that all those pleasant things combine on their own and be bound together as if by some converse force, I virtually went from the frying pan straight into the fire (as the saying goes[22]) and have taken care that they move continuously back and forth between opposites, which should exempt me from a complaint of this sort. Nor do I let my writing go without those elements that are more charming and delightful, not to say alluring, than they are either useful or necessary, since (as Varro says[23]) one thing is adequate for the individual, another for all humanity, and since we seek fair appearance without regard to usefulness, no less, by God, than we seek utility without beauty.

Therefore, just as certain unpolished and raw elements from these chapters, ones that are more chopped than hewn and that lack not only the file but the plane or the rasp,[24] will delight shaggy country bumpkins, so, contrariwise, will a style that is wavy and variegated with parti-colored little tiles captivate fastidious readers, who are depilated and smoothed with pumice,[25] lest,

vocibus, et aequabili vel plausu vel sibilo, aut ad caelum efferar aut
ad humum deiciar. Mediis autem inter hos et neutro notandis
⟨qui⟩[8] quasi quidam diversorum cinnus (ut ait Cicero) satisfaciet,
non uno aliquo excellens et omnium tamen particeps. Nec enim
gustus idem omnibus, sed suum palatum cuique. Tum, credo, et
expuent in convivio quidam pro fastidioso et vesco quod mox in
culina pro suavi liguriant et opimo.

10   Nos ista certe non foro et curiae, sed cubiculo et scholae paravi-
mus, eoque studuimus, nescio an et praestiterimus, ut siquae hic
essent, omnino faciles essent et simplices munditiae, non operosa
et pigmentata lenocinia, color nitorque verus et ingenuus, non
ascitus et ex arcula, congruens habitus et expeditus, non onerosus
et laciniosus.

11   Postremo cuicuimodi exeant, quoquo modo haec accipiantur,
minime profecto recusamus (sed nec opinor evademus) communem illam scribentium fortem male audiendi, sit modo ita
cordi lectoribus. Quin immo isti aleae caput obiectamus, neque
patrocinium respicimus, quod ultro nobis ademimus censura. De-
cernaturque potius in nos, traducamur, vexemur quam non litterarum publica fraus, quarum nobis est honor propriis utilitatibus
antiquior, etiam nostro aliquo vel famae vel otii dispendio redima-
tur. Nam quo ista, quaeso, studiorum communium professio, si
iam ventum ad haec usque est, ut quod officium studiis universi
debemus, cessare omne tamen suspitione degeneri patiamur? Quo
pacto vel durare ultra vel esse iam poterit honestarum litterarum
sinceritas, soluta penitus censura, dum sic aeque omnes invidiam
perhorrescimus? Quanquam (quod ad me attinet) utinam labori
meo non contemptus potius quam invidia debeatur, illud enim

with an outcry coming from both sides, and equal applause or hissing, I either be extolled to the heavens or cast down to the ground. But he will give satisfaction to those who are intermediate between the two and are to be condemned by neither, who, like a mixed drink (as Cicero says[26]), does not excel in some one area but has a share in all. For not everyone will have the same taste, but each will have his own palate. So too, I believe, some folks at a banquet spit out as disgusting and insipid what those back in the kitchen readily lick up as appealing and tasty.

I have, at any rate, not prepared these miscellanies for the pub- 10 lic square and senate house but for the private study and the class-room, and my aim has been—I am unsure whether I have also achieved it—that if an essay is included herein, it will be quite easy to follow and straightforward in its elegance,[27] not painstak-ingly tarted up with rouge, its hue and splendor true and natural, not alien and drawn from a powder box, but dressed appropriately and unencumbered, not ponderous and bundled up.

Finally, in whatever form these chapters may depart and how- 11 ever they may be received, in no way do I shun (nor, I think, will I evade) that fate common to writers of being ill spoken of, if that be the readers' wish. On the contrary, I am baring my neck to just such a risk, and I am not looking to patronage, from which I have voluntarily removed myself by means of criticism. Let me be con-demned, let me be exposed to scorn, let me be harassed, rather than that public harm befall literature—the honor of which has for me priority over any personal advantages—even at the cost of some reputation or leisure of my own. For what good is it, I ask, to pursue general studies professionally if we have already reached the point where we allow the obligation we all owe to such studies to lapse because of an unworthy suspicion?[28] How, in the face of wholly unrestrained criticism, will the integrity of belles lettres be able to endure into the future or exist in the present while we all equally shudder in fear of envy? And yet, for my part, may my

prope in votis est, si modo, quod ait Livius, invidia velut ignis alta petit.

12   Quin agitedum studiorum cultores optimi, pro se quisque alacres, gramen hoc inexpugnabile, quo bonae fruges humanitatis praefocantur, avellite, subnascentesque sacris stirpibus quasi pernitiosissimas hederas et omnem earum sucum lapsibus erraticis exsorbentes abrumpite penitus et detruncate. Non desunt interpolatores veritatis, ne desint quoque redintegratores, existat vindex aliquis, rogo, et patronus periclitantium disciplinarum. Nam ego ut unus e medio quid mihi liberum sit utique experiar. Faciam necne operaepretium post videro. Quorsum tamen fluxerit aut quocunque res ceciderit, aequi boni faciam, planeque malignitatum omnium et obtrectationum venena non devorabo modo sed (quo sum stomacho) etiam concoquam, certus veritatis hunc esse quasi genium, simul atque in publicum appareat, ut odiosa inimicaque sit vulgo.

13   Conniveant igitur alii licet, et dicere verum mussent, ego unus profecto (quidquid erit) non dissimulabo iudicium, non supprimam quae sensero, non indulgebo iam talibus patientiam, sed vel huic libello meo, saltem semilibere, sic insusurrabo: 'Vidi, vidi ipse, libelle, cotidieque video, multa in litteris fieri capitalia: compilari subdole aliena, confingi ad libidinem quae cui commodum, ascribi etiam idoneis quae nec agnoscant, allegari qui non extent auctores, citari quin etiam pro vetustis nullibi comparentis codices, compleri libros omnes operosissimis vanitatibus, falsa pro veris, ascita pro nativis, novicia pro vernaculis, supponi, pollui, adulterari, oblini, incrustari, distorqueri, confundi, praecipitari, interverti

toils not earn greater scorn than envy, for that is my hope, given that, as Livy says, envy, like a fire, attacks the heights.[29]

But come, you leaders in the pursuit of [literary] studies, each one keen on his own behalf, pluck out this weed, which resists extirpation but is strangling the good fruits of humanity, and completely rip it out and lop it off as it sprouts up covertly like ivy that destroys sacred plants and with its wandering tendrils drains all their sap. Those who pervert the truth are not in short supply, but let there also be a supply of those who would revive it; let some champion arise, I pray, and defender of the imperiled disciplines. For as a member of the public, I will at least test what is open to me. I will decide later whether it is worth my while to act or not. But wherever this leads or however the matter turns out, I shall bear it calmly, and not only will I devour the venom of all malicious persons and faultfinders, but will also (insofar as I can stomach it) digest it, convinced that this is, as it were, the essential nature of truth, that as soon as it appears in public, it is hateful and antagonistic to the masses. 12

Though others may be complicit or hesitate to speak the truth, I alone (whatever may happen) will assuredly not cloak my judgment, will not suppress what I think, will no longer bestow patience on such persons, but I will whisper the following, at least semi-freely, to this little book of mine:[30] "I have seen, I have seen with my own eyes, my little book,[31] and every day I continue to see that many capital crimes are being committed in literature: others' works are being plagiarized on the sly, and things are being capriciously invented to suit a man's convenience;[32] things are ascribed to good authors that they do not recognize; nonextant authors are cited. What is more, codices that exist nowhere are cited as old ones;[33] all books are filled with highly elaborate deceits, falsehoods are substituted for truths, foreign for native, the fashionable for the tried and true. Everything is fraudulently introduced, polluted, adulterated, defiled, papered over, distorted, 13

omnia, nulla fide, nullo nec pudore nec iudicio, quodque his omnibus pestilentius, occasione quoque recentis artificii, quamlibet stolidissimas opiniones in mille voluminum traduces momento propagari.'

14   Postremo (ut semel dicam) etiam nunc multos auriculas habere asini. Dicat hic aliquis: Quid tu autem? Fateor equidem, possum falli ut humanus. Sed neminem profecto sciens fallo, et ut mendacium fortasse dico, sic certe non mentior. '"Tum egomet mi ignosco," Maevius inquit.' Immo autem (extra iocum) nec egomet mi ignosco, et si quid indoctius incautiusque protulero, refutari a quovis cupio, refutaturus ipse me, si fuero admonitus. Non enim sic me perverse amo, ut errare alios malim quam innotescere quod errem.

15   Sed ex eorum sum numero et ipse, qui proficiendo scribunt et scribendo proficiunt, ac de isto quidem fors viderit. Illud verissimum, si domi commentarios istos diutius atque in manibus habuissem,[9] et regustare interim ex intervallo licuisset, longe instructiores fuisse eos, locupletiores, adminiculatiores predituros. Videlicet hoc illud est praecipue studiorum genus, quod vigiliis augescat, ut cui subinde ceu fluminibus ex decursu, sic accedit ex lectione minutatim quo fiat uberius. Tum incondita nunc quoque pleraque, ineliquata, indiscussa, non rotunda, non tornata adhuc, sed quae aurem prorsus praeterierint, utpote restrictim cogitata, et ex tempore potius quam a cura, quanquam ex abundanti pene stili negotium curat[10] et elocutionem concinnat, quem cana et veritas et fides praecipue sollicitat.

confounded, hurled down, and purloined, void of good faith, shame, or judgment.[34] And what is more noxious than all these is that by the chance of a recent invention,[35] you can in an instant convert opinions, however stupid, into a thousand books for distribution."

Finally (to say it once and for all), many people still have the ears of an ass.[36] At this point, someone may say, "But what about you?" I admit, of course, that since I am human, I can make a mistake. But I do not intentionally deceive anyone, and though I may say something false, I certainly do not lie. "Then 'I excuse myself,' Maevius says."[37] To the contrary, all joking aside, it is not the case that I excuse myself; rather, if I were to put forward something ignorant or reckless, I want anyone to refute me; I would refute myself if someone were to point out my mistake. For I am not so perversely in love with myself that I would prefer that others err rather than for it to become known that I err.

But I count myself among those who write by making progress and make progress by writing, and fortune will take care of that. But truth be told, if I had had these rough drafts in hand for a longer time at home, and if I had been able to come back to them at an interval, they would be published in a far better equipped, fuller, and better supported form.[38] This is the special mode of the studies: it grows through working long into the night; just as rivers are constantly augmented from a downward course, so each of these studies is increased bit by bit through reading, so that it becomes richer. So then, many of these chapters are even now in disarray, unclear, ill-considered, unpolished, and not yet well-crafted, but they have gone right past the ear, seeing that they are barely thought through, and have been conceived on the spur of the moment rather than carefully[39] — albeit a writer particularly stirred by hoary truth and reliability more than takes care of the business of writing and constructs a fine discourse.

14

15

16   Enimvero ne putent homines maleferiati nos ista, quaeque sunt, de faece hausisse neque grammaticorum transilivisse[11] lineas, Pliniano statim exemplo nomina praetexuimus auctorum, sed honestorum veterumque dumtaxat, unde ius ista sumunt et a quibus versuram fecimus, nec autem quos alii tantum citaverint, ipsorum opera temporibus interciderint, sed quorum nosmet ipsi thesauros tractavimus, quorum sumus per litteras peregrinati, quanquam et vetustas codicum, et nomismatum fides et in aes aut in marmore incisae antiquitates, quae tu nobis, Laurenti, suppeditasti, plurimum etiam praeter librorum varietatem, nostris commentationibus suffragantur.

17   Ut autem vel exemplo doceremus circulatorum praestigias et imposturas omnis esse tollendas, refrenandamque adeo quorumpiam lasciviam, quae iam sicuti cancer late serpit, inaniter de praescripto et licenter egrediendi, nusquam aliquando veteris scripturae testimonium citavimus, ne quid adscripticium, neve quid usquam superducticium praevaleret, quin sua quodque facie repraesentaverimus, et eas apposuerimus notas, unde exquiri penitus usque a stirpe possit auctoritas. Atque ut muneris huius nostri nullae prorsus appendices desiderentur, etiam capita ipsa rerum titulis inclusa brevissimis, sed in quis maior quam pro numero utilitas, concenturiavimus, et ceu brevibus caeris[12] ingentes summas calculatorum more collegimus, quo negligentiae delicati lectoris ipsi potissimum subscriberemus. Proinde sicuti sub Aiacis clipeo Teucer Homericus, ita nos utique sub umbra tui nominis latitantes, centuriatim dabimus in barbaros impressionem. Ita editione subinde aliqua vel aequis vel iniquis mos geretur. Et quadam pensante vice, sicut illis quod osculentur, ita his abunde supparabimus quod mordeant.

But truly, lest idlers fancy that I have drawn my work, whatever   16
it be, from the dregs, and that I have leaped across the bounds of
grammarians, I have provided — right away, following Pliny's example[40] — the names of authors, but only respected and ancient
ones, from whom my work derives its license and from whom I
have borrowed. I have not, however, used the names of authors
who have only been cited by others, whereas their works have been
lost to the ages, but those whose treasures I have personally han-
dled and through whose writings I have roamed, albeit ancient
codices and the reliable record of coins and inscriptions carved in
bronze or marble, which you have supplied to us, Lorenzo, have
vastly supported my writings even besides the variety of books.[41]

But to show by example that all the deceptions and tricks of the   17
hucksters must be eliminated and the wanton desire of certain individuals to depart pointlessly and audaciously from the rule must
be checked, which is already creeping far and wide, like a crab, I
have never cited the testimony of an ancient writing, lest something forged or spurious gain currency, unless I presented each one
in its own form and have appended the marks by which its authority can be rigorously traced all the way back to its origin.[42] And so
that no appendages might be felt to be missing from this work of
ours, we gathered the chapters themselves, which were comprised
under very brief titles, in "centuries" — though here the usefulness
is disproportionate to the number[43] — and, in the manner of an
accountant, I collected huge totals as if on short wax tablets, so
that I could best support the carelessness of the pampered reader.
In the same way that Homer's Teucer hid under Ajax's shield,[44] so
I, lying hidden beneath the shadow of your[45] name, will offer attack against the barbarians century by century. Critics, whether
favorable or otherwise, will thus be humored by some immediate
publication.[46] Just as we shall supply in abundance to the one
group something to cherish, so to the other something to carp at,
by a certain balancing exchange.

18   Mordebunt autem, puto, nostra vel rabiosuli quidam, quos eleganter Cato vitilitigatores appellat, isto potissimum litigandi vitio
veluti morbo laborantes, cerebrosa gens et irritabilis, qui sine
causa, sine discrimine, clausisque (quod aiunt) oculis, quodcunque
nomen adlatrant. Vel qui rursus, advocatione mercennaria vena-
lique sententia, cuicunque semel auctorati atque addicti quasique
dediti mancipio sint, eundem tueri pugnaciter pertinaciterque quo
iure quaque iniuria obstinaverunt. Vel iactanticuli illi et nugivendi,
pleni tumida sed et fatua coniectura, qui seque et sua dumtaxat
etiam sine rivalibus adamant, sibi favent, alios obtrectant. Vel postremo lucifugi quidam veritatis et (ut planius dixerim) blattarii
litteratores, qui defluentibus oculis vereque noctuinis, non diem
tantum sereniorem, sed nec umbram sublustrem satis ferunt. Nam
de illis dubitat nemo quos livoris tinea comest, quos rubigo subro-
dit invidiae, qui gloriam alterius suam penam, felicitatem alterius
suam carnificinam faciunt, qui profectu contabescunt alieno, quos
aegrescens prosperis malevolentia ceu tortor intestinus iugiter ex-
cruciat.

19   Sed et censores item pulpitarii (nec autem de doctis bonisque
nunc agimus) solent plerunque fodicare nos et studiis obstrepere
istis. Etenim pleni ieiunitatis litteras humanioris apud insciam
plebeculam, pene dixerim sollemniter,[13] buccis concrepantibus in-
famant et crassa rusticitate feroculi, quam solam (quod et Hieronymus ait) pro sanctitate habent, sic in eas et earum studiosos
ampullosis proclamationibus infrendentes inspumantesque desae-
viunt, ut facile se declarent etiam Graecos illos improbare et pene
odisse, vere sanctas animas, Basilium, Chrysostomum, Gregorios,

But our *Miscellanies* will, I think, be carped at by those half-   18
crazy persons whom Cato finely calls "captious critics,"[47] who suffer, as if from a disease, from the vice of litigiousness, a hotheaded
and excitable sort, who, for no reason and with no discrimination,
and with (as they say) "their eyes shut,"[48] rail against every detail.
On the other hand, there are those critics whose advocacy is for
sale and whose opinion can be bought and who belligerently and
doggedly persist in defending, through thick and thin, the person
by whom they have been bought and to whom they are bound
over as if by a formal act of property conveyance. Or there are also
petty boasters and self-promoters, full of puffed up and silly conjecture, who highly esteem only themselves and their own works as
unrivaled, who are fans of themselves while disparaging others.[49]
Or finally, there are certain school teachers who flee the light of
truth and (to put it bluntly) remain in the shadows, who, with
eyes that are streaming and in fact light sensitive, can abide neither
the bright light of day nor even the dimly lit twilight. But no one
is in doubt about those who are consumed by the worm of envy
and gnawed at by the blight of jealousy, who turn someone else's
glory into their own punishment, another's joy into their own torture, who waste away at another's progress, whom festering ill will
at others' successes constantly racks like an internal tormentor.[50]

Likewise, critics in the pulpit (though I am not referring here to   19
the learned and good ones) are wont to ridicule us at length and
raise a din against these studies. Indeed, brimming with their own
arid style, they decry humane letters before the ignorant rabble
with, I might almost say, solemnity, ferocious with their noisy
mouths[51] and gross boorishness, which alone (as Jerome also
says[52]) they consider holiness; with their bombastic proclamations
they so rage at humane studies and those engaged in them, gnash-
ing their teeth and foaming at the mouth, that they make no
bones about declaring that they even disapprove and practically
loathe the famous Greeks, truly sacred souls, Basil, Chrysostom,

etiam Latinos, Cyprianum, Ambrosium, Augustinum, Hieronymumque ipsum, et alios id genus nostrae religionis antistites, gentium linguarumque omnium disciplinis, velut opibus Aegyptiorum suffarcinatos. Quo mihi etiam videtur admirabilior deliciae tuae Marianus hic Genazanensis, nec in theologia cuiquam secundus et omnium quos in ecclesia contionantes audivimus non prudentissimus modo sed et facundissimus, cuius neque suspecta populis ad bonam frugem tendentibus eloquentia, quoniam vitae incredibili severitate commendatur, nec e diverso tristis aut reformidabilis austeritas, quoniam poetica delenimenta, pulchramque istam litterarum varietatem, nitorem, delicias, non aspernatur. Ut igitur lana purpuram bona fide potura certis prius inficitur medicamentis, ita litteris, arbitror, doctrinisque talibus excoli animos (quod ait in *Hortensio* Cicero) et ad sapientiam excipiendam imbui praepararique decet.

20   Atqui non tamen ob istos pigebit aut exigere stilo quidquid hoc nostrarum lucubrationum est aut experiri quid concedatur in illos qui fraudes in litterarum negotio concipiunt capitales. Nam et ego Philoxeno ignosco, sicuti Cicero idem ad Atticum scribens, redire in carcerem quam mancipare iudicium praeoptanti, maxime si non praesenti seculo sed quasi aeternitati (prout etiam dictum a Thucydide) servire scriptores convenit. Eoque libri, puto, ipsi monumenta vocantur, quod ad memoriam magis posteritatis incorruptius iudicaturae quam ad ineptam praesentis temporis gratiolam spectare debent.

21   Ergo ut quam maxime (si licebit) haec non extinguatur solum, sed etiam opprimatur improbitas effuse omnia depravantium nec abeat in exemplum trita et prostituta frons atque oris tanta duritia, iam nunc centurias sequentis pro suscepto (arbitror) salutari

and the Gregories, and even the Latins, Cyprian, Ambrose, Augustine, and Jerome himself, and others of that sort—the champions of our religion, stuffed with the disciplines of the heathen and all their languages, as if with the riches of the Egyptians. For this reason your favorite, Mariano of Genzano, seems to me the more remarkable, second to none in theology, and among all those whom I have heard giving sermons in the church, not only the wisest but also the most eloquent. Neither does his eloquence rouse suspicion among people inclined toward uprightness, since he is recommended by the unbelievable severity of his life, nor yet is there a gloomy or dreadful austerity about him, since he does not disdain poetic allurements, literature's attractive variety, elegance, and charms.[53] Therefore, just as wool will reliably accept purple dye if it is first treated with specific chemicals, so too is it appropriate, I think, for minds to be cultivated through such literature and teachings (as Cicero says in his *Hortensius*[54]) and to be steeped in them and prepared to accept wisdom.

And yet I will not for their sakes regret testing with my pen   20
whatever this product of my lucubrations is or finding out what license is granted to attack those who commit capital crimes in literary studies. For I too pardon Philoxenus, as did Cicero in writing to Atticus,[55] that he preferred to return to prison rather than to sell his judgment, especially if it is fitting for writers to serve not so much the present age but, as it were, eternity (as Thucydides also said[56]). For this reason, I believe, books are called "monuments," because they ought to look to the memory of posterity, which will pass a more impartial verdict, than to the foolish popularity of today.

Therefore, not only in order to blot out these trends (if one   21
can) to the fullest extent but also so that the audacity of those who ravage everything far and wide may be put down and this worn and prostituted façade along with its brazen face not become a model, I even now promise more centuries to follow for this ef-

conatu, ne utiquam ad huius primae gustum repromittimus. Quos enim molli nunc articulo tractamus, quos levi et lento bracchio tangimus, fortius dein, puto, prememus atque urgebimus, et contenti paulisper interim praelusoria velitarique pugna, mox viribus collectis toto exercitus robore depraeliabimur. Quin etiam (quoniam tunica propior pallio) vindicabimus audacter et gnaviter a plagiariis ac furunculis interdum nostra et asseremus liberali causa manum. Nostra vero nunc accipi tantum volumus quae labore industriaque ipsi magna principes extudimus, nec expalpari unquam nec extorqueri nobis ea passuri, quamdiu licebit, nostra inquam non eiectamenta, sed pignora. Nam ut haec in medium vice missilium direptui conculcatuique relinquimus, ita illa nobis recipimus et defendimus, haec exponimus, illa et agnoscimus et tollimus, sed ita tamen ut imitari simias nolimus, quae suos dicuntur foetus quamlibet deformes pro formosissimis admirari.

22   Nec erunt, opinor, haec quoque nostra, quanquam levioris operae studia seu ludicra verius, dedecori tibi, Laurenti Medices, cui nunc adscribuntur. Adscribuntur autem non magis adeo ut me gratum beneficiis tuis approbent aut reponant gratiam, quod auxiliarium te, quodque consiliarium habuerunt, quam ut auspicato procedant et ut in iis tui memoria frequentetur, ex quo liber auctoritatem capiens magni celebritate nominis commendetur. Tum cui summa studiorum meorum debetur omnis, ab eo quoque portio ipsa iure incipiet. Et hercule veluti bellaria sint ista secundis accepta mensis, quoniam rectae cenae speciem vicemque graviora illa occupant qualia tibi multa vel Marsilius Ficinus Platonis vel

fort I have taken up, a beneficial one, I believe, though not at all in the same vein as this first one. Those whom I am now handling with a soft finger, and touching with a light and gentle arm, we will then, I think, press and push more strongly. For the meanwhile I will content myself with this preliminary skirmish with light-armed soldiers, but soon I shall collect my forces and fight it out with an army at full strength. What is more (since a tunic is closer than a cloak[57]), I shall in the meantime boldly and zealously claim my works from plagiarists and pilferers and assert ownership in an honorable cause. But I only wish for my work—my pledges,[58] I say, not castoffs—which I have been the first to forge with great toil and exertion, now to be received, though as long as I can, I will never allow it to be coaxed or wrenched from me.[59] For as I am releasing the one group to the public like darts to be pillaged and trampled upon, so I take to myself and defend the other group; the former I expose, the latter I recognize and take up, but only insofar as I refuse to imitate apes, who are said to admire as epitomes of beauty their own offspring, however ugly.

Nor will these studies of mine, despite involving modest effort or, more accurately, something I have been toying with, be, I think, a disgrace to you, Lorenzo de' Medici, to whom they now are dedicated. But they are dedicated equally to prove that I am grateful for the benefits you have bestowed and to give thanks for the fact that you are their helper and counselor, and also so that they may go forth under fair auspices, and that your memory may be celebrated in them, as a result of which my book will be recommended, taking its authority from the renown of your great name. So then, it is right for the apportionment to begin with the man to whom the entire compass of my studies is owed. Good heavens, let these be received like sweets on the second tables because the more substantial fare is taking up the splendid place of the main table—such are the many dishes that Marsilio Ficino, interpreter of Plato, or [John] Argyropoulos of Byzantium, interpreter of

22

Aristotelis interpres Argyropylus Byzantius e philosophiae penu congesserunt. De isto enim praecunctis admirando non Pico iam, sed (ut ipse appellare soleo) Phoenice potius, qui nunc in tua lauru nidificat, tanta mea quidem expectatio est ut ausim Propertio succinere: 'Cedite Romani scriptores, cedite Grai.' Tu vale, patrone iucundissime, et (quod facis) perge favere doctis, perge litteras excitare, perge a situ recipere rem Latinam, ab interitu Graecam, quo tui memoria nominis ab iniuria prorsus oblivionis asseratur.

Aristotle, have heaped up for you from the pantry of philosophy. But concerning the one who is to be admired above all others — no longer "Pico" but rather (as I am wont to call him) "the Phoenix," who is now building a nest in your laurel tree[60] — I have such high expectations that I dare to sing with Propertius: "Yield, Roman writers! Yield, Greek writers!"[61] Fare you well, my most delightful patron, and continue (as you are doing) to show favor to the learned, to inspire literature, to keep Latin culture from neglect and Greek culture from ruin, that the memory of your name may be claimed from wrongful oblivion.

LATINI GRAMMATICI

Servius
Priscianus
Donatus
Acro
Porphyrio
Marcellus
Sex. Pompeius Festus

Iunius Philargyrius
Probus
Gellius
Fulgentius
Pedianus
Persi vatis innominatus
    interpres

POETAE

Vergilius
Ovidius
Lucanus
Lucretius
Valerius Flaccus
Statius
Claudianus
Silius Italicus
Seneca tragicus
Plautus
Terentius
Horatius

Persius
Iuvenalis
Propertius
Tibullus
Catullus
Martialis
Ausonius
Prudentius
Marcianus[14]
Germanicus Caesar
Licentius

HISTORICI

T. Livius
Cornelius Nepos
Cornelius Tacitus
Valerius Maximus

Suetonius
Capitolinus
Eutropius
Ammianus

List of Authors Cited

LATIN GRAMMARIANS

Servius
Priscian
Donatus
Acro
Porphyrio
Marcellus
Sextus Pompeius Festus

Junius Philargyrius
Probus
Gellius
Fulgentius
Pedianus
An anonymous interpreter of
  the poet Persius[62]

POETS

Vergil
Ovid
Lucan
Lucretius
Valerius Flaccus
Statius
Claudian
Silius Italicus
The tragic poet Seneca
Plautus
Terence
Horace

Persius
Juvenal
Propertius
Tibullus
Catullus
Martial
Ausonius
Prudentius
Marcian
Germanicus Caesar
Licentius

HISTORIANS

Titus Livy
Cornelius Nepos
Cornelius Tacitus
Valerius Maximus

Suetonius
Capitolinus
Eutropius
Ammianus

ORATORES

Cicero
Quintilianus

Plinius Iunior
Symmachus

ASTROLOGI

Iulius Firmicus

Hyginius[15]

PHILOSOPHI

Seneca
Censorinus

Boetius
Apuleius

AUCTORES AMBIGUI TITULI

Plinius
Solinus
Cato
Vibius Sequester
Vitruvius
Frontinus

Varro
Macrobius
Columella
M. Iunius Nypsus
Petronius
Faustus

AUCTORES SACRI

Tertullianus
Cyprianus
Lactantius
Hilarius
Ambrosius
Hieronymus

Gaudentius
Augustinus
Rufinus
Sidonius
Item ex iure civili pontificioque
     delibata quaepiam

ORATORS

Cicero   Pliny the Younger
Quintilian   Symmachus

ASTRONOMERS

Julius Firmicus   Hyginus

PHILOSOPHERS

Seneca   Boethius
Censorinus   Apuleius

AUTHORS IN DOUBLE CATEGORIES

Pliny   Varro
Solinus   Macrobius
Cato   Columella
Vibius Sequester   M. Junius Nypsus
Vitruvius   Petronius
Frontinus   Faustus

SACRED WRITERS

Tertullian   Gaudentius
Cyprian   Augustine
Lactantius   Rufinus
Hilarius   Sidonius
Ambrose   Also some selections on civil
Jerome   and pontifical law

GRAECI AUCTORES GRAMMATICI

Eustathius

Pollux

Hephestion

Nica

Suida⟨s⟩

Maximus

Apollodorus

Doxopater[16]

Lucilius

  Tarrhaeus   ⎫ Apolloni

Sophocleus   ⎬ interpretes[17]

Theon   ⎭

Platonius

POETAE

Homerus

Hesiodus

Apollonius

Nonnus

Dionysius

Aeschylus

Sophocles

Euripides

Aristophanes

Pindarus

Callimachus

Theocritus

Triphysiodorus

Lucilius

Evenus

Posidippus

Gauradas

HISTORICI

Herodotus

Thucydides

Plutarchus

Herodianus

Iosepus[18]

Strabo

Pausanias

Dion

Zosimus

Xenophon Ephesius

Diodorus Siculus

Dionysius Halicarnasseus

Laertius

Appianus

Helianus

Heliodorus

Sozomenus

GREEK AUTHORS — GRAMMARIANS

Eustathius
Pollux
Hephaestion
Nica
Suidas
Maximus
Apollodorus

Doxopater
Lucilius
  Tarrhaeus
  Sophocleus
  Theon
Platonius

} interpreters of Apollonius

POETS

Homer
Hesiod
Apollonius
Nonnus
Dionysius
Aeschylus
Sophocles
Euripides
Aristophanes

Pindar
Callimachus
Theocritus
Tryphiodorus
Lucilius
Evenus
Posidippus
Gauradas

HISTORIANS

Herodotus
Thucydides
Plutarch
Herodian
Josephus
Strabo
Pausanias
Dio
Zosimus

Xenophon of Ephesus[63]
Diodorus Siculus
Dionysius of Halicarnassus
[Diogenes] Laertius
Appian
Aelian
Heliodorus
Sozomen

RHETORES

Aristides
Lucianus
Libanius
Aphthonius

Synesius[19]
Nicetes
Nicephorus

MATHEMATICI

Theon
Achilles
Heron

Cleomedes
Aristides Quintilianus

PHILOSOPHI

Plato
Aristoteles
Xenophon
Theophrastus
Heraclitus
Porphyrius
Proclus
Abammon
Iamblichus
Atticus

Dexippus
Philo
Maximus Tyrius
Alexander
Themistius
Sextus
Philoponus
Simplicius
Arrianus

MEDICI

Galenus
Paulus Aegineta[20]

Dioscorides

RHETORICIANS

Aristides

Lucian

Libanius

Aphthonius

Synesius

Nicetes

Nicephorus

MATHEMATICIANS

Theon

Achilles

Heron

Cleomedes

Aristides Quintilianus[64]

PHILOSOPHERS

Plato

Aristotle

Xenophon

Theophrastus

Heraclitus

Porphyry

Proclus

Abammon

Iamblichus

Atticus

Dexippus

Philo

Maximus of Tyre

Alexander

Themistius

Sextus [Empiricus]

Philoponus

Simplicius

Arrian

PHYSICIANS

Galen

Paul of Aegina

Dioscorides

AUCTORES AMBIGUI TITULI

Artemidorus
Iustinianus
Diogenianus

Callistratus
Apostolius[21]
Africanus

AUCTORES SACRI

Paulus
Eusebius
Severianus

Basilius
Theodoretus[22]

Sunt et alii citati veteres prudentes auctoritatis incognitae, sicuti *Poemenicon* scriptor, et Aristophanis, Xenophontis, Aristidae, Euripidi⟨s⟩, Callimachi, Synesique enarratores, sed nec barbari denique Hebraei,[23] Chaldaeique auctores in suis quoque originibus asymboli.

AUTHORS IN DOUBLE CATEGORIES

Artemidorus   Callistratus
Justinian   Apostolius
Diogenianus   Africanus

SACRED AUTHORS

Paul   Basil
Eusebius   Theodoret
Severianus

Other wise ancients of unknown identity, such as the writer of *Shepherds' Tales* (*Poemenica*),[65] have also been cited, as well as commentators on Aristophanes, Xenophon, Aristides, Euripides, Callimachus, and Synesius, and finally not even foreign authors — Hebrew and Aramaic ones — have failed to make a contribution[66] as regards their own origins.

List of Chapters in the First Century

41

45

Caput 57 Quae sint apud Suetonium tetraones, correctumque erratum Plinianis exemplaribus

Caput 58 Origo et ritus ludorum Saecularium, praetereaque ad id alia, citatumque eo Sibyllae oraculum, mox et obiter explicata quaedam, rursusque alia refutata non inutiliter

Caput 59 Non Vergilium sed Ovidium videri Priapei carminis auctorem. Tum versiculum illum qui sit apud Martialem, 'Ride si sapis, o puella, ride,' Nasonis esse proculdubio, sed ex epigrammatis potius quam aut ex *Artibus* aut ex tragoedia *Medea* videri citatum, moxque novum quippiam et mirum de *Medea* Nasonis adscriptum

Caput 60 *Agon* verbum, quo victimarius uti solitus, de[30] quo etiam in *Fastis* Ovidius

Caput 61 Erratum in codicibus Plinianis super cicuta vinoque, quodque mendose apud Macrobium *aconitum* pro *conio*

Caput 62 Qui sint arietini testiculi, qui digitus medi⟨c⟩us[31] apud Tullium

Caput 63 Aliter citari a Varrone Terenti verba quam aut in exemplaribus habeatur aut Donatus agnoverit

Caput 64 Declarati versus Ausoni, sed et Ovidi super choliambo aut scazonte

Caput 65 Qui sit habitus in statuis pacificator, deque eo sentire Statium in prima silva

Defensus a calumnia Cicero super
enarrata vi novi apud Aristotelen vocabuli,
quod est endelechia

1 Argyropylus ille Byzantius, olim praeceptor in philosophia noster, cum litterarum Latinarum minime incuriosus tum sapientiae decretorum disciplinarumque adeo cunctarum, quae cyclicae a Marciano dicuntur, eruditissimus est habitus. Hic et apud Medicem Cosmum, decreto publico patrem patriae, et dein apud Cosmi filium Petrum, nepotemque adeo Laurentium hunc, decus ubique nostrum, patritae simul avitaeque virtutis heredem, suaeque rei publicae columen, insigni fuit et auctoritate et gratia, quibus etiam libros dicavit Aristotelis a se versos in Latinum, sed et ipsum vix adhuc quidem puberem Laurentium dialecticis imbuit eaque philosophiae parte qua de moribus praecipitur. Ceterum (ut homo Graecus) perquam ferebat iniquo animo nobilem illam, nec (ut Theodorus Gaza putat) importunam M. Tulli Ciceronis exclamationem, qua Graeciam verborum interdum inopem, quibus se putat abundare, non eloquentius fortasse quam verius pronuntiavit. Ob id igitur subiratus Latinae copiae genitori et principi Graecus magister etiam dictitare ausus est (quod nunc quoque vix aures patiuntur), ignarum fuisse non philosophiae modo Ciceronem sed etiam (si dis placet) Graecarum litterarum. Vix enim dici potest, quam nos aliquando, idest, Latinos homines, in participatum suae linguae doctrinaeque non libenter admittat ista natio. Nos enim quisquilias tenere litterarum se frugem, nos praesegmina se corpus, nos putamina se nucleum credit.

2 Sed ut ad Argyropylum revertar, oculos ad hunc modum nostri parentis viventis victurique sigillantem, utebatur hoc ille vel

Cicero defended from a false accusation in regard to his explanation of the meaning of a neologism in Aristotle, ἐνδελέχεια

The famous [John] Argyropoulos of Byzantium—my sometime 1
tutor in philosophy, a man with no lack of curiosity about both
Latin literature and the tenets of philosophy and all the rest of the
disciplines that Martianus [Capella] calls "cyclics"[71]—was considered extremely learned.[72] He enjoyed marked influence and favor
with Cosimo de' Medici, "father of his country" by public decree,
then with Cosimo's son Piero, as well as with his grandson Lorenzo, our glory everywhere, heir of his father's and grandfather's
virtue alike, and the pillar of his republic. To them he also dedicated books of Aristotle, which he translated into Latin,[73] but he
also steeped Lorenzo, just barely then into puberty, in dialectics
and the ethical teachings of philosophy. Yet being Greek, he was
vexed at that famous and not, as Theodore Gaza thinks, perverse
proclamation of M. Tullius Cicero, by which he declared—not
perhaps more eloquently than truly—that Greece is sometimes
impoverished in words,[74] in which he thought he himself
abounded.[75] Being for this reason annoyed at the father and leading representative of Latin eloquence, the Greek teacher even
dared to state repeatedly—something that even now my ears can
barely endure—that Cicero was ignorant not only of philosophy
but also (can you believe it?) of Greek. For it can hardly be said
how grudgingly that people [the Greeks] ever grant us, that is,
Latins, a share in their language and learning. For they believe we
have scraps of literature, while they have the fruit, that we have
snippets, they the body, we the shells, they the core.

But to return to Argyropoulos, fixing my eyes with the look of 2
my father when he was alive and about to get the better of me, he

maxime argumento, quod in primo *Tusculanarum quaestionum* scribat Cicero, censere Aristotelen quintam esse quandam praeter elementa naturam, de qua sit mens, verbaque denique ipsius ita legantur: 'Quintum genus adhibet vacans nomine, et sic ipsum animum *endelechian*[36] appellat novo nomine, quasi quandam continuatam motionem et perennem,'[37] sed enim nemo est, aiebat, in Aristotelis lectione paulo frequentior, quin sciat *endelechian* esse potius Aristoteleum verbum, ne utiquam significans quod Cicero putat, continuatam motionem et perennem,[38] sed perfectionem potius aut consummationem quampiam. Nam cum vellet Aristoteles quasi nomenclaturam facere intellectuum suorum, verba ipse quaepiam nova concepit animo, velutique dein peperit, in quis hoc quoque per quod indicatur forma speciesque, cui perfectionem res quaeque suam debeat. Quod enim quidque est, ab hac est *entelechia* potissimum. Cicero autem non quidem hanc Aristoteleam vocem sed aliam prorsus ei contiguam finitimamque similitudinis praestigio falsus enarravit. *Endelechos* enim continuatim mobiliter, continuataque mobilitas *endelechismos*, unde hanc Aristotelis *entelechiam* deduci putavit ille, quae non *d* litteram tamen sed *t* potius habeat in syllaba secunda. Iam auctores contra Ciceronem stare quamlibet magnos Peripateticos adiiciebat. Et ut homo erat omnium (ut tum quidem videbatur) acerrimus in disputando atque aurem (quod ait Persius) mordaci lotus aceto, praeterea verborum quoque nostrorum funditator maximus, facile id vel nobis vel ceteris tum quidem suis sectatoribus persuaserat, ita ut (quod pene dictu quoque nefas) pro concesso inter nos haberetur, nec philosophiam scisse M. Tullium nec litteras Graecas. Enimvero re dein tota diligentius pervestigata, meas esse partis et item cuiuscumque Latini professoris existimavi, Ciceronis gloriam, qua vel maxime contra Graecos stamus, etiam vice capitis omni contentione defensare, quamquam

would make use of this argument in particular, that in the first book of the *Tusculan Questions* Cicero writes that Aristotle thought there was a fifth nature beyond the [other] elements from which the mind derives, and that his own words are as follows: "He [Aristotle] cites a fifth, nameless category and thus calls the soul itself by a new name, *endelechia,* as a certain continuous, perpetual motion."[76] But there is no one, he [Argyropoulos] used to say, even moderately well read in Aristotle, who does not know that *endelechia* is an Aristotelian word that by no means signifies what Cicero thought, a continuous and perpetual motion, but rather a perfection or completion. For when Aristotle wanted to create terminology for his ideas, he coined some neologisms, and then, as it were, brought them to birth, including this one, by which the form and type is expressed to which each thing owes its own perfection. In fact, what each thing is it is most of all as a result of this *entelechia.* Cicero, however, explained, not this Aristotelian word but another one, bordering and neighboring to it, deceived by the similarity.[77] For *endelechos* means "continuously in motion" and *endelechismos* means "continual motion," from which he [Cicero] thought that Aristotle's *entelechia* ("perfection") is derived, which, however, has the letter *t* in the second syllable rather than a *d.* Now he would adduce the great Peripatetics to stand as authorities against Cicero. And since he was the sharpest individual of all (at least as it then seemed) in debate and having washed his ear (as Persius says[78]) with stinging acid, he was especially good at slinging even our own words back at us, and he easily persuaded either us or his other disciples at the time, so that it was conceded among us (a thing that is practically a crime even to say[79]) that M. Tullius knew neither philosophy nor Greek. For indeed upon investigating the entire matter with greater care, I thought that it was incumbent upon me and likewise any Latin professor, to defend with all my heart, even at the price of my head, the glory of Cicero, by which we most of all stand against

illam sua non antiquitas modo sed quaedam prope divinitas extra ictum supraque iniuriam posuit.

3   Iam primum igitur Argyropyli huius apud me quoque non exigui ponderis auctoritas aliis auctoritatibus multoque, arbitror, valentioribus refellenda est, tum ostendendum, ex eo quod obicitur, augeri Ciceronis praeconium, nedum decrescat. Et prodibunt in medium satis (arbitror) quod ad philosophiam modo pertinet idonei Ciceronis laudatores (ut simus interim quam paucissimis contenti) Boetius, Macrobius, et Augustinus. Nam quis Boetio vel in dialecticis acutior, vel subtilior in mathematicis, vel in philosophia locupletior, vel in theologia sublimior? Quem tanti iuniores etiam philosophi, longe (arbitror) omnium perspicacissimi, fecerunt ut Aquinatem Thommam divum hominem magnumque illum Thommae[39] praeceptorem (Deus bone, quos viros!) habere meruerit enarratores, et ab ipsius sententia ne sit ulla quidem pene iam provocatio. Porro de Macrobio, cui, rogo, magis credendum quam laudanti praecipue Boetio? Denique ipsius Augustini tam alte nisa in omnibus ferme disciplinis est auctoritas ut extra omnem sit aleam posita, sic ut ab ea iam ne transversum quidem (quod dicitur) unguem recedi fas habeatur. Etenim tanta ingenii constat eum celeritate viguisse ut quidquid de arte loquendi et disserendi, quidquid de dimensionibus figurarum, de musicis, de numeris praecipitur, etiam sine magna difficultate, nullo hominum tradente, perceperit, tanto dein acumine praestitisse disputandi ut iure in uno isto potissimum totius veritatis niti patrocinium videatur.

4   Consideremus igitur quid hi singuli saltem de Cicerone senserint, quantumque ei tribuerint in philosophia, tum credamus audacter non cuiusvis esse calumniam conflare homini qui fuerit a laudatissimis hominibus tam singulariter laudatus. Boetius itaque non modo sic utitur identidem M. Tulli testimoniis ut ea pro

the Greeks, albeit not only its antiquity but a certain near divinity
has placed it above and beyond any injurious blow.

In the first place, then, the authority of this Argyropoulos, 3
which carries no small weight with me, must be refuted by other
authorities and, I think, much stronger ones, and then it must be
shown that from the objection raised the praise of Cicero, far from
being diminished, is augmented. As pertains to philosophy, to
content ourselves for the moment with as few as possible, Boethius, Macrobius, and Augustine will come forward, I think, as
sufficiently suitable panegyrists of Cicero. For who is sharper in
dialectics, more accurate in mathematics, more authoritative in
philosophy, or more sublime in theology than Boethius? It is he
whom the more recent philosophers, by far the most perceptive of
all (I think), have held to be of such significance that he deserved
to have St. Thomas Aquinas and Thomas's great teacher (good
God, what men!) as commentators,[80] and against his opinion
there is virtually no appeal. Furthermore, in regard to Macrobius,
who, I ask, should be believed more than Boethius when he
praises him?[81] And finally, there is the authority of Augustine
himself that is so highly exalted in just about all disciplines that it
stands beyond all hazard,[82] so that it is now considered wrong to
deviate from it by even as much as (as they say) a fingernail.[83] For
it is certain that he had such a vigorous and quick intellect that
with no human instruction he easily grasped the art of speech and
discourse, geometry, music, poetry, and he excelled with such great
skill in debate that the defense of the whole truth rightly seems to
rest upon him alone.

Let us, then, consider what they individually thought about 4
Cicero, and how much authority they attributed to him in philosophy; then let us boldly believe that it was not anyone's business
to incite false accusations against the man who was praised so
uniquely by the most praised men.[84] Now then, Boethius not only
deploys citations of M. Tullius over and over so as to pose them as

firmissimis et inviolabilibus obiciat argumentis, sed et ipsius *Topicorum* (qui maximus est honor) suscipere interpretationem non erubescit. Macrobius autem sic in unius eiusdem libri vel exigua particula versatur ut nec Platoni comparem facere nec omnibus insignire eum disciplinarum omnium titulis dubitaverit. Denique Augustinus cum in *Academicis*, quanquam sub alterius persona, nunc suum Ciceronem, nunc sapientem appellans, tandem ab ipso inquit in Latina lingua philosophiam et inchoatam esse et perfectam, tum in *Confessionibus* ubi neutiquam personatus, eos ex professo damnat qui linguam Ciceronis mirantur, pectus non ita; quin immo quod affectum mutaverit ipse, quod ad deum preces et vota converterit, quod desideria non eadem quae prius habuerit, quod omnis ei vana spes eviluerit, quod immortalitatem sapientiae quaesierit aestu cordis incredibili, postremo quod surgere iam ceperit ut ad deum reverteretur, cuncta haec esse Ciceronis munus fatetur, unique prorsus illius libro, qui vocaretur *Hortensius*, omnem suae salutis occasionem rettulit acceptam. Non enim ad acuendam linguam liber, inquit, ille offerebatur nec locutionem[40] mihi, sed quod loquebatur persuaserat. Quod isti utinam legissent, qui somnium aegroti nobis Hieronymi vapulantis ad tribunal obiectant, nec illud saltem cogitantes, illum ipsum Hieronymum, cum post repetitam dein statim Ciceronis lectionem periurus a Rufino argueretur, etiam gravissime conqueri, quod sibi ab illo suamet somnia obicerentur.

5   Ceterum (ut ad propositum revertar) vicerit sane vel Argyropylus vel quivis alius Ciceromastix, sed, rogo, istas prius transcendere audeat auctoritatum moles quas opposuimus. Enimvero de Graecis litteris facilior proniorque sententia. Quis enim tam hispida aure, quis tam inimicus veritati qui si pauca modo peneque etiam tumultuaria Graeca verba sparsim adhuc vel in epistolis

his strongest and most unassailable arguments, but he also does not blush to undertake a commentary on Tullius's *Topics* (doing which is the greatest honor).[85] Macrobius, on the other hand, is so engaged with a small part of one of his books that he does not hesitate either to make him the equal of Plato or to distinguish him with a claim to all disciplines.[86] Finally, in his *Academics*, albeit in the guise of another character, Augustine calls him sometimes "his Cicero" and at other times the "wise man"; at length, he says that it was by him that philosophy had been both initiated and brought to perfection in the Latin language. So too in his *Confessions*, when he was not assuming another persona, he openly condemns those who marvel at Cicero's style but not his mind.[87] What is more, that he himself altered his attitude, that he turned his prayers and vows to God, that his desires were not the same as before, that every vain hope became cheap in his sight, that he sought the immortality of wisdom with incredible fervor, and finally that he then began to rise up so as to return to God, he confesses that all these are the gift of Cicero, and he credited his entire opportunity for salvation to a single book of his, the one entitled *Hortensius*. For that book, he says, was not offered to me for sharpening my language or expression, but because he carried the point he was discussing.[88] Would only that those persons had read this who cast in our teeth the dream of Jerome, who was ill and being beaten before the tribunal, and fail to consider this point, that when he was, after repeated reading of Cicero, accused of perjury by Rufinus, Jerome himself complained with great gravity that his dreams were objected to by him.[89]

However (to return to the topic), let either Argyropoulos or   5
some other scourge of Cicero claim victory, but first, I beg, let him dare to cross over that mass of authorities that I have set in his path. For indeed, the opinion concerning Greek is easier and more straightforward. For who has such a tin ear, who is so hostile to truth that if he sniffs a few Greek words poured out in

ipsius olfaciat, quicquam se dicat unquam magis aut elegans aut
Atticum tota quoque Graecia repperisse? Sic ut iure Posidonium,
doctissimum illum hominem, deterruerit a scribendo, iure Graecam nationem Graeco de rebus suis commentario conturbaverit, in
quo se ait libro totum Isocratis myrhothecion atque omnis eius
discipulorum arculas, tum nonnihil etiam Aristotelea pigmenta
consumpsisse. Qua mihi videtur fiducia non minus aliquando
Graecae quam Latinae linguae veluti pomerium protulisse.

6   Sit argumento vel illud (ut uno interim contenti exemplo simus) quod innocentiae vocabulum negat habere apud Graecos
usitatum nomen sed habere ait posse tamen *eulabian*. Tum castigat
interdum quoque ceu segnitiam quorundam apud illos vocabulo-
rum, sicuti cum velle eos ait quidem distinguere sed parum valere
verbo, quod vel in illis probant, quae sunt melancholia et furor, vel
item in eo quod πόνον pro labore confusius illi et dolore pariter
accipiunt, tum melius aliquid nos dicere indicat quam illos, ut
convivium, ut alia, multoque melius quaedam notata esse verbis
Latinis quam Graecis, quod et significat multis locis reperiri, sed
et carere hos ipsos nomine rei cuiuspiam quam maxime habeant
familiarem non dissimulat. Nec ullus eorum tamen quamlibet in-
quirendo se torserit, inepti reperire adhuc aut excogitare vocabulum potuit. Iam vero nonne Apollonius quoque ille Molo, rhetorum omnium sui temporis celeberrimus, audita semel Graeca M.
Tulli sed et extemporali oratione, defixus diu stetisse ac denique
ita mirabundus pronuntiasse dicitur?

Ego vero te quidem, Cicero, cum laudo, tum admiror, sed me
Graecorum fortunae miseret taedetque, quod humanitatis et

disorder and scattered here and there even in Cicero's letters, would declare that he had ever discovered anything more elegant or Attic in the whole of Greece? So much so that he rightly deterred Posidonius,[90] that most learned man, from writing, he rightly caused a sensation among the Greek people with the Greek commentary about his own exploits; he says that in that book he used up all of Isocrates's perfume box and all the little boxes of his students, and some rouge from Aristotle as well.[91] By this self-confidence he seems to me to have extended the bounds of the Greek tongue no less than the Latin.[92]

Let the following serve as proof (to content ourselves for the   6 time being with a single example). He declares that "innocence" has no equivalent among the Greeks but that one could make use of the term "circumspection" (εὐλάβεια).[93] Then he sometimes also criticizes the laziness, as it were, of certain words among them, as when he says that they want to make distinctions but lack power in vocabulary, which they prove as regards the words "melancholy" and "fury,"[94] or again they use *ponos* promiscuously for both "toil" and "pain."[95] Then he shows that we say something better than they do, such as "banquet"[96] and other things, and that certain things are much better denoted by Latin words than Greek, which he also shows is found in many places, but he does not hide the fact that they themselves lack a name for something that is quite familiar. Nor has any of them, however much he might torture himself with investigating, so far been able to discover or think up a word for "inept."[97] Now indeed, is not Apollonius Molo, the most celebrated of all teachers of rhetoric of his age, having once heard an extemporaneous Greek oration by M. Tullius, reported to have stood motionless for a long time and at last to have declared in amazement?

You, Cicero, I both praise and admire, but I feel pity and am sick at heart over the fortune of the Greeks, since the orna-

eloquentiae decora, quae sola nobis reliqua feceramus, ea quoque per te (quantum intelligo) Romanis arrogantur.

Enimvero hoc illius iudicium non Latinus, non ineptus aliquis, sed Plutarchus ipse, Graeco vir ingenio, Romana gravitate, in litteris rettulit. Ergo ad hunc sane modum de scientia ipsius, deque Graecae linguae peritia testatum nobis veteres reliquerunt.

7   Age vero nunc *endelechian* quoque istam pensitemus, seram Ciceronis calumniatricem. Utrum ne istic igitur reprehenditur, quod Aristotelem dixerit adhibuisse Cicero quintam quandam praeter elementa naturam, et sic ipsum animum novo nomine appellavisse? Quod et Alexander Aphrodisieus, Peripateticorum omnium etiam ab Averroe laudatissimus, in egregie subtilibus illis *Naturalium quaestionum* libris ostendit, quos a se lectos divus Hieronymus gloriatur, et Porphyrius in commentario quod in Aristotelis decem genera per interrogationes edidit et responsiones, et Themistius super hos in paraphrasi *De anima* secunda, et Simplicius, ubi Aristoteleum paris argumenti volumen interpretatur, et Quintilianus Aristides in tertio *De musica*, et postremo in epistola quadam sua divus Ambrosius (ut alios interim praetereamus) unanimiter prope significarunt, quamquam de hoc utique, ne in verbis quidem Aristotelis ipsis, ulla dubitatio est. An illud potius culpatur, quod *endelechiae* vocabulum nec suis litteris notaverit, et alium quam Aristoteles intellectum (sicuti supra diximus) accommodaverit?

8   Principio igitur quaero ego ab istis, quonam maxime argumento *entelechian* potius quam *endelechian* scriptum collegerint ab Aristotele. Tam enim verbum novum hoc quam illud, nec minus altero significari animus quam altero potest, nec Aristoteles ipse perfectionem potius quam motionem illam indicari continuam nova voce pronuntiat, crediderint ita sane Porphyrius, Themistius, Simplicius, aut siqui compares.

ments of humanity and eloquence, which alone we had left
to us, these things too are, as far as I can see, being appropriated by you for the Romans.[98]

For indeed this judgment of his was recorded, not by some Latin
or inept person, but by Plutarch himself, a man of Greek genius
and Roman substance. The ancients, then, have left us such testimony about the man's knowledge and skill in the Greek language.

Now let us also consider *endelechia*, Cicero's late, false accuser. Is   7
it criticized that Cicero said that Aristotle had deployed a fifth
nature beyond the [four] elements, and thus called the mind itself
by a new name? This has been shown by Alexander of Aphrodisias, the most highly praised of all Peripatetics even by Averroes,
in those exceptionally subtle books of his, *Questions on Nature*,
which St. Jerome boasts of having read and was unanimously indicated by Porphyry in the commentary that he published in a
question-and-answer format on Aristotle's ten categories, and besides them Themistius in his paraphrase of the second book of *On
the Soul*, and Simplicius, when he expounds on the volume of Aristotle on the same theme, and Aristides Quintilianus in the third
book of his *On Music*, and finally St. Ambrose in a certain letter of
his (to skip over others for now).[99] However, about this point at
least, Aristotle's own words leave no doubt. Or is fault found
rather in the fact that he failed to write the term *endelechia* with its
proper letters, and that he supplied a different sense than Aristotle
(as I said above[100])?

Therefore, in the first place, I ask them on what basis they con-   8
cluded that Aristotle had written *entelechia* rather than *endelechia*.
For this latter term is just as new as the former, and the soul can
be designated no less by the one than the other, nor does Aristotle
himself declare that perfection rather than continuous motion is
expressed by this new word, albeit this is what Porphyry, Themistius, Simplicius, and others like them believed.

9   Quae autem tandem invidia est, etiam Ciceronem aliter quam posteriores opinatum, si stare ipse sic quoque tuerique gradum bene et fortiter potest? Nam sit utra lectio verior, ea quam Cicero agnoscit, an quae apud posteros obtinuit, in incerto adhuc est. Etenim libri omnes Aristotelei, qui tam grandi nunc quidem auctoritate pollent, interpolati plenique multis erroribus olim sunt editi, si fidem Straboni accommodamus, auctori non malo. Siquidem Neleus ille Scepsius, Corisci filius et Aristotelis Theophrastique non solum auditor sed et bibliothecae successor et heres, libros utriusque philosophi Scepsin, hoc est in suam patriam, comportasse universos perhibetur. Hique dein a posteris ipsius, metuentibus videlicet Attalicos reges, librorum istiusmodi studiosissimos, infossi terrae negligenterque habiti diu, tandem aliquando ab Apellicone Teio magna empti mercede dicuntur, sed carie situque (quod necesse fuit) multis exesi et labefacti locis, quos tamen inconsultius supplere Apellicon ipse librorum quam philosophiae studiosior, et pro arbitrio (quemadmodum quidem putabat) emendare ausus, plurimis temeravit erroribus. Hi tamen ad usque Sullae tempora (sicuti Plutarchus memorat) Athenis delitescebant. Nam Peripatetici veteres, ordinariis istis, quibus omnis instruitur philosophia carentes, paucos modo quos vocant exotericos habuerunt, eoque posteriores exquisitius philosophati, quod Aristotelis volumina, quamquam alicubi contaminata, pervolutabant. Quippe L. Sulla bibliothecam Apelliconis istam repertam Athenis, Romam primus transtulit, tum grammaticus Tyrannion et ei pene suppar Andronicus Rhodius, is qui libros etiam *Peri hermenias* negat esse Aristotelis, magna copia libros eius philosophi, tabulis etiam nescio quibus editis invulgarunt.

10   Quocirca nihil est quod iam dubitemus, quin de sinceritate primaeva lectionis istius, praesertim tantillo discrimine, vel libera

Finally, what cause is there for envy that Cicero thought differ- 9
ently from his successors, if he can stand on his own and well and
stoutly defend his ground? For it is still uncertain which of the
two readings is genuine — the one that Cicero recognizes or the
one that held sway among later authors. For all of Aristotle's
books, which now enjoy such great authority, were once published
in interpolated form and full of many errors, if we credit Strabo,
who is not a bad authority. For the famous Neleus of Scepsis, son
of Coriscus and not only a student of Aristotle and Theophrastus
but also successor and heir to their library, is said to have gathered
the books of both philosophers and transported them to Scepsis,
that is, his own homeland. They were then buried by his descendants, who evidently feared the Attalid kings, who were keen on
such books, and negligently kept for a long time; finally, they are
said to have been bought at a great price by Apellicon of Teos, but
they were damaged and degraded in many passages by decay and
neglect (which was inevitable); Apellicon himself, though keener
on books than philosophy, nevertheless inadvisably ventured to
supplement and emend them (as he fancied) at his own discretion,
but he defiled them with a host of errors. These books, nonetheless, lay hidden at Athens down to the time of Sulla (as Plutarch
records[101]). For the ancient Peripatetics, lacking those ordinary
books with which all philosophy is equipped, had only a few
books that they call "exoteric," and their successors philosophized
all the more subtly because they consulted Aristotle's volumes, albeit contaminated in some passages. Of course, L. Sulla was the
first to transport that library of Apellicon's, discovered at Athens,
to Rome. Then the philologist Tyrannion and his near contemporary Andronicus of Rhodes, who denies even that the books *On
Interpretation* are Aristotle's,[102] published the books of that philosopher in quantity, upon publication of certain tables.[103]

Therefore we no longer have any reason to doubt the original 10
soundness of that reading, especially with such a tiny difference,

sit in utramque partem suspitio, vel (si alterutri accedendum) tu-
tius Ciceronem sit praeferri, longe priorem quam Alexander est,
primus ex illa cohorte, quam diximus, Aristotelis enarrator, quem
Severi floruisse temporibus vel ipsius *De fato* significat opus, ae-
qualemque propemodum, seu paulo, credo, maiusculum summis
illis Academicis Origene et Plotino. Quid autem prohibet, quomi-
nus Cicero ipse videre matricem quoque librorum Aristotelis, qui
fuerint ipsius aetate publicati, si non incorruptam, certe (sicuti
diximus) conscribellatam potuerit?

11   Tum et consulto factum ab homine doctissimo crediderim, ut
libero pectoris muro septus, eam novo huic Aristotelis vocabulo
interpretationem iure accommodare sit ausus, quae cum Platonis
in *Phaedro* sententia super animae motu sempiterno atque (ut
Varro inquit) dio consentiret, de qua ipse quoque vel in *Tusculanis
quaestionibus*, vel in sexto *Rei publicae* volumine commeminerit,
quando et Philoponus in *Aristotelis vita*, et Simplicius in commentariis *De anima*, et in extremo *Peri hermenias* libro Boetius ipse,
germanas esse et compares utriusque philosophi sententias asseve-
rant, etiamque libros septem composuisse Porphyrius traditur,
quibus hoc maxime argumentum colligeretur, eandem Platonis
esse prorsus et Aristotelis haeresin. Quod et Picus hic Mirandula
meus in quadam suarum disputationum praefatione tractavit, et
vero verius esse copiosissimo opere (credo) pulcherrimoque per-
vincet (nisi me tamen gustus fefellit), quod de Platonis hac ipsa
quam dicimus et Aristotelis concordia noctes atque dies molitur et
cudit.

12   Ita non modo non errasse in vocabulo isto noster Cicero, sed vel
eruditius aliquanto quam ceteri vel ad suam sectam scripsisse ac-
commodatius intelligetur, ut quod de clarissimi viri doctrina tam

whether we are at liberty to be suspicious of both possibilities, or (if we must choose one over the other) it would be safer for preference to be given to Cicero, who is much earlier than Alexander, the first expounder of Aristotle of the cohort that I mentioned, who flourished, as his own work, *On Fate*, indicates, in the times of Severus, a virtual contemporary of or, I believe, a little older than those supreme Academics, Origen and Plotinus.[104] Moreover, what is to prevent Cicero himself from being able to see the archetype of Aristotle's books, which were published in his own age, if not uncorrupted, at least (as we said) covered with scribbling?[105]

Next, I would also suppose that it was a deliberate act of the learned man, protected by the wall of a free heart, that he rightly dared to supply an interpretation for this neologism of Aristotle's, an interpretation that agrees with Plato's idea in his *Phaedrus* in regard to the perpetual and (as Varro says) divine motion of the soul, which he himself also mentioned, whether in his *Tusculuan Questions* or in book six of the *Republic*, when [John] Philoponus in the *Life of Aristotle* and Simplicius in his commentaries on *On the Soul*, and Boethius himself on the last book of *On Interpretation*, asserted that the thoughts of the two philosophers are similar and siblings, and Porphyry is even said to have composed seven books, in which, above all, this point was argued, that the philosophical school of Plato and Aristotle is the same.[106] My friend [Giovanni] Pico della Mirandola also dealt with this in a certain preface to his *Disputations*,[107] and indeed by his abundant and splendid work, he will, I think, establish (unless my judgment is deceived) as more true than the truth what he is laboring at and hammering out night and day concerning this very harmony we are discussing of Plato and Aristotle.

Thus not only will it be recognized that our friend Cicero did not err concerning that word, but that he wrote either somewhat more eruditely than others or more aptly for his own philosophical school, so that what such good authorities, as we have shown

idonei, quam superius ostendimus, auctores spoponderunt, etiam ipsemet, in quo praecipue diverticulo calumniam patitur, largissime cumulatissimeque praestiterit. Nec autem novum Ciceroni aut inusitatum, calumniam pati a Graecis, quando etiam Didymus sex libros adversus eundem composuit, sillographos imitatus maledicos scriptores, qui tamen libri iudicio doctarum aurium sunt improbati. Sic adversus generosissimum leonem, procul despectis vocibus etiam quidam saepe lucernarii canes baubantur.

: 2 :

Quae sint crepidae *apud Catullum* carpatinae,
*quod probe scriptum vocabulum
perperam mutatur*

1 Valerius Catullus in epigrammate quodam sic ait:

Ista tamen lingua, si usus veniat tibi, possis
Culos et crepidas lingere carpatinas.

Quaesitum vero a multis, explicatum adhuc a nemine, quae sint *carpatinae*, seu *carbatinae*, crepidae. Nam utrunque recte, sed et item *carbasinae* dicitur. Quidam autem plani et tenebriones in litteris, vetere expuncto vocabulo, nescio quas supponunt, aut *cercopythas*, aut *coprotinas* ex hara productas, non schola, vocabula nuda, nomina cassa, et nihili voces. Nos de Graeco instrumento, quasi de cella proma, non despicabilis nec abrogandae fidei proferemus auctoritates, quibus et lectio praestruatur incolumis et interpretamenti nubilum discutiatur.

above, have pledged about the distinguished man's teaching, he himself has also fully and abundantly made good, in particular regarding the divergence about which he has suffered false accusation.[108] Moreover, it is neither new nor unusual for Cicero to endure a false accusation at the hands of the Greeks, when even Didymus wrote six books against him, imitating the sillographi, malicious writers,[109] books which nonetheless were rejected by the judgment of learned ears. Just so, some dogs often bay contemptibly from afar in the dead of night against the noble lion.

: 2 :

What crepidae carpatinae *are in Catullus,*
a word that was written correctly
but has been incorrectly altered

In one of his epigrams Valerius Catullus says the following: 1

Yet, with that tongue of yours, were the opportunity to present itself to you, you could lick asses and leather sandals (*crepidas carpatinas*).[110]

It has been asked by many, but so far explained by no one, what *carpatinae,* or *carbatinae, crepidae* are. Both are correct, but *carbasinae* ("canvas") is also used. Certain literary swindlers and cheats delete the ancient word and substitute some others, either *cercopythas* ("snake-skinned") or *coprotinas* ("dung-covered"),[111] products of the pigsty, not the school, mere words, empty names, signifying nothing. I shall fetch authorities from my Greek toolkit, as if from a pantry, neither despicable nor void of credibility, that thereby both a sound reading may be laid down as a foundation and interpretative clouds be dispersed.

2   Iam primum igitur, Iulius ipse Pollux libro nono ad Commodum Caesarem *carbatinas* esse ait rusticum calciamentum, sic a
Caribus appellatum. Aristoteles vero in secundo *De animalium his-*
toria chamelos calceari carbatinis scribit, ne scilicet in exercitu
longiore itinere fatiscant. Sed et quattuor extant Graece nimisquam libelli elegantes *Poemenicon* titulo, quorum in secundo senex
quidam cum pera et calceis carbatinis introducitur, et Lucianus in
dialogo qui vel *Alexander* vel *Pseudomantis* inscribitur oratores quospiam e Paphlagonia carbatinis calceatos ait. Denique etiam Xenophon Socraticus *Anabaseos* tertio: 'Cum defecissent,' inquit, 'veteres
calcei carbatinas habebant ex recentibus coriis bubulis confectas,'
quem etiam locum, dissimulato tamen auctore, Suidas adducit.
Quin interpres quispiam Xenophontis eiusdem *carbatinas* esse addit barbaricum calciamentum.

: 3 :

Quibus verbis Horatius chamelopardalin significaverit, quaeque
sit eius animantis facies, quibusque etiam nominibus censeatur,
et quo primum tempore visa in Italia

1   Horatius in epistola ad Augustum:

Diversum, inquit, confusa genus panthera chamelo.

Nos olim iam publica praelectione dictavimus videri eum de *cha-*
melopardali, quae vulgo *girafa* dicitur, sentire. Quam enim vocamus
pantheram, Graeci *pardalin*. Et hanc a rege dein ipso Aegypti, qui

In the first place, Julius Pollux himself, in Book 9 of his work   2
dedicated to Commodus Caesar, says that *carbatinae* ("leathers")
are rustic shoes, so called from the Carians.[112] In fact, in the second book of his *On the History of Animals*, Aristotle writes that
camels are shod with leather shoes, so that they may not suffer
fatigue on a long trek with the army.[113] But four elegant little
books are extant in Greek, with the title *Shepherds' Tales* (*Poemenica*), in the second of which an old man with a pouch and wear-
ing leather shoes is introduced, and in his dialogue, entitled either
Alexander or *False Prophet*, Lucian says that some orators from
Paphlagonia wore shoes of leather.[114] Finally, Xenophon the So-
cratic too says in the third book of the *Anabasis*: "After their old
shoes wore out, they had leather shoes made from fresh cowhides,"
a passage that Suidas cites without naming the author.[115] In fact,
some commentator on Xenophon adds that *carbatinae* are barbarian footwear.[116]

: 3 :

*What words Horace used for a camel-leopard, and
what this animal looks like; also, by what other names it is
identified, and when it was first seen in Italy*

In his letter to Augustus, Horace says: 1

A diverse species, a leopard conflated with a camel.[117]

I once said in a public lecture that with *camelopardalis* he seemed to
mean what is commonly called a "giraffe."[118] For what we call a
panthera ("leopard"), the Greeks call a *pardalis*. I saw this when it
had been sent by the then king of Egypt himself, who is called the

Sultanus vocatur, inter munera alia dono missam Laurentio Medici vidimus, non tam meo quam ingeniorum omnium virtutumque patrono.

2   Tantum mirati sumus habere ipsam cornicula, quamquam mas erat, quoniam de his nihil hactenus in veteribus memoriis legebamus. Ceterum Graecus Heliodorus, non dilutae scriptor auctoritatis, libro *Aethiopicon* decimo in hanc ferme sententiam de ea meminit, cum scilicet Hydaspae regi Aethiopum dono datam ab Auxomitarum legatis fabulatur:

> Postremo, inquit, accessere etiam Auxomitarum legati, non vectigales illi quidem, sed amici et federe iuncti, qui benivolentiam rebus prospere gestis indicantes cum alia et ipsi munera obtulerunt, tum imprimis animantem quampiam inusitata specie naturaque, cuius ad magnitudinem chameli proceritas. Color pellisque pantherae, maculis veluti florentibus variegata. Postremae infra alvum partes humi subsidebant, sicuti in leonibus videmus. Humeri pedesque priores, atque item pectus, praeter ceterorum membrorum rationem procera. Tenuis cervix, et quae de reliqua corporis mole in olorinum collum se tenderet. Chamelo caput simile. Maior ipsa pene duplo quam Libyssae struthi, subscriptosque velut oculos torve motans connivebat. Incessus autem longe animantium ceterarum terrestrium vel aquatilium dissimilis, neque enim vicissatim crura simul, sed dextra pariter, dein sinistra utraque agitabat. Cumque iis suspensa proferebat latera, tractu motuque tam facili, ut eam quo vellet tenui capistro vertici devincto, veluti fortissimo vinculo, magister perduceret. Haec ut est conspecta animans, omnem continuo multitudinem obstupefecit, speciesque nomen invenit ex

Sultan, as a gift, among other presents, to Lorenzo de' Medici, a patron not just of me but of all talented and virtuous individuals.[119]

I was very amazed that it had small horns, even though it was a male, since we had so far read nothing about these in ancient records. Yet the Greek Heliodorus, a writer of solid authority, in the tenth book of his *Ethiopian Tales*, speaks of it to this effect, when he explains that it was given by the ambassadors of the Auxomitae as a gift to Hydaspes, king of the Ethiopians: 2

> Finally, the ambassadors of the Auxomitae also approached, who were not tributaries but friends and allies bound by treaty, and who, upon completion of the successful campaign, showed their kindness by offering various other gifts and in particular a creature of unusual form and nature, whose height was as great as that of a camel. Its color and hide were those of a leopard, variegated with spots like flowers. Its hindquarters below the belly sloped down to the ground, just as we see in lions. Its shoulders, front legs, and chest were tall out of proportion to the rest of its body. The neck was thin and elongated itself from the remaining mass of the body like that of a swan. Its head was like a camel's. It was almost double the size of ostriches, and it had eyes painted, as it were, under the eyebrows that it rolled savagely as it blinked. Moreover, it walked with a stride far different from that of other creatures whether terrestrial or aquatic, for it did not move its legs alternating back and forth, but both right legs at the same time and then both left. And when it advanced its flanks suspended by those legs, it was so easily guided and moved that its trainer led it wherever he wanted with a thin halter attached to its head, as if it were a very strong chain. When this animal was seen, it at once astounded the entire crowd, and the species was named from

iis, quae praecipua in corpore, sic ut extempore eam populus chamelopardalin appellaret.

Hactenus Heliodorus.

3   Dion vero Graecus et ipse auctor in tertio quadragesimoque *Romanae historiae* libro, de Caesare narrans, ita ferme scribit:

> Chamelopardalin vero primus ipse Romam adduxit et populo ostendit. Id animal cetera chamelus, crura autem inaequalia habet, posteriora prioribus magis brevia, ut a clunibus attolli sensim, quasi ascendenti simile, incipiat, corpusque reliquum sublime admodum cruribus prioribus sustentatur, sed cervix in altitudinem pene peculiarem se tollit. Colore ipsa maculoso ceu panthera, quo fit ut amborum promiscuo vocabulo censeatur.

Plinius vero de chamelis tractans, hoc quoque addit:

> Harum aliqua similitudo in duo transfertur animalia. Nabun Aethiopes vocant, collo similem equo, pedibus et cruribus bovi, chamelo capite, maculis albis rutilum colorem distinguentibus. Unde appellata chamelopardalis, dictatoris Caesaris circensibus ludis primum visa Romae. Ex eo subinde cernitur aspectu magis quam feritate conspicua, quare etiam ovis ferae nomen invenit.

Consimilia ferme huic etiam Solinus prodidit, quo loco de Aethiopibus.

4   Sed et M. Varro in libro *De lingua Latina* ad Ciceronem:

the special properties of its body, in that the people spontaneously called it a camel-leopard.[120]

Thus far Heliodorus.

Indeed, the Greek Dio, an authority himself, in the forty-third   3
book of his *History of Rome*, when he is speaking about Caesar,
writes to the following effect:

He was the first to bring a camel-leopard to Rome and exhibit it to the people. This animal is in most respects a
camel; but it has unequal legs, with the hind legs shorter
than the forelegs, so that it begins to rise up little by little
from its hindquarters, like a climber, and the rest of its body
is supported at a great height on its forelegs, but its neck
rises to a virtually unique height. In color, it is spotted like a
leopard, as a result of which it is labeled with a name that
combines both animals.[121]

Indeed, when Pliny was discussing camels, he also added this:

A bit of resemblance to these is carried over to two animals.
Ethiopians call a *nabus* an animal that has the neck of a
horse, the hooves and legs of an ox, and the head of a camel,
and is red in color with distinguishing white spots. On account of this it is called a camel-leopard, and was first seen
in Rome at the dictator Caesar's Circus games. Since then it
has been seen at intervals, striking more for its appearance
than its ferocity, and it has, accordingly, earned the name
"wild sheep."[122]

Solinus too gave an account similar to Pliny's, in a passage about
Ethiopians.[123]

But in the book *On the Latin Language* dedicated to Cicero, M.   4
Varro says:

Chamelus, inquit, suo nomine Syriaco in Latinum venit, ut
Alexandrea chamelopardalis nuper adducta, quod erat figura
ut chamelus, maculis ut panthera.

Risi etiam nuper, quia verbum ex Varrone dimidiatum *pardalis*
tantum nescio quis grammaticus in lexicon rettulerat suum, quod
per ordinem litterarum compositum circumfertur. Centum autem
Gordiani principis ludis exhibitas auctore[41] Capitolino feras oves
accepimus.

: 4 :

Quam multa poetarum interpretibus legenda,
quodque satyram Persius de
Alcibiade Platonis *effinxit*

1 Qui poetarum interpretationem suscipit, eum non solum (quod
dicitur) ad Aristophanis lucernam, sed etiam ad Cleanthis oportet
lucubrasse. Nec prospiciendae autem philosophorum modo familiae, sed et iureconsultorum, et medicorum item, et dialecticorum,
et quicunque doctrinae illum orbem faciunt quae vocamus *encyclia*,
sed et philologorum quoque omnium. Nec prospiciendae tantum,
verum introspiciendae magis, neque (quod dicitur) ab limine ac
vestibulo salutandae, sed arcessendae potius in penetralia et in
intimam familiaritatem, si rem iuvare Latinam studemus et insci-
tiam cottidie invalescentem profligare, alioqui semidocta sedulitas
cum magna sui persuasione detrimento ⟨sit⟩,[42] non usui. Plurima
tamen in philosophorum maxime operibus invenias quae sint in
poetarum nostrorum libros ascita, quale videlicet quod etiam

Camel entered Latin with its Syrian name, just as the Alexandrian camel-leopard was recently introduced, since it was in the shape of a camel but with spots like a leopard.[124]

I recently smiled because some grammarian assigned only the truncated word *pardalis* from Varro to his lexicon, which is alphabetically organized and in public circulation.[125] Moreover, I have learned on the authority of Capitolinus that one hundred "wild sheep" were displayed at the games of the emperor Gordian.[126]

: 4 :

How many works must be read by poets' interpreters,
and the fact that Persius fashioned a satire from
Plato's Alcibiades

Whoever undertakes to interpret the poets must have burned the midnight oil, as the saying goes, not only at Aristophanes's lamp but also that of Cleanthes.[127] One must, however, have a look not only at the schools of philosophers but also those of jurists, physicians, and dialecticians, and all who comprise the world of learning that we call "general"[128] — and those of all philologists as well. And these must not merely be viewed from a distance but rather looked into deeply, not just greeted at the doorway or vestibule, as they say, but rather summoned into the inner rooms, and intimate familiarity,[129] if we are keen on advancing Latin culture and beating back the ignorance that is gaining strength every day. Otherwise, endeavor that is only semi-learned, albeit driven by great conviction, would be detrimental rather than beneficial. Still, you may come upon very many elements, especially in the works of philosophers, that have been adopted into the books of our poets,

annos abhinc aliquot Persium publice poetam enarrantes indicabamus.

2   Satyram ipsius quintam, cuius est initium 'Rem populi tractas?,' ad Platonici dialogi qui *Primus Alcibiades* vocatur exemplar veluti deliniatam, sic ut non ea solum, quae de iusto atque iniusto, deque sui cuique notitia Socrates inibi cum Alcibiade agit, delibasse ex eo pudenter, sed locos etiam quospiam, si non magni momenti, certe veneris tamen plenissimos et leporis duxisse indidem Persius intelligatur. Quod genus et illa: 'Dic hoc magni pupille Pericli,' quoniam Socrates quoque ostendit omnium maximum visum Alcibiadi quod ipsi relictus a patre tutor Xanthippi filius Pericles. Sic item: 'Dinomaches ego sum,' ductum ex eo quod apud Platonem sic est: ὦ φίλε παῖ Κλεινίου καὶ Δεινομάχης. Consimiliter quod ait ibidem: 'Tecum habita,' nonne dialogi eiusdem pervidisse videtur voluntatem, siquidem (quod Proclus enarrator affirmat) nihil hic aliud Plato quam litteram Delphicam respexit, monentem, se quisque ut norit? Quod et Picus Mirandula, noster amor, in *Heptaplo* sua, quam mox editurus de septiformi sex dierum geneseos enarratione, pulcherrime tetigit.

3   Haec igitur invenisse aliquando, vel invicem etiam contulisse, non emolumentum modo studiosis, sed et voluptatem pepererit minime vulgarem.

the sort of thing I indicated some years ago in my public lectures expounding the poet Persius.[130]

His fifth satire, which begins "Are you engaged in public af- 2 fairs?,"[131] was, as it were, drawn in outline after the model of Plato's dialogue entitled *Alcibiades* 1 in such a way that Persius may be seen not only to have bashfully culled from it Socrates's conversation there with Alcibiades about justice and injustice and knowing oneself, but also to have drawn from the same source some passages, if not key ones, at least ones filled with grace and charm. An example of that sort is the phrase: "Tell me this, you ward of the great Pericles,"[132] seeing that Socrates also shows that Alcibiades thought it the greatest thing that Pericles, son of Xanthippus, had been left by his father as his guardian. And so again "I am son of Deinomache"[133] was taken from this text of Plato's: "O beloved son of Cleinias and Deinomache."[134] Similarly, when he says in that same passage, "Live in your own house,"[135] does he not seem to have discerned the very intent of the same dialogue, inasmuch as in it (as the commentator Proclus affirms[136]) Plato had nothing else in view than the Delphic inscription that advises that each person know himself?[137] Our beloved [Giovanni] Pico della Mirandola[138] has touched on this most elegantly in his *Heptaplus*, which he is about to publish about the sevenfold account of the six days of creation.[139]

Therefore, to discover these things or contribute to them may 3 not only yield dividends to scholars but pleasure of no vulgar sort.

: 5 :

Qui sit apud Lucretium durateus equus, *quodque legendum apud Valerium Flaccum, non quidem* nox dorica, *sed* durica, *vel* duria *potius, in libro* Argonauticon *secundo*

1 Lucretius in primo *De rerum natura*:

> Nec cum[43] durateus Troianis Pergama partu
> Inflammasset equus nocturno Graiugenarum.

Durateum vocavit equum illum Troianum, ab Epeo fabricatum perite simul et eleganter, quae Graeca vox et poetica ligneum significat, et sane *durateon* vocat hunc etiam Homerus equum libro octavo *Odysseae*[44] sic inquiens:

> Ἀλλ' ἄγε δὴ μετάβηθι καὶ ἵππου κόσμον ἄεισον
> Δουρατέου, τὸν Ἐπειὸς ἐποίησεν σὺν Ἀθήνῃ.

Et item paulo post:

> Δουράτεον μέγαν ἵππον, ὅθ' εἴατο πάντες ἄριστοι,

vulgoque eundem non *durateon*, sed *durion*, communiore lingua, sicuti etiam poeta Aristophanes.

2 At enim Opici homines dictionem sibi incognitam expungere, proque illo, quod est *durateus*, reponere nugamenta quaepiam, vel *dura tuens* vel *dira tenens*, occeperunt. Id ne attentare amplius audeant, visus mihi sum facturus operaepretium, si de isto quoque nonnihil *Miscellaneis* inseruissem.

3 Sed et codicem proxime nobis *Argonauticon* Valeri Flacci perveterem Taddaeus Ugoletus Parmensis, Matthiae Pannoniorum

: 5 :

What a durateus *horse is in Lucretius, and that one must not read* nox dorica *but* durica *in Valerius Flaccus, or rather,* duria, *in the second book of the* Adventures of the Argonauts

Lucretius, in the first book of his *On the Nature of the Universe:* 1

> Nor would the wooden horse, with its nocturnal progeny of Greeks, have set Pergamum ablaze for the Trojans.[140]

He called that famous Trojan horse that had been as skillfully as elegantly crafted by Epeus "wooden" (*durateus*), a Greek poetic word that means "made of wood," and Homer too calls this horse *durateon* ("wooden"), in Book 8 of his *Odyssey*, when he says the following:

> Come now, change [the topic], and sing of the form of the wooden horse that Epeus built together with Athena.[141]

And again a little after that:

> the huge wooden horse, where all the bravest lay hidden,[142]

and generally [they call] the same horse not *durateon* ("wooden") but *durion* ("wooden") in the common language, as the poet Aristophanes does as well.[143]

But ignoramuses[144] have begun to delete the word unknown 2 to themselves, and to replace *durateus* with nonsense, either *dura tuens* ("defending hard things") or *dira tenens* ("holding dreadful things").[145] To put a stop to these audacious attempts, it seemed to me to be worthwhile to include something about this in the *Miscellanies*.

A very learned man, Taddeo Ugoletti of Parma, courtier of 3 Matthias [Corvinus], the most wise and invincible king of the

sapientissimi et invictissimi regis aulicus, homo litteratissimus ostendit, e quo fluxisse opinor et ceteros qui sunt in manibus, cuius in secundo sic est: 'Manet immotis nox durica fatis,' non ut vulgo legitur *dorica*. Quae certo aut vera et emendata lectio, aut (quod suspicor magis) verae proxima, ut quod et usus et vocalitas persuadet, *nox duria* sit apud illum, qua scilicet inclusos utero Danaos, equus ille durius, hoc est idem qui durateus, patefactus ad auras reddiderit. Neque autem diphthongus impediat. Quam enim δούρειος Graece, tam et δούριος.

: 6 :

Quo intellectu Catullianus passer accipiendus,
locusque etiam apud Martialem indicatus

Passer ille Catullianus allegoricos, ut arbitror, osceniorem quempiam celat intellectum, quem salva verecundia nequimus enuntiare. Quod ut credam, Martialis epigrammate illo persuadet, cuius hi sunt extremi versiculi:

> Da mi[45] basia, sed Catulliana,
> Quae si tot fuerint, quot ille dixit,
> Donabo tibi passerem Catulli.

Nimis enim foret insubidus poeta (quod nefas credere) si Catulli passerem denique ac non aliud quippiam, quod suspicor, magis donaturum se puero post oscula diceret. Hoc quid sit, equidem pro stili pudore suae cuiusque coniecturae de passeris nativa salacitate relinquo.

Hungarians,[146] recently showed me a very ancient codex of Valerius Flaccus's *Adventures of the Argonauts* from which I think flowed all the rest [of the codices] that are in circulation,[147] in the second book of which is this: "Wooden night (*nox durica*) remains, with the fates unchanged," not, as is commonly read, *dorica* ("Doric").[148] This reading is definitely either true and free of defect, or is (as I rather suspect) very near the true [reading], so that, as both usage and vocalism argue, *nox duria* ("wooden night") is his text, on which namely that wooden (*durius*), i.e., *durateus*, horse, opened up and restored to the world the Greeks enclosed in its belly. Nor should the diphthong be an obstacle. For in Greek the word is δούρειος ("timbered") as well as δούριος.[149]

: 6 :

How Catullus's sparrow should be understood,
and a passage of Martial is clarified as well

Catullus's famous sparrow[150] allegorically conceals, I think, an obscene meaning that we cannot express while maintaining modesty. Martial persuades me to believe this with an epigram the final verses of which are these:

> Give me kisses but in Catullus's way;
> If they are so many as he said,
> I shall give you Catullus's "sparrow."[151]

The poet would be exceedingly foolish (which is horrid to believe), if he were to say that after the kisses he would finally give the boy Catullus's sparrow and not something else, as I suspect. What this is, for my pen's modesty, I leave to each person's conjecture about the inherent salaciousness of the sparrow.[152]

∴ 7 ∴

Pathicos homines Iuvenalem innuere,
'qui digito scalpant uno caput,'
idque de Calvi poetae versiculis

1   Qui digito scalpunt uno caput.

Sane mollem virum ex eo significari apud Iuvenalem in satyra
nona nemini dubium, sed et Pompeium sic a Clodio notatum Plutarchus indicat in *Pompei vita,* ut illud interim omittam quod in libello quoque eo notam hanc Pompei attigit, cui titulus est: *Quo*
pacto fiat, ut inimici quoque prosint. Quin et Ammianus Marcellinus
Historiae libro XVII Pompei obtrectatores ait etiam hoc in eo ludi-
briosum et irritum observasse, quod genuino quodam more caput
digito uno scalpebat. Ceterum non tam mollis ex his verbis quam
plane pathicus et draucus aliquis designatur. Quod genus homines
in satyra universa Iuvenalis insectatur. Alioqui languidus oppugna-
tor et lenuncidus, vel potius (ut ita dixerim) ficulneus poeta sit
iste, si iam quasi in molles feratur, hactenus in pathicos invectus.
Alludit enim, sicuti mihi videtur, ad Calvi poetae versiculos in
Pompeium, de quis ita est apud Senecam in libris *Oratorum et rhe-*
torum: 'Carmina quoque,' inquit, 'eius, quamvis iocosa sint, plena
sunt ingentis animi; dicit de Pompeio, "Digito caput uno scalpit,
quo credas hunc sibi velle virum."' Hucusque Seneca de Calvo.

2   Quare cum poeta Iuvenalis indicare conaretur confluere Romam pathicos omnis, hoc est eos qui sibi virum vellent, festive id

: 7 :

That Juvenal is hinting at passive homosexuals with the
phrase "those who scratch their head with a single finger,"
as is the case concerning verses of the poet Calvus

Those who scratch their head with a single finger.[153]   1

No one, of course, doubts that an effeminate man is being referred
to by this phrase in Juvenal's ninth satire, but in his *Life of Pompey*
Plutarch points out that Pompey was thus branded by Clodius,[154]
though for now I will ignore that Plutarch also touched on this
mark of infamy of Pompey's in the little book entitled *On Deriving
Benefit from Enemies*.[155] In fact, in Book 17 of his *History*, Ammianus
Marcellinus also says that detractors of Pompey even observed in
him this scornful and pointless mannerism, namely, that he used
to scratch his head with a single finger as a kind of tic.[156] Yet he is
characterized in this excerpt as someone not so much effeminate
as clearly a passive homosexual and an athlete. Those are the sorts
of men Juvenal attacks in his entire satire. Besides, he would be a
feeble assailant and pander, or rather (so to speak) a poet made
of figs, if he were now attacking passive homosexuals as being
merely effeminate. For he alludes, as it seems to me, to the poet
Calvus's verses against Pompey, about which there is this in Seneca's books *On Orators and Rhetoricians*: "His poems, however jolly
they may be, also abound in enormous spirit; he says about Pompey 'he scratches his head with a single finger, so that you may
believe that he wants a man for himself.'"[157] Thus Seneca com-
menting on Calvus.

And so when the poet Juvenal tried to indicate that all the pas-   2
sive homosexuals, that is, those who want a man for themselves,
were flocking to Rome, he drolly hints at this on the basis of an

innuit ex particula Calvi versiculorum, tum quidem (ut est verisimile) notissimorum, per quam consequentia noscitarentur. Deque
his item supra dictis Calvi versiculis sentire Porcium Latronem
declamatione quadam apud eundem Senecam arbitror, qui ita dicat: 'In Cn. Pompeium, terra marique victorem fuit qui carmen
componeret, uno (ut ait) digito caput scalpentem; fuit aliquis qui
licentia carminis tres auratos currus contemneret.' Haec Porcius
Latro.

3   Quoniam autem liber hic Senecae quem adducimus rarissimus
adhuc inventu, propterea quasi novum dignati sumus hunc locum
nostris commentationibus, ne quis exposita nimis forsitan et pro-
culcata velutique in medio iacentia putet rettulisse.

: 8 :

Cur errantium siderum vocabula diebus tributa,
rationesque inibi ordinis
eorum scitu relatuque iucundae

1   Nomina ista dierum de stellarum errantium vocabulis appellata
quam habeant aut originem aut rationem, nusquam sane alibi me
legere quam apud historicum Dionem memini. Cuius ex libro
septimo atque trigesimo sic verba possumus interpretari:

> Nam quod his septem stellis qui planetes vocantur dies assi-
> gnari receptum est, inventum quidem putatur Aegyptiorum.
> Sed in omnes tamen homines haud ita pridem (ut sic dixe-
> rim) vulgari coeptum. Ceterum Graeci veteres (quantum
> equidem sciam) nullo prorsus eam rem pacto cognitam

excerpt from Calvus's verses, that were then (probably) very well known, from which the consequences would be recognized. Then again, I think that [Marcus] Porcius Latro was thinking about these above-mentioned verses of Calvus's in a certain declamation quoted by that same Seneca, since he said this: "There was a man who composed a poem attacking Gnaeus Pompey, conqueror on land and sea, who (as he claimed) scratched his head with a single finger; there was someone who, with poetic license, condemned his three gilded chariots."[158] Thus Porcius Latro.

Moreover, since this book of Seneca's that I am citing is a rarity,[159] I thought this virtually new passage worthy of my book, lest someone think that I have perhaps reported matters too much discussed, trite, and obvious. 3

: 8 :

Why names of the planets have been assigned to the days,
and the reasons for their order there, which are
charming to know and report

I recall reading nowhere else than in the historian Dio the origin 1 or reason that the names of the days were called after the planets. We can translate the words from his thirty-seventh book as follows:

The accepted system whereby the days are assigned to the seven stars that are called planets is thought to have been devised by the Egyptians. But even so, it was not all that long ago (so to speak) that it was spread among all people. Yet the ancient Greeks (as far as I know) did not have any knowledge of this system. But since this custom has become

habuerunt. Quoniam vero cum nationibus aliis, tum Romanis vel maxime, sic mos pervulgatus hic est ut quasi iam patrius videatur, pauca super iis edisseram, et quo pacto, quave causa sic ordinentur, exponam. Duplex igitur audita mihi ratio est, utraque sane haud intellectu difficilis, sed ut ambae tamen inspectionem contineant.

Nam siquis harmoniam quae diatessaron appellatur, qua una vis universa musicae totius contineri creditur, ad stellas has quibus omnis caeli ornatus distinguitur eodem quo feruntur ordine rettulerit; atque ab orbe illo supremo, qui Saturno tribuitur incipiens, omissis duobus sequentibus, quarti denique dominum nuncupaverit, ac dein duos item alios transiliens, septimum adiecerit, eodemque modo progrediens, praesides illorum deos subinde in orbem recensuerit atque ita dies adnumeraverit, deprehendet omnes ratione quadam musica cum caelesti illa distinctione ornatuque congruere. Ceterum haec una est quae fertur ratio.

Altera vero eiusmodi. Si diei noctisque horas a prima statim ceperis numerare, sic ut eam Saturno, dein sequentem Iovi, tertiam Marti, quartam Soli, quintam Veneri, sextam Mercurio, septimam Lunae tribuas, per eam scilicet orbium seriem quae ab Aegyptiis traditur, atque item denuo facias, donec horas quattuor et viginti pertranseas, invenies primam sequentis diei horam Soli cohaerentem. Tum hoc idem in quattuor illis et viginti horis, eadem qua prius ratione, si facias, Lunae primam tertii diei horam conciliabis. Quod si subinde hoc ipsum in ceteris observabis, congruentem plane deum sibi dies quaelibet asciverit.

so widespread among other peoples, and especially the Romans, that it now seems almost ancestral, I will offer a few explanations about the planets and set out how and why they are thus organized. I have heard two reasons, each of which is not at all difficult to understand, but both nonetheless require examination.

For if one applies "harmony," which is called the interval of the fourth, by which alone the universal force of all music is believed to be comprised, to these stars, by which all the beauty of the heavens is divided up in the same order in which they move; and if one begins at the highest orbit, which is assigned to Saturn, skips over the next two, then invokes the lord of the fourth orbit by name, and next passing over another two orbits again, adds the seventh; and if proceeding in the same way, one then includes in the circle the gods presiding over them, and thus enumerates their days, one will find that by a certain musical system all of them coincide with the heavenly pattern and beauty. So this is one account that is given.

The second one is along these lines. If you begin to enumerate the hours of the day and night starting with the first one, attributing it to Saturn, then the next one to Jupiter, the third to Mars, the fourth to the Sun, the fifth to Venus, the sixth to Mercury, and the seventh to the Moon, according to the order of their orbits, as has been passed down from the Egyptians, and likewise if you do it all over again until you have gone through twenty-four hours, you will discover that the first hour of the following day aligns with the Sun. Then if you do this again for another twenty-four hours by the same method as before, you will bring the first hour of the third day into conjunction with the Moon. If you then follow this procedure among the others, each day will have clearly aligned itself to a corresponding god.[160]

Haec Dion, festiva nimis et arguta (ni fallor).

2   Sed quoniam vulgo nunc sabbatum diesque dominicus vetus amisere nomen, cum ceteri etiam nunc retineant, scire studiosos convenit, et hunc Saturni et illum Solis appellatum. Nam de Solis die (quantum equidem nunc recordor) etiam Sozomenus Graecus historicus, etiamque divus Hieronymus, de Saturni autem vel hic ipse Dion libro eodem, vel Frontinus in *Strategematis*, vel item poeta *Elegiarum* Tibullus, vel postremo etiam Tertullianus in *Apologetico*, et Gaudentius in sermonibus commeminerunt. Sed et Faustus Milevitanus, Manichaeorum propugnator ille maximus, ita inquit: placet suscipere sabbatorum otium, et Saturniacis manus insertare catenis. Nec illud omiserim, mutata dierum istorum nomina in quae nunc a Christianis usurpantur auctore Constantino principe, sicut in illius Graeca laudatione meminit Nicephorus.

: 9 :

Quid in litteris Domitio
et quatenus credendum deque illius evidenti
pudendoque errore super voce attegias

1   Dirue Maurorum attegias.

Hoc Iuvenalis hemistichion de satyra quartadecima, quam aut erudite, aut fideliter, aut etiam perspicaciter enarret Domitius, age iam (si vacat) inspiciamus. Sed pauca de homine prius, siquis haec etiam fortasse.

Thus Dio's text, very droll and witty (if I am not mistaken).

But since the Sabbath and the Lord's Day have now commonly 2
lost their ancient names, while the rest [of the days] still retain
[theirs], it is fitting for scholars to know that the former was
named for Saturn and the latter for the Sun.[161] For (so far as I
now recall) even the Greek historian Sozomen as well as St. Jerome made mention of Sunday, whereas Dio himself in the same
book, and Frontinus in his *Stratagems*, and likewise the poet Tibullus in his *Elegies*, and finally also Tertullian in his *Apologeticus*,
as well as Gaudentius in his sermons, all mentioned Saturday.[162]
But Faustus Milevitanus too, that greatest champion of the Mani-
cheans, said: "It is pleasing to take up the leisure of the Sabbaths;
and to insert your hands into Saturn's cuffs."[163] Nor should I skip
over the fact that the names of those days have changed to those
which are now used by Christians by the authority of the emperor
Constantine, as Nicephorus mentions in his Greek eulogy of
him.[164]

: 9 :

What credence should be given to Domizio in literary matters,
and to what extent, and concerning his obvious,
shameful error about the word attegiae

Destroy the huts of the Moors.   1

Come now (if you are at leisure), let us examine how learnedly or
faithfully or even perceptively Domizio explains this half-line of
Juvenal's, from his *Satire* 14.[165] But first, if you please, a few things
about the man.[166]

2   Domitius igitur Calderinus Veronensis, qui decem abhinc annos vita functus, vir fuit acris ingenii multaeque in litteris industriae, Latinae linguae diligentissimus, Graecae non incuriosus, non
prosam condere absurdus, non carmen. Nimium sui tamen (quod
opera ipsius testantur) admirator, ac pro sententia cui semel
adhaeserat, etiam contra verum contumax et refractarius. Tum ob
id in scribendo quoque iactantior, atque omnium prae se contemp-
tor, omnium quam minima occasiuncula cavillator et sine discrimine vellicator. Itaque etiam simultates eum doctissimorum hominum nimio plures exercuerunt, odioque apud eos neutiquam
obscuro laboravit, auctoritatis vulgo tam magnae fuit, ut Romae
inter professores, iuvenis adhuc, primam sibi celebritatem vindica-
verit.

3   Cuius tuendae ac retinendae gratia factum compluries putamus,
ut in suis operibus frontem perfricuerit, et per aequa per iniqua
famam captans, parum ex fide quaepiam rettulerit, nonnulla etiam
male sollers et praestigiosus, speciem quidem primorem veri ha-
bentia, magno credentium dispendio, sententiis ignorabilibus im-
plicuerit, et pulverem (quod aiunt) oculis offuderit, aut sicubi
maior difficultas, nec absistens, nec congrediens, spem lectoris
eluserit. Ita dum nescire se nihil probare contendit, etiam Parthis
aliquoties et Cretensibus mendacior invenitur. Cuius exemplum
secutis aliis quoque in omnes iam litterarum articulos (ut verbis
utar Varronis) haec mali gangrena sanguinolenta permeavit, prae-
cidenda deletili stili parte certatim a doctis omnibus, ne ad vitalia
usque deserpat.

4   Sunt autem editi ab eo grammatici commentarii aliquot, ut in
Martialem Iuvenalemque poetas, quos et Medicibus meis Laurentio Iulianoque fratribus dedicavit, a quibus etiam muneribus est

Now Domizio Calderini of Verona, who departed this life ten   2
years ago, was a man of sharp intellect and great industriousness
as regards literature, a most diligent student of the Latin language
and not incurious of Greek, and facile at composing prose or poetry. Nonetheless (as his works attest) he was overadmiring of
himself, and on behalf of an idea he had once embraced, even in
the face of truth, insulting and belligerent. On that account, he is
a boaster in his writing, a despiser of all in comparison with himself, and a captious critic at the tiniest excuse, and indiscriminately
carps at everything. Therefore all too many feuds with the most
learned of men occupied him, and among them he suffered from a
loathing that they did not at all disguise; but he had such great
authority among the common people that when he was still a
young man, he claimed for himself the foremost fame among professors in Rome.

For the sake of guarding and holding on to this fame, we think   3
that he several times showed himself brazen in his works and,
courting reputation through thick and thin, reported certain things
unreliably, some even cunningly and deceitfully, though they had
an initial semblance of truth; at great cost of those believing him,
he entangled them in ignorant opinions, and (as they say) oc-
cluded their vision,[167] or wherever the difficulty was more serious,
neither shrinking from it nor meeting it head-on, he frustrated the
reader's expectation. And so, while striving to prove that there is
nothing he does not know, he is found to be several times more
mendacious even than the Parthians and Cretans.[168] Since others
are following his example, this bloody gangrene of evil has already
permeated all the joints of literature (to use Varro's words[169]); it
must be energetically obliterated with the blunt end of a stylus by
all the learned, lest it creep all the way to the vital organs.

Moreover, he published some grammatical commentaries, such   4
as on the poets Martial and Juvenal,[170] which he dedicated to
those Medici brothers of mine, Lorenzo and Giuliano,[171] by whom

amplissimis honestatus. Sed et in Stati *Silvulas*, et in epistolam
Sapphus, in *Ibin* quoque Nasonis, edidit quaepiam plena nimirum
bonae frugis, ubi non fucum facit et lectoris credulitatem ludifica-
tur. Ceterum Georgius Merula, vir plane doctus ac diligens, longe-
que quam Domitius in scribendo cautior, et nunc primi fere nominis, non remulo (quod aiunt) sed velificatione plena invectus,
commentariorum illius in Martialem, permultis editis notis, licentiam primus hominis magno veluti passu gradientem prorsusque
iam ferocientem compescuit.

5   Nos quoque dein primae sub flore iuventae, non quidem ut ipsius libros plane de manibus excuteremus, sed ut somniculosam
iuventutem velut in aurem utranque dormientem expergefacere-
mus, in ipso iam tum nostrae professionis tirocinio, sic eundem
leniter quandoque, quasique parcente manu feriebamus, et nunc
idem facturos praefamur, utcunque res feret, quo fides nobis liber-
tasque constet. Neque enim patiemur, quatenus vires suppetent,
impune illudi credulae iuventuti et simplicia ingenia supplantari.
Quoniam autem (ut est apud Plautum) feliciter sapit is, qui periculo alieno sapit, cavebimus ipsi quidem pro virili ne quid in hos
libros, quod non defendi queat auctoritatibus, referamus. Quid
autem ad summam de ipso sentiamus, si vitia virtutibus pense-
mus, et qua parte ingenii maxime stetit aestimemus, vel epigramma
testetur nostrum, quod in ripa Benaci lacus, ipso Domiti natali
solo, Baccius Ugolinus Florentinus atque Angelus Maffeus Veronensis, illius memoriae studiosi, novennium ferme abhinc inciden-
dum saxo curaverunt, quod et hic adscribam:

he was also honored with an abundance of gifts. But on Statius's dear little *Silvae* and on the letter of Sappho,[172] as well as in Naso's *Ibis*, he published some things full of good sense, when he is not playing tricks and mocking the reader's credulity.[173] Yet Giorgio Merula, a man clearly learned and diligent, and far more careful in his writing than Domizio, and now of generally outstanding reputation, not propelled by a little oar (as they say[174]), but attacking under full sail, by means of many published notes, was the first to check the license of the fellow's commentaries on Martial, license gaining ground, as it were, with great strides and already wreaking havoc.[175]

We too, then, in the blossoming of our early adolescence, already in the apprenticeship of our profession, struck him thus gently once or twice and, as it were, with a forebearing hand, not in order to shake his books out of his hands, but in order to wake up sleepy young people with a message for both their ears, and we now declare in advance that we are going to do the same, however the matter may turn out, so that our credibility and liberty may remain in place. For as far as in me lies, I shall neither allow credulous young people to be mocked nor innocents to be tripped up with impunity. However, since (as it says in Plautus) that man is happy in his wisdom who is wise in another man's danger,[176] I myself shall, to the best of my ability, beware of consigning to these books anything that cannot be defended by means of authorities. Moreover, to sum up, let our epigram, which the Florentine Baccio Ugolini and the Veronese Angelo Maffeo, cultivators of his memory, had carved in stone almost nine years ago on the bank of the Lake Garda, Domizio's native soil, attest to what we think of him, if we weigh his flaws against his virtues, and where, in particular, we think he ranked in terms of genius; I shall append it here:

5

Asta, viator, pulverem vides sacrum,
Quem vorticosi vexat unda Benaci,
Hoc mutat ipsum saepe Musa Libethron
Fontemque Sisyphi, ac virecta Permessi,
Quippe hoc Domitius vagiit solo primum,
Ille, ille doctus, ille quem probe nosti,
Dictata dantem Romulae iuventuti,
Mira eruentem sensa de paenu vatum.
Abi, viator, sat tuis oculis debes.

6   Sed nimis multa fortasse de homine, pauca praesertim polliciti, quod eo tamen consilio fecimus, ut offam veluti quampiam grammaticis istis diobolaribus, omnia quasi per nebulam videntibus, obiceremus, qui nihil omnino rectum putabunt, nisi quod ipsi denique tritum diu proculcatumque de suis illis profitentium commentariolis excerpserunt.

7   Ad *attegias* autem quod attinet, ipsius haec Domiti verba sunt:

Alii, inquit, accipiunt lingua Maurorum attegias mapalia significare. Ego potius intelligo hoc significare Mauritaniam ad extremam partem Libyae. Dionysius:

Ad[46] summam Libyen habitant attegias undas,
Alcidae qua sunt statuae, Maurusia plebes.

Haec ille, videns utique meliora, deteriora sequens, volebamque sane ista credere, sed rumor vera negat esse. Dionysium vero citat auctorem Domitius, qui si unquam vocabuli istius mentionem fecisse ullam reperietur, cedam tollamque manum iam tum, meque omnium haberi vanissimum non recusabo. Sed ut omni remota vessica rem putemus ipsam, non sunt Dionysi versus hi, non sunt.

Halt, traveler, you see the sacred dust,
Which a wave of the eddying Garda buffets.
The Muse often takes this in exchange for Libethron
And Sisyphus's font and Permessus's verdant glens.
On this soil Domizio first wailed,
He, that learned one, he whom you have known well,
The one giving lessons to the young of Romulus,
Extracting marvelous thoughts from the bards' storehouse.
Go, traveler, you have paid sufficient debt to your eyes.[177]

But perhaps we have said too much about the man, especially 6
since we promised to say little. We did this nevertheless with the
intent to throw, as it were, a sop to those two-penny grammarians,[178] who, seeing everything as if through a cloud, will not think
anything correct at all except the thing, long since trite and hackneyed, that they themselves have excerpted from the petty commentaries of teachers.

Moreover, in regard to the word *attegiae*, Domizio's own words 7
are as follows:

Others accept that in the language of the Moors *attegiae*
means "huts" (*mapalia*). I understand this, rather, to refer to
Mauritania at the far end of Libya. Dionysius:

At the end of Libya, the Moorish people inhabit attegian
waves,
Where the statues of Alcides are.[179]

These are his words. Though he sees what is better, he follows the
worse,[180] and though I wanted to believe that, rumor denies that
this is true. Indeed, Domizio cites Dionysius as his authority,
who, if he ever is found to have mentioned this word, I shall withdraw and raise my hand,[181] and I shall not object to being considered utterly useless. But in order that we may ponder the point
itself, with all the covering removed, these verses are not, I repeat,

Verum Prisciani potius, quo libello Dionysium poetam de Graeco interpretatur.

8   Corrumpit eos autem Domitius atque depravat. Nam quod apud Priscianum fuit 'ad Tethyos undas,' priore inducta interpolataque scriptura, pro eo supposuit 'attegias undas,' neutiquam (ut arbitror) facturus, si rationem carminis, aut si spatia morasque syllabarum consuluisset, cum vocabulum quod est *attegias* antepenultima porrecta syllaba, contra ipsius quem interpretatur testimonium, tum postrema brevi, contra omnium posuerit auctoritatem. Bene quod extat Dionysius, cuius esse Graecos illius argumenti hos puto versus:

> Ἀλλ' ἤτοι πυμάτην μὲν ἐπὶ γλωχῖνα νέμονται
> Ἀγχοῦ στηλάων Μαυρουσίδος ἔθνεα γαίης.

9   Licet autem evolvas iam totum, videbis ne minimam quidem suspicionem subesse *attegiarum* apud Dionysium, videbis alium citari pro alio, expungi veram scripturam, supponi falsam, rationem syllabarum vel carminis haberi nullam. Et dubitabit aliquis ab ipso iam liberrime dissentire et refutare has nugas, vel si praeiudicata pridem de hominis ingenio doctrinaque opinio causam faciat invidiosiorem?

10   Ceterum *attegias* ipsi vel tabernacula, vel umbracula, vel (si hoc magis placet) mapalia intelligimus, qualia Mauri colunt, qui Numidae a Romanis, ut *Historiae* scriptor Herodianus est auctor. Vocabulum id Rufinus usurpat in libro *Iosepi*[47] *De bello Iudaico* septimo: 'Cum ad festum,' inquit, 'diem venisset, quo attegias in honorem dei componi ab hominibus mos est.' Nam quod Latine Rufinus 'componi attegias' ait, id ipse auctor Iosepus σκηνοποιεῖσθαι dixerat Graece.

are not Dionysius's. They are, rather, Priscian's, in the book in which he renders the poet Dionysius from the Greek.[182]

These, however, Domizio corrupts and distorts. For what in Priscian was *ad Tethyos undas* ("at the waves of the sea"),[183] with the prior reading introduced and inserted, for this he substituted *attegias undas*, not at all what he would do (I think) if he had considered the meter or the quantities and divisions of the syllables, since he posited the word *attegias* with a long antepenult, contrary to the testimony of the very author he interprets,[184] then a short final syllable, contrary to the authority of all. But it is good that Dionysius is extant, whose Greek verses on this theme are, I think, these:

> But indeed, the peoples of the Mauritanian land dwell
> At the last extremity near the pillars.[185]

Moreover, even if you read through the whole work, you will see that there is not the slightest suspicion of *attegiae* in the writings of Dionysius; you will see one author cited in place of another, the correct reading expunged, a false one substituted, no account taken of the syllables or the poetry. And will anyone by now hesitate boldly to dissent from him and refute this nonsense, even if inveterate prejudice about the man's talent and learning make the cause invidious?

I, however, understand *attegiae* as either "tents" or "shelters" or (if one prefers) "African huts," such as the Moors inhabit, whom the Romans call Numidians, for which the historian Herodian is the authority.[186] Rufinus uses this word in Book 7 of his *Josephus's On the Jewish War*: "When he had come to the feast day, when it is the custom for huts (*attegiae*) to set be up by men in honor of God."[187] For Rufinus's Latin version "for huts to be set up" (*componi attegias*), the author Josephus himself has in Greek "for huts to be put up" (*skenopoieisthai*).

: 10 :

De Baptis et Cotytto, deque Cotyttiis,
tum apud Iuvenalem et Horatium
recta indicata lectio enarratioque

1   Cecropiam soliti Baptae lassare Cocyton.

Hunc Iuvenalis versum Domitius expositurus, erraticis (ut ita
dixerim) suspicionibus fibulam laxans, ineptias hallucinatur et nugas meras, Baptas esse inquiens Cereris sacerdotes, Cocyton Cere-
rem, nec, arbitror, hoc unquam dixisset, si quod in homine, non
pudoris dixerim, sed sensus omnino vestigium fuisset. Nos enim
tunc demum credituri, cum quispiam proferetur, quo satis certo
auctore stetur. Sed est hoc familiare huic (agam enim iam liberius)
ut cum nihil explicare possit, implicet, et quidquid obvium sit ar-
ripiat, eoque feratur diffidente conscientia, quo denique ipsum
impetus errabundae opinionis impellit.

2   Nos antiquam comoediam poetae Eupolidis innui suspicamur,
quod veterum excellens auctoritas persuasit. Etenim de ea sic Platonius Graecus auctor, ubi de comoediarum differentiis agit:

ἴσμεν γοῦν τὸν Εὔπολιν ἐπὶ τῷ διδάξαι τοὺς
Βάπτας ἀποπνιγέντα εἰς τὴν θάλατταν ὑπ᾽ ἐκείνων
εἰς οὓς καθῆκε τοὺς Βάπτας.

'Scimus,' inquit, 'Eupolin, quoniam Baptas fabulam docuerit, ab iis
ipsis in mare summersum contra quos Baptas emiserat.' Lucianus

: 10 :

Concerning the Baptae and Cotytto, as well as the Cotyttia;
then a reading and an account in Juvenal and Horace
are shown to be correct

Baptae used to tire out Cecropian Cocyto.[188]   1

When Domizio sets out to explain this line of Juvenal, he loosens
the clasp (so to speak) on erroneous suspicions and dreams up
absurdities and pure nonsense, when he asserts that the Baptae
were priestesses of Ceres and that Cocyto was Ceres, nor, I think,
would he ever have said this, if the man had had a particle, I
would not say of shame, but of sense. For we are only going to
believe it when a reliable authority is cited to vouch for it. But this
is a familiar procedure for him (for I shall now deal with him more
boldly), that when he can offer no explanation, he complicates the
matter, and seizes whatever is to hand, and though his conscience
hesitate, he is swept wherever the force of erroneous opinion
drives him.

We suspect an allusion to an ancient comedy of the poet Eupo-   2
lis, a fact argued by the outstanding authority of the ancients.[189]
The Greek author Platonius says this about it, when he addresses
the differences between comedies:

> We know at any rate that after producing the *Baptae* Eupolis
> was drowned in the sea by those whom he targeted in the
> *Baptae.*

"We know," he says, "that since he produced the play the *Baptae*,
Eupolis was drowned in the sea by those very ones against whom
he had unleashed the *Baptae*."[190] Lucian too in the oration entitled

quoque in ea oratione quae inscribitur *Ad ineruditum multos empti-tantem libros* in hanc ferme sententiam:

> Dic mihi, inquit, etiamne Aeschinis orationem adversus Ti-marchum legis? an vero illa omnia scis, et nosti singula? Aristophanem vero et Eupolin subisti? Baptas integram fa-bulam pellegisti? Tum nihil ex his pertinere ad te putasti? neque ea cum agnosceres erubuisti?

Sed et Hephestion in *Enchiridio* de acatalectis agens, duos citat versiculos ex Eupolidis *Baptis*. Et Suidas unum ex eisdem in voca-bulo quod est *atrypheros*.

3   Iam primum igitur constare opinor, *Baptas* comoediam fuisse veterem et mordacem poetae Eupolidis. Quod autem comoediae argumentum, quae materia per ipsa quae nunc extant vestigia sagaciter indagabitur. Athenienses igitur ea tempestate sacra quae-dam religionesque peregrinas novosque deos asciverant, quibus nocturnae pervigilationes essent institutae, magnorum dein flagi-tiorum causa sicuti Romae Bacchanalia. Sed inter sacra cetera[48] fuere etiam quae dicerentur Cotyttia. Contra haec nocturna Cotyttia scripsisse Eupolin *Baptas* putamus, sed et alios comicos, interque eos Aristophanem quoque, videmus totum hoc genus pervigiliorum et peregrinitatis exagitasse, sic ut Iuvenalis, quae Romae fierent contra ritum cerimoniarum, non dissimilia dicat iis quae Baptae Athenis in nocturnis Cotyttiis patrarent. Cicero in *Legibus* sic ait:

> Quid autem mihi displiceat in nocturnis poetae indicant co-mici. Qua licentia Romae data, quidnam egisset ille qui in sacrificium cogitatam libidinem intulit quo neque impuden-tiam quidem oculorum adici fas fuit?

Against an Ignoramus who Habitually Buys a Lot of Books, speaks to this effect:

> Tell me, do you also read Aeschines's speech *Against Timarchus*? Or indeed do you know all of those things and understand every point? Have you, in fact, taken on Aristophanes and Eupolis? Did you read through the entire play the *Baptae*? So then, did you think that none of this pertains to you? And when you recognized it, did you not blush?[191]

But in his *Handbook*, where he addresses acatalectic verse, Hephaestion cites two lines from Eupolis's *Baptae*.[192] And Suidas cites one of these under the word *atrypheros* ("delicate").[193]

In the first place, then, I think it is established that *Baptae* was   3
an old, caustic comedy by the poet Eupolis. Furthermore, I will keenly track down the theme of the comedy and the subject matter by the traces that still remain. Now at that time the Athenians had adopted certain foreign rites and religious practices and new gods, for whom nocturnal vigils had been established, which were then, like the Bacchanalia at Rome, a cause of great scandal. But among the holy rites there were also included those that were called the Cotyttia. I think that it was against these nocturnal Cotyttia that Eupolis wrote his *Baptae*, but we also see that other comic poets, including Aristophanes, excoriated this entire category of foreign all-night rituals. Hence Juvenal says that the ceremonies performed at Rome contrary to ritual were not dissimilar to those that the Baptae carried out at Athens in the nocturnal Cotyttia. Cicero says the following in *On the Laws*:

> Moreover, the comic poets indicate what displeases me in nocturnal ceremonies. If such license were granted at Rome, what would he have done who introduced deliberate wantonness into a sacrifice which it was impermissible even for an inadvertent glance to see?[194]

Et mox idem:

> Atque omnia nocturna (ne nos duriores forte videamur) in
> media Graecia Diagondas Thebanus lege perpetua sustulit.
> Novos vero deos et in his colendis nocturnas pervigilationes
> sic Aristophanes, facetissimus poeta veteris comoediae, vexat
> ut apud eum Sabazius[49] et quidam alii di peregrini iudicati e
> civitate eiciantur.

Apparet utique de Ciceronis testimonio, cum Aristophanem tum
comicos alios veteres contra novos deos contraque nocturnas pervigilationes aciem stili destrinxisse. Cum vero ex superioribus li-
queat, *Baptas* fuisse comoediam qua turpia et obscena carperentur,
atque hic de Baptis deque nocturnis Atheniensium sacris mentio,
quae nos Cotyttia fuisse appellata declarabimus, quis non intelligat
iam, *Baptas* fuisse denique qua potissimum fabula talia vexarentur?

4   Strabo autem in libro *De geographia* decimo Cotyttia Bendi-
diaque sacra fuisse apud Thracas narrat, ex quibus Orphica sump-
serint originem, deamque nominat Cotyn, cuius faciat Aeschylus
mentionem, tum idem paulo post Athenienses ait multa ex peregrinis sacris accepisse ὥστε καὶ ἐκωμῳδήθησαν, inquit. Sed
et inter cetera quae peregrina ab iis recepta sacra commemorat,
prima enumerat Thracensia, quae supra ostendimus Cotyttia Ben-
didiaque appellari. Liquet igitur Cotyttia ab Atheniensibus sacra
externa coli solita, liquet etiam vexata a comicis, coniectura autem
ducimur, ut cum de *Baptis* hic mentio, quam scimus fuisse Eupolidis comoediam, deque sacris Atheniensium nocturnis, in ea potissimum id genus sacra exagitarentur.

And immediately the same author:

> And (lest we seem too harsh) in central Greece Diagondas of
> Thebes abolished all the nocturnal rites by a perpetual law.
> Indeed Aristophanes, the wittiest poet of Old Comedy, so
> ridiculed the new gods and the nocturnal vigils in their wor-
> ship that in his writings Sabazius and certain other foreign
> gods are condemned and expelled from the city.[195]

It is, in any case, evident on Cicero's testimony that both Aristophanes and other poets of Old Comedy drew the point of their
stylus against new gods and nocturnal vigils. Since indeed it is
clear from the passages above that the *Baptae* was a comedy in
which disgraceful and obscene practices were criticized, and here
there was mention of the Baptae and of the nocturnal rites of the
Athenians, which I shall show were called the Cotyttia, who still
fails to understand that the *Baptae* was the play in which such
practices were excoriated *par excellence?*

Moreover, in the tenth book of his *On Geography*, Strabo ex-   4
plains that the Cotyttia and Bendidia were sacred rites among the
Thracians, from which the Orphic rites took their origin, and he
identifies the goddess as Cotys, whom Aeschylus mentions; then
the same author says a little later that the Athenians accepted
many elements from foreign rites, "with the result that they were
also satirized."[196] But among the rest of the foreign rites that he
says were received by them, he first lists the Thracian ones, which
I showed above were called the Cotyttia and Bendidia. It is therefore clear that the Cotyttia were foreign rites wont to be practiced
by the Athenians; it is also clear that they were pilloried by comic
poets. Moreover, we are led to conjecture that when mention is
made here of the *Baptae*, which we know to have been a comedy of
Eupolis's, and of nocturnal rites of the Athenians, rites of this type
were above all excoriated in it.

5   Ceterum deam quae talibus praeesset ritibus pervigiliisque Cotytto vocatam putamus, a qua etiam recta ratione Cotyttiorum est inclinata appellatio, quae quoniam dea comoediis veteribus defamatissima, ideo Synesius in epistola quadam, cuius principium est: ὁ καὶ τοὔνομα δοῦλος καὶ τὴν προαίρεσιν ad hunc plane modum narrat:

> Ἑρμῇ μὲν καὶ Ἡρακλεῖ τοῖς παλαίστρας ἐφόροις
> οὐδὲ κατὰ μικρὸν πρέπει· Κοτυττοῖ δὲ καὶ τοῖς ἄλ-
> λοις Ἀττικοῖς κονισάλοις νεωκορεῖ.

Quibus verbis significatur eum, de quo in epistola agat, non Mercurio congruere, non Herculi, palestrae[50] praesidibus, sed esse Cotyttus aeditimum ceterorumque apud Atticos despicatissimorum. Quare *Cotytto* legendum, non *Cocyton*, praesertim cum syllabae repugnet quantitas, quae ne tum quidem brevis, cum *t*[51] alterum subtraxeris, ut Domitius praescribit, inscite ille quidem nimis (sit vero venia), nimis inquam inscite negligenterque, qui non cogitaverit primam nominis syllabam non positu modo, cui duntaxat occurrit, sed natura quoque productam.

6   Quidam tamen hanc deam Cotyn maluere quam Cotytto, sicuti Strabo supra, sicuti alibi Synesius[52] idem his verbis:

> θαρρῶν ἀποφαίνου τὸν ἄνδρα ἡμίγυννον αὐτόχρημα
> θιασώτην τῆς Κότυος.

'Audacter,' inquit, 'pronuntia virum eum semimarem statim sodalemque Cotys.' Quem exponens locum Suidas, Cotyn deam coli ait turpium praesidem:

Moreover, I think that the goddess who presided over such rites 5
and vigils was called Cotytto, from whom the name of the Cotyttia derives according to rule. Since she was the most notorious
goddess in Old Comedy, in a particular letter, the beginning of
which is: "The slave both by name and choice," Synesius writes
thus:

> He is not one whit fitting for Hermes and Heracles, over-
> seers of the palaestra, but cleans the temple for Cotytto and
> other Attic demons.[197]

By these words it is indicated that the subject of the letter is not
fitting for Mercury or Hercules, who preside over the wrestling
school, but is a sacristan of Cotytto and the other most despised
gods among the people of Attica. Therefore *Cotytto* must be read
and not *Cocyton*, especially since the length of the syllable is incom-
patible, which is not even short when you subtract the second *t*, as
Domizio prescribes, far too ignorantly (let the truth be pardoned),
far too ignorantly, I say, and carelessly, since he failed to consider
that the first syllable of the name, is not simply lengthened by
position, which at any rate does occur, but also by nature.

Nevertheless, certain persons have preferred this goddess to be 6
Cotys rather than Cotytto, just as Strabo above, just as elsewhere
Synesius likewise, with these words:

> Be bold and at once reveal the effeminate man, a worshipper
> of Cotys.[198]

He says, "Boldly proclaim him at once to be an effeminate and an
associate of Cotys." In explaining this passage, Suidas says that the
goddess Cotys is being worshipped, who presides over obscene
practices:

Unde, inquit, sunt Clisthenae, et Timarchi, et quicunque lucri gratia formam colunt ad infandam libidinem, sicut effeminati, et capillum fingentes universi.

Sed et alibi, credo, invenient quibus haec adiuventur viri docti, si doctrinae studium adhibuerint. Quin apud Horatium quoque in *Epodis* ita legendum existimamus:

Inultus ut tu riseris Cotyttia,

non ut plerique codices *Cocytia*. Et in vetustissimo libro, qui sit Georgi Antoni Vespuccii Florentini, Graece Latineque docti hominis, vocabulum id antepenultima syllaba *t* retinet, non *c*, vestigium, arbitror, unum adhuc integrum verae integraeque lectionis.

: II :

Sententia de Claudiano exposita,
relatu praequam lepidae fabellae,
tum fabella altera non insuavior e Graeco itidem
versa super Venere et rosa

1 Claudianus in libro *De raptu Proserpinae* secundo, de Venere dea rosas purpureas colligente loquens, ita inquit:

Sic fata cruoris
Carpit signa sui.

From this, he says, derive the Clistheneses and Timarchuses, and all who cultivate their beauty for profit and unspeakable lust, like the effeminate and all those who style their hair.[199]

But elsewhere learned men will also, I believe, discover means by which this argument can be aided, if they apply their zeal to learning. In fact, I am of the opinion that in Horace's *Epodes* as well the following should be read:

So that you laugh with impunity at the Cotyttia,

and not, as many codices do, "Cocytia."[200] And in a very old book that belongs to the Florentine Giorgio Antonio Vespucci, a man learned in Greek and Latin, the word retains a *t* in its antepenult, not a *c*—a single still intact vestige, I think, of the true, intact reading.

: II :

A thought from Claudian is expounded by telling a very
charming tale and then another tale no less sweet,
likewise translated from the Greek,
about Venus and the rose

In the second book of his *On the Abduction of Proserpina*, speaking   1
about the goddess Venus gathering crimson roses, Claudian writes
the following:

Having spoken thus, she plucks
The signs of her own gore.[201]

Locus sane videri obscurus poterat, nisi apud Aphthonium in *Progymnasmatis rhetoricis* exposita fabella, sic propemodum:

> Qui rosae pulchritudinem demiratur, plagam Veneris consideret. Amabat Adonin dea, Mars ipsam. Quodque dea foret Adonidi, Veneri Mars erat. Deus deam adamabat, deaque hominem sequebatur. Par cupido, tametsi genus dispar. Perimere Adonin Mars zelotypus tendebat, finem putans amoris Adonidis necem. Ferit Adonin Mars. Accurrit auxilio Venus, festinans in rosas incidit, ac se spinis implicuit. Ita pedem perforatur, qui vulnere manarat cruor de se rosam coloravit. Sic rosa, quae prius candida, quod nunc cernitur facta.

Attigimus ipsi quoque fabellam hanc in *Rustico* nostra versiculo illo:

> Idalio pudibunda sinum rosa sanguine tinguit.

Sed et universam pulcherrime numeris vernaculis complexus Mecenas hic aevi nostri Laurentius Medices, ut in omni virtute, sic etiam in poetica eminentissimus.

2   Nonnus autem poeta mirificus libro primo et quadragesimo Dionysiacon[53] Martem ipsum, cum ab eo fuerit Adonis occisus, in aprum semet vertisse fabulatur, ita de Venere scribens:

> Μούνην δὲ συῶν οὐκ ἤθελε λεύσσειν
> Τερπωλὴν ἅτε μάντις· ἐπεὶ συὸς εἰκόνι μορφῆς
> Ἄρης καρχαρόδων θανατηφόρον ἰὸν ἰάλλων
> Ζηλομανὴς ἤμελλεν Ἀδώνιδι ποτμὸν ὑφαίνειν.

The passage could very well seem obscure, except for a tale set out in Aphthonius, in his *Preliminary Rhetorical Exercises*, approximately as follows:

> Let him who is amazed at the beauty of the rose consider it Venus's wound. The goddess loved Adonis, as Mars loved her. What the goddess was to Adonis, Mars was to Venus. The god was in love with the goddess, and the goddess pursued the man. The passion was equal, even though the category was different. Out of jealousy Mars was trying to kill Adonis, thinking that the death of Adonis would be the end of her love. Mars struck Adonis dead. Venus ran to his aid and in her haste she fell into some roses and became caught in their thorns. In this way she pierced her foot [on a thorn]; the blood that flowed from the wound dyed the rose. Thus the rose, which previously had been white, became what it is now seen to be.[202]

I myself also touched on this tale in my *Rusticus*, in this line:

> The blushing rose tinged her bosom with Idalian blood.[203]

But Lorenzo de' Medici, the Maecenas of our age and so very distinguished in the art of poetry as in every virtue, also took up the whole tale most beautifully in vernacular verse.[204]

Moreover, in the forty-first book of his *Dionysiaca*, the marvelous poet Nonnus tells the story of how Mars turned himself into a wild boar after he killed Adonis, when he writes the following about Venus:

> Only the delights of swine did she [Venus], like a seer, refuse to gaze upon, since Ares, in the form of a boar, with sharp jagged teeth, spewing deadly poison, and mad with jealousy, intended to contrive death for Adonis.[205]

2

Negat his versibus Nonnus delectatam fuisse apris Venerem, quoniam fore cognoverat, ut apri figuram indueret aliquando Mars ac prae[54] zelotypia necaret Adonin. Rosam vero esse alioqui gratam Veneri nec ille tacet lepidissimus epigrammatum vates:

> I felix rosa (inquiens) mollibusque sertis
> Nostri cinge comas Apollinaris,
> Quas tu nectere candidas sed olim,
> Sic te semper amet Venus, memento.

Sed et Vergilius in elegidio quodam suo (cur autem non suum credamus quod omnium sit elegantissimum?) sic ait:

> Sideris et floris est domina una Venus.

3   Ceterum Libanius ille quoque sophista Graecus, nec ulli Atticistarum secundus, ita quodam velut angulo super argumento isto de rosa Veneris lusitat:

> Quo, inquit, tempore iudicem deabus pastorem fabula dedit, male habebat Iunonem, male Minervam quoque, cestus ille Veneris, in quo amabilitas, in quo etiam cupido est. Ita venturas prius in certamen negabant, quam ubi a se Venus medicamentum foret amolita. Sic enim cingulum illud appellabant. Atqui ne vos quidem, Venus aiebat, lenociniis[55] vacuae. Tu diadema aureum crinibus, tu galeam similiter auream geris vertice. Sed enim fucos istos habere per me vobis liceat.[56] Liceat modo per vos ornatum comptumque mihi alium asciscere cinguli vice. Sic morem deabus gerens, ire ad Scamandrum pergit, lectura flores qua se pratum sub ripa explicabat herbidum. Simul aquulae ipsae blandae

In these verses Nonnus declares that Venus took no pleasure in the wild boar since she knew that Mars would one day assume the form of a wild boar and slay Adonis out of jealousy. Indeed, the delightful epigrammatist does not suppress the fact that the rose was in other respects pleasing to Venus:

> Go, happy rose, and with soft garlands
> Wreathe the locks of our Apollinaris;
> Remember to wreathe them one day when they are white,
> So may Venus always love you.[206]

Vergil too says the following in a certain elegy of his (and why should we not believe that it is his, since it is the most elegant of all?):

> Venus alone is mistress of the star and the flower.[207]

Yet the famous Greek sophist Libanius, second to none of the 3
Atticists, also likes to play this way, as if in a private retreat, with the theme of the rose of Venus:

> When legend assigned a shepherd as judge for the goddesses, Venus's famous girdle worried Juno and Minerva too, the girdle which attractiveness and desire inhabit. And so they declared they would not enter the contest until Venus removed her charm—for that is what they called her girdle. And yet you are not free of allurements either, Venus asserted. You [Juno] wear a golden diadem on your hair; you [Minerva] similarly wear a golden helmet on your head. But you may keep those adornments as far as I am concerned. Only let me, with your permission, annex another ornament and embellishment in place of the girdle. Thus humoring the goddesses, she proceeded to go to the Scamander, to pick flowers where the grassy meadow stretched out beside the riverbank. Nearby was a gentle, clear brook, inviting to bathe

perspicuaeque suberant, et ad lavandum illices. Lota ibi dea, statim (qua causa venerat) ornatum quaerebat sibi. Tum nescio qui mire suavis aspirare odor visus. Iam lilia, iam violas legerat dea, cum tamen odor ille magis interim magisque blandiebatur. Pergit aurae flagrantis vestigia subsequi. Videt rosam, visamque naribus admovet, et esse hanc suave olentiae illius matrem cognoscit. Ibi flores aspernata ceteros abicit humi. Tantumque rosis coronata, recepit se ad Idam denuo. Nec autem plus Veneri flos, quam flori Venus conciliare gratiam visa. Adeoque confestim Iuno Minervaque victae, ut ne ipsae quidem pastoris expectarint calculum. Sed adcurrentes utraque sertum crinibus detraxerint, floremque deosculatae ipsum, rursum Veneris capiti reposuerint.

Hactenus de rosa Libanius, cuius tamen linguae Graecanicis pictae coloribus nitidissimum tectorium, nescio an ad unguem nostra ista tumultuaria Latinitas repraesentaverit.

: 12 :

Quomodo inventa purpura,
simul explicatus Nonni locus Graeci poetae

1   Quo pacto inventa sit purpura non alienum fuerit hic referre, vel ut Graeci poetae Nonni locus intelligatur, vel ut fabella praequam lepida, Latinis intacta, noscatur. Est autem apud Pollucem libro *De verbis idoneis ad Commodum* primo, in hanc sententiam:

in. Upon bathing there the goddess immediately began to search for an adornment (since that is why she had come). Then some sort of wonderfully sweet aroma seemed to permeate the air. The goddess had already collected lilies and violets, but in the meantime that aroma charmed her more and more. She continued to follow the tracks of that intense breeze. She saw a rose, and, upon seeing it, moved it to her nostrils and recognized it as the source of that sweet fragrance. At that, she rejected the other flowers, throwing them to the ground. And crowned only with roses, she made her way back to Ida once again. Moreover, the flower won no less favor for Venus than Venus for the flower. Juno and Minerva were so quickly defeated that they did not even await the shepherd's verdict. But running to her, they both pulled down the wreath from her hair and showered that flower with kisses, and they repositioned it again on Venus's head.[208]

So far Libanius on the rose. I rather think that his fresco, extremely elegant with the Greekish colors of his painted language, was represented to a "t" by my improvised Latin.

: 12 :

How purple dye was discovered, along with explanation of a
passage by the Greek poet Nonnus

It is fitting to report here how purple dye was discovered, whether   1
in order to make sense of a passage by the Greek poet Nonnus or
that a quite charming little tale, one untouched by Latin authors,
may become known. Moreover, this is explained in the first book
of [Julius] Pollux's *To Commodus on Suitable Words*, along these
lines:

Tyrii ferunt, inquit, captum amore Herculem nymphae cuiusdam indigenae cui nomen Tyro, sequebaturque eum, inquiunt, canis antiquo more quo dominum canes usque etiam ad contionem comitabantur. Quare canis hic Herculeus, irreptantem scopulis purpuram conspicatus, peresa caruncula sua sibi labra cruore puniceo infecit. Cum igitur ad puellam Hercules adiisset, delectata illa insueta tinctura, quam ceu florentem in eius canis labris aspexisset, affirmavit, sibi cum illo posthac nihil fore, nisi ad se vestem afferret etiam canis illius labris splendidiorem. Quocirca inventa Hercules animante collectoque sanguine munus puellae detulit, primus (ut Tyrii dictitant) auctor puniceae infecturae.

2   Nos igitur in *Rustico* nostra propter hoc ipsum denique concham diximus Herculeam, cum purpuram significaremus. Porro autem Nonni poetae versiculi super hac ipsa fabula, sic in libro quadragesimo Dionysiacon[57] inveniuntur:

Καὶ Τυρίης σκοπίαζε δεδευμένα φάρεα κόχλῳ
Πορφυρέους σπινθῆρας ἀκοντίζοντα θαλάσσης.
Ἧχι κύων ἁλιεργὸς ἐπ᾽ αἰγιαλοῖσιν ἐρέπτων
Ἐνδόμυχον χαροποῖσι[58] γενειάσι θέσκελον ἰχθῦν,
Χιονέας πόρφυρε παρηίδας, ἔνδοθι κόχλου
Χείλεα φοινίξας διερῷ πυρί. τῷ ποτε μούνῳ
Φαιδρὸν[59] ἁλιχλαίνων ἐρυθαίνετο φάρος ἀνάκτων.

The Tyrians tell that Hercules was held captive by love for a certain native nymph whose name was Tyro and a dog followed him around, they say, in the ancient manner in which dogs would accompany their masters all the way to the assembly. This dog of Hercules, then, catching sight of the Murex brandaris creeping over the crags, ate the flesh and stained its lips with the crimson blood. So upon Hercules's approach, the girl, delighted by the unusual color seen so vividly on the dog's lips, asserted that she would have nothing further to do with him, unless he brought her a dress even more resplendent than the lips of that dog. And so Hercules discovered the creature and collected its blood and presented the gift to the girl, according to the Tyrians, the first discoverer of crimson dye.[209]

It was, then, on account of this that in my *Rusticus* I said that the conch shell was "Herculean" when I meant "purple."[210] Moreover, the verses by the poet Nonnus about this very tale are found in Book 40 of his *Dionysiaca* as follows: 2

He discovered a cloth tinged with a Tyrian conch shell
And shooting forth the sea's purple sparks,
Where a dog, fishing along the shoreline and plucking
With joyful jaws the wonderful fish lurking within,
Darkens its snowy cheeks and reddens its lips with the wet fire
From within the conch shell — with this alone
The resplendent cloak of purple-clad kings was one day
    reddened.[211]

: 13 :

Salutis augurium quod sit apud Suetonium

1   Suetonius Tranquillus in *Augusto* sic ait: 'Nonnulla etiam ex antiquis cerimoniis paulatim abolita restituit, ut salutis augurium,' et
cetera. Quod autem foret salutis augurium, video etiam a doctis
aliquot ignorari. Nos eam rem libro septimo trigesimoque Dionis
Historiarum ad hanc sententiam repperimus:

> Tum vero etiam salutis augurium, quod appellant, longo in-
> tervallo fecerunt. Est autem modus augurii quispiam, ut si
> deus permittat, salutem populo poscant, quasi ne salutem
> quidem a dis petere fas, ni prius hoc ipsum di concesserint.
> Observabatur autem dies una quot annis, in qua nullus ad
> bellum proficisceretur exercitus, nemo se contra pararet,
> nemo pugnaret. Quo circa in assiduis periculis, maximeque
> civilibus, neutiquam fiebat. Nam et arduum imprimis, pu-
> ram rebus his omnibus diem servare, et perquam absurdum
> videri poterat, ultro seditionibus detrimenta sibi ipsos incre-
> dibilia conciliare, cum et victis ea res futura esset et item
> victoribus pernitiosa, mox autem salutem a dis immortalibus
> petere. Ceterum tum fieri quidem augurium eiusmodi po-
> tuit. Sed ne id quidem purum processit, quoniam adversae
> quaepiam aves devolarunt unde augurium captum, aliaque
> item signa inauspicata apparuerunt.

2   Idemque etiam libro quinquagesimo scribit, ab Augusto pace
terra marique parta Ianum clusum, neque non salutis augurium
factum, quod ante multis causis[60] fuerat omissum.

: 13 :

What the augury of safety is in Suetonius

In his *Augustus*, Suetonius Tranquillus says the following: "He also   1
restored some of the ancient ceremonies that had gradually lapsed,
such as the augury of safety," etc.[212] But I see that it is unknown,
even by some learned individuals, what the augury of safety is. I
discovered this in Book 37 of Dio's *Histories*, along these lines:

> Then after a long interval they performed the "augury of
> safety," as they call it. This is, moreover, a type of augury
> that is for seeing whether the god allows them to beseech
> safety for the people, as if it were not even right to ask for
> safety from the gods unless the gods had previously granted
> this permission. Moreover, one day was observed every year
> on which no army advanced to war, no defensive measures
> were taken, and no one fought. Hence in the midst of con-
> stant dangers, especially civil ones, no augury was performed.
> For it was especially difficult to keep a day clear of all these
> things, and it would seem quite absurd for them to inflict
> incredible damage on themselves through civil wars, since
> that state of affairs is going to be deadly for both victors and
> vanquished alike, but then beseech safety from the immortal
> gods. Still, they were then able to conduct an augury of that
> kind. But even that did not proceed cleanly, since some unfa-
> vorable birds flew down from where the augury was taken,
> and other inauspicious signs likewise appeared.[213]

And the same author also writes in Book 50 that when Augus-   2
tus had established peace on land and sea, the temple of Janus was
closed, and that the augury of safety was performed, which had
been previously omitted for a variety of reasons.[214]

: 14 :

Naulia quae sint in Ovidi Artibus, *atque inibi de barbaris organorum appellationibus quibus Graeci nostrique utantur, quodque etiam Chaldaei Graeca interim nostraque id genus vocabula non aspernantur*

1   Disce etiam duplici genialia naulia palma
         Vertere, conveniunt dulcibus illa modis.

Naulia diminutivum[61] puto, sive *nablia*, ab illis quae vel *naula* vel *nabla* dicimus. Etenim *b* litteras et *u* ferme pro eisdem positas invicem saepe veteribus monimentis adnotavimus. Suidas etiam *nabla* organi species ait, et idem alio loco: 'Psalterium,' inquit, 'organum est musicum quod naula etiam vocatur.' Quin et Sophoclis versum Plutarchus adducit:

   Οὐ ναῦλα κωκυτοῖσιν, οὐ λύρα φίλα,

libro eo quem super ει Delphico fecit, sed et Theodoretus[62] in *Psalmos* de eo meminit, et Plutarchus in libris *Symposiacis*, ex quo nos in *Nutrice*:

         Non quae duplici geniale resultant
   Naula citata manu.

2   Sunt autem multa organorum barbara nomina, sicuti Strabo narrat libro decimo, inter quae *nabla* quoque enumerantur,[63] hoc est *psalteria*. Sed et illud observavi nuper apud Danielem prophetam, ducente me scilicet in recessus illos et sacra studiorum suorum penetralia Ioanne Pico Mirandula, Graeca etiam quae

: 14 :

What naulia *are in Ovid's* Art of Love, *and also about foreign names for instruments there that the Greeks and our own people use, and the fact that sometimes even the Chaldeans do not reject Greek and Latin words of that kind*

Also learn to play the festive harp (*genialia naulia*) with both   1
        hands;
    It is suited to sweet measures.

I think *naulia* or *nablia* is a diminutive from what we say as either *naula* or *nabla* ("harp"). For I have observed that the letters *b* and *u* are frequently substituted one for the other on ancient monuments.[215] Suidas too says *nabla* is a type of instrument, and likewise in another passage he says: "A cithara is a musical instrument that is also called a *naula* ('harp')."[216] In fact, Plutarch cites a verse from Sophocles —

Neither a harp nor a lyre is friendly to lamentations

— in the book he wrote on the Delphic ει,[217] but Theodoret also mentions it on the Psalms, as does Plutarch in the books of his *Table Talk*, by which I was inspired to write in my *Nurse:*

        Not the harps that resound with merriment
    When played with both hands.[218]

There are, however, many foreign names of instruments, as   2
Strabo explains in Book 10, among which are numbered *nabla*, that is, harps (*psalteria*).[219] But I have recently observed in the book of the prophet Daniel,[220] when Giovanni Pico della Mirandola was guiding me into the recesses and sacred inner sanctums of his studies, that names for such instruments that seem to be Greek

videantur Latinaque adeo istiusmodi organorum nomina, quamquam paulo corruptius, a Chaldaeis quoque auctoribus usurpari,
ut *carna* pro *cornu*, *cathros* pro *cithara*, *sabecca* pro *sambuca*, *psanterin*
pro *psalterio*, *samphonia* pro *symphonia*. Quin Gallus Solomon, ordi-
narius apud Hebraeos enarrator sacrarum litterarum, *nevel* ait esse
Hebraice quod ibi *psanterin*, idest *psalterium*, legatur. Constat autem litteris id nomen tribus[64] נכל, ex quo etiam *navel* in Esaia legitur et Amos, et Graeca dein figura *naulon*, a quo diminut⟨iv⟩um[65]
sit *naulion* hoc Ovidianum. Siquidem noviciae istae sunt notae
quibus Hebraei nunc pro vocalibus utuntur, ut idem et comperit
et ostendit Ioannes Picus Mirandula meus, unus omnium prorsus
ab omni parte beatissimus in opere singulari atque admirando, quo
Psalmos a Septuaginta versos, isto notarum praecipue argumento,
docet Hebraicae veritati respondere, ne iam insultare Iudaeus aut
obicere possit, ea nos in templo singulis canere horis quae ne ipsi
quidem satis versa fideliter existimemus.

3   Denique *genialia* cur dixerit Ovidius, facile noris verba ipsa legens de Scipionis Africani Aemiliani oratione contra legem iudi-
ciariam Corneli Gracci,[66] quae posita sunt in Macrobi *Saturnalibus*,
eorumque principium sic est:

> Docentur praestigias inhonestas, cum cinaedulis et sambuca
> psalterioque eunt in ludum histrionum, discunt cantare quae
> maiores nostri ingenuis probro ducier voluerunt. Eunt, in-
> quam, in ludum saltatorium inter cinaedos virgines puerique
> ingenui.

Sic Scipio.

4   Tum Ambrosius quoque libro ipso *De utilitate ieiunii* tertio, *psalteria* docet adhiberi conviviis, ut libidines incitentur. Sed enim in
comoediis quoque crebra psaltriarum mentio. Porro vocabulum

and Latin are also used, albeit in corrupt form, by Chaldaean[221] authors, such as *carna* for *cornu* ("horn"), *cathros* for *cithara* ("lyre"), *sabecca* for *sambuca* ("a small triangular harp"), *psanterin* for *psalterium* ("harp"), *samphonia* for *symphonia* ("a band of musicians"). As a matter of fact, Gallus Solomon,[222] a regular expounder of sacred literature among the Jews, says that *nevel* in Hebrew is what is there called *psanterin*, that is, *psalterium*. Moreover, it is well known that there is a noun with the three letters נכל, for which *navel* ("lute") is read in Isaiah and Amos,[223] and then the Greek form *naulon*, from which derives this Ovidian diminutive *naulion*. Since the marks that the Jews now use in place of vowels are of recent origin, as my friend Giovanni Pico della Mirandola both discovered and demonstrated—one man blessed in all respects in his unparalleled and admirable work, in which he teaches that the Psalms translated from the Septuagint, especially on the evidence of those marks, correspond to the original Hebrew, lest a Jew be able to scoff or object that every hour we are singing in the church things that we ourselves do not think have been translated faithfully enough.

Finally, you would easily know why Ovid said *genialia* when you 3 read the words from the speech of Scipio Aemilianus Africanus against the judiciary law of Cornelius Gracchus, which were cited in Macrobius's *Saturnalia*, the beginning of which is as follows:

> They are taught dishonest tricks; they go to acting school with catamites and an Asian and a regular harp; they learn to sing the songs that our ancestors wanted it considered a disgrace for freeborn persons to sing. Freeborn boys and girls, I say, go to dancing school among catamites.[224]

Thus Scipio.

Next, Ambrose too in the third book of his *On the Usefulness of* 4 *Fasting*, teaches that *psalteria* are used at banquets, so that sexual lusts may be aroused.[225] But there is frequent mention of harps in

ipsum Hebraicum est, nam Graece *psalterium* dicitur, Latine *lauda-torium*, sicuti divus Hieronymus ait in epistola ad Dardanum, docens in clypei modum quadrati esse formatum chordarum de-cem, quamquam Romanus Emanuel Hebraico commentario in Psalmos, utriculariam[67] putet esse fistulam *nevel*, videlicet etymon sequutus, quod ab utre deduci vocabulum illud apud Hebraeos videatur.

: 15 :

Qui fuerit auctor Sybaritidos, de quo Ovidius,
deque Sybariticis libellis apud Martialem
luxuque item cetero Sybaritarum

1 Ovidius in epistola ad Augustum libro *Tristium* secundo sic inquit:

Nec qui composuit nuper *Sybaritida* fugit.

Quaeritur inter litterarum studiosos, quinam sit is qui *Sybaritida* composuerit, quodve ipsius operis fuerit argumentum.

2 Nos utrumque apud Lucianum deprehendisse videmur in ora-tione quae est *Ad ineruditum qui multos emptitaret libros.* In ea scriptum est ad hanc fere sententiam:

Dic mihi hoc quoque, inquit. Si Bassus ille sophista vester, aut tibicen Battalus, aut cinaedus Hemitheon Sybarita, qui vobis mirificas conscripsit leges, quo pacto insanire oporteat et velle[68] et pati ac facere illa, si horum quispiam nunc leonis pellem circumdatus clavamque tenens incedat, quid? eum ne putes Herculem spectantibus visum iri?

comedies as well. Furthermore, the word itself is Hebrew, for in Greek it is called *psalterion*, and in Latin *laudatorium*, just as St. Jerome says in his letter to Dardanus,[226] where he teaches that it is shaped like a square shield and has ten strings, although in his Hebrew commentary on the Psalms Emanuel of Rome[227] thinks that the *nevel* is a bagpipe, obviously following the etymology, since among the Hebrews that word seems to have been derived from "bag."

: 15 :

Who was the author of the Sybaris, *about whom Ovid wrote, and about the Sybaritic pamphlets in Martial, and likewise the luxury of the Sybarites in general*

In his letter to Augustus, in the second book of his *Tristia*, Ovid 1 says the following:

He who recently composed the *Sybaris* did not go into exile.[228]

Literary scholars investigate who exactly composed the *Sybaritis* and what the content of this work was.

I seem to have discovered both in Lucian, in his oration *Against* 2 *an Ignoramus who Habitually Buys a Lot of Books*. In this, he writes more or less as follows:

Tell me this, too. If Bassus, that sophist of yours, or the flutist Battalus, or the catamite Sybarite Hemitheon, who wrote wonderful laws for you, by which you had to go mad and be willing to submit to and do such things, if anyone of this sort were now to go about, wrapped in a lion's hide and carrying a club, do you think that the spectators will take him for Hercules?[229]

Sed et Philo Hebraeus in *Vita* ipsa *Mose:* 'Comoedias,' inquit, 'et Sybariticas nequitias componentes.' Martialis quoque in libro duodecimo *Epigrammaton* de Sybariticis libellis ita:

> Qui certant Sybariticis libellis,
> Musseti pathicissimos[69] libellos
> Et tinctas sale pruriente chartas,
> Instanti lege Ruffe,[70] sed puella
> Sit tecum tua, ne Talassionem
> Indicas manibus libidinosis
> Et fias sine femina maritus.

3   Hemitheon igitur fuisse videtur, non, ut Domitius ariolatur, Sybaris, a quo vel *Sybaritis,* vel libelli Sybaritici, obscenissimo[71] sint argumento compositi. Notabiles autem sunt imprimis luxu et deliciis Sybaritae, sic ut praecipuos omnium colerent Ionas atque Tyrrhenos, quoniam alteri Graecorum, alteri barbarorum luxuriosissimi. Ab his etiam fabulae Sybariticae, quales ferme apud Aesopum, et proverbium deductum 'Sybarites per plateam,' contra fast⟨u⟩osius[72] ingredientes. Atque haec quidem de Sybaritis aliaque non dissimilia Suidas. Plutarchus autem in *Convivio septem sapientum* morem fuisse scribit Sybaritis mulieres ab usque anno priore ad convivia vocandi, ut veste auroque moliri exornareque per otium se possent. Sed et Maximus Tyrius in dissertatione tertia *De voluptate* primos enumerat Sybaritas inter eos populos, quos vult mollissimos deliciosissimosque videri, neque non Sybariticas etiam saltationes commemorat. Quin idem in dissertatione alia, cui titulus *Quae finis sit philosophiae,* fere in hanc sententiam: 'Crotoniates,' inquit, 'oleastrum adamat, Spartiates armaturam, venationes Cretensis, luxum Sybarites, Ion choros.' Hinc ergo Iuvenalis:

But Philo the Jew said in his *Life of Moses*: "Those who compose
comedies and Sybaritic naughtiness."[230] In Book 12 of his *Epigrams*,
Martial also speaks as follows about Sybaritic books:

> Read, Instantius Ruffus, those salacious little books of Mus-
> setus, which rival the Sybaritic books, their pages tinged
> with salacious seasoning. Yet may your girl be with you, so
> that you not betray your wedding cry with lecherous hands,
> and become a husband without a wife.[231]

Therefore, it seems to have been Hemitheon, not Sybaris, as 3
Domizio [Calderini] conjectures,[232] by whom the *Sybaritis*, or the
Sybaritic books, were composed with obscene content. Moreover,
the Sybarites are famous *par excellence* for their luxury and pleasures, such that they cultivated the Ionians and Etruscans in particular, since the former were the most luxurious of the Greeks,
the latter of the barbarians. From these also the Sybaritic tales
originate, which are mostly found in the works of Aesop, and the
derived proverb, "a Sybarite going through the square,"[233] against
those who walk mincingly. And Suidas says this and similar things
about the Sybarites.[234] Moreover, in his *Banquet of the Seven Sages*,
Plutarch writes that the Sybarites had the custom of inviting
women to banquets a year in advance, so that they could take
pains and adorn themselves with gold and clothing at their leisure.[235] But in his third essay *On pleasure*, Maximus Tyrius numbers the Sybarites first among the peoples he claims seem most
effeminate and most addicted to luxury, and he also mentions
Sybaritic dances.[236] In fact, in another essay, entitled *What is the
Goal of Philosophy?*, the same author speaks to this effect: "the Cro-
toniate is enchanted by the wild olive tree, the Spartiate armor, the
Cretan hunting, the Sybarite luxury, the Ionian a choral dance."[237]
Hence Juvenal:

Nullum crimen abest facinusque libidinis, ex quo
Paupertas Romana perit, hinc fluxit ad Istros
Et Sybaris colles.

Astipulatur et Strabo, qui Sybaritas omni sua felicitate propter
delicias luxumque septuaginta solis diebus fuisse narrat a Crotoniatibus exturbatos, quin dictum quoque Plutarchus Sybaritae
ponit in *Pelopide* negantis mirum facere Spartiatas, qui se in bellis
morti obicerent, ut tantos labores victumque illum quo utebantur
effugerent. Aristoteles autem *Moralium Eudemiorum* primo, Smyn-
diriden quoque Sybaritam comparem Sardanapallo inter voluptua-
rios nominavit.

4   Illud urbanum sane quod Africanus tradit in *Cestis* (sic enim
Graece liber ipsius de re militari inscribitur). Etenim Sybaritas eo
deliciarum venisse narrat, ut equos in convivia introducerent ita
institutos, ut audito tibiae cantu statim se tollerent arrectos, et
pedibus ipsis prioribus vice manuum gestus quosdam chironomiae
motusque ederent ad numerum saltatorios:

> At enim tibicen, inquit, ibi quispiam contumelia affectus
> transfugit ad Crotoniatas hostes, paulo ante praelio supera-
> tos a Sybaritis, et quod e republica foret illorum, pollicetur
> (si fidem modo habeant) sua opera Sybaritarum cunctos
> equites in ipsorum venturos potestatem. Credita res, et belli
> dux creatus a Crotoniatibus tibicen convocat omnis quot-
> quot eiusdem forent in urbe artificii, modulamentumque iis
> indicat, atque ut visum tempus, procedere in hostem iubet.
> Sed enim Sybaritae, fastu praeturgidi quod equitatu super-
> abant, eunt contra praeliumque conserunt. Hic autem re-
> pente dato signo tibicines universi conspirant. Ecce tibi igitur

No crime nor act of lust has been lacking, since
Roman poverty perished; from here Sybaris has flowed
To the people on the Danube and the hills.[238]

And Strabo too lends support, who reports that the Sybarites were cast out of all their happiness on account of their delicacies and luxury within only seventy days by the Crotoniates. Indeed, in his *Pelopidas* Plutarch too cites the saying of a Sybarite who declares it is no wonder the Spartiates expose themselves to death in war, in order to escape such severe hardships and the regimen they employ.[239] Moreover, in the first book of his *Eudemian Ethics*, Aristotle named Smyndirides the Sybarite as the equal of Sardanapallus among voluptuaries.[240]

The tale Africanus relates in the *Cesti* — for thus is his book on 4 military affairs entitled in Greek — is quite charming.[241] For he narrates that the Sybarites advanced to such a pitch of refinement that they introduced their horses into banquets trained in such a way that, upon hearing the tune of a flute, they would immediately rear up and with their forelegs, like hands, produce certain artful gestures and dance moves in rhythm:

> But a flutist there, smarting from an insult, defected to the Crotoniate enemy, who had a short time before been defeated in battle by the Sybarites, and promised that, if they trusted him, by his agency the entire Sybarite cavalry would be placed in their power — an outcome in the interest of their commonwealth. When the Crotoniates lent credence and placed the flutist in charge of the war, he summoned all his fellow flutists from the city and gave them the beat. And when it seemed time, he ordered them to advance against the enemy. But the Sybarites, puffed up with arrogance because they were used to conquering with their cavalry, went to meet them and joined battle. Here, as soon as the signal was given, all the flutists began playing. Behold, as soon as the

confestim modulamine agnito cantuque illo vernaculo, tollunt eriguntque semet in pedes equi Sybaritae, sessoribus excussis, et quod tripudium domi didicerant etiam in acie exhibent. Ita capti omnes equites, sed humi iacentes, omnes equi, sed tripudia repraesentantes.

Tantum de Sybaritis Africanus.

: 16 :

De Aristidae Milesiacis, *de quo sit apud Ovidium,*[73] *deque Milesiorum deliciis*

1 Ovidius idem in eadem ad Augustum epistola sic ait:

Vertit Aristiden Sisenna,[74] nec obfuit illi
Historiae turpes inservisse iocos.

Qui sit hic Aristides, quave libros materia fecerit, magna haesitatio, nos autem studiosam iuventutem ad auctorem Plutarchum delegamus, cuius in M. *Crassi vita* sub hoc propemodum intellectu verba sunt:

Collecto igitur Seleucensium senatui libros Aristidae Milesiacon perquam impudicos ostentavit, nihil in eo mentitus, siquidem re vera fuerant inter Rosci[75] sarcinas reperti. Quod et Surenae praebuit occasionem probri cavillique adversus Romanos, cum ne inter bella quidem continere semet a rebus litterisque huiuscemodi valerent.

Ita Plutarchus.

rhythm and that native song were recognized, the Sybarite horses reared up on their hind legs, shook off their riders, and displayed on the battlefield the triple-time dance they had learned at home. Thus, all the knights were captured, albeit lying on the ground, and all the horses, albeit reenacting the triple-time dance.[242]

This much Africanus on the Sybarites.

: 16 :

About the Milesian Tales *of Aristides, whom Ovid mentions, and about the Milesians' pleasures*

In the same letter to Augustus, Ovid says: 1

> Sisenna translated Aristides, and he was not harmed
>   By inserting off-color jokes into his *History*.[243]

There is great doubt as to who this Aristides is, and on what subject he wrote his books. Let us refer studious young people to the author Plutarch, whose words in the *Life of Marcus Crassus* have this approximate sense:

> Therefore he showed to the assembled senate of the Seleucians the lewd books of Aristides's *Milesian Tales*, being quite truthful in this matter, since they had in fact been found among Roscius's baggage. That also gave Surenas the opportunity to reproach and jeer at the Romans, since they were incapable of abstaining from affairs and literature of this sort, even in the midst of war.[244]

Thus Plutarch.

2   Est autem Surenas apud Persas magistratus nomen, quasi prae-
torem dixeris, quod et Zosimus ostendit. Atque hunc quidem
Plutarchi locum transcriptum plane, sicuti alia pleraque, in Ap-
piani quoque *Historia* deprehendes. Lucianus item in *Amoribus* sub
hoc pene sensu de Aristide:

> Magnopere, inquit, me narratiuncularum tuarum perquam
> impudicarum lepida et dulcis suadela lactavit, ut propemo-
> dum te esse Aristiden, meque sermonibus crederem Milesia-
> cis demulceri.

Quocirca etiam Apuleius epigramma ipsum statim, quod in fronte
Asini sui collocavit, ita exorditur:

> At ego tibi sermone isto Milesio varias fabellas conseram,
> auresque tuas benivolas lepido susurro permulceam.

Ex quo Marcianus:[76] 'Nam certe,' inquit, 'mythos, poeticae etiam
diversitatis delicias Milesias,' et reliqua.

3   Fuere autem Milesii quoque deliciis luxuque notabiles, ex eoque
proverbium Graece fertur: Οἶκοι τὰ Μιλήσια· μὴ γὰρ ἐνθάδε,
hoc est, 'Domi, non hic Milesia,' videlicet in eos qui domesticum
luxum celebrant ubi minus probatur. Nam sic Lacedaemone Milesius hospes audivit, cum delicias patrias extolleret, sicuti etiam
scriptum in Apostoli Byzantii[77] proverbiorum collectaneis. Sed et
Maximus Tyrius idem significat, qui Milesios a vestitu molliore
vocat εὐειμονοτάτους. Ex quo apud Vergilium in *Georgicis*:

> Milesia vellera nymphae
> Carpebant.

Ex quo illud item Horatianum:

Moreover, Surenas is the name of a magistrate among the Per- 2
sians, what you might call a *praetor*, as Zosimus shows.[245] And indeed you will find this very passage of Plutarch, like many others,
clearly transcribed in Appian's *History*.[246] Lucian likewise, in his
Loves, speaks about Aristides in this approximate sense:

> The charming and sweet allurements of your salacious narra-
> tives so thoroughly beguiled me that I almost thought you
> were Aristides and that I was being soothed with Milesian
> conversations.[247]

Hence the epigram that Apuleius prefaced to his *Ass* begins as follows:

> I shall string together an assortment of tales for you in this
> Milesian discourse, and shall delight your kind ears with
> charming murmurings.[248]

Accordingly, Martianus [Capella] says: "For certainly myths, even
the Milesian delights of poetic diversity," etc.[249]

Moreover, the Milesians were also notable for their pleasures 3
and luxury, as a result of which a proverb is circulated in Greek:
"Let Milesian things be at home, but not here," that is [in Latin],
"Milesian things at home, not here," i.e., it is directed at those
who celebrate domestic luxury where it is disapproved. For this is
what a Milesian guest heard at Sparta, when he extolled the pleasures of his homeland, as is also written in the collections of the
proverbs of Apostolius of Byzantium.[250] But Maximus of Tyre indicates the same, who calls the Milesians "extremely well turned
out," because of their softer style of dress.[251] Hence in Vergil's
Georgics:

> The nymphs were carding
> Milesian wool.[252]

From this too derives that verse of Horace's:

139

Alter Mileti textam cane peius et angui
Vitabit chlamydem.

Sunt autem omnino Iones quoque ceteri praequam deliciis habiti
defluentes, quod in veteribus memoriis passim. Ceterum ne hoc
quidem tacitum praeteribimus: 'Veretro solitas uti Milesiacas femi-
nas e corio,' sicuti scriptum etiam apud auctorem Suidam. Quin
item apud eundem legimus a Milesio Cadmo libros compositos
quattuor de solvendis amoribus.

: 17 :

Correctus in tragoedia Senecae locus atque
ex Graeca remotiore fabula declaratus super
Nemiaeo[78] leone

In tragoedia Senecae quae *Hercules furens* inscribitur hic senariolus
legitur:

Sublimis alias Luna concipiat feras.

Alias enim codex habet vetustus ex publica Medicae familiae bibliotheca, non *altas*, ut in vulgariis exemplaribus. Cuius intellectum
loci non temere aliunde quam ex Achille desumpseris, quem auctorem Iulius quoque Firmicus in Matheseon libris et citat et laudat. Is igitur in commentariis Arateis, cum de Luna verba facit, ita
scribit ad verbum:

εἶναι δὲ ἐπ' αὐτῆς οἴκησιν ἄλλην, ποταμούς τε καὶ
ὅσα ἐπὶ γῆς, καὶ τὸν λέοντα τὸν Νεμιαῖον ἐκεῖθεν
πεσεῖν μυθολογοῦσιν,

idest,

CHAPTER 17

The other will avoid a woven cloak from Miletus
More than a dog or a snake.[253]

However, the other Ionians have generally been held to abound in pleasures, as is seen here and there in ancient records. Yet we will pass over not even this in silence: "The Milesian women generally make use of a leather dildo," as was recorded in Suidas.[254] In fact, we likewise read in the same author that four books were composed by the Milesian Cadmus on putting an end to love affairs.[255]

: 17 :

A passage in a tragedy by Seneca corrected and elucidated from a recherché Greek tale about the Nemean lion

In Seneca's tragedy entitled *Hercules Furens*, this iambic senarius is read:

The moon on high conceives other (*alias*) wild beasts.[256]

For an old codex in the public library of the Medici family has *alias* ("other"), not *altas* ("tall"), as in the common copies.[257] You would be rash to take the meaning of this passage from any source other than Achilles [Tatius], an author whom Julius Firmicus both cites and praises in the books of his *Lessons*.[258] He, then, when speaking of the moon in his commentaries on Aratus, writes verbatim:

There is another dwelling upon it [the moon], both rivers and whatever is on the earth, and they invent the tale that the Nemean lion fell from there,[259]

that is [in Latin],

in ea etiam habitari fluviosque esse et cetera, sicut in terra, quin Nemiaeum quoque illinc cecidisse leonem fabulantur.

Ex quo nos in *Nutrice:*

>Nemiaeaque tesqua
>Lunigenam mentita[79] feram.

: 18 :

*Quid sit apud Iuvenalem 'fraterculus gigantis,'
quidque apud alios 'terrae filius,'
ibidemque de Mani vocabulo*

1   Unde fit ut malim fraterculus esse gigantis.

Versum poetae Iuvenalis hunc ex satyra quarta quicunque hacte-nus interpretati sunt haerent in salebra, quantum video, nec enar-rare illi quidem mihi, sed risum captare anilibus fabulamentis, vel derisum potius videntur. Quippe alii gigantas in simias conversos, alii post gigantas a Terra simiam productam in deorum contemp-tum comminiscuntur, frigidiora his alia quae, sicut ille Martialis rhetor, Neronianas thermas refrigerarent. Etenim nullo, quantum intelligam, sensu, nullo (quod sciam) dicuntur tradente has nugas auctore.

2   Mihi fraterculus gigantis significare hominem videtur nullis maioribus ortum, ignoto genere obscuroque, quoniam cuius igno-rabantur parentes, eum vulgo appellare veteres terrae filium con-suevissent. Ex quo Persius:

142

In it there are habitations and rivers and other things, as on earth; in fact, they even tell the tale that the Nemean lion fell from there.

On the basis of this, I wrote in my *Nurse:*

> The wilderness of Nemea lied that the beast
> Was born on the moon.[260]

: 18 :

What the "little brother of a giant" is in Juvenal,
and what the "son of the earth" is in other authors;
and concerning the word Manius *in the same place*

For which reason I would prefer to be the little brother of a 1
giant.[261]

Those who have previously interpreted this line by the poet Juvenal, from the fourth satire, are stuck in a rut, as far as I can see, and they seem to me not so much to explain it as to try to provoke a laugh, or rather ridicule, by telling old wives' tales. Indeed, some made up the story that the giants were turned into monkeys, others that, after the giants, the Earth produced a monkey to show contempt for the gods;[262] other things still more frigid than these would chill Nero's baths, as Martial's rhetorician says.[263] For these things are said without any logic so far as I can perceive, without any source (as far as I know) passing on this nonsense.

It seems to me that the little brother of a giant designates a 2 man born with no forebears, of an unknown and obscure lineage, since the ancients were wont to call him whose parents were unknown a "son of the earth." Hence Persius:

Praesto est mihi Manius haeres
Progenies terrae, quaere ex me quis mihi quartus
Sit pater, haud prompte dicam, tamen adde etiam unum,
Unum etiam, terrae est iam filius.

Vides igitur vel unius auctoritate Persi, terrae filium dici cuius nescirentur parentes, nec adeo putes otiose Manium illic a Persio nominatum. Ut enim omittam quae de Manio scribit Aricino Pedianus,[80] etiam Mani nomen ipsum Graecus auctor Zosimus[81] *Romanae historiae* libro tertio, non quia natus mane, sicuti ceteri, sed a manibus ait appellatum. Quin M. Varronis liber compluries a Marcello citatur *Mani* titulo etiam nescio quid alicubi de funere attingens, ut favere hunc quoque augurer nobis.

3   Cicero item in primo *Epistolarum* volumine *ad Atticum:* 'Sed haec ad te scribam alias subtilius, nam neque adhuc mihi satis nota sunt, et huic terrae filio nescio cui committere epistolam tantis de rebus non audeo.' Sed idem quoque in epistola ad Trebatium sic ait: 'Cn. Octavius—an Cn. Cornelius?—quidem tuus familiaris, summo genere natus, terrae filius,' quod in quibusdam codicibus depravatum, proque eo suppositum *Zerae filius*, cum verior scriptura maneat adhuc in libro pervetere, quondam doctissimi viri Philelphi, nunc Laurenti Medicis, patroni litterarii, simulque in libro altero de vetere (ut apparet) exscripto, qui nunc in bibliotheca publica Medicae familiae. Vides a Cicerone quoque nihilo setius ignotum prorsus hominem terrae appellari filium.

My heir, Manius — a son of the earth —
Is standing ready. Ask me who is my grandfather's
Grandfather. I shall answer, though not at once.
Add one and another one, and he is now a son of the earth.[264]

Therefore you see that it is on the authority of Persius alone that he whose parents are unknown is called a "son of earth," nor should you suppose that Manius was redundantly named there by Persius. For though I shall omit what Pedianus writes to Aricinus[265] about Manius, the Greek author Zosimus, in the third book of his *History of Rome*, also says that the name Manius was given not because he was born in the morning (*mane*), as the rest of the sources say,[266] but from the spirits of the dead (*Manes*).[267] In fact, a book of M. Varro's entitled *Manius* is cited several times by [Nonius] Marcellus, which touches in part on something connected with a funeral, so that I conjecture that he also supports me.[268]

Likewise, Cicero, in the first book of his *Letters to Atticus*: "But I will write this to you in more detail at another time, for so far I have insufficient knowledge, and I dare not entrust a letter about such important matters to this 'son of the earth.'"[269] But the same author says again in a letter to Trebatius: "There is a certain Cn. Octavius — or is it Cn. Cornelius? — a friend of yours, born to the highest station, a son of the earth," which is corrupted in some codices, and in its place *Zerae filius* ("son of Zera") is substituted,[270] although the more accurate text still remains in a very ancient book, one that once belonged to an extremely learned man, [Francesco] Filelfo, but now to Lorenzo de' Medici, a literary patron, and at the same time in another book copied out from an old one (so it seems), which is now in the public library of the Medici family.[271] You see nonetheless that Cicero too calls an unknown man a son of the earth.

3

4   Lactantius etiam *Divinarum institutionum* libro primo his utitur
verbis:

> Minucius[82] Felix in eo libro qui *Octavius* inscribitur sic argu-
> mentatus est: Saturnum, cum fugatus esset a filio in Ita-
> liamque venisset, Caeli filium dictum, quod soleamus eos,
> quorum virtutem miremur, ad quos repentine advenerint de
> caelo cecidisse dicere, Terrae autem quod ignotis parentibus
> natos terrae filios nominemus.

Hactenus Lactantius.

5   Sed et Tertullianus in *Apologetico* de eodem Saturno sic scribit:
'Dictus autem Terrae et Caeli filius, quia ignoti vel ex inopinato
apparentes de caelo supervenisse dicuntur, ut terrae filios vulgus
vocat quorum genus incertum est.'

6   Quare cum hoc praeoptaret homo esse obscurus quam nobilis
Umbricius,[83] quod olim prodigio par erat in nobilitate senectus,
utpote saevientibus in eam Romanis principibus, malle se ait fraterculum gigantis, hoc est, terrae filium, quod (ut ostendimus)
obscurum significat, quam nobilem patriciumque. Gigantes enim
terra editi. Suavius autem fraterculum quam fratrem, ne videretur
vastitatem illam molemque gigantei corporis, sed generis duntaxat
ignobilitatem concupiscere.

Lactantius, too, in the first book of his *Divine Institutes*, uses   4
these words:

> Minucius Felix in the book entitled *Octavius*, argued as fol-
> lows: When Saturn had been put to flight by his son and
> had come to Italy, he was called "son of Heaven," because we
> are wont to say that those whose virtue we admire have
> fallen from heaven to those to whom they have suddenly
> come. On the other hand, we call those born to unknown
> parents "sons of the earth."[272]

Thus Lactantius.

In his *Apologeticus*, Tertullian writes the following about Saturn: 5
"He is called the son of Earth and Heaven because unknown persons or those who appear unexpectedly are said to have arrived out
of the heavens, just as the common folk call those whose lineage is
uncertain 'sons of earth.'"[273]

Therefore, when Umbricius[274] preferred to be obscure rather   6
than a noble, because among the nobility old age was once as rare
as a prodigy, since the Roman emperors were raging against the
nobility, he says that he prefers to be the "little brother of a giant,"
that is, a son of the earth, which (as we demonstrated) means obscure, rather than noble and patrician. For the giants were produced by the earth. Moreover, it was more elegant to say "little
brother" than "brother," so that he would not seem to crave the
hugeness and mass of the giant's body but merely the ignobility of
the family.[275]

: 19 :

Super aspiratione citata quaepiam,
simul enarratum Catulli nobile epigramma

1 Quintilianus libro *Oratoriarum institutionum* primo de aspiratione
agens ita inquit:

> Parcissime ea veteres usi etiam in vocalibus, cum aedos[84]
> ircosque dicebant, diu deinde servatum, ne consonantibus
> aspirarent, ut in Graccis, et in triumpis. Erupit brevi tempore
> nimius usus, ut choronae, chenturiones, praechones adhuc
> quibusdam inscriptionibus maneant. Qua de re Catulli no-
> bile epigramma est.

Haec ille. Putamus autem epigramma citari hoc potissimum.

> Chommoda dicebat, si quando commoda vellet
>   Dicere, et hinsidias Arrius insidias,
> Et tum mirifice sperabat se esse loquutum,
>   Cum quantum poterat dixerat hinsidias.
> Credo sic mater, sic liber avunculus eius,
>   Sic maternus avus dixerat, atque avia.
> Hoc misso in Syriam requierant omnibus aures
>   Audibant eadem haec leniter et leviter.
> Nec sibi post illa metuebant talia verba.
>   Cum subito affertur nuntius horribilis

: 19 :

Some passages are cited on aspiration,
along with an explanation of a famous epigram by Catullus

When Quintilian addresses the topic of aspiration in the first 1
book of his *Education of an Orator*, he says:

> The ancients used it [aspiration] very sparingly even on vow-
> els, since they used to say *aedi* [for *haedi* ("kids")] and *irci* [for
> *hirci* ("goats")], and then for a long time they kept the prac-
> tice of not aspirating consonants, as in the case of *Gracci* [for
> *Gracchi*] and *triumpi* [for *triumphi* ("triumphs")]. Excessive use
> [of aspiration] erupted for a short time, so that *choronae* [vs.
> *coronae* ("garlands")], *chenturiones* [vs. *centuriones* ("centuri-
> ons")], *praechones* [vs. *praecones* ("heralds")] still survive in
> certain inscriptions. There is a well-known epigram by
> Catullus about this matter.[276]

These are Quintilian's words. Moreover, we think that this epigram is being cited in particular:

> Arrius used to say *chommoda*, whenever he wanted to say
>   *commoda* ("benefits"),
> And *hinsidiae* whenever he wanted to say *insidiae* ("plots").
> And then he hoped that he had spoken marvelously,
>   When he had said *hinsidiae* as forcefully as he could.
> I believe his mother said it this way, as did his freeborn uncle,
>   As well as his maternal grandfather and grandmother.
> After he was sent to Syria, everyone's ears found relief,
>   And they heard these same words in a softer, lighter way.
> Nor did they fear such words after that.
>   Then suddenly a horrible report arrived

Ionios fluctus postquam illuc Arrius isset,
    Iam non *Ionios* esse, sed *Hiønios.*

Est vero observandum ut etiam in pronuntiando, quemadmodum in scribendo, vocibus aspires. Quod nunc Graeci tantum in consonantibus, Latini ne in consonantibus quidem retinuerunt.

2   Contra veteres Latini etiam in loquendo vocalibus aspirabant. Ex quo Cicero in *Oratore* ad Brutum ita scribit:

> Quin ego ipse cum scirem ita maiores locutos esse ut nusquam nisi in vocali aspiratione uterentur, loquebar sic ut pulcros, Cetegos, triumpos, Cartaginem[85] dicerem. Aliquando idque sero convicio aurium cum extorta mihi veritas esset, usum loquendi populo concessi, scientiam mihi reservavi.

Sic Cicero. Sed et aureolum vidi equidem nuper apud Laurentium Medicem nomisma cum titulo: TRIUMPUS. Et item argenteum alterum, cum vulgatiore hoc: TRIUMPHUS.

3   Quin A. quoque Gellius in secundo *Noctium Atticarum*[86] testatur veteres *h* litteram, seu spiritum, plerisque vocibus verborum firmandis (ut ipse inquit) roborandisque inseruisse, ut sonus eorum esset viridior vegetiorque. Sed et Priscianus ait aspirationem vocalibus extrinsecus ascribi, ut minimum sonet, consonantibus autem intrinsecus, ut plurimum.

4   Quare si constare tibi Catulliani epigrammatis leporem voles, aspirationem ipsam suo loco, quantum poteris, pronuntiabis. Sed ista video iam sic innotuisse ut aliena fortasse cuipiam videri

That after Arrius had gone there, the Ionian waves,
  Were no longer *Ionii* but *Hionii*.[277]

But it must be noted that you aspirate words in pronouncing them
as you do in writing them. The Greeks have now retained aspiration only on their consonants, the Latins not even on their consonants.

In contrast, the ancient Latins used to aspirate even their vow- 2
els in speaking. Hence Cicero writes to Brutus in his *Orator* as
follows:

> In fact, knowing that our ancestors spoke in such a way that
> they used aspiration nowhere except on vowels, I used to
> speak so as to say *pulcri, Cetegi, triumpi,* and *Cartago* [instead
> of *pulchri, Cethegi, triumphi,* and *Carthago*]. And after some
> time, all too late, when the truth was wrung from me by my
> ears' reproach, I yielded to the people my practice in speak-
> ing and kept that knowledge to myself.[278]

Thus Cicero. I recently saw a gold coin at Lorenzo de' Medici's
house with the legend: "TRIUMPUS."[279] And likewise, I saw
another coin, this one silver, with this more common inscription:
"TRIUMPHUS."

In fact, in the second book of his *Attic Nights*, A. Gellius, too, 3
bears witness that the ancients inserted the letter *h*, or aspiration,
on the vowels of many words for firming them up (as he says) and
strengthening them, with the result that their sound was fresher
and livelier.[280] But Priscian also says that aspiration is added exter-
nally to vowels so as to sound minimally, but added internally to
consonants in order to sound as much as possible.[281]

Therefore if you want to give a correct account of the charm of 4
the Catullan epigram, you will pronounce the aspiration in its
place as strongly as possible. But I see that those things have already become so well known that someone might take them to be

possint. Atqui tamen pene adhuc equidem adulescens coram litteratis aliquot, quos et meminisse arbitror, de hoc ipso loco ad Domitium Florentiae rettuli, qui sic ei statim applausit ut ingenue fateretur se plus eo die ab uno scholastico didicisse quam multis ante annis a quopiam professorum. Scit Aurelius Ariminensis (ut alios omittam), qui nunc Patavi degit, praestanti iuvenis et ingenio et litteratura, quam multos abhinc annos istam de nobis ennarationem Florentiae tum quidem agitans acceperit, quamque sit (ut idem postea Patavi narrabat) nova prorsus ignotaque iam tum visa omnibus, ad quos de ea.[87]

5   Catullum autem plane universum Veronae (scit hoc vir liberrimi ingenii Baccius Ugolinus) intra officinam quampiam, quo nos pluvia coegerat, viris aliquot litteratis pene cogentibus enarravimus, cum quidem illic adesset etiam Guarini propinquus Ioannes Baptista (ni fallor nomine) simulque Dantes quidam Aligherius, quintus, ut aiebat, a Dante Florentino poeta, neque non duo qui tum Veronae non indocti homines profitebantur magnaque itidem scholasticorum manus, ita pronis auribus nostra illa qualiacunque accipientes, ut identidem clamarent demissum caelitus[88] Angelum sibi (sic enim aiebant) qui poetam conterraneum interpretaretur. Neque ob id istorum tamen commemini, quo inventa mea mihi denique uni, nullo in participatum recepto tribui postulem (non enim sic mihi arrogo) sed ne quis forsan alienis laboribus me, quasi corvum aut vulturem relictis ab aquila cadaveribus, putet vesci.

another's property. But when virtually still an adolescent, I reported on this very passage, in the presence of some literary scholars (who I reckon also remember the occasion), to Domizio [Calderini] at Florence, who at once applauded it so strongly that he honestly confessed that he had learned more on that day from one student than for many years from any of the professors. [Giovanni] Aurelio [Augurello] of Rimini (to skip over the others), who now lives in Padua, a young man outstanding in both talent and learning, knows how many years ago he heard that story about me when he was then living at Florence and how new (as the same man afterward related at Padua) and unknown it seemed to all to whom he spoke about the matter.[282]

Moreover, I explained all of Catullus at Verona (Baccio Ugolini, 5 a man of boundless genius knows this) in a certain shop, in which the rain had forced us to take refuge, to some literary scholars who practically placed me under compulsion, when indeed there were present Giovanni Battista (if I'm not mistaking his name), a relation of Guarino's, along with a certain Dante Aligheri, the fifth (as he used to say) from the Florentine poet Dante, as well as two other learned men who were then professors at Verona, and likewise a great band of students, who received our views, whatever their merits, with such eager ears that they repeatedly shouted that an angel had descended to them from heaven (so they said) to interpret an earthly poet.[283] I have not, however, called them to mind to demand that my discoveries be attributed to me alone, with no one allowed a share in them (for I make no such claim for myself) but lest someone suppose that I am feeding on the toils of others like a crow or vulture on corpses left by an eagle.[284]

: 20 :

Emendata apud Suetonium, et enarrata vox haec ascopera

1 Vitiati deprehenduntur Suetoniani codices in *Nerone*. Nam sic utique in omnibus: 'Alterius collo et scopa deligata, simulque titulus: "Ego quod potui, sed tu culleum meruisti."' Nam neque scopa Latine dicitur numero singulari, et si maxime dicatur, nihil tamen commercii scopis et culleo.

2 Sed enim in vetustis exemplaribus vestigium, ut arbitror, extat incolumis veraeque lectionis, hoc modo: 'Alterius collo ascopa deligata.' Quare si litteram penultimam perscripseris, *ascopera* fiet, quod et esse rectissimum puto, siquidem est ascopera sacculus pelliceus, compositumque nomen Graece est ex utre et sacco, de quo vocabulo ita scribit Suidas: ἀσκοπήρα τὸ μαρσίππιον ἤτοι τὸ σακκοπάθνιον.[89] Marsippium significare Suidas *ascoperam* docet. Haec ergo fuit *ascopera* Neronianae statuae collo deligata, cullei symbolum, quoniam matricida. Quod enim culleo parricidae insuuntur qui sit e corio bovis, eius cullei veluti instar quoddam repraesentavit, qui deligavit ascoperam.

3 Iuvenalis de parricida et culleo sic:

Et deducendum corio bovis in mare, cum quo
Clauditur adversis innoxia simia fatis.

: 20 :

Corrections in Suetonius, and the word ascopera explained

Suetonius's codices are found to be corrupt in the *Nero*. For at any rate all of them contain: "A broom is tied about the neck of the other one, and likewise an inscription: 'I got what I deserved, but you earned the leather sack.'"[285] For *scopa* ("broom") is not treated in Latin as singular, and even if it were, there is no connection between a broom and a leather sack.

But there remains in ancient exemplars a trace, I think, of the intact, true reading, along these lines: "A leather pouch (*ascopa*) is tied about the neck of the other one." So if you write out the penultimate letter in full, it will become *ascopera*, which is what I think is correct, since *ascopera* is a small leather sack, and is a compound noun in Greek from "bag" and "sack," about which word Suidas writes as follows: *ascopera*: a little bag or sack.[286] [In Latin] Suidas teaches that *ascopera* means "little bag." This *ascopera*, then, was tied around the neck of Nero's statue, a symbol of the sack, since he was a matricide. For because parricides were sewn into a sack made of cowhide, he who tied on the leather pouch portrayed the likeness of that sack.

Juvenal says the following about the parricide and the sack:

And the man must be thrown into the sea inside a cow's hide,
With whom an innocent ape is enclosed by unlucky fate.[287]

∶ 21 ∶

Quid sit aut minerval *aut minervale munus,*
ex eoque sententiae Iuvenalis et Varronis expositae

1   Quisquis adhuc uno partam colit asse Minervam.

Hoc ex decima Iuvenalis poetae satyra Domitius ita exponit ut
eius neutiquam videatur pervidisse intellectum: 'Minervam partam, idest cuius ludis Quinquatribus, ut posset certare adeptus
est.' Quo quid est absurdius aut inconcinnius? An, quaeso, uno
asse quispiam assequatur, ut certare de eloquentia publice possit?

2   Ceterum minervale munus, quod et minerval dicitur, innuisse
Iuvenalis videri potest, mercedulam magisterii scilicet a scholasticis
dari solitam, potissimumque arbitror ante Quinquatria, per quos
dies pueri vacabant, unde Horatius in extrema epistola:

Ac potius puer ut festis Quinquatribus olim,
Exiguo gratoque fruaris tempore raptim,

sicuti Saturnalibus et Kalendis[90] item mos habuit. Quare de Quinquatribus agens Ovidius in *Fastis* ita inquit:

Nec vos turba feri censu fraudata magistri,
Spernite, discipulos attrahet illa novos.

: 21 :

What a minerval or a minerval gift is, and on that basis the thoughts of Juvenal and Varro are expounded

Whoever still worships frugal Minerva with a single coin.[288]   1

Domizio [Calderini] explains this point from the tenth satire of the poet Juvenal in such a way that he seems not to have understood its sense at all: "He obtained an acquired Minerva, that is, he obtained the privilege of competing in her Quinquatrial Games."[289] What is more absurd or clumsy than this? Might someone, I ask, for a single penny obtain the ability to compete in a public contest for eloquence?

Yet Juvenal may seem to have hinted at a minerval gift, which is   2
also called a *minerval*, a small payment for teaching customarily given by school boys, especially, I think, prior to the Quinquatrial games, during which boys were on holiday, whence Horace in his last letter:

And rather, like a boy once at the Quinquatrial games,
    You are hastily enjoying a small, pleasant bit of time,[290]

just as was likewise the custom at the Saturnalia and Calends. Accordingly, when discussing the Quinquatrial games, Ovid says in his *Fasti*:

You, harsh teachers, now that your band of students has been
        defrauded
    Of their wealth, do not spurn Minerva; she will attract new
        students.[291]

De minervali hoc munere etiam divus Hieronymus ita meminit, in epistolam scribens Pauli ad Ephesios, quod etiam in canonicis decretis invenias:

> Legant, inquit, episcopi atque praesbyteri,[91] qui filios suos saecularibus erudiunt litteris et faciunt illos comoedias legere et mimorum turpia scripta cantare, de ecclesiarum sumptibus forsan eruditos, et quod in corbonam pro peccato virgo vel vidua vel substantiam suam totam effundens quilibet pauper obtulerat, hoc in Kalendarum strenam et Saturnalium[92] sportulam et minervale munus grammaticus et rhetor aut in sumptus domesticos aut in templi stipes aut sordidum convertit in lucrum.[93]

Quas autem Saturnalium sportulas vocat Hieronymus, has nomine absoluto Saturnalicia Tertullianus. Varro quoque in tertio libro *Rerum rusticarum* sic de minervali:

> Axius: Merula mi, inquit, recipe me discipulum villaticae pastionis. Ille: Qui simul ac promiseris minerval, incipiam (inquit), idest caenam.

Ludit enim Merula hic apud Varronem, quoniamque Axius discipulum se velle recipi dixerat, ipse sibi minerval promitti postulat, quasi magistro. Caenam autem iocose minerval appellavit, quia magisterii merces.

3   Ne forte igitur poetae sensus hic erit, eum quoque qui semel praeceptori minerval porrexerit, quod per assem designatur, idest qui paucis diebus rhetori aut grammatico operam dederit, optare totis Quinquatribus, quae festa erant Minervae ingeniorum praesidis, non modicum quippiam, sed eloquium et famam Demosthenis aut Ciceronis.

St. Jerome, too, mentions this minerval gift, when he writes as follows on Paul's letter to the Ephesians, which you may also find in canon law:

> Let the bishops and elders read this [*sc.* Eph. 6.4], who teach their sons secular literature and make them read comedies and sing the obscene literature of mimes, educated at the expense of churches, and what the virgin placed as a sin offering in the basket or the widow or a pauper who poured out all his wherewithal, this the grammarian and rhetorician turned into the lucky gift of the Calends, the little basket of the Saturnalia and the minerval gift or household expenses or church alms or base profit.[292]

Moreover, what Jerome calls the little baskets of the Saturnalia, Tertullian simply calls *saturnals*.[293] Varro, too, in the third book of his *On Agriculture*, says this about a *minerval*:

> Axius: My dear Merula, take me on as your student of villa-based grazing. He: I will begin as soon as you have promised the *minerval*, that is, "scum."[294]

For Merula is jesting in this passage of Varro, and since Axius had said he wanted to be taken on as a student, he demands that a *minerval* be promised to him, as if to the teacher. Moreover, he jokingly called a *minerval* "scum" because it was a teacher's wage.

Therefore, the poet's meaning will perhaps be this: he who has 3 once offered a *minerval* to his teacher, which is designated by a penny, that is, he who has applied himself for a few days to a rhetorician or grammarian, for the whole Quinquatrial celebration, which were the holidays of Minerva as guardian of talented persons, hopes not for something trifling, but for the eloquence and reputation of Demosthenes or Cicero.

: 22 :

Cuiusmodi sint versiculi in quibus (ut ait Martialis)
Echo Graecula recantet

1 Martialis in secundo *Epigrammaton* de supinis quibusdam super-
vacuisque carminibus agens, in quis multus labor, minima laus fa-
ciendis, hoc quoque inter cetera scribit:

Nusquam Graecula quod recantat Echo.

Domitius autem Graeculam accipit echo vocem Graecam inser-
tam, quasi se neget Martialis Graecis uspiam verbis uti in suis
epigrammatis, quod contra deprehenditur.

2 Aut nos igitur coniectura fallit, aut innuuntur versiculi quidam
sic facti ut in extremis responsitationes ex persona ponantur
Echus, sententiam explentes et morem tuentes illius ultima refe-
rendi.[94] Quales etiam vernaculos ipsi quospiam fecimus qui nunc a
musicis celebrantur, Henrici modulaminibus commendati, quos-
que etiam abhinc annos ferme decem Petro Contareno Veneto
patricio, non inelegantis ingenii viro, mire tum desideranti nonnul-
lisque aliis litterarum studiosis dedimus. Sed et extant Graeci
quoque Gauradae cuiusdam antiqui poetae, quos et apponam:

Ἀχὼ φίλα μοι, συγκαταίνεσόν τι· τί;
Ἐρῶ κορίσκας· ἁ δ᾽ ἐμ᾽ οὐ φιλεῖ· φιλεῖ.
Πρᾶξαι δ᾽ ὁ καιρὸς καιρὸν οὐ φέρει. φέρει.
Τὺ τοίνυν αὐτᾷ λέξον ὡς ἐρῶ· ἐρῶ.

: 22 :

What types of lines are those in which (as Martial says)
Greekling Echo repeats

In his second book of *Epigrams*, in discussing certain palindromic   1
and redundant poems, composition of which involves a lot of labor but very little praise, among other things Martial writes:

Since nowhere does Greekling echo repeat.[295]

Moreover, Domizio [Calderini] understands a Greekling echo as
an inserted Greek word, as though Martial were denying that he
ever uses Greek words in his epigrams, whereas the opposite is
found to be the case.

Either my powers of conjecture fail me, or he is hinting at   2
verses composed in such a way that responses are placed at the
ends under the guise of Echo, completing the sense and observing
his custom of repeating the last parts. We ourselves have also written such verses in the vernacular, which were entrusted to the
musical scoring of Heinrich[296] and are now celebrated by musicians, and which about ten years ago we dedicated to Pietro Con-
tarini, a nobleman of Venice, an elegant and talented man, who
was wondrously desirous of them, and to some other literary
scholars.[297] But there are also lines extant in Greek of a certain
ancient poet, Gauradas, which I will set down here:

Beloved Echo, will you do me a favor? . . . favor?
I am in love with a girl, but for me she has no love. . . . love.
But the right moment to act does not itself present. . . .
    present.
So then, tell her that she's the one I desire. . . . desire.

Καὶ πίστιν αὐτᾷ κερμάτων τὺ δός. τὺ δός.
Ἀχὼ τί λοιπὸν ἢ πόθου τυχεῖν; τυχεῖν.

: 23 :

Legendum apud Martialem 'cum compare mulo,' quod
plerique 'cum compare gibbo,' simul
explicata ratio in eo sensusque verior

1 Martialis *Epigrammaton* sexto:

Non aliter ridetur Atlas cum compare gibbo.

Sic enim et vulgo legunt omnes, et pro rectissimo exponunt quicunque sunt in cultu litterarum celebriores. Nos contra in codicibus plerisque veteribus minusque vacillantis auctoritatis et fidei sic
invenimus:

Non aliter ridetur Atlas cum compare mulo.

Mulo inquam, non *gibbo*, neve surdis (quod aiunt) agatur testimoniis, in hac ipsa gentis Medicae bibliotheca publica codex habetur
vetustissimus Langobardis litteris, quem et Domitius olim Florentiae pellegit. Sed et Veronae mihi pagellas quaspiam antiquissimi
item voluminis Bernardinus quidam adulescens, ut tum visus est,
haud illiberalis, Domiti propinquus, commodavit, cum quidem
una esset mecum Baccius Ugolinus, absolutissimi vir ingenii candi-
dissimique, neque non Romae quoque volumen item Martialis
Langobardis characteribus ostendit legendumque nobis indulxit
Bernardinus Valla, vir et carminum studio et iuris scientia et generis nobilitate atque opibus, praetereaque humanitate quapiam non

And to her this pledge of small coins give. . . . give.
Echo, what is left but my desire to achieve. . . . achieve.[298]

: 23 :

In Martial cum compare mulo *must be read, which many
read as* cum compare gibbo; *at the same time, the rationale
for this and the true meaning are explained*

Martial, in the sixth book of his *Epigrams:*   1

Similarly, Atlas is laughed at with his matching hump.[299]

For this is how all commonly read the line, and all the famous
philologists expound it as though it were correct. On the other
hand, in a great many old, authoritative, and trustworthy manuscripts, I have found the following:

Similarly, Atlas is laughed at with his matching mule.

"Mule," I say, not "hump," and lest the case be pleaded on the basis
of mute testimony (as they say),[300] this same public library of the
Medici family contains an extremely old codex in Lombardic
script, which Domizio [Calderini] once perused in Florence.[301]
But also in Verona a certain young man, as he then was, Bernardino, a relative of Domizio, generously lent me some pages of
another very ancient volume,[302] when Baccio Ugolini was with me,
a man of a perfect and kindly nature. At Rome, too, there is yet
another volume of Martial, likewise in Lombardic script, that Bernardino Valla showed me and allowed me to read, a man with enthusiasm for poetry, knowledge of the law, and of a noble and
wealthy family, and one who should, in addition, be celebrated for

vulgari celebrandus. Quin Florentiae item praeter hos alium codicem primae nobilitatis civis Pandulfus nobis Oricellarius semiveterem dedit utendum, in quis utique singulis hanc quam dicimus scripturam reperias. Neque autem diffitear etiam illam superiorem in uno alteroque non plane novo exemplari vidisse me, sicuti in eo quod Romae in Palatina bibliotheca, mediae antiquitatis, et item in altero tum quidem cum legebamus Francisci Saxetti Florentini negotiatoris, nunc autem Taddaei Ugoleti Parmensis, humani doctique viri, qui regi Pannonum Matthiae, regii prorsus animi principi, libros ornamentaque alia Florentiae, nobis ista prodentibus, procurabat. Nam in eo quem mihi nuper doctus utraque lingua vir Bernardus Michelottius ab nescio quo sibi Perusino commodatum dedit inspiciendum, *gippo* scriptum corruptius adnotavi.

2   Quare cum superiorem illam veluti constantem solidamque reperiamus in melioribus scripturam, quaerendum videtur, quid sibi Atlas postulet cum compare mulo, quave causa perinde rideatur, uti Maurus elephanto vehens. Porro Atlantem de Iuvenalis verbis nanum quendam pumilumve fuisse temporibus illis haud ignoratum colligimus. Sic enim inquit:

Nanum cuiusdam Atlanta vocamus.

Ut ex contrario per deridiculum sit Atlas appellatus qui foret pumila statura, sicuti:

Canibus pigris, scabieque vetusta
Turpibus, et siccae lambentibus ora lucernae,
Nomen erit tygris, pardus, leo, siquid adhuc est
Quod fremat in terris violentius.

Sed et muli pumili vel mulae tum in pretio sunt inque deliciis habitae. De quis in distichis idem Martialis:

his uncommon kindness. In fact, beyond these, there is another somewhat old codex in Florence that Pandolfo Rucellai, a citizen of the highest nobility, gave me to use. In each of these manuscripts you will find the reading I speak of. I shall, however, not deny that I also saw that aforementioned reading in one or another not quite new copy, for instance, in a copy of moderate antiquity in the Palatine library at Rome,[303] and likewise in another which, when we read it, belonged to the Florentine merchant Francesco Sassetti, but now to Taddeo Ugoleto of Parma,[304] a humane and learned man, who used to procure books and other prestige goods in Florence, when we produced them, for Matthias [Corvinus], king of the Hungarians,[305] a prince of absolutely regal spirit. For in the codex that Bernardo Michelozzi, a man learned in both languages,[306] recently gave me to look at, which was lent to him by some Perugian, I noted that *gippo* had been written corruptly [*sc.* instead of *gibbo*].

Therefore, since we find the aforementioned reading consistent   2 and firm, as it were, in the better [codices], it seems that we must inquire what Atlas wants with a matching mule, or equally, why he is being laughed at, like a Moor riding on an elephant. Further, we gather from Juvenal's words that Atlas was some sort of dwarf or pygmy well known at that time. For he says:

We call someone's dwarf Atlas.[307]

Hence someone of short stature was called Atlas by reversal for the sake of ridiculing him, as is the case with:

Lazy dogs, filthy with old mange
And licking at the edge of a dry lamp,
They will be named "Tiger," "Leopard," "Lion,"
Or whatever else there is on earth that roars fiercely.[308]

But short mules, or female mules, were then prized and kept as pets. Martial likewise says of them in the distichs:

His tibi de mulis non est metuenda ruina,
　　Altius in terra pene sedere soles.

Si quando igitur nanus hic Atlas mulo consimiliter nano et compare sibi utebatur, verisimile est rideri solitum publicitus, sicuti etiam Maurus niger derisui vulgo, quoties concolorem sibi elephantum inscenderat. Unde inquit idem in primo:

Et molles dare iussa quod choreas
Nigro bellua nil negat magistro.

3　　Convenit autem proposito argumentoque poetae in eum qui, iuvenis et validus et pauper, lectica identidem tamen a sex et ipsis iuvenibus validis pauperibusque gestabatur, atque, ut illi superiores, nihilo ipse setius cunctis deridendi sui dabat occasionem.

: 24 :

*Quaedam super Hecale anu in memoriam data deque
poesi Callimachi, tum ex epigrammatis
Priapeis expositus locus et item
alter apud Statium, quodque vitiose legitur de eo
in Apuleianis codicibus*

I　　Aequalis tibi, quam domum revertens
Theseus repperit in rogo iacentem.

Versiculi sunt hi de Priapeis epigrammatis, per quos aut ego fallor aut Hecale anicula demo⟨n⟩stratur,[95] a qua Theseus olim adulescens hospitio comiter acceptus est. Unde sacrum quoque

From off these mules no tumble must be feared,
    You practically sit higher on the ground.[309]

Therefore, whenever this dwarf Atlas used a dwarf mule like himself, it is likely that he was generally laughed at in public, just as a dark Moor was also commonly laughed at whenever he climbed up on an elephant the same color as himself. Hence the same poet says in his first book:

And the beast, commanded to take light dance steps,
    Does not refuse its black trainer.[310]

Moreover, it suits the intent and argument of the poet against 3
the man who, though a young man both strong and poor, was nonetheless repeatedly carried in a litter by six young men, likewise strong and poor, and like those earlier ones, gave everybody opportunity to laugh at him.[311]

: 24 :

Certain things recorded about the old woman Hecale and
about Callimachus's poem, then a passage from the
Priapean epigrams is explained and likewise another
passage in Statius, and a faulty reading about this
in the codices of Apuleius

Your contemporary, whom Theseus, upon returning home,   1
Found lying on a funeral pyre.[312]

These are lines from the Priapean epigrams, in which either I am mistaken or the little old woman Hecale is referred to, by whom Theseus as a young man was once received with kind hospitality.

Hecalesion per pagos celebre fuit Hecalo Iovi, non sine ipsius Hecales honoribus. Quam etiam Hecalenen[96] diminutiva[97] forma vocabant, quoniam ipsa quoque adulescentem adhuc Thesea salutare aniliter et huiuscemodi excipere diminutivorum blanditiis consuevisset. Quoniam autem proficiscente ad pugnam Theseo sacrum Iovi pro illius reditu voverat, ac priusquam reverteretur, ipsa obiit diem, vicem hanc Thesei iussu pro hospitalitate recepit, sicuti Philochorus memoriae prodidit. Qua de re Plutarchus in *Thesei vita* commeminit.

2   Ceterum de ea iustum poema Callimachus fecit, *Hecalen*[98] nomine, sicuti innuit item versiculus ex notissimo epigrammate:

Μέλπω δὲ γραὸς τῆς φιλοξένου τρόπους.

Multique passim reperiuntur auctores Hecalen citantes Callimachi. Nam et herbas edules enumerat aliquando Plinius quas rustica illa Hecale apud Callimachum apponat, sicuti *crethmon* in libro XXVI, sicuti etiam *sonchon* in XXII, quamvis in novis codicibus *Hecate* sit ibi, non *Hecale,* vestigium autem verae lectionis manet adhuc in antiquis eis qui sunt in publica gentis Medicae bibliotheca. Quin ubi Callimachus in *Apollinis* ait *hymno:*

Ὁ Φϑόνος Ἀπόλλωνος ἐπ᾽ οὔατα λάϑριος εἶπεν,

Οὐκ ἄγαμαι τὸν ἀοιδὸν ὃς οὐδ᾽ ὅσα πόντος ἀείδει,

in eum locum sic interpres propemodum: 'Per haec, inquit, illos accusat qui sic in eum cavillarentur, quasi magnum facere poema non posset. Unde coactus est *Hecalen* facere.' Verba interpretis ita sunt: ἐγκαλεῖ διὰ τούτων τοὺς σκώπτοντας αὐτὸν μὴ

For this reason the Hecalesion festival was celebrated throughout the country districts in honor of Jupiter Hecalus, not without honors for Hecale herself. They also called her Hecalene with a diminutive form,[313] since she used to greet Theseus, still a young man, in the manner of an old woman and to receive him with fawning words containing such diminutives. Moreover, since when Theseus set out for battle, she had pledged a rite to Jupiter for his return, but she died before he returned, she received this recompense by order of Theseus in return for her hospitality, as Philochorus recorded.[314] Plutarch mentioned the fact in his *Life of Theseus*.[315]

Furthermore Callimachus wrote a full-length poem about her, 2 entitled *Hecale*,[316] as this line from a very well-known epigram likewise hints:

I sing of the character of a hospitable old woman.[317]

Many authors are found here and there who cite Callimachus's *Hecale*. For on one occasion Pliny lists edible herbs that the country woman Hecale serves in Callimachus, such as *crethmon* in Book 26 and *sonchon* in Book 22; although the recent codices have *Hecate* there, not *Hecale*, a trace of the true reading still remains in the ancient ones that are in the public library of the Medici family.[318] In fact, when Callimachus says, in his *Hymn to Apollo*:

Jealousy whispered covertly into Apollo's ear,
"I do not admire the bard who does not sing of things as great
    as the sea,"[319]

the commentator on this passage says more or less: "In this way he is accusing the people who railed at him that he could not write a long poem, which is why he was driven to compose the *Hecale*." The commentator's words are as follows [in Greek]: "With these verses he accuses those who jeer at him that he was unable to

δύνασθαι ποιῆσαι μέγα ποίημα· ὅθεν ἠναγκάσθη ποιῆσαι τὴν Ἑκάλην. Hinc nos in *Nutrice*:

> Battiades Hecalen sonat et Marathonia gesta,
> Celsior assueto.

Sed et Statius in extremo *Thebaidos* de hac ipsa:

> Nec fudit vanos anus hospita fletus.

Et Suidas Hecalen ait heroida quampiam esse apud Callimachum.

3 Denique Apuleius in primo *Metamorphoseos* de eadem, puto: 'Si contentus, inquit, lare parvulo Thesei illius cognominis patris tui virtutes aemulaveris, qui non est aspernatus Hecales anus hospitium tenue.' Neque autem ignoro depravatam fere ubique esse scripturam, siquidem non *Hecales anus*, sed *Ales anus* praecerptis aliquot litteris scriptum plerunque invenies, ut in transcursu etiam Apuleianos codices emaculemus, et lectorem veluti superpondio dimittamus onustum.[99]

: 25 :

Quam multa in Epistolis familiaribus
quae nunc habentur Ciceronis praepostera,
tum quem in ordinem restituendae

1 Nactus sum Ciceronis *Epistolarum familiarium* volumen antiquissimum, de quo etiam supra dixi, tum ex eo ipso alterum descriptum, sicuti quidam putant Francisci Petrarchae manu. Descriptum

compose a long poem, which is why he was forced to compose the *Hecale*."[320] From this source, we have in our *Nurse*:

> Battiades [Callimachus] sings of Hecale and the feats of
>   Marathon
> In a loftier than usual style.[321]

But Statius, too, in the last book of his *Thebaid*, speaks about her:

> The hospitable old woman did not pour out her tears in
>   vain.[322]

And Suidas says that Hecale is a heroine in Callimachus.[323]

Finally, Apuleius in the first book of his *Metamorphoses* is talk- 3
ing about the same woman, I think: "If you content yourself with
a tiny household and emulate the virtues of your father's famous
namesake, Theseus, who did not spurn the meager hospitality of
the old woman Hecale."[324] I am aware, however, that the reading
has been corrupted almost everywhere, since you will generally
find not *Hecales anus* ("of the old woman Hecale") but *Ales anus*
written with some letters cut off, with the result that, in passing, I
am even tidying up the codices of Apuleius, and I send the reader
on his way, loaded, as it were, with a surplus.[325]

: 25 :

How the many passages in the Letters to His Friends
*that are now considered Cicero's are out of sequence
and to what order they should be restored*

I came upon a very old volume of Cicero's *Letters to His Friends*, 1
about which I wrote above,[326] and another one copied from it, as
some suppose by the hand of Francesco Petrarch.[327] It can, more-

autem ex ipso liquet multis argumentis, quae nunc omiserim. Sed hic posterior quem dixi codex ita est ab indiligente bibliopola conglutinatus uti una transposita paginarum decuria, contra quam notata sit numeris deprehendatur. Est autem liber in publica gentis Medicae bibliotheca. De hoc itaque uno, quantum coniciam, cuncti plane quotquot extant adhuc *Epistolarum* earundem codices, ceu de fonte capiteque manarunt, inque omnibus praeposterus et perversus lectionis ordo qui mihi nunc loco restituendus quasique instaurandus. Quare adhibe, quaeso, animum, quicunque liberalis has litteras amplecteris.

2 Igitur in libro octavo Caeli epistola ad Ciceronem sic incipit: 'Certe, inquam, absolutus est, me repraesentante, pronuntiatum est, et quidem omnibus ordinibus, sed et singulis in uno quoque genere sententiis. Vide modo, inquis.' Hucusque ordo nondum interpellatus. Quae autem statim sequuntur verba: 'Litteris ostenderis,' et cetera, diversa prorsus a superioribus atque alterius epistolae invenias. Perge porro ab ea ipsa epistola deinceps numerare sequentis ad eam quae sit quarta et vigesima, cuius ita principium: 'Non mehercules. Nihil unquam enim,' quae cum superiore continuatur, ut legas ita: 'Certe, inquam, absolutus est, me repraesentante, pronuntiatum est, et quidem omnibus ordinibus, sed et singulis in uno quoque genere sententiis. Vide modo, inquis. Non mehercules. Nihil unquam enim,' atque ita reliqua subtexe donec ab hac ipsa quam diximus alterius esse epistolae perveneris ad sequentem decimam, cuius hoc initium: 'Sic tu, inquis, Hircium?' quam eo usque lege dum in verba haec incidas: 'Si ullam spem,' quae simul offenderis, totum hoc delebis: 'aut in tecto vitii, cetera mihi probabuntur.' Totum hoc, inquam, delebis aut induces, quoniam aliena plane huic loco. Mox denuo recurres ad ea quae

over, be shown by many arguments, which I skip over for now, that it was copied from it. But this latter codex that I referred to was bound by a careless bookseller in such a way that one gathering of ten folia is found to have been transposed, contrary to the way it was numbered. This book, moreover, is in the public library of the Medici family. More or less all the codices of these *Letters* that are extant have flowed, as I conjecture, from this single one, as if from a spring or fountainhead.[328] And in all of them the order of the text is out of sequence and distorted—which I must now restore and, as it were, refurbish. So pay attention, you who are devoted to these liberal studies.

Now then, Caelius's letter to Cicero, in Book 8, begins as follows: "Yes indeed, I say, he was acquitted, with me representing him—the verdict was announced—and by all the orders and by one vote in each class.[329] See here, you say."[330] Up to here the order of the text has not been interrupted. But you will find that the words that immediately follow, "[if] you show in your letter," etc.,[331] are different from the preceding and belong to a different letter. Then proceed to count from this letter through the ones that follow, up to the twenty-fourth letter,[332] which begins thus, "No, for goodness sake! For nothing ever. . . ."[333] This continues directly from the earlier one, so that you read thus: "Yes indeed, I say, he was acquitted, with me representing him—the verdict was announced—and by all the orders but by a single vote in each class. See here, you say. No, for goodness sake! For nothing ever . . ."[334] and subjoin the rest of the text from the point that I said came from a different letter, until you arrive at the following tenth letter, of which this is the beginning, "'You,' you say, '[handled] Hircius this way?'"[335] Read this straight through until you reach these words, "If any hope . . ."[336] As soon as you come upon them, you will delete this in its entirety: ". . . or defect in the roof, the rest will have my approval."[337] All this, I say, you will delete, or erase, since the words are clearly alien to this passage. You will

posita perperam sunt in illa Caeli, de qua primitus dictum, atque ita continuabis lectionem: 'Si ullam spem litteris ostenderis.' Ita tractim legens ad epistolam pervenies tertiam ab hac et vigesimam, sic videlicet incipientem: 'Duabus eius[100] epistolis respondebo,' clausamque hac fini: 'Si enim nihil est in parietibus aut in tecto vitii, cetera mihi probabuntur,' post eamque statim consequi debet epistola, quae nunc ab illa undecima, sic ordiens: 'Delectaverunt me tuae litterae.'

3   Comprobat hunc ordinem quem posuimus non solum codex uterque, vel ille antiquus vel hic ex eo statim natus, a quo ceteros quoque omnis bibliopolae vitio depravatos liquet, sed intellectus etiam sensusque ipse luce clarior, sic ut acutius inspicienti quidquid usquam prorsus obscuri est ambiguique tollatur.

: 26 :

Versiculi in Fastis *e Graeco super vite et capro,*
tum parodia quaepiam obscurior apud Suetonium

1   Ovidius in primo *Fastorum*:

> Sus dederat poenas, exemplo territus huius[101]
>   Palmite debueras abstinuisse, caper.
> Quem spectans aliquis dentes in vite prementem
>   Talia non tacito dicta dolore dedit.
> 'Rode, caper, vitem, tamen hinc cum stabis ad aras
>   In tua quod spargi cornua possit erit.'

next go back again to the words that were misplaced in Caelius's letter, which I discussed at the beginning, and you will continue the text as follows: "If you offer any hope in your letter."[338] In this way, by reading step-by-step, you will reach the twenty-third epistle from here, that is, the one beginning, "I shall reply to his two letters,"[339] and complete the phrase with this, "If there is no defect in the walls or roof, the rest will have my approval."[340] After this one, the letter ought to follow immediately that is now the eleventh from it, the one beginning: "Your letter delighted me."[341]

This order that I have established is corroborated not only by 3
each codex, whether the old one or its immediate copy—from which it is clear that all the other ones had been corrupted through the fault of the bookseller—but also by the meaning and crystal-clear sense, so that for anyone who examines it keenly whatever is obscure and ambiguous is removed.

: 26 :

Lines in the Fasti *from Greek about a vine and a goat;*
then a rather obscure parody in Suetonius

Ovid, in the first book of the *Fasti*:   I

The pig paid the penalty; terrified by his example,
    You, O goat, ought to have kept away from the vine.
Someone, watching him gnawing on the vine,
    Spoke such words with audible displeasure:
"Gnaw, O goat, at the vine. But when you stand at the altar,
    There will be something from it [the vine] that can be
        sprinkled on your horns."[342]

Nimirum hi duo versiculi de Graeci poetae disticho perquam inclyto festivoque facti, quod in primis celebre fertur et volitat docta per ora virum. Nam cum dixisse quempiam illa memorat, ipsum nimirum auctorem carminis Evenum digito designavit. Loquitur autem in Graecis versiculis vitis ipsa, sic scilicet:

Κἤν με φάγῃς ἐπὶ ῥίζαν, ὅμως ἔτι καρποφορήσω
Ὅσσον ἐπισπεῖσαί σοι, τράγε, θυομένῳ.

Vertit hos nimirum quam potuit ad unguem poeta ingeniosissimus, et sunt tamen in Graeco nonnulla quae noster parum enarrate. Quin si veris concedendum, transmarinam illam nescio quam Venerem ne attigit quidem noster. Quod vitium linguae potius minus lascivientis, quam parum copiosae.

2   Sed quoniam in Graeci huius distichi mentionem incurrimus, afferamus etiam quod apud Suetonium in *Domitiano* est, ut obiter illi quoque non inobscuro loco lucem interpretationis inferamus velutique auctarium demus merce ipsa neutiquam vilius. Verba igitur ita sunt:

Ut edicti de excidendis vineis propositi gratiam faceret, non alia magis re compulsus creditur quam quod sparsi libelli cum his versibus erant:

Κἤν με φάγῃς ἐπὶ ῥίζαν, ὅμως ἔτι καρποφορήσω
Ὅσσον ἐπισπεῖσαι Καίσαρι θυομένῳ.

Quod enim supra vitis capro minitabatur, hoc eadem nunc Caesari, pulcherrima hercules parodia:

Undoubtedly these two verses were modeled on a very famous and
witty distich of a Greek poet, which is especially celebrated and is
circulated by the talk of learned men.[343] For when he mentions
that someone had said this, he pointed, of course, to the very author of the poem, Evenus. Moreover, the vine herself speaks in the
Greek verses, as follows:

> But even if you devour me down to the root, I shall
>   nonetheless bear
>   Enough fruit to pour a libation upon you, goat, when you
>   are being sacrificed.[344]

Of course, the gifted poet translates these lines as precisely as he
could, but there are nonetheless some things in the Greek that our
poet renders none too clearly. In fact, if the truth be told, our poet
did not even touch that certain foreign charm. This is the fault of
a language that is less playful rather than lacking abundance.[345]

But since we happened to mention this Greek distich, let us
also adduce what is in Suetonius's *Domitian*, so that we may in
passing shine the light of interpretation on that obscure passage as
well and, as it were, give a bonus of no less value than the mer-
chandise itself. And so, the words are as follows:

> He is believed to have been compelled to renounce a pro-
> posed edict about cutting down vineyards by nothing other
> than the fact that pamphlets had been scattered about with
> these verses:
>
>> But even if you devour me down to the root, I shall
>>   nonetheless
>>   Bear enough fruit to pour a libation upon Caesar, when
>>   he is being sacrificed.[346]

The same threat the vine previously made to the goat was now
made to Caesar—a very pretty parody, by Jove [Latin version fol-
lows]:

Vel si me, inquiens, ad radicem comederis, tantum tamen vini producam, quantum immolando Caesari possit infundi.

Mos enim veteribus uti capitibus stantium sub ictu cultroque victimarum vinum infunderetur. Sic apud Maronem videlicet:

Ipsa tenens dextra pateram pulcherrima Dido
Candentis vaccae media inter cornua fundit.

Igitur neci Domitianum Caesarem per hos versiculos libelli destinabant, quoniam, ut Suetonius idem scribit:

Ad summam quondam ubertatem vini, frumenti vero inopiam, existimans nimio vinearum studio negligi arva, edixit ne quis in Italia novellaret utque in provinciis vineta succiderentur, relicta ubi plurimum dimidia parte, nec exsequi rem perseveravit.

3   Meminerint autem studiosi nos in hoc invento non uno dumtaxat nomine in commune consuluisse, quoniam in plerisque adhuc Suetoni codicibus, etiamque nonnullis veteribus, non modo Graecos hos versiculos non invenias, sed ne vestigium quidem, ac ne locum etiam quo se recipiant. Sed eos nos quoniam tenebamus iam pridem, utpote lepidissimos, facile mox de obsoletis mendosisque exemplaribus, singulas pensitando, paulatimque nunc agnoscendo, nunc restituendo litteras pervestigavimus.

Even if you eat me down to the root, I shall nonetheless produce enough wine to be able to be poured out upon Caesar, destined for sacrifice.

For the ancients had the custom of pouring out wine on the heads of victims standing ready for the blow of the knife. Thus in Maro:

The fair Dido, holding the bowl in her right hand,
Pours a libation between the horns of a white cow.[347]

Therefore, by these verses the pamphlets destined the Emperor Domitian for death, since, as Suetonius likewise writes:

Once when there was an extreme bounty of wine but a scarcity of grain, he, thinking that the fields [of grain] were being neglected out of excessive enthusiasm for the vineyards, ordained that no one plant any new vineyards in Italy and that vineyards in the provinces be cut down, with, at most, half left. But he did not pursue the matter.[348]

Moreover, scholars will remember that we conferred in detail 3 on this discovery, since in most of the surviving codices of Suetonius, and even in some old ones, not only will you fail to find these Greek verses, but you will find no trace of them, nor will you even find a place where they might be inserted. But since we had kept them in mind for a long time, thanks to their extreme charm, soon we easily tracked them down from obsolete and error-filled copies, by weighing individual letters and now gradually recognizing them, now restoring them.[349]

: 27 :

Verba in Ciceronis epistola ex Enni Medea, *de Graeca Euripidi*

1 Cicero in epistola ad Trebatium:

> Hoc tibi tam ignoscemus nos amici quam ignoverunt Medeae quae Corinthum arcem altam habebant matronae opulentae optimates, quibus illa manibus gypsatissimis persuasit, ne sibi vitio illae verterent quod abesset a patria, nam
>
> Multi suam rem bene gessere et publicam patria procul;
> Multi qui domi aetatem agerent propterea sunt improbati.

Nemo ex his quorum edita sit sententia suspicatus est adhuc, non esse ista plane Ciceronis verba, sed poetae alicuius magis, cui liceret uti vocibus illiusmodi figurisque, ceu sunt illa 'quae Corinthum arcem altam habebant,' et 'matronae opulentae optimates,' neque saltem hoc viderunt, iambos adhuc in his versibus extare integros duos, aliorumque quasi discerpta membra veluti noscitari. Nos haec ex Enni *Medea* verba esse collegimus, non quidem suo prorsus ordine, sed quo commodissimum Ciceroni fuit allegata. Nam cum de Graeca Euripidi versam ab Ennio *Medeam* in Latinum cognovissemus, sententiam protinus horum verborum de ipsa nimirum Euripidi tragoedia (quando illius Ennianae iacturam fecimus) libuit aucupari.

2 Sic igitur in ea fabula, cum matronis Corinthiis loquens inducitur Medea, uti persuadeat non sibi verti vitio oportere quod absit

: 27 :

Words from Ennius's Medea *in a letter of Cicero's,
from the Greek of Euripides*

Cicero, in a letter to Trebatius: 1

> We, your friends, will forgive you this just as much as Me-
> dea was forgiven by the rich aristocratic matrons who held
> the high citadel of Corinth, whom she, with her hands heav-
> ily covered in plaster, persuaded not to impute it to her as a
> vice that she was away from her homeland, for
>
>> Many have conducted their own and public affairs well,
>>   though far from their homeland;
>> Many who led their lives at home have, for that reason,
>>   been tainted with infamy.[350]

None of those whose view has been published has so far suspected
that these are not wholly Cicero's words but rather those of some
poet, who had license to use such words and figures as these, "who
held the high citadel of Corinth," and "rich aristocratic matrons,"
nor did they even see this, that two whole iambs are still embedded in these verses, and, as it were, the scattered limbs of others
are recognized.[351] We inferred that these words are from Ennius's
Medea, though not in their proper order. But they were cited in the
order most convenient for Cicero. For when we had learned that
Medea had been translated into Latin by Ennius from the Greek
play of Euripides, we immediately wanted to investigate the sense
of these words from that very tragedy of Euripides (since we have
lost the Ennian one).

Therefore in this play, when Medea is brought onstage speaking   2
with the Corinthian matrons, in order to persuade them that they
ought not to impute it to her as a vice that she was away from her

a patria, 'Quando multi,' inquit, 'honesti etiam procul a patria, multi contra domi fuerunt inglorii.' Nam male audiebant peregrinae feminae, unde illud comicum: 'Adeon est demens, ex peregrina?' Similiter taceri posse ait Parmeno, Samiam fuisse Thaidis matrem, tunc Athenis victitantis.

3   Versiculos autem Euripidis ipsos ex Medeae persona, nequis fortasse desideret, hic adscribemus:

> Κορίνθιαι γυναῖκες ἐξῆλθον δόμων
> Μή μοί τι μέμψησθ', οἶδα γὰρ πολλοὺς βροτῶν
> Σεμνοὺς γεγῶτας, τοὺς μὲν ὀμμάτων ἄπο
> Τοὺς δ' ἐν θυραίοις·[102] οἱ δ' ἀφ' ἡσύχου[103] ποδὸς
> Δύσκλειαν ἐκτήσαντο καὶ ῥαθυμίαν.

Quod autem diximus poetam Ennium de Graeco vertisse tragoediam Euripidi *Medeam*, partim de verbis Ciceronis coniectamus, qui sic ait in primo *De bonorum malorumque finibus*: 'Quis enim tam inimicus pene nomini Romano est, qui Enni *Medeam* aut *Antiopam* Pacuvii spernat aut reiciat? Qui se iisdem Euripidi fabulis delectari dicat, Latinas litteras oderit?' Partim etiam, quod Ennianae tragoediae principium multis locis, ut a Quintiliano volumine quinto, ut a Cicerone in libro *De fato*, ut item ab aliis auctoribus identidem citatur, sed nusquam tamen longiore tractu quam in *Rhetorico* secundo[104] eiusdem Ciceronis *ad Herennium*. Quod hic ex codicibus variis emendatum subscribimus, ut illustretur obscuritas locis aliquot in lingua Latina oboriens, quoties unus aut alter de eius tragoediae principio versus allegatur, suppresso auctoris nomine simulque intellectu suspenso. Locus ipse apud Ciceronem sic est:

homeland, she says: "For many individuals were honorable even when far from home; many, contrariwise, were inglorious at home." For foreign women had a bad reputation, whence that comic verse: "Is he so crazy? By a foreign woman?"[352] Likewise, Parmeno says it can be kept secret that the mother of Thais, who was then living in Athens, was a Samian.[353]

Moreover, I will add here the very verses of Euripides from 3 Medea's character, lest someone might miss them:

Women of Corinth, I have come out of my house
So that you may not reproach me. For I know many mortals
Become pompous, some out of sight
And others in public view. And others have acquired
A bad reputation for laziness by keeping their feet at rest.[354]

As to the fact that we said that the poet Ennius had translated Euripides's tragedy *Medea* from Greek, we conjecture this in part from the words of Cicero, who says in the first book of his *On the Ends of Good and Evil*: "For who is so hostile to the Roman nation that he would scorn or reject Ennius's *Medea* or Pacuvius's *Antiopa*? Does the man who declares that he delights in the very same plays of Euripides loathe Latin literature?"[355] Partly, too, because the beginning of Ennius's tragedy is cited in many places, such as by Quintilian in his fifth book, by Cicero in his book *On Fate*, and repeatedly by other authors as well, but nowhere at greater length than in the second book of that same Cicero's *Rhetoric to Herennius*.[356] We are subjoining this here, corrected on the basis of various codices, in order to shine light on the obscurity that arises in some passages in the Latin language as often as one or another verse from the beginning of his tragedy is cited, with the author's name suppressed and the sense simultaneously left vague.[357] The passage in Cicero is as follows:

Ne Ennium, inquit, et ceteros poetas imitemur, quibus hoc modo loqui concessum est:

> Utinam ne in nemore Pelio securibus
> Caesa accidisset abiegna ad terram trabes
> Neve inde navis inchoandae exordium
> Coepisset, quae nunc nominatur nomine
> Argo, qua Argivi vecti delecti viri
> Petebant illam pellem inauratam arietis,
> Colchis imperio regis Peliae per dolum.
> Nam nunquam era errans mea domo efferret pedem
> Medea animo aegro, amore saevo saucia.

4   Est autem trabes in versiculo secundo singularis numeri, quemadmodum et Priscianus legit libro septimo. Vetustissimi enim (ut ipse inquit) etiam *trabes* pro *trabs* proferebant. Euripidi vero tragoediae principium si cum Ennianae conferas, feceris, arbitror, operaepretium, quod et subnectam:

> Εἴθ᾽ ὤφελ᾽[105] Ἀργοῦς μὴ διαπτᾶσθαι σκάφος
> Κόλχων ἐς αἶαν κυανέας Συμπληγάδας,
> Μηδ᾽ ἐν νάπαισι Πηλίου πεσεῖν ποτε
> Τμηθεῖσα πεύκη, μηδ᾽ ἐρετμῶσαι χέρας
> Ἀνδρῶν ἀρίστων οἳ τὸ πάγχρυσον δέρος
> Πελίᾳ[106] μετῆλθον· οὐ γὰρ ἂν δέσποιν᾽ ἐμή
> Μήδεια πύργους γῆς ἔπλευσ᾽ Ἰωλκίας,[107]
> Ἔρωτι θυμὸν ἐκπλαγεῖσ᾽ Ἰάσονος.

Let us not imitate Ennius and the rest of the poets, who have license to speak in this way:

> If only a beam of silver fir had not been cut by axes in the
>   grove of Pelion
> And fallen to the earth, and had not the first construction
>   of a ship
> Begun from that point, which is now called by the name
> Argo, sailing on which the select men of Argos
> Searched for that golden fleece of a ram,
> In the empire of Colchis, by the deceit of King Pelias.
> For never would my distracted mistress Medea
> Have set foot out of the house,
> Heartsick, smitten by cruel love.[358]

Moreover, the beam (*trabes*) in the second line is singular in number, as Priscian also reads, in Book 7.[359] For the ancients (as he himself says) used to say *trabes* instead of *trabs*. Indeed, you will, I think, find it worthwhile if you compare the beginning of Euripides's tragedy, which I append below, with that of Ennius: 4

> Would that the ship Argo had not flown
> Through the dark Symplegades to the land of the Colchians.
> Would that the pine tree had never been cut
> And felled in the woodlands of Pelion, nor set
> The hands of the valiant men to rowing, who went
> In search of the golden fleece for Pelias. For then my mistress,
> Medea, would not have sailed to the towered land of Iolcia,
> Her heart smitten with love for Jason.[360]

: 28 :

Panici terrores *qui vocentur,*
eoque locupletissimi citati testes

1   In Ciceronis epistola ad Tironem, quae posita in extremo *Familia-*
rium volumine, sic scriptum est:

Et si Atticus noster, qui quondam me commoveri πανικοῖς
intellexit, idem semper putat nec videt quibus praesidiis
philosophiae septus sim, hercle, quod timidus ipse est,
θορυβοποιεῖ.

Panica vocantur (ut arbitror) a Graecis repentini quidam terrores
et consternationes, quales utique lymphatici metus, usque adeo
inrevocabiles[108] ut non ratione modo sed mente etiam careant.
Quo item verbo Cicero idem utitur in epistola ad Atticum libro
quinto: 'Scis enim,' inquit, 'quaedam πανικά dici.' Facit item Hyginius de panico terrore mentionem, quo loco de Capricorno, his
verbis: 'Hic enim dicitur, cum Iupiter Titanas oppugnaret, primus
obiecisse hostibus terrorem qui panicos dicitur, ut ait Eratosthenes.' Quam fabulam et Germanicus innuit in *Arateo* commentario.
Euripides in *Medea* sic ait:

Καί τις γεραιὰ προσπόλων, δόξασά που
Ἢ Πανὸς ὀργὰς ἤ τινος θεῶν μολεῖν,
Ἀνολόλυξε.

2   Panos autem vocat iras Euripides, sicuti est apud antiquissimum ipsius interpretem: τὰ πανικὰ δείματα, idest panicos terrores, ὅτι τὴν τῶν αἰφνιδίων φόβων καὶ ταραχῶν αἰτίαν τῷ
Πανὶ ἀνατιθέασιν, quoniam, inquit, repentinorum terrorum et
consternationum causam deo Pani tribuunt. Et apud Synesium in

: 28 :

What are called panici terrores, and for that the most reliable witnesses are cited

In a letter of Cicero to Tiro, which is set down in the last book *To* 1
His Friends, the following is written:

> If our friend Atticus, who once thought that I was disturbed
> by "panics," still thinks the same and fails to discern by what
> defenses of philosophy I am hedged about, by Jove, he is
> creating an uproar because he is timid himself.[361]

"Panics" are, I think, what the Greeks call certain sudden terrors
and consternations such as frenzied fears, so incurable that they
are not only unreasonable but even mindless. Cicero likewise uses
this word in a letter to Atticus, in Book 5: "For you know that
certain things are called 'panics.'"[362] Hyginus likewise mentions a
"panic," in a passage concerning Capricorn, with these words:
"When Jupiter was besieging the Titans, he is said to have been
the first to have thrown at his enemies the terror called panic, according to Eratosthenes."[363] Germanicus, too, hints at this tale in
his *Aratea*.[364] Euripides has this to say in his *Medea*:

> An old maidservant, imagining that
> The anger of Pan or some other god was approaching,
> Raised a cry.[365]

Moreover, Euripides calls them the anger of Pan, according to 2
his ancient commentator: *ta panika deimata*, that is, panicky terrors, "because they attribute the cause of sudden fears and confu-
sions to Pan," [in Latin] because they attribute the cause of the
sudden terrors and consternations to the god Pan.[366] And in

libro *De providentia* sic invenio ferme: καὶ πανικοὶ θόρυβοι μεθ᾽ ἡμέραν τὸ στράτευμα κατελάμβανον, et panici tumultus interdiu exercitum occupabant. Quo loco ampliter etiam cuiusmodi essent hi denique terrores explicatur. Quin interpres etiam nescio quis ita verba haec ipsa Synesi enarrat, ut panicos appellari terrores dicat, cum repente in exercitu viri equique perturbantur, nulla comparente causa: 'Solent enim,' inquit, 'feminae vi numinis instinctae Panos orgia clamoribus concelebrare, quibus utpote repentinis metu audientes afficiantur.'

3   Sed et Nicetes Choniates, non aspernabilis omnino inter Graecos auctor, Panicorum meminit phantasmatum in oratione quapiam sua. Theon quoque, Arati poetae interpres, militasse ait Pana deum adversus Titanas, primumque eum videri concham illam tortilem et turbinatam qua pro tuba utuntur invenisse, quae Graece cochlos appellatur, factumque ipsius opera uti se armandi sociis interim fieret copia, dum sonitu quocumque illo qui Panicos vocatur in fugam Titanes agebantur. Sed et Nonnus poeta *Dionysiacon* decimo, furentem describens Athamanta, nunc insano Panos flagello furiatum ait, nunc intra ipsius aures bombum illum insonuisse Panici Saturnii flagelli, verba ita sunt:

Οἰστρηθεὶς Ἀθάμας μανιώδει Πανὸς ἱμάσθλῃ.

Et item:

Ἀεὶ δέ οἱ ἔνδον ἀκουῆς.
Πανιάδος Κρονίης ἐπεβόμβει δοῦπος ἱμάσθλης.

4   Quo autem nunc piaculo Valeri Flacci pulcherrimos poetae versus taceam super hoc ipso positos in libro *Argonauticon* tertio?

Synesius's book *On Providence*, I find this, approximately: ". . . and panicky uproars seized the army during the day," [in Latin] . . . and panicky uproars seized the army by day.[367] In this passage the nature of these terrors is fully explained. In fact, some interpreter explains these words of Synesius, saying that terrors are called panics when the men in an army along with their horses are suddenly thrown into confusion with no apparent cause: "For women," he says, "possessed by the force of a divine power, are wont to celebrate Pan's orgies with shouts which, because of their suddenness, cause the listeners to be gripped by fear."[368]

But Nicetes Choniates, a far from contemptible Greek author, also mentions Pan's phantasms in some oration of his.[369] So too, Theon, a commentator on the poet Aratus, says that the god Pan waged war against the Titans, and that he seems to be the first to have discovered that twisted, cone-shaped conch shell, which they use as a trumpet — which in Greek is called *cochlos* — and by his effort it came about that the allies meanwhile had opportunity to arm themselves while the Titans were being driven to flight by that sound, whatever it is, that is called panic.[370] But in the tenth book of his *Dionysiaca*, the poet Nonnus, too, when describing the raging Athamas, says now he was driven mad by the insane whip of Pan, now the buzzing of Pan's Saturnian whip sounded in his ears; the words are as follows:

Athamas, stung by the maddening whip of Pan.[371]

And again:

And those within always heard the sound.
The crack of the whip of Pan, son of Cronus, sounded.[372]

But how could I atone for the crime of suppressing mention of the extremely beautiful verses of the poet Valerius Flaccus, written on this very topic, in the third book of the *Adventures of the Argonauts*?

Dant (inquit) aethere longe
Signa tubae, vox et mediis emissa tenebris.
'Hostis habet portus, soliti rediere Pelasgi.'
Rupta quies, deus ancipitem lymphaverat urbem
Migdoniae Pan, iussa ferens saevissima matris,
Pan nemorum bellique potens, quem lucis ab oris
Antra tenent, patet ad medias per devia noctes
Setigerum latus et torvae coma sibila frontis.

Vox omnes super una tubas, qua conus et enses,
Qua trepidis auriga rotis nocturnaque muris
Claustra cadunt, talisque metus non Martia cassis
Eumenidumque comae, non tristis ab aethere Gorgo
Sparserit, aut tantis aciem raptaverit umbris.
Ludus et ille deo, pavidum praesepibus aufert
Cum pecus et profugi sternunt dumeta iuvenci.

Quin libro etiam sexto apud eundem barbarus quispiam ad terrorem incutiendum simulacra Panos praetulit:

Hispidus inque dei latuit terrore Lycaei.[109]

Sed et Zosimus[110] historiae Graecus auctor in libro tertio monstroso aspectu quempiam apparuisse pellitum dicit Albanis Romanisque praelium[111] commissuris.

5   Etenim deum Pana belligerum fuisse, vel ex argumento Nonni cognoscimus vel ex Theocriti *Fistula*, nam in ea sunt ista quoque verba de[112] Pane deo:

Οὗ αἴθε πάρος φρένας τέρμα σάκους.

The trumpets send their signals far up to heaven, and a voice sounds forth from the midst of the darkness: "The enemy holds the port; the Pelasgians have made their accustomed return." The quiet is ruptured; the god Pan, doing the savage bidding of his Migdonian mother, has driven the wavering city mad, Pan, ruler of groves and of war. Though the caves contain him from the hours of light, at midnight in the wilderness, his bristly flank and the rustling locks of his savage visage stand revealed.

His voice alone resounds above all the trumpets, at which helmets and swords fall, as does the charioteer from his trembling wheels, along with the nighttime bolts from the walls. Neither the helmet of Mars nor the hair of the Eumenides, nor grim Gorgon scatter such terrors from heaven, nor have they whisked away an army with such darkness. That is mere play for the god when he drives the quaking cattle from their steadings and the fleeing steers trample the thickets.[373]

In fact, in Book 6, too, in the same poet some barbarian bore before him images of Pan to incite terror:

Shaggy, he skulked in the terror of the Lycaean god.[374]

But in his third book, the Greek historian Zosimus says that a monstrous specter clothed in hides appeared to the Albans and Romans as they were about to join battle.[375]

Indeed, we know that the god Pan was belligerent, whether on the evidence of Nonnus or from Theocritus's *Pipe*, for this contains these words about the god Pan:

Whose heart the edge of a shield burned.[376]

Eundemque fuisse Atheniensibus auxilio contra Persas, cum alibi legimus, tum in ea ipsa quam diximus *Fistula*, his verbis:

Ὃς σβέσεν ἀνορέαν ἰσανδέα
Παππoφόνου Τυρίης τ᾽ ἀφείλετο.

: 29 :

Unde sint apud Ovidium
'Teuthrantia turba' Thespi vocatae filiae

Ovidius in *Epistola Deianirae ad Herculem*:

Nec tibi crimen erunt, Teuthrantia turba, sorores,
   Quarum de populo nulla relicta tibi est.

Notissima quidem fabula, etiamque a Diodoro prodita, super Thespi natabus ab Hercule compressis. Cur autem 'Teuthrantia turba' vocentur, hoc tam plerisque incompertum atque ignotum est ut audeant litteratores pro illo *Teuthrantia*, *Thespeia* reponere, nimisquam improbe insciteque. Nos de eo invenimus apud Eustathium Homeri interpretem, ubi maxime *Catalogum* enarrat:

φησὶ δὲ ὁ τῶν Ἐθνικῶν συγγραφεὺς ὅτι κτίσμα ἐστὶν ἡ Θέσπεια Θεσπιάδον· κατὰ δέ τινας Θεσπίου υἱοῦ Τεύθραντος τοῦ Πανδίονος,

ex auctoritate scilicet cuiuspiam, qui de gentibus conscripserit, Thespiam tradit a Thespiade fuisse conditam, sicut autem nonnulli

And we read that he likewise gave assistance to the Athenians against the Persians both elsewhere and in the *Pipe* that we mentioned, with these words:

> Who put an end to the boasting of the one who bore the same name
> As the grandfather slayer and removed him from the Tyrian woman.[377]

: 29 :

Why the daughters of Thespius were called
"the crowd of Teuthras" in Ovid

In *Deianira's letter to Hercules*, Ovid writes:

> I shall not charge you with the sisters, the throng of Teuthras,
> From the group of whom none was left by you.[378]

The tale is indeed well known, and is also related by Diodorus, about the daughters of Thespius, with whom Hercules had sex.[379] But why they are called "the crowd of Teuthras" is so undiscovered and unknown to most people that literary scholars dare to restore *Thespeia* for *Teuthrantia*, quite wrongly and ignorantly.[380] On this, I discovered in Eustathius, a commentator on Homer, where he is explaining the *Catalogue* in particular:

> The author of the *Ethnika* says . . . that Thespeia is the foundation of Thespiades. But according to some [it is the foundation] of Thespius, son of Teuthras, son of Pandion,[381]

that is to say [in Latin], on the authority of someone who wrote about peoples, he relates that Thespia was founded by Thespiades,

scribant, a Thespio Teuthrantis filio Pandionisque nepote. Quare
'Teuthrantia turba' Thespi vocatae filiae ab avo Teuthrante. De-
nique et Aeschylus in tragoedia *Agamemnone* Thespiam urbem
Teuthrantis appellavit.

: 30 :

Vocabula inventu rara nec tamen singularia,
cucuma, proseucha, scruta

1 Vocabula quaepiam sunt ita rara inventu ut si iterum in ea in-
cidamus, ob id fecisse operaepretium videamur, quoniam singularia credebantur. Sicuti est *cucuma* apud Martialem in hoc hemisti-
chio:

Cucumam fecit Otacilius.

Nam sic in *Satyrico* legimus Petroni Arbitri:

Tum illa carnis etiam paululum delibat, et dum coaequale
natalium suorum sinciput in carnarium furca reponit, fracta
est putris sella, quae staturae altitudinem adiecerat, anum-
que pondere suo deiectam super focum mittit. Frangitur
ergo cervix cucumae, ignemque convalescentem restinguit,
atque totam faciem excitato cinere perfudit.

Ex eoque inclinatum diminutivum *cucumion* invenio apud Arria-
num in libris de Epicteto, quo maxime capite περὶ Κυνισμοῦ,
hoc est de Cynica professione, loquitur, atque adeo verba Arriani
ponam: δεῖ αὐτὸν κουκούμιον ἔχειν ὅπου θερμὸν ποιήσει τῷ

but some write that it was founded by Thespius, son of Teuthras and grandson of Pandion. Accordingly, the daughters of Thespius were called "the crowd of Teuthras" after their grandfather Teuthras. Finally, Aeschylus, too, in his tragedy *Agamemnon*, called Thespia the city of Teuthras.[382]

: 30 :

Words that are rarely found but nonetheless not unique:
cucuma, proseucha, *and* scruta

Some words are so rarely found that if we happen upon them a second time, we seem to have done something worthwhile, since the words had previously been believed to be unique. Such is the case of *cucuma* ("kettle") in this half-verse of Martial's: 1

Otacilius made a kettle.[383]

For we read the following in Petronius Arbiter's *Satyricon*:

Then she was nibbling on a little bit of meat, and while she was putting the jowl — as old as she was — back on the meat rack with her fork, the rotten chair that had increased her height broke, and threw the old woman down on the hearth by her own weight. In that way, the neck of the kettle was broken, and she extinguished the fire as it was just gaining strength and got her whole face covered with the stirred up ashes.[384]

I find the diminutive derived from this, *cucumion* ("little kettle"), in Arrian's books about Epictetus, in the chapter in which he speaks in particular "On Cynicism," that is, about the calling of a Cynic, and so I provide Arrian's text: "He needs to have a little kettle with

παιδίῳ ἵν' αὐτὸ λούσῃ, habere, inquit, eum cucumion oportet, ubi calfactet puero, quo ipsum lavet. *Cucumion* dixit Graeca consuetudine quod nos *cucumulam*, non inconcinne.

2   Sed et *proseucha* tantum apud Iuvenalem inveniri vocabulum pro loco mendicabulorum putatur, cum tamen Cleomedes in secundo *Circularis inspectionis* libro, adversus Epicurum disserens, ita propemodum loquatur:

> Ex iis nonnulla e lupanaribus ascita, quaedam simillima his quae in Cerialibus a feminis dictitantur, alia vero ex media proseucha atque ab iis ipsis qui illic mendicant desumpta, Iudaica plane et retrita, longeque etiam reptilibus humiliora.

Sed et *scruta* dixit Horatius quidem semel in hoc versiculo:

> Vilia vendentem tunicato scruta popello.

Dixit iterum, quantum videam, Sidonius Apollinaris libro *Epistolarum* septimo per haec verba: 'Nunc quaedam frivola, nunc ludo apta virgineo scruta donabat.'

: 31 :

Quid significet[113] illud apud Iuvenalem, 'tanquam habeas tria nomina,' quodque manu emissi patronorum sibi nomina imponebant, deque in nomen adoptando ex testamento

1   Et ponere foris, si quid tentaveris unquam
    Hiscere, tanquam habeas tria nomina.

which he can prepare hot water for the child, in order to wash it."
[In Latin] . . . it was necessary for him to have a little kettle in
order to heat water for the boy with which to wash him.[385] By
Greek usage, he elegantly called *cucumion* what we call *cucumula*.[386]

But *proseucha* ("synagogue") is a word thought only to be found 2
in Juvenal for "a place for beggars' equipment,"[387] even though in
the second book of his *Comprehensive Theory*, where he is arguing
against Epicurus, Cleomedes says something like this:

> Of these, some are acquired from brothels, certain ones are
> similar to these that are chanted by women during the festi-
> val of Ceres, but others are drawn from the midst of the
> synagogue and those who beg there, clearly Jewish and well-
> worn, and far more lowly even than reptiles.[388]

But Horace also mentioned *scruta* ("trash"), in this verse:

> Selling vile trash to the rabble wearing tunics.[389]

It was used a second time, as far as I can see, by Sidonius Apollinaris, in the seventh book of his *Letters*, with these words: "He
used to give now certain trifles, now trash suited for girlish play."[390]

: 31 :

What Juvenal's phrase "as if you had three names" means;
and that manumitted individuals used to take the names of
their patrons; and concerning adoption by
assumption of name under a will

And you will be thrown out the door if you ever try 1
To open your mouth as if you had three names.[391]

Sane Domitius idem (nam ceteros omitto interpretes, cum ipso ut praefractiore congredior) Domitius igitur sic hunc ex quinta Iuvenalis satyra locum enarravit:

> Si velles, inquit, loqui quasi tu quoque unus esses ex nobilibus, quasi innuat quod tantum his qui nobiles sunt loqui liceat. Nobilitas enim cognomine, agnomine, et nomine designabatur, C. Iulius Caesar.

Hactenus ad verbum Domitius.

2   Ceterum tria nomina nec soli habebant nobiles, nec universi. Sed hi potius, arbitror, qui e servitio manumittebantur. Quocirca sensus quoque vel ob id acutior atque concinnior, ut convivator ne liberum quidem putet, neve pro libero fari aequum censeat quem sibi convivam vocaverit. Hoc si non auctores haud lubricae fidei comprobant, vincor nihil esse Domitio pensitatius.

3   Artemidorus igitur Ephesius, sive is Daldianus dici mavult, in libro *De somniorum coniecturis* primo, Graece ille quidem, sed ad hanc sententiam: 'Novi autem quendam,' inquit, 'servum hominem qui sibi habere tria virilia visus. Dein vero liber factus eo pacto tria pro uno habuit nomina, duobus assumptis patroni nominibus.' Haec Artemidorus.

4   Septimius quoque Florens Tertullianus in libro *De resurrectione* sic ad verbum:

> Oro te, inquit, si famulum tuum libertate mutaveris, quia eadem caro atque anima permanebunt, quae flagellis et compedibus et stigmatibus obnoxiae retro fuerant, idcirco ne illas eadem pati oportebit? Non opinor. Atqui et vestis albae nitore et anuli aurei honore et patroni nomine ac tribu mensaque honoratur.

Doubtless that same Domizio [Calderini] (I pass over all the other interpreters, since I join battle with him as the most obstinate one) — Domizio, then, explained this passage from the fifth satire of Juvenal in this way:

> If you wish to speak as if you, too, were one of the nobility, as if he hints that only those who are nobles are allowed to speak. For the nobility used to be indicated by one's family name, clan name, and personal name, C. Julius Caesar.[392]

So far Domizio verbatim.

Yet not only nobles had three names, and not all of them did. 2 But it was rather those, I think, who had been freed from slavery. The meaning is also sharper and neater on that account: the host does not even think that the man he invited to be his dinner guest is a free man or entitled to speak as such.[393] If reliable authors fail to confirm this, I yield the point that there is no more considered judgment than that of Domizio.

Now then, Artemidorus of Ephesus, or Daldianus if he prefers 3 to be so called, in the first book of his *On the Interpretation of Dreams*, albeit in Greek, speaks to this effect: "I know a certain slave who dreamed that he had three penises. Then, upon manumission, he thus had three names instead of one, with two names assumed from his patron."[394] This is Artemidorus's text.

In addition, in his book *On the Resurrection*, Septimius Florens 4 Tertullian, says verbatim as follows:

> I ask you, if you have manumitted your slave, since the same flesh and spirit abide which had previously been subject to lashes and shackles and brandings, will they therefore have to suffer the same things? I think not. And indeed he is honored with the splendor of white clothing and with a ring of gold and with the name and tribe of his patron and access to his table.[395]

Hinc illud opinor Persianum: 'Exit Marcus Dama.'

5   Probat morem Cicero quoque *Epistolarum ad Atticum* volumine quarto, sic scribens: 'De Eutychide gratum, qui vetere praenomine novo nomine T. erit Caecilius, ut est ex me et te iunctus Dionysius M. Pomponius.' Sed ut obiter hunc quoque Ciceronis non inobscurum locum interpretemur, nosse oportet etiam morem fuisse ut haeredes testamento in nomen familiamque adoptarentur, sicuti est a Caesare C. Octavius, quemadmodum scribit et Suetonius in *Iulio*. Quocirca post eam diem semper est ille Caesar, ut in epistolis quoque Bruti ad Ciceronem appellatus.

6   Quemadmodum et Q. Scipio collega in consulatu Pompei, qui cum filius Nasicae foret, ex testamento in Metelli Pii genus adoptatus, eius etiam nomine vocabatur, sicuti libro[114] *Historiarum* xxxx scribit Dion. Quare etiam T. Pomponius Atticus heres relictus a Q. Caecilio ex dodrante, sicuti scribit Cornelius Nepos in ipsius *Attici vita*, postea ut est apud Varronem in secundo *De re rustica*, ex T. Pomponio Attico Q. Caecilius Atticus est appellatus. Quare Eutychidem manumissum T. Caecilium Eutychidem vocavit, vetere praenomine suo. Nam T. Pomponius olim dicebatur, novo nomine quod haud pridem Q. Caecilius vocari coeperat. Sic servus Dionysius, M. Pomponius Dionysius vocatus est, ascito Ciceronis praenomine, Attici nomine. Sed et Milesius Alexander, cui Polyhistori cognomentum fuit, Cornelius est etiam a Cornelio Lentulo appellatus, a quo videlicet fuerat manumissus, sicuti quae Suidae dicuntur collectanea testantur.

This, I think, is the source of Persius's famous tag: "He goes out as Marcus Dama."[396]

Cicero, too, evidences this custom in Book 4 of his *Letters to Atticus*, writing: "It is pleasing news about Eutychides, who with your old first name and new gentile name will be T. Caecilius, just as Dionysius is M. Pomponius combined from me and you."[397] But to interpret this opaque passage of Cicero's in passing, one must know that it was also the custom for heirs to be adopted into one's name and family under a will, just as C. Octavius was adopted by Caesar, as Suetonius writes in his *Julius*.[398] And so after that day, he was always called "Caesar," just as he was in Brutus's letters to Cicero.[399]

So too Q. Scipio, a coconsul with Pompey, who, though he was the son of Nasica, upon adoption into the family of Metellus Pius under his will, was also called by his name, as Dio writes in Book 40 of his *Histories*.[400] Accordingly, T. Pomponius Atticus was made heir to three-fourths of his estate by Q. Caecilius, as Cornelius Nepos writes in his *Life of Atticus*, and was afterward, according to Varro in the second book of his *On Agriculture*, called Q. Caecilius Atticus, not T. Pomponius Atticus.[401] For this reason he called Eutychides, upon manumission, T. Caecilius Eutychides, with his own old first name. For he was formerly called T. Pomponius, but just recently began to be called by his new name, Q. Caecilius. Thus the slave Dionysius was called M. Pomponius Dionysius, with Cicero's first name added and Atticus's gentile name. But Alexander of Miletus, whose cognomen was Polyhistor, was also named Cornelius after Cornelius Lentulus, by whom he had evidently been set free, as the collection attributed to Suidas attests.[402]

: 32 :

Restituta Plinianis codicibus abolita pridem
vox, quidque poppysmos *aut* poppysma *significent,*
quodque mos poppysmis
adorandi fulgetras

1 Corrigendus apud Plinium locus, ex libro octavo et vigesimo *Naturalis historiae*, capite secundo, quo tractatur an sit in medendo aliqua vis verborum, subducta enim vox una, qua vetus indicatur consuetudo, vetustiore quoque testimonio comprobata. Sic autem plerique codices habent: 'Fulgetras adorare consensus gentium est.' Sed in vetustis duobus exemplaribus ex ipsa Medicae gentis nobili bibliotheca sic scriptum: 'Fulgetras adorare poppysmis consensus gentium est.' Quam lectionem vel Aristophanes facetissimus poeta confirmat in comoedia cui Σφῆκες inscriptio. Nam apud eum Philocleo quidam senex ita loquitur ut se dicat poppyssantibus (liceat autem sic verbo uti) fulguraturum. Tum interpres antiquissimus morem hunc esse ait uti ad fulgetras poppyssetur. Verba Aristophanis haec sunt: κὰν ἀστράψω ποππύζουσιν. Tum interpres haec: ἔθος ταῖς ἀστραπαῖς ποππύζειν. Quemadmodum ergo apud Iuvenalem Martialemque poetas *poppysma* legitur et *poppysmata*, sic apud Plinium *poppysmis* a casu recto, qui sit *poppysmus*.

2   Est autem facticia de sono vox, id significans, quo maxime nondum perdomitis equis adulamur, uti Maximus in lexico et Nicas item et Suidas. Utitur verbo etiam Sophocles: ποππύζεται ζευγηλάτρις, sicut et Pollux meminit in septimo *Onomasticon*.

: 32 :

A word restored to the manuscripts of Pliny that had vanished long ago; and what poppysmos *and* poppysma *mean; and that there was the custom of acknowledging lightning bolts by smacking one's lips*

There is a passage in Pliny that requires correction, in the second   1
chapter of Book 28 of his *Natural History*, where it discusses
whether there is any healing power in words, for a single word has
been removed, by which an ancient custom is indicated, which is
shown by every old witness. Most codices have, however: "It is the
consensus among the peoples to acknowledge lightning."[403] But in
two ancient exemplars in the famous library of the Medici family,[404] it is written: "It is the consensus among peoples to acknowledge lightning by smacking one's lips." The witty poet Aristophanes confirms this reading in his comedy entitled *Wasps*. For in
Aristophanes, a certain old man Philocleon says that he will flash
lightning for those smacking their lips (if one may so express it[405]).
Then a very ancient interpreter says that it is the custom to smack
one's lips at lightning bolts. This is Aristophanes's text: "and if I
hurl my lightning bolts, they smack their lips"[406] Then the interpreter says this: "It is the custom to smack one's lips at lightning
bolts."[407] Therefore, just as in the poets Juvenal and Martial *poppysma* and *poppysmata* are read, so in Pliny *poppysmis* from the
nominative *poppysmus*.[408]

It is, moreover, an onomatopoetic word, indicating in particular   2
how we greet horses that are not yet tamed, as Maximus says in
his lexicon and also Nicas and Suidas.[409] Even Sophocles uses the
word: "The team driver smacks his lips," as [Julius] Pollux mentions in Book 7 of his *Lexicon*.[410]

3   Quin idem quoque in primo sisti equum poppysmo docet, hoc ipsum usurpans vocabulum quod et Plinius, qui tamen etiam libro eiusdem *Naturalis historiae* quinto trigesimoque sic ait: 'Similis et Nealcem successus in spuma equi similiter spongia impacta sequutus dicitur, cum pingeret poppyzonta retinentem equum.' Dexippus etiam Platonicus philosophus in dialogo quem edidit in Aristotelis *Categorias* ita scribit: ἢ εἴ τις ἄναρθρος ψόφος, ὡς ἐπὶ ποππυσμάτων.

: 33 :

Crambe *quae sit apud Iuvenalem,*
superque ea Graecum proverbium

1   Occidit miseros Cambre repetita magistros.

Hunc Iuvenalis versum Domitius idem Calderinus his verbis enarrat:

Cornelius de declamationibus ita scribit: 'Declamationes aut ex historiis trahebantur, sicuti sane nonnullae usque adhuc, aut ex veritate ac re, si qua forte recens accidisset. Itaque locorum etiam appellationibus additis proponi solebant, et sic certe collectae editaeque se habent.' Cambre igitur inscriptio est declamationis a loco. Nam Cambre oppidum est in Teuthrania Troadis, ut scribit Plinius, et e proxima regione est Lesbos, in qua Mitylenen occupaverunt tyranni, ut auctor est Strabo, Nigessilus et Megarogilus. Alcaeus poeta

Moreover, the same author also informs us in his first book that   3
a horse stops at the smacking of lips, using the very word that
Pliny does, who also says the following in Book 35 of his *Natural
History*: "Such success is said to have attended Nealces in depicting
a horse's foam by a sponge similarly thrown, when he was painting
someone controlling a horse by smacking his lips."[411] Even the
Platonic philosopher Dexippus writes as follows, in the dialogue
he published on Aristotle's *Categories*: "or if any inarticulate sound
like smacking one's lips."[412]

: 33 :

What crambe *is in Juvenal,
and a Greek proverb about it*

Warmed-over cabbage (*cambre repetita*) killed the wretched   I
  teachers.[413]

The same Domizio Calderini explains this verse of Juvenal's with
these words:

> Cornelius [Tacitus] writes this about declamations: "Decla-
> mations used to be drawn from either histories, as indeed
> some still are today, or real-life experience, if perhaps some-
> thing has recently occurred. And so they were customarily
> propounded with the names of places attached, and this, at
> any rate, is the way they have been compiled and published."
> Therefore, *Cambre* is the title of a declamation derived from
> a place. For Cambre is a town in the Teuthrania region of
> the Troad, as Pliny writes, and in the neighboring region is
> Lesbos, where, according to Strabo, the tyrants Nigessilus
> and Megarogilus occupied Mitylene. The poet Alcaeus

eos carmine est insectatus, unde aureum plectrum habuisse
dicitur, auctore Fabio. De tyrannis eiectis Cambre declama-
tio semper erat repetenda a magistris. Haec placet sententia,
ut conveniat cum eo quod dixit:

Cum perimit saevos classis numerosa tyrannos.

Quod alii a Cambro Scytharum rege, cuius meminit Diodorus, Cambren declamationem deducunt, nulla ex parte ac-
commodatum est.

Hactenus igitur Domitius tortuosa prorsus et tergiversanti oratione, cuius ex verbis haec denique colligitur confusa necessitate
sententia, Cambren declamationem ab oppido Teuthraniae appellari, quod et a locis nomina declamationibus imponantur, et
Mitylenen[115] tyranni occupaverint oppidum in Lesbo, ut id poeta
versiculo illo significet:

Cum perimit saevos classis numerosa tyrannos.

2   Nos igitur proponerentur necne a veteribus controversiae, locorum appellationibus additis, non laboramus, quamvis hoc non
Cornelius (ut ipse dicit) sed Suetonius Tranquillus scripserit in
libello quem de claris grammaticis rhetoribusque composuit,
eumque libellum, non ut Corneli, sed ut Suetoni Domitius quoque
ipse superius agnoscit, et suo se laqueo (quod dicitur) implicat,
exponens (ut quidem sibi videtur) versiculum eiusdem satyrae:

Parte alia solum russati pone Lacertae.

3   Iam vero *cambren* (ut quod nunc instat agamus) esse inscriptio-
nem, id nos plane pernegamus. Quin audacter pronuntiamus neque tale quippiam apud idoneos modo scriptores inveniri neque si
maxime inveniatur, idcirco tamen ad tyrannos eos qui Mitylenen

assailed them in his verse, which is why he is said, according
to Fabius [Quintilian], to have had a golden plectrum. The
Cambre declamation about the expulsion of the tyrants had
always to be repeated by teachers. This sense wins approval,
so as to agree with what he said:

When the large fleet crushed the cruel tyrants.

As to the fact that others derive the Cambre declamation
from Camber, the king of the Scythians, whom Diodorus
mentions, this is wholly inappropriate.[414]

So far Domizio, then, with his twisted and equivocating account,
from whose words this inevitably confused opinion is gathered,
that the declamation was called *Cambre* after a town in Teuthrania,
since declamations are named after places, and tyrants occupied
Mitylene, a town on Lesbos, so as for the poet to indicate this
with the line:

When the large fleet crushed the cruel tyrants.[415]

Now then, we are not concerned whether or not debates were   2
set by the ancients with the names of places attached, although it
was not Cornelius (as Domizio says) but Suetonius Tranquillus
who wrote that in the little book that he composed concerning
famous grammarians and rhetoricians, and Domizio himself also
previously recognized this book as being not by Cornelius but by
Suetonius, and hoists himself by his own petard (as the saying
goes)[416] when he expounds (as he thinks) a line of the same satire:

On the other side put only [the patrimony] of Lacerta dressed
in red.[417]

Now (to deal with the present matter) we flatly deny that *cam-*   3
bre is a title. In fact, we boldly assert that nothing of the kind
is found in good writers, and that even if it is found, it should
not on that account be connected with the tyrants who occupied

occupaverint referendum, cum oppidum Cambre non modo non in Lesbo, sed ne in insula quidem sit ulla. Quare (quod pace sua dixerim) nihil hac Domiti commenticia opinione (siquis modo eam diligenter excutiat) dici fingique potest aut absonum magis aut inconcinnum et ridiculum, sic ut sese ipsa nullo impellente subvertat. Neque autem causa fuit cur Mitylenen ad Alcaeum confugeret ut classis numerosa tyrannos perimeret, quando inter primas controversiarum materias tyrannicidarum[116] praemia numerat Cornelius in eo dialogo quem de claris edidit oratoribus. Ita sibi omnia tenebrarum et caliginis genera[117] Domitius offundit, quoties velut e nassa pisciculus nequit exsinuari, quodque Aristotelem facere docet Atticus philosophus non inelegans Platonis propugnator, ut quemadmodum sepia sparso sub oculos ipsos manumque piscatoris suo sibi suco elabitur, ita ille deprehendi metuens, sententias de industria obscuritatibus infuscet, hoc in hunc hominem potius conveniat, nunquam magis quam cum pene tenetur involventem semet obnubilantemque ambagibus et quoddam sicut atramentum perplexitatis intervomentem.

4   Quod autem quidam vir, alioqui doctus et industria sua bene de litteris meritus, in commentario nuper edito de Gambra Anathoque affert ex Probo (ut ipse inquit) Iuvenalis interprete, fateor equidem nec scire me quinam sit hic Probus nec putare eum esse, cuius Gellius aliique ex veteribus meminerint. Fides ergo de eo apud auctorem sit.

5   Mihi tamen quod videtur exponam breviter, nam (ut ait ille nescio qui tragicus) veritatis simplex oratio est. Graecum igitur hoc (arbitror) proverbium Iuvenalis expressit: δὶς κράμβη θάνατος, quo significatur, bis posita crambe mors esse. Crambe autem brassicae genus, ut fastidium videlicet repetitae saepius controversiae denotaret, cum vulgo quoque recalfacta brassica iam

Mitylene, since the town Cambre not only is not on Lesbos but is not on any island. Therefore (let it be said with his permission) nothing can be said or invented more absurd or clumsy and ridiculous than this fanciful opinion of Domizio's (if anyone investigate it carefully), so that it subverts itself without outside influence. Nor was there any reason for him to flee for refuge to Mitylene and Alcaeus in order for a large fleet to crush tyrants, when Cornelius numbers rewards for tyrannicides among the first topics of debates in the dialogue that he published about famous orators.[418] Thus Domizio scatters all manner of darkness and gloom, whenever, like a little fish, he cannot worm his way out of a trap, and as the philosopher Atticus, no inelegant champion of Plato, teaches that Aristotle does: in the same way that a cuttlefish, by spreading its ink, slips out from under the very eyes and the hands of a fisherman, so he, fearing capture, deliberately imbues his thoughts with obscurity.[419] This would fit Domizio even better, who never ties himself in knots and covers himself with clouds of ambiguity and emits, as it were, the black ink of perplexity more than when he is almost caught.

On the other hand, as to what a certain man who is otherwise 4 learned and has earned literary merit through his own hard work, in a recently published commentary, cites from Probus (as he says), an interpreter of Juvenal, concerning Gambra and Anathus,[420] I admit that I do not know who this Probus is, or believe that he exists, though [Aulus] Gellius and other ancients have mentioned him.[421] So concerning him let the author stand surety for his veracity.

Nevertheless, I will briefly explain my view, for (as some tragic 5 poet says[422]) truth's speech is straightforward. So then, Juvenal expressed this Greek proverb, I think: "Cabbage twice is death,"[423] by which is meant, cabbage served twice is death. Moreover, *crambe* is a type of cabbage, so that he indicated disgust with a debate often repeated, since warmed over cabbage has by now commonly

in proverbium fastidii concesserit. Maluit autem Graecum usurpare quam Latinum vocabulum poeta, vel quia tritius id Graecis
quam Latinis proverbium, vel sane quia species etiam quaedam
brassicae proprie appellata *crambe*, tenuioribus (ut est apud Plinium) foliis et simplicibus densissimisque amarior sed effica-
cissima. Ipsius vero Graeci proverbii mentionem Suida⟨s⟩ facit,
ponique etiam in conviviis cramben docet, quod sit ebrietati
contraria, quemadmodum in libro *De re rustica* testatur Cato.

∶ 34 ∶

Vitiose quaepiam in epistola Ciceronis,
deque vocabulo quod est sciamachia

1 Rusticum nimis et illepidum sordidumque adeo plane vocabulum
Ciceronis epistolam occupavit, eam quae est ad Brutum, isto principio: 'Mirabiliter, mi Brute, laetor.' Sic enim in ea legimus: 'Meae-
que illae vehementes contentiones tanquam scientia adnihilatae
esse videantur.' Quod quidam tamen hactenus corrigunt ut dicant
'tanquam si iam adnihilatae esse videantur.' Consulant, quaeso,
eruditi peritique idoneorum verborum veterumque lectionum,
consulant suum quisque iudicium sensumque, ac tum demum
credere audeant adnihilatas contentiones scriptum fuisse a Cicerone.

2 Nos in codicibus duobus Medicae familiae, quorum supra
quoque fidem allegamus (mendose id etiam sed tamen ut erroris
adhuc vestigium non sit abolitum) sic repperimus: tanquam sciamachalaae esse videantur. Quare suspicamur legendum *sciamachiae*.
Sunt enim *sciamachiae* nihil sane aliud quam umbratiles pugnae.

become a proverbial expression for disgust.[424] The poet preferred, however, to use the Greek rather than the Latin word, whether because it is a more common proverb for Greeks than for Latins, or because there is a certain type of cabbage that is properly called *crambe*, more bitter, with delicate (as it says in Pliny[425]) simple and thick leaves, but most efficacious. Indeed, Suidas mentions this precise Greek proverb, and teaches that *crambe* is served even at feasts, because it is an antidote to drunkenness,[426] just as Cato attests in his book *On Agriculture*.[427]

: 34 :

Certain errors in a letter of Cicero's;
and about the word sciamachia

An uncouth, inelegant, and vulgar word has taken hold of a letter   1
of Cicero's, one to Brutus that begins, "I am remarkably pleased, my dear Brutus." For we read in it as follows: "Those vehement speeches of mine seem to have been, like knowledge, reduced to nothing."[428] Certain persons, however, correct this to the extent that they say "as if they seem now to have been reduced to nothing." Please let learned people skilled in good usage and ancient readings take counsel, let each consult his own judgment and good sense and let them only then dare to believe that Cicero wrote "speeches reduced to nothing."

   In two codices of the Medici family, whose testimony we also   2
adduced above,[429] I found the following (this, too, is faulty but nevertheless such that a trace of the error was not yet obliterated): "they seem to be as if *sciamachalaae*." Therefore I suspect that *sciamachiae* ("shadow boxing") must be read. For *sciamachiae* are nothing other than fights with shadows. For Cicero thinks that he

Sentit enim Cicero hoc utique frigere iam se plane in senatu, non succedentibus Bruto rebus, suasque illas vehementis contentiones sciamachias videri.

3   Vocabulum ipsum perquam est elegans apud Graecos et magnopere usitatum. Quin Galenus quoque medicus in libro secundo Ὑγιεινῶν sic ait: μεταβαίνειν δὲ καιρὸς ἐπὶ τὰ ταχέα χωρὶς εὐτονίας καὶ βίας. δρόμοι δ᾽ εἰσὶ ταῦτα καὶ σκιαμαχίαι. Inter celeres exercitationes, quae tamen attentae violentaeque non sunt, etiam cursus adnumerat et sciamachias. Denique vel Eustathius in Odysseae commentario rhapsodiae tertiae de verbo eo sic meminit: Ὁμοίως δὲ καὶ τὸ μὲν ὑπὸ σκιᾷ μαχούμεθα φαῦλον δηλοῖ οὐδέν. οὐ μέντοι καὶ τὸ σύνθετον σκιαμαχεῖν. Et M. Varro satyram unam e suis illis Menippeis *Sciamachiam* inscripsit. Haec enim est apud Gellium vera ex antiquis exemplaribus lectio, non ut quidam etiam scribunt *Criomachia*.

4   Quin paulo etiam supra in epistola eadem Ciceronis vocabulum alterum, quod est ὄργανον, de Graeca scriptura depravatum migravit in Latinam. Nam pro eo quod erat ὄργανον factum iam *optanon*. Neque autem hoc quoque ab ullo hactenus animadvertitur. Quare sic legeris: 'Plane iam, Brute, frigeo. Organon enim erat meum senatus,' ut quo pro organo Cicero proque instrumento utebatur.

is in any case by now simply a spent force in the senate, since Brutus's projects are failing, and his own vehement speeches[430] seem to be shadowboxing.

Among the Greeks, the word itself is quite elegant and much used. In fact, in Book 2 of his *Hygienics*, the physician Galen says the following: "It is time to go over to quick exercises that involve no strain or violence. These include running and shadowboxing."[431] Among the quick exercises, which, however, involve no strain and violence, he includes running and shadowboxing. Finally, even Eustathius in his commentary on the third book of the *Odyssey*, mentions this word as follows: "Likewise, for us to fight under a shadow signifies nothing bad. But not also the compound "to engage in shadowboxing" (*skiamachein*)."[432] And M. Varro entitled one of his Menippean satires, *Shadowboxing*.[433] For this is the true reading in [Aulus] Gellius from the ancient exemplars, not, as certain persons write, *Criomachia*.

In fact, a little earlier in that same letter of Cicero's another word — *organon* ("tool") — has migrated in corrupted form from Greek script into Latin. For instead of *organon*, it has now become *optanon*. Moreover, no one has even noticed this up to now. Therefore, read as follows, "I am, Brutus, now clearly a spent force. For the Senate was my tool," as the thing Cicero was using as a tool and an instrument.[434]

: 35 :

Locus in M. Varronis,
et item alter in Columellae libris Rei rusticae,
defensus a vitio, quaedamque super
Euhemero inibi et Iovis sepulchro et Cretensibus addita,
et locus apud Statium declaratus

1 In M. Varronis libro primo *Rerum rusticarum* mendose legitur illud: 'Arista et *granum* omnibus fere notum, *gluma* paucis. Itaque id apud Ennium solum scriptum scio esse in Ephemeridis versibus.' Nam quod habent etiam qui putantur emendatissimi codices, 'in Ephemeridis versibus,' hoc ego in venerandae vetustatis exemplari e publica gentis Medicae bibliotheca sic invenio: 'in Euhemeri libris versis.' Neque autem dubium est Enni sacram historiam significari a Varrone de Euhemero in Latinum versam, quam videlicet et Lactantius identidem et Eusebius citat et Augustinus. Verba Lactanti de libro *Divinarum institutionum* primo sic habent:

> Antiquus auctor Euhemerus, qui fuit e civitate Messana, res gestas Iovis et ceterorum qui di putantur collegit, historiamque contexuit ex titulis et inscriptionibus sacris, quae in antiquissimis templis habebantur, maximeque in fano Iovis Triphyli, ubi auream columnam positam esse ab ipso Iove titulus indicabat. In qua columna gesta perscripsit, ut monimenta essent posteris rerum suarum.

: 35 :

A passage in M. Varro's books On Agriculture,
*and then another in those of Columella, each protected from
corruption; and some material added in the same place about
Euhemerus, and on the sepulcher of Jupiter, and on Cretans;
and a passage in Statius clarified*

In the first book of M. Varro's *On Agriculture* the following is read   1
erroneously: "'Ear' and 'grain' are known to almost everyone but
'husk' to few. In fact, I know it to have been written only in Ennius, in the verses about Ephemerus."⁴³⁵ As to the fact that even
codices considered quite free of error have "in the verses about
Ephemerus," in an exemplar of venerable age in the public library
of the Medici family, I find the following: "in the translated books
of Euhemerus."⁴³⁶ Nor is there any doubt that a sacred tale of Ennius's, translated from Euhemerus into Latin, is signified by Varro,
one namely which Lactantius cites time and again, as do Eusebius
and Augustine.⁴³⁷ The words of Lactantius from the first book of
the *Divine Institutes* are as follows:

> The ancient author Euhemerus, who was from the city of
> Messana, compiled the exploits of Jupiter and others who are
> considered gods, and wove together a history from com-
> memorative tablets and sacred inscriptions, which were pre-
> served in the most ancient temples, especially in the shrine of
> Jupiter of the Three Tribes, where a commemorative tablet
> indicated that a golden column had been set up by Jupiter
> himself. On this column he set out his exploits in order that
> they might be memorials of his affairs for posterity.⁴³⁸

Hanc historiam interpretatus est Ennius et secutus, cuius haec sunt verba:

> Ubi Iuppiter imperium Neptuno dat maris, ut insulis omnibus et quae loca sunt secundum mare omnibus regnaret.

Dein Lactantius idem locos Enni nonnullos de hac ipsa historia iterum atque iterum adducit, quos equidem brevitati studens praeteribo. Quin ipsius quoque Euhemeri verba Sextus item allegat Empiricus, *Pyrrhoniorum* maxime volumine quarto, vocatumque ait *Atheon*, sicuti Melium Diagoran, Prodicum Ceum, Theodorum Cyrenaicum, complurisque alios, ac de eo quoque Timon Phliasius (ut arbitror) sic ait:

> Εὐήμερος γέρων ἀλαζὼν ἄδικα βιβλία ψύχων.

2   Sed his omissis, illud utique acrius inspiciendum est apud Columellam quoque libro x capite autem tertio, ubi de apibus agitur, bis Homerum citari pro Euhemero in pervulgatis codicibus, quod et vetustissimus indicat liber de privata familiae Medicae bibliotheca, litteris Langobardis exaratus, et item alter e publica eiusdem gentis, quem de vetusto exemplari Nicolaus Nicolus, vir doctus et diligens, sua manu perscripsit, tum et ratio astipulatur, cui nulla resistunt claustra, siquidem apud Homerum fabula nulla istiusmodi de apibus reperitur, ac verisimile est scriptam fuisse ab Euhemero potius, qui Iovis historiam composuerit, cuius apes illae fuisse nutrices praedicantur.

3   Quod autem apud hunc ipsum (ut arbitror) Euhemerum, de quo supra diximus, scriptum reppererat poeta Callimachus in sacra eadem historia, Iovem in Creta vitam consumasse,[118] atque inibi sepulchrum eius esse in oppido Cnoso, in quo sepulchro eius

This history was translated and followed by Ennius, whose words are as follows:

> When Jupiter gave dominion over the sea to Neptune, so that he might reign over all the islands and all the shores next to the sea.[439]

Next, Lactantius likewise repeatedly cites some passages of Ennius from this very history, which I will pass over in the interest of brevity. In fact, Sextus Empiricus, too, cites the words of Euhemerus himself, especially in the fourth book of the *Pyrrhonians*, and says that he was called an atheist, like Diagoras of Melos, Prodicus of Ceus, Theodorus of Cyrene, and several others. And in fact Timon of Phlius (I think) also says this about him:

> Euhemerus, the old imposter, cooling his unrighteous scrolls.[440]

With these matters set to one side, the following point should 2 be explored more keenly in Columella, in Book 10, chapter 3, where he discusses bees: Homer is twice cited in place of Euhemerus in the common codices, which is indicated both by an extremely old book from the private library of the Medici family, one written in Lombardic script,[441] and again another one from the public library of the same family, which Niccolò Niccoli, a learned and careful man, copied out in his own hand from an ancient exemplar.[442] Then again reason, which no barrier resists, lends its support,[443] since no such story about bees is found in Homer, and it is more probable that it was written by Euhemerus, who composed a history of Jupiter, for whom bees are proclaimed to have been the nursemaids.[444]

Moreover, as to what the poet Callimachus had found written 3 in Euhemerus himself (I think), about whom we spoke above, in that same sacred history, that Jupiter spent his life in Crete, and that his sepulcher was there in the town of Cnossus, on which

inscriptum fuerit antiquis litteris Graecis Ζεύς Κρόνου, id est
Latine 'Iuppiter Saturni,' quod hoc, inquam, poeta doctissimus et
scriptum ab illo cognoverat et pro confesso a Cretensibus habitum
testatumque, ob id, opinor, in *Hymno* ipso *ad Iovem:* 'Cretenses,'
inquit, 'semper mendaces, qui sint Iovis sepulchrum fabricati, cum
nunquam ille obierit, perpetuoque sit.' Versus autem hi sunt:

Κρῆτες ἀεὶ ψεῦσται, καὶ γὰρ τάφον ὦ ἄνα σεῖο
Κρῆτες ἐτεκτήναντο, σὺ δ' οὐ θάνες, ἐσσὶ γὰρ αἰεί.

Propterque hoc ipsum denique Statius quoque, opinor, in primo
Thebaidos inquit:

Mentitaque
Manis Creta tuos.

Cyprianus etiam martyr, homo disertissimus, in libro *De origine et
generibus idolorum:* 'Antrum Iovis,' ait, 'in Creta mutitur,[119] et sepulchrum eius ostenditur,' quamquam parum emendate scripta verba
haec in novis codicibus reperiuntur.

4   Porro Cretenses adeo mendaces habiti semper ut Graeco proverbio quod est πρὸς Κρῆτα κρητίζειν nihil aliud significetur
nisi mendacio uti adversus mendacem. Sed et Cretensis illius Epi-
menidis versiculus hic a Paulo etiam Apostolo citatus, atque ob id
etiam sanctificatus est:

Κρῆτες ἀεὶ ψεῦσται, κακὰ θηρία, γαστέρες ἀργοί.

Id significat, Cretenses semper mendaces, malae bestiae, ventres
pigri. Nam versiculi prioris hemistichion de Epimenide sumpsit
Callimachus. Quocirca eleganter etiam hoc Ovidius in *Amoribus:*

sepulcher of his it had been inscribed in ancient Greek letters, "Zeus, son of Cronus," that is, in Latin, "Jupiter, son of Saturn," since the very learned poet recognized, I assert, both that this had been written by Euhemerus and that it had been held to be a fact and attested by the Cretans, he therefore (I think) said in his *Hymn to Jupiter*: "The Cretans are always liars, since they built Jupiter's sepulcher, although he never died and is eternal." These are the [Greek] verses:

Cretans are always liars; for the Cretans built your tomb,
Lord, but you did not die, for you are eternal.[445]

And in my opinion, for this very reason, Statius, too, says in the first book of his *Thebaid*:

Crete lied
About your ghost.[446]

The martyr Cyprian, as well, an eloquent man, says in his book *On the Origin and Types of Idols*: "There are mutterings about the cave of Jupiter in Crete, and his sepulcher is on display,"[447] although these words are found in the new codices in corrupt form.

Furthermore, the Cretans were always held to be such liars that 4
the Greek proverb "to behave like a Cretan to a Cretan"[448] signifies nothing else than to lie to a liar. But this little verse by the famous Cretan Epimenides was even cited by the Apostle Paul, and on that account was even sanctified:

Cretans are always liars, evil beasts, lazy gluttons.[449]

which translates [into Latin] as "the Cretans are always liars, evil beasts, lazy gluttons." For Callimachus appropriated the half-line of the verse above from Epimenides. Accordingly, Ovid elegantly [said] this in his *Loves*:

Cretes erunt testes, nec fingunt omnia Cretes.

Et alibi:

Nota loquor, non hoc quae centum sustinet urbes,
  Quamvis sit mendax, Creta negare solet.

: 36 :

*Solutum hic et enodatum, quod aenigma de Varronis libro
citat Gellius*

Aenigma illud ex Varrone quod Gellius proponit et inenarratum
relinquit, ut legentium coniecturas acuat, equidem soluturum me
meo quoque periculo profiteor. Est autem tale in tribus senariis:

Semel minusne an bis minus sit non sat scio
An utrunque horum, ut quondam audivi dicier
Iovi ipsi regi noluit concedere.

Terminum significare videtur, qui deus concedere Iovi noluit, cum
Capitolium exaugurabatur. Ovidius *Fastorum* secundo:

Quid, nova cum fierent Capitolia? Nempe deorum
  Cuncta Iovi cessit turba locumque dedit.

The Cretans will be my witnesses, and the Cretans do not fabricate everything.[450]

And elsewhere:

What I say is well known — Crete, which supports a hundred cities,
Is not wont to deny this, mendacious though she be.[451]

: 36 :

Here a riddle quoted by Gellius from a book of Varro is solved and explained

The riddle from Varro that [Aulus] Gellius sets out but leaves unexplained, in order to sharpen readers' powers of conjecture, I claim I shall solve, even at my own risk. It is as follows, in three *senarii*:

I am not sure whether it is "once *minus*" or "twice *minus*,"
Or both of these, as I once heard it said that
He refused to yield to King Jupiter himself.[452]

He seems to signify Terminus, the god who refused to yield to Jupiter, when the Capitol was being deconsecrated. Ovid, in Book 2 of his *Fasti*:

What of when the new Capitol came into being? The entire troop
Of the [other] gods yielded, of course, to Jupiter and made way for him.

Terminus, ut veteres memorant, inventus in aede
 Restitit, et magno cum Iove templa tenet.

Dubitat ergo hic scirpi auctor semel minus, an bis minus fuerit an utrunque horum, ex utroque autem, hoc est ex semel et bis, resultat ter. Quare non semel minus, non bis minus, sed Terminus fuit qui Iovi ipsi regi noluit concedere.

: 37 :

Lapsum fede[120] *Servium super
Oaxe fluvio et Creta*

1   Et rapidum Cretae veniemus Oaxem.

Hoc ex prima *Bucolicon* ecloga sic enarrat ad verbum Servius:

Rapidum cretae, inquit, lutulentum, quod rapit cretam. Creta alba terra dicitur, nam Oaxis[121] fluvius est Mesopotamiae, qui velocitate sua rapiens albam terram turbulentus efficitur.

Hactenus ille.

2   Sed enim ego Oaxem Cretae insulae fluvium intelligi crediderim potius. Nam Vibius quoque Sequester Oaxem Cretae fluvium dicit esse, a quo et civitas Oaxia. Quare Apollonius Cretam quoque insulam tellurem Oaxida vocavit in primo *Argonauticon* his verbis:

CHAPTER 37

[Yet] as the ancients tell, when Terminus was discovered in the
house,
He stood firm and occupies the temple together with
mighty Jupiter.[453]

Therefore, this author of the brainteaser is uncertain whether it
was "once *minus*" or "twice *minus*," or both of these, but from both
of them, that is, once plus twice, results thrice (*ter*). Hence it was
neither "once *minus*" nor "twice *minus*" but Terminus who refused
to yield to king Jupiter himself.

: 37 :

*That Servius stumbled disgracefully concerning
the river Oaxis and Crete*

We shall come to the swift Oaxis in Crete.[454]   1

Servius explains this point from the first eclogue of the *Bucolics*
word for word as follows:

"Swift for *creta*," turbid, since it carries chalk (*creta*) away.
White earth is called chalk, for Oaxis is a river of Mesopotamia that is made turbid by carrying away white earth by its
swiftness.[455]

So far Servius.
But I would rather believe that the Oaxis river on the island   2
Crete is understood.[456] For Vibius Sequester, too, says that the
Oaxis is a river on Crete, from which derives the city Oaxia.[457]
Hence Apollonius also called the island of Crete the Oaxian land
in the first book of his *Argonautica*, with these words:

Δάκτυλοι Ἰδαῖοι Κρηταέες οὕς ποτε νύμφη
Ἀγχιάλη Δικταῖον ἀνὰ σπέος ἀμφοτέρῃσι
Δραξαμένη γαίης Οἰαξίδος ἐβλάστησε.

Hoc autem postremum ita Varro transtulit, ille arbitror Atacinus alieni operis interpres:

Et geminis capiens tellurem Oaxida palmis.

Neque vero non convenit rationi, ut qui dispersum iri toto orbe suos populares velit ostendere, de insula quoque in medio, veluti Mediterraneo mari sita, tum autem et de altera toto penitus orbe divisa meminerit.

: 38 :

*Expositum Iuvenalis carmen
contra omnium hactenus sententias
super* laconico *et* pitylismate

1   Qui Lacedaemonium pitysmate lubricat orbem.

Versus hic ex undecima satyra Iuvenalis varie prorsus expositus est hactenus atque (ut arbitror) indiligenter. Nam Domitius *pitysma* dicit esse irrorationem e levi sputo, de verbo *pityo*. Lacedaemonium vero orbem pro anulo accipit, quoniam, inquit, a Lacedaemoniis anulorum usus manavit, ut senatores et equites per anuli mentionem significentur. Porro alter eruditissimus homo, quem tamen nominare parcimus honoris gratia, qua parte ab eo dissentimus, saltationem putat esse Lacedaemoniam, sed ingenue tamen fatetur nihil adhuc de eo se legisse, nisi tantum apud Pollucem mentionem factam Lacedaemoniae saltationis. Tertius denique vir, ipse

The Idaean Dactyls of Crete, whom the nymph
Anchiale once gave birth to in the Dictaean cave,
With both hands grasping the Oaxian earth.[458]

Moreover, Varro of Atax, I believe, that well-known translator of others' work, rendered this last line thus:

And taking the Oaxian earth in both hands.[459]

And certainly it makes sense for one who wants to show that his own people will be scattered across the whole world to mention an island in the middle [of it], given that it was situated in the Mediterranean Sea, but also another island that was "separated from virtually the entire world."[460]

: 38 :

One of Juvenal's poems explained,
contrary to everyone's previous opinions,
regarding the words laconicum *and* pitylisma

He who lubricates the Spartan circle with spit.[461]　　　　　I

So far this verse from the eleventh satire of Juvenal has been explained variously and (in my opinion) carelessly. For Domizio [Calderini] says that *pitysma* is a moistening from a light spit, from the verb *pityo*. But he takes "the Spartan circle" to be a ring, since, he says, the use of rings emanated from the Spartans, so that their senators and knights are identified by mention of their rings.[462] Furthermore, another very erudite man, whom I nonetheless refrain from naming for his honor's sake, insofar as I disagree with him, thinks that it is a Spartan dance, but nonetheless he frankly acknowledges that he has so far read nothing about this other than merely a mention of Spartan dance made in Pollux.[463] Finally, a

quoque doctissimus, trochum intelligit de arbore pinu fabricatum, quod *pitys* dicatur pinus, unde sit *pitysma*.

2   Nos e tribus his opinionibus honorem praefati auctorum nullam plane probamus, principioque negamus orbem Lacedaemonium[122] significare anulum posse, quoniam nusquam legatur anuli originem manasse a Lacedaemoniis. Plinius autem, quem Domitius adducit, tantum ferreo etiam tum anulo Lacedaemone[123] uti refert. Quod si tollitur [non][124] posse Lacedaemonium orbem pro anulo accipi, sicuti certe tollitur, nihil profecto commenticia illa irroratio valebit. Neque tamen a *pityo*, quod nunquam verbum invenias, sed a *pityzo* magis *pitysma* deducetur, quod apud Nicam grammaticum declaratur. Qui vero saltationem putat esse Lacedaemoniam *pitysma*, cum de eo nihil inveniat, facile (ut esse ingenuus consuevit) potiori sententiae cesserit. Quod item facturum credo, qui trochum putat e pinu factum *pitysma* esse, cum nec usquam lectum nec ad rem faciat, et syllabae ratio pugnet, quoniam *pitys* habeat priorem correptam syllabam, ut ex primo liquet etiam Theocriti versiculo.

3   Nos igitur *pitylisma* legendum credimus, ut inscitia librariorum syllabam de medio dempserit, quod haud mirum est in tantis tenebris. *Pitylisma* vero intelligimus exercitationem de qua Galenus excellens medicus in secundo Ὑγιεινῶν libro, quamvis apud eum sit verbum potius *pitylizin*, quam nomen *pitylisma*. Ceterum recte *pitylisma* fit inde etiam usitatissima proportione. Neque adeo incongruum Galeni Graeca verba prius adscribere, dein pro captu nostro interpretari. Cum igitur exercitationum varia genera notet ac de iis etiam doceat quae veloces quidem sed citra intentionem violentiamque sint, inter quas et haec ipsa sit de qua nunc agimus, ita scribit ad verbum:

third man, also very learned, understands a hoop made from a pine tree, on the grounds that pine is called *pitys*, from which derives *pitysma* ("spit").[464]

Though I have paid preliminary respect to the authors, I approve none of these three opinions, and in the first place, I deny that "the Spartan circle" can denote a ring, since it is nowhere read that the origin of the ring emanated from the Spartans. Moreover, Pliny, whom Domizio cites, reports that even then they only used an iron ring at Sparta. If it is eliminated that "the Spartan circle" can be understood as a ring, as it certainly is eliminated, that spurious "moistening" will surely be worthless.[465] Nor, however, does *pitysma* derive from *pityo*, a word you will never find, but rather from *pityzo*, which is elucidated by the grammarian Nicas.[466] As for the one who thinks that *pitysma* is a Spartan dance, since he found nothing about this, he would easily yield to a better opinion (as he is wont to be honest). I believe that he likewise will do so who thinks that *pitysma* is a hoop made of pine, since this is read nowhere and fails to clarify the content, and the quantity of the syllable argues against it, since *pitys* has a short first syllable, as is clear from the first line of Theocritus.[467]

Therefore I think that *pitylisma* should be read, with the result that the scribes' ignorance removed a syllable from the middle, which is hardly astonishing in times of such darkness. Indeed, I understand *pitylisma* as the exercise about which the outstanding physician Galen [wrote], in the second book of his *Hygienics*, although in his work it is the verb *pitylizein* rather than the noun *pitylisma*. Yet *pitylisma* is correctly formed from it by a very common relationship. It is quite appropriate first to set down Galen's words in Greek, then to translate them as I understand them. So when he notes various types of exercises and also teaches about the ones that are speedy but involve no violent straining, which include this very one that we are currently discussing, he writes verbatim as follows:

τὸ δὲ πιτυλίζειν ἐπειδὰν ἐπ᾽ ἄκρων τῶν ποδῶν βε-
βηκὼς ἀνατείνας τὼ χεῖρε κινεῖ τάχιστα τὴν μὲν
ὀπίσω φέρων, τὴν δὲ πρόσω· μάλιστα δὲ τοίχῳ
προϊστάμενοι γυμνάζονται τοῦτο τὸ γυμνάσιον, ἵν᾽
εἰ καί ποτε σφάλλοιντο προσαψάμενοι τοῦ τοίχου
ῥαδίως ὀρθῶνται. καὶ οὕτω δὴ γυμναζομένων λαν-
θάνει τε τὰ σφάλματα καὶ ἀσθενέστερον γίνεται
τὸ γυμνάσιον,

Est, inquit, pitylizin, vel si mavis pitylissare, cum quispiam
summis pedibus ingrediens manus protendit ocissimeque
movet, alteram retrorsum scilicet alteram prorsum, quo potissimum gymnasii genere ad parietes exercentur, ut sicubi
lapsentur, adprehenso mox pariete facile resurgant, atque ita
exercentium lapsus fallunt, et ipsa fit exercitatio inbecillior.

4   Porro Lacedaemonium orbem, laconicum ipsum acceperim, ut
in quo solerent ad eum modum exerceri. Dion *Historiarum* tertio
quinquagesimoque libro laconicum in urbe vaporarium aut sudato-
rium (sic enim interpretari videmur posse quod est apud eum
pyriaterium) ab Agrippa aedificatum tradit. Dein laconicum dicit
appellatum quoniam Lacedaemonii per ea tempora nudi unctique
praecunctis exercebantur. Laconicum istud et Martialis innuit, ita
inquiens:

Ritus si placeant tibi Laconum,
Contentus potes arido vapore
Cruda Virgine Martiaque mergi.

Sed et Columella in libro *De agricultura* primo sic:

Pitylizein is when one walks on tiptoes and moves the arms quickly, with one behind and the other in front; and they perform this exercise especially standing next to a wall, so that if they stumble, they may grab the wall and easily right themselves. And when they exercise in this fashion, the stumbles are avoided and the exercise becomes less strenuous.[468]

[In Latin] *Pitylizein*, or if you prefer, *pitylissare*, is when someone walking on tiptoes extends the arms, and moves them quickly, that is, one behind and the other in front; in this type of exercise they train by preference next to walls, so that if they ever fall, they may at once grab the wall and easily raise themselves up, and thus the participants evade falls and the exercise itself becomes gentler.

Furthermore, I would understand "the Spartan circle" as the *laconicum* itself ("sweat bath" or "sauna"), as the place where they were wont to exercise in this fashion. In the fifty-third book of his *Histories*, Dio records that a *laconicum*, a vapor or sweat bath (for we seem able thus to translate what in his text is *pyriaterium*), was built in the city by Agrippa.[469] Then he says that it was called a *laconicum* since in those days the Spartans used to exercise publicly naked and oiled. Martial, too, hints at such a *laconicum*, saying the following:

> If the style of the Spartans pleases you,
> You can be content with dry air
> And can take a dip in the natural Virginal or Martian
>   waters.[470]

Columella, too, in the first book of his *On Agriculture*, writes as follows:

Attonitique miramur gestus effeminatorum, quod a natura sexum viris denegatum muliebri motu mentiantur decipiantque oculos spectantium. Mox deinde ut apti veniamus ad ganeas cotidianam cruditatem laconicis excoquimus, et exusto sudore sitim quaerimus.

Iam igitur vel ex his Columellae verbis constare cuivis potest quos iam potissimum poeta significet, nempe eos dubio procul, qui diem totum in laconicis istis gymnasiisque contererent uncti nudique. Quare etiam *lubricat* inquit, propter oleum et unguen quo defricti exercebantur. Seneca etiam libro *Epistolarum* septimo *ad Lucilium* nihil aliud prorsus quam laconica insinuat, ita narrans: 'Quid mihi cum istis calentibus stagnis? Quid cum sudatoriis in quae siccus vapor corpora exhausturus includitur? [ut][125] Omnis sudor per laborem exeat.'

5   Restat uti nunc, quoniam *orbem* dixit, etiam doceamus fuisse in orbem constructa laconica, quod ex libro quinto *Architecturae* apud Vitruvium patet in his verbis:

Laconicon sudationesque[126] sunt coniungendae tepidario, eaeque[127] quam latae fuerint, tantam altitudinem habeant ad imam curvaturam hemisphaerii, mediumque lumen in hemisphaerio relinquatur, ex eoque clypeum aeneum catenis pendeat, per cuius reductiones et dimissiones perficietur sudationis temperatura, ipsumque ad circinum fieri oportere videtur, ut aequaliter a medio flammae vaporisque vis per curvaturae rotundationes pervagetur.

We are stunned and amazed at the gestures of effeminate males, because with feminine movement they feign a sex denied by nature to men and deceive the eyes of spectators. Next, so that we may arrive at dining establishments in appropriate condition, we cook out our daily indigestion in sweat baths (*laconica*), and by burning off sweat we develop a thirst.[471]

Now therefore, from these words of Columella's it should be clear to everyone to whom the poet is particularly referring — undoubtedly those who spend all day in those *laconica* and gymnasia, oiled and naked. Hence he uses the word "lubricates," because of the oil and unguent rubbed down with which they engaged in their exercises. In Book 7 of his *Letters to Lucilius*, Seneca, too, hints at nothing else than *laconica*, explaining as follows: "What do I have to do with those hot spas? What with the saunas, in which dry air is enclosed to drain the body? May all sweat be extruded through effort."[472]

It remains now, since he spoke of a circle, for us also to explain 5 that *laconica* were built in a circle, as is clear from Book 5 of Vitruvius's *On Architecture*, in these words:

The *laconicum* and saunas are to be adjacent to the cooling-down room, and they should be just as wide as the height they have at the lowest curvature of the dome. And a window is to be left in the middle of the dome, where there should hang a bronze shield on a chain so that by lowering or raising it the temperature of the sauna can be controlled. Also, it seems that it must be made circular, so that the intensity of the heat and steam may be evenly distributed from the center throughout the rounded spaces of the dome.[473]

: 39 :

Scirpus exsolutus Ausoni vatis
de Cadmi filiabus, Melone, Sepia,
et Cnidiis nodis

1 Scirpum quem Theoni grammatico per dimetros iambos acatalectos proponit ingeniosus et non ineruditus poeta Ausonius, sic nos tentabimus explicare. Sed ipsos prius versiculos adscribamus:

> Aut adsit interpres tuus
> Aenigmatum qui cognitor
> Fuit meorum, cum tibi
> Cadmi nigellas filias,
> Melonis albam paginam
> Notasque furvae Sepiae
> Cnidiosque nodos prodidit.

Ex his autem postremus versiculus libris quidem vulgatioribus mendose legitur, *modos* habens vel *meos* pro eo quod nos reposuimus *nodos*. Sic autem invenio cum in aliis nonnullis tum in libro Iohannis Boccacii manu perscripto, qui nunc in bibliotheca Sancti Spiritus Florentina servatur. Ceterum nec ratio metri patitur alterutrum, vel *modos* vel *meos*, quoniam iambum esse, non pyrrhichium sede illa secunda oporteat.

2 Litteras igitur, Cadmi Phoenicis munus, et papyrum Niloticam et atramentum scriptorium et calamum librarium, litteratoris eius germanum instrumentum, videtur mihi Ausonius sub haec involucra conplicasse. Cadmus enim litteras primus in Graeciam attulit e Phoenice. Testatur Herodotus in *Terpsicore*[128] Phoenicas eos inquiens, qui Cadmo duce venere in Graeciam, litteras vernaculas et patrias, hoc est Phoenissas, ostendisse primitus Graecis, sed fluxu

: 39 :

Explanation of a riddle of the poet Ausonius about the daughters of Cadmus, Melo and Sepia, and the knots of Cnidus

I shall try to explain a riddle that Ausonius, an ingenious and 1
not unlearned poet, propounded to the grammarian Theon, in
acatalectic iambic dimeters. But let us first set down the lines:

> Or may your interpreter assist you,
> Who understood my riddles
> When he revealed to you
> The darkish little daughters of Cadmus,
> The white page of Melo,
> The marks of black *Sepia*,
> And the knots of Cnidus.[474]

Of these, however, the last verse is read in corrupt form in the
more common books, having *modos* or *meos* in place of what we
restored, *nodos* ("knots"). I find it thus not only in several others
but also in a book copied out in the hand of Giovanni Boccacio,
which is now conserved in Florence's Santo Spirito library.[475] But
the meter allows neither *modos* nor *meos*, since it would have to be
an iamb, not a *pyrrhichius* in that second position.

Now then, Ausonius seems to me to have folded together un- 2
der this wrapper letters, the gift of Cadmus the Phoenician, the
papyrus of the Nile, the ink of scribes, and the pen for writing
books, the true equipment of that schoolmaster. For Cadmus was
the first to introduce letters into Greece from Phoenicia. Herodotus attests to this in his *Terpsichore*, saying that the Phoenicians,
who came into Greece with Cadmus as their leader, first showed
the Greeks their native and ancestral, that is, Phoenician, letters,

aetatis ait cum voce notae quoque sensim mutatae. Primique iis
Iones usi. Quare etiam Φοινικήια sunt appellatae. Cadmeas autem se quoque vidisse scribit Herodotus litteras in templo Apollinis Ismenii Thebis in Boeotia, caelatas in tripodibus quibusdam,
de quibus tria citat epigrammata maxime (ut inquit ipse) Ionicis
similes. Quamobrem si veteres Graecae litterarum notae non aliae
quam Phoenicum, Latinae vero non aliae fuere quam Graecorum,
sicut et Plinius indicat, citata ipse quoque Delphica (nam illud *tabula* novicium est et ab ineruditis additum), manifestum est etiam
Latinas litteras non alias esse quam quas a Cadmo didicerimus.
Quare ob id eas Cadmi filias vocat Ausonius, quoniamque atramento minusculae imprimuntur, ideo suaviter *nigellas*. Ob id igitur
Zeno sic in epigrammate:

> Εἰ δέ[129] πάτρα Φοίνισσα, τίς ὁ φθόνος, οὗ καὶ Κάδμος
> Κεῖνος ἀφ᾽ οὗ γραπτὰν Ἑλλὰς ἔχει σελίδα.

Timon quoque Pyrrhonius, ut apud Sextum legimus libro *Pyrrhoniorum* quarto, sic scripsit:

> Γραμματικὴ, τῆς οὔ τις ἀνασκοπὴ οὐδ᾽ ἀνάθρησις
> Ἀνδρὶ διδασκομένῳ Φοινικικὰ σήματα Κάδμου,

Cadmi Phoenicica signa notas litterarum vocitans. Omitto quod
et Suidas, aut Zopyrion potius, Φοινίκεια vocatas litteras ait.
Omitto Plinium ceterosque permultos qui dicant eas a Cadmo in
Graeciam allatas. Nam cum diversi quae legerant apud Herodo-
tum passim meminerint, satis ipsi fecisse videmur, quod ista suae
reddimus auctoritati, nec enim tam numeranda, sicuti putamus,
veterum testimonia sunt, quam ponderanda.

but he says that with the passage of time, as the pronunciation gradually changed, so did the letterforms.[476] The Ionians were the first to use them. That is why they were called Phoenician. Furthermore, Herodotus writes that he too saw Cadmean letters in the temple of Apollo Ismenius at Thebes in Boeotia, carved on some tripods, from which he cites three epigrams especially similar (as he himself says) to those in Ionia. For that reason, if ancient Greek letterforms were none other than those of the Phoenicians and Latin letters were none other than those of the Greeks, as Pliny also indicates, citing the Delphic letter (for *tabula* ["tablet"] is an intrusion added by unlearned people), it is clear that even Latin letters are none other than those we have learned from Cadmus.[477] And so for this reason Ausonius calls them "daughters of Cadmus," and since smallish letters are inscribed with ink, he charmingly calls them "little dark ones" (*nigellas*). For this reason, then, Zeno [writes] as follows in an epigram:

> If his homeland is Phoenicia, what cause for envy there?
>> Whence [came] Cadmus, too, from whom Greece got its
>>> written page.[478]

Timon the Pyrrhonian, too, as we read in Book 4 of Sextus's *Pyrrhonians*, wrote the following:

> Grammar, which is not an object of inquiry or observation
> For a man learning the Phoenician signs of Cadmus,[479]

calling the letterforms of Cadmus Phoenician signs. I skip over the fact that Suidas, or rather Zopyrion,[480] says that letters are called "Phoenician things."[481] I also set aside Pliny and many others who report that they were introduced into Greece by Cadmus.[482] For when various people recall what they read here and there in Herodotus, I think I have done enough by referring those matters to their source, for the testimonies of the ancients must, I think, be not so much added up as weighed.[483]

3 Melonis vero albam paginam ob id ait, quod papyrum Nilus producit, ex quo paginae fiunt candidae. Nilus autem a veteribus Latinis, nondum assuetis Graecae linguae, Melo vocabatur, quemadmodum Pompeius in vocabulo quod est *Alumento* declarat. Quanquam habent plerique codices non *melo* sed *milo,* mendose insciteque. Quare vacillantem (si videtur) auctoritatem adminiculo Servi substentabimus, cuius in primo *Aeneidos* ita verba sunt: 'Sane Atlas Graecum est, sicut Nilus. Nam Ennius dicit Nilum Melonem vocari, Atlantem vero Telamonem.' Sic ille.

4 Denique pro atramento in litterarum formas lito *Sepiam* capimus, etiam apud Persium:

Nigra quod infusa vanescat[130] sepia lympha,

scilicet ob eius piscis ingenium, qui liquorem dicatur atrum profundere, quo fortassis olimque atramentum confieret. Ex quo Marcianus: 'Dehincque nigello pulvere, qui ex favilla confectus vel sepia putaretur, illato per cannulas eadem resanari.' *Furvum* porro nigrum, de quo et furem dici putat Varro. Sed et Horatius ex eo quoque: 'Furvae,' inquit, 'regna Proserpinae.' Et furvas hostias Diti patri Valerius Maximus, sed et ante eum Varro nigras interpretatur.

5 *Cnidios* dein *nodos* accipe, quoniam calami probatiores Cnidii, sicuti Plinius ait libro sextodecimo *Historiae naturalis.* Affectavit autem imitationem Persianam cum dixit nodos, quoniam et ille scripserat:

Inque manus chartae, nodosaque venit harundo.

Indeed, he says that the white page belongs to Melo, since the 3
Nile produces papyrus, from which white pages are made. But the
Nile was called Melo by the ancient Latins, who were not yet familiar with the Greek language, as Pompeius [Festus] explains on
the name *Alumento*.[484] However, many codices erroneously and ignorantly have not *melo* but *milo*. I will, accordingly, support a weak
authority (if so it seems) with the aid of Servius, whose words on
the first book of the *Aeneid* are as follows: "Certainly *Atlas* is
Greek, as is *Nilus*. For Ennius says that the Nile is called *Melo* and
that Atlas is called *Telamon*."[485] So says Servius.

Finally, we take *Sepia* as the ink smeared into the shapes of let- 4
ters, as Persius also has it:

The black ink (*sepia*) fades when water is poured on,[486]

namely, on account of the nature of this fish, which is said to pour
forth a black liquid, by which perhaps ink was once produced.
Hence Martianus [Capella says]: [He showed that children's
speech impediments] "were then healed with a black powder that
was thought to be made from ash or sepia and delivered through
small reeds."[487] Furthermore, *furvum* ("dark") is black, from which
Varro thinks *fur* ("thief") is derived.[488] From this Horace, too,
speaks of "the realms of dark Proserpina."[489] Also, Valerius Maximus, and Varro before him, interpret the dark victims for father
Dis as black.[490]

Next, hear about "the knots of Cnidus," since Cnidian pens are 5
more esteemed, as Pliny says in Book 16 of his *Natural History*.[491]
Moreover, he [Ausonius] aimed to imitate Persius when he said
nodos ("knots"), since he had written:

Paper and a knotty reed [i.e., a pen] came to hand.[492]

∶ 40 ∶

Scirpi simile vatis eiusdem epigramma
emaculatum atque enarratum

Quem nuper vatis Ausoni scirpum enodavimus redegit in mentem
nobis tetrastichon[131] eiusdem facilius intellectu fortasse, siquis et
emaculatum habeat codicem et Graecae litteraturae non sit igna-
rus, ut cui vel alterutrum desit, non minoris sane laboris futurum
quam hoc est aenigma superius. Versus hi sunt:

Lais Eros et Itys, Chiron et Eros Itys alter
  Nomina si scribas, prima elementa adime,
Ut facias verbum quod tu facis, Eune magister.
  Dicere me Latium non decet opprobrium.

Nempe de primis singulorum ipsorum nominum litteris seriatim
inter se coagmentatis Graecum dissultat hoc verbum λείχει, quod
est Latine *lingit,* ut eo verbo (sit autem honor auribus) inguinum
ligurritor Eunus, aut siquid tale addivinas,[132] insinuetur.

: 40 :

*A riddle-like epigram of the same poet is
emended and explained*

That riddle of the poet Ausonius that I just explicated put me in
mind of a four-line poem of his, perhaps easier to understand if
one has both a manuscript free of corruption and is not unac-
quainted with Greek, just as if anyone lacks either of these two, it
will involve no less labor than the preceding riddle. The verses are
these:

> Lais, Eros, and Itys, Chiron and Eros, and Itys again—
>   If you write down these names and take their initials,
> The result is the action that you perform, schoolteacher
>   Eunus.
>   It were unseemly for me to name the shame of Latium.[493]

Of course, from the first letters of the individual names, linked
together in series, this Greek verb jumps out, λείχει, which in
Latin is *lingit* ("he licks"), so that by that verb Eunus is hinted to
be (let the ears be spared!) a licker of genitalia or whatever such
thing you guess besides.

: 41 :

Quod in Digestis *Iustiniani principis*
diem diffusum *male pro eo quod est* diffisum *legitur, ut et
apud* Gellium diffundi *et* definitiones *pro illis*
diffindi *et* diffisiones, *atque inibi
de* Pandectis Florentinis *nonnihil*

1   *Diffisionis* vocabulum et item quod dici solitum in iudiciis *diffindi
diem,* pene iam sublatum e medio atque inscitia quadam improba
importunaque bonis artibus exitiosa iam oblitteratum, restituere
ipsi pro virili conabimur et renovare diligentia nostra. Utitur ista
loquendi figura etiam iureconsultus Ulpianus in libro LXXIIII *Ad
edictum* per haec sane verba, quae posita libro primo *Digestorum*
sunt sub hoc titulo: 'Siquis cautionibus in iudicio sistendi causa
factis non obtemperaverit':

> Siquis (inquit) in iudicio se sisti promiserit et valetudine vel
> tempestate vel vi fluminis prohibitus se sistere non potuit,
> exceptione adiuvatur. Nec immerito. Cum enim in tali pro-
> missione praesentia opus sit, quemadmodum potuerit se sis-
> tere qui adversa valetudine impeditus est, et ideo etiam Lex
> XII Tabularum, si iudex vel alteruter ex litigatoribus morbo
> sontico impediatur, iubet diem iudicii esse diffisum.

Hactenus Ulpianus.

2   *Diffisum* autem legendum, non *diffusum,* quod omnes habent hi
ferme libri qui sunt in manibus. Atqui volumen ipsum Iustiniani
Digestorum seu *Pandectarum,* dubio procul archetypum, in ipsa

: 41 :

That in the Emperor Justinian's Digests *the phrase*
diem diffusum *is read erroneously for* diffisum, *as also
in Gellius* diffundi *and* definitiones *are read instead of*
diffindi *and* diffisiones; *and something in the same place
about the Florentine* Pandects

I shall, to the best of my ability, endeavor to restore and renew by   1
my diligence the word *diffisio* ("postponement") and likewise a
phrase customarily used in court, *diffindi diem* ("the day is postponed"), that by now has almost disappeared and been blotted out
through a certain reckless and misguided ignorance deleterious to
culture. The jurist Ulpian also uses that figure of speech in Book
74 of his *On the Edict* in these very words, which have been placed
in the first book of the *Digests* under this title: "If anyone fails to
comply once pledges have been given for the purpose of appearance in court":

> If anyone has promised to appear in court, but was unable to
> do so because he was prevented by ill health, bad weather, or
> a flood, he is aided by an exemption. Rightly so. For al-
> though one's presence is required by such a promise, how
> could someone be present who is hindered by ill health?
> Therefore the Law of the Twelve Tables directs that the day
> of the trial be postponed (*diffisum*) if a judge or either of the
> litigants is hindered by serious illness.[494]

Thus far Ulpian.
But *diffisum* ("postponed") must be read, not *diffusum* ("ex-   2
tended"), as almost all the books in circulation have. Yet that very
volume of Justinian's *Digests* or *Pandects*, undoubtedly the arche-

Curia Florentina a summo magistratu publice adservatur magnaque veneratione, quanquam raro id, etiamque ad funalia ostenditur. Est autem liber haud quota spoliorum praedaeque Pisanae portio saepe a consultis citatus, maioribus characteribus, nullisque intervallis dictionum, nullis item compendiariis notis, quibusdamque etiam saltem in praefatione velut ab auctore plane et a cogitante atque generante potius quam a librario et exceptore inductis, expunctis, ac superscriptis, cum Graeca epistola Graecoque etiam pulcherrimo hoc epigrammate in prima fronte:

Βίβλον Ἰουστινιανὸς ἄναξ τεχνήσατο τήνδε
Τήν ῥα Τριβωνιανὸς μεγάλῳ[133] κάμε παμβασιλῆι
Οἷά τις Ἡρακλῆι παναίολον ἀσπίδα τεύξας
Ἧι ἐπιμαρμαίρουσιν ἀγάλματα πάντα θεμίστων,[134]
Ἄνθρωποι δ' Ἀσίης τε δορυκτήτου τε Λιβύσσης
Εὐρώπης τε πίθονται ὅλου σημάντορι κόσμου.

Cuius tamen voluminis legendi ac versandi per otium mihi est uni facta copia, Laurenti Medicis opera causaque, qui, vir suae rei publicae princeps, dum studiosis obsequatur, etiam ad haec usque officia se demittit. Igitur in *Pandectis* his, non iam Pisanis ut quondam sed Florentinis, in quibus pura sunt verba nec ut in ceteris plena maculis et scabie, *diffisum* reperio, non *diffusum*.

3   Quod idem apud A. quoque Gellium video depravatum libro qui nunc vulgo tertiusdecimus, cum sit quintusdecimus emendatis codicibus. Nam ubi haec verba legimus: 'Atque in rerum quidem definitionibus comperendinationibusque,' hic ego in codice Gelliano ex bibliotheca publica Medicae familiae, quem vir haud indoctus (ut tum ferebant tempora) sed diligens tamen imprimis Nicolaus Nicolus ex vetustissimo exemplari fideliter pro suo more

type,[495] is kept in public custody in Florence's senate house by its highest magistrate and displayed with great veneration, albeit rarely, and adjacent to a ceremonial candlestand.[496] This book—no trifling portion of the spoils and booty of Pisa[497]—has often been cited by jurists. It is written in majuscule letters, with no breaks between words, and likewise with no abbreviations but with certain elements added, deleted and written above the line, at least in the preface, as if by the author who is thinking about and producing the text rather than a scribe or one taking dictation, and [it is equipped] with a Greek epistle and also this lovely Greek epigram in front:

Emperor Justinian commissioned this book,
Which Tribonian wrought for the great universal king,
Like someone who crafted a glittering shield for Heracles,
By which all the glories of the laws sparkle,
And the people of Asia and conquered Libya
And Europe obey the commander of all the world.

However, the opportunity of reading this volume and studying it at leisure was granted to me alone thanks to and for the sake of Lorenzo de' Medici, who, as leading man of his own republic, while he supports scholars, even condescends to such duties as this. In these *Pandects*, then, no longer, as formerly, Pisan, but now Florentine, in which the text is pristine and not as in the others full of blemishes and rough spots, I find *diffisum* ("postponed"), not *diffusum* ("extended").[498]

I see this same corruption in A. Gellius, in the book that is now commonly the thirteenth, although it is the fifteenth in error-free codices. For where we read these words: "And indeed in the definitions (*definitionibus*) and adjournments of cases," there, in a codex of Gellius from the public library of the Medici family, which Niccolò Niccoli, a man hardly unlearned (relative to the times) but particularly diligent, copied out faithfully, as was his

3

descripserit, ita invenio: 'Atque in rerum quidem diffisionibus comperendinationibusque.' Quod si suspitio libera mi detur, malim credere equidem 'in dierum' quam 'in rerum' veram habuisse et incolumem scripturam. Quin eodem capite Gellius: 'Iussi igitur,' inquit, 'diem diffindi.' Sic enim in eodem codice quod in his pervulgatioribus 'diem diffundi.'

: 42 :

Pollices in favendo premi,
sicut in denegando favorem verti solitos,
ex eoque sententiae Horati, Iuvenalis,
et Prudenti declaratae

1   Horatius in primo *Epistolarum* libro:

Consentire suis studiis qui crediderit te
Fautor utroque tuum laudabit pollice ludum.

'Utroque,' inquit, 'pollice,' Porphyrion, 'hoc est utraque manu, ut sit tropos synecdoche, a parte totum.' Sed ne quem forte veteris scriptoris auctoritas infatuet, ei quoque aurem leviter pervellemus.

2   Scriptum est igitur apud Plinium libro *Naturalis historiae* octavo et vigesimo, in haec verba: 'Pollices, cum faveamus, premere etiam proverbio iubemur.' Ex quo Iuvenalis peritissime illud:

Et verso pollice vulgi,
Quemlibet occidunt populariter,

wont, from a very old exemplar, I find the following: "And indeed in the postponements (*diffisionibus*) of cases and adjournments."⁴⁹⁹ If I have license to venture a suspicion, I prefer to believe that the true and intact reading had *in dierum* ("in [postponement] of dates") rather than *in rerum* ("in [postponement] of cases"). In fact, in the same chapter Gellius says: "Therefore, I ordered the date (*diem*) to be postponed (*diffindi*)."⁵⁰⁰ For in the same codex it is written thus, as in the many common ones, "the date is extended" (*diem diffundi*).

: 42 :

*That thumbs are customarily clenched to show support and
likewise that they are turned down to deny support;
and on this basis ideas of Horace, Juvenal,
and Prudentius are clarified*

Horace, in the first book of his *Letters*:   1

> He who believes that you share his enthusiasms
> Will, like a fan, praise your game with both thumbs.⁵⁰¹

Porphyrio says: "With both thumbs, that is, with both hands, so that the trope is synecdoche, the whole from a part."⁵⁰² But lest the authority of an ancient writer perhaps make a fool of someone, we will also gently tweak his ear.

Now then, in Book 28 of Pliny's *Natural History*, one reads the   2 following: "We are bidden by a proverb to clench our thumbs when we are in support."⁵⁰³ Hence Juvenal says most skillfully:

> Upon the crowd's turn of their thumbs,
> They kill whomever you please to the people's applause,⁵⁰⁴

ceu si verso pollice tollatur favor. Denique etiam Prudentius in heroico *Adversus Symmachum* ita contra Vestales quae muneri gladiatorio intererant declamavit:

> Et quoties victor ferrum iugulo inserit, illa
> Delicias ait esse suas, pectusque iacentis
> Virgo modesta iubet converso pollice rumpi.

Nam ut favere qui pollicem premerent, ita, puto, qui verterent denegare gladiatoribus favorem credebantur.

: 43 :

Quam multas habuerint antiqui diphthongos

1 Diphthongi apud Latinos non plures quattuor perhibentur, cum septem nos eas saltem inveniamus in antiquis vel marmoribus vel nomismatis, quorum nobis copiam ingentem Medices Laurentius suppeditat. Nam praeter illas vulgatissimas, quae sunt *ae, oe, au,* et *eu,* est adeo invenire etiam *ai* et *ei* et item *ou* pro illis *ae, i, u* in veteribus monimentis.[135] Et *ai* quidem pro *ae,* nonnulli cum littera *i,* non *e,* Graecorum more semper efferebant, ut Quintilianus ostendit, quidam singulariter tantum, cum in genitivum vel dativum casum incidissent. Unde etiam *Aimilius* pro eo quod sit *Aemilius* alicubi Romae in antiquis spectationibus adnotavimus. Omnino autem cum supra testudinem Panthei ascendissemus, fragmentum ibi marmoreum cum eiuscemodi scripturae vestigiis offendimus. Ex quo etiam diaeresin videmus factam in illis, quae vel apud

as if support is removed by turning the thumb down. Finally, Prudentius, too, in his heroic poem *Against Symmachus*, declaimed thus against the Vestals who attended a gladiatorial game:

> And whenever a victor inserts his blade in the neck [of his
>   defeated opponent], she
> Says he is her sweetheart, and the modest [Vestal] virgin,
> With her thumb turned down, orders that the breast of the
>   vanquished be ruptured.[505]

For just as those who clenched their thumbs were believed to show support, so, I think, those who turned their thumbs down were thought to deny support for the gladiators.

: 43 :

How many diphthongs the ancients had

In Latin authors there are said to be no more than four diph- 1
thongs, although I find at least seven of them on ancient marble
monuments or coins, a huge supply of which Lorenzo de' Medici
makes available to me.[506] For in addition to the most common
diphthongs, which are *ae, oe, au,* and *eu,* it is also possible to find
ai and *ei,* and *ou* as well, in place of *ae, i,* and *u,* on old monuments.
In fact, some people always pronounced *ai* for *ae,* with the letter *i*
rather than *e,* in the Greek manner, as Quintilian points out,[507]
some of them only in the singular, when they came upon the
genitive or dative case. Thus, when inspecting antiquities in Rome,
I occasionally observed *Aimilius* for *Aemilius.* Indeed, when I had
climbed up onto the vault of the Pantheon, there I came upon a
marble fragment with traces of this same spelling. From this I also
see a diaeresis effected on these words, which are found even in

Vergilium sunt: *aulai, pictai,* et quod nunc mendose legitur *aquai.*
Porro autem diphthongus *ei* frequentius invenitur peneque etiam
in confesso est, quod et nomismata pleraque et marmora vetustissima declarant et argumenta ipsa Plautinarum comoediarum quae
Captivi quaeve item *Menaechmi* inscribuntur. Nam si versuum singulorum primas subinde litteras connectas, *Capteivei* et *Menaechmei*
resultabit, ut sit ubique *ei* diphthongus. Praeterea *fouri,* non *furi,*
legimus in nomismate alio, ut prima syllaba diphthongo produca-
tur, qualis etiam apud Graecos est.

2   Quid autem de eo dicam quod et Quintilianus indicat et nos
aliquando observavimus, ut vocalem producendam geminarent
cum in aureo nomismatio *feelix* per *e* geminum, in aereo autem
Galbae principis *viirtus* per *i* duplex reperiatur? Iam illa ἄκυρος
nonne etiam apud nos in Graecis saltem nominibus, ut in Harpyia, Orithyia, Thyiadeque, reperitur? Ut non iam septem diph-
thongos, sed decem quoque habuisse videri maiores queant.

: 44 :

Pegaseium nectar *legi oportere apud Persium, non* melos

1   Persius in epigrammate quod prohoemii vice fungitur:

> Corvos poetas, inquit, et poetridas picas,
> Cantare credas Pegaseium melos.

Nos in vetustissimo commentario, litteris quas Langobardas vocant perscripto, quod etiam publice nostris auditoribus exhibui-
mus, sic ad verbum invenimus: 'Pegaseum nectar,' in aliis *melos,* ex

248

Vergil: *aulai*, *pictai*, and as is now incorrectly read, *aquai*.[508] Furthermore, the diphthong *ei* is found quite frequently and is almost even acceptable, a fact that is shown by many ancient coins and marble monuments, as well as by the arguments of Plautus's comedies entitled the *Captives* and the *Menaechmi*. For if one connects the initial letters of the individual lines one after another, *Capteivei* and *Menaechmei* leap out, so that the diphthong *ei* is used throughout. Furthermore, we read *fouri* rather than *furi* on another coin,[509] so that the first syllable is lengthened with a diphthong, just as it also is among the Greeks.

But what am I to say about the fact, both shown by Quintilian 2 and occasionally observed by myself, that they would double a vowel that is to be lengthened, since *feelix*, with a double *e*, is found on a gold coin, and the *viirtus* of the Emperor Galba is found with a double *i* on a bronze coin? Now is not that improper [diphthong] also found among us, at least in Greek names, such as Harpyia, Orithyia, and Thyias? Hence our ancestors can be seen to have had not just seven diphthongs, but even ten.[510]

: 44 :

Pegaseium nectar, *not* melos, *ought to be read in Persius*

In the epigram that serves as his preface, Persius says: 1

> You would think that raven poets and magpie poetesses
> Were singing a song of Pegasus.[511]

In an extremely old commentary that was written in so-called Lombardic script and which I publicly showed my students, I have found the following, verbatim: *Pegaseum nectar* ("nectar of Pegasus"), in others *melos* ("song"),[512] from which I judge that the an-

quo existimamus veterem sinceramque scripturam *nectar* habuisse,
noviciam vero et mendosam *melos*. Sed et Pomponius Laetus Romanae princeps academiae,[136] diligentissimus homo antiquitatis,
veterem se habere Persianum codicem multis audientibus affirmavit huic nostrae lectioni suffragantem.

2   Quod et ratio tamen carminis evicerit. Nam cum oporteat no-
vissimum choliambi pedem spondeum poni vel trocheum, *melos*
autem nunquam, neque apud Graecos neque item apud nostros,
nisi brevi priore syllaba accipiatur. Mendum profecto fuerit in
versu, si *melos* admiseris. Nam quod autumant nonnulli λ litteram
vim producendi habere apud Graecos, quod omnino tacuit auctor
metrorum singularis Hephestion,[137] id ego inveniri quidem scio,
sed in obscuris duntaxat quibusdam et ignobilibus schedis,[138]
exemplumque afferri ex Homero, apud quem *heloria* prima intenta
syllaba legamus. Id autem quam frivolum, quam leve sit et nugato-
rium, vel hoc evidentissime declarat, quod usu iam et auctoritate
doctissimi cuiusque receptum est ut id vocabulum apud Homerum
quoque λ duplici notaretur.

3   Ceterum si maxime concesserimus fieri hoc solere aliquando
apud Graecos, non tamen continuo credendum est, illiusmodi
usum licentia Persium Graeca una appellatione, quam vix semel in
tanta scriptorum silva Graeci usurpare ipsi reperiantur, praesertim
cum neque apud Graecos, quantum equidem observaverim, neque
item apud Latinos aliter quam brevi priore syllaba *melos* inveniatur.
Nam quantopere hanc solis concessam Graecis licentiam fugitarint
Latini veteres vel Martialis poeta declarat, cum se de nomine ipso
Earini tantopere torquet, nec sibi saltem pro *Earino* Εἰαρινόν
dicere permittit, vulgata apud Graecos licentia *i* litteram inter-
ponendi, sicut apud Homerum:

ʼΕπ’ ἄνθεσιν εἰαρινοῖσιν.

cient and untainted text had *nectar*, but that the new and erroneous reading is *melos*. But Pomponio Leto, too, head of the Academy of Rome, a scrupulous investigator of antiquity, affirmed before many witnesses that he possessed an ancient codex of Persius that supports this reading of ours.[513]

The poem's meter will also prove this. For although a spondee or trochee must be placed as the last foot of a choliamb, *melos* would never be admitted among either the Greeks or our people, except with a short first syllable. Actually, there would be an error in the verse if you accept *melos*. For as to the fact that some assert that among the Greeks the letter λ had the power of lengthening, about which Hephaestion, the single author on meters, was completely silent, I know that this is found, though only in some obscure and insignificant pages, and I know that an example is adduced from Homer, in whose work we read *heloria* ("prey") with a lengthened first syllable. How trivial, slight, and inconsequential this is, is shown very clearly by the fact that it has been accepted by the usage and authority of all learned persons that this word is also spelled with a double λ in Homer.[514]

Yet, even if we grant that this once regularly occurred among the Greeks, it must nonetheless not immediately be supposed that Persius used a single Greek noun with such license, which the Greeks themselves, among such a welter of writers, are scarcely found to have used once, especially since neither among the Greeks, as far as I have seen, nor among the Latins, is *melos* ever found other than with a short first syllable. For the poet Martial shows how strongly the ancient Latins shunned this license granted to the Greeks alone, when he so tortures himself over the name *Earinos*, nor does he permit himself even to say *Eiarinos* for *Earinos*, by the common license among the Greeks of interposing the letter *i*, as in Homer:

Upon the spring (*eiarinoisin*) flowers.[515]

Atque adeo Martialem ipsum audi:

> Dicunt Iarinon tamen poetae
> Sed Graeci, quibus est nihil negatum
> Et quos Ares Ares licet[139] sonare.
> Nobis non licet esse tam disertis,
> Qui Musas colimus severiores.

Quare nihil dubitandum, quin sit illud *melos* in Persiano versiculo tanquam verruca deformis recidendum restituendumque *nectar*, quod ratio nobis toto capite et vetusta pariter auctoritas adnuerunt.

∶ 45 ∶

Patroclo iuniorem Achillem, contra quam aut
Aeschylus prodiderit aut vulgo existimetur

1 Disseminata inter omnes iam pridem receptaque opinio Patroclum fuisse Achille iuniorem ab eoque velut[140] adamatum, sicut ferme Hylan ab Hercule. Tum innuere hunc ipsum Martialis creditur, sic inquiens:

> Aeacidae propior levis amicus erat.

Quare etiam versiculo cuidam nequissimo ex *Hermaphroditi* libellis vulgo quoque applaudebatur. Ceterum Statius in *Achilleide* parem denique utriusque aetatem[141] praedicat, ita inquiens:

> Insequitur magno iam tum connexus amore
> Patroclus, tantisque extenditur aemulus actis

And indeed hear Martial himself:

> The poets nevertheless say *Eiarinos,*
> But Greek poets, to whom nothing is denied,
> And who have license to say "Ares Ares."[516]
> We do not have license to be so eloquent,
> We who cultivate stricter Muses.[517]

Therefore it should by no means be doubted that *melos* must, like an ugly wart, be cut out of Persius's line, and *nectar* must be restored—to which reason has given full assent and ancient authority as well.[518]

: 45 :

That Achilles is younger than Patroclus, contrary both to what
Aeschylus propounded and is commonly thought

The opinion that has for a long time now been disseminated and   1
received among everyone is that Patroclus was younger than Achilles, and, as it were, beloved by him, just as Hylas was by Hercules. In addition, Martial is believed to hint at him, when he says the following:

> His beardless friend was closer to Aeacides.[519]

Hence even a certain naughty verse from the little books of *The Hermaphrodite* was generally applauded.[520] Yet in his *Achilleid* Statius asserts that the two of them were the same age, when he says the following:

> Patroclus, even then bound by a great love, follows [him],
> And he exerts himself as a rival to such great deeds,

Par studiis aevique modis, sed robore longe,
Et tamen aequali visurus Pergama fato.

2   Plato autem in *Symposio* longe diversum contendit. Nam et
multo iuniorem fuisse Achillem declarat et ipsum potius a Patroclo adamatum, utpote imberbem adhuc, nec Patroclo ipso modo
sed heroibus etiam cunctis formosiorem. Quin ea causa di, inquit,
illum honoribus egregiis affecerunt ut ad insulas fortunatas mitte-
rent, quod amatorem tanti fecerit ut non pro eo solum mori, sed ei
vel immori quam in patria consenescere praeoptaverit.

3   Quin Aeschylum Plato idem ceu nugacem taxat, quod is
quoque Achillem Patrocli fuisse amasium prodiderit, testemque
utriusque aetatis Homerum citat, cuius si quispiam verba (nam
haec utique Plato non posuit) sibi indicari postulat, legat in undecima *Iliados* rhapsodia sub Nestoris persona, quibus cum mandatis
Patroclum filium pater Menoetius ad bella dimiserit.

Equal in endeavors and the measure of his age, but far behind
   in physical strength
And nonetheless destined to see Pergamum with an equal
   fate.[521]

But in his *Symposium* Plato contends that it was far different. 2
For he asserts that Achilles was much younger and that he, rather,
had been beloved by Patroclus, inasmuch as he was still beardless,
and was more handsome not only than Patroclus himself but even
all the rest of the heroes. What is more, the gods, he says, bestowed upon him exceptional honors, so as to send him to the
Isles of the Blessed, because he set such store by his lover that he
not only preferred to die for him, but preferred to die for him
rather than to grow old in his homeland.[522]

In fact, Plato censures Aeschylus as an incompetent, because he 3
also propounded that Achilles had been Patroclus's lover, and cites
Homer as a witness of the ages of both men.[523] If anyone demands
that Homer's words be shown him (for Plato failed to cite them),
he can read them in the eleventh book of the *Iliad*, spoken by the
character Nestor, with the orders with which the father Menoetius
sent his son Patroclus to war.[524]

: 46 :

Cacoethes *apud Iuvenalem tetrasyllabon, non* cacethos, *et
'condita pyxide Lyde,' non 'in ⟨pyxide⟩*[142] *condita' legendum,
simul enarratus apud Marcianum*[143] *locus haud,
arbitror, indiligenter*

1 In septima Iuvenalis poetae satyra sic scriptum:

> Tenet insanabile multos
> Scribendi cacethos et aegro in corde senescit.

Vocabulum autem quod est *cacethos* neque a Graecis uspiam usur-
patur neque a Latinis, sed neque ratio carminis admittit. Quare
cacoethes legendum suspicamur, ut sit quod apud Graecos τὸ
κακόηθες. Eo namque[144] verbo frequentissimo usitatissimoque
mala consuetudo significatur. Quod item in vetusto codice Langobardis exarato litteris repperimus, cuius mihi potestatem legendi
fecit Franciscus Gaddius Florentinus, summi magistratus a secretis
prudens humanusque vir nec litteris incultus.

2 Sed et ille versus ita in eodem:

> Turgida nec prodest condita pyxide Lyde,

quod alibi perperam sic est: 'in pyxide condita Lyde,' ut anum in-
telligas Lyden illiusmodi medicamenta venditantem, crassam et (ut
inquit Plautus) doliarem. Quod et Capella fortasse spectans et fa-
cetissime super ebrio Sileno ludens ita inquit:

> Ac dum movere gressum
> Cupit avocante Lyde.

: 46 :

Quadrisyllabic cacoethes, *and not* cacethos, *must be read in Juvenal; and* condita pyxide Lyde, *not in* pyxide condita, *must be read; at the same time a passage in Martianus is, I think, rather carefully explained*

In the seventh satire of the poet Juvenal, one reads the following: 1

> An incurable itch (*cacethos*) to write has a hold on many
> And endures to old age in a sick heart.[525]

The word *cacethos,* however, is nowhere used either by Greeks or Latins, nor does the meter allow it. Accordingly, we suspect that *cacoethes* must be read, so as to be the Greek τò κακόηθες. For by this very common and much-used word a bad habit is signified. We likewise find this in an old codex written in Lombardic script; I was given the opportunity to read this by the Florentine Francesco Gaddi, a wise and kind man, secretary to the highest magistracy and no stranger to literary culture.[526]

But the following verse reads this way in the same manuscript: 2

> Swollen Lyde is no use, her medicine box hidden.[527]

This is incorrectly found elsewhere as: *in pyxide condita Lyde* ("Lyde, hidden in a medicine box"),[528] so that you take Lyde to be an old hag who sells such cosmetics, fat and (as Plautus says[529]) shaped like a storage jar. But [Martianus] Capella, perhaps also with this in view and wittily joking about the drunken Silenus, says the following:

> And while he wanted to take a step forward,
> With Lyde beckoning.[530]

Nam ut si Cantharae vel Pyrrhiae nomina vel Baucidos inaudias, continuo suffarcinatas tibi et vinosas et pannucias quasdam delectione confinxeris, ita nomine audito Lydes mox hanc Iuvenalis turgidam recordaris, ut mirifice sint inductae ad excutiendos cachinnos personae, vino venas inflatus Silenus et ventriosa Lyde, quae titubantem et lapsabundum etiam (si dis placet) avocet ab irrisu.

: 47 :

Quae Plinius super titulis veterum artificum pendentibus prodiderit, ea de monimentis[145] etiam veteribus agnita Romae, sicutique speciem Vergilianae aegidos

1 Romae nuper in atrio Mellinae domus marmoream quandam veluti basin aspeximus, in qua Graece sic erat: Σέλευκος Βασιλεὺς Λύσιππος ἐποίει. Id Latine valet: 'Seleucus Rex, Lysippus faciebat.' Erat ibi tum nobiscum Iohannes Laurentius Venetus,[146] Summi Pontificis a secretis, homo linguae utriusque doctissimus omniumque istiusmodi quasi lauticiarum studiosissimus. Is igitur nos submonuit, quod et statim arripuimus agnovimusque, non temere illic ἐποίει potius quam ἐποίησεν, hoc est *faciebat* quam *fecit*, siquidem, ut ait Plinius in praefatione librorum *Naturalis historiae*, summi illi artifices etiam absoluta opera pendenti titulo inscripsere, ut Apelles faciebat et Polyclitus, tanquam inchoata[147] semper arte et imperfecta, ut contra iudiciorum varietates superesset artifici regressus ad veniam velut emendaturo quidquid desideraretur, si non esset interceptus. Quare, inquit, plenum

Just as when you hear the names of Canthara or Pyrrhia or Baucis, you immediately conjure up with pleasure some women stuffed with padding, reeking of wine, and shriveled up,[531] so upon hearing the name Lyde, you at once recall this swollen woman in Juvenal, so that the characters are wonderfully brought onstage to produce guffaws, Silenus, his veins popping with wine, and a pot-bellied Lyde, who—would you believe it?—calls him back from ridicule as he staggers and stumbles about.

: 47 :

What Pliny related about open-ended labels of ancient artists
can also be detected as regards ancient monuments at Rome,
as well as the appearance of the Vergilian skin shield

At Rome I recently gazed upon a particular marble base in the   1
atrium of the house of the Millini,[532] on which was written in
Greek: "King Seleucus, Lysippus was making it." The Latin equivalent is: "King Seleucus; Lysippus was making it." With me there
was the Venetian Giovanni Lorenzi, a papal secretary, learned in
both Greek and Latin and very keen on all such elegant goods.[533]
He, then, advised me of a point that I immediately snatched
up and recognized, that ἐποίει was not there by chance rather
than ἐποίησεν, that is, *faciebat* ("was making") rather than *fecit*
("made"), since, as Pliny says in the preface to the books of his
Natural History, even when the work was complete, those supreme
artists inscribed it with an open-ended label, such as Apelles or
Polyclitus was making it, as if the work of art was always begun
but unfinished, so that the artist could have recourse to pardon
in the face of adverse judgments, as if he were about to correct
whatever was found wanting, had he not been interrupted.[534]

verecundiae est illud, quod omnia opera tanquam novissima inscripsere et tanquam aliquid singulis fato sit ademptum. Tria autem, non, ut ille opinatur, amplius absolute[148] traduntur inscripta
'ille fecit,' quae suis locis reddit. Quo apparuit summam artis secu-
ritatem auctori placuisse. Et ob id magna invidia fuere omnia ea.
Ceterum etiam alibi Romae similis inveniri titulos idem Iohannes
Laurentius Venetus asseverabat.

2   Vidimus item, quod etiam his *Miscellaneis* nostris putavimus
inserendum, marmoreum quoddam in urbe eadem Palladis simulachrum gestans aegida squamoso draconum corio contectam, sic
ut extremum ipsius ambitum dracunculi item ad limbi aut fim-
briae vicem circumcluderent. Erat ibi tum nobiscum Iulianus Bo-
noniensis, cui nunc ex re cognomen Antiquario factum, simulque
Georgius Italianus Genuensis, homo rerum abditarum investigator
experientissimus, cum statim Vergilianos versus recordati quibus
eam demum Palladii clypei caelaturam mire expressisse poeta in-
comparabilis videbatur, ita in octavo *Aeneidos* libro scribens:

Aegidaque horrificam turbatae Palladis arma
Certatim squamis serpentum auroque polibant,
Connexosque anguis ipsamque in pectore divae
Gorgona desecto vertentem lumina collo.

Therefore, he said, it is a mark of great modesty that they inscribed all their works as if they were their last and as if something had been removed from each one by fate. However, three works, not more, as he thinks, are reported to have been inscribed in completed form: "he made it (*ille fecit*)," which he reported in their proper places. From this it was apparent that supreme assurance in one's art pleased the author. And on account of this, great envy attached to all of these works.[535] Moreover, the same Giovanni Lorenzi of Venice asserted that similar labels are found elsewhere in Rome.

In the same city we likewise saw — something I thought also 2 had to be included in my *Miscellanies* — a certain marble statue of Pallas that bore a skin shield covered with the scaly hide of snakes in such a way that the little snakes surrounded the perimeter of the thing like a border or fringe. With us there on that occasion was Giuliano of Bologna, who now, on account of this work, enjoys the sobriquet "Antiquarius," as well as Giorgio Italiano of Genoa, a very experienced investigator of recherché subjects, when at once we remembered the Vergilian verses in which the incomparable poet seemed to have wonderfully expressed that engraving of Pallas's shield, when he wrote in the eighth book of the *Aeneid*:

> And vying with each other, they gave finish to the horrifying
>   skin shield,
> Arms of roused Pallas, with the scales of serpents and gold
> And the snakes intertwined and the Gorgon herself on the
>   goddess's breast,
> Rolling her eyes, with her neck severed.[536]

: 48 :

De Megabyzo scripsisse alios, quod Plinius de Alexandro,
ventitare in Apellis officinam solito

1   Plinius Secundus in volumine *Historiae naturalis* quinto et vigesimo[149] ventitare in Apellis excellentissimi pictoris officinam
solitum ait Alexandrum Macedonem, non artificio solum sed
comitate etiam hominis delectatum. Qui et 'in officina,' inquit,
'imperite multa disserenti silentium comiter suadebat, rideri eum
dicens a pueris qui colores tererent.'

2   Hoc quod de Alexandro Plinius scribit, Plutarchus ad Megabyzum rettulit in eo volumine quo disputat quae sint adulatoris et
amici discrimina, cuius si verba Latine interpretemur, haec fere
sunt:

Apelles, inquit, pictor assidenti sibi Megabyzo superque linea et umbra dicere nonnihil tentanti, 'viden,' inquit, 'ut
pueri melida (coloris id genus) terentes tacenti nuper tibi
animos adhibebant, purpuramque demirabantur et aurum.
Sed idem te nunc derident, loqui super iis quae haud didice-
ris incipientem.'

Quin Helianus quoque in libris *Historiae multifariae* ad Megabyzum et ipse, non ad Alexandrum rettulit.

: 48 :

What Pliny wrote about Alexander, others wrote about
Megabyzus, that he was wont to visit Apelles's workshop

In the twenty-fifth volume of his *Natural History*, Plinius Secundus   1
says that Alexander of Macedon was wont to visit the workshop of
the outstanding painter Apelles because he was delighted not only
by the man's art but also by his sociability. "When Alexander
spoke at length but without knowledge in the workshop," Pliny
says, "Apelles politely urged him to observe silence, saying that he
was being derided by the boys who grind the colors."[537]

What Pliny writes about Alexander, Plutarch ascribed to Mega-   2
byzus in the volume where he discusses the differences between a
flatterer and a friend. His words, rendered into Latin, are something like the following:

> Apelles the painter said to Megabyzus when he sat with him
> and attempted to say something about lines and shading,
> "Do you see that the boys grinding out the 'honey' (a sort of
> color) were just now paying attention to you while you were
> keeping quiet, and were admiring your purple and gold, but
> that they are now laughing at you, since you began to speak
> about things you barely know?"[538]

In fact, Aelian himself, in the books of his *Historical Miscellany*,
also relates the story to Megabyzus, not Alexander.[539]

: 49 :

Contentio epigrammatum Graeci Posidippi
et Latini Ausoni super Occasionis imagine,
tum pulcherrima ecphrasis Graeci Callistrati

1 Ausoni poetae celebre est epigramma quo simulachrum describitur
Occasionis, nam sic utique deum quem Graeci Καιρόν appellant
interpretatus est. Sed enim longe miror quid ita Phidiae tribuerit
quod erat Lysippi. Extat adhuc enim Posidippi Graecum comparis
argumenti, de quo suum finxerit Ausonius, quamquam in Graeco
Lysippus Sicyonius artifex, in Latino Phidia⟨s⟩ perhibetur. Porro
autem summis digitis Graecus auctor ingredi, Latinus insistere
dicit rotulae. Talaria uterque adnectit, uterque faciem crine tegit,
uterque occipitium denudat. Novaculam tamen dextra gerit Graecus ille Καιρὸς et Penitentia comes iungitur Latinae Occasioni.
Figurae sunt apud utrunque poetam pariles, plus tamen aliquanto
arrident Graecae, nam in istis omnibus (ut ita dixerim) mangonis-
sandis nescio quo pacto Graeci belliores quam Romani nostri, tum
velut ab antigrapho decidere apographon erat necesse.

2 Sed et Callistrati legimus ecphrasin simulachri eiusdem mire
festivam, qua confirmatur a Lysippo id opus factum publice Sicyo-
niis spectabile. Porro autem ex aere hunc ait esse deum Callistratus, puerumque adhuc primae pubis a capite florulentae ad pedes,
tum formosum eundem, sparsisque favonio crinibus, et multa
frontis gratia, genarumque adeo et corporis totius pulchritudine
Dionyso maxime similem, quin et insistere pilae suspenso gradu,

: 49 :

*A comparison of the epigrams of the Greek Posidippus
and the Latin Ausonius on the image of Occasio;
then a most beautiful description by the Greek Callistratus*

There is a famous epigram by the poet Ausonius, in which he de- 1
scribes an image of *Occasio* ("Opportunity"), for that, at any rate,
is how he translated the name of the god the Greeks call
Καιρός.⁵⁴⁰ But I have long wondered why he attributed to Phidias what was Lysippus's. For there still exists a Greek epigram by
Posidippus on the corresponding subject,⁵⁴¹ modeled on which
Ausonius composed his own, although in the Greek the artist is
called Lysippus of Sicyon, in the Latin Phidias. Furthermore, the
Greek author says that he goes on tiptoes, the Latin one that she
stood on a little wheel. Both authors fasten on winged sandals,
both cover the face with hair, and both strip the hair from the
back of their heads. Nevertheless the Greek Καιρός holds a razor
in his right hand, and Regret is joined as a companion to the Latin
Occasio.⁵⁴² The figures are alike in both poets; nonetheless the
Greek figures are a bit more charming, for in all matters that must
be gussied up (so to speak) for some reason the Greeks are prettier
than our Romans, just as a copy must be inferior to the original.

But we also read Callistratus's marvelously witty description of 2
the same statue, by which it is confirmed that the work, which was
available to the Sicyonians for public viewing, had been done by
Lysippus. Furthermore, Callistratus says that this god was made
out of bronze and was a boy still at the beginning of puberty flowering from his head to his feet,⁵⁴³ then the same beautiful boy,
with a breeze scattering his hair, and with a very lovely face, and
with a beauty in his cheeks and his whole body very much resem-
bling Dionysus's, in fact standing with his step suspended on top

pinnatis pedibus. Sed et capillos idem Callistratus in oculos pueri, genasque deflectens occipitium crinibus liberat. Cetera denique scriptoris huius condimenta et laenocinia delicias festivitates argutiasque transmarinas ex ipso utique petendas auctore arbitror.

3 Fit autem nescio quo pacto, lasciviolas ut istas et electiusculas,[150] quasi textam Mileti chlamydem, cane peius et angui Romana reformidet gravitas. Illud haudquaquam praeterierim, Nicephorum quoque non inelegantem scriptorem Graecum sic ordiri quam de virgine Deipara composuit orationem ut cum super imagine ista, nescio Temporis dixerim an Occasionis loquatur, referat eam ad temporis illius qui sit Graece *chronos* fugacissimam celeritatem.

: 50 :

*Locus in Plinianis exemplaribus emendatus
super nomine Proetidum,
atque inibi de ipsarum furore relata historia*

1 In quinto et vigesimo *Naturalis historiae* libro verba Plini Secundi, quo capite de helleboro tractatur, ita in vulgatissimis codicibus reperiuntur:

> Melampodis fama divinationis artibus nota est; ab hoc appellatur unum hellebori genus melampodion. Aliqui pastorem eodem nomine invenisse tradunt, capras purgari pastore illo animadvertente, datoque lacte earum sanasse Parotidas furentes.

of a ball, and with winged feet. But Callistratus, too, [has] the
boy's hair down in his eyes, and turning his face aside, he makes
the back of his head free of hair. Finally, I think that the other
spices, allurements, delights, charms, and foreign refinements of
this author should be sought from the author himself.

It comes about somehow or other that Roman seriousness re- 3
coils at playful things and little dainties such as these, like the
woven cloak of Miletus, more than at a dog or snake.[544] And I
shall by no means pass over in silence the fact that Nicephorus, an
elegant Greek writer, began an oration that he composed about
the Blessed Virgin in such a way that when he speaks about that
image — should I call it that of Time or Opportunity? — he connects it with the fleeting swiftness of that time which in Greek is
chronos.[545]

: 50 :

Correction of a passage in the manuscripts of Pliny about the
name of the daughters of Proetus, and the story told
in the same place about their madness

In the twenty-fifth book of his *Natural History*, in the chapter that 1
discusses hellebore,[546] the words of Plinius Secundus are found in
the most common codices as follows:

> The reputation of Melampus in the arts of divination is well
> known, from whom one species of hellebore is called melam-
> podion. Some relate that a shepherd (*pastorem*) with the
> same name discovered it: while the shepherd (*pastore*) was
> watching his she-goats, they were purged [by it], and by giv-
> ing them the goats' milk he cured the crazed daughters of
> Parotas (*Parotidas*).[547]

Ceterum non *pastore* sed *pasto*, non *Parotidas* sed *Proetidas* in codice uno vetustissimo ex nobilissima ista Medicae gentis bibliotheca inveniebamus. Sed de *pastore* et *pasto* facile est, sic *Proetidas*, non *Parotidas* legendum manifesta fides, eamque vel indubitatissimam verissimamque esse scripturam, praeterquam quod ratio docet inprimis efficax. (Quid enim sint parotides furentes, aut quid parotidibus, aurium vitio, cum veratro?) Tamen et Dioscorides bonus auctor apertissime declarat, ita scribens:

> Veratrum nigrum, id alii melampodium, alii ectomum, quidam polyrrhizum appellant. Melampodium vero quoniam eo Melampus quidam pastor Proeti furentes filias purgasse videtur atque curasse.

Sic ille.

2 Sed Atheniensis Apollodorus in *Bibliotheca* (nam ita liber eius appellatur) purgationem Proeti filiarum potius ad vatem Melampoda quam ad pastorem refert. Natasque ait ex Proeto et Sthenoboea[151] filias Lysippen, Iphinoen, et Iphianassam, quae ubi primum adoleverint, vexatae insania sunt, seu quoniam (ut scribit Hesiodus) Liberi patris cerimonias non acceperint, sive (quod est apud Acusilaum) quoniam Iunonis contempserint simulachrum.[152] Postea autem quam furere occoeperint, toto Argivorum agro prius errabundas, dein vero etiam per Arcadiam Peloponnesumque universam sui decoris oblitas locis solis excucurrisse, donec Melampus Amythaone filiaque Abantis Idothea natus, vates scilicet et qui primus medicamentis sanare ac purgationibus invenerat, curaturum se virgines spoponderit si pretium sibi pars regni tertia transcriberetur. Cui cum Proetus minime assentiret, videlicet mercede tam immani deterritus, magis magisque in dies gliscere furorem illum virginum coepisse, contagione etiam ad mulieres ceteras

Yet, in one extremely ancient codex from the famous library of the Medici family, we found not "shepherd" (*pastore*) but "eaten" (*pasto*), and not *Parotidas* ("daughters of Parotas") but *Proetidas* ("daughters of Proetus"[548]). The corruption from *pasto* to *pastore* is easy,[549] so there is a clear basis for believing *Proetidas* not *Parotidas* must be read and that this is the indubitable and true reading, besides the fact that reason, our most effective tool, teaches this. (For what are "crazed *parotides*," or what do *parotides*, a defect of the ears, have to do with hellebore?) All the same, Dioscorides too, a good authority, straightforwardly discloses this when he writes the following:

> Black hellebore, that some call melampodium, others ecto-mum, still others polyrrhizum. But melampodium, since a certain shepherd Melampus seems to have purged and cured the crazed daughters of Proetus with it.[550]

So far Dioscorides.

But in his *Library* (for that is the title of his book), Apollodorus 2 of Athens attributes the cleansing of Proetus's daughters to the seer Melampus rather than to a shepherd.[551] He also says that to Proetus and Sthenoboea were born the daughters Lysippe, Iphinoe, and Iphianassa, who, as soon as they grew up, were plagued by insanity, whether because (as Hesiod writes[552]) they refused to embrace the rites of Bacchus or because (as is told in Acusilaus[553]) they insulted the statue of Juno. After they began to rave, they first wandered throughout all the territory of the Argives, and then indeed even ran through Arcadia and the entire Peloponnesus, in desolate places, heedless of modesty,[554] until Melampus, the son of Amythaon and Idothea, daughter of Abas, a seer and the first to discover how to heal by means of medicines and purgatives, vowed that he would cure the young women if a third of the realm were paid over to him as compensation. Since Proetus by no means agreed, deterred by so vast a price, the madness of the girls began to blaze up more and more each day, with the contagion

demigrante, sic ut vulgo suam quaeque domum relinquerent, filios occiderent, ac per solitudines vagarentur.

3 Quare propagante se etiam atque etiam calamitate, cum daturum Proetus postulatam mercedem pacisceretur, iam vero non prius curaturum Melampus ait quam cum alterum tantum agri fratri quoque suo Bianti adiudicaretur. Hic vero metuentem Proetum ne si praesentem condicionem respueret, plus etiam subinde postularetur, consensisse in eam mercedem. Ac tum demum Melampoda valentissimum quemque iuvenum comitem sibi ascivisse, clamoribusque eas atque enthea quadam (sic enim inquit) chorea Sicyona usque de montibus compulisse. Ceterum in persequendo maximam natu Iphinoen extinctam, reliquas purgatione usas resipuisse. Tum Melampodi eas et Bianti Proetum tradidisse, ipsumque dein filium genuisse Megapenthen. Hactenus ferme Apollodorus.

4 Helianus autem nomina Proetidibus in *Omnifaria historia* Elegen facit et Celenen. Sextus porro Empiricus *Pyrrhoniorum* quarto Polyanthum Cyreneum dicere scribit in libro de Asclepiadarum genitura Proeti filias ab Aesculapio fuisse insania liberatas, in quam Iunone irata incidissent. Adicit Ovidius purgamina[153] mentis earum Biantem misisse in Clitorium fontem, cuius potus abstemios faciat. Sed enim qui Probus vulgo putatur, haud improbus omnino Maronis enarrator, et ipse testem citat Hesiodum, fabulamque pene sicut haec est Apollodori, quamquam brevissime, perstringit.

5 Hunc autem in eis errorem fuisse mentis animique boves ut se crederent, quod Vergilius quoque in *Bucolicis* significat, neutiquam videri fabulosum debet, siquidem Paulus Aegineta,[154] medicus

spreading to other women as well, so that women commonly abandoned their homes, killed their children, and roamed about in the wilderness.

Therefore, with the calamity spreading farther and farther, 3 Proetus agreed to pay the price demanded. But now Melampus said that he would not cure them until another territory of the same size was made over to his brother Bias as well. At this point, fearing lest if he reject the present offer, even more be demanded from him in future, Proetus agreed to this price. Then and only then did Melampus enroll all the strongest young men as his companions and drive the young women with shouts and some sort of frenzied dance (for that is what he calls it) all the way down from the mountains to Sicyon. Although the eldest daughter, Iphinoe, died in the pursuit, the rest came to their senses upon using the purgative. Then Proetus gave over his daughters to Melampus and Bias [in marriage], and after that he himself sired a son, Megapenthes. Thus far, in essence, Apollodorus.

Aelian, however, in his *Historical Miscellany* gives the daughters 4 of Proetus the names Elege and Celaene.[555] Furthermore, in the fourth book of his *Pyrrhonians*, Sextus Empiricus writes that Polyanthus of Cyrene says in his book about the origin of physicians that Proetus's daughters had been freed from their insanity by Aesculapius, into which they had plunged as a result of Juno's anger.[556] Ovid adds that for the cleansing of their mind Bias sent [them] to the spring at Clitor,[557] a drink from which makes one abstain from wine.[558] But in fact the man commonly thought to be Probus, a very decent interpreter of Vergil,[559] himself cites Hesiod as a witness and touches on a version of the tale, albeit very briefly, almost like that of Apollodorus.[560]

Moreover, it should by no means be thought mythical that 5 there was this mental defect in them that they believed themselves to be cows — something that Vergil also points out in his *Bucolics* — since Paul of Aegina, a Greek medical author, in discussing

Graecus auctor in tertio *Periodeutico de atra bile* de[que][155] insania ipsa narrans, usu quoque venire ait uti quidam sibi brutae animantes esse vocesque imitari illarum videantur, praetereaque nonnullos arbitrari se vasa esse testacea factos, tum autem ob id metuere ne confringantur.

: 51 :

Cur in Ephesiae Dianae templo
molles appellati honores a Martiale

1 Cur molles dixerit honores in Triviae templo Martialis, hoc est in Dianae Ephesiae, etiam haec afferri possunt, scita (ni fallor) et arguta satis, sed quae tamen interpretes omiserunt. Ac primo quidem de multimammiis[156] possumus dictum existimare. Nam ut divus Hieronymus[157] in epistolam Pauli ad Ephesios scribit, erat Ephesi templum Dianae, et eiusdem in ipso multimammia, idest multarum mammarum, effigies, qua cultores eius decepti putabant eam omnium viventium nutricem. Possumus item ad pompam referre de qua Xenophon Ephesius in primo *Ephesiacorum* libro scribit ad hanc sententiam:

Agebatur autem, inquit, solemne iis locis Dianae festum ab urbe ad templum, quae sunt stadia omnino septem. Celebrare pompam virgines omnis indigenas oportebat, splendide inprimis ornatas. Praetereaque ephebos, Abrocomi aequales, qui tum annum circiter decimum septimum agebat, et cum ephebis aderat velutique primas in ea pompa ferebat. Magna

this insanity in the third book of his *Systematic Study on Black Bile*, says that it is a matter of common experience that certain persons think they have the minds of animals and imitate their sounds, and, in addition, some suppose that they have become pots, and then fear being broken.[561]

: 51 :

Why, in the temple of Diana of Ephesus,
offices are called "effeminate" by Martial

The following reasons, clever and neat, I believe, can be adduced   1
as to why Martial said that offices are effeminate in the temple of
Trivia,[562] that is, in the temple to Diana of Ephesus, but the interpreters have nonetheless failed to note them. In the first place, we
can consider what is said about multibreasted [statues]. For, as St.
Jerome writes on Paul's letter to the Ephesians, there was a temple
of Diana at Ephesus, and in it there was a multibreasted image of
the goddess, that is, one with many breasts, deceived by which her
worshippers believed that she was the nurse of all living beings.[563]
We can likewise point to the parade about which Xenophon of
Ephesus writes in the first book of his *Ephesian Tales*, along these
lines:

> In that region, a ceremonial procession in honor of Diana
> was led from the city to the temple, altogether a distance of
> seven stades. All the young women of the district had to at-
> tend the parade, dressed in their finest splendor. So too, the
> young men of the same age as Habrocomus, who then was
> about sixteen years old, and when he was present with the
> young men, he played, as it were, the leading role in that

autem vis hominum spectaculo intererat, vel popularium vel hospitum, siquidem mos habebat uti in ea celebritate et sponsi virginibus, et ephebis uxores invenirentur. Procedebat ergo ordinatim pompa, primo scilicet sacra, faces, canistra, et suffimenta, tum autem equi canesque et venatoria arma, nonnulla[158] quoque bellica, sed pleraque tamen pacalia, feminarum se quaeque veluti ad amatoris oculos composuerat virginumque ordinem ducebat Anthia.

Sic utique Xenophon scribit, non quidem Atheniensis ille sed alter eo non insuavior Ephesius, qui paulo post etiam ita subdit:

Ut igitur peracta pompa, venere in templum sacrificatum multitudo omnis, atque ibi ornatus pompae solutus omnis. Et convenere eodem viri feminaeque, ephebi et virgines.

2   Non absurdum est autem propter Dianae quoque sacerdotem molles honores audire, de quo etiam nonnihil Domitius ex Strabone. Ceterum Heracliti Ephesii, summi philosophi, scilicet illius qui ex obscuritate librorum Scotinos, hoc est Tenebricosus, appellabatur, quique omnibus humanis actibus illacrimabat, illius, inquam, Heracliti ad Hermodorum extat epistola, qua sic ferme in Ephesios cavillatur:

Quanto Ephesiis meliores lupi atque leones! Non se invicem mancipant, nec aquila aquilam emptitat, nec leoni leo ministrat pocula. Sed neque canem canis exsecat, ut vos deae sacerdotem exsecuistis Megabyzum, metu ne virgini vir

parade. A great number of people attended that spectacle, both locals and visitors, since it was the custom amid that throng for husbands to be found for the young women and wives for the young men. The procession, then, was advancing group by group: first of course were the holy implements, torches, baskets [of offerings], and incense; then came horses and dogs and equipment for hunting, some also for warfare, but most were for peaceful uses. Each of the women had prepared herself as if for the eyes of a lover, and the group of the young women was led by Anthia.[564]

This at any rate is what Xenophon writes — not the famous Athenian but the other no less charming one from Ephesus — who a little afterward appends this:

When therefore the parade was completed, the whole multitude entered the temple to perform sacrifice; and there the entire order of the parade was dissolved. And the men and women and the young men and young women converged on the same place.[565]

Moreover, it is not absurd for the offices to be called effeminate, 2 in view of the priest of Diana, about whom Domizio [Calderini] [cites] something from Strabo.[566] Yet there is a letter of the great philosopher Heraclitus of Ephesus, namely, the famous man who from the obscurity of his books was called "the Dark," i.e., "the Obscure," and who used to weep over all human actions[567] — that Heraclitus's letter, I say, to Hermodorus is extant, in which he jeers at the Ephesians as follows:

How much better are wolves and lions than the Ephesians! They do not enslave one another; the eagle does not buy an eagle, nor does a lion serve poison to a lion. Neither does a dog castrate a dog, as you castrated the goddess's priest Megabyzus, for fear lest a man be consecrated to a virgin,

consecretur, et quo pacto impii adversus naturam, pii sitis adversus simulachrum. Principio enim id agitis, ut dis primus imprecetur sacerdos amissa virilitate. Quin deam quoque impudicitiae velut insimulatis, metuentes ne illi ministretur a viro.

: 52 :

Quae sit apud Martialem 'cornibus ara frequens'

1 In superiori epigrammate locus est hic alter, neutiquam a Domitio, neve ab aliis, quantum videam, cognitus:

> Dissimuletque deum cornibus ara frequens.

Quod enim Domitius Hammonis[159] templum in Libya accipit, nullo pacto procedit. Nam cum hic magnificentissima orbis terrarum aedificia memorentur quaeque inter miracula referrentur, ut ex eorum comparatione amphitheatri praeconium crescat, ridiculum profecto fuerit de templo hic Hammonis audire pauperrimo scilicet, ut Lucanus ait his versibus:

> Ventum erat ad templum, Libycis quod gentibus unum
> Inculti Garamantes habent, stat corniger illic
> Iuppiter, ut memorant, sed non aut fulmina vibrans
> Aut similis nostro, sed tortis cornibus Hammon.

and so that you might be pious to a statue as you are impious to nature. For at the beginning you cause the first priest to curse the gods for the loss of his manhood. What is more, you are, as it were, accusing the goddess of unchastity, by your fear that she be ministered to by a man.[568]

: 52 :

What "the altar densely covered with horns" is in Martial

There is another passage in the above epigram that has been understood neither by Domizio [Calderini] nor by others, as far as I can see: 1

Let the altar densely covered with horns conceal the god.[569]

Insofar as Domizio understands this to be the temple of Ammon in Libya, he has made no progress whatever. For since in this passage the world's grandest buildings are mentioned, the ones which were counted as miracles, so that the praise of the amphitheater may grow by comparison with them, it would actually be ridiculous to hear in this context about the temple of Ammon, since it was extremely poor, as Lucan says in these verses:

They came to the temple, the single one among the Libyan
peoples
That the uncivilized Garamantes possess. There Jupiter stands
with horns
On his head, they say, but without either brandishing
thunderbolts or
Being like our [Roman] Jupiter, but instead Ammon, with
twisted horns.

Non illic Libycae posuerunt ditia gentes
Templa, nec Eois[160] splendent donaria gemmis,
Quamvis Aethiopum populis Arabumque beatis
Gentibus atque Indis unus sit Iuppiter Hammon.
Pauper adhuc deus est, nullis violata per aevum
Divitiis delubra tenens, morumque priorum
Numen, Romano templum defendit ab auro.

Neque autem aut ex Plini aut ex Maronis dictis colliges templum Hammonis apud Nasamonas insigne vel aedificiis vel opibus fuisse, si verba ipsa diligenter utriusque pensitabis.

2   Et quidem mentior nisi ara potius Apollinis in Delo accipienda, quam[161] 'ceratinon bomon' dicunt, inter septem orbis spectacula, sicuti Plutarchus ait, celebrata, quae tantum ex dextris cornibus sine glutino ullo aut vinculo, coagmentata compactaque sit. Hoc autem Plutarchus in eo scribit opusculo, quo tractat utra prudentiora sint aquigena an terrigena animalia. Deque ara eadem sic Ovidius in *Epistola Cydippes ad Acontium* meminit hoc versiculo:

Miror et innumeris structam de cornibus aram.

3   Plutarchus etiam in *Theseo* de ara in Delo scribit, non quidem ex dextris, sed ex sinistris tantum cornibus compacta, quem κερατῶνα βωμόν appellat, nisi mendum sit exemplarium. Laertius quoque Diogenes 'ceratinae arae,' hoc est e cornibus factae, mentionem nonnullam facit in *Pythagorae vita*. Quin et Callimachus poeta in *Apollinis hymno* quadrimum adhuc Apollinem[162] scribit ex cornibus Cynthiadum caprearum quas soror Diana in

The Libyan tribes did not there erect a wealthy
Temple, nor does the temple treasury glitter with eastern
    gems,
Even though Jupiter Ammon is the single god for the
    Ethiopian
People, and for the wealthy nations of Arabia, and for India,
The god is still poor, and holds a temple unstained through
    the ages
By riches; a divinity of old-style character,
He guards his temple from Roman gold.[570]

Moreover, you will not conclude from the statements of either
Pliny or Maro that the temple of Ammon was conspicuous among
the Nasamonians in terms of either its buildings or its riches, if
you carefully weigh the actual words of each.[571]

I am lying unless the altar of Apollo in Delos should rather be 2
understood, the one they call the "horned altar," renowned among
the seven wonders of the world, as Plutarch says, which was joined
together and constructed from right horns alone, without any glue
or chain. Moreover, Plutarch writes this in the little work where
he addresses whether animals born in water or on land have
greater intelligence.[572] And Ovid mentions the same altar in *Cy-
dippe's letter to Acontius*, in this line:

I marvel at the altar built from the huge number of horns.[573]

Plutarch also writes in his *Theseus* about the altar at Delos and 3
that it was built not from right horns but only left ones, which he
calls [in Greek] the "horned altar," if the copies are not faulty.[574]
Diogenes Laertius, too, mentions the "horned altar," that is, the
altar made from horns, in his *Life of Pythagoras*.[575] In fact, in his
Hymn to Apollo the poet Callimachus writes that when Apollo was
only four years old, he constructed an altar from the horns of
Cynthiad she-goats that his sister Diana had slain while on a hunt

venatu occiderat aram compegisse fundamentaque item et parie-
tem e solis struxisse cornibus. Ipsius autem sunt haec verba:

Τετραέτης τὰ πρῶτα θεμείλια Φοῖβος ἔπηξε
Καλῇ¹⁶³ ἐν Ὀρτυγίῃ περιηγέος ἔνδοθι λίμνης.
Ἄρτεμις ἀγρώσσουσα καρήατα συνεχὲς αἰγῶν
Κυνθιάδων φορέεσκεν· ὁ δ᾽ ἔπλεκε βωμὸν Ἀπόλλων.
Δείματο μὲν κεράεσσιν ἐδέθλια, πῆξε δὲ βωμὸν
Ἐκ κεράων, κεραοὺς δὲ πέριξ ὑπεβάλλετο τοίχους.

4   Ob id ergo inquit Martialis 'dissimulet deum,' quasi non iam
dei esse id opus videri queat, quo alterum longe praestantius, hoc
est amphitheatrum, mortali manu factum. Saneque per totum
epigramma signatis usus est verbis argutissimus poeta, qui
Memphin silere iubet, quia barbara, nec iactari vult Babylona labore assiduo, quoniam ipsa quoque iactatio intellectum laboris
habeat. Et negat laudandos ob id honores Triviae, quia molles,
neque enim mollibus praeconia debentur. Negat etiam quae aere
pendeant mausolea, supra aera ipsum, hoc est ad astra usque, ferri
oportere, ut sit hoc epigrammate nihil utique pensitatius.

and that he built the foundation as well as the wall from horns alone. These are his own words:

> At four years of age, Phoebus laid the first foundations
> In beautiful Ortygia within the encircling lake.
> Artemis hunted and brought an unending supply of heads
> Of Cynthiad goats, and Apollo wove an altar —
> Building the foundations with horns, joining together the altar
>   out of horns,
> And throwing up walls round about made of horns.[576]

And so for this reason Martial says, "let it conceal the god," as 4 if it might no longer be possible for this to be seen as the work of a god, since another work far superior to this, i.e., the amphitheater, was made by human hand. And indeed the witty poet used emphatic words throughout the entire epigram, bidding Memphis to hold her tongue, because she is a barbarian, not allowing Babylon to boast over her unremitting labor, since the mere boasting would contain the idea of labor.[577] He denies that the offices of Trivia [Diana] should be praised because they are effeminate, for no public praises are owed to effeminates.[578] He even denies that mausoleums poised in the air should be praised above the air itself, that is, up to the stars,[579] so that nothing is more carefully considered than this epigram.

: 53 :

Quod positum nomen Agamemnonis in M. Tulli
Divinationibus *pro Ulyssis*[164] *est, tum in transcursu locus in*
Epistolis ad Atticum *non inelegans super miniatula caera*
correctus et enarratus

1 Aulus Gellius in *Noctibus* illis suis maxime candidis errorem notat
Ciceronis manifestissimum, non magnae rei, neque errasse eum
miratur, sed errorem non esse postea vel ab ipso animadversum vel
a Tirone suo. Nam cum Homeri versus Cicero quospiam vertat in
Latinum, dicere illos Aiacem scribit apud eum poetam, cum re
vera dicantur ab Hectore. Facit haec A. Gelli libertas ut ne ipse
quidem verear referre in his libris paululum[165] quiddam compar
huic eiusdem Ciceronis, peneque illi superiori germanum et geminum, nisi forte (quod avidius crediderim tanto intervallo) mendum fuerit exemplarium. Quamvis etiam in antiquissimo quoque
libro non dispariliter scriptum inveniamus, nec sane lubricus ex
litterarum vicinitate sit in alterutrum nomen lapsus.

2 Verba sunt Ciceronis in libro *Divinationum* secundo:

Nam illud mirarer si crederem quod apud Homerum Cal-
chantem dixisti ex passerum numero belli Troiani annos au-
guratum, de cuius coniectura sic apud Homerum, ut nos
otiosi vertimus, loquitur Agamemnon:

Ferte viri, et duros animo tolerate labores,
Auguris ut nostri Calchantis fata queamus
Scire, ratosne habeant an vanos[166] pectoris orsus.

: 53 :

That the name of Agamemnon was substituted in Cicero's On
Divination *for that of Ulysses; then, in passing, a not
inelegant passage about the red pencil in his* Letters to Atticus
is corrected and explained

In his markedly candid *Nights*, Aulus Gellius notes what is a very   1
clear error by Cicero, though not one of great import, nor is he
surprised that he made the mistake but that it had not been noticed afterward either by him or his freedman Tiro.[580] For when
Cicero translated some lines of Homer into Latin, he wrote that
Ajax spoke them in the work of this poet, although in fact they are
said by Hector.[581] This candor of Aulus Gellius's removes my inhi-
bition about including in these books a small point similar to this
one, likewise by Cicero, almost the sibling or twin of the one
above, unless perhaps the fault was in the copies (which, after so
great a lapse of time, I am quite ready to believe). However, we
may find a not dissimilar text in every ancient book, nor is a slip
from one name to the other easy because of the closeness of the
letterforms.

The words of the second book of Cicero's *On Divination* are: 2

> For I would be amazed—if I were to believe it—at the fact
> that you said that in Homer Calchas divined the years of the
> Trojan War from the number of sparrows. Concerning his
> conjecture Agamemnon speaks as follows in Homer, as I
> translated in my leisure:
>
>> Bear, men, and endure your harsh toils with courage,
>> So that we can know whether the fates predicted by our
>>   augur Calchas
>> Are confirmed or are vain fancies of his heart.[582]

Ac deinceps versus quoque ceteros Homericos a se conversos exponit. Quod igitur haec Agamemnonem loqui apud Homerum Cicero tradit, si modo ita scriptum Cicero reliquit, hoc neutiquam verum probatur, cum apud Homerum ipsum in secunda *Iliados* rhapsodia non Agamemnon, sed Ulysses istius sententiae versus pronuntiet.

3   Neque est quod quisquam aut stomachetur haec apud Ciceronem quoque deprehendi aut miretur, cum appareat ex ipsius epistolis, nonnunquam huiuscemodi errata memoriae fuisse in Ciceronis libris vel ab Attico vel a Bruto animadversa atque curata. Sicut illud in oratione *Ligariana* de L. Cursidio, quod erratum fatetur esse suum, sed (ut aiunt) inquit μνημονικὸν ἁμάρτημα. Sicuti quod in *Oratore*, arbitror, Eupolin pro Aristophane Cicero posuerat. Dein Atticus Aristophanen pro Eupolide reposuit. Itaque etiam vereri se Cicero dicit aliquando, ne suae syntaxis[167] miniata illius caerula[168] pluribus locis notandae sint.

4   Quod autem incidit ut de miniata caerula meminerimus, corrigendus obiter et interpretandus nobis hic ex epistola ad Atticum libro penultimo locus est, in quo ita scriptum perperam invenitur:

His litteris scriptis me ad syntaxis dedi, quae quidem vereor, ne nimia tua pluribus locis notandae sint, ita sum meteoros et magnis cogitationibus impeditus.

Ego legendum puto: 'ne miniatula caera[169] tua pluribus locis notandae sint,' ut sit intellectus, ad libros componendos, id enim Graece syntaxis, Ciceronem se dedisse. Sed vereri tamen ne miniatula caera ipsius ad quem scribit Attici, quo saepe uteretur emendatore, pluribus locis notandae sint, quoniam meteoros, hoc est suspensus

And then he sets out additional Homeric verses, translated by himself.[583] Therefore, Cicero reports that Agamemnon said this in Homer; if Cicero left it written thus, this would in no way be proven accurate, since in Homer himself, in the second book of the *Iliad*, it is not Agamemnon but Ulysses who speaks verses of this purport.[584]

And it is not that anyone is either annoyed or surprised that this is discovered in Cicero, since it appears from his letters that there were, on occasion, such memory lapses in Cicero's books that were noticed and corrected by Atticus or Brutus. For instance, he acknowledges the passage in the oration *On Behalf of Ligarius* concerning L. Cursidius to have been a mistake on his part, and he said it was (as they say) a "lapse of memory."[585] Again in the *Orator*, I think, Cicero had cited Eupolis in place of Aristophanes.[586] Then Atticus replaced Eupolis with Aristophanes. Therefore, Cicero even says that he was occasionally apprehensive lest his compositions have to be marked in many places by Atticus's red pencil.

Moreover, since mention of his red pencil has cropped up, we must correct and explain in passing a passage in a letter in the penultimate book to Atticus, in which the following is found incorrectly written:

> After finishing this letter I turned to writing books (*syntaxis*); indeed, I fear they will be have to be marked up in many passages by your excessive (*tua nimia*) — I am so on edge and preoccupied with great thoughts.[587]

I think we must read: "they will have to be marked up in many places with your little red pencil (*miniatula caera tua*)," so that the meaning is that Cicero devoted himself to writing books, for that is *syntaxis* ("compositions") in Greek. But he nonetheless fears lest by the red pencil of his addressee, Atticus himself, whom he frequently employed as an editor, they must be marked in many passages, since Cicero was on edge, that is, distracted and preoc-

animi, foret Cicero, et magnis cogitationibus (ut ait) impeditus. Consueverat, opinor, Atticus, siqui parum absolute locus a Cicerone tractaretur, ei loco rubellas caeras affigere, quod nunc quoque solemus. In codice autem, quem fuisse aiunt Francisci Petrarchae primitus, certe Colucci Salutati dein fuit, et post hunc Leonardi Arretini, mox et Donati Acciaioli, virorum suae cuiusque aetatis eruditissimorum, sic adhuc extat: 'ne miniata caeruia[170] tua,' quod si penultimae dictionis penultimam litteram paululum[171] a summo produxeris, hoc est, de *i* littera *l* feceris, omne proculdubio mendum sustuleris. Sed et pervulgatis codicibus sic in extremo rursum volumine epistolarum adhuc earundem legitur: 'Caerulas enim tuas miniatulas illas extimescebam,' ut iam omnis hoc testimonio superior ambiguitas aboleatur.

: 54 :

Ceratinae qui[172] sint apud Quintilianum

1 Ceratinae qui sint apud Quintilianum libro primo, non temere qui tibi explicet invenias. Qui autem Graeca voluerint Latinaque commentaria plane intelligent ratiocinationis inexplicabilis esse eam speciem quae nescio quas ansas atque uncos arte dialecticae perplexitatis inferret. Sic arbitror appellatam a materia ipsa qua uterentur verborum, sicuti est apud Senecam libro *Epistolarum* quinto *ad Lucilium*:

Sederem, inquit, otiosus et eiusmodi quaestiunculas ponens: 'Quod non perdidisti habes. Cornua non perdidisti. Cornua ergo habes,' aliaque ad exemplum huius acutae delirationis concinnata.

cupied (as he says) with great thoughts. If a passage was left unpolished by Cicero, Atticus was wont, I think, to attach red marks to that place, as we also are nowadays wont to do. More-over, in a codex which reportedly belonged originally to Francesco Petrarch, and certainly in turn to Coluccio Salutati, and after him to Leonardo [Bruni] of Arezzo, and most recently to Donato Ac-ciaiuoli — each the most erudite man of his age — the following is still extant: *ne miniata caeruia tua.*[588] If you lengthen the penulti-mate letter of the penultimate word a little from the top, that is, if you create an *l* from the letter *i*, you undoubtedly remove the en-tire defect.[589] But in the common codices, in the last book of the same letters, the following is still read: "For I was in fear of those red pencils of yours," so that now all the previous ambiguity is abolished by this testimony.[590]

: 54 :

What ceratinae *are in Quintilian*

You will not easily find someone to explain to you what *ceratinae*   1
("horned arguments") are in the first book of Quintilian.[591] But those who have studied Greek and Latin books will clearly under-stand that this is a type of irrefutable argument that provides some handles and hooks by the art of dialectical perplexity. I think that it takes this name from the very material of the words they used, as in the fifth book of Seneca's *Letters to Lucilius*:

> I would sit at leisure propounding such petty problems as: "What you have not lost, you have. You have not lost horns; therefore, you have horns," and other things concocted on the model of this extreme silliness.[592]

Sed de hoc item in *Atticis Noctibus* invenias. Cerata autem Graece dici cornua, quis nesciat? Meminit huius etiam Lucianus in *Philosophorum symposio*, sicuti de sorite atque therizonte, sed et in *Dialogo* item *Mortuorum* Castoris et Pollucis, ita ferme inquiens: 'Et cornua inter se producunt, et crocodilos faciunt, et eiusmodi perplexa docent interrogare,' ut ex cornibus scilicet hanc quam diximus ceratinen ratiocinationem, nec ratiocinationem verius quam tendiculam accipias. Quin etiam in dialogo altero cui vel *Somnium* vel *Gallus* est nomen:

> Et docens, inquit, duabus negationibus unam confici asseverationem, noctemque non esse, si dies sit. Interdum etiam cornua mihi esse dicebat aliaque id genus.

2　　Huiuscemodi autem dialecticis in percunctando quaestiunculis, quales frequenter ingeniorum acumen excogitat, etiam Milesius Eubulides plurimum usus, sicut a Laertio Diogene in *Euclidae Megarensis vita* ponuntur, ut Latine conemur interpretari, mentiens, fallens, electra, convelata, acervalis, et ceratinae[173] vel cornea, et item calva. Ex quo in hanc sententiam est apud comicum nescio quem, ut idem prodit Laertius:

> Contumeliosius autem Eubulides ceratinas interrogans, et mendacibus gloriosisque sermonibus oratores versans, abiit Demosthenis habens volubilitatem.

Quem etiam locum Suida⟨s⟩ citavit.

3　　Sed et Zenon ille Cytieus inter cavilla cetera dialecticorum ceratinas item et utidas numerabat, sicuti idem in libro septimo *De vitis philosophorum* prodidit Laertius. Quin hoc ipsum postremo

But you will also find something about this in the *Attic Nights*.[593]
But who is unaware that horns are called *cerata* in Greek? Lucian,
too, mentions this in his *Philosophers' Symposium*, as well as the
heap and the reaper,[594] but he does so also in the *Dialogue of the
Dead* of Castor and Pollux, approximately as follows: "They create
'horns' among themselves, and they make 'crocodiles,' and they
teach how to pose such perplexing questions,"[595] so that from the
"horns" you may understand this "horned" argument we mentioned, nor is it an argument so much as a little snare. In fact,
the name appears in a second dialogue, entitled either *Dream* or
Gallus:

> And he teaches that a single [positive] assertion is made
> from two negative ones — that it is not night, if it is day.
> Sometimes he even used to say that I had horns, and other
> things of that sort.[596]

Moreover, in posing questions Eubulides of Miletus made a   2
good deal of use of nuanced dialectical problems such as clever
folk frequently think up and such as Diogenes Laertius cites in his
Life of Euclid of Megara; to try to translate them into Latin: the liar,
the deceiver, the "electra," the veiled argument, the heap, the
horned problem,[597] and also the "bald" argument.[598] Hence there
are words to this effect in some comic poet, as [Diogenes] Laertius
likewise discloses:

> Eubulides, dripping with contempt, posing his "horned ques-
> tions" and plying the orators with deceitful and boastful talk,
> has gone away with Demosthenic volubility.[599]

Suidas also cited this passage.[600]
But the famous Zeno of Citium also used to include the   3
"horned" (*ceratinas*) as well as the "no one" arguments (*utidas*)
among the other quibbles of the dialecticians, as [Diogenes] Laertius also disclosed in Book 7 of his *Lives of Philosophers*.[601] Lastly,

nobis insinuat Marcianus Capella libro quarto cum inquit: 'Perdita neque[174] unquam cornua fronte ferant.'

: 55 :

Qui sint crocodilitae apud eundem

1 Apud Quintilianum eundem libro item primo etiam de crocodiline mentio fit, obscuro et ipso plerisque ignotoque vocabulo. Ceterum de hoc invenimus apud Aphthoni Graecum enarratorem Doxapatrem,[175] quamvis apud eum *crocodilites* potius, quam *crocodiline*. Quod et verius puto. Verba ipsius ita Latine interpretamur:

> 'Serra,' inquit, 'et crocodilites,' sicuti est in Aegyptiaca fabula: Mulier quaepiam cum filio secundum fluminis ripas ambulabat. Ei crocodilus filium abstulit, redditurum dicens, si verum mulier responderet. Negavit illa fore ut redderetur, atque ob id aequum aiebat reddi.

Hactenus ille. Moxque idem: 'Crocodiliten,' inquit, 'hanc propositionem vocant crocodili huius gratia,' quam etiam πρίωνα, idest serram, vocari a Graecis indicat.

2 Adiuvat Lucianus in dialogo cui titulus *Vitarum venditiones* ita ferme, Chrysippum loquentem inducens eique respondentem quempiam qui se profiteatur emptorem:

Martianus Capella in fact hints at this very point for us in Book 4, when he says: "[Although] they wear on their forehead the horns they never lost."[602]

What crocodilitae *are in Quintilian*

In Quintilian's first book mention is likewise made of a "crocodile 1 puzzle" (*crocodiline*), an obscure word and unknown to many people.[603] Yet we find an explanation of it in Doxopater, the Greek expounder of Aphthonius, although in his works we find, rather than *crocodiline*, the term *crocodilites*, which I consider more accurate. I translate his words into Latin thus:

> "The saw and the crocodile puzzle," as in the Egyptian tale: A woman was walking along the bank of a river with her son. A crocodile snatched her son from her but said that it would return him if the woman would give a truthful reply. She said he would not be returned, and the crocodile said that because of this answer it was fair for him to be returned.

Thus his text. But soon after that he went on to say: "Thanks to this crocodile, people call this proposition a crocodile puzzle," which he indicates is also called by the Greeks a *prion*, that is, a saw.[604]

Lucian provides help in his dialogue entitled *Lives for Sale*, in- 2 troducing Chrysippus as a speaker and someone replying to him who declares himself to be a buyer:

Considera igitur, ait. Estne tibi filius? Quorsum istud? Si forte illum iuxta fluvium errabundum crocodilus inveniat rapiatque, dein redditurum polliceatur cum verum dixeris, utrum reddendus ei videatur necne? Quid eum sentire dices? Rem sane perplexam interrogas.

3   Ex his, ut arbitror, liquet etiam crocodiliten, sicuti supra ceratinen, sophismatos esse parum explicabilis speciem, quo dialectici veteres, potissimumque Stoici, uterentur. Quod genus eleganter Quintilianus exquisitas ambiguitates appellavit.

: 56 :

Cur 'gemino cornu' Martialis dixerit in Spectaculis
ubi de rhinocerote,
deque tauris Aethiopicis

1   Martialis epigramma est in *Spectaculis* de rhinocerote, cuius extremi versus hi sunt:

Nanque gravem cornu gemino sic extulit ursum,
    Iactat ut impositas taurus in astra pilas.

Domitius ita enarrat:

Gemino, inquit, cornu, forti et vehementi. Vergilius: 'Gemino dentalia dorso.' Vel quoniam rhinoceros habet duo cornua, ut apud Pausaniam solum legi, quorum alterum insigni magnitudine ex naribus extat, alterum superne erumpit exiguum sed validissimum.

Consider, then. Do you have a son? — What of it? — If a crocodile were perchance to find him as he was wandering along next to a river and were to snatch him, and then promised to return him if you told it the truth about whether you thought it would have to return him or not, what will you say he intended? — You are asking something truly perplexing.[605]

From this excerpt it is clear, I think, that the "crocodile puzzle," 3 like the horned argument above, [606] is an insoluble type of sophism that the ancient dialecticians, especially the Stoics, used to employ. Quintilian elegantly called this style [of verbal conundrum] "studied ambiguities."

: 56 :

Why Martial said "with twin horn" in his Spectacles
when he was talking about the rhinoceros,
and about Ethiopian bulls

In the *Spectacles*, there is an epigram of Martial's about a rhinoc- 1
eros, of which these are the final verses:

For he lifted a heavy bear with his twin horn,
    As a bull tosses balls up to the stars.[607]

This is how Domizio [Calderini] explains it:

"With twin horn," with a strong and forceful one. Vergil: "a plow beam with a double-humped surface."[608] Or since a rhinoceros has two horns, as I have read in Pausanias alone, one of which is of notable size and protrudes from the nostrils, the other emerges above it, small but extremely powerful.

Fatetur sane Domitius apud unum se Pausaniam legisse rhinoce-
rotem duo habere cornua. Quid autem Plinium, quid Solinum,
quid alios credimus unum rhinoceroti cornu tribuentis duntaxat,
an videlicet ignorasse omnis quod solus animadverterit Pausanias?

2   Quid porro Septimio Florenti Tertulliano respondebimus,
Christianorum omnium quorum quidem Latine opera extent, ut
antiquissimo sic, ausim dicere, in omni pene litteratura diligentis-
simo, qui libro *Adversus Praxeam* tertio verba illa enarrans de Vetere
Instrumento 'Tauri decor eius, cornua unicornis cornua eius, in eis
nationes ventilabit ad summum usque terrae,' 'Non utique,' inquit,
'rhinoceros destinabatur unicornis, nec minotaurus bicornis' et
quae[176] sequuntur.

3   Ceterum de eo Pausanias in *Boeoticis* meminit, neque autem
omnino rhinocerotas duo habere cornua, nam hoc manifesto refelli
poterat, sed tauros dicit esse in Aethiopia, qui rhinocerotes vocentur, ὅτι σφίσιν ἐπ' ἄκρᾳ[177] τῇ ῥινί — sic enim illius verba
sunt — ἓν ἑκάστῳ[178] κέρας καὶ ἄλλο ὑπὲρ αὐτὸ οὐ μέγα, ἐπὶ
δὲ τῆς κεφαλῆς οὐδὲ ἀρχὴν κέρατά ἐστιν, 'quoniam,' inquit,
'illis in summa nare singulis unicum cornu tum aliud supra non
magnum, verum in capite ne initio quidem cornua.'

4   Non igitur Pausanias aut insigni magnitudine alterum cornu,
aut alterum ait esse validissimum. Quod ob id eminiscitur fortasse
Domitius ut his facilius ursus extolleretur. Neque autem de rhinocerote ipso sentit Pausanias, sed, ut diximus, de Aethiopico tauro,
qui similitudine quapiam et ipse rhinoceros a quibusdam vocabatur. Quare nos ita putamus exponendum Martialem, ut ursum videlicet a rhinocerote cornu illo unico elatum eiectatumque sentiat,
gravem gemino cornu, hoc est gravem tauro futurum, cui sunt
cornua gemina, ut cornu sit dativi, non ablativi casus. Nam cum

Domizio admits, of course, that he read in Pausanias alone that a
rhinoceros has two horns. Why, however, do we suppose that
Pliny, Solinus, and others ascribe only a single horn to the rhinoceros, or do we suppose that they were all ignorant of what Pausanias alone noticed?[609]

Furthermore, what will we say in response to Septimius Florens   2
Tertullian, of all Christians whose works are extant in Latin, both
the most ancient and, I daresay, the most diligent in virtually all
literature, who, in his third book *Against Praxeas*, expounding these
words from the Old Testament, "His beauty is that of a bull, his
horns those of a unicorn, with which he shall cast the nations to
the very end of the earth," said: "But certainly, the rhinoceros was
not designed single-horned nor the minotaur two-horned," etc.[610]

Yet Pausanias mentions it [the rhinoceros] in his *Boeotica*; he   3
does not, however, by any means say that rhinoceroses have two
horns, for this could be clearly refuted. But he says that there are
bulls in Ethiopia called rhinoceroses, "because on the tip of their
nose" — for such are his words — "they have one horn each and
another above that one, though not a large one, but on the head
there is no hint of a horn."[611] [In Latin:] "Since each of them has
a single horn on the top of the nose, then another horn above that
one, not large, but not even the beginning of horns on the head."

Therefore Pausanias says neither that the one horn is of notable   4
size nor that the other is extremely strong. Domizio perhaps invents this so that the bear may more easily be lifted by means
of them. Furthermore, Pausanias did not think this about the
rhinoceros proper, but, as we said, an Ethiopian bull, which, on
account of a certain similarity was called by some a rhinoceros.
Therefore I think that Martial must be explained in such a way
that he means that the bear was picked up and thrown by the
rhinoceros with its single horn, heavy for a double horn, that is, it
would be heavy for a bull that has twin horns, so that the word
cornu ("horn") is in the dative case and not the ablative. For even

tauri pilas cornibus ad astra eventilent, extollere ursum tamen non poterant gravem gemino cornu, proptereaque eum mirabilius quamlibet uno cornu rhinoceros extulit.

: 57 :

Quae sint apud Suetonium tetraones,
correctumque erratum Plinianis exemplaribus

1 Tetraones in *Caligula* Suetoni quae sint aves, omnino ignoratur. Verba ipsius haec: 'Hostiae erant phoenicopteri, pavones, tetraones, numidicae, meleagrides, phasianae, quae generatim per singulos dies imolarentur.'

2 Ceterum inventu res erat haud difficilis, nisi Plinianos inemendatissimos haberemus codices. Nam quod apud illum legimus libro decimo *Historiae naturalis*, ubi de anseribus agit: 'Decet Erythrotaonas suus nitor absolutaque nigritia,' hoc in illo vetustissimo Pliniano exemplari de Medicae gentis bibliotheca publica pene legitur emendate, videlicet una tantum commutata littera, qualia multa in vetustis omnibus voluminibus interpolata vocabula. Nam cum ipsa quoque mendosissima plerisque sint locis, vestigia tamen adhuc servant haud obscura verae indagandae lectionis quae de novis codicibus ab improbis librariis prorsus oblitterantur. In eo igitur sic est: 'Decet et traonas,'[179] ut si ordinem duarum primarum litterarum inter se commutes, *tetraonas*[180] dissultet. Quare ita apud illum Politiano auctore legas:

though bulls may throw balls up to the stars with their horns, they nonetheless were unable to lift up a heavy bear on their double horn, and therefore it would be especially marvelous for a rhinoceros to lift it up with one horn.[612]

: 57 :

What tetraones *are in Suetonius; and correction of an error in copies of Pliny*

It is completely unknown what birds *tetraones* are in Suetonius's   1
Caligula. These are his words: "The victims were flamingoes, peacocks, *tetraones*, Numidian and Meleagrian guinea hens, and pheasants, which were all sacrificed kind by kind on their own separate days."[613]

Yet the matter would hardly be difficult to discover, except that   2
we have codices of Pliny that are very corrupt. For what we read in the tenth book of his *Natural History*, where he deals with geese, is: "Its sheen and utter blackness adorn the erythrotaon."[614] In an extremely ancient exemplar of Pliny in the public library of the Medici family,[615] this passage appears in virtually correct form, that is, with only a single letter altered, such as is the case with many words that have been interpolated in all the old books. For even though the books are replete with errors in many passages, they nonetheless still preserve clear traces of the true reading that is sought that have been obliterated from the new codices by incompetent copyists. And so, in this codex it reads as follows: *Decet et traonas*, so that if you switch the order of the first two letters, *tetraonas* leaps out.[616] In Pliny, therefore, on Poliziano's authority, you should read thus:

Decet tetraonas suus nitor absolutaque nigritia. In superciliis cocci rubor. Alterum eorum genus vulturum magnitudinem excedit. Quorum et colorem reddit, nec ulla avis excepto struthochamelo maius corpore implens pondus, in tantum aucta ut in terra quoque immobilis prehendatur. Gignunt eas[181] Alpes et septentrionalis regio.

Hactenus ille de tetraonibus.

: 58 :

Origo et ritus ludorum Saecularium,
praetereaque ad id alia, citatumque eo
Sibyllae oraculum, mox et obiter explicata quaedam,
rursusque alia refutata non inutiliter

1 Erit, arbitror, operaepretium[182] colligere hic etiam Saecularium ludorum originem causamque nominis, et item quot annorum interiecto spatio quotiesque facti, quo ritu, quibusque deis celebrati. Nam et res est ipsa per se cognitu non indigna cui studium modo sit ullum vetustatis, et ad intelligendos poetarum locos nonnullos ingens attulerit adiumentum.

2 Cum igitur bellum inter se Romani Albanique gererent, et utraque in procinctu iam staret acies, extitit repente quidam monstrosa specie, pelle amictus furva, vociferans iubere Ditem patrem deamque Proserpinam fieri sacrum sibi priusquam praelium committeretur. Quo perterrefacti viso Romani protinus aram sub terra aedificarunt, et statim sacrificio facto, pedum xx aggere

Their own sheen and utter blackness adorn grouses (*tetrao-nas*). On their eyebrows is a tinge of scarlet. Another type of them exceeds the size of vultures and replicates their color. No bird, with the exception of the ostrich, puts on more weight, growing so large that, unable to move about even on land, it is [easily] captured. They originate in the Alps and the northern realm.[617]

Thus far Pliny on grouse.

: 58 :

The origin and ritual of the Secular Games,
and other related matters besides; and I go on to cite a
Sibylline oracle; next, certain things are explained in passing,
and others are not unprofitably refuted

It will be worthwhile, I think, to compile here the origin of Secu-   1
lar Games and the reason for their name, as well as how often they were produced and with how many years' interval inserted, by what ceremonial and for which gods they were celebrated. For this matter is worth knowing per se for anyone who has any interest in antiquity, and it will be hugely profitable for understanding some passages of the poets.[618]

So then, when the Romans and the Albans were at war, and   2
each side's battle line was already standing at arms, there suddenly appeared a huge figure cloaked in a dark pelt shouting that father Dis and the goddess Proserpina commanded that sacrifice be made to them before battle was joined. Terrified by this specter, the Romans at once built an underground altar and immediately upon making sacrifice, covered it with a mound twenty feet high

contexerunt, ut esset omnibus praeterquam Romanis ipsis ignorabilis.

3 Sed enim evenit, ut Valesus Valesius, unde nomen et origo Valeriae familiae, clarissimus in gente Sabina et locuples homo rusticae vitae, aram hanc quam diximus ita divinitus invenerit. Erat ei nemus ante villam proceris maxime arboribus, quae statim fulmine ictae conflagrarunt. Nec multo post filii duo et filia correpti pestilentiae morbo ad desperationem usque medicorum laborabant. Cum sese igitur Laribus familiaribus advolvens pater pro liberorum salute suum matrisque puerorum capita devoveret, vox e nemore quod tactum de caelo statim audita, salvos fore eos spondens si, Tiberi ad Tarentum pervecti, calfactam Ditis et Proserpinae foco de fluvio ipso biberent aquam. Quoniam vero longissime abesse Tarentum, scilicet in extrema Iapygia, nec proxime eam urbem reperiri Tiberim ullum fluvium sciebat, spem sibi deterrimam fingebat, etiam inde territus quod inferarum potissimum vox illa potestatum meminisset. Sed impositos nihilo setius in lintrem filios, hostiam pergens,[183] mox ad Campi Martii regionem devexit. Ibi recreare sitientes et aestu febrique laborantes desiderans, qua placidissime amnis labitur, exponit in ripa aegrotos, ac dum tumultuariam sibi tegeticulam concinnat, extincto igniculo, admonetur a gubernatore petendum potius Tarentum (nam ita locus in proximo vocabatur), etenim fumum sese illic aspicere.

4 Tum vero laetior audito Tarenti nomine Valesius deos adorans et salutem sibi liberorum iamiam propemodum bona fide spondens

so that it could not be known to anyone except the Romans themselves.[619]

But it came about that Valesus Valesius, the source of the name 3
and origin of the Valerian family, a man of distinguished Sabine
stock and wealthy in the rustic style, with divine aid discovered the
altar I mentioned in the following way. There was a grove in front
of his house, with trees as tall as can be, which were struck by a
lightning bolt and burned up. And not long afterward his two
sons and daughter were seized and afflicted by pestilence, to the
despair of the physicians. When, therefore, their father fell prostrate before the family Lares and vowed to sacrifice his own life
and that of their mother in exchange for the children's recovery, a
voice was immediately heard from the grove that had been struck
by lightning, pledging that they would be safe if they sailed on the
Tiber to Tarentum and drank water from the river itself that had
been heated on the hearth of Dis and Proserpina. Since he knew
that Tarentum was far distant, that is, in the furthest part of Iapygia [southern Italy], and since he knew that no Tiber river was
found close to that city, he imagined that his prospects were bleak;
he was also frightened because the voice had made particular mention of the powers of the underworld. But nonetheless, after embarking the children on a skiff, he next went down to the region of
the Campus Martius, leading a sacrificial animal. There, as they
were suffering from thirst and fever, he sought to relieve them, and
he set the sick children out on the riverbank, where the river glides
by at its gentlest, and in fact, while he was preparing a small
makeshift mat for himself and after the small flame had gone out,
he was advised by the pilot that he should rather head for Tarentum (for that was the name of the nearby place), and as a matter
of fact he saw smoke rising from there.

Then indeed, upon hearing the name Tarentum, Valesius 4
cheered up and, worshipping the gods and confident in the prospect that his children would at last be safe, he ordered that this be

agi prorsum iubet et illuc maxime navigium appelli. Quo cum pervenisset, haurit aquam festinato de flumine, fretusque omine tenacius arrepto, fumigans ibidem solum, flatu sollicitat in flammam, calfactamque mox aquam porrigit in calice pueris. Succedit autem potui somnus. Vident in quiete illi spongia sibi a nescio quo detergeri morbum, tum praecipi ut Diti patri et Proserpinae furvae ibidem mactarentur hostiae trinoctiumque perpetuum choris et carminibus concelebraretur. Surgunt igitur recuperata valetudine, visumque illud patri renuntiant. Is homo locuples defodi iaciundis alte fundamentis humum iubet. Inventa igitur sic ara est ea quam diximus cum titulo Ditis et Proserpinae. Mactat ille (quod erat iussus) furvas continuo victimas, et trinoctium sacris frequentat, tot enim numero filios media de morte receperat, ex eoque Manius Valerius Tarentinus appellatus, quod a dis manibus in Tarento liberum[184] suorum valetudinem impetravisset. Ad hunc igitur modum quidam tradiderunt.

5   At enim M. Varro libro *De scaenicis originibus* primo:

> Cum multa, inquit, portenta fierent et murus ac turris quae sunt inter portam Collinam et Exquilinam de caelo tacta essent, et ideo libros Sibyllinos Quindecemviri adiissent, renuntiaverunt uti Diti patri et Proserpinae ludi Tarentini in Campo Martio fierent tribus noctibus et hostiae furvae imolarentur.

Hactenus de origine.

done and the boat make for land there. When he had arrived there, he quickly drew water from the river, and clinging tenaciously to the omen he had taken, and causing the ground there to smoke, by blowing he roused it to flame, and next offered the warmed water to the children in a cup. After the drink, sleep followed. In their sleep, they saw the disease being wiped off them by a person with a sponge. Then they were instructed that on the same site dark victims should be sacrificed to father Dis and Proserpina, and for three nights straight there should be celebrations with choruses and songs. The children, then, rose up with health restored and reported the vision to their father. Being wealthy, he ordered that the ground be dug for laying deep foundations. And thus the altar I mentioned was discovered, with the inscription "To Dis and Proserpina." As he had been ordered, he continuously offered up dark victims, and observed the three-night period with rituals, for that is the number of children he had recovered from imminent death. On account of this he was called Manius Valerius of Tarentum, because it was in Tarentum that he had obtained his children's recovery from the gods of the underworld.[620] This is how certain persons have passed the story down.[621]

Marcus Varro, however, in the first book of his *On the Origins of Theatrical Festivals* said:

> Since many portents were occurring and the wall and tower that stand between the Colline and Esquiline gates had been struck by lightning, and therefore the Council of Fifteen had consulted the Sibylline books, they reported back that Tarentine games should take place in honor of father Dis and Proserpina in the Campus Martius for three nights and that dark victims be sacrificed.[622]

So much for the origin [of the games].

6   Saeculares autem, non quia fierent anno vel centesimo denique vel etiam centesimo decimoque nuncupati, quod utrunque sicut assertores habet, ita re ipsa penitus coarguitur, sed ob id magis credi potest, quod plerumque semel hominis aetate fierent, ut multa alia quae rara sunt post saeculum evenire loquentium consuetudo usurpat.

7   Tarentini autem a loco ipso, qui Tarentum[185] ob id vocatur, aut quod ara ibi Ditis patris (quemadmodum supra diximus) in terra occultaretur[186] aut quod ripam Tiberis fluvius eo loco tereret, ex quo etiam Rumon dictus a veteribus et in sacris Serra nominatus, quod ruminaret, hoc est exederet et secaret, ripas. Unde ait Maro:

Stringentem ripas et pinguia culta secantem.

8   Ceterum de temporum intervallis quibus isti ludi referrentur, fides in ambiguo est. Siquidem in *Carmine saeculari* Horatius undenos decies per annos fieri declarat, quod et commentarii Quindecemvirorum et divi Augusti edicta et ipsius denique Sibyllae quod adhuc extat oraculum confirmaverint. Contra vero centesimum redire post annum tam Valerius Antias quam Titus Livius et item M. Varro testati perhibentur. Quod enim legimus apud Herodianum trium spatio aetatum solitos instaurari, vereor ut emendata sit ibi lectio, nostramque ob id e Graeco interpretationem cum venia legendam censeo. Nec autem, si tempora dinumeres, aut quanta intervalla retro fuerint aut quanta esse debeant omnino colligas.

9   Instituti autem primi Saeculares ludi post exactos reges a P. Valerio Publicola, qui primus consul fuit, existimantur. Etenim

Furthermore, the games were called Secular not because they occurred either in the hundredth year or one hundred and tenth year, both of which have their supporters but are refuted by the facts, but, it can rather be supposed, because they occur, for the most part, once in a man's lifetime, just as in common parlance one says that many other things that are rare will occur in the next century.[623]

They are called Tarentine, however, from the place itself, which is called Tarentum either because an altar to father Dis was hidden there in the ground (terra), as we said above, or because the river Tiber wears away (terere) its bank in that place, from which it was called Rumo by the ancients and is called Serra ("saw") in the rituals, because it chews (ruminare), that is, eats away and carves, its banks. Hence Maro [Vergil] says:

[The Tiber] skimming its banks and cleaving the rich fields.[624]

Moreover, in regard to the intervals at which those games were revived, there is doubt as to which account is reliable. In his *Secular Poem*, Horace asserts that they occurred at intervals of one hundred ten years,[625] as the records of the Council of Fifteen, the edicts of the divine Augustus,[626] and finally the still extant oracle of Sibyl herself confirm. But to the contrary, Valerius Antias as well as Titus Livy, and likewise Marcus Varro, are reported to have attested that the games recur after the hundredth year.[627] For as to the fact that we read in Herodian that they were wont to be renewed after a span of three lifetimes, I suspect the text there is not error free, and because of that I think my translation from the Greek should be read with indulgence.[628] But if you count up the times, you would by no means infer either how long the intervals were or ought to be.

Furthermore, the first Secular Games are thought to have been established upon expulsion of the kings by Publius Valerius Publicola, who was the first consul. For when the citizens were suffering

6

7

8

9

laborantibus pestilentia civibus, apud hanc ipsam quam diximus aram publice nuncupatis votis, atrum bovem Diti pro maribus, concolorem pro feminis iuvencam Proserpinae mactavit, ludosque et lectisternia trinoctio fecit, et aram terra, sicut ante fuerat, exaggerata occuluit, inscriptam titulo isto: 'P. Valerius Publicola frumentarium campum Diti et Proserpinae consecravi, et ludos Diti et Proserpinae Romanorum salutis ergo feci.'

10   Secundos autem secundo et quinquagesimo post Romam conditam factos anno admonitu Sibyllinorum[187] carminum tradit Graece Zosimus, missis occupata morbo civitate lectis ad hoc viris qui libros consulerent, ex quorum responso denuo regesta humo apud aram hanc ipsam in extremo Campi Martii, de more sacra et ludi persoluti, restitutaque Romanis iterum est incolumitas. Consulem vero scriptor hic unum dumtaxat, exemplario fortasse mendo, M. Publium Quintium nominavit, cum Censorinus M. Valerium et Spurium Verginium consules prodat. Idemque tertios et item quartos consulum temporibus quos et nominatim citat, auctoritatibus Antiatis Valeri, T. Livi, Varronis, Pisonis, Gelli, et Eminae comprobat factos, etiamque commentarios Quindecemvirum sacris faciundis in testimonium asciscit. At enim quoniam lubricus in propriis nominibus et item in numerorum notis librariorum lapsus, vitiata ista, ni fallor, in Censorini commentario reperies.

11   Ceterum divus Augustus abolitos eos paulatim (sicuti quidam putant) atque intermissos instauravit magno (ut Livius ait) apparatu, L. Censorino et M. Manlio Puellio consulibus, Atteio autem Capitone circumitum spatiumque subiciente, ritum vero sacrorum libris indicantibus Sibyllinis.

under plague, after pronouncing public vows at this very altar that we mentioned, he sacrificed a black bull to Dis for males and a heifer of the same color to Proserpina for females, and he held the games and ritual feasts for three nights, and hid the altar by piling soil up over it, as it had previously been, once the altar had been inscribed with this legend: "I, P. Valerius Publicola, consecrated this field of grain to Dis and Proserpina and held games in honor of Dis and Proserpina for the well-being of the Romans."

Zosimus records in Greek that the second games were held on   10 the advice of the Sibylline poems, in the five hundred second year after the founding of Rome.[629] When the city was held in the grip of plague, picked men were dispatched to consult the [Sibylline] books. On the basis of their response, the earth was again dug up at this very altar at the edge of the Campus Martius, the sacred rites and games were discharged in the customary fashion, and their well-being was once again restored to the Romans. Indeed this writer named—perhaps as a result of a defect in the exemplar—a single consul, Marcis Publius Quintius, although Censorinus records M. Valerius and Spurius Verginius as consuls.[630] He likewise substantiates that the third and fourth [games] were held in the times of consuls whom he cites by name, with Valerius Antias, Titus Livy, Varro, Piso, Gellius, and Hemina as his authorities,[631] and also adduces as evidence the records of the Council of Fifteen for Performing Sacrifices. But since scribes are prone to err in proper names as well as numerical notation, you will find these corruptions, unless I am mistaken, in Censorinus's book.

Yet after they had gradually died out (as some think) and   11 lapsed, the divine Augustus reinstituted the games on a lavish scale, as Livy says,[632] when Lucius Censorinus and Marcus Manlius Puellius were consuls, with Ateius Capito laying out the circumference of the [sacred] space and with the Sibylline books providing the ceremonial for the rites.[633]

12   Porro sextos Claudius se consule IIII et L. Vitellio, quasi antici-
patos ab Augusto nec legitimo tempori reservatos, quamvis ipse in
Historiis suis prodidisse memoretur intermissos eos Augustum
multo post, diligentissime annorum ratione subducta, in ordinem
redegisse, quare vox etiam irrisa praeconis traditur invitantis more
sollemni ad ludos quos nec spectavisset quisquam nec spectaturus
esset, cum superessent adhuc qui spectaverant et quidam histrio-
num producti olim tum quoque producerentur. Etenim Stepha-
nionem, qui primus togatis saltare instituit, utrisque Saecularibus
ludis, Augusti videlicet et Claudi, saltasse accepimus, qui LXXXIII
non amplius anno interfuere, quamvis et postea ille diu vixerit.

13   Septimos Domitianus se XIIII et L. Minutio Rufo consulibus,
computata ratione temporum ad annum, non quo Claudius
proxime, sed quo olim Augustus ediderat. Denique in nomismatis
variis apud Laurentium nostrum Medicem stelographiam quoque
istam vidimus: LVD. SAEC. FEC. COS. XIIII. Ac de his Papi-
nium sentire in silvula ad urbis praefectum Gallicum cui titulus
Soteria iam tum nostris auditoribus ostendebamus, cum volumen
ipsum scilicet abhinc novennium publice interpretabamur. Verba
ita sunt:

> Nec tantum induerint fatis nova saecula crimen,
> Aut instaurati peccaverit ara Tarenti.

Quo loco Domitius noster, quanquam de Tarenti ara disque ipsis
manibus meminit, nihil omnino tamen super Saecularibus istis
suspicatur. Iam vero apud Martialem — quam pene idem suae litteraturae, ne dixerim ingenii quoque obliviscitur — quem scilicet et

Next, Claudius held the sixth games, under the consulship of 12
Lucius Vitellius and himself for the fourth time, as if they had
been celebrated early by Augustus and not reserved for the legitimate time, although he is said to have reported in his own *History*
that long after they had lapsed Augustus had restored them to
order, with the number of years carefully calculated. Therefore it is
said that the proclamation of the crier was ridiculed when, in the
customary form, he invited the people to games that no one had
ever seen or would see again, although persons still survived who
had seen them and certain actors who had previously been brought
onstage were on that occasion brought on once again. We have, in
fact, heard that Stephanio, who first taught Romans to dance, had
danced at both of the Secular Games, that is, the games of Augustus and Claudius, which were not more than eighty-three years
apart, although he lived a long time afterward.[634]

Domitian produced the seventh games, under the consulship of 13
Lucius Minutius Rufus and himself for the fourteenth time, with
the year in which Augustus had once produced them taken as the
standard, not the one used most recently by Claudius. Finally, on
various coins in the collection of our Lorenzo de' Medici, we have
also seen this inscription: "He held the Secular Games as consul
for the fourteenth time."[635] And indeed I showed my students that
Papinius [Statius] expressed an opinion about these in one of his
Silvae to the urban prefect Gallicus, entitled "Soteria" ("present
given for recovery"), when I was publicly lecturing on that book
nine years ago.[636] This is the excerpt:

Only let not the new ages bring on wickedness by the Fates,
Nor the altar of renewed Tarentum sin.[637]

About this passage, although he mentions the altar of Tarentum
and the infernal gods, our Domizio suspects nothing at all about
those Secular Games. Now that same man—how Domizio for-
gets his literature, not to say his talent!—I brilliantly refuted (if I

tunc et cum *Fastos* anno post enarrabamus, luculente (ni fallor) coarguimus. Est autem Martialis epigramma de matrona, quae, puto, binis ludis, Claudi scilicet Domitianique, interfuerat, in eoque etiam hic versiculus:

Bis mea Romano spectata est vita Tarento.

Quo loco parum cordatus homo hic trigesimo quoque anno celebrari sacra ad Tarentum dicit consuesse, quod nec aliquis etiam fando audiverit. Quin idem illos ex quarto eiusdem poetae libro versiculos pertractans:

Hic colat ingenti redeuntia saecula lustro,
Et quae Romuleus sacra Tarentus habet,

etiam posteriorem diiungit a priore, et ut in illo Saeculares ludos, ita in hoc commenticia ista tricenaria sacra putat insinuari. Facit autem Tarenti huius etiam Varro in *Latinae linguae* commentario etiamque vel iterum in *Fastis* Ovidius mentionem. Sed redeo unde digressus.

14   Centesimo decimoque post Domitiani ludos anno instauravit et eos imperator ille Septimius Severus, cuius etiam nunc Romae pulcherrimus spectatur triumphalis arcus, cum filiis Antonino et Geta, Chilone et Vibone consulibus. Quos ludos et vidisse se memorat Herodianus, et Dion aetate sua factos memoriae prodidit.

15   Post Severum negat instauratos Zosimus, quoniam hic annorum centum et decem pene receptus auctoritate ambitus in consulatum Constantini Christiani principis tertium et Licini, quem dein bello ipse vicit, incurrisset. Nos tamen apud Eusebium in *Chronicis* et Eutropium in *Historiarum* libro nono legimus Philippo

am not mistaken) [regarding a passage] in Martial both then and
when we were expounding the *Fasti* the following year.[638] Martial,
then, has an epigram about a matron, who, I think, attended two
sets of games—that is, Claudius's and Domitian's—and in it is
this verse:

> My life was twice approved by Roman Tarentum.[639]

About this passage this not very clever man[640] says that the rites
were usually celebrated every thirtieth year at Tarentum, which no
one has heard said. What is more, dealing with the following lines
from the fourth book of that same poet,

> Let him honor the ages when they return in their mighty cycle,
>   And the rites that Romulean Tarentus keeps,[641]

the same man even severs the latter verse from the former, and
thinks that as in the former the Secular Games are hinted at, so in
the latter are those spurious thirty-year rites.[642] Moreover, Varro
also mentions this Tarentum in his book *On the Latin Language*, as
does Ovid in his *Fasti*.[643] But I return to the point from which I
digressed.

The emperor Septimius Severus, whose lovely triumphal arch   14
is even now seen at Rome,[644] along with his sons Antoninus and
Geta, repeated the games in the one hundred and tenth year after
those of Domitian, when Chilon and Vibo were consuls.[645] Herodian mentions that he watched those games,[646] and Dio recorded
that they had taken place in his own age.[647]

Zosimus says that they were not revived after Severus, since   15
this cycle of one hundred and ten years that is more or less accepted on authority coincided with the third consulate of the
Christian emperor Constantine and Licinius, whom he subsequently conquered in war.[648] Nonetheless, we read in Eusebius's
Chronicles and in Book 9 of Eutropius's *Histories* that when Philip

imperante (quamquam primus fuisse Christianus imperator creditur) millesimum annum Romanae urbis ingenti ludorum apparatu
et spectaculorum fuisse celebratum bestiasque in Circo innumera-
biles interfectas et ludos in Campo Martio theatrales tribus diebus
ac noctibus populo pervigilante concelebratos, quibus ludis Saecularibus etiam dicitur Philippus Iunior, is qui nunquam risisse creditur, patrem Philippum Seniorem petulantius cachinnantem
vultu aversato notavisse.

16   Restat uti de ritu carptim paucula perstringamus. Instantibus
itaque ludis tota Italia praecones missitabantur convocatum ad ludos qui nec spectati nec spectandi iterum forent. Tum aestatis
tempore paucis antequam spectacula edebantur diebus Quindecemviri sacris faciundis in Capitolio et Palatino templo pro sug-
gestu considentes, piamina dividebant populo, quae erant taeda,[188]
sulfur, et bitumen, nec tamen ad ea servis quoque accipienda ius
ullum. Coibat autem populus cum in quae supra rettulimus loca,
tum praeterea in Dianae templum quod erat in Aventino et cuique
triticum, faba, hordeumque dari mos. Tum ad instar Cereris ini-
tiorum pervigilia fiebant.

17   Ubi vero iam advenit festus dies, triduum trinoctiumque sacris
intenti in ripa ipsa maxime Tiberis agitabant. Sacrificia vero Iovi,
Iunoni, Apollini, Latonae, Dianae, praetereaque Parcis et quas vocant Ilithyias,[189] tum Cereri et Diti et Proserpinae suscipiebantur.
Igitur secunda primae noctis hora, princeps ipse, tribus aris ad ripam fluminis extructis, totidem agnos et una Quindecemviri imo-
labant, et sanguine imbutis aris caesa[190] victimarum corpora con-
cremabant. Constructa autem scaena in theatri morem, lumina et

was emperor, even though he is believed to have been the first Christian emperor,⁶⁴⁹ the thousandth year of the city of Rome was celebrated with the most lavish games and spectacles and that innumerable beasts were killed in the Circus, and theatrical games were celebrated in Campus Martius for three days and three nights while the people kept vigil.⁶⁵⁰ At these Secular Games Philip the Younger, who is believed never to have laughed, is even said to have noted, with his face averted, that his father, Philip the Elder, burst into a guffaw.⁶⁵¹

It remains for us to touch selectively on a few points about the rite. And so, when the time for the games approached, criers used to be dispatched throughout Italy to call everyone to games that had not been seen and would not be seen again.⁶⁵² Then during the summer, a few days before the spectacles were produced, the Council of Fifteen for Performing Sacrifices, taking their seats on the Capitol and at the Palatine temple in front of the raised area, distributed the agents of atonement to the people, which were torches, sulfur, and pitch, but slaves had no right to receive these as well. Moreover, the people would come together not only to the places we referred to above but also to the temple of Diana that was on the Aventine hill, and it was the custom for wheat, beans, and barley to be given to each. Then they held an all-night vigil on the model of the initiations of Ceres.⁶⁵³

When the day of the festival arrived, they spent three days and three nights focused on the rites on the bank of the Tiber. Indeed sacrifices were undertaken to Jupiter, Juno, Apollo, Latona, Diana, and the Fates as well, and those whom they call the Ilithyiae, as well as Ceres, Dis, and Proserpina. Accordingly, when three altars had been built on the riverbank, at the second hour of the first night, the emperor himself, along with the Council of Fifteen, sacrificed that number of lambs, and when the altars had been stained with the blood, they burned the bodies of the slain victims. Then after a stage had been built in the style of a theater, fires and

ignes accendi et hymni concini ad hunc usum tum maxime compositi,[191] et item spectacula edi sollemniter solita, data celebranti-
bus hec[192] mercede, tritico, faba, hordeo, quae supra inter universum populum dividi ostendimus.

18   Mane vero Capitolium ascendere, sacra ibi de more agitare, tum
in theatrum convenire ad ludos in honorem Apollinis et Dianae
faciundos consueverunt. Sequenti die nobiles matronae, qua hora
praecipitur ab oraculo, convenire in Capitolium, supplicare deo,
frequentare lectisternia, canere hymnos ex ritu, ⟨ut⟩[193] mos habebat.

19   Tertio denique die in templo Apollinis Palatini ter noveni pueri
praetextati totidemque virgines, patrimi omnes matrimique,
Graeca Romanaque voce carmina et paeanas concinebant, quibus
imperium suum et incolumitatem populi dis immortalibus com-
mendabant.

20   Quod siquis fortasse quaesierit quod genus tunc aut ludorum
fieret aut sacrificiorum, sciat et ludos celebrari omnibus theatris
atque omne genus et sacrificia templis omnibus consuesse, noctu
pariter atque interdiu. Nam de scaenicis et circensibus minime
dubitatur, cum Domitiani ludis histriones interfuisse meminieri-
mus, praetereaque circensium die, quo facilius centum missus
peragerentur, singulos a septenis spatiis ad quina legerimus correp-
tos. Illud utique in Augusto memorabile, qui ludis istis iuvenes
utriusque sexus prohibuit ullum nocturnum spectaculum frequentare, nisi cum aliquo maiore natu propinquorum.

21   Enimvero his prout in mentem de subito venerunt expositis,
iam nec ille vatis Ausoni versiculus ambiguus relinquetur:

torches were lit and hymns sung that had been specially composed for the occasion, and likewise the usual spectacles were solemnly performed, after those celebrating these rites were presented with this reward, wheat, beans, and barley, which we showed above were divided among all the people.

In the morning, they would ascend the Capitoline Hill, make 18 customary sacrifices there, then meet in the theater for the games to be held in honor of Apollo and Diana. On the following day, the noble matrons would meet on the Capitol at the hour prescribed by the oracle, supplicate the god, observe the ritual feasts,[654] and sing ritual hymns, as custom dictated.

Finally on the third day in the temple of Palatine Apollo, three 19 groups of nine boys dressed in fringed togas, and as many young girls, all with their fathers and mothers still living, would sing songs and paeans with Greek and Roman lyrics, by which they entrusted their empire and the security of the people to the immortal gods.[655]

If anyone should ask what types of games or sacrifices were 20 then performed, let him know that games were wont to be celebrated in all the theaters, and all types of sacrifices were wont to be performed in all the temples, by night and day alike. There is scant doubt about the stage plays and circus games, since we mentioned that actors had participated in Domitian's games,[656] and besides on the day of the circus games, we read that, in order for the hundred events to be completed more easily, the individual events were shortened from seven to five spaces each.[657] And in the case of Augustus, it was particularly memorable that he prohibited young people of either sex from attending any nightly spectacle unless accompanied by some older relation.[658]

Now that these things have been expounded as they came to 21 mind, that famous verse of the poet Ausonius no longer remains obscure:

Trina Tarentino celebrata trinoctia ludo,

iam nec obscura apud Horatium ratio extiterit cur Parcas, Ilithyian, Dianamque ex Aventino, cur et puerorum vota et Quindecemviros memoraverit, et item Sibyllinos versus, qui nunc quoque apud eundem Zosimum vetustissimis quidem codicibus citra ulla fastigia, qualesque de industria subiecimus, inveniuntur:

Αλλ οποταν μηκιστοσ ικηι χρονοσ ανθρωποισι

Ζωησ εισ ετεων εκατον δεκα κυκλον οδευων

Μεμνησθαι ρωμαιε και ει μαλα λησεαι αυτου

Μεμνησθαι ταδε παντα θεοισι μεν αθανατοισι

Ρεζειν εν πεδιωι παρα θυμβριδοσ απλετον υδωρ   5

Οππη στεινοτατον νυξ ηνικα γαιαν επελθηι

Ηελιου κρυψαντοσ εον φαοσ ενθα σε ρεζειν

Ιερα παντογονοισ μοιραισ αρνασ τε και αιγασ

Κυανεασ επι ταισ δ ειλειθυιασ[194] αρεσασθαι

Παιδοτοκουσ θυεεσσιν οπη θεμισ αυθι δε γαιηι   10

Πληθομενη[195] χοιροσ συσ θ ιρευοιτο[196] μελαινα

Πανλευκοι[197] ταυροι δε διοσ παρα βωμον αγεσθων

Ηματι μηδ επι νυκτι θεοισι γαρ ουρανιοισιν

Ημεριοσ πελεται θυεων τροποσ ωσ δε και αυτοσ

Ιρευειν[198] δαμαλισ δε βοων δεμασ αγλαον ηρης   15

Δεξασθω νηοσ παρα σευ και φοιβοσ απολλων

Οσ τε και ηελιοσ κικλησκεται ισα δεδεχθω

Θυματα λητοιδησ αιδομενοι[199] τε λατινοι[200]

Παιανεσ κουροισ κουραισι τε νηον εχοιεν

Αθανατων χωρισ δε κοραι χορον αυται εχοιεν   20

Three triple nights each were celebrated with the Tarentine
game,[659]

nor is the reason still obscure why Horace mentioned the Fates,
Ilithyia, and Diana from the Aventine Hill, why the children's
prayers, and why the Council of Fifteen, and likewise the Sibylline
verses,[660] which are now found in that same Zosimus in extremely
ancient codices without any accents, in which form I have deliberately subjoined them:

But whenever the longest span of human life,
Traveling its circuit, reaches one hundred ten years,
Remember this, Roman, even if you are quite forgetful,
Remember to sacrifice all these things to the immortal gods
On the plain beside the immense water of the Tiber,   5
Where it is narrowest, when night comes upon the earth
After the sun has hidden its light, then
Sacrifice dark lambs and kids, things sacred to the all-
   generating Fates.
In addition to them, appease the Ilithyiae,
Who preside over childbirth, with burned offerings, as is right, 10
   and to Earth
Let a pregnant black sow be offered.
But lead white bulls beside the altar of Zeus
By day, and not at night, for to the gods of heaven
There is offering by day; so should you also
Sacrifice. Let the temple of Hera receive the body of a   15
   splendid cow
From you, and let Phoebus Apollo,
Who is also called the Sun, the son of Leto,
Receive equal sacrifices, and let Latin paeans,
Sung by boys and girls, fill the temple
Of the immortal gods. But let the girls have their own separate 20
   chorus

Και χωρισ παιδων αρσην σταχυσ αλλα γονηων
Παντων ζωοντων οισ αμφιθαλησ ετι φυτλη
Αι δε γαμου ζευγλαισ δεδμημεναι ηματι κεινωι
Γνυξ ηρησ παρα βωμον αοιδιμον εδριοωσαι,
Δαιμονα λισσεσθωσαν απασι δε λυματα δουναι   25
Ανδρασιν ηδε γυναιξι μαλιστα δε θηλυτερηισιν
Παντεσ δ εξ οικοιο φερεσθων οσσα κομιζειν
Εστι θεμισ θνητοισιν απαρχομενοισ βιοτοιο
Δαιμοσι μειλιχιοισιν ιλασματα και μακαρεσσιν
Ουρανιδαισ τα δε παντα τεθησαυρισμενα κεισθω   30
Οφρα τε θηλυτερηισι και ανδρασιν ιδρυοωσιν[201]
Ενθεν πορσυνηισ μεμνημενοσ ημασι δ εστω
Νυξι τε πασσυτερηισι θεοπρεπτουσ κατα θωκουσ
Παμπληθησ αγυρισ σπουδη τε γελωτι μεμιχθω.
Ταυτα τοι εν φρεσιν ηισιν αει μεμνημενοσ ειναι   35
Και σοι πασα χθων ιταλη και πασα λατινη
Αιεν υπο σκηπτροισιν επαυχενιον ζυγον εξει.

22   Cur autem non et Latinos eos temptemus reddere, si non eleganter utpote ex temporales, ex fide tamen, servato etiam, quantum liceat, incomptae illius sed venerandae vetustatis colore non-
nullo, aut squalore potius? Igitur ita qui volet eos togatis illis
adhuc quidem rusticanis adscribat:

  Ast ubi iam humanae longissima tempora vitae
  Orbis agens annos referet centumque decemque,
  Sis, Romane, memor (licet alta oblivia temptent)
  Sis memor, ut qua se nimium Tiberina coartat

And the male progeny have their own separate one, but let
    them
Have all their parents living, their stock still flourishing on
    both sides.
On that day let the women subdued by the yoke of marriage
Kneel beside Hera's famous altar
And beseech the goddess. And let them give the means of   25
    expiation to all
The men and women, but especially the latter,
And let them all bring from home whatever is fitting
For mortals to bring as first fruits of their livelihood
As appeasements for the gentle gods [*sc.* of the underworld]
    and the blessed
Heaven dwellers. Let all of them be laid up in store   30
So that you may be mindful and provide therefrom
To the women and men who beseech you. Let there be
On consecutive days and nights a large gathering
At the temples worthy of the gods, and let the solemn be
    mixed with merriment.
Always remember these things in your heart,   35
And the entire land of Italy and of the Latins
Will always bear the yoke of your sovereignty upon its neck.[661]

Why should I not attempt to render these verses into Latin, if   22
not elegantly, since they are done on the spur of the moment, yet
faithfully preserving, insofar as possible, some of the color, or
rather roughness, of uncouth but venerable antiquity? Therefore
let anyone who wants ascribe them to those still rustic Romans:[662]

But when the longest span of human life,
    Guiding its cycles, brings back one hundred and ten years,
Be mindful, Roman (even if deep forgetfulness beset you),
Be mindful, where the bank of the Tiber narrows,

Ripa, feras dis in campo sollemnia sacra,   5
Cum nox atra premit terras tectusque latet sol.
Agnae caprigenumque pecus genitalibus Parcis,
Hostia furva utraeque cadant, tum numina placa
Laeta puerperiis (quod fas fuat) Ilithyias,[202]
Terra suem ferat, et scropham sibi fertilis atram,   10
Sed Iovis ante aram candenti corpore tauros
Luce feri,[203] nam lux superis gratissima divis.
Iunonis templum nitida cervice iuvenca
Imbuat, atque itidem Phoebus placetur Apollo,
Quem vocitant etiam Solem, Latoa propago.   15
Paeanas puerique canant pueraeque Latinorum
In templo. Sed enim pueri pueraeque seorsum
Concelebranto choros, verum haec sit patrima proles
Matrimaque. At nuptae genibus Iunonis ad aram
Oranto innisae, divamque in vota vocanto.   20
Februa quin etiam vir quisque et femina, quanquam
Femina praecipue, accipito. Dehinc aedibus omnes
Primitias vitae placidis placamina divis
(Qua fas est) et caelitibus portanto beatis.
Ante domi tamen illa memor tibi habeto reposta,   25
Quae dare mox usu liceat poscente virisque
Femineoque gregi. Tum digna sedilia divis
Perque dies iuxta et noctes multesima turba
Complento, et lepidis miscento seria ludis.

To perform solemn rites for the gods on the plain,   5
When black night weighs upon the earth and the sun lies
    hidden.
Let lambs and goats fall to the generative Fates,
A dark victim to each, then appease the goddesses
Who delight in childbirth (as is right), the Ilithyiae.
Let the fertile Earth have her pig, a black breeding sow,   10
But slay[663] white bulls before the altar of Jupiter
By daylight, for the daylight is highly pleasing to the upper
    gods.
May a heifer with shining neck redden the temple
Of Juno, and let Phoebus Apollo likewise be appeased,
Whom they also call the Sun, offspring of Leto.   15
Let the boys and girls sing paeans of the Latins[664]
In the temple. But let the boys and girls
Celebrate their choruses separately, and let these young people
Have living fathers and mothers. But let the married women
    pray kneeling
At the altar of Juno, and let them appeal to the goddess in   20
    prayer.
Moreover, let each man and woman, but especially
The women, receive agents of purification. Next let all bring
    from home
The first fruits of their livelihood as appeasements for the
    placid gods
(As is right) and for the blessed denizens of heaven.
Remember, however, to have stored up at home in advance   25
What you may give, when the need arises, to the band of men
And women. Then let a numerous throng fill temples
Worthy of the gods continuously day and night,
And let solemn events be mixed with delightful games.

Quae tibi si stabili sint omnia condita mente,   30
Cuncta tuo Italiae tellus, cunctique Latini
Subdent colla iugo et victoris sceptra timebunt.

‡ 59 ‡

Non Vergilium sed Ovidium videri Priapei carminis auctorem.
Tum versiculum illum qui sit apud Martialem, 'Ride si sapis,
o puella, ride,' Nasonis esse proculdubio, sed ex epigrammatis
potius quam aut ex Artibus aut ex tragoedia Medea *videri*
citatum, moxque novum quippiam et mirum de Medea
Nasonis adscriptum

1 Quae *Priapeia* vocantur epigrammata, Vergilio plerique tribuunt,
inter quos etiam est, arbitror, Servius. Ceterum ego in Senecae libris illis qui iam diu delituerant, nuper in lucem quamquam non
admodum sinceri prodiere, quibusque oratorum et rhetorum sententias, divisiones, colores suasoriarum complectitur (nisi forte
mendosum credamus, quod habetur exemplar unicum) subditicia
esse nec Vergili, sed Ovidi deprehendo. Siquidem illius in volumine secundo verba ita sunt:

> Hoc genus sensus memini quendam praetorium dicere, cum
> declamaret controversiam de illa quae egit cum viro malae[204]
> tractationis, quod virgo esset, et damnavit.[205] Postea petiit
> sacerdotium. 'Novimus,' inquit, 'istam maritorum abstinen-
> tiam, qui etiam si primam virginibus timidis remisere noc-
> tem, vicinis tamen locis ludunt.' Audiebat illum Scaurus,

If all these things are kept firmly in mind,   30
All the land of Italy and of all Latium
Will submit their necks to your yoke and will fear the victor's
    scepter.

: 59 :

*That not Vergil but Ovid appears to be the author of the
Priapean poem. Then that the line in Martial— "Smile, if
you are wise, girl, smile"— is undoubtedly Ovid's but appears
to be cited from an epigram rather than from either his Arts
or his tragedy Medea; and next, something new and surprising
is added about Ovid's Medea*

The epigrams that are called the *Priapea* many people attribute to   1
Vergil, among whom is, I think, even Servius.[665] Yet, in those
books of Seneca's that had been hidden for a long time but have
recently come to light, albeit not in completely pristine condition,
and which include the maxims, divisions, and "spin" of the persua-
sive speeches of orators and rhetoricians (unless perhaps we believe it is faulty, since a single exemplar is to hand),[666] I discover
that they are falsely attributed and that they are not Vergil's but
Ovid's. In fact, these are his words in the second book:

> I remember a certain ex-praetor expressed this sort of idea
> when he was declaiming in a debate about a woman who
> sued her husband for mistreatment, since she was a virgin,
> and got him condemned. Afterward he was a candidate for a
> priesthood. "We are familiar with that sort of husbands' ab-
> stinence," he said, "when they yield the first night to the vir-
> gins, since they are fearful, yet play in nearby places." Among

non tantum disertissimus homo sed venustissimus, qui nul-
lius unquam impunitam stultitiam transire passus est, statim
Ovidianum illud:

> Dum timet alterius vulnus inepta loci.
> Et ille excidit nec ultra dixit.

Huc usque Seneca.

2   Novimus autem hunc esse versiculum in Priapeio epigrammate,
cuius principium est:

> Obscure poteram tibi dicere.

Sed et stilus ipse (ni fallor) et prorsus Ovidiana quaepiam in eis
versibus germana lascivia. Quatenus autem sit huic auctoritati
fidendum, legentium sit iudicium. Nos ut non pro vano scripsimus
hoc, ita nec pro concesso. Certe sic Ovidio convenit etiam in ceteris osceniori, sic Vergilium contra dedecet, a virginea quoque verecundia Partheniam vocatum, titulus istius operis, ut quamlibet
iniurato testi et suspecto, pudeat tamen profecto non credere. Sane
illud in confesso, scripsisse epigrammata quoque alia Nasonem, de
quis versiculum citat hunc Priscianus:

> Larte ferox caeso[206] Cossus opima tulit.

Et apud eundem ludentem legerat sane Quintilianus istud:

> Cur ego non dicam, Furia, te furiam?

Nec alibi certe crediderim quam fuisse in epigrammatis, quem citat hendecasyllabum phalecium[207] Martialis:

> Ride si sapis, o puella, ride.

the listeners was Scaurus, a man not so much eloquent as charming, who never allowed any piece of foolishness to pass with impunity, who immediately quoted the Ovidian tag:

> Since, in her inexperience, she fears a wound in the other
> spot.
> But the other lost his train of thought and said nothing
> more.[667]

So far Seneca.

I know, however, that this is a line in a Priapean epigram, which 2 begins

> I could have told you obscurely.[668]

But the style itself (unless I am mistaken) is Ovid's, and there is in these lines a certain genuine Ovidian wantonness. But let readers judge to what extent one should trust this authority. I have written this neither groundlessly nor taking it for granted. Certainly the title of this work — although it is attested by an unsworn and suspect witness, it would nonetheless be a shame not to believe him[669] — suits Ovid, who is obscene elsewhere, and, on the other hand, is unfitting for Vergil, who was called Parthenias from his virginal modesty.[670] It is admitted that Naso wrote other epigrams as well, from which Priscian cites this verse:

> Fierce Cossus took the spoils from fallen Lars.[671]

And in the same poet at play Quintilian had read this passage:

> Why should I not call you a fury, Furia?[672]

Nor would I believe the phalecian hendecasyllable Martial cites was elsewhere than in the epigrams:

> Smile, if you are wise, girl, smile![673]

3   Nam quod praeceptum respicit aliquod ex *Artibus* Domitius, id
utique vel auctoritate refutatur Marciani Capellae, qui videlicet in
satura pro versiculo Nasonis eum, non pro Martialis agnoscit.
Audivi etiam, qui crederent de tragoedia esse *Medea*, quam Tacitus, quam laudat Quintilianus, et quam fuisse (quod miror) pene
Vergilianis consutam versibus auctor Tertullianus est, et nos in
Nutrice significavimus. Sed hoc mihi non sit verisimile. Quis enim
vel in Graeca uspiam vel in tragoedia Latina phalecios[208] legit, aut
quid omnino tragicum sapit hic versiculus, a tetrica illa gravitate
resiliens penitus atque abhorrens? An vero non et Marcianus ipse
negat propemodum clare de tragoedia hunc esse, si verba modo
ipsius fideliter recitata, diligenter quoque expendantur? An non
ille saturam suam, quod austera et censoria quodque nimium tra-
gici supercilii lusus castigaverat, quasi repercutiens et ad frontem
(quod dicitur) exporrigendam invitans?

Peligni, inquit, de cetero iuvenis versiculo resipisce, et (ni
tragicum corrugaris):

Ride (si sapis), o puella, ride.

'Ni tragicum,' inquit, 'corrugaris,' idest, nisi frontem caperas tragica
severitudine, quod significat rugas[209] tristitia et squalore asperas.
Igitur si de tragoedia sit ipsa versiculus, quo revocare uno maxime
saturam suam poeta hic ab austeritate illa tragica molitur, sane io-
cus hic (ut arbitror) frigidus hibernas cana nive conspuet Alpes.
Iam siquis de sinceritate lectionis istius ambigat, libros velim Marciani vetustissimos inspiciat e publica Medicae gentis Florentina
bibliotheca, sic enim profecto fidem nostram, credo, sua diligentia
adiuvabit.

As to the fact that Domizio regards it as a precept taken from 3
the *Arts*,[674] that [idea] is refuted at any rate by the authority of
Martianus Capella, who in his satire clearly recognizes that it is a
verse by Naso, and not by Martial.[675] I have also heard that there
are some who believe that it was from the tragedy *Medea*, which
Tacitus and Quintilian praise, and Tertullian is the authority for
the fact (which I find amazing) that it was virtually stitched together from Vergilian verses, and which I pointed to in my *Nurse*.[676]
But this would not seem likely to me. For who reads phalaecians
anywhere in either a Greek or Latin tragedy, and what tragic flavor
does this verse have at all, since it recoils from and is at odds with
that grim seriousness? Indeed does not Martianus himself deny
more or less clearly that this is from tragedy, provided his own
words are faithfully read and diligently weighed? Does he not say,
turning back, as it were, his own satire because it was austere and
censorious and had, with an all too tragic air, lambasted play, and
inviting it to smooth out its brow (as the saying goes)?[677]

Come to your senses in accord with another line from the
Paelignian boy and (unless you put on a tragic frown):

Smile, (if you are wise), girl, smile![678]

"Unless you put on a tragic frown," he says, that is, unless you fur-
row your brow with tragic severity, which means wrinkles rough
with sadness and neglect. Therefore, if the line by which alone the
poet is endeavoring to call back his satire from that tragic austerity
were from a tragedy, truly this frigid joke will (I think) sprinkle
the wintry Alps with white snow.[679] If anyone is still wavering
about the soundness of this reading, I would like for him to examine the extremely old books of Martianus from the public library
of the Medici family in Florence,[680] for in this way he will, I believe, support my accuracy with his diligence.[681]

: 60 :

Agon verbum, quo victimarius uti solitus,
de quo etiam in Fastis *Ovidius*

Ovidius in primo *Fastorum:*

> Nominis esse potest succinctus causa minister,
>   Hostia caelitibus quo feriente cadat,
> Qui calido strictos tincturus sanguine cultros
>   Semper agatne rogat, nec nisi iussus agit.

De hoc mactandae victimae ritu deque item verbo quo sacerdotis
minister uteretur, apud unum duntaxat Senecam in libro eodem
Oratorum rhetorumque tertio factam reperio mentionem per haec
verba:

> Deinde cum scholasticorum summo fragore: 'et tu, quisquis
> es carnifex, cum strictam substuleris[210] securim, antequam
> ferias, patrem respice.' Belle deridebat haec Asinius Pollio:
> 'Filius,' inquit, 'cervicem porrigat. Carnifex manum porrigat,
> deinde respiciat ad patrem et dicat, "agon?" quod fieri solet
> victimis!' Sed ioco quoque remoto, aiebat rem verissimam,
> non posse carnificem venire, nisi eo tempore quo iam exorari
> pater non posset.

Haec Seneca. Quo colligitur verbum quo victimarius identidem
utebatur *agon* fuisse, hoc est 'agone?' Quare belle Ovidius:

> Semper agatne rogat, nec nisi iussus agit.

: 60 :

The verb agon, *which the assistant at sacrifices customarily used, and about which Ovid also speaks in his* Fasti

Ovid, in the first book of the *Fasti*:

> [The Agonalia] may be so named because the girded attendant,
>   At whose blow the victim falls in honor of the gods of
>   heaven,
> As he is about to tinge his drawn knife with hot blood,
>   Always asks whether he should strike, and he does not
>   strike unless ordered.[682]

Concerning this sacrificial ritual and the verb that the priest's assistant would use, I find mention made only in Seneca, in the same third book of the *Orators and Rhetoricians*,[683] in these words:

> Then, to great applause of students: "And you, executioner, whoever you are, when you have lifted your drawn ax, before you strike, look back at the father." Asinius Pollio neatly mocked this. "Let the son," he says, "stretch out his neck. Let the executioner stretch forth his hand, then let him look back at the father and say 'Shall I strike?' That is what customarily happens with the victims!" But, all joking aside, he said the truth, that the executioner could not come except when it was no longer possible for the father to plead for mercy.[684]

Thus the text of Seneca. From this it is inferred that the verb the sacrificial assistant repeatedly used was *agon*, that is, *agone* ("Shall I strike?"). Hence Ovid neatly says,

> He always asks whether he should strike, and he does not
>   strike unless ordered.

: 61 :

*Erratum in codicibus Plinianis super cicuta vinoque, quodque
mendose apud Macrobium* aconitum *pro* conio

1   Verba ex epistola Androcidis ad Alexandrum Magnum, clari sa-
pientia viri, vitiose posita in Plinianis his codicibus reperiuntur
hoc modo: 'Vinum potaturus, rex, memento te bibere sanguinem
terrae. Sicuti venenum est homini cicuta, ita et vinum.' Levis profecto sententia nimisque violenta et coacta, addo etiam insipida
falsaque, vinum esse homini venenum, sicuti cicutam. Sed enim in
vetustissimo illo Medicae familiae Pliniano codice, citato a nobis
iam saepe, sic invenias: 'Cicuta homini venenum est, cicutae
vinum.' Nam ut hominem cicuta, sic cicutae virus meri potus ex-
tinguit. Ex eoque persuadere Alexandro nititur Androcides ut
tanquam re potentissima parcius utatur vino, quod veneni venenum sit. Unde non dispari sensu terrae esse sanguinem docuerat.
Quocirca de verbis eius ita Plinius concludit: 'Neque viribus corporis utilius aliud, neque voluptatibus pernitiosius, si modus absit.' Consimiliter etiam idem in libro quinto et vigesimo de cicuta
narrans ut homini exitiosa: 'Remedium est,' ait, 'prius quam perve-
niat ad vitalia vini natura excalfactoria.' Quod idem Dioscorides
prodidit. Divus igitur Ambrosius in libro quem de utilitate ieiunii
composuit: 'Etiam, inquit, maior vis vini quam veneni. Denique

: 61 :

An error in the codices of Pliny regarding hemlock and wine;
and that the word aconitum *stands erroneously instead of*
conium *in Macrobius*

Words from a letter to Alexander the Greek from Androcydes, a   1
man distinguished by his wisdom, are found to have been erroneously cited in the codices of Pliny, as follows: "O king, when you
are about to drink wine, remember that you are drinking the
blood of the earth. Just as hemlock is poisonous to a man, so also
is wine."[685] This is a trivial point, too violent and forced, and I add
also foolish and false, namely that wine is poisonous to a human
being in the same way as hemlock. But in the very old codex of
Pliny belonging to the Medici family, already often cited by us,
you will find the following: "Hemlock is poisonous to a man, wine
is poisonous to hemlock."[686] For just as hemlock kills a man, so a
dose of pure wine kills the poison of hemlock. On this basis, Androcydes tries to persuade Alexander to use wine more sparingly,
for it is a very powerful thing since it is the poison of poison.
Hence he had similarly taught that it [wine] is the blood of the
earth. Accordingly, Pliny concludes the discussion of his words
this way: "There is nothing more useful for the vigor of the body
[than wine], nor anything more pernicious to our pleasures, if
moderation be lacking."[687] Similarly in Book 25 the same author,
relating that hemlock is deadly to a human being, says: "The rem-
edy is [to utilize] wine's heating characteristic before it [hemlock]
can travel to the vital organs."[688] Dioscorides recorded the same
point.[689] Accordingly, in the book that he wrote on the usefulness
of fasting, St. Ambrose said: "The strength of wine is greater than

venenum vino excluditur, non vinum veneno.' Sed et Plutarchus in
Symposiacis libris eadem ferme quae Plinius de cicuta.

2   Tum eum locum, sicutique alios permultos, prope adverbum
conatus exprimere est in *Saturnalibus* Macrobius, quanquam in
omnibus quos quidem hactenus viderim Macrobianos codices, *aconitum* pro *cicuta* reperitur, sicut in vetustissimo etiam Bernardi
Micheloctii, bene litterati hominis et amici nobis. Sed enim opinor
mendum esse id exemplarium, nec enim mihi tam fuisse ineruditum Macrobium persuaserim ut quod esset Graece *conion*, ipse
aconitum verterit. Libentius crediderim Graeco usum vocabulo, sicuti quoque Ambrosius in *Hexahemero conium* dixit, quod ex Basi-
liano paris argumenti libro et tituli *cicutam* Rufinus transtulit. Lubricus autem sane lapsus in *aconitum* de *conio*.

: 62 :

*Qui sint arietini testiculi,
qui digitus medicus apud Tullium*

1   Cicero *Ad Herennium* libro tertio, de memoriae artificio tractans,
ita imaginem quandam instruit: 'Et reum,' inquit, 'ad lectum eius
statuemus, dextra poculum, sinistra tabulas, medico testiculos
arietinos tenentem.' Quo loco video hesitare litteratores quospiam
etiam haud extremae sortis, quid sit quod legimus, 'medico testiculos arietinos tenentem.'

that of poison. In the end, poison is overcome by wine, not wine by poison."[690] But in the books of his *Table Talk*, Plutarch, too, says almost the same about hemlock as does Pliny.[691]

Then Macrobius tried to express this passage virtually verba- 2 tim, just as he did very many others, in his *Saturnalia*,[692] although in all the codices of Macrobius that I have so far seen, the word *aconitum* ("poison") is found rather than *cicuta* ("hemlock"), just as [was the case] even in the old codex belonging to Bernardo Michelozzi, a well-read man and our friend. But I think this is a fault of the exemplars, for I am not persuaded that Macrobius was so uneducated that what in Greek is *conion* he would translate [into Latin] as *aconitum*. I would more readily believe that he used the Greek word, just as Ambrose, too, in his *Hexaemeron*, said *conium*, which Rufinus translated as *cicuta* from Basil's book with the same subject and title.[693] It is certainly an easy error to go from *conium* to *aconitum*.

: 62 :

What arietini testiculi *are,*
and what the "doctor finger" is in Cicero

In dealing with the art of memory in the third book of his *To He-* 1
rennius, Cicero constructs a particular image, as follows: "And let us stand the defendant beside his bed, holding in his right hand a cup and in his left writing tablets, and his *arietini testiculi* (ram's testicles) with his 'doctor.'"[694] Regarding this passage I see that some school teachers, even the better ones, hesitate over "holding his ram's testicles with his 'doctor.'"

2   Medicus autem unus e digitis quinque vocatur, hoc est, ut arbitror, minimo proximus. Porphyrio enim super Horatianum illud ex ultimo sermone:

> Qui siquid forte lateret,
> Indice monstraret digito,

sic ait: 'Hoc ideo, quia certis nominibus singuli digiti appellabantur, et sunt haec nomina: pollex, index, famosus, medicus, minimus.' Quidam vero e Graecis, credo, iunioribus nomina digitorum ῥωμαιστί sic esse scribit: ἀντίχειρ, δεικτικός, ἰατρός, δακτυλιώτης, ὠτίτης, ut si dicas pollex, index, medicus, anularis, auricularis. Quod equidem nec affirmo, nec refello. Tantum notandum medicum ab eo dictum, qui sit medius, aut famosus, non qui minimo proximus. Apud ipsos autem leguntur haec nomina, ἀντίχειρ, λιχανός, σφακελός, ἐπιβάτης, μύωψ.

3   De testiculis autem arietinis legis in vocabulo *scortes* in Festi compendio sic: 'Scortes, idest pelles testium arietinorum, ab eisdem pellibus dicti.' Tantum apud Festum. Sed enim Pedianus sportas, sportulas, sportellas nummum esse ait receptacula, et saccos, sacculos, saccellos, et crumenas et vellera[211] et scorteas et manticas et marsippia.

4   Ut nihil sit dubium quin e digito eo, qui sit minimo proximus, suspensas haberi velit scorteas, hoc est, e testibus arietinis pelliceas crumenas.

One of the five fingers is, however, called the "doctor," that is, I 2
think, the one next to the smallest finger. For Porphyrio on this
passage from Horace's last satire,

> If anything should perhaps escape notice,
> He would point to it with his index finger,[695]

says the following: "This is the case because the individual fingers
were called by specific names, and these names are the thumb,
index, notorious, doctor, and little fingers."[696] Indeed, one of the
younger Greeks, I believe, writes that in the Romaic language[697]
the names of the fingers are as follows: the opposing [to the fingers, i.e., the thumb], the pointer, the doctor, the ring finger, and
the ear finger — as if to call them [in Latin] the thumb, index, doctor, ring, and ear fingers. This I neither affirm nor deny. It must
only be noted that he calls the middle finger or "notorious" the
doctor, not the one next to the little finger. Among them [the
Greeks], moreover, these names are read: the opposing, the licking
finger, the bundle, the passenger, and the gadfly.

On the other hand, you may read about ram's testicles in Fes- 3
tus's compendium under the word *scortes* ("leather bags"), as follows: "Leather bags, that is, skins made of ram's testes, named
from the same skins." So much is in Festus.[698] But [Asconius]
Pedianus says that baskets, little baskets, and miniature baskets
are receptacles for coins, as are sacks, little sacks, miniature sacks,
purses, hides, skins, knapsacks, and pouches.[699]

So there is no doubt that it is by the finger next to the little 4
finger that he intends for the purse to be held suspended, that is,
the leather sack made from ram's testicles.

: 63 :

Aliter citari a Varrone Terenti verba quam aut in
exemplaribus habeatur aut Donatus agnoverit

1   Marcus Varro in libris *De lingua Latina* sic ait: 'Apud Terentium
scortatur, potat, olet unguenta de meo. Scotari est saepius meretri-
culam ducere.' Sic ille, ac deinceps alia in eam sententiam. Ceterum Terentiani omnes ad unum codices non *scortatur* habent, ut
Varro legit, sed *obsonat*. Locus autem in *Adelphis* est:

Obsonat, potat, olet unguenta de meo,

quam lectionem etiam Donatus agnoscit.

2   Quid hic igitur dicemus? Mendumne esse in Terentianis omnibus codicibus, an (quod vix credere ausim) memoriola vacillasse
Varronem quoque ipsum, πολυγραφότατον a Cicerone appellatum, sicuti eundem Ciceronem Gellius deprehendit? Ut fateamur
etiam maximis quibusque ingeniis officere incuriam nonnunquam,
prodesse usquequaque diligentiam.

: 63 :

Words of Terence's are cited differently by Varro than either is
contained in the manuscripts or Donatus read them

In his books *On the Latin Language*, Marcus Varro says the follow- 1
ing: "In the text of Terence [we read] 'he whores, he drinks, he
reeks of perfumes at my expense.' 'To whore' is to engage prosti-
tutes frequently."[700] Thus Varro, and then other words to that effect. Yet not one of the codices of Terence has *scortatur* ("he
whores"), as Varro reads, but rather *obsonat* ("he feasts"). Moreover, the passage in the *Brothers* is:

He feasts, he drinks, he reeks of perfumes at my expense,[701]

a reading that Donatus, too, recognizes.[702]

What, then, are we to say here? That there is an error in all the 2
codices of Terence, or (a thing I would hardly dare to believe) that
Varro himself also suffered from a small lapse of memory, a man
whom Cicero called a "polygraph,"[703] just as Gellius discovered
Cicero to have done?[704] Hence we admit carelessness sometimes
blocks even the greatest geniuses, but that care is wholly beneficial.[705]

: 64 :

Declarati versus[212] Ausoni sed et Ovidi
super choliambo aut scazonte

1 Ausoni poetae sunt trimetri versus ita:

Cui subiugabo de molarum ambagibus,
Qui machinali saxa volvunt pondere
Tripedes caballos, terga ruptos verbere.

Quid hic eum significare opinemur? Nempe, ut arbitror, versus illos qui choliambi vel scazontes appellantur, ut si dixeris claudicantes, quales apud Persium in principio, qualis ille item Martialis, ab ipso nominatim citatus:

Apollinarem conveni, meum scazon.

Est enim scazon trimeter iambicus, senis et ipse constans pedibus, sicuti rectus iambicus, hoc uno[213] dispar, ut etiam scribit Hephestion, quod rectus postremam sedem iambo pyrrhichiove occupat, in[214] antepenultima cunctos accipit pedes quorum modo id metrum sit capax, circa syllabarum quantitates indifferens. Sed claudus hic iambicus clausulam postulat spondiacam vel trochaicam prorsus, penultimum autem pedem, non dissyllabum modo, sed iambum plane vel spondeum. Quod vero ait Hephestion, spondeum recipi sede quinta choliambi, nunquam equidem apud Latinos invenire me commemini. Ipse[215] versiculum hunc adducit Graecum:

Ἐπ' ἄκρον ἕλκων ὥσπερ ἄλλαντα ψύχων.

Et Quintilianus Aristides Graecus auctor in libro *De musica* super iambico loquens trimetro: 'Claudum fieri,' ait, 'quando in extremo

: 64 :

*Verses of Ausonius, and also of Ovid, are clarified
concerning choliamb and scazon*

The following are trimeter lines by the poet Ausonius: 1

To which I shall hitch three-footed horses, taken from
The revolutions of the mill, which turn the millstones
With the weight of the mechanism, their backs abraded by
    flogging.⁷⁰⁶

What are we to suppose that he means here? Surely, I think, the
verses that are called choliambs or scazons, as if you were to say
limping ones, such as those at the beginning of Persius, just like
that of Martial, expressly cited by him:

Greet Apollinaris, my scazon.⁷⁰⁷

For a scazon is an iambic trimeter consisting of six feet each, just
like a proper iamb but different in this one respect, as Hephaestion also writes, that a proper iambic trimeter fills its last place
with an iamb or a *pyrrhichius*,⁷⁰⁸ and admits in the antepenult all
feet which that meter accommodates, without reference to the
quantities of syllables.⁷⁰⁹ But this limping iamb absolutely requires
a spondaic or trochaic closure. Furthermore, it requires that the
penultimate foot not only be disyllabic but definitely an iamb or a
spondee. But I never recall finding among Latin poets what Hephaestion describes, namely that a spondee is accepted in the fifth
position of a choliamb.⁷¹⁰ He cites this Greek verse:

Pulling it up on end as if cooling a sausage.⁷¹¹

In addition, in discussing the iambic trimeter in his book *On Music*, the Greek author Aristides Quintilianus says: "It becomes

spondeum recipit.' Denique Ovidius quoque in priore libro *De amorum remediis* de utroque iambo sic scribit:

> Liber in adversos hostes stringatur iambus,
> Seu celer, extremum seu trahit ille pedem.

2   Sunt autem utrique ad maledicentiam libertatemque facti, truces et cruenti. Quare ob id stringendos etiam ait Ovidius in adversos hostes. Dionysius item Halicarnasseus in libro *De interpretatione* vehemens aut acre metrum esse choliambos ait. Idemque mox Hipponacten, cum lacessere conviciis inimicos vellet, infregisse ait de industria metrum ac pro recto claudum fecisse et abnumerum, hoc est acrimoniae consentaneum convicioque. Nam sicuti dissoluta figura parat acrimoniam, sic (ut ille inquit) dissoluta compositio.

3   Quare *caballos* utique choliambos eos Ausonius nominat, quorum tralationem duxerat ab essedo et vehiculo cui caballi adiunguntur, et ut tardos ostenderet, 'de molarum ambagibus' captos dicit. Praetereaque 'terga ruptos verbere' tum eosdem 'tripedes' vocavit, quia Graece trimetri, quamvis senos habeant pedes, bini[216] quique pro singulis videntur in iambicis capi. 'Qui machinali saxa volvant pondere' propterea dixit, vel ut molas describeret quas versare ipsos indicaverat, vel ut eos violentos ferocesque ostenderet allegoricos, quasi qui lapides ingentes torquent et volvunt in hostem.

4   De trimetro item utroque sic idem Ausonius alibi Graeco versiculo:

> Εἰλιπόδην σκάζοντα καὶ οὐ σκάζοντα τρίμετρον.

limping when it takes a spondee at the end."[712] Finally, in his first book *On the Remedies for Love*, Ovid, too, writes about both types of iamb as follows:

Let an outspoken iamb be drawn against opposing enemies,
    Whether it is quick or drags its final foot.[713]

Moreover, both are made for insult and unbridled speech, grim 2 and gory. Hence Ovid says that they must be drawn against opposing enemies. In his book *On Interpretation*, Dionysius of Halicarnassus likewise says that choliambs are a violent or bitter meter.[714] The same author then says that when Hipponax wanted to provoke his enemies with abuse, he purposely broke the meter and instead of a proper verse he made it limping and lopsided, that is, consistent with acrimony and abuse.[715] For just as a louche appearance paves the way for acrimony, so too does (as he says) a loose composition.

Accordingly, Ausonius labels those choliambs "horses," the met- 3 aphor for which he drew from a chariot and cart to which horses are hitched, and in order to present them as slow, he says they were taken "from the revolutions of the mill." Besides, he described them as having "backs abraded by flogging" and being "three-footed" because in Greek, even though the trimeters have six feet each, they seem to be taken two each instead of one by one in their iambic verses. He said, "those who turn the millstones with heavy machinery," either in order to describe the millstones, which he had indicated they were turning, or in order to show them allegorically to be violent and ferocious, like those who hurl and roll huge rocks at the enemy.

Ausonius likewise speaks of both trimeters elsewhere in a 4 Greek verse in this fashion:

A limping trimeter with shambling gait and a nonlimping
    one.[716]

Quod Latine sic vertas:

Loripedem scazonta et non scazonta trimetrum.

5   De scazontibus eisdem sic in epistola quapiam ex libro quinto apud iuniorem Plinium: 'Proinde aut rumpe moras aut cave ne eosdem istos libellos, quos tibi hendecasyllabi nostri blanditiis elicere non potuerunt, convicio scazontes extorqueant.'

: 65 :

Qui sit habitus in statuis pacificator,
deque eo sentire Statium in prima silva

1   Statius in silvula prima, quae in equum maximum scripta est:

Iuvat ora tueri
Mixta notis belli placidamque gerentia pacem.

Tum idem:

Dextra vetat pugnas.

Quem locum Domitius sic enarrat: '*Dextra vetat pugnas,* hoc est inermis est in statua, vel ad dextram est templum Pacis, quod non placet,' inquit. Ceterum sicuti placet hic sensus, dextra vetari pugnas, quia sit inermis, aut item quod de templo ipso traditur Pacis, quamquam nec auctori quidem placet suo, feram non moleste scilicet huic sententiam meam non probari.

This you may translate into Latin as:

A bowlegged scazon and a nonscazon trimeter.

Regarding the same scazons, [we find] as follows in a letter 5
from the fifth book of Pliny the Younger: "So then, either put an
end to the delays or beware lest my scazons abusively extort from
you the same little books of yours that my hendecasyllables could
not coax you to surrender by flattery."[717]

: 65 :

*What the peacemaking attitude is in statues; and that
Statius had this in mind in his first* silva

Statius, in his precious first *silva*, which was written for a large 1
horse, says:

It is a delight to gaze upon faces that show placid peace
blended with the scars of war.[718]

Then he goes on:

His right hand prohibits battles.[719]

Domizio [Calderini] explains the passage this way: "*His right hand
prohibits battles*, that is, he is unarmed in the statue, or else the
temple of Peace is to his right, which finds no favor." But just as
this interpretation finds favor, that battles are forbidden by his
right hand, since it is unarmed, or likewise what is reported about
the temple of Peace itself, although this finds no favor with its
own author, I would not be annoyed that my opinion fails to meet
with his [Calderini's] approval.

2   Nam ego notari habitum puto qui pacificator in statuis diceretur. De quo ita legimus apud Quintilianum:

> Fit et ille habitus qui esse in statuis pacificator solet, qui inclinato in humerum dextrum capite, brachioque ab aure protenso, manum infesto pollice protendit, qui quidem maxime placet iis qui se dicere sublata manu iactant.

Hactenus Quintilianus.

3   Extat autem adhuc pacificatore habitu (ni fallor) statua illa Romae, quae pro aede Lateranensi inter prima urbis spectacula convisitur.

: 66 :

Locus in Plauti Mustelaria,[217] *et item alter in* Milite, *vindicati a vitio*

1   In *Mustelaria* Plauti locus est mendose scriptus plerisque codicibus, ad hunc sane modum:

> Viden ornamenta in foribus? — Video. — Specta quam[218] arte dormiunt. —
> Dormiunt? — Ille quidem ut convenit volui dicere.

Sed cum de his neque sensus eliciatur ullus et festivum Plauti dictum vitio librariorum pereat, faciam (ut arbitror) operaepretium, si scripturam incolumem de Plautino codice citato a nobis iterum reposuero. Est autem prorsus haec:

I think the attitude is being noted that in statues was called "the   2
peacemaker." Regarding this we read the following in Quintilian:

> That attitude is struck that in statues is wont to be called
> "the peacemaker," which, with the head tilted toward the
> right shoulder and the arm stretched out at ear level, extends
> the arm with the thumb raised. This posture is especially
> favored by those who boast that they speak with their hand
> raised.[720]

Thus Quintilian.

Moreover, there still exists at Rome (unless I am mistaken) a   3
statue in the attitude of the peacemaker, which is seen among the
finest spectacles of the city in front of the Lateran temple.[721]

: 66 :

A passage in Plautus's Haunted House, *and likewise*
another one in his Soldier, *both freed from error*

There is a passage in Plautus's *Haunted House* that is written defec-   1
tively in many codices, in this way:

> Do you see the fastenings on the doors? — I see them. — See
>   how soundly they sleep. —
> Are they sleeping? — Yes, that one, as is fitting, I meant to
>   say.[722]

But since no sense at all can be elicited from them and the Plautine wit is lost through the copyists' fault, it would (I think) be
worthwhile for me to restore the pristine text from a Plautine codex that is being cited by me for a second time.[723] Here it is in
fact:

Viden coagmenta in foribus? — Video. — Specta quam arte
dormiunt. —
Dormiunt? — Illud quidem ut connivent volui dicere.[219]

Nam quia connivere dicuntur qui dormitant, ut apud Cinnam
lectus est versiculus:

Iam gravis ingenti connivere pupula somno,

propterea cum in foribus iuncturas esse minime laxas, id est arta
coagmenta[220] sunt, Tranio servus ostenderet, dormire eas ridicule
prius, dein etiam connivere iocul ariter dicit, ex oculis dormitan-
tium ducta metaphora.

2   Similiter corrigendum puto locum alterum ex Plautino *Milite*,
qui sic vitiose legitur:

Mirus oleo victitare te tam vili tritico.
— Quid iam? — Quia lusciosus. — Verbero, edepol tu quidem
Caecus, non lusciosus.

Nam cum nullus hinc elici sensus queat, legendum arbitror sic:

Mirust lolio victitare te, tam vili tritico,

siquidem hoc ubique idem apud Plautum *mirust* pro *mirum est* reperies. Atqui lolio vitiari oculos etiam ait Ovidius *Fastorum* primo:

Et careant loliis oculos vitiantibus agri.

Notat id Fulgentius quoque non contemnendus grammaticus.
Quare cum Sceledrus servus lusciosum vitiatisque oculis conser-
vum Palaestrionem velit significare, mirum esse ait victitare eum

> Do you see the fastenings on the doors? — I see them. — See
> how soundly they sleep. —
> Are they sleeping? — I meant to say this: they've got their eyes
> closed.

For since sleepers are said to have their eyes closed, as this line
reads in Cinna:

> The eye is already closing, heavy with overwhelming sleep,[724]

for that reason, when the slave Tranio shows that the bolts on the
doors are not loose, i.e., the fastenings are tight, he first facetiously
says that they are asleep, then he humorously adds that they have
their eyes closed, a metaphor drawn from sleepers' eyes.

In similar fashion, a second passage, one in Plautus's *Soldier*,   2
must, I think, be corrected, which reads erroneously as follows:

> It is surprising that you live on olive oil, with wheat so cheap.
> — Why so? — Because you are poor-sighted. — Egads, you
> rascal, indeed you're
> Blind, not just poor-sighted.[725]

For since no sense can be teased out of this, I think one must read
as follows:

> It is surprising that you live on darnel, with wheat so cheap.

In fact, you will find this same *mirust* throughout the works of
Plautus in place of *mirum est* ("it is surprising"). In the first book
of his *Fasti*, Ovid also says that darnel corrupts the eyes:

> And let the fields be free of the darnel grass that corrupts
> the eyes.[726]

Fulgentius, too, a grammarian not to be despised, notes this.[727]
And so when the slave Sceledrus wishes to indicate that a fellow
slave, Palaestrio, is poor-sighted and has flawed vision, he says it is

lolio, cum sit ipsum triticum tam vile, lolio autem victitare eum colligere se vel inde affirmat illudens quod sit lusciosus. Lusciosi porro seu luscicii qui vitium hoc habent oculorum, ut clarius vesperi quam meridie cernant.

: 67 :

Cornicem videri apud veteres Concordiae symbolum, non, ut omnes apud Iuvenalem existimant, ciconiam

1 Pro comperto iam habetur, ciconiam denique esse qua Concordiae repraesentaretur apud priscos effigies, atque ita versiculum Iuvenalis omnes interpretantur:

Quaeque salutato crepitat Concordia nido.

De eo tamen nullum omnino afferunt testimonium quo[221] auctoritatis adminiculo sustentetur.

2 Ego cornicem magis accipio, ductus Heliani Graeci scriptoris testimonio, qui libro *De animalibus* tertio de hac avi sic propemodum scribit:

Cornices, inquit, inter se fidissimae sunt, et cum societatem coierint, maximo se opere diligunt. Neque id genus animalia videat quispiam licenter misceri et temere. Quin hoc quoque dictitant qui res istiusmodi callent, altera extincta, comparem viduam degere. Ceterum id quoque audio, veteres in nuptiis post Hymenaeum cornicem invocare, signumque id concordiae dare iis consuesse, qui liberum quaerendorum

surprising that he lives on darnel, when wheat itself is so cheap, and moreover he asserts that he infers that he lives on darnel from that fact, playing upon his having poor sight. Poor-sighted or partly blind persons are those who have this ocular defect, that they see more clearly in the evening than at midday.

: 67 :

The crow seems to be the symbol of Concord among the ancients, not the stork, as all suppose to be the case in Juvenal

It is considered an established fact that the image of Concord is represented among the ancients by the stork, and that is the way everyone interprets Juvenal's line:

The Concord that rustles when its nest is hailed.[728]

They adduce, however, no testimony at all to support this point with the aid of authority.[729]

I take this, instead, to be the crow, based on the testimony of the Greek writer Aelian, who, in the third book of his *On Animals*, writes about this bird approximately as follows:

Crows are extremely faithful to one another, and when they mate, they love one another tremendously. And no one would see this species of animal mate promiscuously and casually. As a matter of fact, ornithologists regularly assert that when one dies, the other spends the rest of its life as a widow or widower. I hear, too, that the ancients used to invoke the crow after the bridal song [was sung] at weddings, and were in the habit of giving this as a sign of concord to those who were joined together for the sake of having

gratia convenissent. Tum qui sedes avium et volatus obser-
vant inauspicatum esse captantibus auguria dicunt unius tantum cornicis obsequium.

Sic ille. Sed et in nomismatis aureis duobus Faustinae Augustae
manifestam prorsus imagunculam nuper mihi Laurentius Medices
ostendit cum titulo ipso concordiae.

: 68 :

Versus ex Callimacho super crinibus reginae Berenices,
atque inde mendum ex
Catulli exemptum versiculo

1 Elegiam Callimachi de crinibus Berenices inter sidera receptis
mira elegantia vertit in Latinam linguam nobilis poeta Catullus,
quamvis pleraque sint in ea corrupta mendosaque et temere scripta
librariorum inscitia. Sed argumentum ipsius partim apud Hygi-
nium Latinum auctorem, partim etiam apud Theonem neque non
Achillem quoque, Graecos Arati enarratores, invenias, Graeca sane
ipsa Callimachi elegia non extat ad nos, quantum compererim, sed
aetate intercidit.

2 Apud Theonem tamen, Arati eiusdem interpretem, principium
illius tale reperio:

Ἦ με Κόνων ἔβλεψεν ἐν ἠέρι τὸν Βερενίκης
Βόστρυχον, ἢ κείνη πᾶσιν ἔθηκε θεοῖς.

Praetereaque in commentariis super Apollonium Rhodium ex
Lucilio[222] Tarrhaeo, Sophocle,[223] ac Theone collectis, ubi de

children. Then those who observe the nests and flight of birds say that the sight of a solitary crow is inauspicious for those taking auguries.[730]

Thus Aelian. But Lorenzo de' Medici recently showed me a quite clear image of Faustina Augusta on two gold coins with the very legend, Concord.[731]

: 68 :

Verses from Callimachus about the lock of Queen Berenice;
and from that source an error is removed
from a line of Catullus

The famous poet Catullus translated into the Latin language with   1
extraordinary elegance an elegy by Callimachus about a lock of
Berenice that was welcomed among the stars, even though in it
there are many corrupt, faulty, and carelessly written elements due
to scribal ignorance.[732] But although you may find its content
partly in the Latin author Hyginus, partly also in Theon [of Alex-
andria] and Achilles [Tatius] as well, the Greek expounders of
Aratus, Callimachus's Greek elegy itself has not come down to us,
so far as I have determined, but is lost to the ages.[733]

Nonetheless, in the writings of Theon, the interpreter of the   2
same Aratus, I find its opening lines as follows:

> Either Conon caught sight of me, Berenice's lock,
> In the heavens, or she dedicated me to all the gods.[734]

In addition, in the commentaries on Apollonius of Rhodes compiled from Lucillus Tarrhaeus, Sophocles, and Theon, where it

Chalybibus agitur libro secundo, sic adeo est invenire: μέμνηται αὐτῶν καὶ Καλλίμαχος 'Χαλύβων ὡς ἀπόλοιτο γένος²²⁴ τηλόθεν ἀντέλλοντα κακὸν φυτὸν οἵ μιν ἔφηναν.'

3   Ex quo versiculum sic illum legendum quis dubitet: 'Iuppiter ut Chalybon omne genus pereat,' ut sit *Chalybon* Graece dictum? Atque hoc inscite legunt quidam *Telorum,* vulgatissimi codices *celitum* retinent contra etiam metri rationem. Sed hanc scio nostram observationem iam pridem esse pervulgatam, quam tamen a nobis ortam vel ille ipse scit qui vulgavit libenterque etiam fatetur, vir doctissimus undecumque, Picus.

: 69 :

Oarion *sinceriter esse apud Catullum,*
quod Aorion *isti legunt qui bonos violant libros*

In²²⁵ elegia eadem Catulli ex Callimacho *Oarion* legitur pro eo quod sit *Orion.* Quam quoniam integram adhuc inviolatamque dictionem nonnulli temere attentare iam incipiunt, contra hanc sinistram imperitorum audaciam standum mihi est omni (quod aiunt) pede, vel Callimachi eiusdem auctoritate, qui sic in hymno ipso in Dianam etiam nunc extante ait:

Οὐδὲ γὰρ ᾽Ὦτος
Οὐδὲ μὲν 'Ωαρίων ἀγαθὸν γάμον ἐμνήστευσαν.

Sed et Nicander *Theriacon* libro consimiliter:

Βοιωτῷ²²⁶ τεύχουσα κακὸν μόρον 'Ωαρίωνι.

deals in Book 2 with the Chalybes,[735] one may find this: "Callimachus, too, mentioned them: 'so that the race of the Chalybes might die, rising from afar they revealed to him a baneful creature.'"[736]

On this basis, who would doubt that this line must be read as 3
follows, "Jupiter, in order that the entire race of the Chalybes perish," so that *Chalybon* was said in Greek?[737] And though certain ones read this ignorantly as *Telorum*, the most common codices retain *celitum*, even contrary to meter. But I know this observation of mine has long since been widely circulated, which he himself who gave it currency knows and even gladly admits to have originated with me, that most learned man anywhere, [Giovanni] Pico [della Mirandola].

: 69 :

Oarion is the true reading in Catullus, which those who do
violence to good books read as Aorion

In the same elegy of Catullus's from Callimachus, *Oarion* is read for *Orion*.[738] Seeing that some are now beginning thoughtlessly to attack a reading that is still intact and whole, I must put my foot down — both of them! (as the saying goes[739]) — against this wrongheaded brazenness of ignoramuses, by the authority of the same Callimachus, who, in his *Hymn to Diana* — which is still extant — says:

> For neither Otus
> Nor Oarion courted a good marriage.[740]

And similarly Nicander, in his book *Theriaca*:

> Causing a miserable death for the Boeotian Oarion.[741]

Et Pindarus in *Isthmiis*:

Οὐ γὰρ φύσιν Ὠαριωνείαν ἔλαχεν.

Et alibi:

Ὀρειᾶν Πελειάδων μὴ τηλόθι Ὠαρίωνα[227] νεῖσθαι.

Quare putat Eustathius quinto in *Odysseam* commentario, παρὰ τὸ ὀαρίζειν appellatum. Non igitur *Aorion* sed *Oarion* vera lectio.

: 70 :

Cuius in Bruti nomismate symbolum sint pileus et pugiones

Siquis nomisma Bruti reperiat ipsius celatum imagine praetereaque pileo et duobus pugiunculis, ne diutius in explicanda ratione causaque laboret, legat *Historiarum* Dionis librum XLVII. 'Nam ex his,' inquit, 'Brutus significabat ab se et Cassio patriam liberatam.' Sed enim pileum gestari ab his solitum qui libertatem nacti, vulgatius manifestiusque quam ut sit auctoritatibus confirmandum.

CHAPTER 70

And Pindar, in his *Isthmian Odes*:

> For he was not born with the physique of Oarion.[742]

And elsewhere:

> To go to Oarion, not far from the mountain-dwelling
> Peleiades.[743]

Hence in his fifth commentary on the *Odyssey*, Eustathius thinks
that he was named from conversation (*oarizein*).[744] Therefore, the
true reading is not *Aorion* but *Oarion*.[745]

: 70 :

What the skullcap and daggers symbolize on a coin of Brutus

If anyone should find a coin of Brutus engraved with an image of
him and besides a skullcap and two small daggers,[746] lest he toil
for a long time trying to explain the reason and cause, let him read
Book 47 of Dio's *Histories*: "For by these," he says, "Brutus indicated that he and Cassius had liberated their homeland."[747] For
indeed the skullcap used to be worn by those who had obtained
their freedom [i.e., former slaves], a point too common and obvious to require confirmation by authorities.

: 71 :

Quaepiam vulgo legi adhuc apud Maronem
contra regulam contraque rationem metri

1   Pudet referre quam manifestum sed nondum tamen a quoquam
(quod sciam) nisi nobis indicibus animadversum mendum Vergilianis codicibus inoleverit libro *Aeneidos* octavo:

Quod fieri ferro liquidove potestur electro.

Ceterum in volumine illo quod est in intima Vaticana bibliotheca
mire vetustum et grandibus characteribus perscriptum non *potestur*
offendas, sed *potest* usitatius verbum. Quae etiam verior esse lectio
vel inde probatur quod *electrum* ubique prima syllaba longa tam
apud Graecos ponitur quam apud nostros. Neque quidquam interpretes super verbo *potestur* alioqui novo inusitatoque loquuntur.
Haud tamen praeterit me, veteres hoc quoque protulisse, sicut
Pacuvium in *Chryse*, sicut etiam Lucretium, quemadmodum et *po-*
teratur lectum a Nonio Marcello est in Caecilianis A*nnalibus*.

2   Sed et alter locus itidem vitio consimili laborat apud eundem
poetam:

Scaeptra Palatini sedemque petivit Evandri,

cum in volumine eodem non *petivit* trisyllabum, sed *petit* disylla-
bum[228] scriptum inveniatur. Quod et metri vis cogit, alioqui prima
syllaba *Evandri* contra omnem vel rationem vel consuetudinem
brevis foret. Est vero in utroque versu spondeus quinta sede. In
verbo autem *petit* syllaba ipsa posterior, vel quia sit in fine vel quia

: 71 :

Some things are still commonly read in Vergil
contrary to rule and meter

It is a shame to report that so evident an error, but one nonethe- 1
less not yet noticed by anyone (that I know of) except when I have
pointed it out, has developed in the codices of Vergil, in the eighth
book of the *Aeneid*:

> Whatever can (*potestur*) be done with iron or liquid
> electrum.[748]

Yet in the volume in the inner Vatican library that is amazingly
ancient and written in capital letters,[749] you encounter not *potestur*,
but the more usual verb *potest*. That this is also the more accurate
reading is proven by the fact that everywhere, both among the
Greeks and us Latins, *electrum* is written with a long first syllable.
And no interpreters say anything about the verb *potestur*, which is
new and unusual. Nonetheless, it hardly escapes my notice that
the ancients have employed this too, for instance, Pacuvius in his
Chryses as well as Lucretius, just as *poteratur* was read by Nonius
Marcellus in the *Annals* of Caecilius.[750]

But another passage by the same poet likewise suffers from a 2
similar corruption:

> He [Aeneas] made for (*petivit*) the realm of the Palatine and
> the seat of Evander,[751]

although in the same volume not trisyllabic *petivit*, but disyllabic
petit is found to have been written. The force of the meter compels
this, since the first syllable of *Evander* would be short, contrary to
all system and usage. Indeed, in both lines there is a spondee in
the fifth foot. In the word *petit*, the second syllable was rightly

coaluerit una ex duabus, iure producta est. Marcianus autem Capella syllabam docet ubique esse communem quae desinat in *t* litteram, sicut in illo cernimus Vergili:

Nam tibi, Thymbre, caput Evandrius abstulit ensis.

: 72 :

De philyra et lemniscatis coronis

1 Philyra quid sit video nesciri a plerisque, perverseque etiam a nonnullis interpretibus accipi. Nam vocabulo eo sic utitur Horatius in primo *Carminum:*

Displicent nexae philyra coronae.

Et Ovidius item quinto *Fastorum:*

Ebrius incinctus philyra conviva capillos
Saltat,

quo apparet usum ipsius apud veteres in coronamentis fuisse percelebrem.

2 Iam primum igitur si conferas quae super *philyra* Theophrastus in tertio *De plantis* quaeve item Plinius in decimosexto *Naturalis historiae* narrant, facile nimirum cognosces eandem apud nos esse *tiliam* quae *philyra* sit apud Graecos. Ac sic etiam Theodorus Gaza quantumvis homo doctus et diligens interpretatur. Porro autem tuniculae etiam quaedam ex libro ipso tiliae arboris vel ad eius imitamentum factae, quibus aut lemnisci fierent, idest fasciolae de

lengthened, whether because it is at the end or because a single syllable has coalesced from two. Furthermore, Martianus Capella teaches that a syllable that ends in the letter *t* is common everywhere,[752] as we see in this line of Vergil's [regarding the word *caput*]:

For Evander's sword cuts away your head (*caput*), Thymber.[753]

: 72 :

On lime-tree bark and garlands decorated with ribbons

I see that most people do not know what lime-tree bark is, and it is even wrongly understood by some commentators. For in the first book of his *Odes* Horace uses the word this way:

Garlands woven out of lime-tree bark are displeasing.[754]

And Ovid likewise says in Book 5 of his *Fasti*:

The drunken reveler dances about with his hair bound with [A garland of] lime-tree bark.[755]

From this it appears that its use in making garlands was renowned among the ancients.

Now then, in the first place, if you compare what Theophrastus says about the lime tree (*philyra*) in Book 3 *On Plants*, or likewise what Pliny says in Book 16 of his *Natural History*, you will, of course, easily recognize that among us *tilia* is the same as *philyra* among the Greeks.[756] So, too, Theodore Gaza, as learned and careful a man as ever was, translates it.[757] On the other hand, certain thin coverings made from the bark of the lime tree or in imitation of it, from which either *lemnisci* were made, that is, ribbons

coronis pendulae, aut libelli, Graeco vocabulo peculiariter appellatae *philyrae*. Testatur partem ex his eodem libro Plinius his versibus:

> Inter corticem et lignum tenues tunicas multiplici membrana,
> e quibus vincula tiliae vocantur tenuissimaque eorum[229]
> philyrae, coronarum lemniscis celebres, antiquorum honore.

Rursusque idem libro primo atque vigesimo de lemniscis et phily-
ris ita meminit:

> Crassus Dives primus argento auroque folia imitatus ludis
> suis coronas dedit. Accesserunt quoque et lemnisci, quos
> adici ipsarum coronarum honos erat, propter Hetruscos,
> quibus iungi nisi aurei non debebant. Puri diu fuere ii, celare
> eos primus instituit P. Claudius Pulcher, bracteasque etiam
> philyrae dedit.

3   Porro lemniscatas coronas etiam (ni fallor) in nomismatis
Laurenti Medicis identidem videmus, deque his mentio quoque
apud Suetonium, sicuti item a Pompeio Festo lemniscorum vocabulum diligenter exponitur, deque lemniscis itidem nonnihil Tertullianus quoque in libro *De corona militis*. Nicas autem in commentario quem per ordinem litterarum composuit, Graece ille
quidem, sed in hunc ferme intellectum philyram interpretatur:
'Philyra,' inquit, 'planta librum papyro similem habens, ex quo
etiam funes complicant.' Esse autem ductilem philyram lanicii
modo, vel restilem[230] potius, innuit et Tertullianus idem in libello
eo qui *De pallio* inscribitur. Quin Herodianus etiam Graecus auctor olim a nobis in Latinum conversus et Innocentio octavo Ponti-
fici Maximo dedicatus, libro ipso *Historiae* primo mentionem libelli

hanging from a garland, or little books, are specially designated with the Greek word *philyrae*. Pliny attests to some of this in the same book, in these lines:

> Between the bark and wood there are thin covers of multiple layers, ropes of which are called *tiliae* and the thinnest of these, *philyrae*, made famous by the ribbons attached to garlands, an honor bestowed by the ancients.[758]

In his twenty-first book the same author again mentions the decorative ribbons and lime-tree bark in this way:

> Crassus Dives was the first to imitate foliage with silver and gold and bestow the garlands at his games. And they also had decorative ribbons attached to them, which increased the honor of the garlands themselves, in the style of the Etruscans, for whom no ribbons were to be added except gold ones. For a long time these ribbons were unadorned; Publius Claudius Pulcher was the first to begin to cover them, and he even added gold leaf to the lime-tree bark (*philyra*).[759]

Furthermore, we also see ribboned garlands (unless I am mistaken) on coin after coin in Lorenzo de' Medici's collection,[760] and mention of them is made in Suetonius as well, just as likewise Pompeius Festus exactingly explains the word "ribbons," and in the same way Tertullian also has something about ribbons in his book *On the Soldier's Garland*.[761] Moreover, in the book he organized alphabetically, Nicas interprets *philyra* in Greek, but in this general sense: "*Philyra* is a plant that has a bark similar to papyrus, from which ropes are also braided."[762] In addition, the same Tertullian in his little book entitled *On the Pallium* also hints that a lime-bark ribbon is malleable like wool, or rather is rope-like.[763] In fact, the Greek writer Herodian, too, whom I once translated into Latin and dedicated to Pope Innocent VIII, in the first book of his *His-*

3

facit e philyra tenuissima utroque versum replicabili. Sed et Capella Marcianus libro *De Philologiae nuptiis* secundo:

> Cernere erat, inquit, qui libri, quantaque volumina, quot[231] linguarum opera ex ore virginis defluebant. Alia ex papyro quae cedro perlita fuerant videbantur. Alii carbasinis voluminibus implicati libri, ex ovillis multi quoque tergoribus, rari vero in philyrae cortice subnotati.

4   Tum ista quoque Ulpiani verba reperias in titulo *Digestorum* 'De legatis et fideicommissis':

> Librorum appellatione continentur omnia volumina, sive in charta, sive in membrana sint, sive in qualibet alia materia, sed et si in philyra, aut tilia, ut nonnulli conficiunt, aut in alio corio, idem enim erit dicendum.

5   Denique etiam Eustathius in commentario secundo Homericae *Odysseae*, facta prius de nauticis rudentibus mentione, corticem tiliae dicit, quam Graece philyram nominat, plurimam in id genus funium suppeditare materiam. Receptum autem videtur ex eo uti coria quoque singula vel tunicas aut membranulas etiam materiae disparis a tilia philyras vocent aut philuras, *y* Graeca in *u* commutata verteri et pervulgata Latinorum consuetudine, sicuti de papyro agens Plinius libro XIII: 'Praeparantur ex eo, inquit, chartae divisae acu in praetenues sed quam latissimas philuras.' Nam illud utique ad haec enarranda neutiquam pertineat quod idem ait Plinius libro XIIII philyra cocos et polline nimium salem cibis eximere.

tory mentions a little book made out of thin strips of lime bark, folded back and forth in both directions.[764] But in the second book of his *On the Wedding of Philology*, Martianus Capella writes:

> It was possible to observe which books, volumes of what scope, and works in how many languages flowed forth from the maiden's mouth. Some appeared to have been made from papyrus smeared with the tar of cedar.[765] Other books were folded into volumes of cowhide, many also of sheepskin; but a few were written down on lime-tree bark.[766]

Next, you may also discover these words by Ulpian in the *Digests* under the title "On legacies and trusts": 4

> Under the rubric of "books" are contained all volumes whether [they are written] on paper, parchment, or whatever other material, but even if [they are written] on lime bark, or lime wood, as some make them, or on some other covering, it will have to be called by the same name.[767]

And finally, Eustathius, too, in his second commentary on 5
Homer's *Odyssey*, after previously talking about ship's riggings, says that the bark of the lime tree, which he calls *philyra* in Greek, supplies most of the material used for such rope.[768] Moreover, from Eustathius it appears to have been the practice for single hides, coverings, or skins of material unlike limewood to be called *philyrae*, or *philurae*, with the Greek *y* changed to *u* by ancient and common usage of the Latins, just as Pliny says, in Book 13, when discussing papyrus: "Pages are prepared from papyrus when they are divided with a needle into strips (*philurae*) that are very thin but as broad as possible."[769] For the point that the same Pliny makes in Book 14 by no means pertains to explaining these matters, that cooks use lime-tree bark and flour to remove excessive salt from food.[770]

: 73 :

Vocabulum quod est expernata
Catullianis videri exemplaribus reponendum

1   Quod nunc tradituri sumus fortasse a nonnullis ut incertum et
vacillans parumque adhuc exploratum deridebitur et exsibilabitur.
Sed ego mihi de eo dicendum putavi, ne vestigium istud antiquitatis pene iam abolitum, qualecunque sit, extingueretur.

2   Ostendit mihi Romae abhinc quadriennium Manilius Rallus,
Graecus homo sed Latinis litteris adprime excultus, fragmentum
quoddam Sexti Pompei Festi (nam ita erat in titulo) sane quam
vetustum, sed pleraque mutilatum praerosumque a muribus.
Quod me magnopere tenuit, siquidem reliquiae[232] illae qualescunque ex integro ipso volumine superabant quod auctor Festus
composuerat, non ex hoc autem compendiario quod nunc in manibus, coactum violenter et decurtatum, scilicet ab ignobili et indocto
quodam nec isto quoque nomine satis bene de litteris merito.
Nonnullas quoque ex eodem fragmento Pomponius Laetus, vir
antiquitatis et litterarum bonarum consultissimus, sibi pagellas
retinuerat, quas itidem legendas mihi describendasque dedit. Ex
lectione igitur ea suspicatus utique sum verbum me Catullianum
quasi postliminio in suas sedes revocaturum.

3   Siquidem ubi exponitur in hoc compendiario vocabulum *supper-*
nati, quod eos significare ostendit quibus femina sunt succisa in
modum suillarum pernarum, atque ex Ennio versus allegatur:

His pernas succidit iniqua superbia Poeni,

: 73 :

It seems that the word expernata
should be restored to copies of Catullus

What we are now about to relate will perhaps be ridiculed and   1
hissed off the stage by some as being uncertain, feeble, and half-
baked. But I think that I must say something about it, lest a vestige of antiquity, whatever its character, almost already effaced, be
blotted out.

Four years ago in Rome, Manilio Rallo, a Greek but exception-   2
ally cultivated in Latin literature, showed me a certain fragment of
Sextus Pompeius Festus (for so the title states) that, albeit quite
ancient, was mutilated in many places, having been gnawed at the
edges by mice. This powerfully captured my attention, since those
remnants, whatever their character, survived from the original volume that the writer Festus had composed, and not just from this
abridgment that is now in circulation, so violently compressed and
shortened by a certain obscure and ignorant individual who failed
to serve literature well in that respect. Pomponio Leto, a man expert in antiquity as well as belles lettres, had also retained for
himself some precious pages from the same fragment, which he
likewise gave to me to read and copy.[771] And so, on the basis of
this reading I suspected that I could in any case restore a word of
Catullus's, as if by *postliminium*, to its home.[772]

For when the word *suppernati* ("hamstrung") is explained in this   3
abridgment, which shows that it denotes those persons whose
thighs have been cut through like swine hams, and the line from
Ennius is adduced,

The Carthaginians, haughty and wicked, hamstrung them,[773]

hoc utique loco vetus codex circumrosam plane habet expositio-
nem, sed ita tamen ut appareat ex reliquiis[233] litterarum male co-
haerentibus, Catullum quoque post Ennium adduci citarique eum
versiculum, qui nunc mendose sic legitur:

> Infossa Liguri iacet separata securi.

4   Nam ut de carminis residuo nihil mihi arrogem temere, videbar
sane tum syllabatim quaeque olfactans etiam pro explorato afferre
posse *expernata*[234] legendum in eo, non *separata*, quantum ex paucis
illis poteram veluti minutalibus aut ramentis colligere, quantumque etiam vel ex oblitteratis pene iam vestigiis ariolari. Quod
si cui pendere adhuc veri fides videtur, at pendeat equidem malo
quam aut cadat aut iaceat. Nos aliquod in eo certe (nec arbitror
iniuria) ponimus firmamentum.

: 74 :

Historia non illepida super Zeusi pictore et Helena

Zeusis ille pictor Heracleotes adprime nobilis etiam Helenae
pinxit imaginem Crotoniatibus nimisquam laudatam, de qua Cicero in *Rhetoricis contra Hermagoran* luculentissime scripsit. Sed
quod obiter in Heliani libris *Omnifariae historiae* superioribus annis
apud Iohannem Laurentium Venetum, magnae quidem in Pontificia Curia auctoritatis nec minoris tamen in litteris eruditionis, sed
et emunctae naris hominem, Romae legimus, id nobis neutiquam
indignum visum quod hic etiam legeretur:

> Neminem, ait, spectatum Zeusis admittebat, nisi qui manu-
> pretium dedisset.

Ex quo vulgo etiam tunc Helena meretrix vocitata, quoniam
quaestuaria.

in this passage in any case, the old codex has an explanation that has been gnawed at all around, but nonetheless in such a way that it appears from the remnants of the badly cohering letters that Catullus, too, is cited after Ennius, and this line is adduced, which now reads faultily as follows:

> She lies buried, severed (*separata*) by a Ligurian ax.[774]

While making no rash claim about the rest of this poem, by   4
sniffing out each point syllable by syllable, I seem able to assert confidently that *expernata*[775] must be read in this text, not *separata* — so far as I could infer from these few chopped bits or shavings, as it were, and divine from traces now nearly obliterated. But if someone finds that the truth still hangs in the balance, I prefer that it hang in the balance than either fall or be defeated. At any rate, I place a degree of support on this (and, I think, rightly).

: 74 :

A charming story about the painter Zeuxis and Helen

The famous painter Zeuxis of Heraclea painted a highly praised image of Helen for the inhabitants of Croton, about which Cicero wrote brilliantly in his *Rhetorical Treatise against Hermagoras*.[776] But what we read in earlier years in passing in the books of Aelian's *Historical Miscellany*, at the home in Rome of the Venetian Giovanni Lorenzi, a man of influence in the pontifical curia and of no less learning in literature, but also with discriminating taste[777] — this seemed to us worthy to be read here as well:

> Zeuxis used to admit no one to look at [the painting], unless he had paid him a fee.[778]

Hence even then Helen was commonly called a prostitute, since she was for hire.

: 75 :

Emendata vox in Ibide,
simul explicata sententia neutiquam nota hactenus

1 Enarravit Domitius libellum Nasonis *In Ibin,* praefatus ex Apollo-
doro se, Lycophrone, Pausania, Strabone, Apollonio aliisque Graecis etiamque Latinis accepta scribere. Multa in eo commentario
vana ridiculaque confingit et comminiscitur ex tempore commodoque suo, quibus fidem facit aut se frontem penitus amisisse aut
'tam magnum sibi fuisse intervallum inter frontem et linguam'
(sicut ait quidam) 'ut frons comprimere linguam non potuerit.'
Furor est adhuc aliquos tam caecos istius hominis inveniri ama-
tores, ut ad ista nondum suos qualescunque oculos adaperiant.
Furor est profecto, furor, dare occasionem impudentiae ceteris fo-
vendo errores etiam alicuius, quoniam fuerit interdum sententiae
non poenitendae. Sed quid istis facias litterationis, non litteraturae, magistris, qui nullo magis quam talibus nugis supercilia tollunt ut cochleae cornua, quorumque plumbea prorsus ingenia,
quam magis excoluntur, tam magis obrutescunt?[235] At enim ne
penitus ludamus operam, dissimulatis his quos sua facit vilitas
contemnendos, exsequemur reliqua propositi.

2 Mihi igitur ille unus locus inter ceteros movere stomachum solet, qui sic mendose nunc legitur:

Utque loquax in equo est elisus guttur Agenor,
   Sic tibi claudatur pollice vocis iter,

: 75 :

A word corrected in the Ibis,
along with explanation of an idea previously misunderstood

Domizio [Calderini] wrote a commentary on Naso [Ovid]'s little 1
book *Against Ibis*, prefacing it by saying that his writing was based
on materials taken from Apollodorus, Lycophron, Pausanias,
Strabo, Apollonius, and other Greeks, as well as Latin writers.[779]
But in this commentary, he fabricated many groundless, ridiculous
things, and he contrived them on the spur of the moment and at
his own convenience, by which he proves either that he completely
lost his mind or that there was "such a tremendous gap between
his head and tongue" (as someone says) "that his head was unable
to control his tongue."[780] It is madness that some admirers of the
man are still found, so blind that they have not yet opened their
eyes, whatever their sharpness, to these things. It is madness, madness, I say, to give others scope for brazenness, while encouraging
the errors of someone else, since he was in the meantime unrepen-
tant in his attitude. But what will you do with those teachers of
reading and writing—not literature—who raise their eyebrows,
like a snail its horns, at nothing so much as such nonsense and
whose absolutely leaden intellects increasingly collapse the more
they are cultivated. But lest we completely foil our task, we will
ignore those persons whose vulgarity makes them despicable and
pursue our remaining project.

Among all the others a single passage is wont to turn my stom- 2
ach, which nowadays is erroneously read as follows:

And just as Agenor, being garrulous inside the horse, had his
    throat choked,
  So may the path of your voice be closed with a thumb,[781]

ubi sic ait Domitius: 'Agenor lapsu equi inserta ori manu extinctus est.' Itane tandem, vir doctissime? Sed oro te, mi Domiti, Graecum profer, si potes, aut Latinum modo idoneum fabulae istius auctorem, nec recusabo iam quin me non dixerim gregales aut admiratores tui, sed viri quoque litterati quibus hic labor exsudat, pro indoctissimo iam, proque etiam impudentissimo damnent, et quidem cunctis suffragiis, quoniam a te dissentiam.

3   Mihi sane recta esse et emendata scriptura videtur, si rationi libera coniectura sit, non *Agenor* sed *acerno*, ut de Anticlo dictum accipiamus, de quo est etiam apud Homerum libro quarto *Odysseae*. Nam cum ad equum illum Troianum, trabibus contextum gravidumque militibus, impulsu numinis accessisset Helena, voces imitari uxorum cuiusque occoepit, ut inibi delitescentium desideria evocaret, refricaret memoriam, responsa tentaret elicere. Sed enim reliquis patientiam silentiumque praestantibus, cum solus Anticlus in respondendi lubrico articuloque iam foret, statim est ab Ulysse[236] praeventus, et manibus impressis suffocatus. Itaque intercepto, vel interstructo potius indicio periculum depulsum. Ceterum Tryphisiodorus quoque Graecus auctor in poemate, quo de Ilio capto[237] scribit, Anticlum hunc Ortygiden appellat, uxoremque eius nominat Laodamian, ita inquiens:

Ὀρτυγίδης δ' Ἄντικλος, ὃν αὐτόθι τεθνειῶτα
Ἵππῳ[238] δακρύσαντες ἐνεκτερέϊξαν Ἀχαιοί.

Et idem alibi sic:

Ἄντικλος δ' ὅτε κέντρον ἐδέξατο Λαοδαμείης
Μοῦνος ἀμοιβαίην ἀνεβάλλετο γῆρυν ἀνοίξας
Ἀλλ' Ὀδυσεὺς κατέπαλτο

where Domizio says the following: "Agenor was killed by a hand inserted in his mouth when the horse fell."[782] Is that really so, learned man? But I beg you, my Domizio, cite, if you can, a suitable Greek or even Latin authority for this tale, and I will pose no further objection if, I will not say your cronies or admirers, but even educated men, for whom this work is being sweated out, condemn me — even unanimously — as unlearned and even brazen, because I dissent from you.

If reason has scope for conjecture, not *Agenor*, but *acerno* ("of 3 maple") seems to me the correct and error-free text,[783] so that we may understand that this was said about Anticlus. There is something about him in Homer as well, in the fourth book of the *Odyssey*.[784] For when Helen had approached that famous Trojan horse, woven together from beams and pregnant with soldiers, by an uncanny impulse, she began to mimic the voices of the wives of each man, so as to rouse the longing of those hidden within, revive the memory, and try to elicit responses. But though the others maintained patient silence, when Anticlus alone was on the point of replying, he was at once forestalled by Ulysses, who laid hands on him and suffocated him. And so the danger was averted, with the evidence intercepted, or rather blocked. The Greek author Tryphiodorus, too, in the poem in which he writes about the capture of Ilium, calls this Anticlus "Ortygides," and names his wife Laodamia, saying the following:

> And Anticlus Ortygides, whom the Achaeans wept for
> And slew on the spot within the horse.[785]

And elsewhere the same poet says the following:

> And when Anticlus alone, goaded by Laodamia,
> Started to shout out a response and opened his mouth,
> Odysseus leaped upon him[786]

et alia. Deinceps addit per quae fabula omnis similiter ut ab Homero versibus permultis explicatur. Sed et nos in *Ambra* sic attigimus:

> Indiciique metu praeclusum pollice fauces
> Anticlon Ortygiden.

4   Consimilia vero istis apud Domitium multa, quae facile arguant quo fuerit illius processura licentia, praesertim sic invitata favoribus imperitorum, nisi morari apud superos adhuc quidem iuvenis desisset.

: 76 :

Non 'Antilochum ab Hectore' sed aliter videri legendum in prima Heroidum

1   In prima *Heroidum* Nasonis epistola sic legitur:

> Sive quis Antilochum narrabat ab Hectore victum.

Sed victum necatumque ab Hectore Antilochum profecto neutiquam reperietur. Quare aut *Amphimachum* crediderim legendum aut non 'ab Hectore' sed 'Memnone.' Constat enim ex tertiadecima Homeri rhapsodia occisum ab Hectore Amphimachum Cteati filium, qui de Graecis ducibus unus etiam in Catalogo numeratur. Constat item interfectum a Memnone filium Nestoris Antilochum.

and so forth. Then he adds a lengthy exposition of the entire tale in a way similar to Homer. But I, too, touched upon it in my *Ambra* as follows:

> Anticlus Ortygides, his throat strangled shut by [Odysseus's]
>   thumb
> For fear he would give them away.[787]

Indeed, there are many things similar to these in Domizio,   4 which easily show how far his license would have gone, especially when egged on by the support of the ignorant, had he not, while still a young man, ceased to tarry in the upper world.[788]

: 76 :

It seems that not "Antilochus [vanquished] by Hector" but something else must be read in the first letter of the Heroides

In the first letter of Naso [Ovid]'s *Heroides*, one reads the fol-   1 lowing:

> If someone related that Antilochus was vanquished by
>   Hector.[789]

But it will, in fact, nowhere be found that Antilochus was vanquished and killed by Hector. Therefore I believe that either "Amphimachus" [rather than "Antilochus"] or else not "by Hector" but "by Memnon" must be read. For it is well known from the thirteenth book of Homer that the man slain by Hector was Amphimachus, son of Cteatus, who alone of Greek leaders is also enumerated in the Catalogue.[790] It is also well known that Antilochus, son of Nestor, was killed by Memnon.[791]

2   Quamobrem ut in eo, quod obtinuerat hactenus mendum deprehenditur manifestarium, sic his a nobis ita pro tempore suffec-
tis, quae, lector, velim boni consulas, aliqua, ni fallor, gratia si non
veritatis, at certe verisimilitudinis, assentatur.

: 77 :

Quo argumento dicendum Vergilius, *non* Virgilius

1   *Vergilius* dicendumne sit an *Virgilius*, ut nunc vulgo loquuntur, hoc
est cum vocali secunda, an cum tertia potius in prima syllaba,
video adhuc inter eruditos ambigi. Ceterum ut ego *Vergilium* dicam magis per *e*, quod iam placere quibusdam per nos etiam doctis incipit, quam *Virgilium* per *i*, quod vulgo nimis obtinuit, in
causa sunt veterrima aliquot monumenta nostrae observationi pa-
trocinantia, quae libens equidem subiciam propter propudiosos
nescio quos et eruginis plenos, odio omni fastidioque dignissimos,
qui quanquam semper elementarii sunt, vindicare tamen inter in-
doctos fautores audent sibi censuram litterarum, sic ut istam
quoque qualemcunque nostram vetustatis deprehendendae ac re-
vocandae (si liceat) diligentiam studiumque non cavillentur modo,
sed et ita reprehendant acerbe quasi flagitium facere putent quod
his otium oblectemus vel (ut ipsi magis contemptim) quod ob haec
otio nostro invideamus, dum in rebus adeo frivolis et levibus operam sumimus, quasique tempus, rem pretiosissimam, in superva-
cua erogamus.

Accordingly, as in this passage an obvious error that has held its   2
ground until now has been detected, so may agreement be granted
to these points provisionally supplied by me. I would wish, reader,
that you look on them indulgently with some gratitude, I think, if
not for their truth, at least for their probability.[792]

: 77 :

Why we should say Vergil *rather than* Virgil

I see it is still debated among the learned whether we should say   1
Vergil or *Virgil*, as people now commonly say, that is, with the second vowel [*e*] or rather with the third vowel [*i*] in the first syllable.
But the reason I prefer to say *Vergil* with an *e*, which through my
efforts is now beginning to find favor with certain learned men,
rather than *Virgil* with an *i*, which has commonly held the field all
too much, is that there are some extremely old monuments that
defend my observation and which I shall gladly subjoin[793] on account of some shameful individuals beset with mental decay, who
are most deserving of all loathing and contempt, and who, even
though they will always only be at a rudimentary level, nonetheless
dare to arrogate to themselves among their unlearned supporters a
license to critique literature. Hence they not only scoff at my diligence, such as it is, and zeal for discovering and (if possible) restoring antiquity, but even sharply condemn it, as if they think it a
disgrace that we delight our leisure by these means, or (as they
themselves say more contemptuously) because we begrudge our
own leisure on account of these studies, while we take pains over
such frivolous and trivial matters and, as it were, spend our time —
our most precious commodity — on superfluous concerns.

2 Qui tamen si legissent aliquando maximos viros de singulis quoque litteris integra volumina composuisse, ac ne Caesarem quidem ipsum veritum in hanc tenuitatem descendere, darent fortasse mihi veniam, non occupatissimo homini, si quando inter altiora studia etiam res istiusmodi tractarem, parvas quidem sed quibus etiam magna iuventur. Neque enim reprehendi me iure puto, si haec etiam, sed haec sola consecter ad quae non ut ab otio ad studium sed ut a studio ad otium me refero, et in quae non tam feror ex professo quam casu incido, ceu si litoribus ex commodo inambulans, conchas interim colligam securus. Neque tamen in id ego supercilium subduco, nec inde me censeri facile paterer ut qui non apinas modo haec esse et tricas, ut in proverbii ludicro est, verum etiam pene nihil et novi et fateor. Sed tamen hoc ipsum tam nihil praestat agere quam longas ad ipsorum fortasse exemplum trahere oscitationes et grunnire in ceno turpiter, aut quam omnino nihil agere ne nihil prorsus agendo male discamus agere. Reddenda igitur testimonia sunt nobis, necubi fides claudicet ac ne quid non in expedito sit noscere volentibus.

3 Invenies igitur Volsinis mensam quampiam marmoream, vetustissimis peneque exoletis characteribus intra aedem Christinae[239] virginis, quae pro ara est Apostoli Petri, ubi VERGILI legitur. Invenies etiam Sutri nomen hoc *Vergilius* ita notatum in mensa item lapidea, qua videlicet et ipsa intra aedem Virginis vice utuntur altaris. Idque nos utrunque non sine aliquot arbitris etiam de proximo inspeximus. Neque enim antiquarum duntaxat inspectionum auriti testes sed et oculati esse concupivimus.

4 Quin in *Pandectis* quoque his quae nunc Florentiae publice asservantur, libro ipso Iustiniani principis archetypo, non aliter quam

Nonetheless, if they had ever read that the greatest men even   2
composed entire books about individual letters [of the alphabet]
and not even Caesar himself was afraid to descend to this detail,
they would perhaps grant leave to me, a not extremely busy man,
if ever I were amid higher studies to treat matters of this sort,
small to be sure, but by which great things may be assisted. For I
believe that I am not rightly criticized for pursuing on the side —
but would be for pursuing exclusively — matters for which I do not
recall myself from leisure to study but from study to leisure and to
which I am not driven by professional concern but hit upon by
chance, as if I were to gather seashells while strolling at my leisure,
carefree on the beach.[794] Nonetheless, I do not raise my eyebrow at
this or suffer my reputation to be based on being a man who does
not only know and confess that these matters are worthless trifles,[795] as in the proverbial jest, but even that they are virtually
nothing. But it is nonetheless better to do this nothing than, on
their model, to take huge yawns and grunt disgracefully at dinner[796] or than to do nothing at all lest by doing nothing we learn
to do badly. Therefore, we must render up our testimonies, lest
our credibility be hampered and lest there be an impediment to
those who wish to find out.

Now then, you will find a particular marble tablet at Bolsena   3
that has very old and almost faded letters inside the church of the
virgin martyr Christina, which serves as an altar of the Apostle
Peter, and on it "of Vergil" is read. You will also find at Sutri the
name *Vergil* so written on a stone tablet, this, too, within a church
of the Virgin and used as an altar. I have inspected both close up
with some witnesses. For in inspecting antiquities we wanted to be
not just "ear witnesses" but eye witnesses.[797]

In fact, in the *Pandects* as well, the ones which are now pre-   4
served publicly in Florence, in the very archetype of the emperor
Justinian,[798] that name is inscribed with no letter other than *e*,[799]

per *e* notatur id nomen, sicuti etiam in volumine Maroniano litteris maioribus perarato quod[240] Romae in intima Vaticana bibliotheca mire vetus ostenditur. Praetereaque commentarium Tiberi Donati nunc in manibus habet Landinus, homo et eloquens et eruditus, et Florentiae iam diu doctor bonarum litterarum celebratissimus, cui se praeceptori adulescentiae meae rudimenta magnopere debent, et qui nunc in professione quasi dixerim collega, locata iam in tuto sua sibi fama, nobis adhuc in stadio laboriosissime[241] decertantibus ita favet ut quidquid ipsi laudis acquirimus, quasi suum sibi amplecti atque agnoscere videatur. Is igitur (ut diximus) commentarium Tiberi Donati habet in manibus et ipsum grandioribus notatum vetustis characteribus, cuius auctoritas hoc haud dubium reliquerit. Quod item in codice Divi Augustini *De civitate dei* ex publica Medicae familiae bibliotheca neque non in Columellae ex privata eiusdem gentis, litteris utroque Langobardis exarato, tum in Senecae *Epistolarum* libro pervetere, cuius mihi copiam fecit Nicolaus Micheloctius, Laurenti Medicis a secretis, elegantis homo ingenii, multisque item aliis venerandis antiquitate voluminibus, identidem nunc Iacobo Modesto Pratensi, familiari nostro et studiorum adiutori, nunc aliis item nostris auditoribus, utcunque aut res ferat aut exigatur, ostendimus.

5   In collectaneis autem quae nuperrime ad Laurentium Medicem Iucundus misit, vir unus, opinor, titulorum monimentorumque veterum supra mortales ceteros non diligentissimus solum sed etiam sine controversia peritissimus, relata quoque invenio elogia duo quae Romae (sicut ille indicat) in marmoribus inveniuntur: TI. VERGILIVS DONATVS, et iterum: C. PAPIRIVS CESTVS VERGILIAE OPTATAE[242] VXORI SVAE BENEMERENTI DE SE.

just as it is in a volume of Maro written in capital letters, an uncommonly old one that is displayed at Rome in the inner library of the Vatican.[800] In addition, a commentary by Tiberius Donatus is now in the hands of [Cristoforo] Landino, an eloquent and erudite man, for a long time the most celebrated teacher of literature in Florence, to whose teaching my youthful beginnings owe a great debt, and who is now, as it were, a colleague in the profession. With his own reputation already secure, he so supports me as I struggle laboriously on the racetrack that he seems to embrace and acknowledge whatever praise I obtain as if it were his own.[801] He [Landino], then, has (as we said) a commentary by Tiberius Donatus, and it is written with rather large old letters, the authority of which scarcely leaves this [sc. the orthography Vergil] in doubt. Likewise, we have repeatedly shown this same thing, now to Jacopo Modesto of Prato, a friend of ours and an assistant in our studies, and at other times also to other students of ours, whenever the matter may arise or be required, in a codex of St. Augustine's City of God in the public library of the Medici family, and also in one of Columella found in the private library of the same family, each written in Lombardic script, and again in a very old book of Seneca's Letters,[802] access to which was granted to me by Niccolò Michelozzi, secretary to Lorenzo de' Medici, a man of elegance, and also in many other volumes venerable for their antiquity.

Moreover, in the collections that were recently sent to Lorenzo 5 de' Medici by [Giovanni] Giocondo—in my estimation the one man beyond all other mortals who is not only the most assiduous student of ancient inscriptions and monuments but also indisputably the most skilled—I find two epitaphs reported which are found at Rome (as he indicates) on marble monuments: "TIBERIUS VERGILIUS DONATUS," and again: "GAIUS PAPIRIUS CESTUS, TO HIS BELOVED WIFE VERGILIA, WHO SERVED HIM WELL."

6   Quamvis autem monimenta ista, tanta saeculorum vetustate roborata, mihi satis ad praesidium sint, attamen res ipsa quoque astipulatur et ratio. Nam sicuti a vere dictae Vergiliae stellae, sic a Vergiliis ipsis vel item a vere proprium hoc nomen crediderim inclinatum potius hercle quam a *virga*, quod quidam nugantur *laurea*. Nam id cum apud auctorem minus idoneum inveniatur, tum refellitur hoc ipso quod multi ante hunc editum poetam eodem sunt appellati nomine. Quandiu igitur aut non testimonium gravius aut non ratio valentior exhibetur, utique a vetusta magis consuetudine quam a nova inscitia standum est, 'unde haec sartago loquendi venerit in linguas.' Etenim magna pars iuniorum caligamus ad veri conspectum.

7   Quin (ut reliqua exsequar) *Verginius* quoque nomen huic finitimum, non *Virginius* in marmoreo nuper labro pro aede ipsa Divae Mariae Maioris insculptum Romae animadvertimus.

: 78 :

Additam falso negationem primo
Digestorum *volumine, quo capite de officio*
proconsulis agitur et legati

Paulus iurisconsultus libro secundo *Ad edictum* ita scribit: 'Legatus mandata sibi iurisdictione iudicis dandi ius habet.' Sed haec verba in primo *Digestorum* volumine, quo capite de officio proconsulis et legati tractatur, addita perperam negatione in plerisque codicibus

Moreover, although these monuments, reinforced by their great   6
antiquity, lend me sufficient protection, the fact is, nonetheless,
also supported by reason. For just as the Vergilian stars are named
after the spring (*ver*),[803] so from the Vergilian [stars] themselves,
or likewise from the spring (*ver*) I should think this name derives — by heaven! — rather than from *virga* ("rod") that some persons falsely claim to be *laurea* ("a laurel branch"). For this, on the
one hand, would be found in an unsuitable author, and, on the
other, is refuted by the fact that many were called by the same
name before this poet was born. Therefore, as long as no weightier
testimony or more cogent reason is produced, one must rather
stand by ancient usage than modern ignorance, "whence this linguistic jumble has come to our tongues."[804] For we younger persons are for the most part in a fog when it comes to viewing the
truth.

In fact (to finish up the topic) we recently noticed the name   7
Verginius — a near neighbor to our name — not *Virginius* carved on a
marble basin in front of the Church of Santa Maria Maggiore in
Rome.[805]

: 78 :

A negation mistakenly added in the first volume of the
Digests, *in the chapter that addresses the duty of*
a proconsul and a legate

In his second book *On the Edict*, the jurist [Iulius] Paulus writes
the following: "A legate with jurisdiction delegated to him holds
the right of naming a judge." But in a good many codices you will
find this text in the first book of the *Digests*, in the chapter that
treats the duty of a proconsul and a legate, with a negation mistak-

invenias, sic videlicet: 'Legatus mandata sibi iurisdictione iudicis dandi ius non habet.' Ceterum in *Pandectis* istis Florentinis, quas etiam archetypas opinamur, negatio prorsus est nulla. Quo fit ut interpres legum Florentinus Accursius, mendosum et ipse nactus codicem, pene dixerim miserabiliter se torqueat.

: 79 :

Cur Lysimachi[243] regis facies in nomismatis cornigera

Lysimachi[244] regis facies in nomismatis cornigera. Causa eius apud Appianum in *Syriacis*. Namque ait ab eo ferum taurum de sacrificio Alexandri Magni vinculis elapsum, retentum manibus ambabus et occisum. Atque ob id, inquit, προστιθέασιν ἐπὶ τοὺς ἀνδριάντας ἐπὶ τῷδε τὰ κέρατα, quod significat: ob id eius statuis denique apponi cornua.

: 80 :

Fabula ignotior de Tiresia et Pallade,
qua sensus aperitur Propertianus

1   Propertius in libro *Elegiarum* quarto sic ait:

  Magnam Tiresias aspexit Pallada vates,
    Fortia dum posita Gorgone membra lavat.

enly added, namely thus: "A legate with jurisdiction delegated to him does not hold the right of naming a judge."[806] Yet in those Florentine *Pandects*, which I even consider to be the archetype,[807] there is no negation. Hence the Florentine legal scholar Accursio,[808] who had chanced upon a faulty codex, torments himself, I might almost say, wretchedly.

: 79 :

Why the image of King Lysimachus on coins is horned

The image of King Lysimachus is horned on coins. The reason for this is found in Appian, in his *Syrian War*. For he says that when a wild bull intended for sacrifice for Alexander the Great once slipped free from its chains, he restrained it with both hands and killed it. And on account of this, he says, "they added horns to his statues," which means [in Latin] "for this reason, horns were added to his statues."[809]

: 80 :

A little known tale of Tiresias and Pallas, by which the meaning of a Propertian text is revealed[810]

In Book 4 of his *Elegies*, Propertius says the following: 1

The seer Tiresias gazed upon the great Pallas
    While she was bathing her mighty limbs, with the Gorgon
    laid aside.[811]

Extat adhuc hymnus Callimachi poetae cui titulus Εἰς λουτρὰ τῆς Παλλάδος, in quo fabula Tiresiae multis elegiacis versibus in hanc ferme sententiam tractatur: fuisse nympham quampiam Thebis cui nomine Chariclo, Palladi prae ceteris gratam, matrem Tiresiae. Sed cum se Pallas aliquando et Chariclo item in Heliconio Hippocrene nudae per aestum lavarent, ac tum casu venator Tiresias ad eundem fontem sitiens accessisset, Minervam scilicet imprudens nudam conspicatus statimque oculis est captus. Nam ita Saturniis legibus cautum, inquit, ut qui deum invitum cernat, ingenti mercede cernat. Cui simile quippiam de dearum conspectu etiam Abammon Aegyptius in epistola scribit ad Porphyrium philosophum, quam tamen existimat Proclus Iamblichi potius esse quam Abammonis. Ex quo Vergilius:

Transque caput iace, ne respexeris.

Quod et Leucothea Homerica monuit Ulyssen.

2   Sed ut illuc, unde abii, redeam. Cum in hanc Tiresias calamitatem incidisset, mota lacrimis Chariclus nymphae Pallas et vatem eum et longaevum et post obitum quoque prudentem sapientemque praestitit, et baculo insuper donavit quo veluti duce vestigiis inoffensis graderetur. Quod et nos in *Ambra* sic attigimus, cum de poeta loqueremur Homero:

Baculum dat deinde potentem
Tiresiae magni, qui quondam Pallada nudam
Vidit et hoc raptam pensavit munere lucem,
Suetus inoffensos baculo duce tendere gressus.

Et item sic in *Nutrice* Tiresian periphrasticos insinuavimus:

A hymn by the poet Callimachus entitled *On the Bath of Pallas* is still extant.[812] In it, the tale of Tiresias is treated in many elegiac verses along these basic lines: there was a particular nymph in Thebes by the name of Chariclo, who was favored by Pallas above all others, and was the mother of Tiresias. But once in the summer when Pallas and Chariclo were bathing naked in Helicon's spring, Hippocrene, and then by chance Tiresias, who was out hunting and thirsty, drew near to that same spring, he, of course inadvertently, caught sight of Minerva naked, and was instantly blinded. For the sanction was imposed by Saturn's laws, she said, that if anyone saw a god against his will, he would see at a heavy cost. Abammon of Egypt, too, wrote something similar to this about looking upon goddesses, in a letter to the philosopher Porphyry, which however Proclus attributes to Iamblichus rather than Abammon.[813] Hence Vergil:

> Cast [them] over your head, and do not look back.[814]

This warning was also given by Homer's Leucothea to Ulysses.[815]

But to return to the point from which I digressed: when Tiresias had fallen into this disaster, Pallas, moved by the tears of the nymph Chariclo, made him a seer and long lived and possessed of foresight and wisdom even after death,[816] and gave him a staff besides, so that, with this guide, as it were, he could walk with feet unobstructed. When we discussed the poet Homer, we touched on this in the *Ambra*, as follows:

> Then he [Achilles] gives him [Homer] the powerful staff
> Of the great Tiresias, who once saw Pallas naked,
> And compensated for the loss of his sight with this gift,
> Inured to guiding his feet unobstructed by means of the
>   staff.[817]

And likewise in our *Nurse*, we hinted at Tiresias periphrastically as follows:

Quid cui post visos nudatae Palladis artus
Cernere nil licitum?

Quin hinc apud Nonnum libro quinto *Dionysiacon* ita exclamans
inducitur Actaeon ut felicem Tiresian dicat, qui citra mortem,
tantum amissis oculis, Minervam aspexerit[245] nudam, quae etiam
lumen ademptum in animum ipsius transtulerit, atque adeo sic
ait:

Ὄλβιε Τειρεσία· σὺ μὲν ἔδρακες ἐκτὸς ὀλέθρου
Γυμνὸν ἀναινομένης οἰκτείρμονος εἶδος Ἀθήνης.

Et paulo post:

Ζώεις σῶν βλεφάρων ὀλέσας φάος, ὑμετέρων δὲ
Ὀφθαλμῶν ἀμάρυγμα νόῳ μετέθηκεν Ἀθήνη.

3   Hactenus autem super hoc poetae loco scripseramus, cum nobis Picus noster Mirandula, quasi Cynthius alter, in illo ipso quo
iam haec imprimenda fuerant articulo, aurem vellit et admonuit ut
elegiam quoque ipsam Callimachi, quae videlicet una extat apud
Graecos (quantum equidem sciam) sed et rarissima est inventu,
subiceremus, et quamquam spatiis iniquis exclusi temporis, vertere
eam quoque tamen in Latinum temptaremus. Ego vero, qui nec
scribere alieno stomacho libenter soleo nec extemporalitati satis
confido, non distuli tamen id onus quoquomodo subire, quoniam
cum quid a me Picus exigit, nec licet mihi nescire quod nesciam
nec non posse quod nequeam, vel quod homini me carissimum
sentio, vel quod plus eum videre in rebus meis quam me ipsum
mihi persuadeo. Vertimus igitur pene ad verbum et, quod Graece

[Why mention] the man permitted to see nothing
After the sight of Pallas's nakedness?[818]

Moreover, in Book 5 of his *Dionysiaca*, Nonnus introduces Actaeon exclaiming that he pronounces Tiresias fortunate, since without dying, having lost merely his sight, he saw Minerva naked, who even transferred the lost light to his mind, and furthermore he says the following:

O fortunate Tiresias, you gazed upon the naked beauty of
Athena against her will
But, since she was compassionate, without your destruction.[819]

And a little further on:

You are alive although you lost the sight of your eyes,
And Athena transferred the sparkle of your eyes to your
mind.[820]

We had written this much about this passage of the poet's, 3 when our friend Pico della Mirandola, like another [Apollo] Cynthius, at that very time when these things were to be printed, plucked our ear and advised[821] us to subjoin Callimachus's elegy itself, which clearly is the one extant among the Greeks (as far as I know) but is extremely rare, and also, though hampered by too little time, attempt nonetheless to translate it into Latin as well. Indeed, though I am not used to writing willingly at another's pleasure nor am I sufficiently confident in my extemporaneous composition, nonetheless I did not by any means hesitate to take up this burden, since, when Pico demands something from me, I do not have license not to know what I do not know or to be unable to do what I cannot do, whether because I understand that I am extremely dear to him, or because I am convinced that he has greater insight into my powers than I have myself. Therefore, I have translated practically word for word, which in Greek is called

dicitur παρὰ πόδα, non sensu modo sed numeris etiam, quod est difficillimum, coloribusque servatis. Tantumque nunc admonemus lectorem, paucula videri mihi adhuc mendosa in Graecis exemplaribus, quae non erat pudoris nostri corrigere, sed et septimum ipsum a fine versiculum, reliquo uno duntaxat vocabulo, exolevisse, quem nos tamen Latinum pro coniectura suffecimus.

4   Illud item scito (est opus): nostrum hoc esse interpretamentum et a nobis denique fluxisse priusquam in ullius commentariis ebulliret, quod et *Silvae* per se ipsae, quas citavimus, tot abhinc annos editae probabunt, quarum videlicet alteram magno sumus olim conventu publice multis excipientibus interpretati. Sit ergo nostri iuris quod nostri fuit muneris, ne quarta omnino luna (sicuti proverbium fertur) nati credamur, ut aliis tantummodo ad Herculis exemplum laboremus.

5   Iam illud quoque miror, cur et Domitius et alii quidam post illum, quocunque momento, quacunque occasione scribere audeant hoc aut illud imitatione Callimachi dictum fuisse a Propertio, cum praeter hymnos pauculos nihil prorsus extet ad nos poetae istius, nec autem plane quidquam quod amoris argumenta contineat.

6   Sed aures ad Callimachi iam versiculos subscriptos veteri more sine ullis accentiunculis arrigamus.[246]

> καλλιμαχου εισ λουτρα τησ παλλαδοσ
>
> οσσαι λωτροχοοι τασ παλλαδοσ εξιτε πασαι
> εξιτε. ταν ιππων αρτι φρνασσομεναν
> ταν ιεραν εσακουσα. και α θεοσ ευτυκοσ ερπει.
> ξουσθε νυν ω ξανθαι ξουσθε πελασγιαδεσ
> ου ποκ αθαναια μεγαλωσ απενιψατο παχεισ   5
> πριν κονιν ιππειαν εξελασαι λαγονων
> ουδ οκα δη λυθρωι πεπαλαγμενα παντα φερουσα

παρὰ πόδα ("exactly"),[822] not by the meaning alone but even in verse, which is very difficult, with its qualities preserved. Now I merely alert the reader that there seem to me to be still a few little errors in the Greek exemplars,[823] which it would exceed my modesty to correct, but that the seventh verse from the end has disappeared, with only a single word remaining, which I have nonetheless supplied in Latin through conjecture.

Know this as well—a necessary point: this is my translation, and it flowed from me before it bubbled up in anyone's books, a fact which the *Silvae* themselves, which I cited, published so many years ago,[824] will prove, of which I once translated the second in a large public assembly with many people taking notes. So let that be my property which is my handiwork, lest I be thought no more than a quarter moon old (as the proverb has it), so that I toil only—after the model of Hercules—for others' benefit.[825]

I am also surprised that both Domizio [Calderini] and others following him, at any time, on any occasion, dare to write that this or that was said by Propertius in imitation of Callimachus, although apart from a few hymns, nothing of that poet is left to us, nor anything at all on an amatory subject.

But let us now prick up our ears for the Callimachean verses written below in the ancient style, without any accents.[826]

On the Bath of Pallas by Callimachus

Come forth, all bathing attendants of Pallas, come forth all. I have heard the sacred mares already neighing, and the goddess is prepared and is approaching. Make haste now, fairhaired daughters of Pelasgus, make haste. Athena has never washed her great arms (5) until she has wiped the dust from her horses' flanks, not even when she came, spattered with gore, bearing all the arms from the wicked Earthborn ones

τευχεα των αδικων ηνϑ απο γηγενεων²⁴⁷
αλλα πολυ πρατιστον υφ αρματοσ αυχενασ ιππων
λυσαμενα παγαισ εκλυσεν ωκεανω   10
ιδρω και ραϑαμιγγασ. εφοιβασεν δε παγεντα
    παντα χαλινοφαγων αφρον απο στοματων
ω ιτ αχαιιαδεσ και μη μυρα μηδ αλαβαστρωσ.
    συριγγων αιω φϑογγον υπαξονιον²⁴⁸
μη μυρα λωτροχοοι ται παλλαδι μηδ αλαβαστρωσ.²⁴⁹   15
    ου γαρ αϑαναια χριματα μικτα φιλει.
οισετε μηδε κατοπτρον. αει καλον ομμα το τηνασ.
    ουδ οκα τ αν ιδαν φρυξ εδικασσεν²⁵⁰ εριν.
ουδ εσ ορειχαλκον μεγαλα ϑεοσ ουδε σιμουντοσ
    εβλεψεν διναν εσ διαφαινομενην   20
ουδ ηρη. κυπρισ δε διαυγεα χαλκον ελοισα
    πολλακι ταν αυταν δισ μετεϑηκε κομαν
α δε δισ εξηκοντα διαϑρεξασα διαυλωσ
    οια παρ ευρωται τοι λακεδαιμονιοι
αστερες. εμπεραμωσ ετριψατο λιτα λαβοισα   25
    χριματα τασ ιδιασ εκγονα φυταλιασ.
ω κωραι.²⁵¹ τοδ ερευϑοσ ανεδραμε πρωιον οιαν²⁵²
    η ροδον η σιβδησ κοκκοσ εχει χροιην²⁵³
τωι και νυν αρσεν τε κομισσατε μουννον ελαιον
    ωι καστωρ ωι και χριεται ηρακλεησ   30
οισετε και κτενα οι παγχρυσεον ωσ απο χαιταν
    πεξηται²⁵⁴ λιπαρον σμαξαμενα²⁵⁵ πλοκαμον
εξιϑ αϑαναια παρα τοι καταϑυμιοσ ιλα
    παρϑενικαι μεγαλων παιδεσ ακεστοριδαν
ωϑανα. φερεται δε και α διομηδεοσ ασπισ   35

[Giants], but first she released her horses' necks from the chariot and washed their drops of sweat in the streams of Ocean (10) and has cleaned all the compacted foam from their bit-champing mouths. Go, daughters of Achaea, bring no myrrh or jars of perfume (I hear the sound of the naves from under the axle), attendants, bring no myrrh or jars of perfume for Pallas (15) (for Athena is not fond of mixed ointments), and bring no mirror: her face is always fair. Not even when the Phrygian [Paris] was judging the contest on Ida did the great goddess look at a mirror or the clear wave of the Simois [River], (20) nor did Hera; but the Cyprian [Aphrodite] often took the shining bronze [mirror] and twice rearranged the same lock of hair. But Athena, after running twice sixty double-stades, like the Spartan stars [Castor and Pollux] beside the Eurotas [River], rubbed herself down expertly, (25) taking simple ointments, the offspring of her own tree [the olive], and a ruddiness spread over her, girls, the kind of color an early rose or the seed of pomegranate has. Therefore bring now only the masculine olive oil, with which Castor and Heracles rub down; (30) bring her a comb of solid gold as well, so that she may comb out her shiny hair, once she has cleansed it.

Come forth, Athena, a pleasing band stands ready, the virginal daughters of the great Acestorides, Athena, and the shield of Diomedes (35) is being carried, as Eumedes taught

ωσ εθοσ αργειων τουτο παλαιοτερον
ευμηδησ εδιδαξε τειν κεχαρισμενοσ ιρευσ
    οσ ποτε βουλευτον γνουσ επι οι θανατον
δαμον²⁵⁶ ετοιμαζοντα φυγασ²⁵⁷ τεον ιρον αγαλμα
    ωιχετ εχων, κρειον δ εισ οροσ ωικισατο   40
κρειον οροσ. σε δε δαιμον απορρωγεσσιν εθηκεν
    εν πετραις, αισ νυν ουνομα παλλατιδεσ
εξιθ αθαναια περσεπτολι χρυσεοπηληξ
    ιππων και σακεων αδομενα παταγωι.
σαμερον υδροφοροι μη βαπτετε. σαμερον αργοσ   45
    πινετ απο κραναν μη δ απο των ποταμων
σαμερον ω δωλαι τασ καλπιδασ ησ φυσαδειαν
    η εσ αμυμωνην οισετε ταν δαναω
και γαρ δη χρυσωι τε και ανθεσιν υδατα μιξασ
    ηξει φορβαιων ιναχοσ εξ ορεων.   50
ταιθαναι το λοετρον αγων καλον. αλλα πελασγε
    φραζεο μουκ εθελων ταν βασιλειαν ιδηισ
οσ κεν ιδηι γυμναν ταν παλλαδα ταν πολιουχον
    τωργοσ εσοψειται τουτο πανυστατιον.
ποτνι αθαναια συ μεν εξιθι μεσφα δ εγω τι   55
    ταισδ ερεω. μυθοσ δ ουκ εμοσ αλλ ετερων
παιδεσ. αθαναια νυμφαν μιαν εν ποκα θηβαισ
    πουλυ τι και περι δη φιλατο ταν εταραν
ματερα τειρεσιαο και ου ποκα χωρισ εγεντο
    αλλα και αρχαιων ευτ επι θεσπιεων   60
†τηπι κορωνειασ†²⁵⁸ η εισ αλιαρτον ελαυνοι
    ιππουσ βοιωτων²⁵⁹ εργα διερχομενα,²⁶⁰
ηπι κορωνειασ ινα οι τεθνωμενον αλσοσ
    και βωμοι ποταμωι κειντ επι κουραλιωι

this ancient Argive custom, a priest pleasing to you, who once, upon learning that the people were plotting death for him, fled with your holy statue and settled on Mount Crion, (40) Mount Crion; and he established you, goddess, on the sheer rocks that now are called Pallatides. Come forth, Athena, sacker of cities, with helmet of gold, delighting in the clatter of horses and shields. Today, water bearers, do not dip [your pitchers]; (45) today, Argos, drink from springs and not from the river; today, slave women, bring your pitchers to Physadia or Amymone, the daughter of Danaus. For Inachus will mix his waters with gold and blossoms and come from the nurturing mountains (50) bringing a fair bath for Athena. But Pelasgian, take care lest you unwittingly see the queen. Whoever sees the naked Pallas, protector of cities, will see this Argos for the last time. Lady Athena, (55) come forth while I tell something to these girls. Children, the tale is not mine but that of others.

Athena once loved one nymph in Thebes far more than her companions, the mother of Tiresias, and was never apart from her, but whenever she would drive her team to ancient Thespiae, (60) †to Coronea†[827] or Haliartus, passing through the Boeotians' fields, or to Coronea, where her fragrant grove and altars are situated beside the Curalius River,

πολλακισ α δαιμων μιν εωι επεβασατο διφρωι   65
  ουδ οαροι νυμφαν ουδε χοροστασιαι
αδειαι τελεθεσκον οθ ουχ αγειτο χαρικλω
αλλ ετι και τηναν δακρυα πολλ εμενε
καιπερ αθαναιαι καταθυμιον ευσαν εταιραν
  δη ποτε γαρ πεπλων λυσσαμενα περονασ   70
ιππω επι κραναι ελικωνιδι καλα ρεοισα⟨ι⟩²⁶¹
  λωντο. μεσαμβρινα δ ειχ ορος ασυχια
αμφοτεραι λωοντο. μεσαμβριναι δ εσαν ωραι
  πολλα δ ασυχια τηνο κατειχεν οροσ.
τειρεσιασ δ ετι μουνοσ αμαι κυσιν αρτιγενεια   75
  περκαζων ιερον χωρον ανεστρεφετο.
διψασασ δ αφατον τι ποτι ρροον ηλυθε²⁶² κρανασ
  σχετλιοσ ουκ εθελων δ ειδε τα μη †θεμιδεσ²⁶³
τον δε χολωσαμενα περ ομωσ προσεφασεν αθανα
  τισ σε τον οφθαλμωσ ουκετ αποισομενον   80
ω ευηρειδα χαλεπην οδον αγαγε δαιμων
  α μεν εφα. παιδοσ δ ομματα νυξ εβαλεν.²⁶⁴
εσταθη δ αφθογγοσ εκολλασαν γαρ ανιαι
  γωνατα. και φωναν εσχεν αμηχανια
α νυμφα δ εβοησε.²⁶⁵ τι μοι τον κωρον ερεξασ   85
  ποτνια. τοιαυται δαιμονεσ εστε φιλαι.
ομματα μοι του²⁶⁶ παιδοσ αφειλεο. τεκνον αλαστε
  ειδεσ αθαναιασ στηθεα και λαγονασ
αλλ ουκ αελιον παλιν οψεαι ω εμε δειλαν
  ω οροσ ω ελικων ουκετι μοι παριτε   90
η μεγαλ αντ ολιγων επραξαο δορκασ ολεσσασ
  και προκασ ου πολλασ φαεα παιδοσ εχεισ

many a time the goddess set her upon her chariot; (65) neither the nymphs' conversation nor their choral dances held
any charm unless Chariclo took the lead. But many tears
awaited her nonetheless, even though she was Athena's favorite companion. For one day they unpinned their gowns
(70) at the fair-flowing horse's spring on Helicon and bathed;
and the mountain was in the grip of a midday quiet. Both
were bathing, and it was noontime, and great quiet covered
the mountain. Tiresias, still alone, with his dogs, his cheeks
just (75) ripening with down, was traversing the sacred place.
Perceiving an overpowering thirst, he came to the stream of
the fountain, wretch, and unwittingly saw the forbidden
sight. Filled with anger, Athena nonetheless addressed him:
"What demon led you on this difficult path, (80) son of
Everes, never destined to recover your sight." She spoke, and
night drove out the boy's eyes. He stood speechless, since
misery held his knees fast and helplessness blocked his voice.
But the nymph raised a cry: (85) "What have you done
to my child, mistress? Goddesses, are you these kinds of
friends? You have taken away my son's eyes. Cursed son, you
have seen the breast and flanks of Athena, but you will never
see the sun again. O wretched me, O mountain, O Helicon,
never more to be trodden by me, (90) truly you have exacted
a great price for small things; you have lost a few gazelles and
roe deer, but you have my son's eyes." The mother embraced

α μεν²⁶⁷ αμφοτεραισι φιλον περι παιδα λαβοισα
ματηρ μεν γοερων οιτον αηδονιδων
αγε βαρυ κλαιουσα. θεα δ ελεησεν εταιραν   95
και μιν αθαναια προσ τοδ ελεξεν εποσ
δια γυναι μετα παντα βαλευ παλιν οσσα δι οργαν
ειπασ. εγω δ ου τοι τεκνον εθηκ αλαον
ου γαρ αθαναιαι γλυκερον πελει ομματα παιδων
αρπαζειν. κρονιοι δ ωδε λεγοντι νομοι   100
οσ κε τιν αθανατων οκα μη θεοσ αυτοσ εληται²⁶⁸
αθρησηι μισθωι τουτον ιδειν μεγαλωι
δια γυναι το μεν ου παλιναγρετον αυθι γενοιτο
εργον επει μοιραν ωδ επενευσε λινα
ηνικα το πρωτον νιν εγειναο. νυν δε κομιζου   105
ω ευηρειδα τελθοσ οφειλομενον
οσσα μεν α καδμηισ εσ υστερον εμπυρα καυσει
οσσα δ αρισταιοσ τον μονον ευχομενοι
παιδα τον αβαταν ακταιωνα τυφλον ιδεσθαι
και τηνοσ μεγαλασ συνδρομοσ αρτεμιδοσ   110
εσσεται. αλλ ουκ αυτον οτε δρομοσ αι τ εν ορεσσι
ρυσευνται ξυναι ταμοσ εκηβολιαι.
οπποταν ουκ εθελων περ ιδηι χαριεντα λοετρα
δαιμονοσ. αλλ αυται τον πριν ανακτα κυνεσ
τουτακι δειπνησευντι. τα δ υιεοσ οστεα ματηρ   115
λεξειται δρυμωσ παντασ επερχομενα
ολβισταν ερεει σε και εναιωνα γενεσθαι
εξ ορεων αλαον παιδ υποδεξαμεναν
ω εταρα τωι μη τι μινυρεο. τωιδε γαρ αλλα
τευ χαριν εξ εμεθεν πολλα μενευντι γερα   120
μαντιν επει θησω νιν αοιδιμον εσσομενοισιν

her dear son and drew out the lament of mournful nightingales, sobbing deeply. But the goddess took pity on her companion, (95) and Athena spoke these words to her: "Madame, take back all you have said in anger. I did not make
your son blind. For it is not Athena's pleasure to take away
children's sight; but the laws of Cronus stipulate as follows:
(100) 'Whoever sees any of the immortals when the god
himself does not choose, sees him at a great price.' Madame,
what is done cannot be revoked, since the threads of the
Fates spun it thus when you first gave birth to him. But now,
(105) son of Everes, take the debt that is owed. How many
burned offerings will the daughter of Cadmus later sacrifice,
how many will Aristaeus, praying to see their only son, the
youthful Actaeon, blind. He will be the running companion
of great Artemis, (110) but their running and hunting together in the mountains will not save him when he, albeit
unwittingly, sees the goddess's lovely bath; but then his
bitches will feed on their former master, and his mother will
scour all the thickets (115) and collect her son's bones. She
will say that you were born most blessed and fortunate, since
you have taken your boy back from the mountains blind.
Companion, do not lament, since for your sake many other
honors await him from my bounty: (120) I shall make him a
prophet revered by posterity, a thing greater than any other.

η μεγα των αλλων δη τι περισσοτερον
γνωσειται δ ορνιθασ οσ αισιοσ. οι τε πετονται
ηλιθα και ποιων ουκ αγαθαι πτερυγεσ
πολλα δε βοιωτοισι θεοπροπα πολλα δε καδμωι   125
χρησει και μεγαλοισ υστερα λαβδακιδαισ.
δωσω και μεγα βακτρον ο οι ποδασ εσ δεον αξει
δωσω δε βιοτου τερμα πολυχρονιον
και μονοσ ευτε θανηι πεπνυμενοσ εν νεκυεσσι
φοιτασει. μεγαλωι τιμιοσ αγεσιλα   130
ωσ φαμενα κατενευσε το δ εντελεσ ωι κ επινευσηι
παλλασ. επει μωναι²⁶⁹ ζευσ το γε θυγατερων
δωκεν αθαναιαι πατρωια παντα φερεσθαι
λωτροχοοι. ματηρ δ ουτισ ετικτε θεαν
αλλα διοσ κορυφα. κορυφα διοσ ωι κ επινευει   135
†θυγατηρ²⁷⁰
ερχετ αθαναια νυν ατρεκεσ. αλλα δεχεσθε
ταν θεον ω κωραι τωργοσ οσαισ μελεται
συν τ εναγοριαι συν τ ευγμασι συν τ ολολυγαισ
χαιρε θεα. καδευ αργεοσ ιναχιου.   140
χαιρε και εξελαοισα και εσ παλιν αυτισ ελασσαισ
ιππουσ και δαναων κλαρον απαντα σαω.

7   Iam nostros quoque legito qui male collocare bonas horas volet,
attamen cum venia quaeso et conniventibus oculis.

Politiani Ex Callimacho In Palladis Lavacra

Ite foras agedum, quaecunque liquentibus undis
    Membra lavaturae Pallados, ite foras.
Ipsa venit. Fremitus sacrorum audimus equorum,
    Ite agedum flavae, o ite Pelasgiades.
Non prius ingentes lavit sibi diva lacertos,   5

He will know the birds: which one is auspicious and which ones fly in vain and which ones' flights are ill-omened. He will pronounce many oracles for the Boeotians, (125) many for Cadmus and others later on for the great Labacids. I shall also give him a great staff, which will guide his feet as needed, and a limit of life stretching for many years, and when he dies, he alone will possess intelligence among the dead and be honored by great Agesilas [i.e., Hades]." (130)

Upon speaking thus, she nodded, and what Pallas assents to with a nod is fulfilled, since Zeus granted to Athena alone among his daughters to have all her father's prerogatives, bath attendants, and no mother bore the goddess, but the head of Zeus. To whatever the head of Zeus nods assent (135) . . . the daughter.[828] Athena is now certainly coming. Receive the goddess, girls, all who care for Argos, with fair speech, prayers, and cries. Hail, goddess. Take care for Inachian Argos. (140) Hail when you drive your team forth and when you return again, and preserve the entire inheritance of the Danaans.

Now let anyone who wishes to invest good hours in a bad cause 7 read my verses as well, but please with indulgence and eyes half closed.

Poliziano's Translation from Callimachus, *On the Bath of Pallas*

Come forth, then, maids, who are to bathe the limbs of Pallas in the clear water, come forth! She herself is coming. We hear the neighing of the sacred horses. Come, then, fair-haired daughters of Pelasgus. The goddess does not wash

Ilia quam abstersit pulvere cornipedum.
Nec tum quando armis multa iam cede cruentis
    Venit ab iniustis horrida terrigenis,
Tum quoque equum subducta iugis fumantia colla
    Perfudit largi fontibus Oceani,   10
Dum sudor guttaeque putres, dumque omnis abiret
    Spuma oris circum mansa lupata rigens.
Ite o Achivae, sed non unguenta aut alabastros,
    Audio certe ipso stridulum ab axe sonum.
Palladi lotrices, non unguenta aut alabastros   15
    Nulla etenim divae huic unguina mista placent.
Ferte nec huic speculum, vultu est pulcherrima semper.
    Nam nec in Ida olim iudice sub Phrygio
Se vel orichalco magna haec dea vel Simoentis
    Spectavit, quanquam vertice perspicuo,   20
Nec Iuno, sed sola Venus se splendido in aere
    Vidit, eandem iterum disposuitque comam,
Bis sexaginta spatiis verum incita cursu.
    Stellae apud Eurotan ceu Lacedaemoniae,
Perfricuit tantum pingui se diva liquore   25
    De baccis, arbor quem sua protulerat.
O puerae, emicuit rubor illico matutinus[271]
    Quem rosa, quem grano Punica mala ferunt.
Ergo marem nunc tantum olei quoque ferte liquorem,
    Quo se unguit Castor, quo Amphitryoniades.   30
Ferte etiam solido ex auro quo pectine crines
    Explicet et pinguem caesariem dirimat.
Exi age iam, o Pallas, praesto tibi virgineus grex,
    Natae magnorum carus Acestoridum.
O Pallas quin iam clypeus Diomedis et ipse   35
    Fertur, ut Argivum mos vetus obtinuit.
Eumedes docuit, meditans tibi grata sacerdos,
    Cum in se composito cerneret interitu

her mighty arms (5) until she has wiped the dust from the
flanks of her horses. Not even when she came fouled with
arms dripping with much gore from [battle with] the wicked
Earthborn ones [Giants]: even then she doused the steaming
necks of her horses, bowed beneath the yoke, in the streams
of abundant Ocean (10) until the foul drops of sweat and all
the foam compacted round about the champed bits of their
mouths disappeared. Come, Achaean maids, but no unguents or jars of perfume—I hear the whirring sound from
the very axle—bathing attendants of Pallas, (15) no unguents
or jars of perfume, for no mixed unguents please this goddess. And bring her no mirror: her face is ever beautiful. For
once upon a time on Mt. Ida, when the Phrygian [Paris] sat
in judgment, neither did this great goddess contemplate herself in a mirror, or in the swirl of the Simois [River], trans-
lucent though it be, (20) nor did Juno, but Venus alone
looked at herself in the shining bronze [mirror] and rearranged the same curl, but she [Athena] ran twice sixty laps
at top speed. Just like the Spartan stars [Castor and Pollux]
at the Eurotas [River], the goddess rubbed herself down
only with the rich liquid (25) from the berries that her
own tree had produced. Girls, a morning ruddiness shone,[829]
such as neither the rose nor pomegranates with their seed
produce. So now bring only the masculine olive oil, with
which Castor and the son of Amphitryon [Hercules] anoint
themselves. (30) Bring also the comb of solid gold that
with it she may untangle her locks and part her thick hair.
Come forward now, Pallas! Your dear band of maidens is
at hand, daughters of the great Acestorides. Pallas, now the
shield of Diomedes is being carried [in procession], (35)
as the ancient Argive custom has held. Eumedes so instructed, a priest showing favor to you, when he perceived
that an evil fate was approaching, a plot having been formed

Ire malam sortem, fugit quippe ille tuamque
    Ad montem Crion substulit effigiem,   40
Ad montem Crion, tum abruptis imposuit te
    Cautibus, hasque vocant nunc quoque Pallatidas.
Exi age, quae expugnas urbes, cuique aurea cordi
    Cassis, equumque fremor cum sonitu clypeum.
Vos hodie undiferae ne tinguite, vos hodie, Argos,   45
    Fontibus ex ipsis, non fluviis bibite.
Vos hodie, ancillae, ferte urnas ad Physadean,
    Aut ad Amymonen, progeniem Danai.
Namque auro et multis permixtus floribus[272] undas
    Defluet e laetis Inachus ipse iugis   50
Et purum feret huic laticem. Cave tu ergo Pelasge,
    Ne nudam imprudens aspicias dominam.
Aspiciet nudam qui Pallada quae tenet urbem,
    Ultra iam hoc Argos cernere non poterit.
Iam veneranda exi Pallas, dum quiddam ego istis   55
    Dicam, nec meus hic sermo sed alterius.
Unam olim, o puerae, Thebis dea Pallas amabat
    Nympham prae cunctis quas habuit comites,
Matrem Tiresiae, nunquamque fuere seorsum,
    Sed sive ad verterum moenia Thespiadum   60
†Sive Coroneas†,[273] seu tenderet illa Haliarton
    Boeotum visens vecta iugis populos,[274]
Sive Coroneas, ubi pulcher odoribus halat
    Lucus, ubi ara ipsi Curalium ad fluvium,
Saepe illam curru secum dea vexit eodem,   65
    Nullaque nympharum colloquia aut thyasi
Grata fuere satis, nisi praeforet ipsa Chariclo.
    Verum et ei multae debitae erant lacrimae,
Quamvis cara comes magnae foret usque Minervae.
    Nam se olim peplis utraque depositis   70
Dum lavat in lymphis Heliconidos Hippocrenes,

against him, he fled and removed your image to Mt. Crion, (40) to Mt. Crion; then on the sheer crags he placed you, and even now they call them the Pallatides. Come forward, Lady, sacker of cities, delighting in the golden helmet, the neighing of horses with the clashing of shields. Water-bearing women, today do not dip your pitchers, Argos, (45) drink today only from the fountains, not the rivers. Today, maidservants, bear your pitchers to Physadea or to Amy-mone, daughter of Danaus. For Inachus himself, mingled with gold and many a flower, will roll his waves from the joyful ridges (50) and bring pure liquid for Athena. Beware, then, Pelasgian, of unwittingly seeing the lady naked. Any man who sees Pallas, upholder of the city, naked, will no longer be able to see this Argos. Go forth now, venerable Pal-las, (55) while I tell these people something, and this tale is not mine but that of another.

At Thebes once upon a time, girls, Pallas loved one nymph above all her other companions, the mother of Tiresias, and they were inseparable. Whether she was bound for the walls of ancient Thespiae (60) †or Coronea†, or driving her char-iot to Haliartus to view the Boeotian peoples, or to Coronea, where the fair grove is fragrant with perfume, where her altar stands beside the Curalius River, many a time the goddess conveyed her with herself in her own chariot, (65) and no conversations or dances of the nymphs held any charm un-less presided over by Chariclo in person. But dear as she might be as companion to the great Minerva, many a tear was in store for her. When one day both had laid aside their gowns (70) and were bathing in the waters of Heliconian

Utque die vacuus mons tacet in medio,
Dum lavat ergo utraque et mediae sunt tempora lucis,
    Dumque est in toto plurima monte quies,
Tiresias unus canibus comitantibus ibat   75
    Per loca sacra, levi flore genas nitidus,
Immensamque sitim cupiens relevare, petito
    Fonte, videt quae non cernere fas homini.
Hic irata licet sic illum affata Minerva est:
    'Quis te non ullis iam rediturum oculis,   80
O Everida malus haec deus in loca duxit?'
    Sic ait, at pueri lumina nox pepulit.
Astitit, obticuit, dolor illi ut glutine vinxit
    Genua, sonum tenuit vocis inops animus.
At nympha exclamans, 'Quid nato,' ait, 'o dea, factum est?   85
    Nunquid vestra, deae, talis amicitia?
Lumina mi pueri rapuisti! Pectora nate
    Vidisti infelix Pallados iliaque,
At non et solem cernes iterum! Heu misera! O mons,
    O Helicon, rursum non peragrande mihi,   90
Magna nimis parvis mutas, qui lumina nati
    Pro cervis paucis dorcadibusque[275] habeas.
Sic puerum ambobus carum complexa lacertis
    Mater flebilium carmen aedonidon
Triste gemens iterat. Sed enim miserata Minerva   95
    Tunc sociam, verbis talibus alloquitur:
'Dia,' inquit, 'mulier, verte haec quae protulit ira:
    Non per me captus luminibus puer est.
Nam pueris auferre oculos haud dulce Minervae,
    Verum Saturni legibus haec rata sunt,   100
Ut quicunque deum aspiciat, nisi iusserit ipse,
    Mercede ingenti scilicet aspiciat.
Dia igitur mulier, fieri haec infecta nequit res,
    Quippe ita Parcarum fila voluta manu,

Hippocrene, and when the empty mountain was silent at midday, when both of them were bathing, then, and the time was midday, and deep silence enveloped the entire mountain, Tiresias was passing alone, with his dogs at his side, (75) through the sacred places, his cheeks gleaming with a light [beard] flowering, wishing to relieve an enormous thirst, he made for the fountain and saw what it is forbidden for a man to see. At this, Minerva, though angered, addressed him thus: "What demon led you to this spot, (80) son of Everes, destined never to return with seeing eyes?" So she spoke, and night drove out the boy's eyes. He stood there in silence, and distress bound his knees as if with glue, his helpless mind restrained the sound of his voice. But the nymph exclaimed, "Goddess, what has happened to my son? (85) Is this the nature of your friendship, goddesses? You have snatched my boy's eyes! Unhappy son, you have seen the breast and flanks of Pallas, but you will never see the sun again! Alas, wretched me! O Mt. Helicon, destined never again to be trodden by me, (90) you have taken all too great a price for small things, since you have my son's eyes in recompense for a few deer and gazelles." Embracing her dear boy with both arms, the mother repeats the song of the mournful nightingales, groaning sadly. (95) But Minerva then took pity on her companion and addressed her with these words: "Lady," she said, "turn back these words prompted by anger: your boy has not been blinded by me. For Minerva takes no pleasure in taking away children's sight, but this has been decreed by Saturn's laws, (100) that whoever looks upon a god, unless he has himself commanded it, sees at a great price. Lady, this thing cannot be undone, since the thread was thus spun by the hand of the Fates already when your

Editus ut primum puer est. Sed tu accipe contra,   105
    O Everida, quod maneat pretium.
Munera Cadmeis pro quanta adolebit in ignes,
    Quanta et Aristaeus, votaque suscipient,
Natus ut impubes Actaeon, unicus illis,
    Tantum oculis careat, namque erit et Triviae   110
Concursor, sed non cursus, non aemulus illum
    Tela arcus iaciens montibus eripiet,
Cum divam (licet invitus) se fonte lavantem
    Viderit, at fiet qui modo erat dominus
Esca suis canibus. Sed enim nemora omnia lustrans   115
    Dum genetrix nati colliget ossa sui,
Tunc te felicem, tunc dixerit esse beatam,
    Cui mons vel caecum reddiderit puerum.
Parce queri, mea grata comes, nam plurima contra
    Huic ego te propter praemia contribuam.   120
Esse dabo egregium vatem, quem protinus omnis
    Perpetuo celebret nomine posteritas,
Cognoscet volucrum quae prospera, quaeque volatu
    Irrita, cuius item triste sit augurium.
Plurima Bœotis[276] oracula, plurima Cadmo   125
    Hic canet, et magnis plurima Labdacidis.
Huic ingens baculum dabo, quod vestigia ducat
    Qua velit, huic vitae tempora longa dabo.
Mox et honoratus Diti, colet infera regna
    Inter et extinctos unicus hic sapiet.   130
Adnuit his Pallas dictis, quodque adnuit illa
    Perficitur: soli Iuppiter hoc tribuit
Natarum e turba, quae sint patris omnia ferre,
    Lotrices; mater nulla deam peperit,
Immo Iovis vertex; vertex Iovis omnia nutu   135
    Perficit, et natae prorsus idem licitum est.[277]

boy was born. But son of Everes, hear, on the other hand, (105) the price that awaits you. What great gift offerings will the daughter of Cadmus consign to the flames. what great ones will Aristaeus, and what vows would they take on, in order for their boy Actaeon, their only child, merely to be without his eyes. For he will be a running companion of Diana, (110) but not the running, not the competitive archery in the mountains will save him, when he has seen (albeit unwittingly) the goddess bathing in the spring, but their former master will become food for his own dogs. But when his mother is scouring all the groves (115) and gathering her son's bones, she then will pronounce you lucky and blessed, to whom the mountain returned your boy, blind though he be. Boon companion of mine, cease to lament, for I will for your sake grant him many a prize in compensation. (120) I will grant him to be an outstanding seer, whose name all posterity will forever celebrate. He will know by their flight which birds are favorable, which useless, and which present baleful auspices. He will chant many an oracle for the Boeotians, many for Cadmus (125) and many for the great Labdacids. I shall give him a great staff to guide his steps where he will, and I shall grant him a long duration of life. Then he will inhabit the lower realms, honored even by Dis, and he alone will have wisdom among the dead." (130)

Pallas nodded in confirmation of these words, and what she nods to is accomplished: Jupiter granted this to her alone of his band of daughters, to have all of her father's powers, bath attendants; no mother bore the goddess, but the forehead of Jupiter; the (135) forehead of Jupiter accomplishes all things with a nod, and the same is permitted to his daughter.[830]

En vere nunc Pallas adest. Eia ergo puellae
   Quis Argos curae est, ite deam accipite
Cumque bonis verbis et cum prece cumque ululatu.
   Salve, o diva, urbem protege et Inachiam.   140
Salve hinc abscedens, iterumque huc flecte iugales,
   Ac rebus Danaum sis, precor, auxilio.

: 81 :

De Ocno et asello,
quodque apud Propertium mendose legitur orno

1 Apud Propertium eundem quarto *Elegiarum* libello ita duo versiculi leguntur:

Dignior obliquo funem qui torqueat Orno,
   Aeternusque tuam pascat, aselle, famem.

Diu, fateor, animum meum stimulaverat ac pupugerat quidam quasi scrupulus, donec eum codex vetustus evellit, quem mihi Bernardinus Valla, celeber iureconsultus et primae homo nobilitatis, Romae abhinc ferme quinquennium commodavit, ubi non *orno*, sed *ocno* legi, legisseque me statim duobus eruditissimis iuvenibus ostendi qui me domi commodum salutaverant. Liquet autem insinuari a Propertio Socraticae illius picturae argumentum, de qua sic Plinius libro *Naturalis historiae* quinto et trigesimo narrat: 'Et piger,' inquit, 'qui appellatur Ocnos spartum torquens quod asellus arrodit.' At enim piger hic Ocnus (ut video) multorum invitamentis vagus repente factus et desultor, cotidie iam sedes mutat.

Lo, Pallas is now truly at hand. Go, then, girls who love Argos, welcome the goddess with words of good omen, with a prayer and with wailing. Hail, goddess, protect the city, and the land of Inachus. (140) Hail when you depart hence and turn your yoke-bearing horses this way again, and, I beg you, give aid to the fortunes of the Danaans.

: 81 :

Concerning Ocnus and the donkey; and that orno is mistakenly read in Propertius

Likewise in Propertius, in the fourth book of his *Elegies*, two lines   1
read as follows:

> He was more deserving than sly Ornus to twist your rope,
> You ass, and forever feed your hunger.[831]

For a long time, I acknowledge, a certain little stone had, as it were, goaded and pricked my mind, until that irritation was plucked out[832] by an old codex that the famous jurist Bernardino Valla, a man of the highest nobility, lent me nearly five years ago in Rome, in which not *orno* but *ocno* is read, which I at once showed I had read to two learned young men who had paid their respects to me at my home. Moreover, it is clear that Propertius was hinting at the subject of a painting by the famous [painter] Socrates, about which Pliny writes in Book 35 of his *Natural History*: "There is also a lazy man, who is called Ocnos, twisting a rope that an ass is gnawing on."[833] Yet, this slothful Ocnus (as I notice) because of many enticements has suddenly become a wanderer and transient and changes his abode daily.

2   Quapropter ut certo in siliquastro conquiescat aliquando, petenda fides est ab eo maxime codice quem citavimus, hoc est (ut vere dixerim) a stirpe de qua istius coniecturae pullulavit occasio. Sic enim quivis intelliget, ne utiquam me mihi asserere aliena sed mea duntaxat, inque meis libris nil prius esse fide.

: 82 :

Quod in Digestis *titulo 'De edendo' legatur 'ad alium,'*
legi 'ad album' convenire

In titulo 'De edendo,' qui secundo *Digestorum* volumine legitur, verba Ulpiani sunt ita libro quarto *Ad edictum*: 'Eum quoque edere Labeo ait, qui producat adversarium suum ad album et demonstret quid dictaturus est.' Sic etenim scriptum in *Pandectis* ipsis Florentinis. Atqui codices omnes qui sunt in manibus non *ad album*, sed *ad alium* habent. Unde multa videlicet Accursi hesitatio. De albo autem praetoris intelliges.

: 83 :

De Harpocrate

1   Epigramma est Catulli:

Laelius audierat patruum obiurgare solere,
    Si quis delicias diceret aut faceret.

Therefore in order that he may finally rest easy in a fixed seat, I   2
must seek the truth above all from this codex that I cited, that is
(to tell the truth), from the root from which the opportunity for
this conjecture sprouted. In this way everyone will understand that
I do not claim others' property but only my own and in my books
nothing has priority over the truth.[834]

: 82 :

In the Digests, *under the title "On Publishing," what is
read as* ad alium *should be read as* ad album

Under the heading "On Publishing," which one reads in the second book of the *Digests*, the words of Ulpian, in his fourth book
On the Edict, are as follows: "Labeo says that he is also publishing
who brings his adversary to the album and shows what he is going
to dictate."[835] For it is written this way in the Florentine *Pandects*
themselves.[836] Yet all codices in circulation have *ad alium* ("to another") rather than *ad album* ("to the album"). Hence Accursio's
great hesitancy [about the text].[837] This should, moreover, be understood as the praetor's album.[838]

: 83 :

Concerning Harpocrates

There is an epigram of Catullus's: 1

Laelius had heard that his uncle was in the habit of scolding
   If anyone were to speak of or engage in carnal pleasures.

411

Hoc ne ipsi accideret, patrui perdespuit ipsam
    Uxorem, et patruum reddidit Harpocratem.
Quod voluit fecit, nam quamvis irrumet ipsum
    Nunc patruum, verbum non faciet patruus.

Quaesitum diu quinam is foret Harpocrates de quo mentionem et
hoc loco faciat Catullus et item in altero epigrammate, sic inquiens:

Si quidquam tacito commissum est fido ab amico,
    Cuius sit penitus nota fides animi,
Me unum esse invenies illorum iure sacratum,
    Corneli, et factum me esse puta Harpocratem.

Nos tamen et Venetiis et item Veronae (quod diximus) abhinc
annos octo ferme de eo studiosis aliquot publice responsitavimus,
quorum nunc testor fidem conscientiamque, si cui forte aliena
adscribere ac non mea potius mihi videor vindicare.

2   Plutarchus igitur in libro quem de Iside fecit et Osiride Harpocraten scribit ex Iside ipsa natum et Osiride, qui cum illa iam
mortuus rem habuerit, sed natum tamen praematuro partu debili-
tatisque cruribus. Porro editum eundem circa brumae tempus minus absolutum et rudem, praeflorentibus puta, praevirentibusque
terrae faetibus, quocirca etiam lentis primitias illi offerri. Neque
tamen inquit aut imperfectum esse deum aut infantem aut denique legumen aliquod existimandum, sed rudis imperfectique
sermonis minimeque articulati praesidem quendam potius ac
moderatorem. Ex quo etiam digito labra comprimit, argumentum
taciturnitatis et silentii. Quin mense eo quem vocant Mesorem

Lest this happen to himself, he fucked his uncle's wife
  And made a Harpocrates of his uncle.
Whatever he wanted, he did, for however much fellatio he
    now receives
  From his uncle, the uncle will not utter a peep.[839]

It has long been investigated who this Harpocrates was whom Catullus mentions both in this passage and in another epigram, as follows:

If something has been entrusted in confidence by a faithful
    friend,
  Who is known to be loyal through and through,
You will find that I am deservedly consecrated as one of those,
  Cornelius, and consider that I have become a
    Harpocrates.[840]

Nevertheless, we have publicly replied to some students in both Venice and likewise Verona (as we said) around eight years ago concerning this, whose good faith and conscience I now call to witness as to whether I appear to ascribe alien property to anyone and not rather claim my own.[841]

Now Plutarch, in his book *On Isis and Osiris*, writes that Harpocrates was born of Isis herself and Osiris, who was already dead when he lay with her, but that he was born nonetheless, prematurely and lame. Moreover, he was born at the winter solstice, imperfect and undeveloped, when the fruits of the earth were, for instance, "preblooming" and "preripening," for which reason the firstfruits of the lentil are offered to him. Nonetheless, he did not say that the god was either imperfect or an infant, or finally that he must be thought to be some sort of legume, but he presides over and moderates undeveloped, imperfect, and inarticulate speech. For this reason he also presses his finger to his lips, a symbol of taciturnity and silence. In fact, in the month that they call

primitias leguminum offerentes ita dictitant, 'lingua fortuna, lingua daemon,' deque Aegyptiacis arboribus persicam inprimis ei sacratam ferunt, quod fructus cordi, frons linguae persimilis. Hactenus ex Plutarcho de Harpocrate, carptim vellicatimque et per intervalla.

3   Meminit eiusdem Lucilius quoque poeta Graecus in epigrammate ad Dionysium, monens ut siquem habeat inimicum, nec Isin ei nec Harpocraten aut qui caecos deus faciat iratos precetur, cogniturum quid deus, quid Simo valeat. Sed et Tertullianus in *Apologetico* sic ait:

> Serapidem et Isidem et Harpocratem cum suo cynocephalo
> Capitolio prohibitos inferri, idest curia deorum pulsos, Piso
> et Gabinius consules, non utique Christiani, eversis etiam
> aris eorum, abdicaverunt, turpium et otiosarum superstitio-
> num vitia cohibentes; his vos restitutis summam maiestatem
> contulistis.

M. autem Varro in libro *De latina lingua* ita scribit: 'Caelum et Terra, hi dei idem qui Aegypti Serapis et Isis, et si Harpocrates digito significat ut taceas.' De hoc igitur intellexit Ovidius libro *Metamorphoseon* nono:

> Sanctaque Bubastis, variisque coloribus Apis
> Quique premit vocem digitoque silentia suadet.

Et item Augustinus libro *De civitate dei* undevigesimo:

> Et quoniam (inquiens) fere in omnibus templis ubi coleban-
> tur Isis et Serapis, erat etiam simulachrum quod digito labiis

Mesor,[842] those offering up the firstfruits of legumes recite the following: "Tongue is luck! Tongue is god!" and from the Egyptian trees they bring the peach, which in particular is sacred to him because its fruit is like the heart, its leaf like the tongue. Up to here has been from what Plutarch says about Harpocrates, excerpted and abridged.[843]

The Greek poet Lucilius, too, mentions Harpocrates in an epigram to Dionysius, warning that if he has any enemy, he should curse him neither to Isis nor Harpocrates, nor any god who blinds angry men, and he will then understand what a god is able to do and what Simo can do.[844] But in his *Apologeticus* Tertullian says:

> The consuls Piso and Gabinius, who were not on any account Christians, in the course of suppressing the vices of base, superfluous superstitions, condemned Serapis and Isis, as well as Harpocrates with his dog-headed baboon, who were forbidden to be brought into the Capitol, that is, they were expelled from the curia of the gods, with their altars overturned as well. You have restored them and conferred the highest majesty on them.[845]

Moreover, Marcus Varro, in his book *On the Latin Language*, writes: "Sky and Earth, the same gods who in Egypt are Serapis and Isis, even if Harpocrates signals with his finger for you to be quiet."[846] Ovid therefore knew about this in the ninth book of his *Metamorphoses*:

> Sacred Bubastis, and Apis with variegated colors,
> And [Harpocrates] who constrains the voice and urges silence
>   with his finger.[847]

And similarly, Augustine writes in Book 19 of his *City of God*:

> Since generally in all the temples where Isis and Serapis were worshipped, there was also a statue that, with a finger

415

impresso admonere videretur, ut silentium fieret, hoc significare idem Varro existimat ut homines eos fuisse tacerent.

Hactenus Augustinus.

4   Sed in epistola Abammonis Aegyptii ad Porphyrium, quam aut
in Graecam vertisse orationem aut certe composuisse Platonicus
Iamblichus existimatur, de deo quodam veluti secundo fit mentio
cui nomen Aegyptiaca lingua fecerit *Icheon*: hunc ostendit silentio
coli oportere. Quod idem etiam de summi dei cultu prolixe Porphyrius ἐν τῷ περὶ ζώων ἀποχῆς. Quin David item propheta
psalmum ita quempiam inchoat:

לך דומיה תהלה אלהים בציון[278]
Lecha dumiggia theilla elohim be ziggion.

Id Latine significat: 'Tibi silentium laus, deus in Sion.' Quod aliter
tamen interpretes Septuaginta verterunt, hoc est: 'Te decet hymnus, deus in Sion.' Quare Harpocratem, puto, Aegyptii suis adhibebant sacris qui silentio colendum ostenderet summum deorum.
Plinius quoque de Harpocrate in libro *Naturalis historie* XXXIII
hactenus meminit: 'Iam vero etiam Harpocratem statuasque Aegyptiorum numinum in digitis viri quoque portare incipiunt.'

5   Ut ergo ad Catullianum Laelium[279] redeamus, scite ille quidem,
ne obiurgaretur a patruo, posthabita illius quam comprimebat
uxore, ipsum iam cepit irrumare patruum eoque pacto tacere coe-
git, quoniam loqui fellator non potest.

pressed to its lips, seemed to admonish one to keep silent, which Varro takes to indicate that they should suppress the fact that they were human beings.[848]

Thus far Augustine.

But in the letter from Abammon of Egypt to Porphyry, which 4 the Platonic philosopher Iamblichus is thought either to have translated into Greek or at any rate to have composed, mention is made of a certain second god to whom he gave the name, in the Egyptian language, of Icheon, and he shows that he [Icheon] must be worshipped in silence.[849] Porphyry said the same in detail about the worship of the supreme god in his treatise *On Abstinence from [Eating] Animals.*[850] In fact, the prophet David also begins a particular psalm in this way [in Hebrew]:

לך דומיה תהלה אלהים בציון
Leha dumia tehila elohim bezion.[851]

In Latin this means: "Silence is praise to you, God in Zion." Nonetheless, the Seventy Translators have rendered this differently, to wit: "A hymn is fitting for you, God in Zion."[852] That, I think, is why the Egyptians adopted Harpocrates in their sacred rites as their supreme god, because he showed that one must worship in silence. Pliny, too, mentions Harpocrates in Book 33 of his *Natural History:* "Now men too are beginning to wear on their fingers [rings with images of] Harpocrates and statues of Egyptian gods."[853]

To return, then, to Catullus's Laelius: in order not to be scolded 5 by his uncle, having set aside his wife, with whom he used to have intercourse, he now cleverly began to have oral sex with his uncle and in this way forced him to keep silent, since a fellator cannot speak.

: 84 :

De libertinis qui vocentur dediticii

1   *Institutiones* hae quae vocantur in iure civili, Iustiniani principis
nomine editae sed a Triboniano tamen doctisque aliis viris compo-
sitae, etiam Graece scriptae sub eodem prorsus intellectu reperiuntur, nisi quia ritus quidam consuetudinesque Romanorum veteres
uberius aliquanto et laxius in Graeco ipso quam in Latino codice
referuntur, ut peregrinis hominibus atque a Romanorum more
consuetudineque alienis res tota penitus innotesceret. Sed quod de
libertinis iis qui dediticii vocabantur strictius breviusque in nostris
Institutionibus, non alienum visum est ex Graeci voluminis sententia
prolixius hic atque ob id etiam dilucidius explicare.

2   Qui igitur apud antiquos manumittebantur, modo maiorem et
iustam libertatem consequebantur et fiebant cives Romani, modo
minorem, et Latini Iuniani ex lege Iuni Norbani fiebant, qui illorum quasi sectae fuerit inventor atque auctor, modo etiam infe-
riorem, et fiebant ex lege Aelia Sentia dediticii. Nam si quisquam
⟨qui⟩[280] diu servitutem servierat supplicium ex delicto dedisset, ut
aut inscriptus fuisset, hoc est ut notas et stigmata inusta fronti
accepisset, aut in publicum carcerem coniectus aut ex delicto ver-
beratus, et se deliquisse confessus fuisset, dein gratia inita a domino[281] manumitteretur, libertinus dediticius vocabatur, ad exemplum videlicet peregrinorum dediticiorum. Nam cum aliquando
peregrini quidam Romanorum vectigales elatis animis bellum repente adversus eosdem suscepissent, tum victi vi, abiectis armis se

418

: 84 :

Concerning the freedmen who are called dediticii

The so-called *Institutes* in the civil law, which were published under   1
the name of the Emperor Justinian but were in fact composed by
Tribonian and other learned men, are found to have been written
with the same content in Greek as well, except that some rituals
and ancient customs of the Romans are described a bit more fully
and loosely in the Greek codex than in the Latin one, so that the
whole subject matter might become known to foreigners and those
alien to Roman custom and practice. But since the freedmen who
were called *dediticii* were discussed more concisely and briefly in
our *Institutes*,[854] it seemed not inapposite to explain them here at
greater length, and hence more clearly, based on the sense of the
Greek text.

So then, among the ancients those who were set free sometimes   2
attained greater, proper liberty and became Roman citizens, but at
other times they attained a lesser degree of freedom and became
"Junian" Latin citizens under the law of Junius Norbanus, who
was the creator and sponsor of their sect, as it were,[855] sometimes
an even a lower type of freedom, and they became *dediticii* under
the Aelian Sentian Law. For if anyone who had long been enslaved
had paid a penalty for a crime so as either to be inscribed, that is,
to receive marks and tattoos branded onto the forehead, or to be
cast into public jail, or flogged for the crime, and confessed that he
had committed the offense, and then, upon winning favor, would
be set free by his owner, he was called a *dediticius* freedman, evidently on the model of foreign prisoners of war. For whenever any
foreign tributaries of the Romans became arrogant and suddenly
rebelled against them but were then conquered by force, threw
away their arms, and surrendered to the victors, they were treated

victoribus dedidissent, hactenus humane tractati sunt a Romanis, ut vitam quidem impetrarent, sed hac velut ignominia notarentur, ut dediticii deinceps vocati sint, quia se dedidissent. Quare etiam libertinorum hoc genus dediticii sunt ab Aelio Sentio nuncupati, ut qui in admittendo crimine velut iidem fuissent, eodem quoque nomine appellarentur.

: 85 :

Cuiusmodi apud Iuvenalem Cereris ludi accipiantur,
deque Cerialium auctore Memmio

1 Iuvenalis in *Satyra* quartadecima sic ait:

Ergo omnia Florae
Et Cereris licet et Cybeles aulaea relinquas.

Nemo ex iis poetae huius interpretibus super ludis Cereris quippiam locutus, non quo nomine appellarentur, non quae fierent in eis, non item a quo primitus celebrati, non ubi de his facta mentio. Quae singula tamen a boni doctique interpretis officio non abhorrebant. Quocirca totum id nobis sarciendum, ne curae istius nostrae scrupulositas in parvulis etiam momentis desideretur.

2 Ludi igitur Cereris, quorum hic est memoria, Cerialia dicti, quibus equorum cursus in Circo celebrabantur, primusque eos C. Memmius aedilis curulis fecit. Cornelius Tacitus in libro *Historiarum* sextodecimo, de Nerone principe loquens: 'Tandem,' inquit, 'statuere Circensium ludorum die qui Cereri celebratur exsequi

humanely by the Romans in that they were granted their lives. But they were branded, as it were, with this mark of infamy, that they were henceforth called *dediticii* ("prisoners of war"), since they had surrendered. This class of freedmen were, accordingly, called *dediticii* by Aelius Sentius,[856] so that those who, by confessing a crime, had been, as it were, the same, were also called by the same name.

: 85 :

What kinds of games of Ceres are understood in Juvenal;
and about Memmius, who originated the festivals of Ceres

Juvenal says in his fourteenth satire: 1

> So you may leave behind all the theater curtains
> Of Flora, Ceres, and Cybele.[857]

Not one of the commentators on this poet has said anything about the games of Ceres—not the name by which they used to be called, not what happened in them, also not by whom they were first celebrated, nor where they are mentioned.[858] Nonetheless, these individual items were not alien to the duty of a good and learned commentator. Therefore I need to repair this entire defect, so that my scrupulous care may not be found wanting even in trivial matters.

The games of Ceres, then, which are recalled here, were called   2
the *Cerealia*, for which horse races were attended by great crowds in the Circus, and which were first held by the curule aedile Gaius Memmius. In the sixteenth book of his *Histories*, speaking about the emperor Nero, Cornelius Tacitus says: "Finally, they decided to carry out their designs on the day of the Circus games that is celebrated in honor of Ceres, because though Caesar rarely went out

destinata, quia Caesar rarus egressu, domoque aut hortis clausus, ad ludicra Circi ventitabat.' Et paulo post: 'Utque Circensium Cerialium ludicrum pluribus equorum[282] cursibus celebraretur.' Ovidius in quarto *Fastorum*:

> Circus erit pompa celeber numeroque deorum,
> Primaque ventosis palma petetur equis.
> Hic Cereris ludi, non est opus indice causa.

Dion quoque *Historiae* scriptor in libro secundo et quadragesimo narrat, potito iam rerum Caesare, aediles tum primum duos ex patriciis, quattuor ex plebe creatos. Sed duos illos superiores a Cerere fuisse denominatos, idque ab illo initio scribit ad suam usque aetatem permanere. Idemque etiam Dion libro septimo quadragesimoque ante devictum Brutum evenisse ait ut aediles plebei gladiatorum certamina pro equorum cursibus Cereri exhibuerint.

3   Praeterea Laurentius Medices, vir omni laude praecellens, nomismata compluria nobis ostendit quae faciem viri barbatam et intonsam habeant, cum duplici titulo: 'Quirinus' et 'C. Memmi,' altrinsecus autem Cereris imagunculam draconibus vehentem, cum titulo huiusmodi: 'Memmius aed. cur. Cerialia preimus fecit,' ubi etiam *preimus*, non *primus*, cum diphthongo in priore syllaba notatum observavimus. Hunc nos putamus autem C. ipsum Memmium fuisse, qui praetor cum L. Domitio fuerit, quique Caesari obiecerit etiam ad cyathum et vinum Nicomedi stetisse cum reliquis exoletis, quique eundem Caesarem asperrimis orationibus laceraverit, mox reconciliatus etiam suffragatorem in petitione consulatus habuerit. De quo sic in epistola ad Atticum Cicero libro quarto: 'O virum, o civem! Memmium Caesaris omnes opes

and stayed shut up at home or in his gardens, he regularly attended the Circus games."[859] And a little later: "And so that the Circus games of the Cerealia might be celebrated with more horse races . . ."[860] Ovid, in Book 4 of his *Fasti*:

> The Circus will be crowded with a parade and a complement
> of gods,
> And first prize will be sought by horses swift as the wind.
> Here are the games of Ceres; there is no need to point out the
> reason.[861]

In the forty-second book of his *Histories*, Dio, too, tells that, when Caesar was already lord of the world, he appointed aediles for the first time, two from among the patricians and four from the plebs.[862] But he named the former two after Ceres, and he writes that this continued from this beginning all the way to his own lifetime. Dio likewise says, in Book 47, that before the defeat of Brutus it came about that the plebeian aediles sponsored gladiatorial contests in place of horse races in honor of Ceres.[863]

Moreover, Lorenzo de' Medici, a man preeminent in every virtue, has shown me a good many coins that have the face of a bearded and long-haired man, with the double legend "Quirinus" and "of C. Memmius," and on the reverse they bear a small image of Ceres being conveyed by snakes, with this legend, "Memmius, curule aedile, first produced the Cerealia." There we also observed that not *primus* but *preimus* was written, with a diphthong in the first syllable.[864] I think, moreover, that this was the very Gaius Memmius who was praetor with Lucius Domitius, and who charged Caesar with being the cupbearer of Nicomedes with other catamites, and who excoriated the same Caesar in bitter speeches, yet who was soon reconciled and even enjoyed his support in his candidacy for the consulate.[865] Cicero writes about this Memmius in a letter to Atticus in his fourth book: "O man, o citizen! All Caesar's resources are strengthening Memmius; they have paired

confirmant, cum eo Domitium consulem iunxerunt, qua pactione epistolae committere non audeo.' Ad eumque, puto, vel certe ad filium liber poetae Lucreti *De rerum natura* scriptus, siquidem et dignitas hominis et tempora congruunt, nisi tamen arbitrari malumus filium potius eiusdem C. Memmi, cognominem patri, aedilem curulem tum factum a Caesare.

: 86 :

De fluctu decimo seu decumano,
cuius permulti poetae meminerunt

1 Ovidi poetae versiculi sunt in primo *Tristium* volumine:

Qui venit hinc fluctus, fluctus supereminet omnes,
    Posterior nono est undecimoque prior.

Decumanum intelligit fluctum, qui fieri maximus dicitur, sicuti ova quoque decumana dicuntur quae maxima. Nam et ovum decimum maius nascitur. Ex hoc scuta quoque decumana, quae essent amplissima sunt appellata. Et decumana in castris porta ab hoste aversa, sicutique decumanus in agro limes ab oriente ad occasum non mihi propterea videtur dictus, quoniam quasi duocimanus, ut M. Iunius Nypsus opinatur, id enim nimis durum et coactum, sed quoniam longissimus et maximus. Nam cardo ipse iam dimidiatus decumano, scilicet anticipante, consideratur. Sed de fluctu decimo sive decumano etiam in undecimo *Metamorphoseon*[283] poeta idem meminit his verbis:

the consul Domitius with him,[866] by what agreement I dare not commit to a letter."[867] To him, I think, or certainly to his son, the book of the poet Lucretius, *On the Nature of the Universe*, was addressed,[868] since the man's rank and date coincide, unless we nonetheless prefer to think that the son of the same C. Memmius, a homonym of his father, was then made curule aedile by Caesar.[869]

: 86 :

On the tenth or "decuman" wave,
which many poets have mentioned

These are lines by the poet Ovid in the first book of his *Tristia*:   1

> Hence comes the wave, the one that towers over them all:
>   It is after the ninth but before the eleventh.[870]

He is referring to the tenth (*decumanus*) wave, which is said to be the biggest, just as with eggs, the biggest are said to be decuman. For the tenth egg laid is bigger. From this the shields that are largest are called "number tens."[871] And the decuman gate in a camp is the one facing away from the enemy, just as the decuman boundary in a field, which lies from east to west, seems to me to have been so called, not because it is, as it were, *duocimanus* ("placed in two piles"), as M. Iunius Nypsus thinks, for that is too hard and forced, but because it is longest and largest.[872] For the baseline itself is thought to have been already halved by the *decumanus*, namely by prior action. But the same poet also speaks in Book II of the *Metamorphoses* about a tenth or decuman wave, with these words:

Vastius insurgens decimae ruit impetus undae.

Et Silius Italicus libro XIIII:

> Non aliter Rhodopes Boreas a vertice[284] preceps,[285]
> Cum sese immisit decimoque volumine pontum
> Expulit in terras.

Sed et Seneca in tragoedia *Agamemnone:*

> Haec onere sidit, illa convulsum latus
> Summittit undis, fluctus hanc decimus tegit.

2   Valerius etiam Flaccus *Argonauticon* secundo sic ait:

> Quanta quoties et Palladis arte
> Incassum decimae cecidit tumor arduus undae.

Lucanus quoque in quinto *Pharsaliae:*

> Haec fatum decimus, dictu mirabile, fluctus
> Invalida cum puppe levat.

Ut vel hoc ipsum notabile sit atque insigne, tantopere decimum istum fluctum velut a conspirante poetarum choro celebrari.

CHAPTER 86

The surging force of a mighty (*decima*) wave crashes down
   with greater destruction.[873]

And Silius Italicus, in Book 14, says:

Just as when the north wind, rushing down from the peak of
   Rhodope,
Plunges and with immense (*decimo*) volume,
Blasts the sea onto the land.[874]

But in his tragedy *Agamemnon* Seneca, too, says:

This [ship] sinks under its own weight, that one exposes
Its battered side to the waves, and an enormous (*decimus*) wave
   inundates another.[875]

In Book 2 of the *Adventures of the Argonauts* Valerius Flaccus,   2
too, says:

How many times by what art of Pallas
Has the towering swell of a huge (*decimae*) wave fallen in
   vain.[876]

And Lucan as well, in the fifth book of his *Civil War*:

After he [Caesar] said that, a huge (*decimus*) wave — wondrous
   to tell! —
Lifted him up, along with his disabled ship.[877]

Hence this very thing is noteworthy and significant, that the tenth
wave is so highly celebrated by, as it were, a chorus of poets in
unison.

: 87 :

Quod erat in Ciceronis epistola vocabulum philotheoron,
corruptum dein improbe in nomen quod est Philocteten

1   In Ciceronis epistola ad Trebatium cuius initium: 'In *Equo Troiano*
scis esse in extremo "sero sapiunt,"' ita scriptum fere cunctis exemplaribus invenitur: 'Deinde quod in Britannia non minus quam
Philocteten te praebuisti, plane non reprehendo.' Diu me torseram
maceraveramque eliciendo sensu de verbis his, neque procedebat.
Quorsum enim de Philoctete hic Cicero?

2   Sed enim postea codicem illum vetustissimum Laurenti Medicis opera sum nactus quem et superius citavi, minus multo quam
ceteri deformatum, inquinatum, perversum, conturbatum. Nam in
eo sic erat: 'Deinde quod in Britannia non minus philotheorum te
praebuisti, plane non reprehendo.' Nam *philotheorus* is est, qui
spectationum studiosus, qualem se Trebatius in Britannia praebue-
rat, dum praelium fugitans, otio se asserit in armis mediis. Ex quo
Ciceroni materia ioci et cavilli.

: 87 :

That the word philotheoros *was in a letter of Cicero's, but
then was wrongly corrupted to the name Philoctetes*

In Cicero's letter to Trebatius, the beginning of which is "You 1
know that in *The Trojan Horse*, at the end are the words 'they are
wise too late,'" in virtually all copies one finds the following written: "Then, I do not at all blame you for showing yourself not less
than Philoctetes in Britain."[878] For a long time I had racked my
brain and tormented myself, trying to tease some sense out of
these words, but there was no progress. Why on earth was Cicero
writing about Philoctetes here?

But afterward, through the effort of Lorenzo de' Medici, I came 2
upon the very ancient codex that I cited above,[879] one much less
distorted, contaminated, corrupted, and confused than the others.
In it [the wording] was: "Then, I do not at all blame you for showing yourself no less a sight-seeing enthusiast in Britain." For a
philotheorus is someone who is a sight-seeing enthusiast, such as
Trebatius had shown himself to be in Britain, who, while fleeing
battle, laid claim to leisure in the midst of armed conflict. This
was the source of Cicero's jests and jeers.[880]

: 88 :

Unde illud tractum 'fuimus Troes,'
quaeque extent in litteris super
Lacedaemoniorum choro et cantico

1 'Fuimus Troes,' hic loquendi color tam efficax, de consuetudine chori illius Lacedaemonii ductus quasique in adagium ascitus. Nam ut est scriptum apud Plutarchum in libello cui sic est titulus, *Quo pacto laudare se quispiam citra invidiam valeat*, chorus erat Lacedaemoniorum trifarius, senum, puerorum, iuvenum. Canebant autem senes ita: ἄμμες ποτ᾽ ἦμεν ἄλκιμοι νεανίαι, quo significabant fuisse quondam se robustos iuvenes. Pueri vero sic: ἄμμες δέ γ᾽ ἐσσόμεσθα²⁸⁶ πολλῷ κάρρονες, ex quo se futuros longe his meliores profitebantur. Iuvenum autem cantio haec: ἄμμες δέ γ᾽ εἰμέν. αἱ δὲ λῆς²⁸⁷ αὐγάσδεο, indicans ipsos iam id esse quod vel illi fuissent vel hi futuros sperarent, eiusque rei paratos facere periculum.

2 Quod item scriptum in Diogeniani collectaneis, consimile proverbium de Milesiis ponit Aristophanes in comoedia *Pluto*: πάλαι ποτ᾽ ἦσαν ἄλκιμοι Μιλήσιοι, ut iam non esse eos viros fortes intelligamus quos olim fuisse dicamus. Hoc intellectu Cicero de coniuratis agens 'vixerunt' inquit, extinctos ea voce nescio quo pacto significantius declarans minusque multo invidiose quam si plane dixisset occisos.

: 88 :

The source of the famous expression "we were Trojans,"
and literary survivals about
the chorus and song of the Spartans

"We were Trojans," this palliative, so effective, was derived from   1
the custom of the Spartan chorus and has acquired quasi-
proverbial status.[881] For as Plutarch wrote in the little book entitled *How To Praise Oneself without Incurring Envy,* the Spartans'
chorus had three divisions: old men, boys, and young men. Moreover, the old men used to sing as follows: "We were once strong
young men," by which they indicated that they had once been ro-
bust young men. But the boys sang: "We shall be much braver," by
which they avowed that they would be far better than they. However, the song of the young men was this: "We are [such now]. If
you wish, take a good look!" indicating that they were at present
what the one group had been and the other group hoped to be,
and that they were prepared to put that to the test.[882]

A similar proverb about the Milesians is likewise included in   2
Diogenianus's collections[883] and was cited by Aristophanes in his
comedy *Wealth:* "The Milesians were once strong long ago," so that
we understand that they are no longer the brave men we say they
once were.[884] In this sense, Cicero said of the conspirators, "they
have lived," by that word declaring somehow more poignantly that
they were dead, and far less invidiously than if he had frankly said
that they had been killed.[885]

: 89 :

Quod Servius grammaticus Bucolicos Maronis versus tam
mendose legit quam falso enarrat,
notataque ibi et relata quaedam super initiandis
pueris superque dis aliquot veterum,
maximeque geniis et iunonibus

1 In *Bucolicis* Vergilianis hi duo sic versiculi leguntur:

> Incipe, parve puer, cui non risere parentes,
> Nec deus hunc mensa, dea nec dignata cubili est.

Quos enarrans Servius, haud inceleber grammaticus, et veram lectionem (quod eius pace dixerim) contaminat et fabulam sibi ex tempore commodoque suo confingit, contra omnem veterum auctoritatem. Neque enim *cui*, sed *qui* legendum, hoc est non casu dativo singularique numero sed plurali nominativo, quanquam utrobique apud veteres eadem vox iisdemque notata litteris, sicuti in primo Quintiliani *De institutione oratoria* non oscitans lector inveniet. Ex quo etiamnum versiculus in VII Valeri Flacci *Argonaticon* libro:

> Curaque cui profuga forsan tenet alta carina.

Etiamnum, inquam, iste versiculus *cui* retinet, non *qui*, tam scilicet in vetustissimo codice de quo reliqui fluxere, quam in his quoque pervulgatioribus. Quod autem dicimus *qui* legendum, non *cui*, docet idem Quintilianus in nono, figuram esse declarans hic in numero sic ut plurali singularis subiungatur: 'Ex illis enim,' inquit,

432

: 89 :

That the philologist Servius reads the verses of Vergil's
Bucolics as erroneously as he explains them, and certain
things noted and related there about initiating
children and about several gods of the ancients,
in particular the geniuses and junos[886]

In Vergil's *Bucolics* one reads these two verses in this form: 1

> Begin, little boy, on whom (*cui*) his parents have not smiled,
> Neither has a god deemed him worthy of sharing his table nor
> a goddess of her bed.[887]

When Servius, that famous philologist, was explaining these lines,
he both corrupted the true reading (let this be said with his permission) and fabricated a tale on the spot and for his own convenience, contrary to every ancient source.[888] For the text must read
not *cui* but *qui*, that is, not in the dative case and singular number
but in the nominative plural, even though among the ancients in
both cases it is the same word, spelled with the same letters, as the
attentive reader will discover in the first book of Quintilian's *Orator's Education*.[889] Hence a line in the seventh book of Valerius Flaccus's *Adventures of the Argonauts* still has:

> . . . and love [for him], who (*cui*) perhaps is sailing on the
> high seas in flight.[890]

That line, I say, still retains *cui*, not *qui*, both in a very old codex,
from which the others derived,[891] as well as in the more common
codices. Moreover, as to the fact that we say that *qui*, not *cui*, must
be read, Quintilian teaches this in Book 9, showing that here is a
figure of number such that the singular follows the plural: "Of

'qui non risere, hunc non dignata.' Quis autem dubitet, quin de Vergilianae lectionis incolumitate Quintiliano credendum sit potius quam Servio, praesertim qui manum quoque Vergili citet aliquando et Ciceronis? Quocirca manifestum est quod diximus, mendose locum a Servio adduci.

2   Fabulam autem sibi eundem ex proposito commodoque finxisse quis non videat, cum nusquam ob id praecipitatum fuisse Volcanum legamus quoniam deformis natus quoniamque ei non Iuno arriserit? Etenim poeta Homerus ob id ait, quod matri contra Iovem patrem suppetias tulerit. Natus enim ex Iove et Iunone secundum Homerum Volcanus, licet ex Iunone sola fingat Hesiodus in *Theogonia*, sicuti ex solo Iove Minerva dicitur. Unde ἀπάτωρ a Theocrito vocatur in aenigmatio cui βωμός inscriptio. Quare parentes ad Iovem Iunonemque vix satis etiam proprie referentur. Sed et illud sane quam frigide Servius idem quod neque admissum ad epulas deorum Volcanum dicit neque divinos honores meruisse, quem Varro etiam inter selectos deos numerat septimum. Tum ne processerit quidem vel isto pacto quod molitur Servius, quando non ob id ait praecipitatum quod haud riserit, sed quod ipsi haud arrisum. Viderimus, utrumne ipse mox credibiliora suspicer, certe iam Servius verissimis revincitur.

3   Et quidem sic ego legerim, sic enarraverim. Parentes Salonini pueri, de quo nunc agitur, ut sit parentes vocandi casus, hunc qui non risere neque deus mensa dignatus neque dea cubili, hoc est nec genius nec iuno vitalibus auris dignum putavere hunc, ex illis qui non risere, ut sit figurate dictum, Quintiliano teste, pro eo quod est 'hunc qui non risit' vel 'qui e numero est eorum qui non

434

those who have not smiled, she has not deemed *him* worthy."[892] Furthermore, who would doubt that one must trust Quintilian on the soundness of a reading of Vergil rather than Servius, particularly since on occasion he cites autograph copies of Vergil and Cicero?[893] Therefore our claim is abundantly clear, that the passage was erroneously cited by Servius.

Moreover, who fails to see that he fabricated the tale for his 2 own purpose and convenience, since nowhere do we read that Vulcan was cast down [out of heaven] because he was born deformed and because Juno had not smiled on him? For the poet Homer says it was because he gave his mother aid against his father Jupiter.[894] For according to Homer, Vulcan was born of Jupiter and Juno, though Hesiod in the *Theogony* invents that he was born from Juno alone, just as Minerva is said to have been born from Jupiter alone.[895] That is why he is called "fatherless" by Theocritus in the riddle poem entitled "Altar."[896] Therefore the "parents" are not properly connected with Jupiter and Juno. But Servius was likewise lame in saying that Vulcan neither was admitted to the feasts of the gods nor merited divine honors, whom Varro even counts as seventh among the select gods.[897] Then again, not even that point would succeed which Servius labors over so much, when he claims that Vulcan had been cast down, not because he scarcely smiled but because they barely smiled upon him. We shall see whether I, in turn, will offer a more credible hypothesis, but Servius at any rate is already refuted by cogent arguments.

The following is the way I would read and interpret the passage. Parents of the boy Saloninus,[898] — who is now being discussed, so that *parentes* is in the vocative case — this boy who have [*sic*] not smiled, neither has a god deemed worthy of a table nor a goddess of a bed, that is, neither a genius nor a juno thought him worthy of vital breath, being among those who have not smiled, so that it is said figuratively, on Quintilian's testimony, instead of "him who *has* not smiled," rather "who is among those who have

risere.' Credebatur enim habere quisque suum deum suamque deam, hoc est suum genium suamque iunonem vitae praesides. Hos igitur indicavit Maro *catexochen*. Mensa enim genio convenit, ut 'funde merum genio,' iunoni lectus. Quod Iunius quoque Philargyrius docet, hunc ipsum ita interpretans locum: 'Pueris,' inquit, 'nobilibus editis, in atrio Iunonis Lucinae lectus ponitur Herculis mensura.' Sed et apud Varronem lectum est, initiari pueros Educae, Potinae, et Cubae, divis edendi, potandi, et cubandi, ubi primum a lacte et cunis transferunt. Quam Varronis auctoritatem Donatus in *Phormionem* Terentianam adducens, etiam hunc ipsum citavit Maronis versiculum, atque idem Probum quoque rettulit adnotasse. Mensa igitur et lectus argumenta vitalitatis, quod initiis ipsis adhiberentur. Ceterum habet homo suam sibi ridendi proprietatem. Qui vero non rideat ei qui potest esse 'vita vitalis,' ut ait Ennius? Deum vero deamque ad has referre Varronis Educam, Potinam, Cubamque nequeas, quod hae feminae omnes, ut Augustinus etiam in libro *De civitate dei* sexto declaravit. Sed nec ad Pilumnum ratione pari et Pitumnum, coniugales deos, ⟨de⟩[288] quibus ut ait Varronem scribere Marcianus in secundo libro *De vita patrum*: 'Natus si erat vitalis, simul ab obstetrice fuerat sublatus et in terra stratus, ut esse rectus auspicaretur, sternere etiam in aedibus lectum consueverunt.'

4   Restat igitur, uti quod de genio et iunone diximus, auctoritatum quoque tibicinibus fulciatur. Plinius itaque *Naturalis historiae* primo: 'Cum singuli,' inquit, 'ex semet ipsis totidem deos faciant, genios iunonesque adoptando sibi.' Seneca *Epistolarum ad Lucilium* undevigesimo: 'Ita tamen,' ait, 'hoc seponas volo ut memineris

not smiled." For each person was believed to have his own god or
her own goddess, that is, his own genius or her own juno presiding over their life. Maro [Vergil] therefore pointed to them *par
excellence*. A table befits the genius, as in "Pour the wine for the
family god (*genio*),"[899] a bed befits the juno. Junius Philargyrius,
too, teaches this, interpreting this specific passage as follows:
"When noble children were born, a bed of Juno Lucina, of Herculean size, is placed in the atrium."[900] In Varro, too, one reads that
as soon as they transfer them from nursing and the cradle, children are initiated to Educa, Potina, and Cuba, the divinities of
eating, drinking, and sleeping.[901] Donatus on Terence's *Phormio*,
adducing Varro's authority, also cited this very verse of Maro's and
reported that Probus also indicated the same in a note.[902] The table therefore and the bed are proofs of vitality since they were applied to the very beginnings. Moreover, human beings have laugh-
ter as their own special characteristic.[903] How can there be "vital
life," as Ennius says,[904] in one who does not smile? But one may
not refer "god and goddess" to these entities of Varro's, Educa,
Potina, and Cuba, since these are all female, as Augustine also
pointed out in his sixth book *On the City of God*.[905] But by the
same token one may not refer them to Pilumnus and Pitumnus,
the gods of marriage, about whom, as Martianus [Capella] says,
Varro writes in Book 2 of his *On the Life of Parents*: "If he had been
born full of life, once he had been held up by the midwife and laid
out on the ground, so that his auspices might properly be taken,
they were also wont to make up a bed in the house."[906]

It remains, then, to support what I have said about the genius   4
and juno with the props of authorities. And so Pliny says in the
first book of his *Natural History*: "Since individuals create from
themselves just as many gods by adopting geniuses and junos for
themselves."[907] In the nineteenth book of his *Letters to Lucilius*,
Seneca says: "Yet I want you to put this aside in such a way as to

maiores nostros, qui crediderint, Stoicos fuisse. Singulis enim et genium et iunonem dederunt.' Unde, arbitror, Iuvenalis:

Et per Iunonem, inquit, domini iurante ministro.

Hoc enim reprehendit satyricus poeta quod non per genium, sed per iunonem domini minister iuraret, videlicet more muliebri. Quocirca sic illa apud Petronium Arbitrum Quartilla loquitur:

Iunonem meam iratam habeam, si unquam meminerim virginem fuisse. Nam infans cum paribus inquinata sum, et subinde prodeuntibus annis maioribus me pueris applicui donec ad hanc aetatem perveni. Hinc etiam puto natum proverbium illud, dicatur ut posse taurum tollere qui vitulum sustulerit.

5   Ceterum si detur modo, non iniquam plane a nobis peragi reprehensionem labascereque iam commentum istud Servianum quod antea quam[289] talia prodebamus pro indubitato obtinuerat, reliqua in medium (ne nobis blandiamur) libera opinaturis relinquemus.

: 90 :

Qui vir Theodorus Gaza quantumque tamen lapsus in Aristotelis Problemate *verso*

1   Non recuso quin sub censuram sub aleamque veniat qualecunque hoc erit de quo scribam, dum ne sint in hoc albo duae mihi maxime suspectae litterariae pestes, inscitia invidiaque, dum ne quis mihi *amusoteros* (ut verbo utar quo Symmachus), dum ne quis

remember that our ancestors, who were believers, were Stoics. For to each individual they assigned a genius or a juno."[908] From this, I think, derives Juvenal's verse:

And while the servant swears by his master's juno.[909]

For the satirist criticizes the fact that the servant swore not by the genius, but the juno of his master, that is, according to the custom of women. And so Quartilla speaks as follows in Petronius Arbiter:

May my juno be angry with me if I ever remember having been a virgin. For as a child I was defiled by mates, and then as the years advanced, I turned my attention to older boys, until I arrived at my current age. I think this is the origin of the well-known proverb, which says he can lift a bull who has lifted a calf.[910]

But if it only be granted that I have engaged in no unfair critique and that that comment of Servius's, which had held the ground as beyond cavil before I published these things, is now torn to pieces, I shall (lest I flatter myself) leave the rest open for others to judge.[911]

: 90 :

What a great man Theodore Gaza was, and yet how greatly he erred when translating one of Aristotle's Problems[912]

I do not object to whatever I write here being subjected to the hazard of criticism provided that ignorance and envy, the two plagues of literature that I most suspect, be excluded from the list of jurors, provided that no philistine (as Symmachus put it[913]),

opicus, dum ne quis durus et contumax et in hominis verba quam in veri fidem iuratus contingat iudex. Quod si iudices etiam nuncupandi, non Tarentinos equidem et Consentinos et Siculos mea ista legere, sicuti sua quaedam Lucilius, sed Latinos homines, Graecae litteraturae[290] non ignaros, non Iunium Congum[291] volo, sed Scipionem, sed doctissimum omnium Persium, atque Rutilium, hoc est, siqui sunt illis compares, macti prudentia ingenio doctrinaque viri, ad quorum iudicium iure sit elaborandum. Qualis, puta, si liceat, is ipse est qui mihi instrumenta studiorum tam multa otiumque altissimum suppeditat, avis atavisque potens, Medices Laurentius, Florentinae reipublicae columen, cuius cum iudicium illud circumspectissimum et naturalem quandam mentis altitudinem maximae quaeque in actu rerum vel civitates experiuntur vel principes, tum eundem in litteris et humanitatis ac sapientiae studiis, ei denique non admirantur, qui non penitus, ut ipsi qui non introrsus inspexerunt.

2   Qualis est item Iohannes Picus hic meus e Mirandulanis principibus, absolutissimum naturae opus, a quo philosophia Latine iam meditans loqui, summum, puto, fastigium accipiet. Quales praeterea duo illi, sed una devincti amoris copula, Veneti patricii sunt Hermolaus Barbarus, barbariae hostis acerrimus, qui Latinae philosophiae velut arma instrumentumque verborum sic aut aure diligentissima terget aut incude nova fabricatur, ut ob ipsius industriam iam nunc pene in isto quidem genere vel nitore vel copia vivamus ex pari cum Graecis, et Hieronymus Donatus, vir nescio utrum gravior an doctior an etiam humanior, certe omni lepore affluens, omni venustate, cuius tamen ob id vereor ne levior cuiquam censura videatur quoniam me pulcherrimo carmine sed et epistola una atque altera mire laudavit. Licet enim tantum boni de

boorish, insensitive, and insulting person, sworn to defend an individual's words rather than the plain truth, be empaneled as juror. But if jurors are to be appointed, I do not want the Tarentini and Consentini and Sicilians to read these words of mine, just as Lucilius did not want them to read his, but Latins schooled in Greek literature, not Junius Congus but Scipio or Persius, the most learned of all,[914] and Rutilius, that is, if there are any like them, men extolled for wisdom, talent, and learning, to meet the standard of whose judgment one may rightly take pains — such as, for instance, if I may, the man who supplies me with so many tools and deep leisure for my studies, a man of distinguished forefathers and ancestry, Lorenzo de' Medici, pillar of the Republic of Florence, whose prudent judgment and innate loftiness of intellect in the administration of affairs both the greatest cities and princes have experienced, and [only] persons who have not contemplated deeply or inwardly fail to marvel that he is the same in literature and humane and philosophical studies.

Such is likewise my friend Giovanni Pico, scion of the princes 2 of Mirandola,[915] the most perfect work of nature, from whom philosophy, which was already practicing speaking Latin, will, I think, receive its crown. Such also are two distinguished noblemen of Venice, joined by a single bond of love, Ermolao Barbaro, fiercest enemy of barbarism, who, with his sedulous ear, is either wiping clean the verbal arms and equipment, as it were, of Latin philosophy or forging it with a new anvil,[916] so that thanks to his diligence, in that genre we are already, in terms of elegance and richness of expression, more or less on an equal footing with the Greeks;[917] and Girolamo Donà, a man who excels, I know not whether in authority, learning, or humanity, but certainly abounding in every charm and grace. I fear, however, that someone may hold his judgment to be less weighty because he has bestowed remarkable praise upon me in a pretty poem and in one or two letters.[918] Though it may be a shame to believe such a good report

me ipso, qui multum a tolerabili, nedum a perfecto, absum, pudeat credere, magis tamen tanto viro pudet non credere talia de me, sic (ut apparet) ex animo affirmanti. Quare istis quidem paucis aut eorum (siqui sunt) consimilibus, dum nostra haec, qualiacunque sunt, arriserint, floccipendo iam nunc imagines penitus umbrasque larvarum, quibus natura esse dicitur (ut sancti viri verbis utar) terrere parvulos et in angulis garrire tenebrosis.

3   Theodorus igitur Gaza, vir Graecus et, ut doctis etiam videtur, eruditissimus, Aristotelis *Problemata* vertit in Latinum. Sed in quo Problemate quaeritur cur homines, qui ingenio claruerunt, vel in studiis philosophiae, vel in republica administranda, vel in carmine pangendo, vel in artibus exercendis, melancholicos omnes fuisse videamus, et alios ita ut etiam vitiis atrae bilis infestarentur, in eo manifestius utique (ni fallor) insigniusque extitit interpretis erratum quam ut excusari iam dissimularive possit. Nam cum illic exempla subiiciat Aristoteles heroum qui laborasse dicantur atra bile, primumque de Hercule agat, fuisse illum nimirum tali habitudine signis argumentisque colligit[292] istiusmodi, quod et comitialis morbus sacer ab eo sit dictus, et filios occiderit vecors, ut in Senecae tragoedia tractatur, et antequam obiret, scatentium ulcerum eruptione laboraverit, unde illa, puto, Nessea[293] tunica venerit in fabulam, nam hoc quoque vitium atrae bilis est. Ex quo etiam Lysandro Lacedaemonio proxime ante obitum genus id, inquit, ulcerum emersit.

4   Theodorus itaque, quod ad filios et ad ulcera Herculis attinet, ita denique interpretatur: 'Puerorum quoque,' inquit, 'motio mentis idem hoc explicat et eruptio ulcerum quae mortem interdum antecedit,' cum sit ita Graece: καὶ ἡ περὶ τοὺς παῖδας ἔκστασις καὶ ἡ πρὸ τῆς ἀφανίσεως αὐτοῦ ἐν τῇ ἑλκῶν ἔκφυσις γενομένη. Neque autem dubitem ex usu esse, antequam ipsi

about me, who am far removed from the tolerable, to say nothing of the perfect, nevertheless it is a greater shame not to believe so great a man when he makes such (apparently) sincere assertions about me. So then as to those few or those like them (if any there be), since they sneer at this work of mine,[919] whatever its character, I now rate them as specters or shadows of ghosts, for whom it is said to be natural (to use the words of a sacred man) to terrorize children and chatter in gloomy corners.[920]

So then, Theodore Gaza, a Greek and a most erudite one, as it appears even to scholars, translated Aristotle's *Problems* into Latin.[921] But in the Problem in which it is queried why we see that men of genius who were distinguished either in philosophy or statesmanship or poetry or in the arts, were all melancholic, and that others were such as to be damaged by black bile,[922] a translator's error arose that is too flagrant (if I am not mistaken) and egregious to be able to be excused or covered up. For when in that passage Aristotle cites examples of heroes who are said to have been afflicted by black bile, he first discusses Hercules; he infers that he was such a type from such signs and evidence: that epilepsy was named the sacred disease after him, that he slew his children in madness — the subject of Seneca's tragedy — and before he died he suffered from an outbreak of suppurating sores, the source, I believe, from which the famous tunic of Nessis passed into legend, for this, too, is a symptom of black bile. As a result of this, he says, such sores also appeared on Lysander of Sparta just before his death.[923]

Theodore, then, translates as follows as regards the children 4 and sores of Hercules: "The mental distraction of children and the eruption of sores which sometimes precede death disclose the same phenomenon [i.e., melancholia]," although in Greek it is as follows: "both his frenzy regarding his children and the outbreak of sores in the ($ \dot{\epsilon}\nu\ \tau\hat{\eta} $) prior to his death." I would, however, not doubt that it is useful, before I translate the passage myself, to

locum vertimus, perpendere diligentius quid sibi illud velit ἐν τῇ, quod ille dissimulat, quaeve de praepositione articuloque illo abiuncto sententia elici possit. Et quidem ego sic arbitror legendum corrigendumque ἐν Οἴτῃ, ut sit ad verbum sensus: Et in liberos suos pavor, seu mavis dicere mentis excessus, et ante obitum ipsius in Oeta ulcerum eruptio. Quod autem *pavorem* maluimus aut *mentis excessum* vertere quam, ut iste, *motionem mentis*, quae Graece sit *ecstasis*, auctorem sequimur in priore quem Psalmorum probat interpretem Pictaviensis Hilarius, in posteriore Hieronymum, qui tamen alicubi solitarium quoque illud *excessus* Latine pro illo *ecstasis* reddidit. Nam *pavorem* Cicero quoque metum definit esse mentem loco moventem. Sed de nomine alias. Nunc quod instat.

5   Profert exempla Aristoteles per quae manifestum fiat Herculem quoque atra bile vexatum, sicuti dein Aiacem, Bellerophontem, ceterosque ostendit, ut sensus, ordo, ratio, praetereaque veritas inexpugnabilis et vinci nescia, nostrae prorsus interpretationi suffragentur. Quorsum enim hic de pueris mente motis in mediis agatur heroibus, aut quae magis aetas a bile hac atra quem furorem dicimus quam puerilis abest? Quid autem generalem hanc ulcerum ante obitum eruptionem accipit, quod neque verba significant Aristotelis et plane illius proposito voluntatique contrarium, nempe qui probare nitatur ex argumentis quibuspiam atque exemplis, non pueros, non quoslibet atra bile, sed heroas maximosque viros inquietari? Quin illud etiam diligentius cogitandum, sacerne tantum morbus, ut Aristoteles ait, an etiam Herculeus, quod de suo Theodorus adicit, appelletur. (Atque locum eundem male versum a Petro etiam Aponensi, cui cognomentum ex re Conciliatori factum, naturae rerum ac medicinae consultissimo, sed, ut tum fuere tempora, parum linguae utriusque perito homine, minus

weigh carefully the function of ἐν τῇ ("in the"), which he conceals, or what thought can be elicited from the preposition and detached article.[924] I for one think that ἐν Οἴτῃ ("on Oeta") must be read and introduced as a correction, so that the literal sense is: "And his frenzy toward his children," or if you prefer, "his derangement, and the outbreak of sores prior to his death on Oeta."[925] In that we preferred to render the Greek *ecstasis* as "frenzy" (*pavor*) or "derangement" (*mentis excessus*), rather than "mental distraction" (*motio mentis*), as he did, we are following, in the former case, the translator of the Psalms whom Hilary of Poitiers approves,[926] in the latter, Jerome, who, however, has elsewhere rendered *ecstasis* in Latin by "derangement" (*excessus*) alone.[927] For Cicero, too, defines frenzy as fear that moves the mind from its normal state.[928] But we shall deal with the noun another time. Now the present matter.

Aristotle cites examples by which it becomes clear that Hercu- 5
les, too, was afflicted by black bile, just as he shows that Ajax, Bellerophon, and others were, so that sense, order, reason, and truth, which is unassailable and invincible, support our interpretation. What is the point of discussing children who are mentally unbalanced in the midst of heroes, or what age is further removed from the black bile that we call frenzy than childhood? What of the fact that he understands this to be a general outbreak of sores before death, which is not indicated by Aristotle's words and is clearly opposite to his thesis and intent, since he is trying to prove with some evidence and examples not that children or any persons at random are troubled by black bile, but heroes and great men?[929] In fact, this too ought to be considered more carefully, whether it is only called the sacred disease, as Aristotle says, or also the Herculean disease, as Theodore adds on his own. (I am less indignant that the same passage was badly translated by Pietro d'Abano,[930] who as a result of his action earned the sobriquet "the Harmonizer,"[931] a man expert in natural science and medicine but, as the times then were, less skilled in both languages.) Theodore, more-

equidem indigner.) Is autem errantem suo semet indicio prodit in commentario quodam super haec ipsa *Problemata* composito. In eas enim se coniecerat angustias ut explicare nil possit, ac 'stuporem sive' quod ait ipse 'congelationem quae pueris accidat denominari inde' cogatur dicere, hoc est (ut arbitror) ab Hercule. Quod ego illi tum dedero cum denominationis istius vox quaepiam indidem pronuntiabitur.

6   Sed enim Theodori causam facile iam quivis impulsam, prostratam, constrictam sciat, etiam si nihil adiciamus. Quin ipse, credo, si revivisceret et de hoc admoneretur, neutiquam pro recto defenderet, si plus vero daret quam studio potius, ut in duodecim scriptis adsolet, quoniam moti semel peniteret, concedi sibi postularet ut calculum reduceret. Nec autem nos haec de eo notaremus, si non plurimi faceremus. Non enim sic dementis otii sumus ut incolumi dignitate nostra velimus eo abuti contra recentem nimiumque iam trivialium nugamentorum proventum, contraque ista, pene dixerim, mendicabula et propudia garrulorum, nescio risune explodenda magis an silentio dissimulanda, quo perpetuo ignobiles inter suas ineptias delitescant.

7   Hoc autem duntaxat attulimus, non quidem obstrigilandi quod dicitur causa, sed admonendi potius studiosos qui scribendi onus hoc laboriosissimum pariter invidiosissimumque susceperint, nequid unquam de intentione remittant, neu parcant industriae operaeque, neve indulgeant sibi aut oneri cedant. Circumspiciant undique, librent, pensent, exigantque singula, nihilque non olfactent, non excutiant, non examinent, non castigent etiam atque etiam, ac sub incudem saepius revocent, consulantque interim vel minus eruditos, et tenuiorum (ut ita dixerim) viriculas non aspernentur, quando ita ferme comparatum est ut in alienis erratis lyncei simus,

over, betrays that he went astray in his judgment in the commentary he composed on these same *Problems*. He got himself into such difficulties that he can explain nothing and he is compelled to explain that "the stupor or," as he says, "the frozenness that befell the children is named from this," that is (I believe), from Hercules. I will grant him this if any hint of that name will be cited from the same passage.

But anyone may easily realize that Theodore's case has already 6 collapsed, been overthrown, and blocked, even if I were to add nothing else. Indeed, if he were to rise from the dead and were advised about this, he would, I think, hardly defend its correctness if he attaches greater value to truth than to partisanship, as is the custom when playing draughts, when someone regrets a move, he demands that he be allowed to withdraw the piece.[932] I would not have stigmatized these points concerning him if I did not think a great deal of him. For I do not have such an extravagant abundance of leisure that I would wish to abuse it [by arguing], even with my dignity intact, against the recent, excessive harvest of trifles and nonsense and against, I might almost say, the shameful beggars' tools of chatterboxes — I know not whether they should be laughed offstage or covered over with silence so that ignoble persons may lie forever hidden amid their follies.

I have raised this point not for the sake of causing destruc- 7 tion,[933] so to speak, but rather to warn scholars who have taken up this burden of writing that is laborious and invidious alike not to give up their plan and neither to spare their hard work nor to indulge themselves or give way to the burden. Let them look about on all sides, balance, weigh, let them test points one by one, let them sniff out, investigate, examine, criticize everything again and again, and let them often bring things back under the anvil, sometimes let them even consult unlearned persons[934] and not despise the modest strength of lesser persons (so to speak), since it is generally the case that we are lynx-eyed as regards others' errors

in nostris lippi caecique, ac non videamus, ut Catullus ait, 'manticae quod in tergo est.' Sed in primis caveant hoc tamen qui scribunt, ne dum nimis ad vota laudum properant, cruda adhuc in publicum sua studia propellant.

8   Illud in Theodoro mirari me fateor, quid ita scripserit in praefatione librorum *De animalibus* Aristotelis, quibus unis praecipue commendatur, adiutum sese a nullo, nec certare adeo cum ceteris interpretibus, quos, inquit, vincere nullum negotium est, cum libros eosdem sic Georgius Trapezuntius ante ipsum luculente verterit ut vel redditis quae apud veteres invenerat vel per se denuo fictis excogitatisque vocabulis, Latiam prorsus indolem referentibus, vitio factum nostro primus, opinor, iuniorum docuerit cur ipsi minus multas quam Graeci rerum appellationes habeamus. Hos igitur si quis libros diligenter legerit, minus profecto Gazam laudabit pene illius vestigiis insistentem. Quin si homo erit ingenuus, credo, stomachabitur sic a Theodoro dissimulatum per quem maxime profecerat, sic habitum pene contemptui ludibrioque cuius potissimum laboribus insidiabatur. Nobis vero etiam fortasse habebit gratiam, quod ista reddere suis auctoritatibus contendamus. Nam quantum sibi Georgius in eo placuerit opere vel illa de praefatione verba significant, quibus sese libros eos Latinis ait non minus elegantis emendatosque dare quam apud Graecos habeantur. Sed et hoc ad se trahere Theodorus conatur, ut item quae de mensibus Graece prodidit, ex huius potissimum de qua loquimur interpretationis prohoemio sublegantur. At enim fuere (sicut apparet) acerbissimae inter hos Graecos inimicitiae, sicut in grammatico quoque suo commentario Theodorus Georgium vocet hunc *Pornoboscon*, quod alentem scorta significat, alludens, arbitror, ad Georgium veterem grammaticum, cui cognomentum Graeci *Choeroboscon* dixere.

but bleary-eyed and blind to our own, and as Catullus says, we fail to see "the bag on our own back."[935] But writers should be especially wary lest in their haste to fulfill their hopes of praise they push their studies, still raw, into the public forum.

I confess that in Theodore's case I am surprised at what he 8 wrote in the preface to Aristotle's books *On Animals*, for which alone he is particularly commended, that he was helped by no one and does not vie with other translators, whom, he says, it is easy to defeat,[936] although before him George of Trebizond had translated the same books[937] so brilliantly that by means of the renderings that he had found in the ancients and the words he himself had coined and thought up that recall a Latin character, he was, I think, the first of the younger authors to show that it was by our own fault that we have fewer names for things than the Greeks do. Therefore, if anyone should read these books carefully, he will surely not praise Gaza, who is virtually walking in his footsteps. In fact, if the man be honest, he will, I think, be disgusted that Theodore has thus covered up the man thanks to whom he made the greatest progress and held him in such contempt and made such sport of him whose labors he treacherously attacked. Perhaps he will even be grateful to me for striving to restore these things to their proper authors. For the words from the preface show what great pleasure George took in that work, in which he says that he is giving these books to the Latins in no less polished and error-free form than they have among the Greeks.[938] But Theodore attempts to appropriate even this for himself, just as what he published in Greek about the months[939] is stolen from the proem of this translation we are discussing. But there were (obviously) intensely bitter quarrels between these Greeks, as for instance in his *Grammar* Theodore calls our George *Pornoboscus*, which means brothel keeper,[940] playing, I think, on the ancient grammarian George, to whom the Greeks attached the sobriquet *Choeroboscos* ("swineherd").[941]

9   Cetera porro, quae Theodorus hic edidit, ubi modo non repe-
tundarum sit accusandus, sicut eruditione diligentiaque non
carent, ita sunt (ut mihi quidem videtur) ad examen quoddam
strictius curiosiusque revocanda. Nos hoc loco nec doctorum nitida nomina temptamus apud imperitorum decolorare iudicia, nec
tamen dissimulare quid in quoque desideremus aut inhonoratum
transire volumus cui veritas patrocinetur. Ut autem habere stilum
quam maxime ingenuum paratumque volumus, ita quam minime
accusatorium, quam minime licentiosum et noxium. Nec enim
tam vafritiam profitemur quam exhibemus industriam.

10   Quid autem nos olim de doctrina aestimaverimus ingenioque
Theodori Graecis aliquot et Latinis epigrammatis testati sumus,
quorum nunc unum dumtaxat, idque Graecum, subiciemus, 'siquis
tamen haec quoque, siquis captus amore leget.' Igitur sic est:

Κεῖτο μέγας ποτ᾽ ἀγὼν Γαζῇ Θεοδώροιο ἄμφι
  Μούσαις τ᾽ Αὐσονίαις ἠδ᾽ Ἑλικωνιάσι.
Ταῖς μὲν γὰρ γενεήν, ταῖς δ᾽ αὖ θρεπτήρι᾽ ὄφειλεν·
  Ἑλλὰς γὰρ τέκε τόν γ᾽, Αὐσονίη δ᾽ ἔτραφεν.
Ἴσον δ᾽ ἀμφοτέρων σοφίῃ γλώττῃ τ᾽ ἐκέκαστο.
  Τὸν δ᾽ οὔτ᾽ αὐτὸς ζῶν, οὔτ᾽ ἂρ ἔκρινε θανών·
Ἀλλὰ καὶ Ἰταλίης μεγάλη ἐπὶ Ἑλλάδι κεῖσθαι
  Εἵλετο, ὄφρα κλέος ξυνὸν ᾖ ἀμφοτέραις.

The other things that this Theodore published, insofar as he is 9
not to be arraigned for recovery of stolen property, are not devoid
of learning and care, but should (I think) be subjected to strict
and careful scrutiny. In this place I am not attempting to defame
the glittering names of learned men in the judgment of the inex-
pert nor, however, do I wish to conceal what I find wanting in each
or to pass over a dishonored person whom truth defends.[942] Moreover, I wish to have a pen at the ready that is, on the one hand, as
honest as possible, on the other, one that is as little as possible
prone to accuse, take liberties, or do harm. For I do not so much
claim cleverness as put hard work on display.

I have borne testimony to what I once thought about the learn- 10
ing and talent of Theodore in some Greek and Latin epigrams, of
which I now subjoin only one, a Greek one, "in case anyone who is
a captive of love will read it."[943] Here it is, then:

There was once a great contest for Theodore Gaza among
    The Muses of Italy and Greece.
To the latter he owed his lineage, to the former his nurture,
    For Hellas gave him birth, Italy reared him
He was equally distinguished in the wisdom and language of
        both.
    Neither alive nor dead did he decide the contest.
But he chose to be buried in Italy's Magna Graecia,
    So as to be a glory common to both.[944]

: 91 :

Quo pacto vir idem Graece transtulerit quod est apud
Ciceronem Suadae medulla, *positique Eupolidos versus de*
Pericle, tum indicatum quibus denique dea
Pitho Latinis appellationibus censeatur

1   Libellum Ciceronis aureolum *De senectute* Theodorus idem Gaza
non incommode profecto nec infeliciter vertit in Graecam linguam. Sed est in eo quoque (nequid gravius dixerim) paulo nonnunquam indiligentior. Illud interim pro argumento sit, quod ubi
ait strictim Cicero M. Cethegum ab Ennio *Suadae medullam* dictum, vocabulum illud *Suadae medulla* μελίγηριν Theodorus, quasi
tu dixeris dulciloquum, interpretatur, cum Cicero idem in *Bruto*
locum hunc Enni verbaque sic ampliter exponat:

Suadae medulla, inquit, Pitho quam vocant Graeci, cuius
effector est orator, hanc Suadam appellavit Ennius. Eius autem Cethegum medullam fuisse vult, ut quam deam in Pericli labris scripsit Eupolis sessitavisse, huius hic medullam
nostrum oratorem fuisse dixerit.

Hactenus in *Bruto* Cicero. Quo apparet utique non intellectum a
Theodoro locum. Neque enim μελίγηριν debuerat, sed πειϑοῦς
μυελόν interpretari. Neque id pluribus tamen arguemus, quia
verborum disceptationis res non est arbitro eius et cognitore
Marco Tullio.

2   Quoniam autem M. Tullius etiam Eupolin citat, qui deam
scripserit hanc persuadendi sessitavisse in Pericli labris, quam

: 91 :

How the same man translated Suadae medulla *in Cicero into Greek and Eupolis's verses about Pericles are cited; then it is shown by what Latin names the goddess Peitho is identified*

The same Theodore Gaza translated Cicero's golden little book *On* 1 *Old Age* into Greek beneficially and not without felicity.[945] But in this he is also (to put it mildly) sometimes a bit careless. For now, let this stand as the evidence, that where Cicero says in passing that Marcus Cethegus was called by Ennius *Suadae medulla* ("the marrow of persuasion"), Theodore renders *Suadae medulla* as *meligerin*, as if you were to say "speaking sweetly,"[946] although in his *Brutus* the same Cicero fully explains this passage of Ennius and his words as follows:

> The heart of persuasion (*Suadae medulla*), what the Greeks call *Peitho*, which an orator creates — this is what Ennius called *Suada* ("Persuasion"). Moreover, he claims that Cethegus was the marrow (*medulla*) of this, so that he said that our orator was the marrow of that goddess who, Eupolis wrote, habitually sat on the lips of Pericles.[947]

Thus Cicero in the *Brutus*. From this it is apparent that Theodore failed to understand the passage. For he had to translate not *meligerin* ("speaking sweetly") but *peithous muelon* ("marrow of persuasion"). Nor shall we argue this at greater length, because there is no scope for debating over words when Marcus Tullius is judge and advocate of the case.

Since, however, Marcus Tullius also cites Eupolis, who wrote 2 that this goddess of persuasion used to sit on the lips of Pericles,

Pitho vocet ipse, Suadam vero Ennius, agedum (si placet) ipsos ex Eupolidos Δήμοις (id enim comoediae nomen) versiculos subiciamus, gratum puto futurum studiosis, si ceu spicilegium racemationemque faciamus, aut si tabulas veluti quaspiam ex hoc litterarum naufragio collectas in corpus aliquod restituamus. Sunt autem quos inveniamus hi:

Κράτιστος[294] οὗτος ἐγένετ᾽ ἀνθρώπων λέγειν
Ὁπότε παρέλθοι, ὥσπερ οἱ ἀγαθοὶ δρομεῖς
Ἑκκαίδεκα ποδῶν, ᾖρει λέγων τοὺς ῥήτορας·
Ταχὺς λέγειν μέν,[295] πρὸς δέ γ᾽ αὐτοῦ τῷ τάχει
Πειθώ τις ἐπεκάθιζεν ἐπὶ τοῖς χείλεσιν—
Οὕτως ἐκήλει—καὶ μόνος τῶν ῥητόρων
Τὸ κέντρον ἐγκατέλιπε τοῖς ἀκροωμένοις.

Neque autem istos Eupolidis poetae versus ex ipsius statim fontibus hausimus, ut cuius opera aetate interciderint, sed eorum partim ex interprete quopiam Aristidae rhetoris accuratissimo, partim ex epistola Plini Iunioris accepimus. Quin Aristides ipse ⟨in⟩[296] oratione quae *Pro Pericle* inscribitur, comici eiusdem testimonium advocans, ita loquitur: μόνου δὲ Πειθώ τις ἐπεκάθιζεν ἐν τοῖς χείλεσιν.

3　　Quam autem vocavit Ennius *Suadam*, puto eandem *Suadelam* Horatius:

Sed bene (inquit) nummatum decorat Suadela Venusque.

Neque enim assentiam Porphyrioni Veneris id epitheton existimanti. Nam Cicero in libro *De oratore* tertio cum de Pericle loquatur, Leporem maluit nuncupare quam Suadam, sic inquiens:

whom he himself calls *Peitho* but Ennius calls *Suada*, come, let us (if you please) append those very lines from Eupolis's *Demes* (for that is the name of the comedy); I think it will be appreciated by scholars if we glean, as it were, the ears of corn and form them in a cluster, or if we gather up some planks from this literary shipwreck and restore them to some sort of body.[948] Moreover, these are the verses we find:

> This man proved to be the mightiest speaker of all
> Whenever he went forward to speak, like good runners
> In the sixteen-foot race, with his speech he cleared away the
>   orators;
> His speech was swift, but besides his speed
> A certain Persuasion sat upon his lips —
> He so charmed them — and he alone of the speakers
> Left behind a goad in his audience.[949]

Furthermore, we did not draw these verses of the poet Eupolis directly from his own fount, since his works were lost to the ages, but we have received a portion of them from a certain very careful expounder of the orator Aristides, and another portion from a letter of Pliny the Younger. In fact, Aristides himself, in the oration that is entitled *On Behalf of Pericles*, calling upon the testimony of the same comic poet, says this: "A sort of Persuasion peculiar to him sat upon his lips."[950]

Moreover, I think Horace called *Suadela* the goddess whom Ennius called *Suada* ("Persuasion"): 3

> But *Suadela* and Venus adorn the well-off.[951]

For I disagree with Porphyrio, who thinks that this is the epithet of Venus.[952] For in speaking about Pericles in his third book *On the Orator*, Cicero preferred to call her *Lepos* ("Charm"), rather than *Suada*, saying the following:

Cuius in labris veteres comici, etiam cum illi maledicerent, quod tum Athenis fieri licebat, Leporem habitasse dixerunt, tantamque in eo vim fuisse, ut in eorum mentibus qui audissent quasi aculeos quosdam relinqueret.

Contra autem Quintilianus ne enuntiare quidem istius deae Latinum ausus nomen, ita in decimo scribit *Oratoriarum institutionum:*

Et quod de Pericle veteris comoediae testimonium est in hunc transferri iustissime possit, in labris eius sedisse quandam persuadendi deam.

4   Porro Marcianus, modo Suadam, modo Pitho nuncupat. Nos eandem in poematis *Manto Ambraque* nostris modo Suadam, modo Leporem, videlicet Ennium Ciceronemque secuti.

: 92 :

Qui sint apud Livium causarii

Livius in septimo *Ab urbe condita:* 'Tertius,' inquit, 'exercitus ex causariis senioribusque a T. Quintio scribatur, qui urbi moenibusque praesidio sit.' *Causarii* qui sint non temere qui tibi explicet invenias. Sed id ex verbis tamen Ulpiani iureconsulti libro sexto *Ad edictum* facile colliges. Ea sunt in tertio scripta *Digestorum* volumine, quo titulo de his agitur qui notantur infamia. Verba ita sunt:

On his lips the ancient comic poets—even when they were slandering him, as was then permissible to do in Athens—said *Lepos* used to dwell and he had such power that he left behind, as it were, certain goads in the minds of those who had listened to him.[953]

Quintilian, however, not even daring to utter the name of that goddess in Latin, writes thus in the tenth book of his *Orator's Education*:

And that what is attested by Old Comedy about Pericles can with full justice be transferred to him [*sc.* Xenophon], that a certain goddess of persuasion sat on his lips.[954]

On the other hand, Martianus [Capella] sometimes calls her 4 *Suada* ("Persuasion"), at other times *Peitho*.[955] In my poems *Manto* and *Ambra*, I sometimes call her *Suada*, at other times *Lepos* ("Charm"), that is, following the style of Ennius and Cicero.[956]

: 92 :

Who the causarii *are in Livy*

In the seventh book of *From the Founding of Rome*, Livy says: "Let a third army be enlisted by T. Quintius from among the *causarii* and the elderly, to defend the city and walls."[957] You will not readily find someone to explain to you who the *causarii* are. But you will easily infer it from the words of the jurist Ulpian, in Book 6 of his *On the Edict*. They are written in the third book of the *Digests*, under the title dealing with those who are branded with infamy (*infamia*). The words are as follows:

'Ignominiae causa missum,' hoc ideo adiectum est, quoniam multa genera sunt missionum. Est honesta, quae emeritis stipendiis vel ante ab imperatore indulgetur, et causaria, quae propter valetudinem laboribus militiae solvit.

Ex quibus verbis ratiocinari possumus causarios proprie dici milites valetudinis causa missos.

⁙ 93 ⁙

Vindicata Iustiniani principis praefatio quaepiam a vitiis mendisque aliquot

Pudet me saeculi nonnunquam istius in quo sum natus, indocti nimis et arrogantis, versantem animo identidem quae monstra rerum verborumque libros etiam ipsos legum quibus regimur occupaverint, sicuti quod nuper dubium ridens an stomachans adnotabam in epistola Iustiniani, quae posita est ante *Digestorum* libros, Theophilo, Dorotheo, Theodoro, Isidoro, et Anatolio, et Thalleleo, et Cratino viris illustribus, antecessoribus, et Salaminio viro disertissimo scripta. Nam cum doceat illic imperator anni quarti studiosos Graeco vocabulo *lytas* appellatos et item quinti *prolytas*, ut in *Pandectis* extat illis archetypis, cuncta nunc habent exemplaria *hircos* in priore, *coloritas* in posteriore loco, nihili vocabula sed quae tamen ab Accursio pro maxime idoneis enarrentur. Quin primi anni auditores non *dispondii* (quod vulgo), sed *dupondii*, sicut in

"Having been discharged because of disgrace": this has been added, since there are many types of discharge. There is the honorable discharge, for those who have completed their term of service or who were granted early discharge by the emperor, and there is the *causaria* discharge, which released one from military service on the ground of ill health.[958]

From these words we can deduce that soldiers dismissed on the ground of ill health are properly called *causarii*.

: 93 :

The preface of the emperor Justinian defended from several corruptions and errors

I am embarrassed for this ignorant and arrogant age in which I was born, as I ponder what monstrosities of content and language have seized the very books of the laws by which we are governed. Take, for instance, what I noted recently, wavering between merriment and disgust, in Justinian's letter placed at the head of the books of the *Digests*, written to Theophilus, Dorotheus, Theodorus, Isidore, and Anatolius, as well as Thalleleus and Cratinus, *illustres* and *antecessores*,[959] plus that most eloquent man, Salaminius. For although the emperor informs us there that fourth-year students were called by the Greek term, *lytai,* and likewise fifth-year students *prolytai*,[960] as is attested in the famous archetype of the *Pandects*,[961] nowadays all exemplars have *hirci* ("goats") in the earlier passage and *coloritae* in the later one, meaningless words but nonetheless ones that are explained by Accursio as especially suitable.[962] In fact, first-year students were called not *dispondii*, as in common parlance, but *dupondii* ("two-penny folk"), as I find in the

archetypis invenio, tam frivolo, ut idem ait, quam ridiculo cognomine appellabantur. Sed et in eadem epistola (ut in transcursu hoc quoque ostendam) desiderantur verba de sexta *Iliados* rhapsodia, cum Glaucum et Diomedem nominat imperator inter se dissimilia permutantes. Etenim post id verbum sequi statim debet hic Homeri versus, si archetypo credimus:

Χρύσεα χαλκείων ἑκατόμβοια ἐννεαβοίων.

: 94 :

Lepidum Severiani commentum
de lunae factura et solis, deque menstruis diebus et annuis

1   Percurrimus aliquando ego et Picus hic Mirandula, nunquam satis homo laudatus, subsicivis horis antiquos enarratores Instrumenti Sacri Veteris, Graecos maxime Diodorum, Philonem, Gennadium, Aquilam, Origenem, Basilium, Didymum, Isidorum, Apollinarem, Severianum, alios id genus compluris, quorum ille sicutique Latinorum sententias omnis quam diligentissime cum Iudaeorum et Chaldaeorum interpretum conferens opinionibus, nihil non eventilat et pensiculat, unde modo aut veritas elici aut obscuritas tolli aut roborari fides aut refelli possit impietas. Sed quod apud Severianum superioribus diebus, auctorem luculentum, memini nos legere visum est haud indignum quod in hunc acciperetur gregem.

2   Solem factum a Deo primitus et lunam legifer Hebraeus prodit, quarta mox ut orbem inchoaverat die, qui tamen, quoniam alterum diei, nocti alteram praefecisset, etiam illum in orientis credi

460

archetype, an appellation, as the same author says, as frivolous as it is ridiculous.[963] But in the same letter (to demonstrate this, too, in passing) words from the sixth book of the *Iliad* are missing, when the emperor cites Glaucus and Diomedes making an unequal exchange.[964] For this line of Homer's ought to follow immediately after this word, if we trust the archetype:

> The worth of one hundred oxen in gold for the worth of nine oxen in brass.[965]

: 94 :

A charming thesis invented by Severianus on the creation of the moon and sun, and on the days of the months and years

On one occasion Pico della Mirandola—a man never praised enough—and I in our spare time were skimming the ancient commentators on the Old Testament, in particular the Greeks Diodorus, Philo, Gennadius, Aquila, Origen, Basil, Didymus, Isidore, Apollinaris, Severianus, and several others of that sort. Comparing their views and all those of the Latins as carefully as possible with the opinions of the Jewish and Chaldean commentators, there was nothing he failed to winnow and weigh from which either the truth could be elicited or by which obscurity could be banished or faith reinforced or impiety refuted. But what I remember we read in previous days in Severianus—a brilliant author—seemed worthy to be admitted to this flock.[966]

The Hebrew lawgiver relates that the sun and moon were created by God in the first place, then on the fourth day, when he had begun the world, since he had put one of them in charge of the day and the other of the night, it can also be supposed that he had

potest, hanc in occidentis posuisse confinio. Nec autem debuit (quemadmodum quidem hic opinatur) sic a principio statim lunam fingere Deus ut detrimento affecta, ut decerpta, ut gracilescens, ut discriminata, ut inanis, ut diluta, ut exhausta foret lumine, qualem nunc esse eam vel nascentem vel intermestruam vel senescentem vel in coitu vel in ipso quoque deliquio videmus, quin orbe pleno potius integroque circulata, non gibbosa, non praetumida, non sinuata, non corniculans, non dividua, non silens. Etenim ista dein multiformitas temporum erat et noctium et dierum velut intervallaris et discriminatrix futura.

3   Quocirca edito recens et matutinos ingrediente carceres sole, luna prorsus e regione metam[297] finitoris radebat occiduam, munifex tum primum orbis et in suo quasi dixerim tirocinio. Sed ut ad occidentem sol ipse circumactus est, etiam invicem pervecta luna suo curriculo est ad orientis collimitium. Sic igitur audientes dicto, diei pariter praefuerunt noctique. Cur autem non se tum potius quartae lunae facies exhibuerit, quota est edita die? Quoniam summum, inquit, luna quarta tenere occidentis limitem nequivisset. Ita rotundata specie, plenoque prorsus ore quintamdecimam pro quarta exhibens, undecim sibi dies velut arrogaverat, ac totidem plane diebus luna solem natura praevertitur. Ex quo fit ut soli etiam iure dies illos undecim luna quasi bona fide restituat. Nam cum sit undetriginta et semissis dierum menstruus lunae calculus, dissultat hinc annarius duodecim mensium numerus e diebus omnino CCCLIIII. Quae summa undecim sibi alios agglutinans, quos a primordio luna sicut auctarium praesumpserat, annum constituet hunc solarem CCC et LXV dierum.

4   Tantum Severianus, lepidiore tamen, puto, quam veriore commento, quo etiam crescere in immensum possit fabularis illa de

placed the sun on the border of the east and the moon on that of the west. However, God ought not (as he at least thought) to have created the moon at the very beginning such as to be affected by loss, plucked at, attenuating, divided up, empty, pale, and drained of light, as we now see it to be whether waxing, at midmonth, or waning or in conjunction or in eclipse, but rather circular with a full and intact orb, not with a hump, not protuberant, not hollowed out, not horned, not divided, not silent. For that subsequent multiplicity of form was a function of times and was to be, as it were, the separator and divider of nights and days.

Therefore when the sun has just been born and enters the barriers of morning, but the moon was gone from the region and touching the western finishing line,[967] then the world was bestowing its gifts for the first time and was, so to speak, in its apprenticeship. But when the sun itself has been driven round to the west, the moon in turn has also been carried on its course to the boundary of the east. In obedience therefore to the command, they held equal charge over day and night. But why did the face of the fourth moon not then appear, the number of the day on which it was created? Because, he says, the fourth moon was incapable of reaching the western boundary. Thus, appearing rounded and, with full face, it showed the fifteenth day instead of the fourth, having annexed, as it were, eleven days. In nature, the moon clearly precedes the sun by so many days. For this reason it comes about that the moon properly restores those eleven days to the sun, as if in good faith. For since the monthly total of the moon is twenty-nine and a half days, this yields over twelve months the annual number of 354 days altogether. When this total attaches to itself the other eleven days, which the moon had taken in advance as a kind of bonus at the beginning of time, it will constitute the solar year of 365 days.

So far the invention of Severianus, more charming, I think, than true. By this account, the legendary hyperbole about the an-

Arcadum vetustate superlatio, qui *proselenoe*, quod est *antelunares*, appellati, si fuerit in confesso diebus esse undecim lunam, non tam mundo ipso quam initiali quoque die maiusculam.

: 95 :

Graecum elegans adagium super xeniis Digestorum *exemplaribus restitutum*

Libet in gratiam iureconsultorum restituere Graecum quoque proverbium, sublatum plane de ipsorum libris sed integrum adhuc in archetypo, sicut in epistola quapiam divi Severi et imperatoris Antonini reperitur; ea citatur ab Ulpiano in primo *De officio proconsulis*, eodemque titulo ponitur in *Digestorum* libro primo. Verba sunt haec epistolae, quae quoniam elegantissima et plena bonae frugis, ediscenda iis censeo qui rempublicam gesturi:

Quantum, inquit, ad xenia pertinet, audi quid sentimus. Graecum proverbium est: οὔτε πάντα, οὔτε πάντοτε, οὔτε παρὰ πάντων. Nam valde inhumanum est a nemine accipere, sed passim vilissimum est, et per omnia avarissimum.

Sic illi. Porro Graeca verba possis ad hunc interpretari modum: 'Nec omnia, nec passim, nec ab omnibus.'

tiquity of the Arcadians, who were called *proselenoi*, i.e., prelunarians,[968] would grow out of all bounds, if it were admitted that the moon was eleven days older not than the world itself, but even than the first day.

An elegant Greek proverb about gifts is restored to copies of the Digests

I want to restore a Greek proverb to the favor of jurists, one that was clearly removed from their books but is still intact in the archetype, as is found in a certain letter of the divine Severus and the emperor Antoninus, which is cited by Ulpian in his first book *On the Duty of the Proconsul*, and placed under the same title in the first book of the *Digests*. These are the words of the letter, which, since they are extremely elegant and full of good sense, I think ought to be learned by heart by those who intend to engage in public affairs:

> As pertains to gifts, hear what we think. The Greek proverb is: "neither everything, nor every time, nor from everyone." For it is inhuman to accept nothing from anyone, but utterly base to do so indiscriminately, and extremely greedy to take everything.[969]

So they wrote. You can, however, translate the Greek words in this way: "Not everything, nor every time, nor from everyone."

: 96 :

Quanta in muribus salacitas,
et Aeliani verborum interpretamentum, atque inibi locus apud
Martialem correctus et enarratus

1 In septimo *Epigrammaton* vulgatis quidem codicibus ita est apud
Martialem:

Nam cum me vitam, cum me tua lumina dicis.

Sed enim vetustissimi quique sic habent:

Nam cum me murem, cum me tua[298] lumina dicis.

Quod tamen a nullo est hactenus animadversum aut emendatum.

2 Quaeri vero potest quo intellectu puella blandiens amatori murem eum vocet. An eodem quo etiam passerculum solet, quia
mures quoque perhibentur salacissimi, sicuti scriptum invenio
libro Aeliani duodecimo *De animalium proprietate*, verbis ad hanc
sententiam?

Ferunt autem mures, inquit, salacissimos esse, testemque
adducunt Cratinum, scilicet in *Fugitivis:* 'Age nunc tibi de se-
reno adversus mollitiem muris fulgurabo Xenophontis.' Sed
enim feminam quoque murem narrant ad veneria esse prae-
rabidam. Rursumque apud Epicratem in *Choro*, fabula enim
haec Epicratis est: 'Postremo subiit me detestabilis lena,[299]
deierans per Puellam, per Dianam, per Phersephattam, esse
vitulam, esse virginem, esse pullam indomitam. At illa cavus
erat murinus.' Superiectione eam salacissimam dicere voluit
cum cavum prorsus murinum vocitavit. Et Philemon: 'Mus

: 96 :

How salacious mice are;
a translation of a text of Aelian; and on this point a passage
in Martial is corrected and explained

In the common codices of the seventh book of Martial's *Epigrams*, 1
one reads the following:

> For when you call me your life, when you call me your
> eyes . . .[970]

But all the most ancient codices have this:

> For when you call me mouse, when you call me your eyes . . .

But so far this has not been noticed or emended by anyone.

But one could ask what was in the girl's mind when, flattering 2
her lover, she calls him a mouse. Is it the same thought by which
she would call him her little sparrow? — since mice are also said to
be salacious,[971] as I find recorded in the twelfth book of Aelian's
On the Characteristics of Animals, in words to this effect:

> Moreover, they say that mice are very salacious, and they cite
> Cratinus as a witness, specifically in his *Fugitives:* "Come now,
> I shall flash lightning for you out of a clear sky at the licen-
> tiousness of Xenophon the mouse."[972] But they also say that
> a female mouse is exceedingly randy. Again, in Epicrates's
> *Chorus* (for this is Epicrates's play): "At last the loathsome
> bawd approached me, solemnly swearing by the Girl, by Di-
> ana, by Phersephatta, that she is a heifer, a virgin, an un-
> tamed filly. But she was a mousehole."[973] He meant to say
> hyperbolically that she was randy when he called her a mouse
> hole. And Philemon says: "A white mouse, when someone—

albus, cum quis eam, sed pudet fari. Clamavit adeo statim
detestanda lena, ut saepe latere non esset.'[300]

Hactenus Aelianus, auctoritatibus etiam magni nominis comico-
rum succenturiatus.

: 97 :

Automaton *legendum in Suetonio quod nunc vulgo* aut ornatum, *quidque ea voce significetur*

1 Locus apud Suetonium in *Claudio* ita perperam legitur in plerisque
voluminibus: 'Si aut ornatum aut pegma vel quid tale aliud parum
cessisset,' cum veri integrique sic habeant codices: 'Si automaton
vel pegma.' Inspice vel Bononiae librum ex divi Dominici vel item
alterum Florentiae ex divi Marci bibliotheca quam gens Medica
publicavit, veterem utrunque, sed et utroque vetustiorem quem
nunc ipsi domesticum possidemus, ut taceam compluris alios ne
fortassis ambitiosior et nimius citandis testimoniis deprehendar:
ubique hanc nimirum posteriorem scripturam invenies. Apparet
ergo *automata* appellari solita, quae ita mechanici fabricabantur ut
sua sponte efficere quippiam velut ignara causa viderentur. Qualia
nunc aut horologia sunt aut versatiles quaepiam machinae, in quibus imagunculas occulta vi cursitantes ludibundasque miramur.
Quales etiam vel fontes vel ignes ipsi, quodam artificioso tempera-
mento specieque nova, certis intervallis aquas flammasve iacu-
lantes. *Automatum* enim velut ultroneum et spontale possumus
Latine interpretari. Sic Homerus in secunda rhapsodia venisse ad
dapem Menelaum dicit *automaton*, sponte sua significans, non

but I am ashamed to say. The detestable bawd immediately raised such a cry that it was impossible to be hidden by the hedge."[974]

Up to this point, Aelian, fortified by the authority of famous comic poets.

: 97 :

What is now commonly read in Suetonius as aut ornatum *should be read as* automaton; *and what this word means*

In Suetonius's *Claudius*, there is a passage that reads thus incorrectly in many books: "If either an adorned thing or a scaffold or anything else of that sort had failed,"[975] whereas the true, intact codices have: "If an automated thing, or a scaffold . . ." Look at a book in the San Domenico library at Bologna or another one in the San Marco library in Florence, which the Medici family opened to the public, both of them old, or another one even older than these two, one that I now have at home,[976] not to mention many others, lest I perhaps be caught citing testimonies ostentatiously and excessively: everywhere you will, of course, find this latter reading. It appears, then, that the things that mechanics constructed in such a way that they seemed to do something on their own as if with an unknown cause were wont to be called *automata*. Such things now include clocks or machines with moving parts, where we marvel at little images running and playing by a hidden force. Such include fountains or fires of a new type, which, by artificial regulation, shoot water or flames at fixed intervals. For we can translate *automaton* into Latin as "self-powered" and "spontaneous." Thus, in the second book [of the *Iliad*] Homer says that Menelaus came to dinner *automatos*, meaning he came of his own

cuiuspiam vocatu, quasi a semet impulsum, sicut Eustathius quoque exponit, qui deinde ait a iunioribus αὐτόματα vocari, quae[301] forte quadam fiant, quasi μάτην, hoc est, temere, καὶ ὡς ἔτυχεν. Et paulo post idem sic addit propemodum: 'Talis autem sententia etiam illa mechanicorum nominavit automata.'

2 Ceterum philosophus Heron in *Pneumaticis* aquam exprimi ait in sublime *automaton*, idest spontalem, de sphaera concava, quam describit, sicuti cornicem quoque confingit quae se ad aviculas itidem fictas convertat αὐτομάτως. Quin aediculam quoque docet construere, cuius accenso igni fores item αὐτομάτως, idest sponte, aperiantur, extincto cludantur, ut omnia quo diximus intellectu sint audienda.

: 98 :

Persi locus et item Senecae declarati, deque manumittendis festuca servis et circumactu

Persius in satyra sexta sic ait:

Non in festuca lictor quem iactat ineptus,

ubi poeta diligentissimus manumissum hominem ex vetere consuetudine significavit. Est enim a Plutarcho traditum in libello *De his qui sero puniuntur a deo* morem fuisse Romanis ubi quempiam manumitterent, ut eius corpori tenuem festucam inicerent. Ex quo illud apud Plautum in *Milite*:

Quid ea, ingenua an festuca facta? Serva an libera est?

accord, not invited by anyone, as if on his own impulse,[977] as Eustathius also explains, who then says that younger authors call *automata* things that occur by some chance, as if in vain (*maten*), that is, randomly and by happenstance.[978] And a little later, the same author adds, approximately: "This idea has also provided the name *automata* of mechanical things."[979]

Moreover, in his *Pneumatics*, the philosopher Heron says that   2 water is spurted skyward *automaton*, that is, spontaneously, from a concave sphere, which he describes, just as he also constructed a crow that turns to other likewise artificial birds spontaneously (*automatos*). In fact, he also tells that he constructed a little house whose doors would open *automatos*, that is, spontaneously, when a fire is lit, and would close when the fire is extinguished, so that everything should be understood in the aforementioned sense.[980]

: 98 :

Passages of Persius, and Seneca, too, are clarified; and about manumitting slaves by rod and by being turned about

In his sixth satire Persius says:

Not with the ceremonial rod that a silly lictor brandishes.[981]

Here the very exacting poet referred to a man's manumission according to an old custom. For Plutarch related in his small book *Concerning Those Who Receive Late Punishment from God* that whenever they freed someone, the Romans had the custom of touching his body with a thin rod.[982] Hence this point in Plautus's *Soldier*:

What about her? Is she freeborn or has she been made such by the rod? Is she a slave or free?[983]

Quoniam autem et circumagebantur qui libertatem nanciscebantur, fortasse ut ostenderetur licere iam ipsis pro suo arbitrio quorsum vellent moveri, quod et supra dixerat Persius:

> Verterit hunc dominus, momento turbinis exit
> Marcus Dama.

Et a praetore plerunque vindicta liberabantur, propterea et *iactat* inquit et *lictor*. Nam lictores seni praetoribus apparebant. Circumagi autem solitos qui manumitterentur etiam Seneca docet in octava primi libri *Ad Lucilium* epistola:

> Philosophiae, inquit, servias oportet, ut tibi contingat vera libertas. Non differtur in diem, qui se illi subiecit et tradidit, statim circumagitur. Hoc enim ipsum philosophiae servire libertas est.

Circumagitur, hoc est manumittitur liberaturque.

: 99 :

Cur muri partem disicere,
quod ait Suetonius, hieronicae soliti

Suetonius in *Nerone*: 'Reversus,' inquit, 'e Graecia Neapolin, quod in ea primum artem protulerat, albis equis introiit, disiecta parte muri, ut mos hieronicarum est.' Ita ille. Nemini autem est dubium, sacrorum certaminum victores *hieronicas* appellari. Sed moris istius

In addition, since those who were obtaining their liberty were also turned about, perhaps to demonstrate that they were now free to go wherever they wanted at their own discretion, as Persius had also said above:

If his master turns him about, with this spin he goes out as Marcus Dama.[984]

And for the most part they were set free by a ceremonial act by the praetor; hence he says both "brandishes [the rod]" and "lictor." For six lictors attended each of the praetors. Moreover, in the eighth letter of the first book *To Lucilius*, Seneca also teaches that those who were being freed were customarily turned about:

You must serve philosophy in order to experience true freedom. He who has subjected and surrendered himself to philosophy is not put off but is immediately turned about. For this very thing, being a slave to philosophy, is freedom.[985]

He is turned about, that is, he is freed and liberated.

: 99 :

Why the victors in the sacred games are wont to shatter a part of the city wall, as Suetonius says

Suetonius says in his *Nero:* "Upon his return from Greece, he entered Naples, since there he had first demonstrated his art, on white horses through a shattered part of the city wall, as is the custom for the victors in the sacred games (*hieronicae*)."[986] Thus Suetonius. Moreover, no one doubts that the victors in the sacred contests are called *hieronicae*. But so far I find the basis for this

causam tantum adhuc invenio apud Plutarchum libro *Symposiacon* secundo in hanc sententiam:

> Quod autem (inquit) victoribus curru vehentibus permissum, partem muri dividere atque deicere, hunc sane habet intellectum, non magnopere civitati muro opus esse, viros habenti qui pugnare possint et vincere.

: 100 :

Quae sint apud Maronem silentia lunae, quaeve
tacita virgo apud Horatium, superque iis
Serviana et Acroniana refutatae sententiae

1 Vergilius *Aeneidos* secundo: 'Tacitae,' inquit, 'per amica silentia lunae.' Servius igitur:

> Sciendum autem est, ait, septima luna captam esse Troiam, cuius simulachrum apud Argos est constitutum. Hinc est quod dicit: 'Oblati per lunam.' Et alibi: 'Per caecam noctem.' 'Tacitae lunae' aut more poetico noctem significat, aut physica ratione dixit. Nam circuli septem sunt Saturni, Iovis, Martis, Solis, Veneris, Mercuri, Lunae. Et primus, hoc est Saturni, vehementer sonat, reliqui secundum ordinem minus. Sicut audivimus in cithara, cuius ultima chorda minus sonat.

Hactenus Servius.

2 Libenter igitur ab eo quaesierim cur amica luna latere ac fallere conantibus, aut num lunam quoque silentem apud M. Catonem et

custom only in Plutarch, in the second book of his *Table Talk*, to this effect:

> The fact that victors were allowed to divide and demolish part of the wall and ride through in their chariots surely has this significance, that a city has no great need of a wall if it has men who can fight and conquer.[987]

: 100 :

What the silences of the moon are in Vergil, or who the
silent virgin is in Horace; and the views of
Servius and Acro on these matters are refuted

In the second book of the *Aeneid*, Vergil says: "Through the 1 friendly silences of a quiet moon."[988] Servius then:

> Moreover, it should be known that it was during the seventh moon that Troy was captured, a likeness of which was set up at Argos. Hence his words: "Appearing under the moonlight."[989] And elsewhere: "Through the blind night."[990] "Silent moons": he either signifies the night in poetic style, or spoke by physical allegory. For the seven orbits are those of Saturn, Jupiter, Mars, the Sun, Venus, Mercury, and the Moon. And the first one, that is, Saturn's, sounds loudly and the others less according to their order—just as we have heard on the lyre, whose last string sounds less.[991]

Thus Servius.

So then, I should like to ask him why the moon is friendly to 2 those who are trying to hide and deceive, or whether he would refer the silent moon in M. Cato or again in Pliny to this same

item apud Plinium ad eandem referat harmoniam planetarum. Quod autem citharae ultimam chordam sonare ait minus, hoc ita denique procedet, si ultimam non iam pro ima, sed pro summa capiat, quae Graece *hypate* vocatur, unde gravior excitatur sonus, sicuti ab extima altera et tenuissima, quam equidem libentius ultimam dixerim, acuta vox profertur, quae plus sonare ob id videtur quia prorsum tenditur, ut in libro *De musica* secundo scribere ait Theophrastum Porphyrius in commentariis illis, quos in *Harmonica* Ptolemaei scriptos reliquit: 'Sicuti gravis ob id,' inquit, 'minus auditur quia circa diffunditur.' Quod autem et apud Macrobium legimus et item apud alios, Saturni orbem, cuius conversio sit concitatior, edere acutissimum sonum, minime hoc, arbitror, a Platone vel in *Timaeo* vel in *Republica* probabitur, qui tardissimum scribit esse Saturni orbem, quanquam hoc fortasse ad longiorem sui cursus ambitum referetur. Sed Aristoteles certe in libro secundo *De caelo* tardiores ob id ait esse superiores orbes, quod impetu stelliferi octavi orbis magis retardentur. Ut ergo vel Alexandri vel Simplici vel item iuniorum de eo opinionem praetermittam, si veram plane Macrobi sententiam vis colligere, ad cursum referas diurnum, qui sine dubio celerrimus in supremis et concitatissimus invenietur.

3   Sed nos hac ablegata commenticia (ut arbitror) Servi minimeque necessaria subtilitate, potius accipimus 'tacitae lunae silentia' lunam ipsam, quam vocant silentem, hoc est minime tum quidem lucentem, ut latere insidiae magis possent, pulchra nimirum et eleganti tralatione[302] ab auribus ad oculos. Nam sicuti silentio nihil auditur, ita nihil tenebris cernitur. Plinius igitur libro *Naturalis historiae* sextodecimo diem inquit coitus lunae ab aliis 'silentia lunae,' ab aliis *interlunium* appellari. Tum idem libro duodevi-

harmony of the planets. But as for the fact that he says that the last string of the lyre sounds less, this will be so if one understands that the last one refers not to the lowest but the highest, which in Greek is called *hypate* ("highest"), from which a deeper sound is produced, just as from the second to the end and thinnest, which I would gladly call the last, a sharp sound is produced, which seems to be louder, since it is made quite taut, as in his commentaries on Ptolemy's *Harmonics*, Porphyry says Theophrastus wrote in his second book *On Music*: "Just as the low sound is less audible, because it is diffused all around."[992] But what we read in Macrobius and others, that the circuit of Saturn, whose revolution is more rapid, produces the sharpest sound, will scarcely, I think, be approved by Plato in either his *Timaeus* or *Republic*, who writes that the circuit of Saturn is the slowest, although this will perhaps be attributable to the longer route of its circuit.[993] But in the second book of his *On the Heavens*, Aristotle at any rate says that the higher orbits are slower because they are slowed down more by the impact of the eighth star-bearing orbit.[994] To pass over the opinion about this, whether of Alexander or Simplicius or others more recent, if you wish to infer the true opinion of Macrobius, you should refer it to the daily course, which will without doubt be found to be the most rapid and impetuous in the heavens.[995]

But setting aside this (in my view) contrived and unnecessary subtlety of Servius's, I take "the silences of the quiet moon" to be the moon itself, which they call silent, that is, then giving off the least light, so that ambushes can be better hidden, with a pretty and elegant metaphor from the ears to the eyes. For just as in silence nothing is heard, so in darkness nothing is seen. Accordingly, in Book 16 of his *Natural History*, Pliny says that the day of the new moon is called by some "the silences of the moon" and by others "the interlunar day."[996] Then, in Book 18, the same author says: 3

477

gesimo: 'Et hoc,' ait, 'silente luna seri iubent.' M. Cato etiam in libro *De re rustica* nunc stercus evehi luna silenti, nunc item silente luna ficos, oleas, mala, piros inseri, postremo etiam prata primo vere iubet eadem luna silente stercorari. Ridiculum autem fuerit aut haec Catoniana Plinianaque referre ad siderum musicam, aut in vetustissima usuque receptissima locutione desiderare istiusmodi ambages.

4   Equidem lunam hic silentem, ut dixi, pro minime tum lucente acceperim, quod fuerat tempus Graecis observandum. Neque ita tamen interpretor ut ad vivum resecem atque ipsum denique lunae coitum plane intelligam, cum nox tota tenebricosa, nam hoc utique refellitur, quoniam poeta mox ait: 'Oblati per lunam.' Nondum igitur luna lucebat, cum illi a Tenedo sub vesperam navigabant. Sed lucere tum coepit, cum iam urbem occupaverant. Non igitur aut sera fuerit aut pernox luna tum nec lunae quidem omnino coitus, sed tempus, arbitror, potius quamdiu illa non luceret. Etenim plura saepe quam videatur vox apud poetas aliqua complectitur. Ob hoc igitur illud in nostra *Rustico*:

Quidque silens moneat, quidque intermenstrua Phoebe.

Nec absurde tamen, praeter epitheti rationem temporariam, lunae acceperis amica silentia, quoniam in auspiciis quoque silentium vocari Cicero scribit quod omni vitio caret.

5   Iam apud Acronem quam pulchrum, quam ingeniosum, qui enarrans Horati locum libro *Carminum* secundo,

"And they bid that this [*sc.* fodder crops] be sown when the moon is silent."[997] In his book *On Agriculture*, M. Cato, too, orders that manure be carried out under a silent moon, and under a silent moon too figs, olives, apples, and pears be grafted, and finally he also orders that the meadows be fertilized at the beginning of spring, likewise under a silent moon.[998] Moreover, it would be absurd either to relate these passages from Cato and Pliny to the music of the stars or to look for such subtleties in this very old and commonly used expression.[999]

In this context, I would, as I said, interpret the silent moon as 4 one that is casting the least light, which was the time the Greeks had to wait for. I do not, however, interpret in such a way as to cut into living flesh and understand it to be the new moon itself, when the whole night is dark, for this is refuted because the poet soon says: "appearing under the moonlight."[1000] Therefore the moon was not yet shining when they were sailing at dusk from Tenedos. But it began to shine, after they had already taken the city. Therefore, it was then neither a late nor an all-night moon, nor indeed a new moon, but rather, I believe, a time during which the moon was not shining. For in the poets a word often encompasses more than might appear. For this reason, therefore, there is this in our *Rusticus*:

What warning would a silent Phoebe ("moon") give, or a new
     moon.[1001]

It would, however, not be absurd for you to interpret "the friendly silences of the moon" apart from a temporal explanation of the epithet, since Cicero writes that in the case of auspices what is free of any defect is called silence.[1002]

Now how pretty, how ingenious is the point in Acro, who, in 5 explaining a passage from Horace in the second book of his *Odes*,

Dum Capitolium
Scandet cum tacita virgine pontifex,

tacitam virginem intellexit quasi claram sacerdotii nobilitate, et ut
hoc ineptis persuadeat, auctoritate etiam abutitur Maronis, qui
dixerit: 'Tacitae per amica silentia lunae,' ceu si tacita luna sit hic
etiam pro clara accipienda. Videlicet non et apud Dionysium
saltem *Romanae historiae* auctorem, et apud Plutarchum aliosque
permultos Acro legerat ignorari prorsus ab omnibus, quibus denique vel sacris vel simulacris Vestales virgines tuendis praeforent,
ut ob hoc ipsum quod praestabat silentium tacita vocetur virgo,
Troianam soli cui fas vidisse Minervam.

⟨*Coronis*⟩[303]

1 Sed ut hic liber, quanquam sic quoque nimis longus, aliqua tamen
veluti coronide cumuletur et nihil sit omnino inrepercussum, scire
lectorem volumus, posteaquam de magno quasi populo iam tum
anno superiore centuriam hanc unam, sicuti nunc est, nisi tantum
pauculis subinde (ut fit) interspersis flosculis, adornaveramus et
spectandam publice amicis aliquot exhibueramus, emanasse in vulgus fabulam non satis certo auctore, quae susurris aures istiusmodi
compleverit:

Nihil esse mirum si quaedam nova et insignia vel antea dic-
taverit Politianus vel nunc referre in litteris incipiat, olim iam
istaec omnia diligentissime perscripta a Nicolao Perotto, qui
fuerit Sipontinus pontifex, in eo maxime libro, cui titulum
fecisset *Copiae cornu*. Nam quoniam plurimum auctoritate

480

As long as the priest
Will climb the Capitol with the silent virgin,[1003]

understood the silent virgin as one distinguished by the nobility of
the priesthood, and in order to persuade philistines of this point,
he even abuses the authority of Vergil, who said: "Through the
friendly silences of the silent moon,"[1004] as if here, too, a silent
moon should be taken to be a bright moon. Evidently, Acro had
not read in Dionysius, the author of the *History of Rome*, or in
Plutarch or many others that it was unknown by absolutely everyone what rites or images the Vestal Virgins were in charge of pro-
tecting, so that because of the very silence that she maintained, she
is called the silent virgin, to whom alone it was allowed to see the
Trojan Minerva.[1005]

⟨Epilogue⟩

So that this book, although already overlong, may nonetheless be   1
crowned with a sort of colophon, and so that everything be turned
back on my opponents, I would like readers to know that after I
had adorned this single "century," out of, as it were, a great popula-
tion, in its current form the year before last — except that (as hap-
pens) a very few little flowers were inserted here and there — and
had submitted it for public examination to a few friends, a story
was leaked to the public without any definite source, which filled
people's ears with whisperings of this sort:[1006]

> It is no wonder that Poliziano has either previously said cer-
> tain new and noteworthy things in public lectures or that he
> is now beginning to set them down in writing, since all these
> things were already long ago most scrupulously written out
> by Niccolò Perotti, who was archbishop of Siponto, in par-
> ticular in that book of his entitled *Cornucopiae*.[1007] Since Lo-
> renzo de' Medici, to whom this book is dedicated (so said

(sic enim quicunque illi aiebant) apud Urbinatem ducem, cui dicatus is liber Medices suus Laurentius, et gratia valet, per eum videlicet operis istius, et quidem archetypi, facta est Politiano potestas. Ergo ille nunc rapinator, ut hunc semel inuncavit librum, velut instar quoddam virgulae divinae, publicam prorsus materiam privati iuris facit et ut alter Aesopi gracculus aliena superbit pluma.

2   De his itaque per aliquot iam conciliabula iactatis eventilatisque rumusculis, cum mihi nescio quid, ut est officiosissimus homo, Robertus noster Salviatus renuntiasset, non litterarum modo, sed litteratorum quoque omnium velut alba linea magnus amator, agnovi statim Invidiae mores, quae dum cui nocere molitur, in omnia sese vertit et, ut ille apud Licentium Proteus,

Spumat aper, fluit unda, fremit leo, sibilat anguis.

3   At enim quod ad ipsius ictus occallueram, non sum propterea studiis iratus meis, tantum laboris tali mercede rependentibus, nec ipse me damnavi quod non hanc teterrimam pestem desidia magis placassem, nec ut nonnulli forsitan cupiebant, concerpsi librum, sed eum potius seposui paululum et omissa in praesens edendi cura, tantumque sulcis velut intercisivis, ita librum nonnunquam sicut hortum rigans, pleniorem tamen cogitatum velut a siliquis ad panes, hoc est a ludicris ad philosophiae seria transtuli.

4   Sic igitur versare altiora quaepiam animo studia et operae gravioris institui, quae suo et ipsa tempore (si lecta potenter erit res) in publicam utilitatem, quo magis argutatoribus istis oculi doleant, apparebunt. Etenim ego tenera adhuc aetate sub duobus excellen-

those persons, whoever they are), has great influence and favor with the Duke of Urbino, thanks to him Poliziano obtained access to his [Perotti's] work, and indeed the archetype. So then, that pillager, once having laid hold on that book, like a magic wand, is making private property public[1008] and like a second Aesopian jackdaw is priding himself in another's plumage.[1009]

Therefore when Roberto Salviati, a most dutiful friend and a great lover not only of literature but of all men of letters without exception, reported something to me concerning those rumors that had already been bruited about and aired in some small gatherings, I instantly recognized the ways of Envy, which, when it strives to harm someone, turns to every device and, like the famous Proteus in Licentius,   2

> The wild boar froths, the wave flows, the lion roars, the snake hisses.[1010]

But because I had hardened myself to Envy's blows, I did not become angry with my studies that were repaying so much labor with such a price, nor did I condemn myself for not appeasing this foul pest with idleness, nor, as perhaps some desired, did I tear up my book, but instead I set it aside for a while and with the intent of publication suspended for the present and merely watering my book from time to time, like a garden, with some furrows, as it were, inserted, I nonetheless transferred my fuller thinking as if from pods to bread,[1011] i.e., from games to the serious work of philosophy.   3

So I began to ponder some loftier studies involving more serious work. These, too, will appear at their proper time for the public benefit (if the content be closely read), so that these sophists' eyes may feel greater pain. For ever since I was a quite young man I have devoted my labor to the two philosophies under the   4

tissimis hominibus, Marsilio Ficino Florentino, cuius longe felicior quam Thracensis Orphei cithara veram (ni fallor) Eurydicen, hoc est amplissimi iudicii Platonicam sapientiam, revocavit ab inferis, et Argyropylo Byzantio, Peripateticorum sui temporis longe clarissimo, dabam quidem philosophiae utrique operam, sed non admodum assiduam, videlicet ad Homeri poetae blandimenta natura et aetate proclivior, quem tum Latine quoque miro ut adolescens ardore, miro studio versibus interpretabar.

5   Postea vero rebus aliis negotiisque prementibus sic ego nonnunquam de philosophia, quasi de Nilo canes, bibi, fugique donec reversus est in hanc urbem maxime Laurenti Medicis cum benivolentia tum virtutis et ingenii similitudine allectus princeps hic nobilissimus Ioannes Picus Mirandula vir unus, an heros potius, omnibus fortunae, corporis, animique dotibus cumulatissimus, utpote forma pene divina iuvenis et eminenti corporis maiestate, perspicacissimo ingenio, memoria singulari, studio infatigabili, tum luculenta uberique facundia, dubium vero iudicio mirabilior an moribus. Iam idem totius philosophiae consultissimus, etiamque varia linguarum litteratura et omnibus honestis artibus supra veri fidem munitus atque instructus.

6   Denique ut semel complectar, nullo non praeconio maior. Is igitur continuo me, cum quo partiri curas dulcissimas et nugari suaviter interdum solet, et quem sibi studiorum prope assiduum comitem (qui summus honor) adlegit, is me instit⟨u⟩it[304] ad philosophiam, non ut antea somniculosis, sed vegetis vigilantibusque oculis explorandam, quasi quodam suae vocis animare classico. Quocirca talem ego illum tantumque vel auctorem nactus vel ducem, neutiquam occasioni defui, quin occurri potius et arripui, sic ut assiduo propemodum summorum tractatu auctorum, velut

guidance of two excellent individuals, the Florentine Marsilio Ficino, whose lyre, far more fortunate than that of the Thracian Orpheus, has summoned back the true Eurydice (if I am not mistaken) from the underworld, that is, the Platonic wisdom of his outstanding judgment,[1012] and [John] Argyropoulos of Byzantium, by far the most distinguished of the Peripatetics of his time — but not uninterruptedly, for I was by nature and age more inclined toward the charms of the poet Homer, whom I then translated into Latin verse with the marvelous passion of a young man, and with marvelous zeal.[1013]

Afterward, however, when other affairs and business exerted pressure, I sometimes took sips from philosophy, as dogs do from the Nile,[1014] and I went into exile[1015] until, by the particular kindness of Lorenzo de' Medici and lured by his similar virtue and talent, the most noble prince, Giovanni Pico della Mirandola, a unique man, or rather a hero, abounding in all endowments of fortune, body, and mind, a young man of almost divine beauty and majestic person, with an insightful nature, singular memory, indefatigable zeal, not to mention a brilliant and abundant eloquence — equally remarkable for his judgment and his character — returned to this city. He is likewise already expert in all of philosophy, and incredibly fortified and equipped with the literature of various languages and every honorable art.

To sum up, he is greater than any encomium. He, then, immediately chose me as the almost constant companion of his studies (which was the greatest honor) and is wont to share with me his sweet attention and now and then indulge in pleasant banter.[1016] He began to rouse me, as if by the trumpet of his voice, to explore philosophy — not, as before, with drowsy eyes, but with vigorous and wakeful ones. Accordingly, once I had found a man of such quality and greatness as an authority or guide, I did not miss the opportunity but ran and seized it, so that, by virtually uninterrupted contact with the greatest authors, I might be seen, as if by

attrito crebrius silice, pauculas saltem veri scintillas videar excudisse tantumque flammae rapuisse fomitibus, ut in nocte caeca et illuni iamiam mihi aliquid profecto fulgoris sublucescat.

7   Sed ecce tibi interim, dum totus in hoc ego, repente *Cornu* istud in vulgus. Fit concursus. Est in manibus. Effunditur. Excutitur. Quid multa? Calumnia me liberat. Vidisses continuo nonnullorum vultus lugubre quiddam tacentes et, quod antea nunquam soliti, nescio tum quo pacto (sicut ille apud Platonem Thrasymachus) erubescentes. Sed isti quidem *Cornu*, quanquam certe non vacuo, quid inesse tamen viderim non est huius temporis indicium. Tantum constiterit impraesentiarum non idem spectasse me quod eius voluminis auctorem, nec par utrique destinatum praestitutumque fastigium. Quod sicubi locos eosdem pro renata forte uterque tractavimus (id autem incidere alicubi fuit necesse) crassior tamen inter nos quam inter Piramum Thisbenque paries. Argumento sit interim vel illa Iuvenalis *Cotytto*, quae tamen apud ipsum *Cocytos* est, de qua tanquam de paupere regno cum Domitio digladiatur, vel 'ara' item Martialis 'frequens cornibus,' vel *philyra*, vel siquid aliud istiusmodi quod optes cum meis manipularibus accensisque committere.

8   Quin illud evenit ut hoc ipso quo *Miscellanea* cessabant intervallo centum quaedam adnotationes, doctae me hercules (quis enim neget?) et laboriosae, ab homine amicissimo nobis, nec huius ignaro propositi, tum bene etiam litterato, non sine benevola grataque nostri mentione publicarentur. In quis unum casu, credo, vel alterum pari ferme atque apud nos argumento, compluscula certe germana illorum propemodum, quae vel cum *Fastos* Nasonis abhinc novennium ferme, vel postea cum Flacci *Satyras* interpretabamur, quanta norunt omnes frequentia publico auditorio dicta-

repeatedly striking flint, to strike out at least a few little sparks of
truth and to catch enough fire in the kindling to enlighten me
somewhat in this now all but dark and moonless night.

But lo and behold! While I was wholly absorbed in this project,   7
that *Cornucopiae* is suddenly published. People make a beeline. It is
circulated — widely — and scrutinized. To cut a long story short,
the slander evaporates. You would immediately have seen some
people's faces observing a baleful silence and somehow or other — a
novel experience for them — like Plato's notorious Thrasymachus,
blushing.[1017] But my view of the content of that *Cornucopiae* —
since there certainly is some — is not something to be disclosed at
this time. For present purposes, let it merely be laid down that I
have not contemplated the same purpose as the author of that
volume, and the two of us have pursued and achieved different
goals. If in the circumstances we have perchance sometimes dealt
with the same passages (which now and then inevitably occurred),
the wall between us is thicker than that between Pyramus and
Thisbe.[1018] For now, let Juvenal's *Cotytto* serve as proof, who, however, in his [Perotti's] pages is *Cocytos*, about whom, as if over an
impoverished kingdom, let him fight it out with Domizio [Calde-
rini],[1019] or Martial's "altar dense with horns" (*frequens cornibus*),[1020]
or lime-tree bark (*philyra*),[1021] or any other such thing that you
may wish to join battle with my troops and auxiliaries.

In fact, it came about that during the interval when the *Miscel-*   8
lanies were idle one hundred annotations were published, learned
ones, by Jove! (for who would deny it?), and much toiled over, by
a good friend of mine,[1022] who was not unaware of this project and
is very learned, including a kind and gratifying mention of myself.[1023] Among these perhaps one or two are, I believe, on more or
less the same topic as my chapters. A few are virtual siblings of the
things that almost nine years ago, when we were interpreting Ovid's *Fasti* or later Horace's *Satires*, I had said in a well-attended
public lecture, as everyone knows.[1024] I would swear (if need be)

veramus. Persancte (si sit opus) deierem, tenens aram, cogitasse me statim, si non de meo, certe de communi iure concedere amico penitus, nec aliquid ex eis agnoscere, quorum sibi ille titulum, haud, opinor, iniuria, vindicavisset.

9   Non enim sic fastu turgeo, sic mihi ipse faveo, ut videri velim tam docti hominis in aliquo doctor, ne mihi illud in os iaciatur: 'sus Minervam.' Sed quoniam sic ea se principem demum repperisse narrabat, ut ignorata prorsus (ita, credo, putavit) et inenarrata ad eam diem ceteris asseveraret, coactus, fateor, sum — quod et ipse pro ea quam profitetur humanitate facile patietur — simpliciter ingenueque professionem meam suspitionibus istis communis ignorantiae absolvere. Nam sicut haberi iure vel incivilis possim vel arrogans, si non ei quoque qui tam sit et diligens et eruditus domi et ista et meliora nasci putem (quandoquidem medio posuit Deus omnia campo), sic e diverso patrocinium famae deserere non solum dissoluti, sed etiam (ni fallor) in semet ipsum pene crudelis videri possit.

10   'Et pereant,' Donatus aiebat, 'qui ante nos nostra dixerunt.' Nos ei prospera faustaque precamur et cupimus qui nostra post nos aut invenit, aut certe dixit. Tantum rogamus ne pigeat in eorum consortium quae tanto ante, tam multi sub nobis exceperunt, et in quibus pro virili parte laboravimus, etiam nos sicuti partiario admittere, ne non amicorum sint (quod ait Euripides) cuncta communia.

FINIS

very solemnly, holding an altar,[1025] that I planned immediately to yield to my friend, if not my own, at any rate a joint right, and not recognize any of the things to which he had, rightly, I think, claimed ownership.

For I am not so puffed up with arrogance, I am not such a fan 9 of myself, that I wish to seem in any matter the teacher of so learned a man, lest the proverb be cast in my teeth: "A pig [teaches] Minerva."[1026] But since he kept repeating that he was the first to discover these things, so that he asserted to others that they were unknown (so, I believe, he thought) and unexplained until this day, I have, I confess, been compelled—which he, in view of the kindness he professes, will take in good part—simply and straight-forwardly to absolve my profession from those suspicions of common ignorance. For just as I might rightfully be considered uncivil or arrogant if I were to suppose that one who is so diligent and erudite could not produce those things and better ones on his own (since God has set everything within reach of all), so, on the other hand, to desert the defense of my reputation could appear not only the act of a careless man but even (if I am not mistaken) almost cruel to myself.[1027]

"Cursed be those," [Aelius] Donatus used to say, "who have ex- 10 pressed our thoughts before we did!"[1028] We pray and desire prosperous and fortunate things for him who has discovered or at least expressed our thoughts after we did. We ask only that he not begrudge admitting us to share those things which so long before so many have received from us, and on which we toiled to the best of our ability, lest not all things be common to friends (as Euripides says[1029]).

THE END

Note on the Text and Translation

The text of the *Centuria I* presented in this volume rests primarily on the one Poliziano himself saw through the press (Florence, 1489 = *Fl.*), some copies of which contain his own printed corrections (*Emendationes* = *Em.*), subsequently added to the original imprint.[1] The corrections in *Em.* are supplemented by readings from two copies of that edition in Harvard's Houghton Library, which contain further manuscript corrections. The first copy has a few unsystematic corrections in Poliziano's own hand, dated 1491: Inc 6149A (*Corr.*).[2] The second copy has rather more numerous corrections, in the hand of Bartolomeo Fonzio: Inc 6149B (*Corr-B*).[3] Fonzio's readings are occasionally cited for comparison in the Notes to the Text. Readings worth considering are occasionally found in the 1498 Aldine *Omnia opera*, edited by Poliziano's student Pietro Crinito (*Ald.*). According to Joseph Dane's study of a single line of Poliziano's translation of a poem by Callimachus (1.80.7, line 27), *Ald.* likely contains at least some readings based on corrections of Poliziano subsequent to *Em.*[4] In addition, a second edition of Poliziano's complete works was published by Nicolaus Episcopius the Younger at Basel in 1553 (*Bas.*); this mostly follows the 1498 edition but on occasion has other readings worth citing. Finally, an edition was prepared in 1981 by Hideo Katayama, thoroughly classicizing in orthography, based on *Fl.*, *Ald*, and *Bas.* It is quoted here for the occasional conjecture (*Kat.*).

We do not claim that the present edition is a critical one, since such an enterprise would require inspection of all surviving copies of *Fl.*, given the Quattrocento practice of issuing editions (especially those containing Greek) with handwritten corrections or textual integrations made "in house" by publisher's assistants and/or by the author and his friends. This practice essentially extended to the world of print longstanding practices relating to the *correctio* of manuscript codices intended for informal distribution networks.[5] Over sixty surviving copies of *Fl.* are recorded in the Incunabula Short Title Catalogue of the British Library, of which an unknown number have handwritten corrections and notes.[6]

Centuria II, written in Poliziano's own hand, was discovered in 1961 by Vittore Branca in manuscript 1 of the Fondazione Giorgio Cini in Venice (hence referred to as FGC 1). Branca and Manlio Pastore Stocchi published a critical edition with introduction, facsimile, and subsidiary transcription in 1972 (= BPS) as well as an *editio minor* (in fact a photo reprint in a reduced format) in 1978; Alan Cottrell has recollated the manuscript. For this material we have, with very few exceptions, followed the text of Branca and Pastore Stocchi, but with occasional changes in punctuation.

Our notes are indebted to those of *Kat.* and *BPS* but considerably supplement and in a few cases correct them. Abbreviations of classical works, when not indicated in the list of abbreviations given at the head of the Notes to the Translation, follow those in *The Oxford Classical Dictionary*, ed. S. Hornblower and A. Spawforth, 4th ed. (Oxford, 2012), which is also consultable online through Oxford Reference.

Though Poliziano was interested in orthography (cf. *I* 43), holding strong views, for example, on the spelling of Vergil's name (cf. *I* 77), in both *Centuriae* he often failed to adhere consistently to a single spelling (flagrant examples: *II* 44 and 45: *decus[s]-* and *Dossenn[i]us*). Many of these inconsistencies are no doubt owing the team of Poliziano's friends who helped correct *Fl.* for the press.[7] However, modern readers are used to consistency, and so we have regularized some common words in fairly close proximity to avoid causing annoyance (e.g., *ceterum*, not *caeterum*; *auctor*, not *autor*); we have also imposed *prehendo* and related forms without special notice, though *praeh-* is regularly found in *Centuria I* (following the practice of the time, e.g., in Calderini's *Comm. in Mart.*). As to proper names, we have followed Poliziano's orthography where his preferences are clear, but this entails a certain amount of inconsistency (e.g., the author Aelian is spelled both "Aelianus" and "Helianus" in various passages of both *Centuriae*, and we have generally allowed that to stand. However, we have altered "Agellius" of *Centuria II* to "Aulus Gellius": since the author is clearly referred to as "Gellius" in *Centuria I* (list of grammarians, *I* 19, 36, etc.), one assumes that Poliziano would have made this correction when seeing the manuscript of *Centuria II* through the press.[8] On the other hand, he refers several times to the author of the *Astronomica* as Manlius and never as Manilius, so we have let that spelling

stand (as do Branca and Pastore Stocchi); similar cases are Tryphisio-dorus and Hyginius in the *Centuria I*.[9]

As to other changes to the text, Poliziano wrote Latin with fluency but without much inclination to go back over what he had written and correct errors. Thus errors in Latinity are still found in the printed version of *Centuria I* (not to mention the manuscript of *Century II*), which he surely would have corrected had he been aware of them. Since our mandate is to produce an intelligible text that lends itself to translation, we have made such adjustments as needed (with appropriate indications in the Notes to the Text). We have also on occasion emended to bring quotations into line with the quoted authors' attested texts, on the assumption that Poliziano quoted from memory or was misled by the abbreviations in his own notes (unless, of course, Poliziano's point depends on the reading he cites).[10] For comprehensive codicological details of FGC 1, including canceled passages, marginalia, and the like, reference should be made to the edition of Branca and Pastore Stocchi. The paragraph divisions in both *Centuries* are our own (in *Century II* often following Branca and Pastore Stocchi), following the requirements of this I Tatti series. We have observed ordinary modern typographical conventions for printing quoted Greek, except for the poetic texts cited in *I* 58 and 80, for which Poliziano specified a different procedure (see *ad locos*). In the Latin text, single quoted words appear in italic, quotations of more than one word within quotation marks (unless presented as indented block quotations).

This work has not been translated as a whole into any language, as far as we are aware. Poliziano's writing is vigorous and pungent, redolent of comedy and satire.[11] As part of his project of reviving antiquity, he is keen to insert archaic words so as to give them a new lease on life.[12] The series mandate is to produce a text that reads smoothly as English but that is in recognizable contact with the Latin on the facing page. We have sought, accordingly, to convey some of the flavor of the original, including the "nervous *gravitas*" that has been singled out as Poliziano's special attribute.[13]

SIGLA

Ald.   *Omnia opera Angeli Politiani et alia quaedam lectu digna* (Venice: Aldus Manutius, 1498)

Bas.   *Angeli Politiani opera* (Basel: Nicolaus Episcopius Iunior, 1553)

BPS   Angelo Poliziano, *Miscellaneorum centuria secunda, edizione critica,* ed. Vittore Branca and Manlio Pastore Stocchi (Florence: Fratelli Alinari, 1972)

Corr.   autograph corrections made by Poliziano in Harvard University, Houghton Library, Inc 6149(A), a copy of *Fl.*

Corr-B   autograph corrections and notes made by Bartolomeo Fonzio in Houghton Inc 6149(B)

Em.   *Emendationes.* A bifolium inserted in some copies of *Fl.* containing a printed list of errata compiled by Poliziano to the typeset text.

FGC 1   Fondazione Giorgio Cini ms. 1, the autograph of *Centuria II*

Fl.   Angelo Poliziano, *Miscellaneorum centuria prima,* 1st ed. (Florence: Antonius Miscominus, 1489)

Kat.   *Miscellaneorum centuria prima Angeli Politiani,* ed. Hideo Katayama, in idem, "A Study of the *Miscellanea*" [in Japanese], in *Gogaku Bungaku Ronbunshu* [*Research Report, Faculty of Literature*], no. 7 (Tokyo: University of Tokyo, 1981 [1982]), 167–428

NOTES

1. We have used the copy of *Em.* bound into the front of Houghton Inc 6149A; it is a bifolium printed on one side. According to Dane, "*Si vis archetypas,*" 13, 17, *Em.* was produced several months after the date of the colophon in *Fl.,* September 19, 1489 (but before December), after Poliziano was made aware, thanks to critical readers, of errors in *Fl. Em.* is

included in none of the copies of *Fl.* currently online (ProQuest Early European Books has three copies, all from BNCF), as far as we are aware. The colophon specifies that the printer worked from the author's archetype: "Impressit ex archetypo Antonius Miscominus. . . . Florentiae Anno Salutis MCCCCLXXXIX Decimotertio kalendas octobris." For the meaning of *archetypus* in the humanist book, see Rizzo, *Il lessico filologico*, 308–17.

2. See the entry on Poliziano's autographs by Alessandro Daneloni in *ALI-Q*, 1:305. Inc 6149A is a presentation copy for Poliziano's friend Alessandro Sarti, carrying the autograph inscription: "Monumentum & pignus amoris: Mcccclxxxxi Die Maij vi Bononie, Ego Angelus Politianus: Quoniam vis Archetypas habere nugas." The phrase "monumentum et pignus amoris," is from Vergil, *Aen.* 5.538; the line "Si vis archetypas habere nugas" is from Martial 7.11.4, the last line of a four-line epigram that may be rendered: "You make me correct my little books with my own pen and hand, Prudens. Oh, how excessively you approve and love me, wanting to have an original of my trifles!" (Loeb translation). As is well known, Sarti was part of the group of friends responsible for collecting materials for publication in the posthumous *Ald.*

3. See Daneloni on Fonzio autographs in *ALI-Q* 1:177. A number of Fonzio's corrections are simply integrations of *Em.* into his own copy.

4. "*Si vis archetypas*," 18: "Such a sequence [of changes to the poem] suggests not only that the Aldine edition is set up from hand-corrections made subsequent to the errata sheet, but also that the contemporary hand-corrections in the Houghton, Huntington and other copies may be Politian's own."

5. See Dane, "*Si vis archetypas*," who mentions copies at the Huntington Library, Yale, the University of Illinois, the British Library, and the Bodleian Library with contemporary corrections that appear to go beyond the simple integration of the corrections in *Em.* Daneloni in *ALI-Q*, 1:305–12 lists four copies of *Misc.* with sparse manuscript corrections by Poliziano. In general, on the contemporary practice of *correctio* in manuscripts and in printed books, see Rizzo, *Il lessico filologico*, 268–76, and

Pontani's remarks in Poliziano, *Liber epigrammatum graecorum*, lxxviii–lxxix.

6. A letter of Jacopo Gherardi to Poliziano describes the work of an editorial team consisting of Girolamo Donati, Jacopo Antiquario, Giorgio Merula, and others "concerned for your reputation," to hand-correct "around 70" copies of *Fl*.: see Dane, "*Si vis archetypas*," 19–20.

7. The colophon of *Fl*. states: "Familiares quidam Politiani recognovere. Politianus Ipse nec Horthographian se ait, nec omnino alienam praestare culpam." ("Edited by some friends of Poliziano. Poliziano himself says that he takes responsibility neither for the orthography nor for others' errors.") *Em*. adds a rather defensive note, in which Poliziano tries to shift blame for mistakes in Greek accents and other errors on to the printers and editors: "Siqui uel desint uel perperam notati sint in grecis dictionibus accentus, eos eruditi uel restituant uel emendent pro iudicio. Siqua etiam preter hec mendosa, lector, inuenies, que properantes oculos nostros subterfugerint, ea quoque pro tuo iudicio emendabis, nec quicquid putabis nostrum quod parum sit rectum. Errata autem omnia uel impressoribus adscribes, uel curatoribus. Nam si mea esse hic errata ulla credes, tunc ego te credam cordis habere nihil." ("If there should be any accents lacking or incorrectly indicated in the Greek, the learned may either restore them or emend them as they see fit. If you will find any mistakes beyond these, reader, that escaped our hasty eye, you will correct them too in accordance with your own judgment, and not impute to us anything that may be less than correct. You will set them down either to the printers or the editors. For if you think any of these errors here are mine, I for my part may then believe you to be lacking in judgment.")

8. We have not specially noted these changes in the Notes to the Text.

9. *Fl*. numbers chapters with lowercase Roman numerals, which may be a choice of the printer. FGC 1 uses Arabic numbers for the individual chapters. In accordance with current ITRL style, we use Arabic numbers throughout.

10. Cf. Grafton, *Joseph Scaliger*, 1:139–40.

11. Cf. Rizzo, "Il latino."

12. Revival of antiquity: *I* 80; introduction of archaic vocabulary: *I* Pref. 6 and n. 15.

13. *Sc.* by Giovanni Ponte, "La *gravitas nervosa* del Poliziano," in Secchi Tarugi, *Poliziano nel suo tempo*, 107–15.

Notes to the Text

❧❦❧

1. invidia magna *Fl.*: *corrected by us*

2. at] ac *Kat.*

3. quis] quibus *Kat.*, *but this form of the ablative plural is often used; cf., e.g.,* §17 *below*

4. Clementis quidem Alexandrini commentaria *Em.*: Clementis quidem romani pontificis, apostolicique viri commentaria *Fl.*

5. stromatis *Em.*: stromata *Fl.*: Στρωματεῖς *Ald.*

6. alabastrus *Em. and Corr.*: alabastus *Fl.*

7. extimabitur *Fl.*: *corrected by Bas.*

8. qui] *supplied by us*

9. habuissem *Bas.*: hahuissem *Fl.*

10. curat *Em. and Corr.*: currat *Fl.*

11. transilivisse *Fl.*: transiluisse *Ald.*

12. caeris] ceris *Bas.*

13. solemniter *Ald.*: sollenniter *Fl.*

14. Marcianus *Fl.*: Martianus *Bas.*

15. *So spelled throughout.*

16. Doxopater *Kat.*: Doxapater *Fl.*

17. *Some copies of Fl. have a hand-drawn bracket indicating Lucilius [sic] Tarrhaeus, Sophocleus, and Theon as the "Apolloni interpretes"; cf. 1.68.2 and note.*

18. Iosepus] Iosephus *Ald.*, *but see I 19.1 on aspirated consonants, I 9.10, etc.*

19. Synaesius] *corrected by Bas.* (cf. §19 *and I 10.5*)

20. Aegynita *Fl.*, *corrected by Bas.* (cf. II 42.5)

21. *Omitted by Corr-B and Ald.*

22. Theodoritus] *corrected by Kat.*

23. Haebraei] *corrected by Bas.*

24. est *chapter title:* sit *Fl. in this place*

25. quicque *Fl., corrected from the chapter title*

26. Euripidi *Fl.:* Euripidis *Bas. (but in I 27* Euripidi *appears thrice as a genitive,* Euripidis *once)*

27. *The title of the chapter has* sit.

28. pyxide] *supplied by us (cf. I 46.2).*

29. Ulyxis *Fl., standardized to* Ulyssis *per Misc. II*

30. de] *to be deleted (with* usus est *understood)? But so also in chapter title.*

31. medicus *chapter title in body of text:* medius *Fl. in this place*

32. Mostellaria *Bas. (but see I 66)*

33. Zeusi *also I 74: expect* Zeussi *or* Zeuxi

34. *Corr-B, and implied by Em. of chapter title in body of work:* Seleuci *Fl.*

35. Aeliani *chapter title:* Heliani *Fl. in this place*

36. endelechian *Em.:* entelechian *Fl.*

37. perennem *Cicero:* peremnem *Fl. (a hypercorrection; see I Pref. 19,* sollenniter)

38. perennem *Cicero:* peremnem *Fl.*

39. Thomam . . . Thomae *Ald.*

40. eloquutionem *Bas., perhaps rightly*

41. auctore *for consistency:* autore *Fl.*

42. sit] *added by Bas. (cf. I 7.1)*

43. cum] clam *Lucretius*

44. Odysseae *(per Cent. II):* Odisseae *Fl.*

45. mi] mihi *Bas.*

46. Ad] Sed *Priscian*

47. Iosephi *Bas. here and below*

48. cetera *(standardized for consistency):* caetera *Fl.*

49. Sabazius *Corr-B:* Sabadius *Fl.*

50. palaestrae *Bas.*

51. t *Bas.*: c *Fl.*

52. Synesius *per* §23: Synaesius *Fl. in this place*

53. τῶν διονυσιακῶν *in margin Corr-B*: Dionysiacon *Fl. (underlined for omission in Corr-B)*

54. pre *Fl.*

55. laenociniis *Fl.*

56. liceat] licet?

57. τῶν διονυσιακῶν *in margin Corr-B*: Dionysiacon *Fl. (struck out in Corr-B)*

58. χαροπῆσι *Ald. (but this can be a two-termination adjective)*

59. φαιδρὸς *Fl.*

60. multis causis] *expect* multis de causis

61. dimminutivum *Fl.*

62. Theodoritus *Fl.*

63. numerantur *Bas.*

64. *Corr. (space left in Fl. to be filled in by hand, possibly in printer's shop, as was done by Poliziano himself in Corr.)*

65. diminutum *Fl.*: *corrected by us (cf. §1 above)*

66. Gracchi *Bas.*

67. utriculariam *Corr.*: utticulariam *Fl.*

68. velle *Bas.*: velli *Fl.*

69. pathicisimos *Fl.*

70. Rufe *Fl.*

71. oscenissimo *Fl.*: *corr. Bas.*

72. fastosius *Fl.*: *corr. Bas.*

73. apud Ovidium] *expect* apud Ovidium mentio

74. Sisenna] Gisena *Fl.*

75. Rosci *Plutarch*: Rusci *Fl.*

76. Martianus *Bas.*

77. Apostoli Byzantii *Fl.*: Zenodoti *for* Apostoli Byzantii *Ald.*

78. Nemeaeo *Bas. and* Nemaeum *and* Nemeaeaque *below (but cf. I 85 Cerialia)*

79. mentita *Em. and Corr.*: mentitam *Fl.*

80. Pedianus *Fl.*: Pompeius *Corr-B*

81. Sozimus *Fl.*: *corrected by us; see list of Greek historians above,* I 16.2

82. Minucius *Kat.*: Minutius *Fl.*

83. Umbricius *Fl.*: Iuvenalis *Corr-B*

84. edos *Fl.*: *corrected by Bas.*

85. Carthaginem *Fl.*: *corrected by Ald.*

86. Acticarum *Fl.*

87. *sc.* egit; *cf. I 28.1*: quo loco de Capricorno, *etc.*

88. celitus *Fl.*

89. σακκοπάτιον *Ald.*

90. Kalendis (*for consistency with* Kalendarum *below [Fl.]*): Calendis *Fl. in this place*

91. presbyteri *Bas.*

92. Saturnalium] Saturnalitiam *Jerome*

93. sordidum convertit in lucrum] in sordida scorta convertit *Jerome*

94. regerendi *Fl.*: *corrected by us*

95. demostratur *Fl.*

96. Hecalenem *Fl.*

97. dimminutiva *Fl.*

98. Hecalem *Fl.*

99. onustum *Bas.*: hon- *Fl.*

100. tuis *Cicero.*

101. huius *Ovid.*: horum *Fl.*

102. δ' ἐν θυραίοις *Corr-B*: δὲ θυραίους *Fl.*

103. ὑσύχου *Fl.*

104. Rhetorico secundo] *sc.* libro

105. ὄφελ᾽ *Fl.*

106. Πελία *Fl.*

107. Ἰωλκίας] Ἰωλκίδος *Ald.*

108. irrevocabiles *Bas.*

109. lycaei *Corr.*: lycei *Fl.*

110. Sozimus *Fl.*: *corrected for consistency (cf. list of Greek historians, I 16.2 and 58.10)*

111. praelium *Ald. (for consistency)*: prelium *Fl.*

112. de *Corr.*: da *Fl.*

113. significet: *cf. list of chapter titles*: sit *Fl., Ald. in this place*

114. libro *Fl.*: in libro *Bas. (cf. I 32.3 etc.)*

115. Mytilenen *Ald. (here and below)*

116. tyrannicidiarum *Fl.*

117. ingenia *Fl.: corrected by us*

118. consummasse *Fl.: corrected by Ald.*

119. mutitur] visitur *Migne in PL*

120. fede *Fl.*: foede *Bas.*

121. Oaxis] Oaxes *Servius*

122. Lacedaemoinum *Fl.*

123. Lacedemone *Fl.*

124. non] *deleted by us; cf. similar error at I 17*

125. ut] *omitted by Seneca*

126. sudationesque *Vitruvius*: sudationes quae *Fl.*

127. eaeque *Vitruvius*: aeque *Fl.*

128. Terpsicore *Fl.*: Terpsichore *Ald.*

129. Εἰ δὲ *Bas.*: Οἶδε *Fl.*

130. quod infusa vanescat] sed infusa vanescit *Persius*

131. tetrastichon *(for consistency) Bas.*: tetrasticon *Fl.*

132. addivinas *Corr.*: ad divinas *Fl.*

133. μεγάλω *Fl.*

134. Ἦι *omitted in Bas.*

135. monumentis *Bas.*

136. achademiae *Fl.*: *corrected by Bas.*

137. Hephaestion *Bas.*

138. scedis *Fl.*: *corrected by Bas.*

139. licet] decet *Martial (hence* quos, *rather than* quibus)

140. velut] vel?

141. etatem *Fl.*

142. pyxide] *supplied by us (cf. §2)*

143. Martianum *Bas.*

144. nanque *Fl.*: *corr. Bas.*

145. monumentis *Bas.*

146. nobiscum Iohannes Laurentius *Corr.*: nobiscum Graece Latineque vir doctissimus et istiusmodi lauticiarum diligentissimus Iohannes Laurentius *Fl.*

147. incohata *Fl. (but cf. I 94.2)*

148. adsolute *Fl.*

149. vigesimo *Fl.*: trigesimo *Corr-B*

150. electatiunculas *Fl.*: *corrected by us*

151. Sthenoebia *Fl.*

152. simulacrhum *Fl.*

153. purgamina *Fl.*: purgamine *Ald. (but cf. Ovid, Met. 15.327–28: purgamina mentis in illas misit aquas)*

154. Aeginita *Fl., corrected by Bas. (cf. II 42.5)*

155. que] *deleted by us*

156. multimammiis statuis?

157. Hieroymus *Fl.*

158. nonnullorum *Fl.*: *corrected by us (cf. contrasting* pleraque)

159. Ammonis *Bas. here and throughout with this name*

160. Aeois *Fl.*: *corrected by Bas.*

161. quam *Bas.*: quod *Fl., Ald.*

162. Appollinem *Fl.*

163. Καλῆ *Fl.*

164. Ulyxis *Fl. here and below*

165. paululum *for consistency*: paullulum *Fl.*

166. vanos *Cicero*: veros *Fl.*

167. syntaxis] *id est* συντάξεις (*cf.* I Pref. 3 Stromatis, *etc.*)

168. cerula *Bas. here and below*

169. cera *Bas. here and below*

170. ceruia *Ald.*

171. pollulum *Fl.*

172. quae *Bas. here and below (but cf.* LSJ *s.v.* κερατίνης)

173. ceratine *Fl., corrected by Bas.*

174. neque *Mart.*: ne qua *Fl.*

175. *sc.* Doxopatrem

176. que *Fl.*

177. ἄκρα *Fl.*

178. ἑκάστω *Fl.*

179. trabonas *Fl.*

180. tetrahonas *Fl.*

181. eas] eos *Pliny*

182. operaeprecium *Fl.*

183. pergens *Em.*: primo *Fl.*

184. liberum *Fl.*: liberorum? (*cf. §3 above but also §§62.3 [nummum] and 67.2 [liberum]*)

185. Tarentus *Fl.*: *corrected by us (cf. §13 below, where the masculine is correct)*

186. ocultaretur *Fl.*: *corrected by Ald.*

187. sibyllinorum *Em. and Corr.*: sibyllorum *Fl.*

188. taeda *Bas.*: teda *Fl.*

189. Ilythyias *Fl. here and in §22 (but cf. §21)*

190. caesa *Bas.*: cesa *Fl.*

191. hymni . . . compositi *Ald.*: hymnos . . . compositos *Fl.*

192. hac *Bas.*: haec *Fl.*

193. ut] *supplied by us; Bas. changes* matronae *to* matronas *earlier in the sentence, but cf. I 51.1, where* mos habebat *is construed with* uti *plus subjunctive*

194. ειλειϑνειασ *Fl.*: *corrected by Ald.*

195. πληϑομενηι *Fl.*: *corrected by Ald.*

196. ιρευοιτο *Ald.*: ιερευοιτο *Fl.*

197. Παλλευκοι *Ald.*

198. ιρευειν *Ald.*: ιερευειν *Fl.*

199. αειδομενοι *Ald.*

200. λατινοισ *Ald.*

201. ιδριοωσιν *Bas.*

202. Ilythyias *Fl. (but cf. §21)*

203. feri *Em.*: imola *Fl.*

204. male *Fl.*: *corrected by Bas.*

205. damnavit *Sen.*: damnata *Fl.*

206. ceso *Fl.*: *corrected by Bas.*

207. phaletium *Fl.*: *corrected by Bas.*

208. phaletios *Fl.*: *corrected by Bas.*

209. rugarum *Fl.*: *corrected by us*

210. sustuleris *Bas.*

211. vellera ("hides") *restored by us (T. Stangl, the editor of ps.-Asconius Pedianus's commentary on Cicero's speeches [Vienna, 1912], adopts Francesco Robertello's unattested* vellereae*)*: velleas *Fl.*

212. vesus *Fl.*

213. iambicus hoc uno *Em.*: iambicus sed hoc uno *Fl.*

214. occupat, in antepenultima *Corr-B*: occupat, sed in antepenultima *Fl.*

215. commemini. Ipse *Em.*: commemini. Sed ipse *Fl.*

216. nam bini *Fl.*: *corrected by us*

217. Mustelaria *Fl. (here and below)*: Mostellaria *Kat.*

218. quam *Plautus (and Fl. below)*: qua *Fl.*

219. dicere *Em. and Corr.*: dicete *Fl.*

220. id est arta coagmenta *restored by us*: id enim coagmenta *Fl.*

221. quod *Fl.*: *corrected by us*

222. Lucilius *Fl.*: Λουκίλλου *in Laur. 32.9, Poliziano's probable source*

223. Sophocleo *Fl.*: *corrected by us*

224. *For the sake of meter* γένος *must be transposed so as to follow* Χαλύβων.

225. n *[sic] Fl.*

226. βοιωτω *Fl.*

227. Ὀαρίωνα *Fl.*: *corrected by Ald.*

228. dissyllabum *Fl.*: *corrected by Kat.*

229. vocantur tenuissimaque eorum *(referring back to* vincula*)* Pliny: evocantur, tenuissimae earum *Fl.*

230. restilem *restored by us (cf. Tertullian. l.c.:* in restis pristinae modum*)*: netilem *Fl.*

231. quot *Martianus (albeit the tradition is divided)*: quod *Fl.*

232. relliquiae *Fl.*

233. relliquiis *Fl.*

234. expernata *Em. and Corr.*: suppernata *Fl.*

235. obb- *Fl.*

236. Ulyxe *Fl.*

237. capta *Fl.*: *corrected by Bas.*

238. ἴππω *Fl.*

239. Christine *Fl.*: Christianae *Bas.*   Volsinis: *sc.* Volsinii

240. qui *Fl.*: *corrected by Bas. (cf. Branca and Pastore Stocchi, "La Biblioteca Vaticana,"* 142)

241. stadio laboriosissime *Em. and Corr.*: studio laboriosissimo *Fl.*

242. OPTIMAE *Bas., perhaps rightly (at least as regards the original inscription)*

243. Lysimachi *doubtfully Em.*: Seleuci *Fl.*

244. Lysimachi *doubtfully Em.*: Seleuci *Fl.*

245. aspexit *Kat.*

246. *We have retained the style of Fl.: no accents, capitals, or* ς, ι *adscript rather than subscript, and punctuation as in the original.*

247. γηιγενεων] *corrected by Bas.*

248. υπαξονιων *Bas.*

249. αλαβαστρωσ *Corr-B*: αλαστρωσ *Fl.*

250. εδικασσεν *Corr-B*: εδικασεν *Fl.*

251. κωραι *Corr-B*: κοραι *Fl.*

252. οιαν *Corr-B*: οιον *Fl.*

253. χροιην *Corr-B*: χροινη *Fl.*

254. πεξηιται] *corrected by Ald.*

255. σμαξαμενα *Corr-B*: σμασαμενα *Fl.*

256. δαμον *Corr-B*: δαιμον *Fl.*

257. φυγας *Corr-B*: φυγαι *Fl.*

258. *Apparently repeats the phrase in line 63; editors either mark a lacuna here or attempt a conjectural supplement.*

259. βοιωτον *Em.*: *corrected by Corr-B*

260. ηπι . . . διερχομενα om. Fl.: supplied by Em.

261. ρεοισα Fl.: corrected by Ald.

262. ειλυϑε] corrected by Ald.

263. θεμιτα FE of Callimachus

264. εβαλεν] ελαβεν is often substituted, but cf. R. Renehan, "Curae Calli-macheae," Classical Philology 82 (1987): 240–54, at 248

265. εβοασε Ald.

266. του] τω Ernesti

267. Ald. inserts επ after μεν for meter

268. εληιται] corrected by Ald.

269. μωναι] μοναι Fl.

270. ϑυγατηρ] the rest of the line is lost

271. O puerae emicuit rubor illico matutinus Ald. and other corrected copies of Fl. (for the evolution of Poliziano's later corrections to this line, see Dane, "Si vis archetypas," 18): O puerae emicuit rubor haud mora matutinus Em.: O puerae sed enim rubor emicuit matutinus Fl.

272. floribus Em. and Corr.: floridus Fl.

273. Sive Coroneas] modern editors posit a lacuna or propose conjectures on the assumption of a repetition from v. 63

274. Boeotum visens vecta iugis populos Em.: Vecta iugis, visens Boeotiae populos Fl.

275. dorcadibusque Em. and Corr.: dorcalibusque Fl.

276. Boeotis] corrected by Ald.

277. This is the conjectural supplement Poliziano mentioned at §19 above.

278. Corr-B: the Hebrew text is added in the margin in Fl. It is uncertain whose hand added the Hebrew. Perhaps Poliziano intended, as at I 14.2, that space be left blank for insertion of the Hebrew; Fl., however, leaves no space for an insertion. Ald. and Bas. both have the Hebrew characters as the line above the Roman.

279. lelium Fl.: corrected by Ald. (cf. §1).

280. qui] added by us

281. domino *Em. and Corr.*: Domitio *Fl.*

282. equorum *Tacitus*: equitum *Fl.*

283. Methamorphoseon *Fl.*

284. vertite *Fl.*

285. praeceps *Bas.*

286. ἐσόμεσθα] *corrected by Ald.*

287. λης] *corrected by Kat.*

288. de *added by us (haplography after* deos)

289. antequam *Ald.*

290. litterature *Fl.*: *corrected by Ald.*

291. Congum] Congium *Fl., perhaps a perseverative error after* Iunium

292. colligit *Ald. (for sequence of tenses)*: collegit *Fl.*

293. Nessea *Bas.*: Nexea *Fl.*

294. κράτιστος. *Em. and Corr.*: κρτάτιστος *Fl.*

295. ταχὺν λέγεις μὲ *Fl.*

296. in *supplied by us*

297. maetam *Fl.*

298. cum me tua *Martial*: tu cum mea *Fl. in this place*

299. laena *Fl. here and below*: *corrected by Bas.*

300. est *Fl.*: *corrected by us*

301. que *Fl.*

302. translatione *Bas.*

303. *Coronis* (= "Epilogue"), *inferred from §1, is not a heading in the early printed texts, though this section is separated by space from chapter 100*

304. institit *Fl.*: *corrected by Bas.*

Notes to the Translation

ॐ§॰ॐ

ABBREVIATIONS

Abbreviations of works by ancient authors follow those of the *Oxford Classical Dictionary*, 4th ed. (also online), with exceptions and additions noted below. Authors in square brackets are considered pseudonymous by modern scholarship.

Achilles Tatius, *Isag.*	Achilles Tatius, *Isagoge in Arati Phaenomena*
[Acro], *Comm. Hor. Carm.*	[Acro], *Commentarii in Horatii carmina*
Aelian, *NA*	Aelian, *De natura animalium*
Aelian, *VH*	Aelian, *Varia Historia*
ALI-Q	*Autografi dei letterati italiani: Il Quattocento*, vol. 1, ed. Francesco Bausi, Maurizio Campanelli, Sebastiano Gentile, James Hankins (Rome: Salerno Editrice, 2013)
Anth. Pal.	*Anthologia Palatina* (= *Palatine Anthology*)
Anth. Pal. sup.	*Epigrammatum Anthologia Palatina cum Planudeis et appendica nova*, ed. E. Cougny (Paris: Firmin Didot, 1890), 3:390–426
Appian, *B Civ.*	Appian, *Bellum civile* (= Books 13–17 of *Hist. Rom.*)
Appian, *Hist. Rom.*	Appian, *Historia Romana*
Artemidorus, *Onir.*	Artemidorus, *Onirocritica*
Averroes, *Ph. Comm.*	Averroes, *Commentarii in Aristotelis libros Physicorum*
BAM	Milan, Biblioteca Ambrosiana
Barbaro, *Castigationes*	Ermolao Barbaro, *Castigationes Plinianae*, ed. Giovanni Pozzi, 4 vols. (Padua: Antenori, 1973–79)
BAV	Vatican City, Biblioteca Apostolica Vaticana

Beroaldo, *Annotationes*	Filippo Beroaldo the Elder, *Annotationes centum,* ed. L. A. Ciapponi (Binghamton, NY: Medieval and Renaissance Texts and Studies, 1995)
Beroaldo, *Comm. in Suet.*	Filippo Beroaldo, *Commentationes in Vitas XII Caesarum Suetonii* (Bologna: Benedictus Hectoris, 1493) and subsequent editions
BML	Florence, Biblioteca Medicea Laurenziana
BNCF	Florence, Biblioteca Nazionale Centrale
Boethius, *Comm. in Cic. Top.*	Boethius, *Commentaria in Topica Ciceronis*
CAG	*Commentaria in Aristotelem Graeca,* 23 vols. (Berlin: Reimer, 1883–1909)
Calderini, *Comm. in Iuv.*	Domizio Calderini, *Commentaria in Juvenalem*
Calderini, *Comm. in Mart.*	Domizio Calderini, *Commentaria in Martialem*
Calderini, *Comm. in Ov. epist. Sapphus*	Domizio Calderini, *Commentaria in Ovidii epistolam Sapphus*
Calderini, *Comm. in Ov. Ibin*	Domizio Calderini, *Commentaria in Ovidii Ibin*
Calderini, *Comm. in Stat. Silv.*	Domizio Calderini, *Commentaria in Statii Silvas*
Calderini, *In Ov. Her.*	Domizio Calderini, *In Ovidii Heroides*
CCL	*Corpus Christianorum. Thesaurus patrum Latinorum.*
Comm. Fast.	Poliziano, *Commento inedito ai Fasti di Ovidio,* ed. F. Lo Monaco (Florence: Leo S. Olschki, 1991)
Comm. Pers.	Poliziano, *Commento inedito alle Satire di Persio,* ed. L. Cesarini Martinelli and R. Ricciardi (Florence: Leo S. Olschki, 1985)

Comm. Selv.	Poliziano, *Commento inedito alle Selve di Stazio,* ed. L. Cesarini Martinelli (Florence: Leo S. Olschki, 1978)
CPG	*Corpus poetarum Graecorum*
CSEL	*Corpus Scriptorum Ecclesiasticorum Latinorum*
CTC	*Catalogus translationum et commentariorum: Medieval and Renaissance Latin Translations and Commentaries, annotated lists and guides,* ed. Paul Oskar Kristeller, F. Edward Cranz, Virginia Brown, Greti Dinkova-Bruun with James Hankins and Julia Gaisser, 11 vols. to date (Washington, D.C.: The Catholic University of America Press, 1960–2011; Toronto: Pontifical Institute of Mediaeval Studies, 2014–16); ACLS Humanities eBook and Project Muse
DBI	*Dizionario biografico degli Italiani* (Rome,1960–); cited from the online edition (without pagination) at Treccani.it
Donatus, *Comm. Ter. Adel.*	Donatus, *Commentum in Terentii Adelphos*
Donatus, *Comm. Ter. An.*	Donatus, *Commentum in Terentii Andriam*
Donatus, *Comm. Ter. Eun.*	Donatus, *Commentum in Terentii Eunuchum*
Donatus, *Comm. Ter. Phorm.*	Donatus, *Commentum in Terentii Phormion*
Eustathius, *Comm. Hom. Il.*	Eustathius, *Commentarii in Homeri Iliadem*
Eustathius, *Comm. Hom. Od.*	Eustathius, *Commentarii in Homeri Odysseam*
Eutropius, *Brev.*	Eutropius, *Breviarium historiae Romanae*
Festus, *De verb. sign.*	Sextus Pompeius Festus, *De verborum significatu*

FGE	*Further Greek Epigrams*, ed. D. L. Page (Cambridge: Cambridge University Press, 1981)
FGrH	*Die Fragmente der griechischen Historiker*, ed. F. Jacoby et al. (Berlin: Weidmann, 1923–)
Firmicus, *Math.*	Firmicus Maternus, *Matheseos libri VIII*
FRH	*The Fragments of the Roman Historians*, ed. T. J. Cornell et al. (Oxford: Oxford University Press, 2013)
FRL	*Fragmentary Republican Latin: Ennius: Dramatic Fragments, Minor Works*, ed. S. M. Goldberg and G. Manuwald (Cambridge, MA: Harvard University Press, 2018)
Galen, *Simpl. medic.*	Galen, *De simplicium medicamentorum facultatibus*
GRF	*Grammaticae Romanae fragmenta*, ed. H. Funaioli (Leipzig: Teubner, 1907)
ITRL	The I Tatti Renaissance Library (Cambridge, MA: Harvard University Press, 2001–)
Jerome, *Comm. in Eccl.*	Jerome, *Commentarius in Ecclesiastem*
Jerome, *Comm. in Epist. ad Ephesios*	Jerome, *Commentarii in Epistolam ad Ephesios*
Jerome, *Comm. in Ezech.*	Jerome, *Commentarii in Ezechielem*
Jerome, *Hebr. quaest. in Gen.*	Jerome, *Hebraicae quaestiones in libro Geneseos*
Keil, *Gramm. Lat.*	H. Keil, *Grammatici Latini*, 8 vols. (Leipzig: Teubner, 1855–1923); Cambridge Books Online
LSJ	*Greek-English Lexicon*, ed. H. G. Liddell and R. Scott, revised and augmented by H. S. Jones (Oxford: Oxford University Press, 1940)
Lucian, *Iud. Voc.*	Lucian, *Iudicium vocalium*

Maximus Tyrius, *Diss.*	Maximus Tyrius, *Dissertationes*
Merula, *Enarr. Juv.*	Giorgio Merula, *Enarrationes satyrarum Juvenalis* (Venice: G. di Pietro, 1478) and later editions
Merula, *In Mart.*	Giorgio Merula, *Adversus D. Calderini commentarios in Martialem* (Venice: G. di Pietro, 1478) and later editions
Misc. I	Angelo Poliziano's *Miscellaneorum centuria prima* (*First Century of the Miscellanies*)
Misc. II	Angelo Poliziano's *Miscellaneorum centuria secunda* (*Second Century of the Miscellanies*)
MRI	A. M. Migliarini, *Monete romane imperiali*, 2 vols. (Florence, 1852)
MRR	T. R. S. Broughton, *Magistrates of the Roman Republic*, 3 vols. (New York-Atlanta: American Philological Association, 1951–86)
Nicas, *Etym. magn.*	Nicas, *Etymologicum magnum*
Nonius, *De comp. doct.*	Nonius Marcellus, *De compendiosa doctrina*
OCD	*Oxford Classical Dictionary*, ed. Simon Hornblower, Anthony Spawforth, and Esther Eidinow, 4th ed. (Oxford: Oxford University Press, 2012) and online via Oxford Reference
OCT	Oxford Classical Texts
ODB	*Oxford Dictionary of Byzantium*, ed. A. Kazhdan, 3 vols. (Oxford: Oxford University Press, 1991)
OLD	*Oxford Latin Dictionary*, ed. P. G. W. Glare (Oxford: Clarendon Press, 1982)
ORF	*Oratorum Romanorum fragmenta liberae rei publicae*, ed. H. Malcovati, 4th ed. (Turin: Paravia, 1955)
Oribasius, *Coll.*	Oribasius, *Collectionum medicarum reliquiae*

Otto	A. Otto, *Die Sprichwörter und sprichwörtlichen Redensarten der Römer* (Leipzig: Teubner, 1890)
PCG	*Poetae comici Graeci*, ed. R. Kassel and C. Austin, 7 vols. to date (Berlin-New York: De Gruyter, 1983–)
PG	*Patrologia Graeca*, ed. J.-P. Migne, 161 vols. (Paris: Migne, 1857–66) and online
PL	*Patrologia Latina*, ed. J.-P. Migne, 221 vols. (Paris: Migne, 1844–91) and online
Porphyrio, *Comm. Hor. Epist.*	Pomponius Porphyrio, *Commentum in Horatii Epistolas*
Porphyrio, *Comm. Hor. Serm.*	Pomponius Porphyrio, *Commentum in Horatii Sermones*
Porphyry, *Isagoge et in Arist. Cat. Comm.*	Porphyry [of Tyre], *Isagoge et in Aristotelis Categorias Commentaria*
Probus, *Scholia Bern. Vergil. Bucol.*	Probus, *Scholia Bernensia in Vergilii Bucolica*
Proclus, *Comm. in Plat. Alc. I*	Proclus, *Commentarium in Platonis Alcibiades I*
RE	*Paulys Realencyclopädie der classischen Altertumswissenschaft*, ed. G. Wissowa, K. Mittelhaus, K. Ziegler, 83 vols. (Stuttgart: J. B. Metzler, 1893–1980)
RRC	M. H. Crawford. *Roman Republican Coinage*, 2 vols. (Cambridge: Cambridge University Press, 1974)
Scholia Ap. Rhod. Argon.	*Scholia in Apollonii Rhodii Argonautica*
Scholia Ar. Nubes	*Scholia in Aristophanis Nubes*
Scholia Ar. Vesp.	*Scholia in Aristophanis Vespas*
Scholia Arat. Phaen.	*Scholia in Arati Phaenomena*
Scholia vet. Hes. Op.	*Scholia vetera in Hesiodi Opera et Dies*
Scholia Xen. Anab.	*Scholia in Xenophontis Anabasim*

Seneca, *Agam.*	Seneca the Younger, *Agamemnon*
Seneca, *Herc. fur.*	Seneca the Younger, *Hercules furens*
Servius, *Comm. Aen.*	Servius, *Commentarii in Aeneidem*
Servius, *Comm. Bucol.*	Servius, *Commentarii in Vergilii Bucolica*
SH	*Supplementum Hellenisticum*, ed. H. Lloyd-Jones and P. Parsons (Berlin: De Gruyter, 1983)
Simplicius, *In libros De anima*	Simplicius, *Commentaria in libros Aristotelis De anima*
SSR	*Socratis et Socraticorum reliquiae*, ed. G. Giannantoni, 4 vols. (Naples: Bibliopolis, 1990)
Strabo	Strabo, *Geographica*
Suetonius, *Gram. et rhet.*	Suetonius, *De grammaticis et rhetoribus*
SVF	*Stoicorum veterum fragmenta*, ed. J. von Arnim, 4 vols. (Leipzig: Teubner, 1903–24)
TLG	*Thesaurus linguae Graecae*, online resource, University of California, Irvine
TLL	*Thesaurus linguae Latinae* (Leipzig: Teubner, 1900–) and online
TrGF	*Tragicorum Graecorum fragmenta*, ed. B. Snell, 5 vols. (Göttingen: Vandenhoeck & Ruprecht, 1971–2004)
TrRF	*Tragicorum Romanorum fragmenta*, vol. 2, *Ennius*, ed. G. Manuwald (Göttingen: Vandenhoeck & Ruprecht, 2012)
Ullman-Stadter	B. L. Ullman and Philip A. Stadter, *The Public Library of Renaissance Florence: Niccolò Niccoli, Cosimo de' Medici and the Library of San Marco* (Padua: Antenore, 1972)
Valerius Flaccus, *Argon.*	Valerius Flaccus, *Argonautica*

Varro, *Antiq. rerum div.*	Varro, *Antiquitates rerum divinarum*
Vibius Sequester, *De flum.*	Vibius Sequester, *De fluminibus, fontibus, lacubus, nemoribus, paludibus, montibus, gentibus quorum apud poetas mentio fit*

PREFACE

The Preface performs several tasks at once. It begins and ends, as expected, with a nod to the dedicatee, Lorenzo de' Medici. The middle pursues two projects, a *praemunitio*, or advance fortification of his case to meet potential criticism, and a critique of the times. Poliziano had already been subjected to searing attacks by Fonzio (cf. Paolo Viti, "Poliziano e Fonzio: motivi e forme di una polemica," in Fera and Martelli, *Agnolo Poliziano*, 527–40) and clearly anticipated more of the same from him and/or others. He defends himself from charges of impure motives (§2), choice of an unacceptable literary form (§§3, 7–8), focus on minutiae (§4), and obscure language (§§5–6). He claims to be seeking a mean between the overrefined and the crude (§§9–10). After declaring himself willing to submit to the reader's judgment, adopting a satirist's *indignatio*, he launches a fierce attack on the dishonest practices of literary scholarship of the day. Presenting himself as a reformer, he contrasts his own attitude and procedures. One can also meet criticism by exposing the critics. Poliziano distinguishes several types — the faultfinders, the mercenary, the self-regarding, the schoolmasters, who will see some of their doctrines exploded (e.g., *Misc. I* 43 and 77), and the ignorant clergy, to whom he offers learned models, present and past, and the idea that the liberal arts should serve as a propaedeutic to theology (§19). Toward the end of the argumentative section, he returns emphatically to the point that one of his purposes in publishing is to reclaim his work from plagiarists, and he threatens to deal with them more harshly in future installments (§§1, 21). The Preface concludes by setting the author into the context of Lorenzo's circle, claiming to provide merely the dessert table, not the main feast, which has been offered or is in prospect from the philosophical authors (§22). In painting this black-and-white picture of

different styles of scholarship—his own versus that of (unnamed) others—without any shades of gray, Poliziano was virtually inviting the criticism he ostensibly seeks to avert, and it did indeed come; see Fera, "Il dibattito."

1. Pfeiffer, *History*, 2:45 n. 5, queries whether this was the first use of the word for "a literary work of mixed contents." Grazzini, "Osservazioni," 157–62, argues that the title was inspired by *miscellanea* at Juvenal 11.20 but admits that the culinary reference there does not shed light on Poliziano's usage. More strikingly Juvenalian is Poliziano's occasional adoption of a tone of *indignatio* (Juvenal 1.79).

2. A quotation of Juvenal 1.80.

3. Quintilian, *Inst.* 5.11.41. Erasmus later cites this proverbial expression: *Adagia* 1.10.91.

4. What Poliziano has in mind becomes clearer at *I* 9.2, 4–5, where he speaks of Calderini taking advantage of the credulity of students and other readers.

5. Here and below in §21 and *I* Epil. 7, Poliziano's "centuries," which may have seemed a mere organizational convenience, like the arrangement of the proverbs in centuries by the Greek paroemiographers, take on a military aspect as a tool of his polemics; cf. Perosa *apud* Grazzini, "Osservazioni," 161 n. 21.

6. The flat end of the stylus was used for smoothing out, or erasing, the marks made by the sharp end.

7. Aelian, *VH*, and Aulus Gellius, *NA*.

8. Clement of Alexandria, *Strom*.

9. A student of Aristotle's and author of Ἁρμονικά στοιχεῖα, ed. H. S. Macran (Hildesheim: Olms, 1990).

10. The title Σύμμικτα is attested for Aristoxenus by Porphyry, *In Harmonica Ptolemaei*, p. 80.18 Düring = Aristoxenus fr. 128 Wehrli. Poliziano could also have cited the *Miscellanea* of Theodore Metochites, whose commentary on Aristotle's *Physics* he later adduces (*II* 53.9).

11. Poliziano will be thinking of Caesar's *De analogia*, Varro's *De lingua Latina*, Marcus Valerius Messalla Rufus's (nonextant) work on augury,

perhaps Cicero's discussion of prose rhythm in *Orator*, and Quintilian's discussion of grammatical matters in Book 1 of *Inst*. He reverts to this point, again invoking the precedent of Caesar, at I 77.2. On Poliziano's defense of descending to details, cf. Godman, *From Poliziano*, 80–83.

12. An allusion to the expansion of the Senate, attributed either to Tarquinius Priscus or to Brutus as first consul of the Republic, the "lesser families" contributing the new senators; cf. Cicero, *Rep.* 2.35; Livy 1.35.6; Tacitus, *Ann.* 11.25.

13. That is, his critics will change their minds about what is common usage once they have become acquainted with the full range of literature. It was, in fact, precisely on the ground of obscure vocabulary that Merula launched some of his bitterest attacks on *Misc.* I (*apud* Perotto Sali, "L'opuscolo inedito," 160). On Poliziano's enrichment of the Latin language, cf. Rizzo, "Il latino," 117–22.

14. Cicero, *Acad.* 2.2 (p. 21.8–9 Plasberg).

15. A scholar might not be expected to cultivate archaisms, but Poliziano's move results from his position as a keen student of archaic diction (cf. II 23.1) and the fact that he shares the humanist impulse to restore antiquity generally (cf. on I 80.6).

16. Poliziano returns in detail to the topic of qualified judges at I 90.1.

17. That is, the content will make the reading worthwhile in spite of stylistic peculiarities.

18. Cyprian, *Epist.* 74.9.

19. See I Epil. 4–5.

20. See on I 4.

21. The opposition of sweet and savory recurs at §22, where the *Miscellanea* as a whole are categorized as the former (in contrast to strictly philosophical works).

22. A proverbial expression also referred to in Tertullian, *De carne Christi* 6.1; Erasmus, *Adagia* 1396.

23. Varro, *Ling.* 8.31.

24. Poliziano describes the process of literary revision in terms drawn from the carpenter's trade: lacking major revision as well as minor polishing; see further Rizzo, "Il latino," 92–94.

25. Cf. the total depilation practiced by the overrefined Tarentines (*II* 49.3). Poliziano's dichotomy of overrefined and rustic potential readers may have been inspired by Aristophanes, *PCG* F 706, cited by Sextus Empiricus, *Adv. math.* 1.228, which Poliziano transcribed in his notebook (Munich, Bayerische Staatsbibliothek, Clm 798, ff. 69r–70) in 1488 shortly before writing this Preface; cf. Rizzo, "Il latino," 96–97.

26. Cicero, *Orat.* 6.21. Poliziano cites the text with the weakly attested reading *cinnus amborum*, rather than *vicinus amborum* ("neighboring both"); he takes *cinnus* in the sense "a kind of drink mixed from many liquids" (Nonius, *De comp. doct.*, p. 62 Lindsay); cf. Rizzo, "Il latino," 96.

27. "Straightforward in its elegance" (*simplex munditiis*) is borrowed from Horace, *Carm.* 1.5.5.

28. The point is left vague here but elaborated at *I* Epil. 1–3.

29. Livy 8.31.7.

30. With "semi-freely," Poliziano adopts the alienated tone of Cicero's letters to intimate friends under Caesar's dictatorship; cf. *Att.* 13.31.3.

31. Alludes to Persius, *Sat.* 1.120.

32. The "capital crimes" and arbitrary invention correspond to the description of Calderini's procedure at *II* 5.2–4.

33. Cf. *II* 10.1–2 (Calderini).

34. This description matches the methods of Calderini repeatedly criticized in *Misc. I* (9.3, 7–9; 10.1 and 5; 15.3; 21.1; 22.1; 31.1–2; 33.1–3; 38.1–2; 52.1–2; 56; 58.13; 59.3; 65.1; 75.1–2 and 4;, 80.5) and *II* (see above) but could also apply to Beroaldo, who is criticized but not named in the Epilogue, §§8–9; cf. P. De Capua, "Poliziano e Beroaldo," in Fera and Martelli, *Agnolo Poliziano*, 506–25, at 515–17. See also the remarks on Giorgio Valla (who is not named) at *I* 33.4.

35. That is, the printing press, much exploited by Calderini; see p. xxiii n. 2.

36. Cf. Persius 1.121.

37. Hor., *Sat.* 1.3.23.

38. The following notes point out various slips on Poliziano's part, mostly mistaken references as a result of citing from memory.

39. This is one of several passages in which Poliziano seeks to shield his work from criticism by emphasizing its hastily improvised (*ex tempore* or *tumultuaria*) character; cf. *I* 11.3, 80.3; *II* 46.4; Fiaschi, "Traduzioni," 42–43. Ex tempore composition was also regarded in Lorenzo's circle as a sign of brilliance or inspiration.

40. Pliny, *HN* 1, *init.*, listing book by book the authors who served as his sources. Contrast *I* 75.1, where Poliziano mocks Calderini's claims about sources; similarly, *II* 5.3.

41. Poliziano's exploitation of these materials to provide historical context gives his scholarship greater depth than that of his contemporaries; cf. Koortbojian, "Poliziano's Role," 270.

42. On the new standards Poliziano set for accurate use and citation of sources, cf. Grafton, "On the Scholarship," 160–62. An example is *I* 91.2, where he explains how he arrived at his reconstruction of a passage of Eupolis's Δῆμοι.

43. That is, the work's value should not be measured by the number of chapters.

44. Homer, *Il.* 8.266–67, 271–72.

45. *Sc.* Lorenzo's. Contrast §11, where Poliziano seems to stand on his own.

46. Very little of Poliziano's learned work—only three of the *Sylvae*—had been published prior to the appearance of *Centuria I* in 1489 (cf. Godman, *From Poliziano*, 93; *Sylvae*, ed. Fantazzi in ITRL 14), and he felt that others were in the meantime publishing ideas taken from his public lectures (cf. §1 and Epil. 8–9); hence the pressure he felt.

47. *M. Catonis praeter librum De re rustica quae extant*, ed. H. Jordan (Leipzig: Teubner, 1860), 80, *apud* Pliny, *HN* Praef. 32.

48. Cf. Otto s.v. *oculus* 7.

49. Cf. I 9.2–3 (Calderini).

50. One suspects Poliziano may be thinking of Fonzio, an inveterate critic of his, who had been disappointed that the younger man was appointed to a professorship ahead of him; see further Ciapponi, "Bartolomeo Fonzio."

51. For tensions between humanists and clergy at this time, cf., for example, H. D. Jocelyn, "Politian and the Study of Ancient Comedy," in Secchi Tarugi, *Poliziano*, 319–31, at 330.

52. *Epist.* 52.9: "Let not a rustic and simple brother account himself sacred if he knows nothing."

53. On the Augustinian friar and preacher Mariano Pomicelli (1450–98), a client and supporter of Lorenzo, cf. Daniela Gionta's entry in *DBI* s.v.

54. Cicero, *Hortensius* fr. 92 Grilli.

55. Cicero, *Att.* 4.6.2; in the marginal note in his copy (Paris, Bibliothèque Nationale de France, Rés. Z.121, 64r), Poliziano notes that Philoxenus preferred to return to the quarries rather than praise Dionysius's tragedy; cf. Juren, "Les notes," 249.

56. Thucydides 1.22.

57. Proverbial; cf. Plautus, *Trin.* 1154. The sense is that one will value, and hence fight for, what is closest to one.

58. *Sc.* of what is yet to come.

59. *Sc.* by false claimants to authorship.

60. Poliziano puns on *picus* (= woodpecker), as he had at *Epist.* 2.10.3 (ed. S. Butler in ITRL 21, 118–19 = *Opera* 1:24), whereas the "laurel tree" (*laurus*) alludes to Lorenzo (Laurentius), with the relation of protégé and patron expressed with a different image than at §17 above. After being embroiled in controversy over his *900 Theses*, some of which were declared heretical by Pope Innocent VIII, Pico took up residence in Florence in the second half of 1484, where he remained, with several interruptions, until the death of Lorenzo. On him, see Franco Bacchelli's entry in *DBI*

s.v. Orvieto, *Poliziano e l'ambiente Mediceo*, 103–18, offers a survey of the relations of Poliziano and Pico.

61. Propertius 2.34.65.

62. *Sc.* Cornutus; see on *I* 44.

63. Poliziano does not have a category for novelists and thus treats Xenophon of Ephesus and Heliodorus as historians; it is surprising, however, that Xenophon of Athens is not included here (albeit he appears among the philosophers).

64. Primarily an author on music, though his work does make some connections with mathematics.

65. That is, Longus; see on *I* 2.

66. *Asymboli*, a word discussed in detail at *II* 43.

67. A civil status; literally, "having surrendered."

68. Tutelary gods of the head of household and his wife.

69. *Sc.* Theodore Gaza.

70. Soldiers invalided out of service.

I

71. Martianus Capella 9.998. On the "cyclics," see note on *Misc. I* 4.1.

72. John Argyropoulos (1415–87) attended the Council of Florence as a member of the Greek delegation (1439–44) and converted to Catholicism at that time. After the Ottoman conquest, he took refuge in Italy in 1456, where he continued his career as a teacher in Padua, Florence, and Rome and translated a number of Aristotle's works; Poliziano also mentions him as his teacher in philosophy at *I* Epil. 4. Though he was factually correct on ἐντελέχεια (see below), Argyropoulos's attack on Cicero was an "egregious error" in view of the orator's high standing in Italy, as is acknowledged by Geanakoplos, *Greek Scholars*, 112. On him, see further E. Bigi's entry in *DBI* s.v. Argiropulo, Giovanni.

73. For a list of Argyropoulos's translations of Aristotle, cf. E. Garin, "Le traduzioni," 82–86.

74. Comparison of the two vocabularies to the advantage of Latin: Cicero, *Caec.* 51; *Fin.* 1.3.10 and 3.15.51; *Tusc.* 2.15.35, 3.5.10, and 10.22; Cicero's own abundance of words: *Att.* 12.32.3.

75. *Aristotelis et Theophrasti Historiae . . .* Theodoro Gaza interprete (Lugduni: Gulielmus Rouillius, 1552), preface, p. 6.

76. Cicero, *Tusc.* 1.10.22 and 26.65.

77. Argyropoulos's distinction of the two words is essentially correct, but the confusion of the words in *end-* and *ent-* arose in antiquity (cf. LSJ s.vv.). Reflecting this confusion, Cicero assumes ἐνδελέχεια and makes this the basis of his interpretation of Aristotle's doctrine of the soul along Platonic lines (as Poliziano hints: §11 below). This chapter, emphasizing argument from authorities in the medieval manner, does not show Poliziano at his best. It is, however, placed programmatically at the beginning so as to situate him (in spite of his philhellenism) firmly on the Latin side of the Greek-Latin cultural divide.

78. Persius 5.86.

79. Cf. the similar formulation about Cicero at *II* 39.2.

80. Thomas's teacher, Albertus Magnus, discussed Boethius, *Opuscula sacra* III in his *De bono* q1, a7; in his youth Thomas wrote commentaries on *Opuscula sacra* I and III; see further Christophe Erismann, "The Medieval Fortunes of the *Opuscula sacra*," in *The Cambridge Companion to Boethius*, ed. John Marenbon (Cambridge: Cambridge University Press, 2009), 155–77, at 161–62 and 175 nn. 33 and 35. Thomas also wrote a commentary on Boethius's *On the Hebdomads*; cf. Aquinas, *An Exposition of the* On the Hebdomads *of Boethius*, trans. J. L. Schultz and E. A. Synan (Washington, D.C.: Catholic University of America Press, 2001).

81. Boethius, *In Isagogen Porphyrii commenta* (CSEL 48), 31–32.

82. An echo of Pliny, *HN* Praef. 7 apropos of Cicero.

83. Cf. Otto s.v. *unguis* 4.

84. An allusion to Cicero, *Fam.* 5.12.7.

85. Boethius, *Comm. in Cic. Top.* (PL 63, 1040D–1173B).

86. Poliziano refers to the comparison of Plato and Cicero at the beginning of Macrobius's commentary on the "Dream of Scipio," a section of Book 6 of the fragmentary *De republica,* and especially to his comment at its conclusion that Cicero included all three "parts" of philosophy (ethics, physics, logic) and that therefore there was nothing more perfect ("nihil hoc opere perfectius": 2.17.15–17).

87. Augustine, *Contra academicos* 1.3.7 (Licentius is the speaker), and *Conf.* 3.4.7.

88. Paraphrase of Augustine, *Conf.* 3.4.7.

89. Rufinus, *Apologia (Contra Hieronymum)* 2.7; Jerome, *Contra Rufinum* 1.30. For humanist reactions in the Renaissance to the famous dream of Jerome, in which he was condemned by the Supreme Judge for being a Ciceronian, see Eugene F. Rice, Jr., *Saint Jerome in the Renaissance* (Baltimore, 1985), passim.

90. Cicero, *Att.* 2.1.2.

91. Cicero, *Att.* 2.1.1.

92. Cf. Caesar *apud* Pliny, *HN* 7.117.

93. Cicero, *Tusc.* 3.8.16.

94. Cicero, *Tusc.* 3.5.11.

95. Cicero, *Tusc.* 2.15.35.

96. Cicero, *Fam.* 9.24.3.

97. Cicero, *De orat.* 2.4.17–18.

98. Plutarch, *Cicero* 4.5.

99. [Alexander of Aphrodisias], *Quaest.* (= *Problemata*), CAG sup. 2.2, pp. 44.21, 54.20, 77.9, etc.; Jerome, *Ep.* 50.1 (where he speaks in general of reading Alexander's commentaries), and *Contra Rufinum* 1.20; Porphyry, *Isagoge et in Arist. Cat. Comm.,* CAG 4.1, p. 55.20–24; Themistius, *Paraphrasis in libros Aristotelis de anima,* CAG 5.3, pp. 39.19–23, 40.2–3, 41.8–22, 43.23–24; Simplicius, *In libros De anima,* CAG 11, p. 4.19–20 and p. 4.38–5.1, p. 105.7ff.; Aristides Quintilianus, *De musica* 3.11 (= p. 111.6–10 Winnington-Ingram); Ambrose, *Epist.,* Classis I 34 (81), PL 16.1119C.

100. *Sc.* §2.

101. Plutarch, *Sulla* 26.1.

102. Boethius, *Comm. in Arist.* Περὶ ἑρμηνείας, 2nd ed., p. 11.13ff. Meiser, also citing Alexander's refutation (in referring to "books," Poliziano takes account of the spurious appendix); Simplicius, *In Categorias commentarium*, CAG 8, p. 379.8–12.

103. Strabo, 13.1.54.

104. Alexander of Aphrodisias, *De fato*, CAG sup. 2.2, p. 164.1.

105. That is, marred by Apellicon's supplements and "corrections." This is, as E. Garin, "ἐνδελέχεια," 180, notes, Poliziano's most interesting move, applying his knowledge of textual transmission in general, the history of the text of the Aristotelian corpus in particular, and the relative chronology of the authorities to bolster Cicero's position; cf. also Wilson, *From Byzantium*, 120–21. Barbaro, *Castigationes*, on *HN* 5.202 disagreed, citing Lucian, *Iud. voc.* 10, to argue that the spelling with *t* was original (for Poliziano's reaction, cf. *Epist.* 12.1 = *Opera* 1:164).

106. Plato, *Phdr.* 245 c–e; Varro, *Antiquitates rerum divinarum* fr. 13 Cardauns; Cicero, *Tusc.* 1.23.53, and *Rep.* 6.27–28 (= 31–32 Powell); perhaps a reference to the *Vita Aristotelis Marciana* (in Marcianus Graecus 257, 13th century), ed. with commentary by O. Gigon (Berlin: De Gruyter, 1962), where at vv. 135–45 the claim is raised that Aristotle polemicized not against Plato, but those who wrongly interpreted Plato (the basis for Poliziano's attribution to Philoponus is unclear, albeit Philoponus also tended to harmonize the two philosophers; cf. Ingemar Düring, *Aristotle in the Ancient Biographical Tradition* [Göteborg: Acta Universitatis Gothoburgensis 63, 1957], 332–36); Simplicius, *In libros De anima*, CAG 11, pp. 246.17–47.15; Boethius, *Comm. in librum Arist.* Περὶ ἑρμηνείας 2:80.2–9 Meiser; Porphyry, Περὶ τοῦ μίαν εἶναι τὴν Πλάτωνος καὶ Ἀριστοτέλους αἴρεσιν ζ' (cited by Suidas s.v. Πορφύριος).

107. Pico della Mirandola, Preface to *De ente et uno* (*Opera* 1:241), which was published with dedication to Poliziano toward the end of 1490 (it was meant to be part of a larger work harmonizing the Academy and Peripatos); cf. also *Opera* 1:124 (*Apologia*).

108. That is, *endelechia* vs. *entelechia*.

109. Didymus, pp. 399–400 Schmidt; Poliziano is thinking of the *Silloi*, satirical writings of Timon of Phlius, who flourished in the third century BCE; cf. citation at *II* 43.4.

2

110. Catullus 98.3–4.

111. The latter was A. Partenio's conjecture (Brescia: Boninus de Boninis, 1485); cf. Gaisser, *Catullus*, 72.

112. Julius Pollux, *Onom.* 7.88.

113. Aristotle, *HA* 2.499a29–30.

114. Longus, *Daphnis et Chloe* 2.3.1; Lucian, *Alex.* 39. For the former, Poliziano used BML, ms. Conv. Soppr. 627 (2nd half of the 13th century), where the title reads Λόγου ποιμενικῶν περὶ Δάφνιν καὶ Χλόην. Hence not taking the first word as an author's name, he cites it as an anonymous work.

115. Xenophon, *Anabasis* 4.5.14; Suidas s.v. καρβάσιναι.

116. Perhaps a modern commentator; the extant ancient scholia on Xenophon, *An.* 4.5.14, merely say that it is a type of shoe.

3

117. Horace, *Epist.* 2.1.195.

118. Perhaps Poliziano made the observation when he lectured on Homer and poetry in general in 1486–87; cf. Maïer, *Ange Politien*, 427.

119. The giraffe arrived in Florence in connection with an embassy bearing various gifts on November 9, 1487; see further Franz Babinger, "Lorenzo de' Medici e la corte ottomana," *Archivio storico italiano* 121 (1963): 305–61, at 351.

120. Heliodorus, *Aethiopica* 10.27.

121. Dio Cassius, *Hist. Rom.* 43.23.1–2.

122. Pliny, *HN* 8.69.

123. Solinus 30.19.

124. Varro, *Ling.* 5.100.

125. A reference to Giuniano Maio, *De priscorum proprietate verborum* (1st ed., Naples, 1475), on the limitations of which cf. Ricciardi, "Angelo Poliziano, Giuniano Maio," 283–84.

126. *Historia Augusta* 20 (*The three Gordians*), 33.1; Capitolinus's text gives the figure ten, however.

4

127. That is, of both literature and philosophy, Aristophanes, Athens' greatest comic playwright (d. ca. 385 BCE), standing for the former, Cleanthes, the successor to Zeno as head of the Stoic school (263–232), for the latter (possibly suggested to Poliziano by the allusion to him at Persius 5.64). But for Poliziano's desire to profile himself as a champion of Latin culture, this would have been an appropriate "programmatic" essay to lead off the book, since it embodies his method of explicating texts by drawing on varied, unexpected sources.

128. With *orbis doctrinae* ("world of learning"), Poliziano renders the Greek ἐγκύκλιος παιδεία (general education preliminary to professional studies). Pliny too refers to "those subjects comprised in what the Greeks call 'encyclic education'": *HN* Praef. 14. Cf. also Quintilian, *Inst.* 1.10.1; Godman, *From Poliziano*, 116.

129. Seneca, *Ep.* 49.6.

130. *Sc.* the lectures of 1484–85; cf. Maïer, *Ange Politien*, 426. The point is implicit in the way Poliziano introduces Persius with reference to the dictum "know thyself": *Comm. Pers.*, 3–5.

131. Persius 4.1 (Poliziano seems to count the Prologue as one of the satires).

132. Persius 4.3.

133. Persius 4.20.

134. Plato, *Alc. I* 105d2.

135. Persius 4.52.

136. Proclus, *Comm. in Plat. Alc. I* 4–5 and 9–10.

137. Plato, *Alc. I* 129a.

138. See on *I* Epil. 6.

139. Pico della Mirandola, *Opera* 1:29; the *Heptaplus* was also published in 1489.

5

140. Lucretius 1.476–77 (the protasis is "if there were no matter"; the cause of the Trojan War, Paris's love for Helen, is the previous example).

141. Homer, *Od.* 8.492–93.

142. Homer, *Od.* 8.512.

143. Aristophanes, *Av.* 1128.

144. *Opici*, originally = "Oscans," came to be applied to uncultured or boorish people generally; cf. *OLD* s.v.; Merula, *Ennar. Juv.* 3.207; Poliziano applies it specifically to those ignorant of Greek; cf. *II* 37 and 53; *Epist.* 11.5.

145. The better of the two conjectures, *dira tenens*, is found in the margin of Naples, Biblioteca Nazionale, ms. IV E 51 (N), known as the Farnesianus and once owned by Pomponio Leto; cf. V. Pizzani, "Angelo Poliziano e i primordi della filologia lucreziana," in Secchi Tarugi, *Poliziano*, 343–55, at 354. Poliziano had borrowed a copy of Lucretius from Leto and kept it for four years, albeit this was not N, but perhaps its exemplar; cf. M. D. Reeve, "The Italian Tradition of Lucretius," *Italia medioevale e umanistica* 23 (1980): 27–48, at 39–40.

146. This powerful ruler (1443–90) began collecting books circa 1460 and ultimately assembled a library that was second in size only to that of the Vatican. Taddeo Ugoletti was his librarian from 1471. Corvinus also patronized scholars, and Poliziano cultivated him with a dedication, never made public, of the *Nutricia* in 1486; see further Godman, "Poliziano's poetics," 113–24; idem, *From Poliziano*, 76 and n. 234; Branca, *Poliziano*, 125–33.

147. As at *I* 1.10, Poliziano uses the concept of the archetype without the term *archetypus*; see below on *I* 41.2.

148. Valerius Flaccus, *Argon.* 2.572. The codex is now identified with certainty as BML, Plut. 39.38, an autograph of Niccoli; cf. Schmidt, "Poliziano," 243–44; Branca, *Poliziano*, III and 121 n. 15. See further *II 2*.

149. Poliziano's conjecture is accepted by modern editors.

6

150. Catullus 2 and 3.

151. Martial 11.6.14–16.

152. This, the most famous or notorious Renaissance interpretation of Catullus, is atypical of Poliziano and was anticipated forty years previously by Pontano based on the same epigram of Martial's; see further Gaisser, *Catullus*, 75–77. Poliziano cross-refers to this chapter at *I 96.2*.

7

153. Juvenal 9.133.

154. Plutarch, *Pomp.* 48.7.

155. Plutarch, *De capienda ex inimicis utilitate* 6 = *Mor.* 89e.

156. Ammianus Marcellinus 17.11.4.

157. Seneca rhetor, *Controv.* 7.4.7, quoting Calvus fr. 18 Courtney.

158. Seneca rhetor, *Controv.* 10.1.8.

159. Though excerpts were published in Naples in 1475, the full text of the *Suasoriae* and the *Controversiae* only appeared in Venice in 1490; see L. Annaeus Seneca maior, *Oratorum et rhetorum sententie, divisiones, colores*, ed. L. Håkanson (Leipzig: Teubner, 1989), xvi. Poliziano is likely to have used BAV, ms. Vat. lat. 3872 (10th century).

8

160. Dio Cassius 37.18.1–19.3.

161. Poliziano actually has this reversed, attributing the latter (the Lord's day) to Saturn, the former (the Sabbath) to the Sun.

162. Sozomen, *Hist. eccl.* 2.30.4, 7.19.8, etc.; Dio Cassius 37.17.3; Frontinus, *Str.* 2.1.17; Tibullus 1.3.18; Tertullian, *Apologeticus* 16.11; Gaudentius, *Sermo* 1 (ed. P. Galearchus [Augsburg: Adami & Veith, 1757], p. 24).

163. Faustus Milevitanus, *apud* Augustine, *Contra Faustum Manichaeum* 18.2.

164. There appears to be no such reference in an oration of a Nicephorus so far published.

9

165. Juvenal 14.196.

166. Domizio Calderini of Verona (1446–78) was the most important philologist of the generation prior to Poliziano. His wide reading enabled him to expand the base of authorities used in philological discussion. By his early death, at age thirty-four or thirty-five, he had published commentaries on Juvenal, Martial, Statius's *Silvae*, and Ovid's *Sappho* and *Ibis*, as well as an edition of three Quintilianic declamations. The young Poliziano was impressed by his work and glad to receive his commendation (*I* 19.4), but as he matured he became aware of the man's flaws, especially his tendency to perpetrate fraud in the heat of controversy. Our chapter offers not a balanced assessment but an almost schizophrenic contrast of a teenager's hero-worship and a mature scholar's disapproval of the methods of a predecessor. On Calderini, see further Dunston, "Studies"; Dionisotti, "Calderini"; A. Perosa's entry in *DBI* s.v.; Campanelli, *Polemiche e filologia*.

167. Quintilian, *Inst.* 2.17.21, quoting Cicero on his defense of Cluentius.

168. For Cretan mendaciousness cf. *I* 35 below.

169. Varro, *De vita populi Romani* 4, fr. 123 Riposati cited by Nonius, *De comp. doct.*, pp. 168–69 Lindsay (Poliziano has substituted "literature" for "the people").

170. Calderini, *Comm. in Mart.* (Rome, March 22, 1474), the earliest printed humanist commentary on a classical author; *Comm. in Iuv.* (Venice, April 24, 1475).

171. These dedications of major works by an author pursuing a career as a papal secretary in Rome are unexpected and reflect the close alliance that Cardinal Pietro Riario was establishing between Rome and Florence; the assignment of the *Statius* to a different dedicatee (Rome, August 13, 1475) marks the end of the flirtation. See further Dionisotti, "Calderini," 169–71.

172. These two works were special favorites of Poliziano's, to which he devoted lectures, students' versions of which have been published; see Bibliography.

173. Domizio Calderini, *Comm. in Stat. Silv.*, *Comm. in Ov. epist. Sapphus* (both Rome, 1475); *Comm. in Ov. Ibin* (Rome, 1474).

174. Ammianus Marcellinus 18.5.6.

175. Merula, *Enarrationes Satyrarum Iuvenalis* and *Adversus Domitii Calderini commentarios in Martialem* (both Venice, 1478). By singling out Merula (1430/31–94) as the first to challenge Calderini, Poliziano clearly hoped to win his goodwill or at least neutralize his opposition. He did, however, criticize Merula without naming him (cf. on *I* 29, 67.1, 85.1). Hence in spite of Poliziano's attempts to smooth ruffled feathers (*Epist.* 11.5), Merula went on to write scathing attacks on Poliziano and his *Miscellanea*, albeit they remained unpublished at his death; see Perotto Sali, "L'opuscolo." On him, see further A. Daneloni's entry in *DBI* s.v. Merlani, Giorgio.

176. Rather, Terence, *Haut.* 209–10: *hoc / scitumst: periclum ex aliis face tibi quod ex usu siet* ("This is the clever course: make a trial by others of what is to your advantage").

177. Poliziano, *Epigr. Lat.* 82, ed. Knox, ITRL 86, p. 99.

178. On the epithet "two-penny" (*diobolaris*), see below, *II* 58.

179. Calderini, *Comm. in Iuv.* 14.196; Alcides = Hercules.

180. Ovid, *Met.* 7.20–21.

181. That is, in token of defeat.

182. Barbaro, *Castigationes*, on *HN* 6.126 claimed (without citing evidence, as Poliziano points out in *Epist.* 12.1) that the translator was not Priscian

but Rhennius Fannius; on the etiology of Barbaro's error, cf. G. B. Parks, "Dionysius Periegetes," *CTC* 3 (1976): 21–61, at 31.

183. Priscian, *Interpretatio ex Dionysio De orbis situ* 174.

184. That is, Juvenal 14.196.

185. Dionysius Periegetes, *Periegesis* 183–84.

186. Herodian 7.9.1. Poliziano had translated this work into Latin in 1487; see below, I 47, n. 533.

187. Josephus, *BJ* 6.300 (not Book 7); similarly 1.73.

10

188. Juvenal 2.92. Cecropian = Athenian, since Cerops was the first king of Athens.

189. In fact, in his note on Juvenal 2.92, Merula had already suggested a reference to Eupolis's *Baptae* and cited commentators on Aristophanes.

190. Eupolis, *Baptae PCG* test. v = Proleg. de com. I 13 (p. 3 Koster). Poliziano had familiarized himself with this material in preparing the remarks on the history of comedy prefaced to his lectures on Terence's *Andria*, probably composed in the years 1484–85; cf. Poliziano, *La commedia antica*, xii–xiii, with apparatus of sources on pp. 5 and 8–9.

191. Lucian, *Ind.* 27.

192. Hephaestion, *Enchiridion* 4.6 = *PCG* F 76.

193. Suidas s.v. ἀτρύφερος = *PCG* F 78.

194. Cicero, *Leg.* 2.15.36. The reference is to the intrusion of P. Clodius Pulcher on the rites of the Bona Dea in 61 BCE.

195. Cicero, *Leg.* 2.15.37; cf. Aristophanes, Ὧραι, *PCG* test. ii and F 578.

196. Strabo 10.3.16, citing Aeschylus, fr. 57 Radt, and 10.3.18.

197. Synesius, *Epist.* 32 (= 45 Garzya).

198. Synesius, *Calvitii encomium* 21 (a paraphrase, not an exact quotation).

199. Suidas s.v. Κότυς.

200. Horace, *Epod.* 17.56.

11

201. Claudian, *De raptu Proserpinae* 2.122–23.

202. Aphthonius, *Progymnastica* 2.

203. Poliziano, *Rusticus* 183.

204. Lorenzo de' Medici, *Canzoniere* 136.5–8.

205. Nonnus, *Dion.* 41.208–11. Poliziano's discovery of Nonnus in BML, Plut. 32.16, a collection of Greek poets assembled by Maximus Planudes in 1280 and owned by Filelfo prior to its acquisition by Lorenzo, marked an epoch in the reception of that poet, previously unknown in Italy. He probably recognized Nonnus as the author toward the end of 1482, based on the account at Agathias, *Historiae* 4.23.5–6; see Fryde, *Humanism*, 181; Francesco Tissoni, "The Reception of Nonnus in Late Antiquity, Byzantine, and Renaissance Literature," in Domenico Accorinti, ed., *Brill's Companion to Nonnus* (Leiden: Brill, 2016), 691–713 at 201–3.

206. Martial 7.89.

207. [Vergil], *De rosis nascentibus* 18. The poem is now attributed to Ausonius. Lines 49–50 were the model for Herrick's "Gather ye rosebuds." Poliziano wrote a short commentary on the poem (see Bibliography).

208. The Διάλεξις περὶ ῥόδου was rediscovered by Leopardi in a Barberini codex (currently BAV, ms Barb. gr. 240) but not published until G. Boissonade, *Anecdota nova* (Paris: Apud Dumont, 1844), 346ff., attributing it (after Mai) to Choricius of Gaza on rhythmical grounds; see further Perosa and Timpanaro, "Libanio (o Coricio), Poliziano e Leopardi," 423–24.

12

209. Pollux, *Onom.* 1.45–47.

210. Poliziano, *Rusticus* 298.

211. Nonnus, *Dion.* 40.304–10.

13

212. Suetonius, *Aug.* 31.4.

213. Dio Cassius 37.24.1–25.1.

214. Dio Cassius 51.20.4.

14

215. *Ars Am.* 3.327–28. The variation in spelling reflects the sound change by which in the Hellenistic period the voiced plosive (*b*) was replaced by the spirant (*v*); cf. Robert Browning, *Medieval and Modern Greek*, 2nd ed. (Cambridge, 1983), 26–27.

216. Suidas s.vv. νάβλα, φατήριον.

217. Sophocles fr. 849 Radt *apud* Plutarch, *De E apud Delph.* 21 = *Mor.* 394b.

218. Theodoret, *Quaestiones in libros Regnorum et Paralipomenon*, PG 80.552, 681, 700 (*bis*), 752, 809, 813, 816, 852 (not on the Psalms, according to TLG); Plutarch, *Quaest. conv.* 2.4 = *Mor.* 638c; Poliziano, *Nutricia* 171–72 (referred to throughout *Misc. I* as "the Nurse" [*Nutrix*], a working title; by *Misc. II* it had been published under the title *Nutricia*, which is the citation form there; cf. Godman, "Poliziano's poetics," 121–22).

219. Strabo 10.3.17.

220. Daniel 3:5, 7, 10, 15.

221. That is, Aramaic.

222. Solomon Gallus is almost certainly Solomon ben Isaac, an eleventh-century French exegete of the Torah better known as Rashi, quite familiar to Christians. The passage in question refers to his commentary on Ps. 33:2 (in the Hebrew numbering). Pico worked on a commentary on the Psalms but never finished it. (We thank Brian Copenhaver and Fabrizio Lelli for identifying Solomon Gallus with Rashi.)

223. Isaiah 5:12, 23:16; Amos 6:5.

224. Macrobius, *Saturnalia* 3.14.6, citing Scipio Aemilianus, ORF 21 F 30. The citation is a bad mistake (not committed by Macrobius); it should be Tiberius Sempronius Gracchus (Poliziano seems to have confused the fact that Gracchus's mother was a Cornelia).

225. Ambrose, *De Elia et ieiunio* 15.54.

226. [Jerome], *Ep.* 23.8 (*PL* 30, 221C).

227. Immanuel ben Solomon (Immanuel Romano, 1261–1328).

15

228. Ovid, *Tr.* 2.417. *Sybaritica* is read by editors.

229. Lucian, *Ind.* 23.

230. Philo Judaeus, *De vita Moysi* 1.1.3.

231. Martial 12.95.

232. Calderini, *Comm. in Mart.* 12.96 of his edition (=12.95), leaves open whether the name was derived from a poet Sybaris or from the city ("vel a Sybari poeta vel a Sybari urbe").

233. Erasmus, *Adagia* 479.

234. Suidas s.v. Συβαριτικαῖς καὶ Συβαρικαῖς, mentioning, besides the proverb, the connection between Sybaritic tales and Aesopian tales, on which see further Doxopater, *In Aphth.* 2.162.15–66.7 Walz.

235. Plutarch, *Septem sapientium convivium* 2 = *Mor.* 147e.

236. Maximus of Tyre, *Diss.* 32.3 (dances) and 10 (enumeration), 37.4 (dances).

237. Maximus of Tyre, *Diss.* 29.1.

238. Juvenal 6.294–96.

239. Strabo 6.1.13; Plutarch, *Pel.* 1.3.

240. Aristotle, *Eth. Eud.* 1.1216a16–18.

241. A mistake; the *Cesti* are a miscellany dealing only in part with military affairs.

242. Sextus Julius Africanus, Κεστοί ("Charmed Girdles") 1.11.

16

243. Ovid, *Tr.* 2.443–44 = Sisenna *FRH* 26 T 12.

244. Plutarch, *Crass.* 32.4.

245. Zosimus 3.15.5. On Poliziano's knowledge of Zosimus, see on I 58.4.

246. Appian, *B Civ.* 2.3.18 Loeb = 2.18.65–66 Viereck (narrative of Crassus in Syria; Poliziano is mistaken, however: Plutarch's anecdote is not repeated here).

247. Lucian, *Amores* 1.

248. Apuleius, *Met.* 1.1.

249. Martianus Capella 2.100.

250. Michael Apostolius 12.37; similarly, Zenobius 5.57 and Gregory II of Cyprus, *Proverbia* (Leiden, 1653), 2.82.

251. Maximus of Tyre, *Diss.* 32.10.

252. Vergil, *Georg.* 4.334–35.

253. Horace, *Epist.* 1.17.30–31.

254. Suidas s.v. Κάδμος.

255. Ibid.

17

256. Seneca, *Herc. fur.* 83.

257. This is the famous "codex Etruscus" (= E, BML, Plut. 37.13, late 11th century), the leading representative of the E class; cf. R. J. Tarrant in Reynolds, *Texts*, 379.

258. Firmicus Maternus, *Math.* 4.17.2.

259. Achilles Tatius, *Isag.* 21.

260. Poliziano, *Nutricia* 568–69. "The beast" is the Nemean lion.

18

261. Juvenal. 4.98. This chapter is anticipated in essentials at *Comm. Pers.* 6.56–57, where this line is cited together with Cicero's epistolary use of "son of the earth" (albeit misattributed to the *Letters to Brutus*) and the suggestion that *Manius* derives from the *manes*.

262. G. Valla ad loc. was the commentator who claimed that Earth produced the monkey after the Giants to show contempt for the gods.

263. Martial 3.25.2–3.

264. Persius 6.56–59.

265. This appears to be a corruption of the name of Artorius (Rufus), the dedicatee of Pompeius Festus's abridgment of Verrius Flaccus; cf. P. L. Schmidt in Sallmann, *Die Literatur*, 240–41. Poliziano's mistake, confusing Pompeius Festus with (Asconius) Pedianus, the commentator on Cicero, was caught by Fonzio (*Corr-B*).

266. For example, Varro, *Ling.* 9.60 and fr. 259 Astbury.

267. That is, after the death of the father. Festus, *De verb. sign.*, p. 135 Lindsay; Zosimus 2.3.2.

268. Var. fr. 258 Astbury, cited by Nonius, *De comp. doct.*, p. 237 L.

269. Cicero, *Att.* 1.13.4.

270. Cicero, *Fam.* 7.9.3.

271. On these two manuscripts, see below on I 25.1.

272. Lactantius, *Div. inst.* 1.11, summarizing Minucius Felix, *Octavius* 23.9–12. Poliziano cites Minucius Felix via Lactantius because the *editio princeps* of the former only appeared at Rome in 1543 (as Book 8 of Arnobius); see further Minucius Felix, *Octavius*, ed. B. Kytzler (Stuttgart and Leipzig: Teubner, 1992), v.

273. Tertullian, *Apologeticus* 10.9–10 (Poliziano skips some of the text).

274. Poliziano mistakenly attributes this speech to Umbricius, the speaker in *Satire* 3; the error was again caught by Fonzio (*Corr-B*).

275. In fact, Poliziano's point already appears in essentials in the Carolingian scholium on Juvenal 8.44; cf. Grazzini, "Osservazioni," 172.

19

276. Quintilian, *Inst.* 1.5.20.

277. Catullus 84.

278. Cicero, *Orat.* 48.160.

279. Did Poliziano draw this conclusion from a gold coin with the legend TRIVMP AVG, or did he mistake silver for gold (a denarius of Papius Celsus)? See further Gionta, *Iconografia*, 31.

280. Aulus Gellius, *NA* 2.3.1.

281. Priscian, *Inst.* 1.24.

282. The point is that if this interpretation was a novelty in Padua at that time, the treatment of the poem by the Paduan professor Giovanni Calfurnio in his edition (Vicenza, 1481) was subsequent to Poliziano's; cf. Gaisser, *Catullus*, 69–70. Giovanni Aurelio Augurello (1441–1524) was a humanist poet who made the acquaintance of Ficino and Poliziano in Florence, frequented humanist circles in Padua and Venice, and later wrote a didactic poem on alchemy dedicated to Leo X.

283. "Angel," of course, plays on his name, Angelo.

284. Battista Guarino's son, Alessandro, had ascribed the doctrine on aspirates in Catullus 84 to his father; hence this narrative claiming priority, on which see also Godman, *From Poliziano*, 95–96. In this case and in four of the other six passages of *Misc.* I dealing with Catullus, Poliziano's positions were adumbrated by the annotations in his copy of the *editio princeps* (Venice, 1472); see further Gaisser, *Catullus*, 69–78. Poliziano's critics Fonzio and Avanzio were quick to charge that he had taken the doctrine from Pontano, *De aspiratione*; cf. Ciapponi, "Bartolomeo Fonzio," 172. He takes a similar line on his claims versus those of others, at *I* Epil. 9.

20

285. Suetonius, *Ner.* 45.2. "The other one," *sc.* of Nero's statues. This is the sack in which convicted criminals were sewn before being thrown into the sea and drowned.

286. Suidas s.v. ἀσκοπήρα. Barbaro, *Castigationes*, on *HN* 36.24.1, disagreed, preferring *ascopa* on the basis of St. Jerome's usage (Vulgate, Judges 10:5); Poliziano discusses the disagreement in *Epist.* 11.1 (= *Opera* 1:165); see also Fera, *Una ignota*, 219–20 n. 2. The latest editor of Suetonius's *Lives*, R. A. Kaster (Oxford, 2016), prints *ascopa* in the text, referring to *TLL* 2:772.10–20.

287. Juvenal 13.155–56. Sometimes other animals were sewn into the sack with the convicted criminal; see further F. Egmond, "The Cock, the Dog,

the Serpent, and the Monkey: Reception and Transmission of a Roman Punishment, or Historiography as History," *International Journal of the Classical Tradition* 2 (1995): 159–92.

21

288. Juvenal 10.116.

289. Calderini, *Comm. in Iuv.* ad loc. The Quinquatrial festival was celebrated annually for five days beginning March 19 in honor of Minerva; see further H. H. Scullard, *Festivals and Ceremonies of the Roman Republic* (London: Thames and Hudson, 1981), 92–94.

290. Horace, *Epist.* 2.2.197–98.

291. Ovid, *Fast.* 3.829–30.

292. Jerome, *Comm. in Epist. ad Ephesios* 6.4 (PL 26.574A). Cf. Gratian, *Decretum* I, Dist. 37, c. 5.

293. Tertullian, *De fuga in persecutione* 13.

294. Varro, *Rust.* 3.2.18. The explanation "that is, scum," is probably an intrusive gloss.

22

295. Martial 2.86.3.

296. Probably Heinrich Isaac, a Flemish composer (ca. 1450–1517) who migrated to Florence in 1485 and found employment with Lorenzo de' Medici, with whom he developed a close relationship. Isaac set to music Poliziano's famous lament for the death of Lorenzo, *Quis dabit capiti meo aquam*, for which see Poliziano, *Greek and Latin Poetry*, ed. Knox, ITRL 86, 170–173. Isaac's setting of Poliziano's "echo" song, *Che fai tu, Ecco*, is lost; see Blake Wilson, "Heinrich Isaac among the Florentines," *The Journal of Musicology*, 23.1 (2006): 97–152, at 114 n. 43. For the text, see Poliziano, *Poesie italiane*, ed. S. Orlando (Milan: Rizzoli, 1976), 193.

297. Poliziano, *Rispetti spicciolati* 1, in *Rime*, ed. Delcorno Branca.

298. *Anth. Pal.* 16.152.

299. Martial 6.77.7.

300. Cf. Otto s.v. *testimonia*, citing Cicero, *Flac.* 4.9–10 (reading *testimonium mutum*, not *mutuum*).

301. This is the first of several references in the *Miscellanea* to Lombardic script, a designation dating to the eleventh century for South Italian minuscule or Beneventan script. Poliziano regularly uses it as a sign that a particular codex is old and therefore carries weight as a witness. See further Rizzo, *Il lessico*, 122–26. The codex of the San Marco library mentioned here is now lost; cf. Ullman-Stadter no. 947; Branca, *Poliziano*, III. Poliziano knew that Calderini had used it, since he himself had brought it to the older scholar's attention as he prepared his commentary on Martial in 1473; cf. *II* 10.2. It certainly belonged to the β family; cf. Saggese, "Poliziano," 186–88.

302. The reference is to Calderini's nephew, Bernardino Messanello. These unbound pages were surely inherited from Calderini and seen by Poliziano on his visit to Verona in early 1480 (cf. *I* 19.5); cf. Saggese, "Poliziano," 188–89.

303. Also cited at *II* 10.2; it is unidentified, but belonged to the γ family and was probably written in the fourteenth century; cf. Saggese, "Poliziano," 194.

304. This is identified as BAV, ms. Vat. lat. 3294 (= V, 10th century), belonging to the γ family; cf. Saggese, "Poliziano," 190 and n. 33 with literature.

305. See on *I* 5.

306. On Poliziano's relations with the brothers Bernardo and Niccolò Michelozzi (also mentioned at *I* 61 and 77), cf. Branca, *Poliziano*, 37–41 with attached notes. Niccolò was the private secretary of Lorenzo de' Medici.

307. Juvenal 8.32.

308. Juvenal 8.34–37.

309. Martial 14.197.

310. Martial 1.104.9–10.

311. Sebastiano Timpanaro, "*Atlas cum compare gibbo*," *Rinascimento* 2.3 (1951) 311–18 = *Contributi di filologia e di storia della lingua latina* (Rome: Ateneo & Bizzarri, 1978), 333–43, reviews the problem, showing that Poliziano was right to first inquire what should count as the correct text. Poliziano knows, however, only a part of the manuscript tradition and hence arrives at a wrong result (*gibbo* is surely correct, *mulo* a banalization); Calderini correctly interpreted *gibbo* as a camel. Poliziano also errs in deriving from Juvenal 8.32ff. license to interpret Atlas as a dwarf. His point stands, however, that the humor arises from the similarity of, not the difference between, the items compared. Cf. also Dionisotti, "Calderini," 164–65; A. Viti, "Per la storia," 420–21 n. 150.

24

312. *Priapea* 12.3–4.

313. Not an ancient Greek diminutive form (cf. A. Debrunner, *Griechische Wortbildungslehre* [Heidelberg: Winter, 1917], §§291–96, 326–27, 391, 397–99), but perhaps Poliziano is thinking of modern Greek diminutives, such as *paidi* from *paidion*.

314. Philochorus, *FGrH* 328 F 109.

315. Plutarch, *Theseus* 14.2–3.

316. Callimachus, *Hecale*, ed. A. S. Hollis, 2nd ed. (Oxford: Oxford University Press, 2009).

317. *Epigr. adespoton* (Callimachus, *testimonium* 23 Pfeiffer = 13 Hollis) 5.

318. Pliny, *HN* 26.82 and 22.88. The reference is to BML, Plut. 82.2, 13th century = no. 792 Ullman-Stadter and Florence, Biblioteca Riccardiana, ms. Ricc. 488, 10th century = no. 793 Ullman-Stadter; cf. Branca, *Poliziano*, 112 and 121 n. 11.

319. Callimachus, *Hymn* 2.105–6.

320. *Scholia Call. Hymn* 2.106.

321. Poliziano, *Nutricia* 426.

322. Statius, *Theb.* 12.582.

323. Suidas s.v. Ἑκάλη.

324. Apuleius, *Met.* 1.23 (the stingy Milo offering hospitality to Lucius).

325. The emendation both of *Priapea* 12.3–4 and of Apuleius, *Met.* 1.23 had already been proposed by Beroaldo, *Annotationes*, 72. However, Sabellico claimed priority based on a public presentation at the Venetian Academy; cf. Barbaro, *Castigationes*, on *HN* 22.18.1, with Pozzi's note.

25

326. *Misc. I* 18.3.

327. The older manuscript is BML, Plut. 49.9 = M, ninth century, sometimes thought to have been copied at a school related to the court of Louis the Pious; the derivative manuscript is BML, Plut. 49.7 = P, a copy made for Salutati at Milan, not by Petrarch; cf. R. H. Rouse in Reynolds, *Texts*, 138–39. D. Speranzi, "Poliziano, i codici di Filelfo, la medicea privata. Tre schede," in P. Viti, *Cultura e filologia*, 51–68, at 64–68, clarifies the early history of the codex in Italy. The codex also contains the hands of Leonardo Bruni, Niccolò Niccoli, and Chrysoloras; see J. Hankins in *ALI-Q* 1:86.

328. Not true; modern editors recognize witnesses independent of M; see further Cicero, *Epistulae ad familiares*, ed. D. R. Shackleton Bailey (Cambridge: Cambridge University Press, 1977), 1:4–20.

329. A reference to the three categories of citizens comprising the jury-panels of the late Republic: the senators, the knights, and the *tribuni aerarii* (a group which, like the knights, had to meet a property qualification).

330. Cicero, *Fam.* 8.2.1.

331. Cicero, *Fam.* 8.9.3.

332. That is, the twenty-four letters, beginning with 8.9 and concluding with 9.15.

333. Cicero, *Fam.* 8.2.1.

334. Cicero, *Fam.* 8.2.1.

335. Cicero, *Fam.* 8.9.1.

336. Cicero, *Fam.* 8.9.3.

337. Cicero, *Fam.* 9.15.5.

338. Cicero, *Fam.* 8.9.3.

339. Cicero, *Fam.* 9.15.1 (a corrupt reading; it should be, "I shall reply to your two letters").

340. Cicero, *Fam.* 9.15.5.

341. Cicero, *Fam.* 9.16.

26

342. Ovid, *Fast.* 1.353–58.

343. A reminiscence of Ennius fr. 46.2 Courtney: *volito vivos per ora virum* ("I fly living on men's lips").

344. *Anth. Pal.* 9.75, already cited in *Comm. Fast.*, on 1.357.

345. This is in line with Poliziano's view that Latin has ample vocabulary (*I* 1.6; but see also *I* 90.8) but lacks playfulness (*I* 49.3).

346. Suetonius, *Dom.* 14.2.

347. Vergil, *Aen.* 4.60–61.

348. Suetonius, *Dom.* 7.2.

349. This is the first example of one of Poliziano's favorite moves: restoring a Greek word or phrase embedded in a Latin text that has been corrupted or has disappeared altogether. For other examples, cf. *I* 34, 93, 95, and *II* 31; Rizzo, *Il lessico*, 295–99.

27

350. Cicero, *Fam.* 7.6.1; the two verses printed as such = Ennius, *Medea* 219–20 Jocelyn = *TrRF* and *FRL* F 90, where a version of "rich . . . Corinth" is also included.

351. Poliziano will return to the image of parts scattered and needing to be reassembled at *I* 91.2 and at *II* 1.1 and 31.2.

352. Terence, *An.* 469 (Simo, on learning that his son Pamphilus has promised to rear the child that Glycerium, the eponymous "woman from Andros," is about to bear).

353. Terence, *Eun.* 108.

354. Euripides, *Med.* 214–18.

355. Cicero, *Fin.* 1.2.4.

356. Quintilian, *Inst.* 5.10.84; Cicero, *Fat.* 15.35; [Cicero], *Rhet. ad Her.* 2.22.34. The attribution of the latter work to Cicero was first challenged by the Venetian Raffaele Reggio (ca. 1440–1520) in 1491; cf. J. J. Murphy and M. Winterbottom, "Raffaele Reggio's *Quaestio* Doubting Cicero's Authorship of the *Rhetorica ad Herennium*: Introduction and Text," *Rhetorica* 17 (1999): 77–87. The text is translated in Aldus Manutius, *Humanism and the Latin Classics*, ed. John N. Grant, ITRL 78 (Cambridge, MA, 2017), 272–85; see also Grant's commentary ad loc. In a marginal note to his copy of *Rhet. Her.* (Munich, Bayerische Staatsbibliothek, 2° Inc. c. a. 467, 10v), Poliziano had written the text of the lines and noted the correspondence to the Nurse's speech at the beginning of Euripides's play; cf. Hunt, "Three New Incunables," 253.

357. One such quotation, without indication of source or author, could be found in Leonardo Bruni's well-known treatise on translation, *De recta interpretatione*, ed. P. Viti in *Sulla perfetta traduzione* (Naples: Liguori Editore, 2004), 80, where, discussing the practice of literary allusion, Bruni states that the phrase is used to allude to the origin and primeval causes of evil.

358. Ennius, *Medea*, vv. 208–16 Jocelyn = *TrRF* and *FRL* F 89, where see notes. Grafton, "On the Scholarship," 175, justly comments, "This identification marks the beginning of the resurrection of early Latin poetry."

359. Priscian, *Inst.* 7.40.

360. Euripides, *Med.* 1–8.

28

361. Cicero, *Fam.* 16.23.2.

362. Cicero, *Att.* 5.20.3.

363. Hyginus, *Poet. Astr.* 2.28 Viré, citing *Eratosthenis Catasterismorum reliquiae*, ed. C. Robert (Berlin: Weidmann, 1878), 149.

364. Germanicus, *Arati Phaenomena* vv. 554–57.

365. Euripides, *Med.* 1171–73.

366. *Schol. Eur. Med.* 1172 (Poliziano cites the Greek [here within quotation marks] and then gives the Latin equivalent).

367. Synesius, *De providentia* 2.1 = p. 109, l. 17 Terzaghi (again, Greek in quotation marks followed by Latin equivalent).

368. Suidas s.v. Πανικῷ δείματι.

369. Nicetas Choniates, *Historia* 271.39 van Dieten (not in an oration).

370. *Schol. Arat. Phaen.* 283.

371. Nonnus, *Dion.* 10.4.

372. Nonnus, *Dion.* 10.12–13.

373. Valerius Flaccus, *Argon.* 3.43–57.

374. Valerius Flaccus, *Argon.* 6.533.

375. Zosimus 2.3.1 (this is reported in context below at *I* 58.2).

376. Theocritus, Σῦριγξ, *Anth. Pal.* 15.21.4.

377. Theocritus, Σῦριγξ, *Anth. Pal.* 15.21.9–10. The riddles are explained in the scholia ad loc.: the Persian (*Perseus* in Greek) is the homonym of Perseus, who killed his grandfather, Acrisius; Europa, born in Tyre, is "the Tyrian woman."

29

378. Ovid, *Her.* 9.51–52.

379. Diodorus Siculus 4.29.3, 5.15.1.

380. Merula (per Perotto Sali, "L'opuscolo," 172–73) acknowledges the change as his (though he cites *Thespieia* as the form he promoted) but says that he recognized his mistake; cf. R. Fabbri, "Per la polemica Poliziano-Merula," in Fera and Martelli, *Agnolo Poliziano*, 551–56, at 556.

381. Eustathius, *Comm. Hom. Il.* 266.4–7 on *Il.* 2.498, citing Stephanus of Byzantium s.v. Θέσπεια (the quotation skips over an intervening phrase in the text).

382. Aeschylus, *Supp.* 549 (not *Agamemnon*).

30

383. That is, he built a small bath, in contrast to Torquatus's elegant bath, described in the previous line: Martial 10.79.4.

384. Petronius 136.1–2.

385. Arrian, *Epict. diss.* 3.22.71.

386. A comparison of Greek and Latin diminutive suffixes.

387. Juvenal 3.296.

388. Cleomedes, *De motu circulari corporum caelestium* 2.1.166.499–502 Todd.

389. Horace, *Epist.* 1.7.65.

390. Sidonius Apollinaris, *Epist.* 7.2.6. This particular chapter is evidently based on one of the lists that Poliziano kept; see above, pp. x–xi.

31

391. Juvenal 5.126–27.

392. Calderini, *Comm. in Iuv.* ad loc. In view of the example, this appears to be Calderini's meaning, though the *cognomen* and *agnomen* are essentially the same (the name of a branch of the family or attribute added to the family name), and the *praenomen* (personal name) is missing.

393. Modern commentators follow this interpretation; cf., for example, Juvenal, *Satires, Book 1*, ed. S. M. Braund (Cambridge: Cambridge University Press, 1996), 297.

394. Artemidorus, *Onir.* 1.45.

395. Tertullian, *De resurrectione carnis* 57.

396. Persius 5.78–79. Cf. I 98.1.

397. Cicero, *Att.* 4.15.1.

398. Suetonius, *Jul.* 83.2.

399. *Ad Brut.* 1.16.6, a barbed reference to him as "your Caesar"; elsewhere Brutus calls him Octavius.

400. Dio Cassius, *Hist. Rom.* 40.51.2–3.

401. Nepos, *Att.* 5.2; Varro, *Rust.* 2.2.2.

402. Suidas s.v. Ἀλέξανδρος ὁ Μιλήσιος. However, Servius Danielis on Vergil, *Aen.* 10.388, implies that the gentile name resulted from enfranchisement by Sulla.

32

403. Pliny, *HN* 28.25.

404. See further on *I* 57.

405. Poliziano hesitates because he has coined a new Latin word, *poppyssans*, on the analogy of Greek.

406. Aristophanes, *Vesp.* 626.

407. *Scholia Ar. Vesp.* 626.

408. Juvenal 6.584; Martial 7.18.11.

409. Maximus and Nicas are Poliziano's way of referring, respectively, to the *Etym. Symeonis* and *Etym. magn.* (here s.v. πόππυσμα). Of the former he possessed a copy that passed to the Medici library to replace books that he had borrowed but were stolen at the time of his death (BML, ms. S. Marc. 303 = C, end of 13th century); cf. R. Reitzenstein, *Geschichte der griechischen Etymologika* (Leipzig: Teubner, 1897), 260; Branca, *Poliziano*, 115. For Poliziano's mistake on the authorship of the latter, cf. Fabricius in *Etym. magn.*, ed. Gaisford, xiv. Cf. also Suidas s.v. ποππύσματα.

410. Sophocles, fr. 878 Radt; Pollux, *Onom.* 7.185.

411. Pollux, *Onom.* 1.210; Pliny, *HN* 35.104: that is, the sponge hit the painting in such a way that the horse's foam seemed to be depicted.

412. Dexippus, *Dialogus in Aristotelis Categorias* (CAG 4.2) 11.17.

33

413. Juvenal 7.154.

414. Calderini, *Comm. in Iuv.*, citing Pliny, *HN* 5.126; Strabo 13.2.3; Quintilian, *Inst.* 10.1.63, alluding to Horace, *Carm.* 2.13.26–27; for Alcaeus's attack on a tyrant (Pittacus, not the ones named by Calderini),

see fr. 348 Voigt; Juvenal 7.151. The reference to a king of the Scythians named Camber in Diodorus is fictitious (Diodorus claims that they were ruled by queens: 2.44).

415. Juvenal 7.151.

416. Cf. Otto s.v. *laqueus* 1.

417. Suetonius, *Gram.* 25.5; Juvenal 7.114 (at Rome the charioteers formed teams distinguished by different colors).

418. Tacitus, *Dial.* 35.5.

419. Atticus fr. 7.13 des Places = Eusebius, *Praep. ev.* 15.9.13.

420. *Iuvenalis Saturae, cum commentariis Georgii Vallae* (Venice, 1485), alluding on Juvenal 7.154 to a proverb on Cambra and Anathus and citing Probus as his authority.

421. Aulus Gellius, *NA* 1.15.18 and often. Poliziano denounces the citation of bogus sources at *I* Pref. 13. He lists Probus as one of his sources after his Preface (and cites him at *I* 50.4), so he evidently denies not the existence of Probus, but his authorship of a commentary on Juvenal; indeed, the *scholia Pithoeana* attributed to Probus go back no further than the fourth century; cf. Hanslik, *RE* VIIIA 1.212.49–55, citing the older literature; Grazzini, "Osservazioni," 171 n. 36. For Giorgio Valla, cf. the chronology of his life and works by G. Gardenal appended to *Giorgio Valla tra scienza e sapienza*, ed. V. Branca (Florence: Olschki, 1981).

422. Euripides, *Phoen.* 469.

423. Cf. Suidas s.v. κράμβη, schol. Juvenal 7.154.

424. Cf. Otto s.v. *crambe*.

425. Pliny, *HN* 20.79.

426. Suidas s.v. κράμβη.

427. Cato, *De re rustica* 156.1.

34

428. Cicero, *Fam.* 11.14.1.

429. See above, *I* 25.

430. That is, the *Philippics*.

431. Galen, *De sanitate tuenda* 2.10.1 (= CMG v. 5, pt. 4.2.64.1–2).

432. Eustathius, *Comm. Hom. Od.* 1459.53 on *Od.* 3.118.

433. Varro, *Sat. Men.*, fr. 506 Astbury, cited by Aulus Gellius *NA* 13.23.4.

434. Cicero, *Fam.* 11.14.1.

35

435. Varro, *Rust.* 1.48.2.

436. No. 794 Ullman-Stadter, now lost.

437. Eusebius, *Praep. ev.* 2.2.52–62; Augustine, *De civ. D.* 6.7 and reference to the doctrine at 7.27.

438. Lactantius, *Div. inst.* 1.11.33–34, 35.

439. Cf. Ennius, *Var.* fr. 107 Vahlen = *FRL Euhem.* 2 = Lactanctius, *Div. inst.* 1.11.32.

440. Sextus Empiricus, *Adv. math.* 9.51, citing Callimachus fr. 191.11 Pfeiffer (not Timon).

441. This is identified as BAM, L 85 sup., second quarter of the ninth century (= A), brought to Italy by Poggio, and in fact written in an insular, not Lombardic script; see *L. Iuni Moderati Columellae Res rustica*, ed. R. H. Rodgers (Oxford: Clarendon Press, 2010), vi.

442. Another lost manuscript (= no. 795 Ullman-Stadter). Niccolò Niccoli (1365–1437) was a Florentine book collector and copyist who belonged to the circle of Cosimo de' Medici; see his biography by Concetta Bianca in *DBI* (2013).

443. The passage illustrates the twin pillars of philology as practiced by Poliziano and the humanists generally: authority (*auctoritas*), that is, of the best witnesses, and reason (*ratio*). Cf. below, I 44, 50, and 77; Rizzo, *Il lessico*, 293–95.

444. Columella, *Rust.* 9.2.3.

445. Callimachus, *Hymn* 1.8–9.

446. Statius, *Theb.* 1.278–79.

447. Cyprian, *De idolorum vanitate* 2.

448. Plutarch, *Aem.* 23.6; the idea is first attested by the Cretan philosopher Epimenides of Cnossus, who proposed a logical self-referential paradox: Epimenides 3 B 1 Diels-Kranz.

449. Titus 1:12.

450. Ovid, *Am.* 3.10.19.

451. Ovid, *Ars am.* 1.297–98.

36

452. Varro, *Ling.* 2 (fr. 35 Funaioli), cited by Aulus Gellius, *NA* 12.6.2.

453. Ovid, *Fast.* 2.667–70.

37

454. Vergil, *Bucol.* 1.65.

455. Servius, *Comm. Bucol.* 1.65.

456. Poliziano loses sight of the fact that Servius offers the interpretation of *creta* as the proper name ("Crete"), rather than "chalk," in his *Comm. Bucol.* 2.24.

457. Vibius Sequester, *De flum.* 114.

458. Apollonius Rhodius, *Argon.* 1.1129–31. The Idaean Dactyls are magicians of metallurgy.

459. P. Terentius Varro Atacinus, *Argonautica* 1, fr. 5.2 Courtney.

460. Echoing Vergil, *Ecl.* 1.66, referring to Britain.

38

461. Juvenal 11.175.

462. Calderini, *Comm. in Iuv.* ad loc.

463. Merula, *Enarr. Juv.* ad loc.

464. *Iuvenalis Saturae cum commentariis Georgii Vallae* (Venice, 1486).

465. Poliziano may have refuted the interpretation of the "Spartan circle" as a ring, but it does not follow that Calderini's interpretation of *pitysma* is untenable. In fact, Poliziano will revert to it himself in a letter to Merula probably to be dated to March 1494 (*Epist.* II.6); cf. Lo Monaco, "On the Prehistory," 63–65.

466. In fact, *Et. magn.* 697.58 (for the form of reference cf. on I 32) has an entry for πυτίζω but cites no derivatives from it.

467. Theocritus, *Id.* 1.1.

468. Galen, *De sanitate tuenda* 2.10 (= CMG v. 5, pt. 4.2.64.8–13).

469. Dio Cassius 53.27.1.

470. Martial 6.42.16–18.

471. Columella, *Rust.* I praef. 15–16.

472. Seneca, *Ep.* 51 (5.10).6.

473. Vitruvius, *De arch.* 5.10.5. The conjecture of the unattested *pitylisma* for *pitysma* was (rightly) rejected by Fonzio (as well as by modern editors); he also challenged the interpretation of the "Spartan circle" as a vapor bath on the ground that such facilities were open to all, not to just a few wealthy people; cf. Ciapponi, "Bartolomeo Fonzio," 170–71. For the current interpretation, cf. E. Courtney, *A Commentary on the Satires of Juvenal* (London: Athlone, 1980) ad loc., who sees the "Spartan circle" as an inlay of black or green marble (the former from Taenarus, the latter from Taygetus) and *pytissare* as "the wine-taster's habit of savoring a sip of wine and then spitting it out," for which he cites Terence, *Haut.* 457.

39

474. Ausonius, *Epist.* 13.71–77.

475. This copy perished in the Santo Spirito fire; cf. R. Weiss, "Ausonius in the Fourteenth Century," in R. R. Bolgar, *Classical Influences on European Culture* A.D. 500–1500 (Cambridge: Cambridge University Press, 1971), 67–72, at 71 with n. 2.

476. Herodotus 5.58.1 and 59.

477. Pliny, *HN* 7.210.

478. *Anth. Pal.* 7.117.5–6, from Diogenes Laertius 7.30 (Poliziano misattributes: the epigram describes Zeno but is by Zenodotus).

479. Sextus Empiricus, *Adv. math.* 1.53, quoting Timon, an expositor of Pyrrho.

480. Poliziano assumes that the author is the same man who compiled a glossary for the letters α–δ that was then continued by Pamphilus; cf. Suidas s.v. Πάμφιλος.

481. Suidas s.v. Φοινικήϊα γράμματα.

482. Pliny, *HN* 7.192.

483. Cf. Cicero, *Off.* 2.22.79. This move may seem to us routine, but at the time it was a revolutionary break from the traditional method of piling up authorities; cf. Grafton, "On the Scholarship," 163–64.

484. Paulus Diaconus, *Excerpta* from Festus, *De verb. sign.*, p. 16 Lindsay: "Alumento was said instead of Laumedon by the ancient Romans, as yet unversed in the Greek language."

485. Servius, *Comm. Aen.* 1.741; Ennius, *Inc.* 43 Vahlen = *FRL* Ennius, unidentified works F 40a.

486. Persius 3.13.

487. Martianus Capella 3.224: that is, pen and ink.

488. Varro, *Antiquitates rerum divinarum* 14, fr. 194 Cardauns.

489. Horace, *Carm.* 2.13.21.

490. Valerius Maximus 2.4.5; Varro as above; cf. also Festus, *De verb. sign.*, p. 74 Lindsay. See below, I 58.4.

491. Pliny, *HN* 16.157.

492. Persius 3.11.

40

493. Ausonius, *Epigrammata* 85.

494. Justinian, *Digest* 2.11.2.3.

495. The term *archetypus* was already used by Cicero in the sense of an author's original manuscript (*Att.* 16.3.1). It is also used for the source of the other copies or for a model copy. Cf. Rizzo, *Il lessico*, 308–17. Here Poliziano infers the status as archetype by a different method from *I* 25, not from the avoidance of shared errors of descendants, but from the internal evidence of the codex itself; cf. Grafton, "On the Scholarship," 167–69. Whether the Florentine *Pandects*, as they are known, were in fact the archetype is doubted by modern scholars, but the manuscript does appear to be very early, possibly written during the reign of Justinian. The manuscript has notes in the hand of Leonzio Pilato, who must have consulted it when it was still in Pisa.

496. Of the grand type customarily set at church altars to signify dignity and importance. The book was kept in the chapel of the Signoria, Florence's highest magistracy, on the top floor of what is now the Palazzo Vecchio.

497. That is, taken in the aftermath of the Florentine occupation of Pisa in 1406. The volume was regarded as a civic trophy.

498. On the Florentine *Pandects*, Poliziano's special access to and assessment of them, see also *Epist.* 10.4 = *Opera* 1:140–41; Branca, *Poliziano*, 182–92.

499. Aulus Gellius, *NA* 14.2.1. The reference is evidently to BNC, Conv. soppr. J.IV.26 (= N), copied by Niccoli in or just before 1431, perhaps from a ninth-century exemplar; cf. P. K. Marshal in Reynolds, *Texts*, 179.

500. Aulus Gellius, *NA* 14.2.11.

42

501. Horace, *Epist.* 1.18.65–66.

502. Porphyrio, *Comm. Hor. Epist.* 1.18.66.

503. Pliny, *HN* 28.25.

504. Juvenal 3.36–37.

505. Prudentius, *Contra Symmachum* 2.1097–99.

43

506. On Lorenzo's collections, kept at his palace on the Via Larga and in the "sculpture garden" adjacent to Piazza San Marco, see Laurie S. Fusco, *Lorenzo de'Medici: Collector and Antiquarian* (Cambridge: Cambridge University Press, 2006).

507. Quintilian, *Inst.* 1.7.14.

508. Vergil, *Aen.* 3.354 (*aulai*), 9.26 (*pictai*), 7.464 (*aquai*).

509. This looks like a misunderstanding or misremembrance; there is no other evidence for such a spelling (cf. *TLL* s.v. *fur*), and it is doubtful that a thief would be commemorated on a coin.

510. This chapter should be read in conjunction with Priscian, *Inst.* 1.50 (= Keil, *Gramm. Lat.* 2.37.8). Priscian states not that there are four diphthongs *tout court*, but four in current use (37.13). He is also aware of the *ai* diphthong and gives the examples *aulai* and *pictai* (37.17). As to *ei*, he merely states that it is not currently used in Latin (40.10). He is also well aware of *yi* in Greek names (37.11–12). Poliziano's contribution, less innovative than it might seem at first sight, is to call attention, on the basis of his epigraphical studies, to the use of *ee* and *ii*. But the fact that *ou* remains doubtful (see above) together with his admission that *ee* and *ii* may be a graphic convention for representing long vowels undermines his claim about the total number of diphthongs.

44

511. Persius Pr. 13–14. An allusion to Hippocrene, a spring on Mt. Helicon, which reputedly gushed forth when Pegasus struck his hoof on the ground there.

512. This is the reading of Cornutus on Persius, Pr. 14: here the transmission is divided, like Poliziano himself, between *Pegaseium* and *Pegaseum*; cf. *Commentum Cornuti in Persium*, ed. W. Clausen and J. E. G. Zetzel

(Munich and Leipzig: Saur, 2004), app. ad loc. Possibly the manuscript he used was Munich, Bayerische Staatsbibliothek CLM 23577 (11th century = M), which lacks the title (hence Poliziano does not cite the author). He refers to his public lectures on the satires of Horace and Persius in 1484–85; cf. Maïer, *Ange Politien*, 426. This interpretation appears in a nutshell at *Comm. Pers.*, p. 23.

513. One suspects that Leto's codex is now BAV, Arch. S. Pietro H 36 (= B), end of the ninth century, which carries the reading in question. On the eccentric Leto and his Academy of Rome, see Maria Accame, *Pomponio Leto: Vita e insegnamento* (Tivoli: Tored, 2008), as well as the papers collected by C. Cassiani and M. Chiabò, eds., *Pomponio Leto e la prima Accademia Romana* (Rome: Roma nel Rinascimento, 2007); the website www.repertoriumpomponianum.it gives much useful information about him and his circle.

514. Both Poliziano and the targets of his criticism are mistaken: ἑλώρια (*Il.* 1.4) and its other forms are not found in Homer with a lengthened first syllable or a double λ.

515. Homer, *Il.* 2.89.

516. That is, with the first vowel successively long and short to fit the meter.

517. Martial 9.11.13–17.

518. For these "twin pillars" of Poliziano's philology, cf. on *I* 35. In fact, modern editors adopt *nectar*.

45

519. Martial 11.43.10. "Closer" (*propior*) *sc.* than Achilles's concubine Briseis, mentioned in the previous verse (if the reading is sound; Housman conjectured *potior* ["preferable"]).

520. Antonio Beccadelli, *Hermaphroditus* 1.7.12, ed. H. Parker, ITRL 42 (Cambridge, MA, Harvard University Press, 2010), 12.

521. Statius, *Achil.* 1.174–77.

522. Plato, *Symp.* 179e–80a.

523. Plato, *Symp.* 180a.

524. Homer, *Il.* 11.786–87.

46

525. Juvenal 7.51–52.

526. Of earlier commentators, both Calderini and Merula print the vulgate *cacethos* (the latter clung stubbornly to his reading; cf. Poliziano,
Epist. 11.10 = *Opera* 1:155); Giorgio Valla, however, has the quadrisyllabic
form. One wonders whether he anticipated Poliziano or if the latter
would regard this as a case when his view leaked out and was plagiarized
(cf. I Pref. 13). The manuscript referred to has been identified as BAV,
Vat. lat. 3286 (11th centuty), written in Beneventan script; cf. Rizzo, *Il
lessico*, 124–25. For Francesco Gaddi (1441–1504), see the entry of Vanna
Arrighi in *DBI* 51 (1998); Poliziano refers to Gaddi's role as secretary to
the Otto di Practica, an important Florentine magistracy.

527. Juvenal 2.141.

528. This reading is also presupposed by the comments of Calderini,
Merula, and Valla ad loc., all of whom took Lyde to be a spider.

529. Plautus, *Pseud.* 659.

530. Martianus Capella 8.805.10–11.

531. Canthara is a nurse in Terence, *Ad.* act 3, scene 2, the name sugges-
tive of a large drinking cup (*cantharus*). Pyrrhia was an old slave woman
in a comedy by Titinius (inc. XXI Ribbeck), alluded to by Horace (*Epist.*
1.13.14 with [Acro] ad loc.). Baucis is the poor but pious old woman in
the story recounted by Ovid (*Met.* 8.631); for Persius, she is the type of
shriveled old age (*pannucia Baucis*: 4.21).

47

532. By the *domus Mellina* Poliziano must mean Tor Millina near Piazza
Navona in Rome, the dwelling of the important Roman family of the
Millini (or Mellini).

533. This encounter was presumably during Poliziano's visit to Rome as a member of a Florentine embassy to congratulate Pope Innocent VIII on his election; it was at this time that he was commissioned to translate Herodian; cf. *I* 72.3. On Lorenzi, who was named Vatican librarian the following year, cf. Branca and Pastore Stocchi, "La Biblioteca Vaticana," 145–46 with literature in n. 9.

534. Michelangelo, who as a young man, like Poliziano, belonged to Lorenzo de' Medici's *familia*, about a decade after the publication of the *Miscellanea* signed his famous "Pietà" (1498–99) MICHAELANGELUS BONAROTUS FLORENTINUS FACIEBAT. Did he remember Poliziano discoursing on this subject at Lorenzo's table?

535. Poliziano paraphrases Pliny, *HN* Praef. 26–27.

536. Vergil, *Aen.* 8.435–38. This chapter is unusual in taking its starting point from observations of antiquities on Poliziano's recent trip to Rome (presumably the one in 1488). It shows two different relations of monument to text: Pliny's preface shows the reason for the form of the artists' inscriptions, whereas the Gorgon is the concrete embodiment of a Vergilian *ekphrasis*, "in effect 'illustrated' Vergil"; see further Koortbojian, "Poliziano's Role," 271–72 (source of the quoted words).

48

537. Pliny, *HN* 35.85 (the citation error was caught by Fonzio; see the note on the text).

538. Plutarch, *Quomodo adulator ab amico internoscatur* 15 = *Mor.* 58d–e; cf. *De tranquillitate animi* 12 = *Mor.* 471f–72a.

539. Aelian *VH* 2.2. Megabyzus is not a personal name here but the title of the (castrated) high priest of Artemis of Ephesus (see *I* 51 below); cf. Kroll, *RE* XV 1.122.8–12. Pliny knew of paintings of Alexander by Apelles and another anecdote connecting the two (*HN* 35.86–87 and 93–94). The story seems likely to have migrated from the less to the more famous figure.

49

540. Ausonius, *Epigr.* 12.

541. *Anth. Pal.* 16.275.

542. Nicephorus Blemmydes, *Basilikos andrias* 143–44 offers an allegorical interpretation of the iconography of Lysippus's statue, which Poliziano might have been expected to cite, had he known it.

543. Callistratus, *Descriptiones* 6.

544. Allusion to Horace, *Epist.* 1.17.30–31: "The other [a Cynic philosopher] will avoid the woven cloak of Miletus more than a dog or a snake."

545. An allusion to the unpublished speech Εἰς τὸν εὐαγγελισμὸν τῆς ὑπεραγίας Θεοτόκου by Nicephorus Gregoras, the beginning of which is reported to be similar to two passages in his *History* (v. 2, 633 ~ 1053 ed. Bonn.); see further G. L. Kittredge, "'To Take Time by the Forelock,'" *Modern Language Notes* 8 (1893): 230–35, at 230–31.

50

546. A plant used in antiquity to treat mental illness.

547. Pliny, *HN* 25.47.

548. Proetus was a mythical king of Tiryns.

549. In good Latin one would not expect *pastor* to appear in the sentence in both the ablative and the accusative case.

550. Dioscorides, *De materia medica* 4.162.

551. [Apollodorus], *Bibl.* 2.26–29 (= 2.2.2 Loeb).

552. *Fragmenta Hesiodea*, fr. 37 Merkelbach–West.

553. Acusilaus, *FGrH* 2 F 28, cited by [Apollodorus] *Bibl.* 2.26.

554. That is, they ran about naked, as Aelian explains (next note).

555. Aelian, *VH* 3.42.

556. Sextus Empiricus, *Adv. math.* 1.261, citing Polyanthus, *FGrH* 37 F 1a.

557. A city of Arcadia.

558. Ovid, *Met.* 15.322–328 (Poliziano wrongly takes Ovid's phrase "the son of Amythaon" [325] to refer to Bias, rather than to Melampus). On this spring, cf. also *II* 31.4.

559. "Decent" (*probus*) is a pun on the name of the scholar.

560. Probus, *Scholia Bern. Vergil, Bucol.* 6.48.

561. Vergil, *Bucol.* 6.48–51; Paulus Aegineta 3.4.1 (= CMG 9.1:156.16–19).

51

562. Martial, *Spect.* 1.3. Though *honores* ("honors, offices") is the transmitted text, Scaliger conjectured *Iones* ("Ionians"), which has won universal acceptance; the line thus reads: "Let the effeminate Ionians not be praised for the temple of Trivia."

563. Jerome, *Comm. in Epist. ad Ephesios*, Prol. (*PL* 26, 441A).

564. Xenophon of Ephesus, *Ephesiaca* 1.2.2–5.

565. Xenophon of Ephesus, *Ephesiaca* 1.3.1.

566. Calderini on Martial, *Spect.* 1.3 makes the essential point, citing Strabo 14.1.23.

567. For Heraclitus's epithet, cf. Cicero, *Fin.* 2.5.15, as well as George L. Kustas, *Studies in Byzantine Rhetoric* (Thessaloniki: Patriarchal Foundation for Patristic Studies, 1973), 80–81; Juvenal 10.28–30 contrasts, without naming them, Democritus and Heraclitus as the laughing and crying philosophers.

568. Heraclitus, *Epist.* 9.4. Like most extant collections of philosophers' letters, the corpus attributed to Heraclitus was written by a sophist of Roman imperial date. Though Poliziano could deal critically with such materials (cf. *Letters* 1.1, ed. Butler, ITRL 21, pp. 4–5, attributing the "letters of Phalaris" to Lucian), he does not do so here or at *I* 61 apropos of the alleged letter of Androcydes to Alexander.

52

569. Martial, *Spect.* 1.4. Calderini on Martial, *Spect.* 1.4.

570. Lucan, *Bellum civile* 9.511–21.

571. Pliny, *HN* 5.31, 49, and 50; 13.102 and 111; Vergil, *Aen.* 4.198–202.

572. Plutarch, *De sollertia animalium* 35 = Mor. 983e.

573. Ovid, *Her.* 21.99.

574. Plutarch, *Thes.* 21.2.

575. Diogenes Laertus 8.13.

576. Callimachus, *Hymn* 2.58–63.

577. A strained interpretation; in fact, *Assyrius* ("Assyrian," cj. Alciatus) is generally accepted for *assiduus* ("constant"), so the line would read "Let not Assyrian labor boast of Babylon."

578. For Poliziano's discussion of eunuchs at the temple of Diana, see the preceeding chapter.

579. The ancients distinguished the lower air (*aer*) from the upper air (*aether*), the medium of the stars; see further Martin Schmidt, *Die Erklärungen zum Weltbild Homers und zur Kultur der Heroenzeit in den bT-Scholien zur Ilias* (Munich: Beck, 1976), 75–81.

53

580. Aulus Gellius, *NA* 15.6.1.

581. Homer, *Il.* 7.89–91; Cicero, *De gloria* 2, fr 2 Garbarino.

582. Cicero, *Div.* 2.30.63 ~ Homer, *Il.* 2.299–300.

583. Cicero, *Div.* 2.30.63–64 ~ Homer, *Il.* 2.301–30.

584. Poliziano first recorded this observation in a marginal note in his printed copy of the text (Munich, Bayerische Staatsbibliothek, 2° Inc. c. a. 467, 304r) that is "virtually an early draft" of the first half of this chapter: Hunt, "Three New Incunables," 258–59.

585. Cicero, *Att.* 13.44.3, referring to Cicero, *Lig.* 33, where Cursidius is mentioned as present at the trial, though, in fact, he was already dead.

586. Cicero, *Orat.* 9.29; for correction of the error, cf. Cicero, *Att.* 12.6a.1.

587. Cicero, *Att.* 15.14.4.

588. This is BML, Plut. 49.18 (M) of the year 1392/93; see R. H. Rouse in Reynolds, *Texts*, 137; Juren, "Les notes," 238. It was a member of the Δ branch, which carries the cited reading; see Shackleton Bailey's apparatus on Cicero, *Att.* 15.14(402).4.

589. That is, *ceruia* becomes *cerula*.

590. Cicero, *Att.* 16.11.1.

54

591. Quintilian, *Inst.* 1.10.5. This and the following chapter no doubt reflect the kinds of issues dealt with in Poliziano's lectures on Quintilian in the 1480–81 academic year; cf. Maïer, *Ange Politien*, 423.

592. Seneca, *Ep.* 49.8; the sentence is part of the protasis of an unreal condition; the sentence starts as follows: "I would seem insane if amid the commotion of war . . ."

593. Aulus Gellius, *NA* 18.2.9.

594. Lucian, *Symp.* 23.

595. Lucian, *Dial. mort.* 1.2. The dialogue is, however, between Diogenes and Pollux, and the subject of the verb is "philosophers"; Castor is not mentioned.

596. Lucian, *Gallus* 11.

597. For this, both Greek and Latin forms are given.

598. Diogenes Laertius 2.108. To summarize:

> The heaping argument inquires how many grains of sand are needed to make a heap. By repeated additions, eventually a heap seems to result without any single action being the identifiable cause.
>
> The "reaping" (or "mowing") argument involves a false contingency. "If one will reap . . ." = If this, then perhaps this or perhaps that, but only the "this" will be true, the "perhaps" false. The argument is thus an assertion in the guise of a logical conclusion.
>
> The "horns" argument involves an invalid conclusion from an inadequately defined (or negative) premise, as explained here.
>
> The "crocodile" puzzle involves the closing off of logical options; cf. the next chapter.
>
> The "liar" puzzle presents someone who claims to be a liar. But if he is indeed a liar, he is telling the truth.
>
> The "electra" puzzle refers to Electra not recognizing her brother Orestes. She fails to recognize him because of her false presumption that he would not return to her without revealing himself.

The "veiled" puzzle involves ambiguous terms. One may "know" ("be acquainted with") an individual but not "know" ("recognize") him because he is veiled or hooded.

The "no one" argument supports a conclusion by arguing against a "straw man," a position advocated by no one but easy to counter.

The "bald" argument is the reverse of the "heaping" argument. If a man with hair has one hair subtracted, then he still has hair and is not considered bald. By repeated such actions, sufficient hair is eventually removed for him to be described as bald but without a single identifiable causal action.

599. Com. adesp. *PCG* v. 8 F 149, cited by Diogenes Laertius 2.108. Eubulides of Miletus was a philosopher of the Megarian school and a teacher of Demosthenes.

600. Suidas s.v. ῥομβοστωμυλήθρα.

601. Diogenes Laertius 7.44.

602. Martianus Capella 4.327.

55

603. Quintilian, *Inst.* 1.10.5.

604. Scholia anon. on Hermogenes of Tarsus, *Stat.* 7:163.4–10 and 14–16 Walz (not Doxopater).

605. Lucian, *Vit. auct.* 22.

606. Discussed in the previous chapter.

56

607. Martial, *Spect.* 22.5–6.

608. Vergil, *Georg.* 1.172 (as the translation suggests, Vergil has "double" [*duplici*], not "twin" [*gemino*]).

609. Pliny, *HN* 8.71; Solinus 30.21.

610. Tertullian, *Adversus Marcionem* 3.18.3 (= CSEL 47, 406.18–21), quoting Deuteronomy 33:17, *cornua unicornis* ("horns of a unicorn"), for which

the Septuagint has κέρατα μονοκέρωτος, the Latin Vulgate *cornua rinocerotis*. Tertullian thus assumes the equivalence of rhinoceros and unicorn, which later appears in the Vulgate, which is Poliziano's point.

611. Pausanias 9.21.2.

612. Another strained interpretation; in fact, rhinoceroses come in both one- and two-horned varieties (cf. Wikipedia s.v.), a possibility not entertained by Poliziano (his experience with a giraffe might have made him more cautious; cf. *I* 3.2).

57

613. Suetonius, *Calig.* 22.3.

614. Pliny, *HN* 10.56.

615. Poliziano cites what is now BML, Plut. 82.1 (= no. 791 Ullman-Stadter), a twelfth- or thirteenth-century manuscript that Cosimo de' Medici purchased in 1430 on the advice of Niccolò Niccoli; it, together with Plut. 82.2 (= no. 792 Ullman-Stadter), was previously cited at *I* 32.1 and will be again on *I* 61.1; cf. P. Viti, "Poliziano e Plinio," 158 and 163.

616. Barbaro, *Castigationes*, on *HN* 10.15, would later argue for *tetragones* as the reading generally attested in older codices; see further Fera, *Una ignota*, 109–10 n. 4.

617. Pliny, *HN* 10.56.

58

618. Poliziano gives examples in §§20–21. For this chapter, readers should refer to the detailed discussion and commentary in Megna, *Poliziano*, to which the following notes are indebted.

619. This account corresponds to Zosimus 2.3.1–2.

620. See *I* 18.2.

621. That is, Zosimus (n. 619) and Valerius Maximus 2.4.5, cited partly verbatim. Poliziano was usually happy to trumpet his discoveries, but here he does not (his failure to do so earned him Merula's dry criticism; cf. Perotto Sali, "L'opuscolo," 177). In fact, on a trip to Rome he had

found Zosimus's *Historia nova* in cod. Vat. 156, and, on his urging, Lorenzo arranged to borrow it and have it copied. The codex was probably sent covertly with the aid of Luigi Lotti da Barberino, hence Poliziano's discretion. See further Megna, *Poliziano*, 50–56.

622. Varro, *De scaenicis originibus* 1 fr. 1 Popma (*GRF* 70, p. 216), cited by Censorinus 17.8.

623. The point is borrowed virtually verbatim from Censorinus 17.12–13.

624. Vergil, *Aen.* 8.63. The two etymologies are from Festus, *De verb. sign.*, p. 478 Lindsay (cf. the reconstruction by Pighi, *De ludis*, 61) and Servius, *Comm. Aen.* 8.63, respectively; Poliziano could also have cited the etymology from the Sabine word for "soft"; cf. II 49.3 with note.

625. Horace, *Carm. saec.* 21–24.

626. The records and edicts are referred to by Censorinus 17.9. Pighi, *De ludis*, 73–75, collects the extant testimonia for Augustus's games; in addition, the acts of Augustus's games, preserved on an inscription in Rome, have been edited with commentary by B. Schnegg-Köhler, *Die augusteischen Säkularspiele* (Munich-Leipzig: Saur, 2002).

627. Valerius Antias, *FRH* 25 F 26 = Censorinus 17.10; Livy, *Per.* 19 (where the reference is supplied by modern editors); Varro as above (where Poliziano omitted the last clause, giving one hundred years as the interval).

628. Herodian 3.8.10 ~ *Opera* 1:345. Because Herodian's text contradicts the rest of the tradition, Poliziano suspects that it is defective, but he let the "error" stand in his translation, rather than attempt to emend it; see further Megna, *Poliziano*, 100–101 n. 2.

629. That is, in 252 BCE: Zosimus 2.4.1–2; cf. Livy, *Per.* 49. It follows that Valesius's celebration of the games was in the regal period; perhaps for that reason it was omitted from the numeration.

630. §§9–10 ~ Zosimus 2.3.3–4.1; editors since Mendelssohn assume a lacuna prior to Μάρκου Ποπιλίου. Poliziano was misled by the damaged text at Censorinus 17.10 to think that Valerius and Verginius were consuls for the second, rather than the first set of games. It is not clear

where he found *Quintius*, which is ordinarily a gentile name, not a cognomen.

631. From Censorinus 17.11. For Valerius Antias and Livy, see above; Varro = *GRF* 308, p. 324; Piso, *FRH* 9 F 41; Cn. Gellius *FRH* 14 F 30; Cassius Hemina *FRH* 6 *F 40.

632. Livy cited by Censorinus 17.9.

633. §11 ~ Zosimus 2.4.2, again referred to vaguely (*quidam*); see on §4.

634. §§12–13 *init.* ~ Pliny, *HN* 7.159; Claudius's games were held in 47 CE. The figure eighty-three reproduces an error in Pliny's manuscript tradition (it should be sixty-four).

635. There was, in fact, one example in Lorenzo's collection (*MRI* 1: no. 1401); see Gionta, *Iconografia*, 32.

636. *Sc.* 1480–81; cf. Maïer, *Ange Politien*, 423. The chronology is emphasized to establish priority over the treatment of the Secular Games in Beroaldo, *Annotationes*, 23. Megna, *Poliziano*, 40–42 and 109 n. 1, suspects that the following broadside against Calderini may be a smokescreen to obscure Poliziano's real target.

637. Statius, *Silvae* 1.4.17–18.

638. Calderini's error is pointed out at *Comm. Selv.* 316–17, but not in the commentary on the *Fasti*.

639. Martial 10.63.3, epitaph of a lady, only women of the nobility of good repute being allowed to participate.

640. Poliziano alludes to (and negativizes) Ennius's characterization of the jurist Sextus Aelius (*Annales* fr. 329 Skutsch).

641. Martial 4.1.7–8. From the toponym Tarentum, the poet has created the name of the (supposed) eponymous hero of the games; see *Publii Ovidii Nasonis Fastorum libri sex*, ed. and trans. with comm. by J. G. Frazer, (London: Macmillan & Co., 1929), 2:195–96.

642. Cf. Megna, *Poliziano*, III n. 1, quoting relevant notes by Calderini. Censorinus 17.2 already condemned the idea that thirty years could comprise a *saeculum*.

643. The reference at Varro, *Ling.* 5.31, is actually to the Calabrian Tarentum (on the heel of the Italian "boot"). The Ovidian reference is to *Fast.* 1.510; this and the passage in Martial are both cited at *Comm. Selv.* 316.

644. Cf. Koortbojian, "Poliziano's Role," 271: "When the ancient monuments . . . survived intact . . . they held eloquent — and *visible* — testimony to the ancient past the humanists sought to restore." Though this example is decorative, cf. *I* 65.3 for such a reference forming a functional part of the argument.

645. ~ Zosimus. 2.4.3, except that Poliziano substitutes *Vibo* for *Libo* as the name of the second consul.

646. Herodian 3.8.10 ~ Poliziano, *Opera* 1:345.

647. The extant text of Dio fails to mention the Secular Games produced in his own lifetime by Septimius Severus; the information derives from a note in the upper margin of BAV, ms. Vat. gr. 156, f. 27v; cf. Megna, *Poliziano*, 55 with Table I.

648. Zosimus 2.7.2. The joint consulate of Constantine and Licinius was, however, in 313, only 109 years after Severus's games.

649. So Orosius 7.20.2 (the reference is to Philip the Arab [r. 244–249]).

650. Eusebius, *Chron.*, under the year 246; Eutropius, *Brev.* 9.3.

651. [Victor], *Epitome* 28.3, albeit the name Philip the Younger derives from Eusebius/Eutropius (previous note).

652. See above, §12.

653. Poliziano added the reference to the rites of Ceres here to cover a lacuna in Zosimus (see Cicero, *Leg.* 2.35–36). He cross-refers to this passage in his lecture on Suetonius, *Cal.* 54.2; cf. Fera, *Una ignota*, 130.

654. The "ritual feasts" (*sc.* for the gods: *lectisternia*) involved preparing special couches for them; this feature, absent from Zosimus, is borrowed from Valerius Maximus 2.4.5, where it is part of the rites celebrated by Valesius and by Valerius Publicola; see further Megna, *Poliziano*, 119 n. 2.

655. §§16–19 ~ Zonaras 2.5.1–5.

656. Perhaps he means Claudius's games; cf. §12.

657. See Suetonius, *Dom.* 4.3, with Fera, *Una ignota*, 276.

658. Suetonius, *Aug.* 31.4.

659. Ausonius, *Griphus ternarii numeri* 34.

660. Horace, *Carm. Saec.*: the Fates, 25; Ilithyia, 14; Diana, the Aventine, the vows, the Council of Fifteen, 69–72; Sibylline verses, 5.

661. Zosimus 2.6.

662. For this characterization of the Romans prior to exposure to Greek culture, see above, *I* 39.3.

663. "Slay" was originally expressed in this verse by *imola*, which, in his *Emendationes*, Poliziano changed to *feri* in light of Battista Guarini's objection on metrical grounds (the *i* of *imola* should be long, rather than short). Poliziano attempted to justify this as an imitation of the archaic color of the verse (*Epist.* 1.20.3 = *Opera* 1:14 = *Letters*, ed. Butler, ITRL 21, 64–65), but the fact that he hastened to make this change and another in verse 27 of his version of Callimachus at *I* 80 suggests that this *apologia* is disingenuous; cf. Megna, *Poliziano*, 75–76.

664. But for the Greek original, this line could be more easily taken as "Let the boys and girls of the Latins sing paeans."

59

665. Servius, *Comm. Aen.* pr., p. 1.14–15 Rand et al.

666. See the last note on *I* 7.

667. Seneca rhetor, *Controv.* 1.2.22; *Priapea* 3.8.

668. *Priapea* 3.1.

669. He perhaps refers to Boccaccio, whose copy of the corpus (BML, Plut. 33.31 [= A], ca. 1340), was and remains the oldest one extant. How and where Boccaccio discovered these poems remains unclear; cf. *Priapées*, ed. and trans. Louis Callebat (Paris: Les Belles Lettres, 2012), lxv.

670. Servius, *Comm. Aen.* pr., p. 1.9 Rand et al.

671. Priscian, *Inst.* 5.13; Ovid, *Epigr.* fr. 3 Courtney. "Spoils" renders *opima*, the spoils taken by a general from the general on the other side, defeated in single combat.

672. Quintilian, *Inst.* 9.3.70.; Ovid, *Epigr.* fr. 4 Courtney.

673. Martial 2.41.1; Ovid, *Epigr.* fr. 6 Courtney.

674. Calderini on Martial 2.41.1. Cf. the advice *against* laughing (if one has bad teeth) at *Ars am.* 3.279–80 (the meter should also have cautioned Calderini against the idea).

675. Martianus Capella 8.809.

676. Tacitus, *Dial.* 12.6; Quintilian, *Inst.* 8.5.6; Tertullian, *De praescriptionibus haereticorum* 39, who, however, speaks of the *Medea* of Hosidius Geta, not Ovid; Poliziano, *Nutricia* 449.

677. That is, to stop frowning.

678. Martianus Capella 8.809.

679. Cf. Furius Bibaculus fr. 15 Courtney, quoted by Quintilian, *Inst.* 8.6.17, and alluded to by Horace, *Sat.* 2.5.41.

680. BML, ms. San Marco 343 (12th century), no. 893 Ullman-Stadter.

681. Discussion of the authorship of the *Priapea* continues; cf. the review of the problem by Callebat, (as above, n. 669), xxv–xxxii, who concludes that there was a single author and that he was close in style and language to Martial.

60

682. Ovid, *Fasti* 1.319–22. At *Comm. Fast.* 1.317 Poliziano cites different etymologies for the *Agonalia*, from Varro and Festus.

683. A lapse of memory: the same work is cited as in the previous chapter, but neither citation is from the third book.

684. Seneca rhetor, *Controv.* 2.3.19.

61

685. Pliny, *HN.* 14.58. The letter circulated under the name of Androcydes, the personal physician of Alexander the Great, is apocryphal; see on §51.2.

686. See above, on *I* 57.2.

687. Pliny, *HN* 14.58.

688. Pliny, *HN* 25.152.

689. Dioscorides, *Mat. med.* 4.78.

690. Ambrose, *De Elia et ieiunio* 14.52.

691. Plutarch, *Quaest. conv.* 3.5 = *Mor.* 653a; cf. *De garull.* 14 = *Mor.* 509d–e.

692. Macrobius, *Sat.* 7.6.5; the latest editor of the *Saturnalia*, R. A. Kaster (Oxford: Clarendon Press, 2011), argues ad loc. that Macrobius has, in fact, confused *conion* and *aconitum*.

693. Ambrose, *Hexaemeron* 3.9.38 (= CSEL 32.1, p. 84.9); Basil, *Hexaemeron* 5.4 (PG 29.101B). It was Eustathius, not Rufinus, who translated the *Hexaemeron* into Latin; Poliziano seems to have been misled by the attribution in the manuscript that is now BML, ms. Fiesol. 44; cf. P. Viti, "Poliziano e Plinio," 168.

62

694. [Cicero], *Rhet. ad Her.* 3.20.33.

695. Horace, *Sat.* 2.8.25–26.

696. Porphyrio, *Comm. Hor. Serm.* 2.8.26.

697. That is, Modern Greek.

698. Festus, *De verb. sign.*, p. 443 Lindsay. In the marginal note of his copy of *Rhet. Her.* (Munich, Bayerische Staatsbibliothek, 2° Inc. c. a. 467, 18v), Poliziano copied Festus's entry beside this passage, adumbrating the approach taken here; cf. Hunt, "Three New Incunables," 253.

699. [Asconius], *Comm. Cic. Verr.* 1.8.22 (p. 212.7 Stangl).

63

700. Varro, *Ling.* 7.84.

701. Terence, *Ad.* 117.

702. Donatus, *Comm. Ter. Ad.* 117.

703. Cicero, *Att.* 13.18. The word means "someone who writes many things," not, obviously, polygraph in its modern sense.

704. Gellius, *NA* 15.6.1, already discussed at *I* 53.

705. Here Poliziano does not apply the principle of *I* 89 that the author closer to the original has greater evidential value (in this case, Varro than Donatus), nor does he consider that Varro is citing the passage specifically for the verb *scortari*, for which he then offers an etymology. Since the two words are not similar in appearance, this may be a case of deliberate substitution. The explanation may lie in a phenomenon relatively recently identified, that is to say, interference by actors in the early stages of the transmission of dramatic texts; cf., for example, D. L. Page, *Actors' Interpolations in Greek Tragedy, Studied with Special Reference to Euripides'* Iphigenia in Aulis (Oxford: Clarendon Press, 1934), esp. 118 on alteration of words. Possibly a shortening for performance was involved, whereby v. 117 was reconfigured on the model of v. 102 (*scortari neque potare*) so as to eliminate v. 118, where *amat* covers the activity of *scortari*.

64

706. Ausonius, *Epist.* 25.33–35 = 19(b).33–35 Green. The antecedent of the relative is the "chariot (*essedum*) filled with heroic verses" mentioned in the previous line.

707. Persius Pr.; Martial 7.26.1. This chapter is adumbrated at *Comm. Pers.* 21–22, where the citations of Martial, Ovid, Ausonius (twice), and Pliny recur.

708. A foot consisting of two short syllables.

709. Hephaestion, *Ench.* 5.4.

710. Ibid.

711. Hipponax, fr. 84.17 West.

712. *Sc.* an iambic or a choliambic line: Aristides Quintilianus, *De musica* 1.25.

713. Ovid, *Rem. am.* 377–78. Poliziano makes the same mistake at *Comm. Pers.* 22 (*Rem. am.* comprises a single book).

714. Actually, Demetrius, *De elocutione* 301.

715. Ibid.

716. Ausonius, *Epist.* 10.31 = 8.31 Green.

717. Pliny the Younger, *Epist.* 5.10.2 (to Suetonius).

65

718. Statius, *Silv.* 1.1.15–16. This chapter is a much condensed version of what Poliziano offered his students; cf. *Comm. Selv.* 90–95. On Poliziano's concept of a *sylva*, promotion of the quasi-Greek spelling with a *y*, and his own imitations of Statius's poems, which inspired a new genre of European poetry, see van Dam, "Wandering the Woods," esp. 45–49.

719. Statius, *Silv.* 1.1.37.

720. Quintilian, *Inst.* 11.3.119.

721. Poliziano draws his crowning argument from his observation of Marcus Aurelius's statue at Rome; cf. Koortbojian, "Poliziano's Role," 270–71. The statue stood before the Lateran Palace in Rome from the eighth century until 1538, when it was relocated as part of Michelangelo's redesign of the Capitoline Hill.

66

722. Plautus, *Mostellaria* 829–30. A pun: *arte*, "soundly" of sleep, can also mean "closely" in reference to door fastenings.

723. An apparent lapse of memory; Poliziano has not previously cited a Plautine codex. One suspects that he may have in mind BNCF, Conv. Soppr. J I 12 (San Marco 228) = no. 918 Ullman-Stadter (pp. 66–67), a copy made by Niccolò Niccoli and often copied subsequently; on this codex, cf. also Questa, *Per la storia*, 6 and 38 with n. 34.

724. Gaius Licinius Calvus, fr. 11 Courtney (not Cinna).

725. Plautus, *Mil.* 321–23.

726. Ovid, *Fast.* 1.691.

727. Fulgentius, *Expositio sermonum antiquorum* 13.

67

728. Juvenal 1.116.

729. This is the opinion of Merula, *Enarr. Juv.* ad loc., followed by Valla; Poliziano repeats the point about lack of authority at *Epist.* 11.10 (= *Opera* 1:155).

730. Aelian, *NA* 3.9.

731. Poliziano has in mind a coin with a bust of Faustina, the wife of Marcus Aurelius, on the obverse and the legend CONCORDIA with the image of a bird on the reverse (*MRI* 1: no. 3347); cf. Gionta, *Iconografia*, 32 with Tav. Xb.

68

732. Catullus, *Carm.* 66.

733. Hyginus, *Poet. astr.* 2.24; Achilles, *Isag.*, p. 41.22 Maass (= Call. fr. 387.2 Pf.). The attributions of the fragmentary commentaries on Aratus to Theon of Alexandria and Achilles Tatius are now considered doubtful.

734. *Schol. Arat. Phaen.* 146; Call. fr. 110.7–8 Pfeiffer ~ Catullus 66.7–8.

735. A people of the southeastern coast of the Black Sea known to legend as the first ironworkers.

736. *Schol. Ap. Rhod. Argon.* 2.373–76a, citing Call. fr. 110.48–49 Pfeiffer. The "baneful creature" is iron. Poliziano is likely using the famous codex of Apollonius, BML, Plut. 32.9, which contains the scholia attributed to the three commentators mentioned.

737. Catullus 66.48. On Poliziano's conjecture, which has been generally accepted, and his assumption, here and in the following chapter, of a literal rendering of Callimachus, see Peter Bing, "Reconstructing Berenike's Lock," in Most, *Collecting Fragments*, 78–94, at 78–79.

69

738. Catullus 66.94.

739. Cf. Otto s.v. *pes* 3.

740. Callimachus, *Hymn* 3.264–65. A striking euphemism: both assaulted Artemis and were punished accordingly.

741. Nicander, *Theriaca* 15.

742. Pindar, *Isthm.* 3/4.67.

743. Pindar, *Nem.* 2.11–12.

744. Eustathius, *Comm. Hom. Od.* 1535.52 on *Od.* 5.274.

745. Though challenged by Marullo, *Oarion* was defended by Scaliger and maintains its place in modern editions; see further Grafton, "Joseph Scaliger's Edition," 166–67.

70

746. The famous issue of 43/42 BCE; cf. *RRC* 518, 741, and plate 508/3; *MRI*, no. 1061; Gionta, *Iconografia*, 33 and Tav. 11a.

747. Dio Cassius 47.25.3.

71

748. Vergil, *Aen.* 8.402.

749. BAV, Vat. lat. 3867, fifth century, the "codex Romanus" (= R); cf. Branca and Pastore Stocchi, "La Biblioteca Vaticana," 142 and n. 2, as well as 155 on the reference to the *Bibliotheca pontificia* as the "inner" library (so referred to also at *II* 23.4).

750. Pacuvius, *Chryses* fr. 85 Schierl = 98 W. cited by Nonius, *De comp. doct.* 817 Lindsay; Lucretius 3.1010; L. Coelius Antipater *FRH* 15 F 4 cited by Nonius, *De comp. doct.* 817 Lindsay (not Caecilius).

751. Vergil, *Aen.* 9.9.

752. That is, either long or short, depending on its specific context. In fact, Martianus Capella 3.278 does not list a syllable ending in *t* as a common syllable; rather, he claims that the *t* shortens, and he cites *caput* as an example (279 = p. 77.16–17 Willis).

753. Vergil, *Aen.* 10.394, where –*put* is treated as long: Conington remarks ad loc.: "Virg. has extended to a substantive ending in 't' a liberty which he usually only allows himself in the case of third persons of verbs."

72

754. Horace, *Carm.* 1.38.2.

755. Ovid, *Fast.* 5.337. Poliziano's lectures on the *Fasti* (in 1481–82; cf. Maïer, *Ange Politien*, 424) comprised the essential points, including citation of Pliny, *HN* 16.65 and 21.6, Ulpian, Theophrastus, Festus, Suetonius, "Nicas," and Herodian; only Horace, Eustathius, and Pliny, *HN* 13.74 and 24.3 were added for this version; cf. *Comm. Fast.*, 389–91.

756. Theophrastus, *Hist. pl.* 3.10.4–5; Pliny, *HN* 16.65.

757. On Theodore Gaza, see further *I* 90–91 below, where Poliziano takes a rather different line. For his rendering of *philyra* as *tilia* see, for example, Theophrastus, *Hist. pl.* 1.10.1 = Theodore 1.16 (cited from the edition of Basel: Heredes Cratandri, 1550).

758. Pliny, *HN* 16.65.

759. Pliny, *HN* 21.6.

760. The reference is too vague to enable an identification; cf. Gionta, *Iconografia*, 33 and n. 2.

761. Suetonius, *Ner.* 25.2; Festus, *De verb. sign.*, p. 102 Lindsay; Tertullian, *De corona* 12.4.

762. *Etym. magn.* s.v. φίλυρα; for Poliziano's mode of reference, see on *I* 32.2.

763. Tertullian, *De pallio* 3.5.2.

764. Herodian 1.17.1; on Poliziano's translation (= *Opera* 1:314–92), first published in Bologna, 1493, see on *I* 47.1.

765. Used as a preservative; cf. *OLD* s.v. *cedrus* 2.

766. Martianus Capella 2.136.

767. Ulpian, *To Sabinus* 24 in *Digest* 32.52 proem.

768. Eustathius, *Comm. Hom. Od.* 1453.7 on *Od.* 2.426.

769. Pliny, *HN* 13.74.

770. Pliny, *HN* 24.3.

73

771. Leto was in possession of the fragment by 1469/70, the date of his commentary on Lucan; cf. P. L. Schmidt in Sallmann, *Die Literatur*, 245.

For the history of Festus's text in the Renaissance, cf. Grafton, *Joseph Scaliger*, vol. 1, chapter v. On Pomponio Leto see *I* 44, n. 513. Manilio Cabacio Rallo (ca. 1447–ca. 1522), born in Greece, probably at Mistra, was a humanist scholar and poet associated with the circle of Leto and held the bishopric of Monemvasia. Cf. Hans Lamers, "Manilio Cabacio Rallo," online in the *Repertorium Pomponianum*.

772. A formal process under Roman law by which one who had been a prisoner of war could be reinstated in his property and other rights; cf. A. Berger, *Encyclopedic Dictionary of Roman Law*, Transactions of the American Philosophical Society n.s. 43.2 (Philadelphia, 1953) s.v. *postliminium*. In question is the so-called Codex Farnesianus (Naples, Biblioteca Nazionale, ms. IV.A.3 = N, mentioned above, *I* 5, n. 145), the sole witness to Festus's text apart from the abridgment created in the late eighth century by Paul the Deacon; cf. P. K. Marshal in Reynolds, *Texts*, 162–63, and for Poliziano's study of it in Leto's circle, see Alessandro Moscadi, *Il Festo Farnesiano* (Florence, 2001), xiv–xvii.

773. Festus, *De verb. sign.*, p. 396.22–29 Lindsay; Ennius, *Ann.* fr. 287 Skutsch.

774. Catullus 17.19.

775. As his *Emendationes* show, Poliziano first contemplated *suppernata* but then changed to the otherwise unattested *expernata*—a mistake. Though Poliziano does not fully explain his reasoning, he evidently thought the sounds of the first two letters of *separata* had been transposed, thus yielding *exparata*; he then further modified *par* to *pern* so as to create *expernata* on the analogy of Ennius's *suppernata*. In any case, modern editors accept *suppernata* as the correct reading in Catullus.

74

776. Cicero, *Inv. rhet.* 2.1.1. Poliziano styles this work "against Hermagoras" because of the polemics at 1.6.8, 9.12, and 51.97.

777. See on *I* 47.1. The allusion is to Hor. *S.* 1.4.8 (of Lucilius).

778. Aelian, *VH* 4.12. For *manupretium* ("fee"), see *II* 23.

75

779. Calderini, *Comm. in Ov. Ibin*, Preface 12. On Poliziano's polemical technique, turning this claim of Calderini's into an indictment, see Grafton, *Joseph Scaliger*, 1:23–24 and 235 n. 47.

780. Augustine, *Contra Iulianum haer. Pelag. defensorem* 1.20.

781. Ovid, *Ibis* 569–70 = 567–68 OCT.

782. Calderini, *Comm. in Ov. Ibin*, l. 569.

783. Modifying *equo* ("the wooden horse"), the reading adopted by modern editors.

784. Homer, *Od.* 4.274–89.

785. Tryphiodorus, Ἅλωσις Ἰλίου 178–79.

786. Tryphiodorus, Ἅλωσις Ἰλίου 476–78.

787. Poliziano, *Ambra* 436–37.

788. For Calderini and his dates, cf. on I 9.

76

789. Ovid, *Heroides* 1.15.

790. Homer, *Il.* 13.183–87, 2.620–21. The "Catalogue" is the epic Catalogue of Ships in *Il.* 2.494–759, where Amphimachus is mentioned in lines 620–21.

791. Homer, *Od.* 4.186–88.

792. The text remains controversial: the most recent critical edition, that of H. Dörrie (Berlin-New York: De Gruyter, 1971), retains the transmitted text on the assumption of an Ovidian error (shared by Hyginus, *Fab.* 113); others (Goold, Knox) adopt Housman's *ab hoste revictum* ("laid low by the enemy") for *ab Hectore victum* ("defeated by Hector").

77

793. After an *apologia* expanding the point about minutiae made at I Pref. 4, Poliziano goes on to treat the question of whether to spell *Vergil*

or *Virgil* as a historical problem to be decided by the oldest available evidence. Hence pride of place is given to ancient monuments and among texts, to the archetype of the *Pandects* and the Vatican Vergil.

794. An allusion to the leisure activity of the hero Scipio Africanus and his friend Laelius, reported in Valerius Maximus 8.8.1 and Cicero *De orat.* 2.22, and cited in the most famous educational tract of the Renaissance, Pier Paolo Vergerio's *De ingenuis moribus* (cap. 69) as an example of justified leisure; see *Humanist Educational Treatises*, ed. C. Kallendorf, ITRL 5 (Cambridge, MA, 2002), 82–85.

795. For "worthless trifles" (*apinas . . . et tricas*) cf. Martial 14.1.7.

796. Poliziano, *Silvae* 3.615–16 (*Ambra*), ed. Fantazzi, ITRL 14, 106–9: *sus . . . aliam ex alia poscit grunnitibus escam* ("with its grunts the pig seeks one bit of food after the other").

797. An allusion to Plautus, *Truculentus* 489; cf. II 32.4.

798. See above, I 41.2.

799. *Digest* 1.8.6.5.

800. See above, I 71.1 with note.

801. On Landino (1424–98), see Roberto Cardino, *La critica del Landino* (Florence: Sansoni, 1973), esp. 48–50, contrasting Landino's emphasis on the literary value of the classics with Poliziano's historicist approach to philology. Poliziano's picture of collegial relations may be a bit idealized, or they may have improved since 1482, when Landino moved to prevent his younger colleague from scheduling lectures at the same time as his own; cf. Verde, *Lo Studio Fiorentino*, 2:27.

802. The Augustine would match no. 230 Ullman-Stadter, with text from the midde of Book 2 to the end; for the Columella see on I 35.2; the Seneca will surely be BML, Plut. 76.50 (= L), first third of the ninth century.

803. The "Vergilian stars" are the Pleiades; for the etymology from the spring (*ver*), cf. Festus, *De verb. sign.*, p. 510 Lindsay.

804. Persius 1.80–81.

805. On the history of the problem, cf. J. M. Ziolkowski in *The Virgil*

Encyclopedia, ed. R. F. Thomas and J. M. Ziolkowski, 3 vols. (Chichester: Wiley-Blackwell, 2014), s.v. Virgil, spelling of.

78

806. *Digest* 1.16.12.

807. See above, I 41.2.

808. Francesco Accursio (1184–1263), a glossator and jurist of the Bologna school.

79

809. Appian, *Hist. Rom.* 11 (*Syriaca*).9.57 Loeb = 11.57.294 Viereck-Roos. Appian's anecdote pertains to Seleucus, to whom Poliziano attributed it in the first printed edition, but then he changed the reading to Lysimachus in the *Emendationes*. Moreover, Lysimachus's coins depict not himself, but Alexander with the iconography of Zeus Ammon, no doubt with the suggestion that he was Alexander's legitimate successor; see further Helen S. Lund, *Lysimachus: A Study in Early Hellenistic Kingship* (London-New York: Routledge, 1992), 163–64. In his *Emendationes*, aware of the conflict of the text with the coinage, Poliziano shows some perplexity and says the question requires further study.

80

810. This chapter heading was evidently not adjusted to reflect the change of plan indicated at §3.

811. Propertius 4.9.57–58.

812. Callimachus, *Hymn* 5.

813. Proclus's attribution to Iamblichus is found in a scholium by Michael Psellus, which was copied before the beginning of the work in Rome, Biblioteca Vallicelliana, ms. F 20 of the mid-fifteenth century; see M. Sicherl, "Michael Psellos und Iamblichus De mysteriis," *Byzantinische Zeitschrift* 53 (1960): 8–19. Cf. Iamblichus, *Myst.* 2.4 on epiphanies, though without specific reference to goddesses, Iamblichus emphasizing that the deity is incorporeal.

814. Vergil, *Bucol.* 8.102.

815. Homer, *Od.* 5.349–50.

816. That is, among the dead.

817. Poliziano, *Ambra* 289–92.

818. Poliziano, *Nutricia* 236–37.

819. Nonnus, *Dion.* 5.337–38.

820. Nonnus, *Dion.* 5.341–42. This is in contrast with Actaeon's own fate, since he was transformed into a deer and dismembered by his own dogs after he saw Artemis naked.

821. Giovanni Pico's role in encouraging the poet is compared to Apollo's at Callimachus, *Hymn* 2.105ff.

822. περὶ πόδα, "around the foot," that is, "fitting exactly," the two prepositions being often confused.

823. It has been thought that the lost final part of BML, Plut. 32.45 (= Pfeiffer's D, 15th century) was Poliziano's source for this text; cf. Fryde, *Humanism*, 181. Tissoni, "Angelo Poliziano," 119, seeks to vindicate Poliziano's use of the plural here by arguing that he may also have used BAM S 31 sup. (Martini and Bassi, *Catalogus codd. graec. Ambros.*, no. 734), with which Poliziano shares the erroneous reading ποτιρροον at verse 77; since the reading of Laur. Plut. 32.45 is unknown, however, the matter remains in doubt.

824. He cross-refers to his verses cited at §2, which adumbrate the interpretation at §§1–2 *init*. The claim about publication rests in part on *edo* having the sense "make public," rather than "publish in a printed edition," since the *Nutricia* would not appear in print until 1491; cf. Godman, "Poliziano's Poetics," 121, and *From Poliziano*, 91–92. However, the *Ambra*, which contains the clearer reference, was published soon after November 4, 1485; cf. Fantazzi in ITLR 14, xii.

825. See *II* 34.6 with note.

826. How did Poliziano infer that written accents were not used in the most ancient texts (cf. Pfeiffer, *History*, 1:180–81)? Merely from old manuscripts such as the Zosimus he used (cf. *I* 58.4), or did he draw the

conclusion from disputes over accents recorded in Homeric commentaries, such as that of Eustathius? In any case, he omits accents from continuous poetic texts as part of the "restoration of antiquity" he pursued in common with other humanists (cf. I 77.1), but not from individual words, phrases, or sentences he cites.

827. See "Notes to the Text."

828. This is the damage Poliziano alluded to at §3, most of line 136 having been lost.

829. Poliziano revised this line in response to criticisms of the prosody of *matutinus* ("morning") so that the *a* would be short, rather than long, a point criticized both by Marullo in an epigram and by Battista Guarini; cf. Fera, "Il dibattito," 340–43.

830. This is the conjectural supplement Poliziano mentioned at §3.

81

831. Propertius, *Elegiae* 4.3.21; *orno* is a variant reading cited in T (= BAV, ms. Vat. lat. 3273, written in 1427); the more common reading is *oeno*; see further Heyworth's apparatus ad loc.

832. The language here is modeled on Cicero, *Rosc. Am.* 2.6.

833. Pliny, *HN* 35.137. Poliziano's spelling of the name alternates between -*os* and -*us*.

834. In the interval between the composition and the publication of *Misc. I* (see Epil. 8), Beroaldo in his *Annotationes* published the reading *Ocno* in Prop. 4.3.21 as if it were his own conjecture. It is now thought that, as Poliziano implies, Beroaldo must have derived it from the same codex, namely, N, a twelfth-century manuscript formerly of Naples, now Wolfenbüttel, Herzog August Bibliothek, ms. Gudianus 224; see further Ricciardi, "Testo di Properzio," 117–19. Hence Poliziano identifies the source of his reading and defends himself against any imputation of plagiarism. The critique of Beroaldo is by implicit contrast with his own truthfulness.

82

835. *Digest* 2.13.1.1.

836. For their possible status as archetype, see I 41.

837. For Accursio, see on I 78.

838. *Sc.* of eligible jurors.

83

839. Catullus 74.

840. Catullus 102.

841. Cf. *I* 19.5, where the trip and presentation at Verona were mentioned. It was while in Venice that he studied the Codex Bembinus of Terence; see on *II* 43.

842. *Mesorē* in Plutarch; Poliziano seems to take this in the sense "reaper" (*messor*).

843. Plutarch, *De Iside et Osiride* 19, 65, 68 = *Mor.* 358e, 377b–c, 378c, paraphrased.

844. *Anth. Pal.* 11.115.

845. Tertullian, *Apologeticus* 6.8.

846. Varro, *Ling.* 5.57.

847. Ovid, *Met.* 9.691–92.

848. Augustine, *De civ. D.* 18.5 (not Book 19), citing Varro, *Antiq. rerum div.* fr. 46a Cardauns.

849. Iamblichus, *Myst.* 8.3.

850. Porphyry, *Abst.* 2.34.

851. Psalms 65:2. The transliteration in Poliziano's text has been regularized here.

852. Septuagint, Psalms 64:1 (the same verse as in the preceding note; the different numbering reflecting the Hebrew vs. Greek verse divisions).

853. Pliny, *HN* 33.41.

84

854. Justinian, *Institutiones* 1.5.

855. Poliziano misunderstands the nomenclature of Roman laws: this one was carried in 19 CE under the consulship of M. Junius Silanus and L. Norbanus Balbus and hence bears both their names; cf. Groag, *RE* s.v. Norbanus 8.

856. Poliziano again misunderstands the designation: in fact, the law takes its name from the two consuls of 4 CE, Sextus Aelius Catus and C. Sentius Saturninus; cf. v. Rohden, *RE* s.v. Aelius 35.

85

857. Juvenal. 14.262–63.

858. Another implicit criticism of Merula, who commented laconically, *Cereris: Cerealia festa* ("of Ceres: the Cerealia festival"). Merula's spelling of the name of the festival is preferred (cf. *OLD* s.v.), though Poliziano spells *Ceri-*, which we retain for his text but not the English translation.

859. Tacitus, *Ann.* 15.53.

860. Tacitus, *Ann.* 15.74.

861. Ovid, *Fast.* 4.391–93. Poliziano cites this passage together with the two preceding ones from Tacitus on *Fast.* 3.786 (*Comm. Fast.*, p. 301).

862. Dio Cassius 43.51.3 (not Book 42). It is surprising that Poliziano takes this to be the creation of the aedileship, rather than its expansion; see further above, xx.

863. Dio Cassius 47.40.6.

864. Cf. *I* 43.1. Two silver coins have been identified as the possible basis of Poliziano's observation, *MRI* nos. 1352 and 1353, including the spelling *preimus*; see further Gionta, *Iconografia*, 35. *Preimus* is, however, a false archaism, given that the word takes its origin from **prīs-mos*; cf. M. Leumann, *Lateinische Laut- und Formenlehre* (Munich: Beck, 1977), 317.

865. On Memmius's praetorship in 58, cf. *MRR* 2:194. For his attacks on Caesar's relations with Nicomedes, king of Bithynia, cf. *ORF* no. 125 frr. 7–10, esp. 8 = Suetonius, *Jul.* 49.2.

866. Here Poliziano relies on a corrupt text: it should be "the consuls paired Domitius with him," reading *consules*, not *consulem*.

867. Cicero, *Att.* 4.15.7 (July 27, 54); Cicero explains the corrupt bargain at *Att.* 4.17.2.

868. Lucretius 1.26 and 42 and 5.8. The sparse references have given rise to the suspicion that Lucretius became disenchanted with this potential patron; if so, Memmius's plan to demolish Epicurus's house at Athens may have been a factor; cf. Cicero, *Fam.* 13.1.

869. The matter is more complex: the moneyer C. Memmius, who issued the coins of 56 BCE, was the nephew of the more famous C. Memmius, whose victory in Pontus in 58 is commemorated on one of them. The depiction of Ceres commemorates the first celebration of the Cerealia in or before 211 by a forebear of the moneyer; see *RRC* 451–52 with plates 427/1 and 2.

86

870. Ovid, *Tr.* 1.2.49–50.

871. Paulus, *Fest.* p. 62 Lindsay (*decumana ova*); Lucilius fr. 1217 Warmington.

872. Hyginus, in *Corpus Agrimensorum Romanorum*, ed. C. Thulin (Leipzig: Teubner, 1913), p. 132.13–17. Poliziano's view on the etymology is the one that prevails today; cf. O. A. W. Dilke, *The Roman Land Surveyors: An Introduction to the* agrimensores (New York: Barnes and Noble, 1971), 231–32. The derivation from *duo* is ancient (combatted by Frontinus, in *Corpus Agrimensorum*, ed. Thulin, pp. 11.15–12.2), but it is not clear why Poliziano attributes it to Nypsus, in whose extant work it does not appear; see M. Iunius Nypsus, *Fluminis variatio, limitis repositio*, ed. J. Bouma (Frankfurt am Main: Lang, 1993), index s.v. *decimanus*.

873. Ovid, *Met.* 11.530.

874. Silius Italicus, *Pun.* 14.121–23.

875. Seneca, *Agam.* 501–2.

876. Valerius Flaccus, *Argon.* 2.53–54.

877. Lucan, *B. civ.* 5.672–73.

87

878. Cicero, *Fam.* 7.16.1.

879. *I* 25.

880. Modern editors read φιλοθέωρον.

88

881. Vergil, *Aen.* 2.325. Poliziano does not, in fact, identify the source of the phrase, as he supposes, but offers parallels for euphemistically expressing a present state by reference to a past one that no longer obtains. Vergil's phrase is different in that an entire ethnic identity is negated, not just certain attributes.

882. Plutarch, *De se ipsum citra invidiam laudando* 15 = *Mor.* 544e.

883. *Sc.* of proverbs: Diogenianus 2.30.

884. Aristophanes, *Plut.* 1002, 1075; cf. Diogenianus 5.3.

885. Plutarch, *Cic.* 22.2.

89

886. For criticism of an erroneous explanation by Servius, cf. *I* 37 and 100.

887. Vergil, *Bucol.* 4.62–63.

888. Servius, *Comm. Bucol.* 4.62. Cf. the similar criticism of Calderini at *I* 75.1.

889. Quintilian, *Inst.* 1.7.27.

890. Valerius Flaccus, *Argon.* 7.129. The correct reading (*qui*) is first found in the second printed edition (Florence, 1491); cf. Ehlers's apparatus ad loc.

891. See further *II* 2 with notes.

892. Excerpted from Quintilian, *Inst.* 9.3.8–9. Quintilian's codices present *cui* in the quotation, but his context clearly implies *qui*, as Poliziano saw.

893. Quintilian, *Inst.* 1.7.20.

894. Homer, *Il.* 1.590–91; but Servius's account receives support from 18.395–97.

895. Homer, *Il.* 1.577–79; Hesiod, *Theog.* 927–28.

896. *Anth. Pal.* 15.26.7 (by Dosiadas, not Theocritus).

897. Varro, *Antiq. rerum div.* fr. 229 Cardauns *apud* August., *De civ. D.* 7.2 (actually, Varro counts him as eighth among the select gods).

898. Saloninus was the son of C. Asinius Pollio, a name commemorating his father's capture of Salona in Dalmatia; see Servius, *Comm. Bucol.* 4.1. He died in infancy.

899. Persius 2.3.

900. Servius, *Comm. Bucol.* 4.63 (= p. 88, col. I, ll. 5–8 Thilo-Hagen); Poliziano found the attribution to Philargyrius in BML, Plut. 45.14; see Thilo-Hagen, xi.

901. Cf. Varro, *Catus vel De pueris educandis*, fr. X p. 249 Riese = Nonius, *De comp. doct.* 155 Lindsay s.v. *Edusam* [sic] *et Potinam.*

902. Donatus, *Comm. Ter. Phorm.* 49.

903. Aristotle, *Part. an.* 673a8.

904. Ennius, *Ann. op. inc.* 18 Skutsch = *FRL* 8 cited by Cicero, *Amic.* 6.22.

905. Augustine, *De civ. D.* 6.9 (naming only Educa and Potina).

906. Varro, *De vita populi Romani* 2, fr. 81 Riposati = Nonius, *De comp. doct.* p. 848 Lindsay. Here Poliziano errs both in citing Martianus (Capella) instead of Nonius and in citing *De vita patrum*, rather than *De vita populi Romani.*

907. Pliny, *HN* 2.16 (not the first book).

908. Seneca, *Ep.* 110.1.

909. Juvenal 2.98.

910. Petronius, 25.4–6; for the proverbial phrase, cf. Otto s.v. *taurus* 1.

911. Poliziano seems to sense that his negative case is stronger than his positive one. His service here is to have corrected Quintilian's quotation of *Bucol.* 4.62 to *qui* from *cui*, against Quintilian's codices but inferred

from his context. This move makes an ancient variant available. Modern editors accept *qui* but emend *parentes* to *parenti* (J. Schrader), since *ridere* + acc. should mean "laugh at." Poliziano's application of the lore of the tutelary *genius* and *iuno* has not found favor, however. For discussion, cf. W. Clausen, *A Commentary on Virgil: Eclogues* (Oxford: Clarendon Press, 1994), 144.

90

912. This chapter has been edited with an English translation in Monfasani, "Angelo Poliziano." The notes here are indebted to this study.

913. Symmachus, *Epist.* 1.14.2.

914. Lucilius fr. 632–34 Warmington *apud* Pliny, *HN* Praef. 7; cf. fr. 635 Warmington, cited by Cicero, *De or.* 2.6.25 and *Fin.* 1.3.7.

915. On the relation of Giovanni and his nephew Gianfrancesco Pico della Mirandola with the Medici at this period, cf. Patrizia Salvadori, "I signori della Mirandola, Firenze e i Medici," in P. Viti, *Pico, Poliziano,* 287–302.

916. Cf. Vergil, *Aen.* 7.625–26; *arma requirunt. / pars levis clipeos et spicula lucida tergent*; Horace, *Carm.* 1.35.38–39: *nova incude* ("new anvil").

917. Ermolao Barbaro (b. Venice 1454, died of plague at Rome 1493); the *Castigationes Plinianae* date from 1492; Poliziano praises his learning at *II* 20.1 and laments his death at *II* 5.2. See further V. Branca, "L'umanismo veneziano alla fine del Quattrocentro: Ermolao Barbaro e il suo circolo," in *Storia della cultura veneta* 3/1 (Vicenza: N. Pozza, 1980), 123–75; on his method, cf. Pozzi in Barbaro, *Castigationes,* 1:lxi–xcvi, esp. xcv–xcvi. Poliziano assumes the ancient complaint of the "poverty of the native [Latin] language" (Lucretius 1.832, 3.260). Monfasani, "Angelo Poliziano," 249, notes Poliziano's emphasis on the Latin form of the contribution of both Pico and Barbaro.

918. Poliziano, *Epist.* 2.11 = *Letters,* ed. Butler, ITRL 21, 120–23 = *Opera Omnia* 1:25 (from Donà, dated June 8, 1485). The poem appears to be the modified version of Theocritus, *Id.* 9.33–35 cited in the letter. The three men to whose judgment Poliziano appeals in this passage play the same

role of "literary triumvirate" (*triumviris . . . litterariis*) at *Epist.* 2.10 = *Letters*, ed. Butler, ITRL 21, 119.

919. Cf. *I* 77. Monfasani, "Angelo Poliziano," 246, suggests that this refers to Bartolomeo Fonzio, who is known to have criticized Poliziano prior to publication of *Misc. I*.

920. Jerome, *Hebr. quaest. in Gen.*, Praef. *sub fin.* = CCL 72, p. 2.16–17.

921. A native of Thessaloniki, Theodore Gaza (1408/10–75) went to study in Constantinople, where he made the acquaintance of Filelfo and other Italians, contacts that paved the way for his immigration to Italy, where he pursued a varied career in teaching and translation; see further C. Bianca's entry on him in *DBI* s.v. Gaza, Teodoro. He translated [Aristotle], *Problemata* in 1453–54; cf. Monfasani, *George of Trebizond*, 150 n. 79.

922. *Sc.* Problem 30.

923. Paraphrase of [Aristotle], *Problemata* 953a10–21.

924. That is, detached from a noun.

925. Cf. Wilson, *From Byzantium*, 121: "Politian saw that the transmitted text must be adjusted so as to include a reference to Mount Oeta, which can be achieved by the addition of two letters. His idea is confirmed by the best manuscripts, which seem not to have been available at the time."

926. Benjamin the Younger, from Hilary of Poitier, *Tractatus super Psalmos* 67.27 = CSEL 22.302.20 (per Monfasani).

927. Psalms 30:23, 67:28.

928. Cicero, *Tusc.* 4.8.19.

929. Poliziano's critique is on target; cf. Monfasani, "George of Trebizond's Critique," 286, who points out that Gaza "completely ignores the fact that the text is supposed to be about Hercules and not some vague group of children or ulcers in general."

930. Pietro de Abano (d. 1316), translator of [Aristotle] *Problemata* and other works.

931. That is, his attempt to harmonize philosophy and medicine: *Conciliatio differentiarum philosophorum et medicorum* (Mantua: Septemcastrensis & Burster, 1472).

932. The game of draughts was played on a board divided into twelve sections (hence referred to here as *duodecim scripta*). On permission to withdraw a play, cf. Cicero, *Hortensius* fr. 32 Grilli.

933. Poliziano's phrase derives from Varro, *Rust.* 1.2.24.

934. Cf. Cicero, *Off.* 1.41.147, who recommends consulting those who are learned or have practical experience (*usu peritos*).

935. Catullus 22.21.

936. *Aristotelis et Theophrasti Historiae* (Lugduni: apud Gulielmum Rouillium, 1552), p. 4 of Theodore's preface to Pope Nicholas V: "Fuit quidem studium mihi certandi, non cum interpretibus illis, quos vincere nullum negocium est, sed cum Aristotele ipso" ("I was keen to compete, not with those translators, whom it is easy to defeat, but with Aristotle himself").

937. Aristotle, *De animalibus*, translated by George of Trebizond in 1452 (cf. Garin, "Le traduzioni," 77), published Venice, 1476.

938. George of Trebizond, *Collectanea Trapezuntiana: Texts, Documents and Bibliographies of George of Trebizond*, ed. John Monfasani (Binghamton: State University of New York, Medieval and Renaissance Texts and Studies 25, 1984), 299 §4.

939. Gaza's claim, in the same passage cited above; his *De mensibus* was published in 1470; cf. M. V. Anastos, "Pletho's Calendar and Liturgy," *Dumbarton Oaks Papers* 4 (1948): 183–305, at 190. Cf. George of Trebizond, *Collectanea Trapezuntiana*, 299–300 §§6–7.

940. The word is not found in printed editions of Gaza's *Grammar* but is in some manuscripts of the work; possibly it was deleted by Gaza himself before publication; see further Monfasani, "Angelo Poliziano," 250–51 and n. 30.

941. A ninth-century Byzantine grammarian; see further R. Browning in *ODB* s.v.

942. On Gaza's manipulations of the text of the *Problemata*, his dispute with George of Trebizond, and Poliziano's attitude, cf. Monfasani, *Greeks and Latins*, VI, at 206–11 and 240 n. 49–50. On the evidence of our passage, Poliziano must have been familiar with George's more accurate rendering (in BML, Plut. 89 sup. 84; see Garin, "Le traduzioni," 80 n. 1),

published in 1476 (see above); for a different view, see J. Monfasani, *Greek Scholars between East and West in the Fifteenth Century* (Farnham and Burlington: Ashgate, 2016), XIII, 277–78. Poliziano may, however, be unfair in assuming that Gaza knew the commentary George had produced, but not yet published, the year before he started on his own.

943. Vergil, *Bucol.* 6.9–10.

944. Poliziano, *Liber Epigrammatm graecorum* 13, in *Greek and Latin Poetry*, ed. Knox, ITRL 86, 198. Greek epigrams 15 and 16 also celebrate Gaza, as well as nos. 71–72 in his book of Latin epigrams.

91

945. Theodore Gaza, *M. Tulli Ciceronis liber De senectute in graecum translatus*, ed. I. Salanitro (Leipzig: Teubner, 1987), p. 37.24.

946. Ennius, *Annales* 308 Skutsch, cited by Cicero, *Sen.* 14.50, where see Powell's note.

947. Cicero, *Brut.* 15.59.

948. He thus performs a service on the Greek side corresponding to the reconstruction of Ennius's *Medea* at I 27. For the metaphor of a shipwreck, cf. A. C. Dionisotti, "On Fragments in Classical Scholarship," in Most, *Collecting Fragments*, 1–33, at 26–28. The metaphor of reconstitution from *disiecta membra* reappears at II 1.1 and 31.2.

949. Eupolis, Δῆμοι, PCG F 102.

950. Aristides, *Orat.* 3.51 (p. 309.9 Lenz-Behr); *Scholia graeca in Aristides*, ed. W. Dindorf (Leipzig: G. Reimer, 1829), 3:472.29; Pliny the Younger, *Ep.* 1.20.17. Poliziano stands out from contemporaries by his care in delineating the intermediate sources used; cf. Grafton, "The Scholarship," 161–62.

951. Horace, *Epist.* 1.6.38.

952. Porphyrio, *Comm. Hor. Epist.* 1.6.38.

953. Cicero, *De or.* 3.34.138.

954. Quintilian, *Inst.* 10.1.82.

955. Martianus Capella 9.888 (*Suada*); 9.906 (*Pitho*).

956. Poliziano, *Manto* 307 (*Suada*); *Nutricia* (not *Ambra*) 506 (*Lepos*).

92

957. Livy 6.6.14, where see Oakley's note.

958. Ulpian, *Digest* 3.2.2.2.

93

959. *Illustris* and *antecessor* are formal titles for senators and law professors, respectively (see further *ODB* s.vv.); the latter is discussed in detail at *II* 56.

960. *Digest, Constitutio 'Omnem'* 5.

961. See *I* 41.

962. This is now Poliziano's third dig at the hapless Accursio; see above, *I* 78 and 82.

963. *Digest, Constitio 'Omnem'* 2. Poliziano returns to the topic at *II* 58, explaining the meanings of the names.

964. *Digest, Constitutio 'Omnem'* 11.

965. Homer, *Il.* 6.236.

94

966. Severianus, *In mundi creationem orat.* 3 in *PG* 56.448–49 (Joannes Chrysostomus).

967. The metaphor is drawn from the racecourse, the barriers (*carceres*) being the starting point, with the finishing line at the end of the day.

968. For the Arcadians' claim to be older than the moon, see, for example, Aristotle, fr. 591 Rose; Ovid, *Fast.* 5.89–90; Plutarch, *Quaest. Rom.* 76 = *Mor.* 282a; Lucian, *Astr.* 26; *Scholia Ar. Nubes* 398c; and *Scholia Ap. Rhod. Argon.* 4.263–64b.

95

969. *Digest* 1.16.6.3.

96

970. Martial 11.29.3 (not Book 7).

971. For the sparrow, see I 6.

972. Cratinus, *Drapetides*, CPG F 58.

973. Epicrates, CPG F 8; the Girl (Kore) and Phersephatta (Persephone) are two names for the same goddess, mocking the speaker's ignorance.

974. Philemon, CPG F 65; Aelian, *NA* 12.10.

97

975. Suetonius, *Claud.* 34.2.

976. The San Marco codex is plausibly identified as BML, Plut. 68.7 (Kaster's L, 12th century, 2nd half), Poliziano's own codex as BML, Plut. 64.8 (Kaster's F, 12th century, 2nd half); the Bolognese codex remains unidentified. See further Fera, *Una ignota*, 33–50. The Library of San Domenico was the library of the Dominican order, which had responsibility for teaching theology in the University of Bologna.

977. Homer, *Il.* 2.408.

978. Eustathius, *Comm. Hom. Il.* 247.28 on *Il.* 2.408 (the editor, M. van der Valk, cites examples ad loc. from Menander).

979. Ibid.

980. Hero, *Pneumatica* 1.10 and 16.

98

981. Persius 5.175 (not the sixth satire).

982. Plutarch, *De sera numinis vindicta* 4 = *Mor.* 550b. There is a bare reference to Plutarch ("as in the margin of the manuscript") at *Comm. Pers.*, 121, where the point about the lictors assigned to praetors also appears.

983. Plautus, *Mil.* 961.

984. Persius, 5.78–79. "Marcus Dama," that is, with a new *praenomen*; cf. *I* 31.4.

985. Seneca, *Ep.* 8.7.

99

986. Suetonius, *Ner.* 25.1.

987. Plutarch, *Quaest. conv.* 2.5.2 = *Mor.* 639e.

100

988. Vergil, *Aen.* 2.255.

989. Vergil, *Aen.* 2.340.

990. Vergil, *Aen.* 2.397.

991. Servius, *Comm. Aen.* 2.255.

992. Theophrastus, *De musica* lib. 2, F 716.63 Fortenbaugh, *apud* Porphyry, *In Ptol. Harm* 1.3.

993. Macrobius, *In somn.* 1.19.3 and 2.4.4; Plato, *Tim.* 38d–39a, *Resp.* 617a–b.

994. Aristotle, *De caelo* 2.10 (291a29–b10).

995. Simplicius, *In lib. De caelo* (CAG 7) 474.7–75.8, citing Alexander's views.

996. Pliny, *HN* 16.190.

997. Pliny, *HN* 18.314.

998. Cato, *De re rustica* 29, 40.1, 50.1.

999. As in the discussion of the spelling *Virgil* vs. *Vergil* (*I* 77), Poliziano sets the phenomena firmly into an historical context that eliminates the competing hypothesis.

1000. Vergil, *Aen.* 2.340.

1001. Poliziano, *Rusticus* 461.

1002. Cicero, *Div.* 2.34.71.

1003. Horace, *Carm.* 3.30.8–9 (not Book 2).

1004. [Acro], *Comm. Hor. Carm.* 3.30.9.

1005. Dionysius of Halicarnassus., *Ant. Rom* 2.66.6; Plutarch, *Cam.* 20.6.

[EPILOGUE]

1006. Godman, *From Poliziano*, 92, thinks that the rumors of plagiarism were circulated by Poliziano's friends. This conclusion is not inevitable, however: certainly, his friends were the ones shown the manuscript, but Beroaldo was privy to the plan (below, §8), and word of its existence could well have leaked to members of the general public. The only friend known to have been familiar with *Misc. I* prior to publication is Pico, who was hardly the soul of discretion (cf. *I* 80.3 and 68.3). Since the rumor served to enhance the reputation of Perotti and reduce that of Poliziano, supporters of the former might have been expected to circulate it.

1007. Niccolò Perotti (1429–80), *Cornu copiae seu linguae Latinae commentarii*, a vast commentary on Martial completed in 1478 but not published until after his death in 1489; it is now available in the eight-volume edition prepared by J.-L. Charlet and M. Fumo (Sassoferrata: Istituto internazionale di studi piceni, 1989–2001). Cf. F. Stok, *Studi sul Cornucopiae di Niccolò Perotti* (Pisa: ETS, 2002); M. Pade, "Niccolò Perotti's *Cornu copiae*: Commentary on Martial and Encyclopedia," in M. Pade (ed.), *On Renaissance Commentaries* (Hildesheim: Olms, 2005), 49–63.

1008. This looks like a reframing, with addition of plausible political details, of the feud carried on during their lifetimes by Perotti and Calderini that issued in Calderini's defense against charges of plagiarism: *Defensio cum recriminatione in calumniatorem commentariorum Martialis* (Rome, 1474).

1009. Aesop, *Fabulae Aesopicae* 103.

1010. Licentius, *Carmen Licentii ad Augustinum praeceptorem* v. 20 *apud* Augustine, *Ep.* 26 (*Ad Licentium*).

1011. Cf. Horace, *Epist.* 2.1.123: "he lives on pods and second-rate bread."

1012. On Poliziano's relations with Ficino, cf. V. Branca, "Tra Ficino 'Orfeo ispirato' e Poliziano 'Ercole ironico,'" in *Marsilio Ficino e il ritorno di*

Platone. Studi e documenti, ed. G. C. Garfagnini (Florence: Olschki, 1986), 459–75; for a brief overview, Orvieto, *Poliziano*, 69–74.

1013. Homer, *Il.* 2–5, rendered into Latin in the 1470s at the request of Lorenzo de' Medici (= *Opera* 2:431–523).

1014. That is, hastily, for fear of crocodiles: Phaedrus 1.25.3–4.

1015. Poliziano's exile in Emilia, Lombardy, the Veneto, and Mantua (1479–80) resulted from a quarrel with Clarice, wife of Lorenzo the Magnificent, over his methods as tutor of young Piero; cf. Giovanni Battista Picotti, *Ricerche umanistiche* (Florence: Nuova Italia, 1955), esp. 45–47 and 77 (Poliziano's *apologia*); more briefly Tateo, *Lorenzo de' Medici*, 136.

1016. This passage might perhaps be adduced in support of the thesis of A. Lee, *The Ugly Renaissance* (London: Hutchinson, 2013), 3–4, that Poliziano and Pico were lovers.

1017. Plato, *Resp.* 350d.

1018. Cf. Ovid, *Met.* 4.55–166.

1019. Cf. *Misc. I* 10.5; Perotti, *Cornu copiae*, on Martial 1.6.258 and 276.

1020. Cf. *Misc. I* 52; Perotti, *Cornu copiae*, on Martial 1.1.77 (referring the phrase to the temple of Ammon).

1021. Cf. *Misc. I* 72; Perotti, *Cornu copiae* on Martial 1.3.370 (deriving *folia* from *philurae*).

1022. Beroaldo, *Annotationes*. For a possible dispute over priority between Beroaldo and Poliziano, see on *I* 81.

1023. A reference to Beroaldo, *Annotationes* 32.8, to which he also alludes in his manuscript comments on Beroaldo's book; cf. Lo Monaco, "Polizano e Beroaldo," 156. Poliziano may have mentioned his plan for the *Miscellanea* when Beroaldo visited him on Easter 1486, but that need not imply that he borrowed the idea of the *Annotationes centum* from Poliziano; cf. the editor Ciapponi on Beroaldo, *Annotationes*, 17.

1024. The lectures on the *Fasti* occurred in the academic year 1481–82, those on Horace's *Satires* 1484–85; cf. Maïer, *Ange Politien*, 424 and 426.

1025. On the mock solemnity of this passage, cf. Krautter, "Angelo Poliziano als Kritiker," 316.

1026. Cicero, *Acad.* 1.18; *Fam.* 9.18.4.

1027. The accusation of plagiarism is muted here in contrast to Poliziano's angry first reaction to Beroaldo's book, *In Annotationes Beroaldi*, a copy of which is preserved in Munich, Bayerische Staatsbibliothek, ms. Clm 754; see further Ciapponi on Beroaldo, *Annotationes* 25–28; Lo Monaco, "Poliziano e Beroaldo."

1028. Jerome, *Comm. in Eccl.* 1.9/10 (*CCSL* 72.257.232–34), quoting his former teacher Donatus and citing Terence's remark that nothing is now said that has not already been said (*Eunuchus* 41).

1029. Euripides, *Or.* 735.

Bibliography

༖ຉ༖

EDITIONS AND TRANSLATIONS OF
POLIZIANO'S WORKS

COMMENTARIES ON CLASSICAL TEXTS

Appunti per un corso sull'Odissea. Editio princeps dal Par. gr. 3069. Edited by Luigi Silvano. Hellenica 37. Alessandria: Edizioni dell'Orso, 2010.

La commedia antica e l'Andria di Terenzio: Appunti inediti. Edited by Rosetta Lattanzi Roselli. Istituto Nazionale di Studi sul Rinascimento, Studi e testi, 3. Florence: Leo S. Olschki, 1973.

"Il Commento del Poliziano al carmine [Ausonii] *De rosis.*" Edited by Manlio Pastore Stocchi. In *Miscellanea di studi in onore di Vittore Branca,* vol. 3, *Umanesimo e Rinascimento a Firenze e Venezia,* 397–422. Florence: Leo S. Olschki, 1983.

Commento inedito all'Epistola ovidiana di Saffo a Faone. Edited by Elisabetta Lazzeri. Istituto Nazionale di Studi sul Rinascimento, Studi e testi, 2. Florence: Leo S. Olschki, 1973.

Commento inedito ai Fasti di Ovidio. Edited by Francesco Lo Monaco. Istituto Nazionale di Studi sul Rinascimento, Studi e testi, 23. Florence: Leo S. Olschki, 1991.

Commento inedito alle Georgiche di Virgilio. Edited by Livia Castano Musicò. Istituto Nazionale di Studi sul Rinascimento, Studi e testi, 18. Florence: Leo S. Olschki, 1990.

Commento inedito alle Satire di Persio. Edited by Lucia Cesarini Martinelli and Roberto Ricciardi. Istituto Nazionale di Studi sul Rinascimento, Studi e testi, 11. Florence: Leo S. Olschki, 1985.

Commento inedito alle Selve di Stazio. Edited by Lucia Cesarini Martinelli. Istituto Nazionale di Studi sul Rinascimento, Studi e testi, 5. Florence: Leo S. Olschki, 1978.

Una ignota Expositio Suetoni *del Poliziano.* Edited by Vincenzo Fera. Messina: Centro di Studi Umanistici, 1983.

OTHER WORKS

Della Congiura dei Pazzi (Coniurationis Commentarium). Edited by Alessandro Perosa. Miscellanea erudite, 3. Padua: Antenore, 1958.

Liber epigrammatum graecorum. Edited by Filippomaria Pontani. Edizione nazionale dei testi umanistice, 5. Rome: Edizioni di Storia e Letteratura, 2002.

Greek and Latin Poetry. Edited and Translated by Peter A. Knox. I Tatti Renaissance Library 86. Cambridge, MA: Harvard University Press, 2018.

Lamia: Praelectio in Priora Aristotelis Analytica. Edited by Ari Wesseling. Leiden: Brill, 1986.

Lamia: Text, Translation, and Introductory Studies. Edited by Christopher S. Celenza. Leiden and Boston: Brill, 2010.

Letters. Vol. 1: Books I–IV. Edited and translated by Shane Butler. I Tatti Renaissance Library 21. Cambridge, MA: Harvard University Press, 2006.

Miscellaneorum centuria prima. Florence: Antonius Miscominus, 1489.

Miscellaneorum centuria prima Angeli Politiani. Edited by Hideo Katayama, in idem, "A Study of the *Miscellanea*" [in Japanese], in *Gogaku Bungaku Ronbunshu* [*Research Report, Faculty of Literature, University of Tokyo*], 7 (1981 [1982]): 167–428.

Miscellaneorum centuria secunda. Edited by Vittore Branca and Manlio Pastore Stocchi. 4 vols. Florence: Fratelli Alinari Istituto di edizioni artistiche, 1972.

Miscellaneorum centuria secunda. Editio minor. Edited by Vittore Branca and Manlio Pastore Stocchi. Florence: Leo S. Olschki, 1978. Photo-reprint in smaller format of previous.

Opera omnia et alia quaedam lectu digna. Venice: Aldus Manutius, 1498.

Opera omnia. Edited by Ida Maïer. 3 vols. Turin: Bottega d'Erasmos, 1970–71.

Oratio in expositione Homeri. Edited by Paola Megna. Edizione nazionale dei testi umanistici, 7. Rome: Edizioni di Storia e Letteratura, 2007.

L'Orfeo del Poliziano, con il testo critico dell'originale e delle successive forme teatrali. Edited by Antonia Tissoni Benvenuti. Padua: Antenore, 1986.

Rime. Edited by Daniela Delcorno Branca. Florence: Presso l'Accademia della Crusca, 1986.

Les silves. Texte traduit et commenté. Edited by Perrine Galand. Paris: Les Belles Lettres, 1987.

Silvae. Edited by Franceso Bausi. Istituto Nazionale di Studi sul Rinascimento, Studi e testi, 39. Florence: Leo S. Olschki, 1996.

Silvae. Translated by Charles Fantazzi. I Tatti Renaissance Library 14. Cambridge, MA: Harvard University Press, 2004.

Stanze, Fabula di Orfeo. Edited by Stefano Carrai. Milan: Mursia, 1988.

Sylva in scabiem. Edited by Alessandro Perosa. Rome: Edizioni di Storia e Letteratura, 1954.

SECONDARY LITERATURE

Baños, Pedro Martín. "De *Virgilius* a *Vergilius*: Poliziano y la bibliografía de Antonio de Nebrija." *Revista de filología española.* 87, no. 1 (2007): 79–102.

Barbaro, Ermolao. *Castigationes Plinianae.* Edited by Giovanni Pozzi. 4 vols. Padua: Antenori, 1973–79.

Bigi, Emilio. "Ambrogini, Angelo." *DBI* s.v.

——— . *La cultura del Poliziano e altri studi umanistici.* Pisa: Nistri-Lischi, 1967.

Branca, Vittore. "Datazione della seconda centuria dei *Miscellanea* di Angelo Poliziano." In *Italian Studies presented to E. R. Vincent,* edited by C. P. Brand, K. Foster, and U. Limentani, 92–100. Cambridge: W. Heffer and Sons, 1962.

——— . "La incompiuta seconda centuria dei Miscellanea di Angelo Poliziano." *Lettere italiane* 13 (1961): 137–77.

——— . *Poliziano e l'umanesimo della parola.* Turin: Einaudi, 1983.

——— . "Il Poliziano nello Studio fiorentino: nuove notizie e nuovi dati." In *Mélanges offertes à Julien Cain,* 2:181–86. Paris: Hermann, 1968.

Branca, Vittore, and Manlio Pastore Stocchi. "La Biblioteca Vaticana nella *Seconda Centuria* dei *Miscellanea* di Angelo Poliziano." In *Mélanges Eugène Tisserant,* 6:141–59. Vatican City: Bibliotheca Apostolica Vaticana, 1964.

Calderini, Domizio. *Commentarioli in Ibyn Ovidii.* Edited by Luca Carlo Rossi. Florence: Edizioni del Galluzzo, 2011.

Campanelli, Maurizio. "Angelo Poliziano e gli antichi manoscritti di Marziale." *Interpres* 17 (1998): 281–308.

_____. *Polemiche e filologia ai primordi della stampa: Le* Observationes *di Domizio Calderini*. Rome: Edizioni di Storia e Letteratura, 2001.

Cesarini Martinelli, Lucia. "De poesi et poetis: uno schedario sconosciuto di Angelo Poliziano." In *Tradizione classica e letteratura umanistica: Per Alessandro Perosa*, edited by R. Cardini, E. Garin, L. Cesarini Martinelli, G. Pascucci, 455–87. Rome: Bulzoni, 1985. Photo-reprint in *Umanesimo e filologia*.

———. "In margine al commento di Angelo Poliziano alle *Selve* di Stazio." *Interpres* 1 (1978): 96–145. Photo-reprint in *Umanesimo e filologia*.

———. *Umanesimo e filologia*. Edited by Sebastiano Gentile. Clavis 3. Pisa: Edizioni della Normale, 2016.

Ciapponi, Lucia A. "Bartolomeo Fonzio e la prima centuria dei *Miscellanea* del Poliziano." *Italia medioevale e umanistica* 23 (1980): 165–77.

Cottrell, Alan. "Renaissance Codicology: Poliziano's Early Practice of a Modern Discipline." *Manuscripta* 41, no. 2 (July 1997): 110–26.

Dane, Joseph A. "*Si vis archetypas habere nugas*: Authorial Subscriptions in the Houghton Library and Huntington Library Copies of Politian, *Miscellanea* (Florence: Miscomini 1489)." Harvard Library Bulletin, n.s. 10.1 (Spring 1999): 12–22.

Daneloni, Alessandro. *Poliziano e il testo dell'*Institutio Oratoria. Messina: Università degli studi di Messina, Centro interdipartimentale di studi umanistici, 2001.

Dionisotti, Carlo. "Calderini, Poliziano e altri." *Italia medioevale e umanistica* 11 (1968): 151–85.

Dunston, John. "Studies in Domizio Calderini." *Italia medioevale e umanistica* 11 (1968): 71–150.

Fera, Vincenzo. "Il dibattito umanistico sui *Miscellanea*." In Fera and Martelli, *Agnolo Poliziano*, 333–59.

———. "Tra Poliziano e Beroaldo: L'ultimo scritto filologico di Giorgio Merula." *Studi umanistici* 2 (1991): 7–41.

Fera, Vincenzo, and Mario Martelli, eds. *Agnolo Poliziano, poeta, scrittore, filologo*. Atti del Convegno Internazionale di Studi Montepulciano, 3–6 novembre 1994. Florence: Le Lettere, 1998.

Fiaschi, Silvia. "Traduzioni dal greco nei *Miscellanea*: Percorsi di reflessione." In P. Viti, *Cultura e filologia*, 33–50.

Fryde, E. B. *Humanism and Renaissance Historiography*. London: Hambledon Press, 1983.

Gaisser, Julia Haig. *Catullus and His Renaissance Readers*. Oxford: Clarendon Press, 1993.

Gardenal, Gianna. *Il Poliziano e Suetonio: Contributo alla storia della filologia umanistica*. Facoltà di lettere e filosofia, Università di Padova. Vol. 53. Padua: Leo S. Olschki, 1975.

Garin, Eugenio. "L'ambiente del Poliziano." In *Poliziano e il suo tempo*, 2–39.

——. "Ενδελέχεια e Έντελέχεια nelle discussione umanistiche." *Atene e Roma* 3 (1937): 177–87.

——. "Le traduzioni umanistiche di Aristotele nel secolo XV." *Atti e Memorie dell' Accademia Fiorentina di Scienze Morali La Colombaria* 16 (1947–50): 55–104.

Geanakoplos, Deno John. *Greek Scholars in Venice*. Cambridge, MA: Harvard University Press, 1962.

Gionta, Daniela. *Iconografia erodianea. Poliziano e le monete di Lorenzo*. Progetto Poliziano: Cultura e Contesto, 1. Messina: Università degli studi di Messina, Centro interdipartimentale di studi umanistici, 2008.

Godman, Peter. *From Poliziano to Machiavelli: Florentine Humanism in the High Renaissance*. Princeton: Princeton University Press, 1998.

——. "Poliziano's Poetics and Literary History." *Interpres* 13 (1993): 110–209.

Grafton, A. *Defenders of the Text: The Traditions of Scholarship in an Age of Science, 1450–1800*. Cambridge, MA: Harvard University Press, 1991.

——. *Joseph Scaliger: A Study in the History of Classical Scholarship*. Vol. 1, *Textual Criticism and Exegesis*. Vol. 2, *Historical Chronology*. Oxford: Clarendon Press, 1983–93.

——. "Joseph Scaliger's Edition of Catullus and the Traditions of Textual Criticism in the Renaissance." *Journal of the Warburg and Courtauld Institutes* 38 (1975): 155–81.

——. "On the Scholarship of Politian and Its Context." *Journal of the Warburg and Courtauld Institute* 40 (1977): 150–88.

Grazzini, Stefano. "Osservazioni sulla *Lectura Iuvenalis* di Poliziano." In P. Viti, *Cultura e filologia*: 153–76.

Hankins, James. "The Dates of Leonardo Bruni's Later Works (1437–1443)." *Studi medievali e umanistici* 5–6 (2007–8): 11–48.

Hunt, Jonathan. *Politian and Scholastic Logic: An Unknown Dialogue by a Dominican Friar*. Florence: Leo S. Olschki, 1995.

——. "Three New Incunables with Marginalia by Politian." *Rinascimento* 24 (1984): 251–59.

Juren, Vladimir. "Les notes de Politien sur les Lettres de Cicéron à Brutus, Quintus et Atticus." *Rinascimento* 28 (1988): 234–56.

Koortbojian, Michael. "Poliziano's Role in the History of Antiquarianism and the Rise of Archaeological Methods." In Secchi Tarugi, *Poliziano*, 265–73.

Krautter, Konrad. "Angelo Poliziano als Kritiker von Filippo Beroaldo." *Res Publica Litterarum* 4 (1981): 315–30.

——. "Der 'grammaticus' Poliziano in der Auseinandersetzung mit zeitgenössischen Humanisten. Zur Entwicklung der Philologie aus den 'studia humanitatis.'" In *Die Antike-Rezeption in den Wissenschaften während der Renaissance*, edited by August Buck and Klaus Heitmann, 103–16. Weinheim: Verlag Chemie, 1983.

Kraye, Jill. "Cicero, Stoicism and Textual Criticism: Poliziano on Κατόρθωμα." *Rinascimento*, series 2, 23 (1983): 79–110. Reprinted in eadem, *Classical Traditions in Renaissance Philosophy*. Variorum Collected Studies Series (Aldershot and Burlington, VT, 2002), no. II.

Lo Monaco, Francesco. "On the Prehistory of Politian's *Miscellaneorum centuria secunda*." *Journal of the Warburg and Courtauld Institutes* 52 (1989): 52–70.

——. "Poliziano e Beroaldo. Le *In Annotationes Beroaldi* del Poliziano." *Rinascimento*, series 2, 32 (1992): 103–65.

Maïer, Ida. *Ange Politien: La formation d'un poète humaniste (1469–1480)*. Travaux d'Humanisme et Renaissance, 81. Geneva: Librarie Droz, 1966.

——. *Les Manuscrits d'Ange Politien. Catalogue descriptif*. Travaux d'Humanisme et Renaissance, 70. Geneva: Librairie Droz, 1965.

Martelli, Mario. *Angelo Poliziano: Storia e metastoria*. Lecce: Conte, 1995.

———. "La semantica di Poliziano e la *Centuria Secunda* dei *Miscellanea*." *Rinascimento*, series 2, 13 (1973): 21–84. Reprinted in idem, *Angelo Poliziano: Storia e metastoria*.

Megna, Paola. *Le note del Poliziano alla traduzione dell'Iliade*. Progetto Poliziano: L'Opera, 1. Messina: Università degli studi di Messina, Centro interdipartimentale di studi umanistici, 2009.

———. "Per la fortuna umanistica di Quinto Smirneo." *Medioevo Greco: Rivista di storia e filologia bizantina* 14 (2014): 121–62.

———. *Poliziano e la storiografia bizantina: il cap. LVIII dei primi Miscellanea*. Progetto Poliziano: L'Opera, 2. Messina: Università degli studi di Messina, Centro interdipartimentale di studi umanistici, 2012.

Monfasani, John. "Angelo Poliziano, Aldo Manuzio, Theodore Gaza, George of Trebizond, and Chapter 90 of the *Miscellaneorum Centuria Prima* (with an edition and translation)." In *Interpretations of Renaissance Humanism*, edited by Angelo Mazzocco, 242–65. Leiden-Boston: Brill, 2006. Reprinted in idem, *Renaissance Humanism, from the Middle Ages to Modern Times*. Variorum Collected Studies Series. Farnham, Surrey: Ashgate, 2015, item VIII.

———. *George of Trebizond: A Biography and a Study of His Rhetoric and Logic*. Leiden: Brill, 1976.

———. "George of Trebizond's Critique of Theodore Gaza's Translation of the Aristotelian *Problemata*." In *Aristotle's* Problemata *in Different Times and Tongues*. Leuven: Mediaevalia Lovaniensia ser. 1, v. 29, 2006: 275–94.

———. *Greeks and Latins in Renaissance Italy: Studies on Humanism and Philosophy in the Fifteenth Century*. Aldershot: Ashgate, 2004.

Most, Glenn W., ed. *Collecting Fragments/Fragmente sammeln*. Aporemata, 1. Göttingen: Vanderhoeck & Ruprecht, 1997.

Orvieto, Paolo. *Poliziano e l'ambiente Mediceo*. Rome: Salerno Editrice, 2009.

Perosa, Alessandro. "Codici di Galeno postillati di Poliziano." In *Umanesimo e Rinascimento. Studi offerti a Paul Oskar Kristeller*, 75–109. Florence: Leo S. Olschki, 1980.

———. *Un commento inedito all'Ambra del Poliziano*. Rome: Bulzoni, 1994.

———. *Studi di filologia umanistica: I. Angelo Poliziano.* Edited by Paolo Viti. Rome: Edizioni di Storia e Letteratura, 2000.

Perosa, Alessandro, and Sebastiano Timpanaro. "Libanio (o Coricio), Poliziano e Leopardi." *Studi Italiani di Filologia Classica* 27–28 (1956): 411–25.

Perotto Sali, Laura. "L'opusculo inedito di Giorgio Merula contro i *Miscellanea* di Angelo Poliziano." *Interpres* 1 (1978): 146–83.

Pesenti, Giovanni. "Diario odeporico-bibliografico inedito del Poliziano." *Memorie R. Istituto Lombardo di Scienze e Lettere* 23 (1916): 229–39.

Pfeiffer, Rudolph. *History of Classical Scholarship.* Vol. 1, *From the Beginnings to the End of the Hellenistic Age.* Vol. 2, *From 1300 to 1850.* Oxford: Clarendon Press, 1968–76.

Pico della Mirandola, Giovanni. *Opera omnia.* 2 vols. Basel: Heinrich Petri, 1572–73. Reprint, Hildesheim: Olms, 1969.

Pighi, Giovanni Battista. *De ludis saecularibus populi Romani Quiritium libri sex.* 2nd ed. Amsterdam: Schippers, 1965.

Poliziano e il suo tempo. Atti del IV Convegno internazionale di studi sul rinascimento. Florence: G. C. Sansoni, 1957.

Questa, Cesare. *Per la storia del testo di Plauto nell'umanesimo.* Vol. 1, *La "recensio" di Poggio Bracciolini.* Rome: Quaderni Athena, 1968.

Reynolds, L. D., ed. *Texts and Transmission: A Survey of the Latin Classics.* Oxford: Clarendon Press, 1983.

Ricciardi, Roberto. "Angelo Poliziano e il testo di Properzio." In P. Viti, *Cultura e filologia,* 113–51.

———. "Angelo Poliziano, Giuniano Maio, Antonio Calcillo." *Rinascimento,* series 2, 8 (1968): 277–309.

Rizzo, Silva. "Il latino del Poliziano." In Fera and Martelli, *Agnolo Poliziano,* 83–125.

———. *Il lessico filologico degli umanisti.* Sussidi eruditi, 26. Rome: Edizioni di Storia e Letteratura, 1973.

Rosen, K. "Two copies of the First Edition of Politian's *Miscellaneorum centuria prima.*" In *Ecumenismo della cultura,* vol. 1: *Teoria e prassi della poetica dell'Umanesimo—Onoranze a Giovanni Boccaccio,* edited by G. Tarugi, 93–100. Atti del XII Convegno internazionale del Centro di Studi Umanistici, Montepulciano, 1975. Florence: Leo S. Olschki, 1981.

Rubinstein, Nicolai. "Il Poliziano e la questione delle origini di Firenze." In Secchi Tarugi, *Poliziano*, 101–10.

Saggese, P. "Poliziano, Domizio Calderini e la tradizione del testo di Marziale." *Maia: Rivista di letterature classiche*, series 2, 45 (1993): 185–95.

Sallmann, Klaus, ed. *Die Literatur des Umbruchs von der römischen zur christlichen Literatur, 117 bis 248 n. Chr.* Handbuch der lateinischen Literatur der Antike. Edited by R. Herzog and Peter L. Schmidt. Vol. 4. Munich: Beck, 1997.

Schmidt, Peter L. "Poliziano und der italienische Archetyp der Valerius-Flaccus-Überlieferung." *Italia medioevale e umanistica* 19 (1976): 241–56.

Secchi Tarugi, Luisa, ed. *Poliziano nel suo tempo. Atti del VI Convegno internazionale (Chianciano-Montepulciano, 18–21 luglio 1994).* Florence: Franco Cesati, 1996.

Sharples, Robert W. "Natural Philosophy in the Peripatos after Strato." In *Aristo of Ceos: Text, Translation and Discussion*, edited by William W. Fortenbaugh and Stephen A. White, 307–27. New Brunswick, N.J.: Transaction Publishers, 2006.

Stork, Peter, Tiziano Dorandi, William W. Fortenbaugh, and Johannes M. van Ophuijsen. "Aristo of Ceos: The Sources, Text, and Translation." In *Aristo of Chios: Text, Translation, and Discussion*, edited by William W. Fortenbaugh and Stephen A. White, 1–177. New Brunswick, NJ: Transaction Publishers, 2006.

Tateo, Francesco. *Lorenzo de' Medici e Angelo Poliziano*. Rome: Laterza, 1996.

Tissoni, Francesco. "Angelo Poliziano, *Miscellanea*, I, 80." In *Filologia e storia litteraria. Studi per Roberto Tissoni*, edited by C. Caruso and W. Spaggiari, 117–25. Rome: Edizioni di Storia e Letteratura, 2008.

Van Dam, Harm-Jan. "Wandering the Woods again from Poliziano to Grotius." In *The Poetry of Statius*, edited by J. J. L. Smolenaars, H.-J. van Dam, and R. R. Nauta, 45–64. Mnemosyne Supplements, 306. Leiden-Boston: Brill, 2008.

Vasoli, Cesare. "Il Poliziano maestro di dialettica." In *Poliziano e il suo tempo*, 161–72.

Verde, Armando F. *Lo Studio Fiorentino 1473–1503: Ricerche e documenti*. 6 vols. Florence: Istituto Nazionale di Studi sul Rinascimento, 1973–2010.

Viti, Anastasia. "Per la storia del testo di Marziale nel secolo XV. I Co-
mentarii in M. Valerium Martialem di Domizio Calderini." Eikasmos 15
(2004): 401–34.

Viti, Paolo, ed. Cultura e filologia di Angelo Poliziano. Traduzioni e commenti.
Florence: Leo S. Olschki, 2016.

——. Pico, Poliziano e l'umanesimo di fine Quattrocento. Exhibition cata-
logue, Biblioteca Medicea Laurenziana, 4 novembre–31 dicembre 1994.
Centro Internazionale di Cultura "Giovanni Pico della Mirandola,"
Studi Pichiani 2. Florence: Leo S. Olschki, 1994.

——. "Poliziano e Plinio: Il cap. 61 della I centuria dei Miscellanea." In
La Naturalis Historia di Plinio nella tradizione medievale e umanistica,
edited by Vanna Maraglino, 153–69. Bari: Cacucci, 2012.

Wesseling, Ari. "Poliziano and Ancient Rhetoric." Rinascimento, series 2,
30 (1990): 191–204.

Wilson, N. G. From Byzantium to Italy: Greek Studies in the Italian Renaissance. 2nd ed. London: Bloomsbury Academic, 2017.

General Index

❧✦❧

Abammon of Egypt, 385, 417
Abas (seer), 269
Academics, 73
Academy, 527n107; Roman, 251,
    557n513; Venetian, 544n325,
    546n356
Acciaiuoli, Donato, 287
Accursio, Francesco (Bolognese
    jurist), 383, 411, 459, 580n808,
    592n962
Acestorides, daughters of, 391, 401
Achaea, daughters of, 391
Achaean/Achaean, 371, 401
Achilles, 45, 253–55, 385, 557n519
Achilles Tatius, 141, 351, 574n733;
    Isagoge, 538n259, 574n733
Acrisius, 547n377
Acro. See [Helenius Acro]
Actaeon, 387, 397, 407, 581n820
Acusilaus of Argos, 269, 560n553
Adonis, 117, 119
Aeacides, 253
Aelian (Claudius Aelianus), 5, 55,
    467–69; Historical Miscellany,
    263, 271, 367, 519n7, 559n539,
    560nn554–55, 577n778; On the
    Nature of Animals, 349–51, 467–
    69, 574n730, 593n974
Aelian Sentian Law, 419
Aelius Catus, Sextus, 584n856
Aelius Sentius, 421
Aeneas, 357

Aeschines, 109
Aeschylus, 45, 111, 253–55,
    534n196; Agamemnon, 195; Sup-
    pliants, 547n382
Aesculapius, 271
Aesop/Aesopian, 133, 483,
    537n234; Fabulae Aesopicae,
    595n1009
Africa/African, 105
Agamemnon, 47, 283–87
Agathias, Histories, 535n205
Agenor, 369, 371
Agesilas (Hades; deity), 399
Agonalia (festival), 329, 570n682
Ajax, 17, 283, 445
Albans, the, 191, 299
Albertus Magnus, 525n80
Alcaeus, 205–7, 209, 549n414
Alcibiades, 85
Alcides (Hercules), 103, 533n179.
    See also Hercules
Alexander of Aphrodisias, 477,
    561n568; On Fate, 73, 527n104;
    Questions on Nature, 69, 526n99
Alexander Polyhistor of Miletus,
    201
Alexander the Great, xix, 47, 263,
    331, 383, 559n539, 570n685,
    580n809
Alexandria/Alexandrian, viii, 83
Alighieri, Dante (descendant of
    the poet), 153

Maximus of Tyre (*continued*)
Pleasure, 133; *What Is the Goal of
Philosophy?*, 133
Medea, 181, 183, 185
Medici: collection, xvii, xviii, xx,
xxi; family, vii, xiv, 588n915; library, xxv n28, 141, 145, 163, 169,
173, 203, 211, 215, 217, 243, 269,
297, 327, 331, 379, 469, 549n409
Medici, Cosimo de', 59, 551n442
Medici, Giuliano de', 99
Medici, Lorenzo de', vii, xii, xiv,
xvii, xxi, xxv n28, xxvii n46,
3–25, 59, 79, 99, 117, 145, 151,
243, 247, 309, 351, 361, 379, 423,
429, 441, 481, 485, 518, 522n39,
522n45, 523n53, 523n60,
535n205, 541n296, 542n306,
556n506, 559n534, 566n621,
567n635; *Canzoniere*, 535n204
Medici, Piero di Lorenzo de', 59,
596n1015
Mediterranean Sea, 225
Megabyzus, 47, 263, 275, 559n539
Megapenthes, 271
Megarian school, 564n599
Megarogilus, 205
Melampus, 267, 269, 271, 560n558
Meleagrian, 297
Melo, 45, 233–37
Memmius, Caius, xx, 53, 421–25,
584n865, 585nn868–69
Memnon, 373
Memphis, 281
Menelaus, 469
Menippean satires, 213

Menoetius, 255
Mercury (deity), 113. *See also*
Hermes
Mercury (planet), 95, 475
Merula, Giorgio, xiv, xxvi n36, 101,
159, 520n13, 533n175, 534n189,
547n380, 553n465, 558n526,
558n528, 565n621, 584n858;
*Against Domizio Calderini's Com-
mentaries on Martial*, 533n175;
commentary on Juvenal,
530n144, 533n175, 552n463,
574n729
Mesopotamia, 223
Mesor (month), 415
Messana (city), 215
Messanello, Bernardino, 163,
542n302
Metellus Pius, 201
Metochites, Theodore, *Miscellanea*,
519n10
Michelangelo Buonarotti, 573n721;
Pietà, 559n534
Michelozzi, Bernardo, 165, 333,
542n306
Michelozzi, Niccolò, 379, 542n306
Migdonians, 191
Milan, 544n327
Miletus/Milesian, xvi, 39, 137–41,
141, 431; woven cloak of Mile-
tus, 267, 560n544
Millini (Mellini) family, 259,
558n532
Minerva (deity), 119, 121, 157, 159,
385, 387, 403, 405, 435, 481,
489, 541n289. *See also* Athena

Tiber (river; Rumo, Serra), 301,
305, 313, 317, 319
Tibullus, Albius, 532n162; *Elegies*,
97
Timarchuses (plural), 115
Time, 267
Timon of Phlius, 217, 235,
528n109, 554n479
Tiresias, 53, 383–409
Tiro (secretary to Cicero), 123,
187, 283
Titans, 187, 189
Titinius, 558n531
Titus (biblical book), 219, 552n449
Torah, 536n222
Torquatus (character), in Martial,
548n383
Tranio, 347
Trebatius Testa, Gaius, 145, 181,
429
Tribonian, 243, 419
Trivia, 273, 281, 561n562
Troad, 205
Trojan Horse, 87, 371
Trojan Horse, The, 429
Trojan War, 283, 530n140
Troy/Trojan, 53, 87, 431, 475, 481
Tryphiodorus, 371, 578nn785–86
Tuscany, vii
Tyrannion, 71
Tyre/Tyrian, 123, 193, 547n377

Ugoletti, Taddeo, 87, 165, 530n146
Ugolini, Baccio, 101, 153, 163
Ulpian (Domitius Ulpianus; jurist), 363, 576n755; *On the Duty
of the Proconsul*, 465; *On the*

Edict, 241, 411, 457; *To Sabinus*,
576n767. See also *Digests*
Ulysses, 47, 283–87, 371, 385. *See
also* Odysseus
Umbricius, 147, 539n274
Urbino, duke of, 483

Valerian family, 301
Valerius, Manius, of Tarentum,
303, 307
Valerius Antias, 305, 307,
566n627, 566–67nn630–31
Valerius Flaccus Setinus Balbus,
Gaius, *Argonautica*, xiii, 37, 87–
89, 189–91, 427, 433, 531n148,
547nn373–74, 585n876,
586n890
Valerius Maximus, 237, 554n490,
565n621, 568n654, 579n794
Valerius Messalla Corvinus, Marcus, 5
Valerius Messalla Rufus, Marcus,
519n11
Valerius Publicola, Publius, 305–
7, 568n654
Valesius, Valesus, 301–3, 566n629,
568n654
Valla, Bernardino, xiv, 163, 409
Valla, Giorgio, 538n262, 558n526,
558n528
Varro (Marcus Terentius Varro),
xix, 5, 9, 41, 43, 49, 73, 99,
157–59, 213, 221–23, 225, 237,
305, 307, 337, 417, 435, 437,
539n268, 554n490, 566n627,
570n682, 572n705; *Manius*, 145;
Menippean Satires, 551n433; *On*

Publication of this volume has been made possible by

The Myron and Sheila Gilmore Publication Fund at I Tatti
The Robert Lehman Endowment Fund
The Jean-François Malle Scholarly Programs and Publications Fund
The Andrew W. Mellon Scholarly Publications Fund
The Craig and Barbara Smyth Fund
for Scholarly Programs and Publications
The Lila Wallace–Reader's Digest Endowment Fund
The Malcolm Wiener Fund for Scholarly Programs and Publications